The GIS Applications Book

Examples in Natural Resources:
a compendium

edited by William J. Ripple

American Society for Photogrammetry and Remote Sensing

The world population has tripled in the last 70 years and is expected to double from 5.7 billion people in the next 40 years. Rates of change in land status and ecosystem health have been accelerating with this population growth. This acceleration in the rates of change places a greater and greater value on the timeliness and the quality of spatial data and spatial models. Today, it is apparent that geographic information systems (GIS) are being chosen to meet these needs. Although the use of GIS by scientists and resource managers is still in its infancy, research scientists are starting to use GIS to do spatial modelling for developing an understanding of natural patterns and processes. We are also now seeing examples of how GIS can be used for making policy decisions based on simulating various future land management scenarios.

The application of GIS in the natural resources is rapidly changing, with much of the information on this topic residing in the periodical literature. The objective of this book is to bring together recent information on various applications of GIS in the natural resources. This book contains an international collection of articles primarily from refereed journals that were published within the last five years. The articles were selected from respected GIS, natural resource, and science journals. This book can be used as a textbook supplement for university level courses in GIS. It can also be used as a reference for geographers, foresters, hydrologists, soil scientists, engineers, wildlife biologists, planners, and ecologists.

The book is divided into 9 sections. Each section begins with a brief overview and a few suggestions for additional reading. Section 1 provides an introduction with information on the role of GIS in natural resources, technological developments, and definitions of commonly used GIS terms. Sections 2 through 9 include articles on GIS applications in various natural resource disciplines including environmental modelling and assessment, soils, water resources, forestry, landscape ecology, wildlife, land use, and biological diversity. The book ends with a selected bibliography on GIS applications in the natural resources, and sources of GIS information, and an author index.

As GIS applications mature, we will study patterns and processes across a huge range of scales from the patch, to the landscape, the region, the continent, and to the entire globe. An holistic view will be required while using GIS in order for us to better understand the earth system, how it functions, and how it can be managed. Fritjof Capra talks about the systems view with the interrelatedness and interdependence of all phenomena in his book Belonging to the Universe. He states, "In the old paradigm it was believed that in any complex system the dynamics of the whole could be understood from the properties of the parts. In the new paradigm, the relationship between the parts and the whole is reversed. The properties of the parts can be understood only from the dynamics of the whole. Ultimately, there are not parts at all. What we call a part is merely a pattern in an inseparable web of relationships." In order for GIS to become a complete success, it will need to be viewed as a technology and a science that assists in understanding these relationships for sustaining and improving life on earth. This can only be accomplished by scientists using GIS in making discoveries about nature and through GIS truly supporting human decisions made by resource managers and policy makers.

William J. Ripple
Oregon State University
Department of Forest Resources
Environmental Remote Sensing Applications
Laboratory (ERSAL)
July 1994

*Instead of production, primarily, we have to think of
sustainability. Instead of dominating nature, we have to
acknowledge that nature is our source and best teacher. Instead
of understanding the world in parts, we need to think about the
whole.*

WES JACKSON

This book is dedicated to Barbara Lee and to my father, John.

ACKNOWLEDGMENTS

Great appreciation is offered to Ann Bacon for her many hours of assistance in bringing this book to publication.

THE GIS APPLICATIONS BOOK:
Examples in Natural Resources

TABLE OF CONTENTS

SECTION 3
SOILS

SECTION 4
WATER RESOURCES

SECTION 5
FORESTRY

SECTION 6
LANDSCAPE ECOLOGY

SECTION 7
WILDLIFE

SECTION 8
LAND USE

SECTION 9
BIOLOGICAL DIVERSITY

SECTION 1

Introduction

Overview

The focus of this section is to set the stage for the various applications in the rest of the book by providing an overview of the evolution of GIS in natural resource analysis. In the first paper, Berry and Ripple trace the emergence and role of GIS in natural resources with special emphasis on forestry by discussing historical developments, current applications, and future trends. In the second paper, Dangermond explores where GIS technology is going and a range of possible futures for natural resource management. The final paper by Kessler provides definitions of common words and phrases typically encountered by GIS users.

Suggested Additional Reading

Aronoff, S. 1989. Geographic Information Systems: A Management Perspective. WDL Publications, Ottawa, Canada.

Berry, J. K. 1993. Beyond Mapping: Concepts, Algorithms and Issues in GIS. GIS World Publishers, Fort Collins, CO.

Maguire, D. J., M. F. Goodchild, and D. W. Rhind (eds.). 1991. Geographic Information Systems: Principles and Applications. John Wiley and Sons, New York, New York.

Ripple, W. J. (ed.) 1989. Fundamentals of Geographic Information Systems: A Compendium. American Society for Photogrammetry and Remote Sensing, Bethesda, Maryland.

EMERGENCE AND ROLE OF GIS IN NATURAL RESOURCES

by

Joseph K. Berry and William J. Ripple

Information is the cornerstone of effective decisions, regardless of discipline or level. The modern office has evolved from typewriters, slide rules and file cabinets to word processors, spreadsheets and database management systems. The increasing complexity of both data and issues has fueled the transition. Natural resource information is particularly complex as it requires two descriptors—where is what. For hundreds of years the link between the two descriptors has been the traditional, manually drafted map. Its historical use was for navigation through unfamiliar terrain and seas, with emphasis on accurate location of physical features.

More recently, analysis of mapped data for decision-making has become an important part of resource planning. This new perspective marks a turning point in the use of maps—from one emphasizing physical descriptors of geographic space, to one of interpreting mapped data, and finally, to spatially characterizing appropriate management actions. This movement from "where is what" (descriptive) to "so what" (prescriptive) mapping has set the stage for revolutionary concepts in resource planning and management. It has extended information systems from an inventory focus to an analytical focus.

Modern geographic information systems (GIS) provide a means for quantitative modeling of spatial relationships. In one sense, this technology is similar to conventional map processing involving paper maps and drafting aids, such as pens, rub-on shading, rulers, planimeters and transparent sheets for light-table overlays. In another sense, these systems provide a radically new analytic toolbox for addressing complex issues in entirely new ways.

HISTORICAL OVERVIEW

Natural resource analysis is inherently a spatial endeavor. In framing any resource plan, it is difficult to anticipate the potential long-term spatial effects of a plan's assumptions and policies. It is a formidable challenge to survey and incorporate a diverse set of opinions, in a manner consistent with the analysis process. These uncertainties and complexities create a need for more useful and timely information, expressed in spatial terms. The use

In press, *The Literature of Forestry and Agroforestry*, Chapter 6, Volume 7, J. Lassoie and P. McDonald, Eds., Cornell University Press, Ithaca, New York.

of manual overlay mapping techniques to relate multiple spatial factors was popularized in the late 1960's (McHarg 1969). The following excerpt (Hendler 1973) depicts the process.

> "...The water systems map, vegetation map, soils map, and noise/visual impact map are placed over each other, taking care to see that the features of each map overlay one another exactly. ...The entire bundle is then placed over a strong light source, such as a window. ...Certain areas on the property will show through lighter than other areas. These lighter areas represent those portions of the property which have fewer restrictions on them. ...A tracing of the outlines of the light areas is then made. ..."

Since the 1960's, decision-making has become increasingly quantitative, and mathematical models have become commonplace. Two factors inhibited the full use of these techniques in natural resources. First, spatial analysis involves tremendous volumes of data. Manual cartographic techniques allowed manipulation of these data, however, they were inherently limited by their non-digital nature. Traditional statistics and mathematics enable quantitative analysis, but the shear magnitude and detail of the digital data sets were prohibitive for the geographic information systems of that time.

Early recognition of these limitations led to stratified sampling techniques developed in the early part of this century. These techniques treat spatial considerations at the onset of analysis by dividing geographic space into analysis units that are assumed to be homogenous. Most often, these parcels are manually delineated on an appropriate map, and the "typical" value for each parcel is determined. Analysis results are assumed to be uniformly distributed throughout each parcel. The area-weighted average of several parcels statistically characterize the typical response for an entire region. Mathematical modeling of forested systems followed a similar approach of spatially aggregating variation in model variables. Most ecosystem models, for example, identify level and flow variables presumed to be typical for vast geographic expanses.

The fundamental concepts of a comprehensive spatial statistics and mathematics have been described for many years by both theorists and practitioners (Brown 1949, Steinitz et al. 1976, Shelton and Estes 1981). The representation of spatial data as a statistical surface is indicated in most cartography texts (Robertson et al. 1978, Cuff and Matson 1982). A host of quantitative and analytical techniques are present in manual cartography. Muehrcke and Muehrcke (1980), in an introductory text, outline a set of cartometric techniques allowing quantitative assessments of spatial phenomena.

Until modern computers and the digital map, many of these concepts were limited in their practical implementation. The computer has provided the means for both efficient handling of voluminous data and the numerical analysis capabilities that are required. From this perspective, the current revolution in GIS is rooted in the digital nature of the computerized map. The complementary fields of systems analysis and GIS share this new perspective. Systems analysis for forest planning has been widely applied during the past two decades. Obvious needs in forest planning include assembling information for the variety of land resources found in a planning area, calculating the effect of various alternative treatments or practices on these land resources, and determining whether or not any combination of treatments could meet various output goals. The objective of such an exercise is generally stated as "meeting the output goals in a least-cost fashion." These output goals can be either by internal staff groups or by public interest groups. The resultant allocation of land treatments to various land units becomes a major part of the forest plan. The analytical problem is readily stated as a linear programming problem, and in fact linear programming is the most commonly used systems analysis technique for forest planning (Jameson 1993).

EARLY GEOGRAPHIC INFORMATION SYSTEMS

The continued use of systems analysis for natural resource plans seems certain, and the laws that lead to the use of these techniques are not likely to change. The amount of information to be processed, the intensity of the calculations, and continued public interest in the world's natural resources require a well designed and well documented procedure. What is changing is how GIS's organize, handle and analyze data.

In the early 1970's, GIS focused on <u>computer mapping</u> to automate the cartographic process. The points, lines and areas defining geographic features on a map are represented as an organized set of X,Y coordinates. These data form input to a pen plotter which can rapidly redraw the connections at a variety of scales and projections. The mapping programs of SYMAP and Odyssey developed at the Harvard Laboratory for Computer Graphic's and Spatial Analysis are examples of this pioneering work. An obvious advantage of computer mapping is the ability to change a portion of the map and quickly redraft the entire area. Updates to resource maps which could take weeks, such as a forest fire burn, can be done in a few hours. The less obvious advantage is the radical change in the format of mapped data—from analog inked lines on paper to digital values stored in computers.

During the early 1980's, the change in format and computer environment of mapped data were exploited. <u>Spatial database management systems</u> were developed that linked computer mapping capabilities with traditional database management capabilities. In these systems, identification numbers are assigned to each geographic feature, such as a timber harvest or habitat parcel. These ID's are used as entry points into a database of information describing the composition and condition of each parcel. For example, a user is able to point at any location on a computer generated map and instantly retrieve information about the location. Alternatively, a user can specify a set of conditions, such as a specific forest and soil combination, and direct the result of the database search to be displayed as a map.

During the early development of GIS, two alternative data structures for encoding maps were debated. The <u>vector</u> data model closely mimics the manual drafting process by representing map features as a set of lines which, in turn, are stored as an organized series of X,Y coordinates. An alternative structure, termed the <u>raster</u> data model, establishes an imaginary grid over a project area, then stores resource information for each cell in the grid. The early debate attempted to determine the universally best structure. The relative advantages and disadvantages of both were viewed in a competitive manner which failed to recognize the overall strengths of a GIS approach encompassing both.

By the mid-1980's, the general consensus within the GIS community was that the nature of the data and the processing desired determines the appropriate data structure. These considerations can be summarized as:

	FAVORING VECTOR	FAVORING RASTER
Data Nature:	Lines Real	Lines Artificial
	Data Certain	Data Probablistic
Processing:	Descriptive Query	Prescriptive Analysis
	Computer Mapping	Spatial Statistics
	Spatial DBMS	Spatial Modeling

The realization of the duality of mapped data structure had significant impact on geographic information systems. From one perspective, resource maps form sharp boundaries which are best represented as lines. Property ownerships, timber sale boundaries, and haul road networks are examples where the lines are real and the data are certain. Other maps, such as soils, site index, and slope are interpretations of terrain conditions. The placement of lines identifying these conditions are subject to judgement, statistical analysis of field data, and broad classification of continuous spatial distributions. From this perspective, the sharp boundary implied by a line is artificial and the data itself is probablistic.

The recognition of the need for both data structures focused attention on data exchange issues. Early programs incorporating both vector and raster data, such as MOSS/MAPS by the U.S. Fish and Wildlife Service, heralded the way for modern commercial systems such as GenaMap/GenaCell by Genesys and ARC/INFO/GRID by Environmental Systems Research Institute (ESRI). These systems provide an integrated processing environment for a wide variety of mapped data. In forestry applications, it allows remotely sensed, digital elevation, roads, and vegetation maps to co-exist in the same computing environment.

The increasing demands for mapped data focused attention on data availability, accuracy, and standards. Hardware vendors continued to improve digitizing equipment, with manual digitizing tablets giving way to automated scanners in many GIS facilities. A new industry for map encoding and database design emerged, as well as a marketplace for the sales of digital map products. Regional, national, and international organizations began addressing the necessary standards for digital maps to insure compatibility among systems.

SPATIAL ANALYSIS AND MODELING

As GIS continued its evolution, the emphasis turned from descriptive query to prescriptive analysis of maps. For the greater part, early GIS concentrated on automating the cartographic process. If an analyst had to repeatedly overlay several maps on a light-table, an analogous procedure was developed within the GIS. Similarly, if repeated distance and bearing calculations were needed, the GIS was programmed with a mathematical solution. The result of this effort was GIS functionality that mimicked the manual procedures in his or her daily activities. The value of these systems was the savings of automating tedious and repetitive operations.

By the mid-1980's, the bulk of descriptive query operations were available in most GIS systems. A comprehensive theory of spatial analysis began to emerge. The dominant feature of this theory is that spatial information is represented numerically, rather than in analog fashion as inked lines on a map. These digital maps are frequently conceptualized as a set of "floating maps" with common registration, allowing the computer to "look" down and across the stack of digital maps. The spatial relationships of the data can be summarized (database queries) or mathematically manipulated (analytic processing).

Because of the analog nature of traditional map sheets, manual analytic techniques are limited in their quantitative processing. Digital representation, on the other hand, makes a wealth of quantitative as well as qualitative processing possible. The application of this new theory to natural resources is revolutionary. Its application takes two forms—spatial statistics and spatial modeling.

Spatial statistics has been used by the geophysicist and statistician for many years (Davis 1973, Ripley 1981, Cressie 1991). This field of statistics seeks to characterize the geographic distribution, or pattern, of mapped data. They describe the spatial variation in the data, rather than assuming a typical response, or numeric average, to be uniformly distributed in space. For example, field measurements of snow depth can be made at several sample plots within a watershed. Traditionally, these data are analyzed for the average depth (and standard deviation) to characterize the entire watershed. Spatial statistics, on the other hand, uses both the location and the measurement value at the sample plots to generate a map of relative snow depth throughout the watershed.

If the measurements are repeated a month later, change detection analysis (simple subtraction of the two maps) can be employed to determine a map of the change in snow depth. The full impact of this "map-ematical" treatment of maps on GIS is yet to be determined. The application of such concepts as spatial correlation, statistical filters, and map uncertainty await their translation from other fields, such as geophysics, environmental sciences, and quantitative geography. It is certain that spatial statistics has the potential to radically alter our current concepts and procedures in forest mensuration.

Spatial modeling, on the other hand, has many examples of assisting resource professionals in defining and evaluating spatial considerations in land management (Ripple 1987). For example, forest managers can characterize timber supply by considering the relative skidding and log-hauling accessibility of harvesting parcels. Wildlife managers can consider such factors as proximity to roads and relative housing density in order to map human activity and incorporate this information into conventional wildlife habitat maps. Forest planners can assess the visual exposure of alternative sites for a facility or clearcut to sensitive viewing locations, such as roads and scenic overlooks.

Just as spatial statistics has been developed by extending concepts of conventional statistics, a spatial mathematics has evolved. This "map algebra" (Tomlin 1990) uses sequential processing of mathematical primitives to perform complex map analyses. It is similar to traditional algebra in which primitive operations (e.g, add, subtract, exponentiate) are logically sequenced on variables to form equations. But in map algebra, entire maps composed of thousands or millions of numbers represent the variables.

Most of the traditional mathematical capabilities plus an extensive set of advanced map processing operations are available in modern GIS packages (Berry 1993). With spatial modeling, the spatial coincidence and juxtapositioning of values among and within maps create new operations such as masking, proximity, and optimal paths. The set of map analysis operators can be flexibly combined through a processing structure similar to conventional mathematics. The logical sequence involves:

- retrieval of one or more maps from the database,
- processing that data as specified by the user,
- creation of a new map containing the processing results,
- and storage of the new map for subsequent processing.

This cyclical processing is similar to "evaluating nested parentheticals" in traditional algebra. For example, in the simple equation $A = (B-C)/B$, the variables B and C are first defined and then subtracted, with their difference stored as an intermediate solution. The intermediate value, in turn, is retrieved and divided by variable B to derive the value of the unknown variable A. This same structure provides the framework for spatial modeling, but the variables are represented as spatially registered maps. The numbers contained in the solution map (in effect, solving for map A) are a function of the input maps and the map analysis operations performed.

This mathematical structure forms a conceptual framework easily adapted to a variety of resource applications in a familiar and intuitive manner. For example, the equation discussed above is used in calculating percent change. If variables B and C are the snow depth maps derived by spatial statistics noted above, the resultant map would be the percent change in snow depth between the two periods. In a similar manner, a map of percent change in timber value for an entire ownership tract may be expressed in such commands as:

COMPUTE ((NEWVALUE.MAP - OLDVALUE.MAP) / OLDVALUE.MAP) * 100
    FOR VALUECHANGE.MAP

[This and the following example commands are in pMAP (Professional Map Analysis Package) language, a PC-based system developed by Spatial Information Systems.]

Within this model, data for current and past timber values for each forest parcel are derived by spatially evaluating tree growth and econometric models. The model might be extended to provide coincidence statistics, such as:

CROSSTABULATE HABITAT.MAP WITH VALUECHANGE.MAP

for a table summarizing the spatial relationship between the wildlife habitat map and changes in timber values. Such a table shows which habitat parcels experienced the greatest increase in timber valuation.

The basic model might be extended to include such geographic searches as:

RENUMBER VALUECHANGE.MAP FOR BIGINCREASES.MAP
    ASSIGN 0 TO -100 THRU 19
    ASSIGN 1 TO 20 THRU 100

The BIGCHANGES search isolates those areas that experienced more than 20 percent change in timber value—a 1 assigned to locations with big increases; 0 assigned to all other changes.

Early map analysis efforts found foresters using GIS technology like a city tax assessor. Information about map parcels were retrieved, evaluated and a decision rendered based on the "repackaging" of existing mapped data similar to the above discussion. As systems matured, entirely new analytic capabilities became part of the GIS toolbox. For example,

RADIATE ROAD.MAP OVER ELEVATION.MAP COMPLETELY
    FOR EXPOSURE.MAP

creates a map of the visual connectivity of the road network. The relative visual exposure to roads throughout a project area is mapped, with locations that are more frequently seen from roads receiving higher exposure values. In turn, this information may be summarized for each potential harvest unit by:

COMPOSITE HARVESTS.MAP WITH EXPOSURE.MAP AVERAGE
    FOR AVGEXPOSURE.MAP

Similarly, a map of effective proximity to roads considering harvester operability can be derived by:

SPREAD ROAD.MAP THRU BARRIERS.MAP FOR PROXIMITY.MAP

then summarized for each potential harvest unit by:

COMPOSITE HARVESTS.MAP WITH PROXIMITY.MAP AVERAGE
    FOR AVGPROXIMITY.MAP

In this example, every location receives a value indicating how far it is from the nearest road (on average), considering intervening barriers, such as streams and excessively steep slopes (THRU BARRIERS.MAP). In effect, this new technique uses a "rubber ruler" that bends around actual barriers to harvester movement, resulting in a more realistic measurement of harvesting access.

A simple harvesting suitability model might combine the visual exposure and effective proximity maps to identify those locations having low values on each by:

INTERSECT AVGEXPOSURE.MAP WITH AVGPROXIMITY.MAP
    ASSIGN 1 TO 0 THRU 20 AND 0 THRU 5
    FOR BESTAREAS.MAP

This command isolates the most suitable harvest units that have low exposure indices (0-20) and are relatively close (0-.5km.) to roads.

The GIS "toolbox" contains many more advanced analytic concepts, such as optimal path routing and landscape diversity, shape, and pattern, which are radically changing how foresters characterize natural resources. These new tools and modeling approach to natural resource information combines and extends record-keeping systems and decision-making models into effective decision support systems.

GIS APPLICATIONS IN FORESTRY AND NATURAL RESOURCES

There is currently a lot of activity and support for GIS in natural resources. For example, the British Columbia Ministry of Forestry and Lands has an operational GIS for managing their lands and making policy decisions on forest harvesting, reforestation, environmental assessment and recreation planning. On the other hand, most other natural resource GIS activities are only at the database creation, or other basic inventory and query stages. We have not yet seen widespread use of GIS for making policy decisions based on simulating various future land management scenarios.

It seems that operational use of GIS in natural resources has lagged behind other areas such as facilities management and urban applications. One reason for this is that GIS users in the natural resources have had problems in acquiring timely and accurate databases over very large geographic areas. For example, nearly all natural resource applications need an accurate vegetation layer, but these data are typically very difficult to obtain. Advances in the field of remote sensing should help alleviate this problem in the future. Reviews are available on how remotely sensed data can be used as an information source for GIS in forest and natural resource management (Trotter 1991, Lachowski et al. 1992). Lachowski et al. 1992 described procedures and examples of how remote sensing and GIS are used to support all phases of resource management within the USDA Forest Service. The authors illustrate an ever-widening use of aerial photographs, satellite imagery, airborne video, and global positioning systems (GPS). They also discuss how GIS has become important in the Forest Service for monitoring forest plans, vegetation mapping, and old-growth modeling, and range allotment monitoring. Also, recent advances in GPS in providing three dimensional coordinates for any location should greatly assist the development of GIS for natural resource assessment.

Additional readings on GIS applications in forestry and natural resources can be obtained by referring to the two 1992 special issues on GIS in the Journal of Forestry, volume 90, numbers 11 and 12, and several books including GIS Applications in Natural Resources edited by Heit and Shorteid (1991), a volume on GIS applications in resource management (Ripple 1987), a volume on fundamentals of GIS (Ripple 1989), and a two volume, sixty chapter book on GIS principles and applications (Maguire et al. 1991). Other examples of GIS applications in forestry, as found in recent journal articles, can be divided into four categories including forest inventory, forest harvesting, forest fire modelling, and forest ecology.

Forest Inventory

The mapping of old growth forests in the Pacific Northwest forests is an important recent GIS application in forestry since the future management of these lands hinges upon accurate inventory data. Congalton et al. (1993) described the process involved in creating a GIS database for more than 30 million acres of national forest land in Oregon and Washington. Maclean et al. (1992) demonstrated how remote sensing and GIS were used to analyze changes in timber stand conditions over time. GIS has also been used to predict the distribution of tree species using digital terrain data with other environmental variables (Davis and Goetz 1990).

Forest Harvesting

The wood products industry can benefit from innovative uses of GIS technology. For example, Brinker and Jackson (1991) used a GIS to study a regional wood procurement problem in Louisiana. They assessed the current competition for pulpwood and located wood supply sources. Baskent and Jordon (1991) used the geographic distribution of stand development types and changes over time to model timber harvesting, wood supply, and wildlife habitat in New Brunswick. The Indonesian government has demonstrated how GIS can be applied to forest harvesting and management in the design of logging roads, forest monitoring, and forest land allocation (Susilawati and Weir 1990).

Forest Fire Modelling

Hamilton et al. (1989) have suggested that GIS can be used to provide a wildfire management probability model using data layers such as fuels, topography, weather, structures, water availability, and access routes. The effects of wind during a forest fire were illustrated in a GIS by Zack and Minnich (1991). Differences in burn severity were related to post-fire vegetative cover in Michigan using GIS (Jakubauskas et al. 1990).

Forest Ecology

Iverson et al. (1989) reviewed how remote sensing can provide increased information on forested ecosystems in the areas of:

1) Mapping forest types
2) Detection of forest changes
3) Study of forest succession
4) Assessment of stand structure
5) Assessment of physiological parameters
6) Assessment of forest productivity

Another indepth review, provided by Johnson (1990), described a variety of ecological applications for analyzing spatial and temporal phenomena with GIS. In the field of landscape ecology, both Pastor and Broschart (1990) and Ripple et al. (1991) demonstrated how to use GIS to characterize forest landscape patterns to study the relationships between patterns and underlying ecological processes or wildlife habitat dynamics. Other wildlife applications with GIS include analyzing grizzly bear sightings (Agee et al. 1989), predicting the presence or absence of red squirrels (Pereira and Itam 1991), and the study of long term landscape alterations by beaver (Johnston and Naiman 1990).

The forestry GIS examples discussed above serve to illustrate an impressive potential for GIS in natural resources. GIS applications in the future will involve a more functional and integrated system for spatial analysis. GIS will help provide a holistic view which will be required in order for us to better understand the natural systems and how they function.

GIS IN THE U.S. FOREST SERVICE

One of the most compelling challenges facing resource managers today is how to identify, measure, and monitor the cumulative effects of forest practices. In meeting these challenges, the U.S. Forest Service has outlined an ambitious plan to incorporate GIS and other computer technologies into a fully integrated resource information management system. The Forest Service has recognized the need for automating natural resources data for a long time. The earliest efforts were with Project INFORM in the 1970's which was developed on a large mainframe computer with limited availability to the field units. By the early 1980's, it was clear a readily available computer-based GIS capability was needed. Since 1984, under Project FLIPS, the Forest Service has automated everything in its office environment from words, to mail, to time and attendance reports. This microcomputer experience brought all their offices into the computer age and has greatly contributed to the agency's overall computer literacy. However, resource information management, and GIS in particular, were not part of this procurement.

In 1988, a plan was initiated for implementing a system combining Office Automation, Database Management, Network, and GIS technologies. The Project 615 procurement is scheduled for award in early 1994. The new workstation platform and software tools will allow for the storage, retrieval, analysis, and presentation of information about land based resources, as well as management direction and activities. It will also provide all of the office automation and database capabilities of their current system in a fully integrated GIS environment. This means that a resource manager can begin a report in a word processing package, access tabular data from the DBMS, cut/paste a map from the GIS, and send the result by electronic mail to a colleague all without leaving the word processing environment. It is estimated the GIS tools can serve 50 percent of the workload at ranger districts and forest science labs, 33 percent of the workload at forest supervisor's offices and research stations, and 10% of the workload at regional offices and the Washington headquarters office.

These capabilities, however, do not come without a price, both literally and figuratively. The Forest Service anticipates an investment of US $1.2 billion over the eight year life of the project, with $400-600 million going for hardware and software and the remainder for data conversion and support. During this period, thousands of resource and related maps will be digitized and entered into the GIS by Forest Service and contract personnel. The project recognizes that this electronic environment requires a new level of information organization and discipline in its management and use, as well as dramatic changes in the work patterns of resource professionals. The first year of the project will be a "pilot year" to capture user experiences and test the new system as they are implemented. The pilot year will address areas of concern such as configuration management planning, system sizing, network optimizing, information management standards, interoffice information transfer, data communications with existing systems, conversion of existing data and applications, and development of "standard" GIS products. These findings will likely define the GIS of the future.

FUTURE TRENDS

The 1990's will build on the cognitive basis, as well as the data bases, of current geographic information systems. The system analysis models of the 1970's documented how forest actions are determined and how plans are developed. They focused attention on the analysis process and translated the constraints and objectives of forest management into mathematical terms. These models can be executed for a variety of 'scenarios' which provide the forester with an understanding of the impacts of alternatives. However, a major limitation of this approach is the lack of spatial specificity, as landscape descriptors must be aggregated over large geographic areas. These aggregated statistics lose the unique character of individual forest parcels, thereby confounding the actual on-site implementation of forest plans.

In the 1980's, GIS technology captured this unique spatial character into modern natural resource information systems. Initially, these systems simply addressed drafting and management of inventory data. With the recognition of the digital nature of the mapped data, applications of GIS became increasingly quantitative. Complex spatial models, from wildfire behavior to harvest scheduling and wildlife habitat, were developed using an approach analogous to traditional math and statistics. These applications are constructed by logically sequencing basic map analysis operations (analytical toolbox) on spatial data (maps) to solve specific application equations (spatial models). However, the unknowns of these equations are represented as entire maps defined by thousands of numbers. This 'map-ematics' forms a conceptual framework for spatial modeling and the next step in GIS.

The technology is at a threshold that is pushing beyond mapping, management, and modeling to spatial reasoning and dialogue (Berry 1991). In the past, analysis models have focused on management options that are technically optimal—the scientific solution. Yet in reality, there is another set of perspectives that must be considered—the social solution. It is this final sieve of management alternatives that most often confounds resource decision-making. It uses elusive measures, such as human values, attitudes, beliefs, judgement, trust and understanding. These are not the usual quantitative measures amenable to computer algorithms and traditional decision-making models.

The step from technically feasible to socially acceptable options is not so much scientific and econometric modeling, as it is communication. Basic to effective communication is involvement of interested parties throughout the decision-making process. This new participatory environment surrounding GIS has two main elements—consensus building and conflict resolution. Consensus building involves technically-driven communication and occurs during the alternative formulation phase. It involves the resource specialist's translation of the various considerations raised by a decision team into a spatial model. Once completed, the model is executed under a wide variety of conditions and the differences in outcome are noted.

From this perspective, a single map of a forest plan is not the objective. It is how maps change as the different scenarios are tried that becomes information. "What if avoidance of visual exposure is more important than avoidance of steep slopes in siting a new haul road? Where does the proposed route change, if at all?" Answers to these analytic queries focus attention on the effects of differing perspectives. Often, seemingly divergent philosophical views result in only slightly different map views. This realization, coupled with active involvement in the decision-making process, can lead to group consensus.

If consensus is not obtained, <u>conflict resolution</u> is necessary. This socially-driven communication occurs during the decision formulation phase. It involves the creation of a "conflicts map" comparing the outcomes from two or more competing uses. Each management parcel is assigned a numeric code describing the actual conflict over the location. A parcel might be identified as ideal as a wildlife preservation, a campground and a timber harvest. As these alternatives are mutually exclusive, a single use must be assigned. This assignment, however, involves a holistic perspective which simultaneously considers the potential assignments of all other locations in a project area.

Traditional scientific approaches are rarely effective in addressing the holistic problem of conflict resolution. Most are linear models, requiring a succession, or cascade, of individual parcel assignments. The final result is strongly biased by the ordering of parcel consideration. Even if a scientific solution is reached, it is viewed with suspicion by the layperson. Modern geographic information systems provide an alternative approach involving human rationalization and tradeoffs. This process involves statements like, "If you let me harvest this parcel, I will let you set aside that one for wildlife preservation." The statement is followed by a persuasive argument and group discussion. The dialogue is far from a mathematical optimization, but often closer to an effective solution. It uses the information system to focus discussion away from broad philosophical positions to a specific project area and its unique distribution of conditions and potential uses.

CONCLUSION

Planning and management have always required information as the cornerstone. Early geographic information systems relied on physical data storage and manual processing. With the advent of the computer, most of these data and procedures have been automated during the past two decades. Concurrently, the focus of these systems have extended from descriptive (inventory) to prescriptive (analysis) applications. As a result, resource information processing has increasingly become more quantitative. Systems analysis techniques developed links between descriptive data of the forest landscape to the mix of management actions which maximizes a set of objectives. This mathematical approach to resource management has been both stimulated and facilitated by modern information systems technology. The digital nature of mapped data in these systems provide a wealth of new analysis operations and a comprehensive ability to spatially model complex resource issues. The full impact of the new data form and analytical capabilities is yet to be determined. Resource professionals are challenged to understand this new environment and formulate new applications. It is clear that geographic information systems have, and will continue, to revolutionize the resource decision-making environment.

References

Agee, J.K., S.C.F. Stit, M. Nyquist, and R. Root. 1989. A Geographic Analysis of Historical Grizzly Bear Sightings in the North Cascades. Photogrammetric Engineering and Remote Sensing 55(11):1637-1642.

Baskent, E.Z. and Jordan, G.A. 1991. Spatial Wood Supply Simulation Modelling. For. Chron. 67(6):610-621.

Berry, Joseph K. 1993. Beyond Mapping: Concepts, Algorithms and Issues in GIS. Fort Collins, Colorado: GIS World Publishers.

Berry, Joseph K. 1991. "GIS in Island Resources Planning: a Case Study in Map Analysis," in Geographical Information Systems. D. Maguire, et. al. (eds.) New York: John Wiley, Chapter 55.

Brinker, Richard W., Ben D. Jackson. 1991. Using a Geographic Information System to Study a Regional Wood Procurement Problem. Forest Science. Vol. 37. No. 6. pp. 1614-1631.

Brown, L. A. 1949. The Story of Maps. Boston: Little, Brown and Company.

Congalton, R.G., K. Green, and J. Teply. 1993. Mapping Old Growth Forests on National Forest and Park Lands in the Pacific Northwest from Remotely Sensed Data. Photogrammetric Engineering and Remote Sensing 59(4):529-535.

Cressie, N. 1991. Statistics for Spatial Data. New York: Wiley & Sons.

Cuff, D. J. and M. T. Matson. 1982. Thematic Maps. New York: Methuen.

Davis, F.W. and S. Goetz. 1990. Modelling Vegetation Patterns Using Digital Terrain Data. Landscape Ecology 4(1):69-80.

Davis, John C. 1973. Statistics and Data Analysis in Geology. New York: Wiley & Sons.

Hamilton, M.P., L.A. Salazar, and K.E. Palmer. 1989. Geographic Information Systems: Providing Information for Wildland Fire Planning. Fire Technology 25(1): 5-23.

Heit, M. and A. Shortreid (ed.). 1991. GIS Applications in Natural Resources. GIS World, Fort Collins, Colorado.

Hendler, B. 1973. Subdividing the Wetlands of Maine. Land Use Information Series II. Maine Land Use Regulation Commission, Augusta, Maine. August.

Iverson, R., L. Graham, and A. Cook. 1989. Applications of Satellite Remote Sensing to Forested Ecosystems. Landscape Ecology 3(2):131-143.

Jakubauskas, M.E., P.L. Kamlesh, and P.W. Mausel. 1990. Assessment of Vegetation Change in a Fire Altered Forest Landscape. Photogrammetric Engineering and Remote Sensing 56(3):371-377.

Jameson, D.A. 1993. Forest and Forestry. *In* McGraw-Hill Yearbook of Science and Technology. McGraw-Hill Inc., New York, New York. pp. 150-151.

Johnson, Lucinda B. 1990. Analyzing Spatial and Temporal Phenomena Using Geographical Information Systems: A Review of Ecological Applications. Landscape Ecology Vol. 4. No. 1. pp. 31-43.

Johnston, Carol A. and Robert J. Naiman. 1990. The Use of a Geographic Information System to Analyze Long-term Landscape Alteration by Beaver. Landscape Ecology 4(1): 5-19.

Lachowski, Henry, Paul Maus, and Bruce Platt. 1992. Integrating Remote Sensing with GIS: Procedures and Examples from the Forest Service. Journal of Forestry 90(12): 16-21.

Maclean, Ann L., David D. Reed, Glenn D. Mroz, Gary W. Lyon, Thomas Edison. 1992. Using GIS to Estimate Forest Resource Changes: A Case Study in Northern Michigan. Journal of Forestry. Vol. 90. No. 12. pp. 22-26.

Maguire, D.J., M.F. Goodchild, and D.W. Rhind (eds.). 1991. Geographical Information Systems: Principles and Applications. John Wiley and Sons, New York, New York.

McHarge, I. L. 1969. Design with Nature. Garden City: Doubleday/Natural History Press.

Muehrcke, P. C. and J. O. Muehrcke. 1980. Map Use: Reading, Analysis and Interpretation. J. P. Publications, Madison, Wisconsin. pp. 192-250.

Pastor, John, Michael Broshart. 1990. The Spatial Pattern of a Northern Conifer-Hardwood Landscape. Landscape Ecology. Vol. 4. No. 1. pp. 55-68.

Pereira, Jose M.C., Robert M. Itami. 1991. GIS-Based Habitat Modeling Using Logistic Multiple Regression: A Study of the Mt. Graham Red Squirrel. Photogrammetric Engineering & Remote Sensing. Vol. 57. No. 11. pp. 1475-1486.

Ripley, Brian D. 1981. Spatial Statistics. Wiley & Sons, New York.

Ripple, William J., (ed.). 1987. Geographic Information Systems for Resource Management: A Compendium. American Society of Photogrammetry and Remote Sensing. Bethesda, Maryland.

Ripple, W.J. (ed.). 1989. Fundamentals of Geographic Information Systems: A Compendium. American Society for Photogrammetry and Remote Sensing, Bethesda, Maryland.

Ripple, W.J., G.A. Bradshaw, and T.A. Spies. 1991. Measuring Forest Landscape Patterns in the Cascade Range of Oregon. Biological Conservation 57(1):73-88.

Robertson, A., R. Sale and J. Morrison. 1978. Elements of Cartography. New York: John Wiley and Sons, 4th edition.

Shelton, R. L. and J. E. Estes. 1981. Remote Sensing and Geographic Information Systems: An Unrealized Potential. Geo-Processing 1(4): 395-420.

SIS, Inc. 1993. pMAP User's Manual. Spatial Information Systems. Springfield, Virginia. 2nd edition.

Steiitz, C. F., P. Parker and L. Jordan. 1976. Hand-Drawn Overlays: Their History and Perspective Uses. Landscape Architecture 66: 444-455.

Susilawati, S. and J.C. Weir. 1990. GIS Applications in Forest Land Management in Indonesia. ITC Journal 3:236-244.

Tomlin, C. Dana. 1990. Geographic Information Systems and Cartographic Modeling. Prentice Hall: Englewood Cliffs, New Jersey.

Trotter, Craig M. 1991. Remotely-sensed Data as an Information Source for Geographical Information Systems in Natural Resource Management: A Review. Int. J. Geographical Information Systems 5(2):225-239.

Zack, J.A. and R.A. Minnich. 1991. Integration of GIS with a Diagnostic Wind Field Model for Fire Management. Forest Science 37(2):560-573.

Where is the technology leading us?

by Jack Dangermond

Abstract

With GIS technology now about 25 years old, it is appropriate to consider where GIS use may be leading us, with special reference to natural resource management uses and considering forest management in particular. After beginning with a consideration of where GIS technology is going, and with mention of several important related technologies, the paper considers the range of problems and of possible immediate futures for natural resource management generally, and for forest management in particular. The role of GIS in natural resource management is taken up next. Some comments on who determines where GIS technology will go in the future are offered. The paper concludes with a consideration of where GIS technology may lead natural resource management in the next decade and just after the turn of the century.

Résumé

Compte tenu que la technologie des systèmes informatisées de références spatiales existe depuis 25 ans, il est approprié de considérer où peuvent nous mener les SIRS, tout spécialement dans le domaine de la gestion des ressources naturelles et en particulier selon l'aspect de l'aménagement forestier. Après avoir étudier en premier lieu où se dirige la technologie SIRS, tout en mentionnant quelques-unes des plus importantes technologies qui s'y rattachent, cet exposé considère l'étendue des problèmes ainsi que les possibilités immédiates dans le cas de la gestion des ressources naturelles en général, et de l'aménagement forestier en particulier. Le rôle du SIRS dans la gestion des ressources naturelles est étudié par la suite. Quelques commentaires se rapportant à qui détermine où l'application de la technologie SIRS sera utilisée dans l'avenir, sont présentés. Cet exposé se termine sur l'évaluation de la direction que pourrait prendre la technologie SIRS dans la gestion des ressources naturelles au cours de la prochaine décennie et tout juste au début du prochain siècle.

Introduction

The first uses of automated means for processing geographically referenced data occurred about 25 years ago.

With the extremely rapid recent growth in the use of this technology in many fields, including forestry and natural resource management, it is appropriate to consider the implications of its use, and in particular, where the technology may be leading its users in the foreseeable future, perhaps ten years from now, and beyond.

This paper considers the future of the technology itself, of GIS applications to natural resource management, and of forest management as an example of a particular area of natural resource management which uses GIS extensively.

Where GIS Technology is Going

The most important fact to bear in mind about GIS and related technologies is the rapid growth which is occurring in their use. It is likely that by about the year 2000 there will be a million users of GIS technology. This assumes annual growth rates of between 25 and 40 per cent; the field has been experiencing such rates for a number of years.

The continuing rapid developments in processing speed, storage density, wide-band communications technology and other areas of hardware technology guarantee that the costs to acquire GIS capabilities will continue to fall and system performance will continue to rise.

GIS technology provides the means for integrating many kinds of spatial data, either through conversion, capture from existing hardcopy products, or referencing other kinds of data to a map. These sorts of integration capabilities will increase and GISs will be able to bring together increasingly diverse kinds of spatially referenced data from an ever wider variety of source media.

Environmental Systems Research Institute, 380 New York Street, Redlands, California 92373.
This paper was originally published in the proceedings of GIS '91 Symposium.

GIS technology will also continue to grow easier to learn and to use because additional efforts and computer power will be devoted to the user interface and to making all kinds of GIS functions easier to do.

Actual testing and the growing acceptance of GIS technology both indicate that GIS technology is becoming more reliable and more cost effective. As a result, governments and large corporations are investing heavily in acquiring the technology. Once acquired, the use of the technology usually expands, sometimes very rapidly.

With gradual improvements occurring in scanning and related technologies, and greater understanding of how to automate previously existing data, larger investments are being made in the creation of digital databases for GIS use. This makes further investments ever easier to justify, so that rapid increases in the size and number of digital databases can be expected in the years just ahead, as international events and budgets permit.

In the years just ahead, global GIS databases of various kinds are going to become available, probably in a few years on global networks.

If numbers of students are considered, training programs in GIS technology are growing even more rapidly than the field itself. This means that there will be many more people, with at least basic knowledge of GIS, available for employment in the next few years than has been the case in the past. Related to this growth is an equally rapid growth in the technical literature in the field, with many new publications now occurring in book form and many new introductory and intermediate level textbooks just now becoming available.

As the number of people in the GIS field increases, the number of firms offering specialized consulting, contract programming, analysis, data capture, rent-a-tech, and other GIS services will continue to expand.

All of these developments are producing a rising interest in GIS technology and increased optimism about what it may be capable of doing for its users.

Related Technologies

It is also important to recognize that GIS technology is closely allied with various other technologies, such as remote sensing and other data capture technologies, communications, image processing, and the like. So if we are trying to see where the technology is leading us, we also have to take these other technologies into account.

Because most of these technologies are considerably more mature than is GIS, less profound short term change is likely to occur in them, but as they advance, so too, will GIS and some important developments in these related areas can be anticipated in the middle and longer term.

Where Natural Resource Management May be Going

It is not this author's aim or function to predict the future of natural resource management generally or of forest management in particular. Such an effort is obviously outside of his competence. But in order to indicate where GIS technology may be leading users in the natural resource management fields, it's necessary to speculate about the possible range of developments in these fields and how GIS-technology may relate to them.

Forests present, in some ways, a critical, even a paradoxical case of natural resource management efforts because they are simultaneously one of the most carefully conserved of natural resources as well as one of the most extensively used as a source of goods for sale.

Forest management is especially important because forests, unlike some other natural resources, are a potentially renewable resource. But forest management policies and practices which a few decades ago were generally well accepted are becoming controversial today.

As a result, forests, which a few decades ago represented an almost idyllic remoteness in the minds of most people around the world, are now becoming frontlines in economic, international trade, environmental, political and other types of controversies.

The interrelations between forests and such global issues as loss of habitat and species diversity, acid precipitation, and possible global warming through rising levels of carbon dioxide, are drawing increased attention to the importance of the world's forests. Managed as wilderness, recreational resources, resorts, watersheds, preserves, parks, greenbelts, shelter belts, or for related kinds of purposes, forests are attracting the attention of rapidly growing numbers of people around the world. Managed for sawn timber, a growing variety of forest products, paper products, fuel wood, or other commercial purposes, forests continue to engage the attention of most national and sub-national governments and many organizations in industry and commerce.

International commerce in timber, forest products and paper is, if anything, more important and more complex today than previously, while international efforts to preserve rainforests, old growth and ancient forests are growing in intensity.

In many less developed countries forests represent, often simultaneously, the chief source of fuel, a major national resource, a major export, and a major impediment to the expansion of agriculture. The removal of forests often leads to rapid loss of soil fertility, to rapid erosion, to desertification, and ultimately, to worsened human habitability and a lessened chance of human survival.

It is inevitable that in such a setting, forest management policies and practices in all parts of the world are coming under intense scrutiny.

When other kinds of natural resources are considered, such as minerals, rangeland, water, and so on, the associated problems faced by natural resource policy makers, decision makers and managers grow proportionately more diverse. Depletion rates, pollution, rehabilitation, and other issues not common in forest management come to the forefront.

In sum, the problems faced by natural resource managers at the present time are complex and difficult and becoming more so with each passing year.

Perhaps this is because we are recognizing that natural resources are finite and we are moved to do something more to preserve them; perhaps it is because we have better information about natural resources and a clearer scientific understanding of the processes which create and sustain them; perhaps it is the times we live in. Whatever the reason, the trend is clear: faced with increasingly difficult situations, policy makers, decision makers and managers are looking for tools to assist them, and they are turning to GIS technology with that in mind.

Role of GIS in Natural Resource Management

GIS technology has been associated with the mapping and management of natural resources, including forests, from the inception of its use some twenty-five years ago. Canada was one of the first countries in the world to make use of a large GIS for natural resource management as well as other purposes.

The uses to which GIS technology has been put in managing natural resources are well illustrated by some of the uses it has in forest management and forestry.

GIS continues to be used for simply automating the making of forest maps (automated cartography). At the present time, it can be truly said that GIS techniques produce maps which are equal to or superior to those produced by manual means. The evidence for this is the number of governmental and commercial cartographic organizations which are going over to GIS approaches to map production.

In importance just behind the production of conventional kinds of maps is the production of various kinds of thematic maps in an attempt to clarify users' understanding of the natural resources situation with which they must deal. The production of GIS-derived reports and statistics is probably equally important, especially for monitoring and management related purposes.

Many organizations make use of the modeling capabilities of their GIS software to analyze natural resources issues. Beginning with simple models and simulations, these organizations, over time and with the support of basic scientific research and better theoretical understanding, are creating more sophisticated and more reliable models. Some models simply automate the calculation of timber yields, help locate such land uses as haul roads or recreational facilities, help select timber for harvest or conservation, identify sensitive habitat for preservation, or are used to analyze possible alternatives approaches to managing a timber stand or forest. As confidence is gained in these applications, more complex and powerful applications of GIS modeling are likely to follow.

Some of these more complicated modeling efforts are already underway; these attempt to predict where forest fires are likely to start and how they are best suppressed, what the effect of acid precipitation and other environmental insults will be on forests, and how rapidly certain wooded areas will become desert. Aspatial, process models are being combined with GISs to address the critical questions of how economic, meteorologic, hydrologic and other processes interact with geographically disposed natural resources.

Because GIS technology, when combined with Database Management System (DBMS) technology and with various data gathering techniques, makes it much easier to create and maintain comprehensive information about natural resources, many issues, which were not approached systematically in the past because the data were too costly to gather or the analysis too time consuming, are now being addressed explicitly. Instead of having to identify, fund, and staff a special study for each new problem, the existence of GISs makes it much easier to deal with special problems by means of query and reporting efforts not too much different from other kinds of routine management operations.

The combining of GIS technology with expert systems (based on principles of artificial intelligence), the use of Global Positioning System (GPS) technology to enhance data capture for GIS systems, and the use of image processing to provide more rapid updating of GIS databases are all examples of the interaction between GIS technology and other modern technologies with which it is often associated.

What remains to be seen, in this area of GIS application as in all others, is the extent to which GIS technology can do more than just help organize and rationalize policy making, decision making and management, important as that would be if it were accomplished. What remains to be seen, and what is potentially most important about GIS technology, is whether GIS technology can make an important contribution to the solution of the problems which have been sketched out about; in short, whether GIS technology can make a difference in natural resource management, whether that difference is measured by profits, healthier forests, conservation, habitat rehabilitation, or in some other way.

What Determines and Who Decides Where GIS Technology is Going?

A critical question in every applied technology field is "Where is the technology going?" The answer to it should determine the directions in which research and development are to go, it should determine marketing strategies for the future, and it should determine investment policies. A reliable answer to that can be of enormous value. But there are so many uncertainties and so many factors to take into account that any answer to such a question is an educated guess at best, and unforeseen events, from the introduction of a new product to the outbreak of a war, can overturn even the most carefully calculated estimates.

GIS technology is driven as much, or probably more, by user wants as it is by developments in the fundamental underlying technologies. At ESRI, for example, we listen very closely to our users and customers as we lay our development plans each year. So while it seems entirely reasonable to ask a supplier of technology to guess what the users of the technology are going to want at some time in the future,

it is a question which many suppliers would much rather be asking of their customers.

Beyond user needs and user wants, one also must consider what the capabilities and limits of the supporting technologies are or seem to be, what research promises for the future, what new and emerging technologies may offer, what resources can be brought to bear, how fast the field is growing, and myriad other factors.

Two kinds of answers to the question will be given here: a fairly straightforward projection for the middle term, the next 5-10 years, and a vision of the period just after the turn of the century.

Where the Technology May Lead in the Next Decade

While improvements in technology may seem the most important elements of change in GIS technology within the next decade, this is not likely to be so. What is most likely to be important within the next decade is the rapid spread of GIS technology to new users.

At the present time, there are probably fewer than 100 000 users of GIS technology in the entire world; at the end of the decade, there are likely to be a million users. For every organization that has the technology now, ten may have it in the year 2000. The impact of GIS technology will be felt as these organizations move from manual analysis of geographic data to automated analysis. Moreover, these organizations will do so with an enormously richer base of experience than was the case for the earlier users of GIS technology. Really effective GIS technology, incorporating DBMS technology, only became widely available in the mid-1980's, and until the late 1980's, only a handful of organizations used the technology. But in the 1990's there will exist a very large experience base from the thousands of organizations which have been using GIS technology, often for a decade or more.

Data capture techniques will continue to improve slowly and this improvement, coupled with pressures for including more kinds of data and for wider geographic coverage, will fuel the increases in available GIS data resources. All these new users will thus have a much richer store of data available to them as they begin GIS use.

Within the next decade information about natural resources will be increasingly integrated and access to it will continue to move down through every natural resource organization. Organizations which deal with international forest management issues will begin to get access to global databases which contain the kinds of information they need. Commonly used databases will be up to two orders of magnitude larger than they are today and will be readily accessible through networks of varying spatial extent. This will mean that organization-wide, forest-wide, state-wide, nation-wide and applications even larger in scope will be easy enough to do that many will want to make their plans on these scales.

Models will grow in usefulness and become more widely accepted as decision support tools. The number of software organizations providing such models as a product, or performing GIS modeling and analysis for clients, will increase. These models will increasingly incorporate process and temporality as well as spatial data and their attributes.

Finally, practical and useful applications of expert systems, acting with GIS databases, will begin to come into use in natural resource management; at first, these will provide very specialized functions, quite possibly in forestry, but over time, as the expert systems prove their usefulness, their use will inevitably increase and change the way in which some management tasks are approached.

Where the Technology May Lead Us Just After the Turn of the Century

The question of where GIS technology 'is leading us' is not quite the same as 'where is the technology going to go', and the author will take advantage of that difference in this last section.

This section is considerably more speculative than the previous parts of this paper. It may be that neither the author nor those who read this section will live to see the natural resource management environment which it envisions. But one failure of those who predict the future is that they are often too conservative. This section tries to avoid that fault.

Sometime after the turn of the century, manual digitizing will, at last, give way to completely automated means of data capture, and organizations will begin to augment their current digital data with baseline data from much older hardcopy maps. This and other related developments will force much greater emphasis on efforts to standardize and integrate various types of data. Organizations specializing in this area, perhaps working on contracts jointly funded by many organizations, both public and private, are likely to arise as a result. New kinds of GIS workstations will need to be devised to support their efforts.

Remote sensing technology will continue incremental improvements and be coupled with data gathered by the first of a wave of ultraminiature sensing devices which will, later in the century, give rise to the 'instrumented universe': a universe where sensors, based on silicon chips or some related technology, will be broadcast through the natural areas of the world and will telemeter their data, via satellites, to various collection centers around the world.

Global GIS-based models with limited predictive capabilities will be used to provide routine kinds of predictions for limited geographic areas, such as more precise predictions of flooding following local precipitation. Global meteorological and atmospheric models will be more closely integrated with GIS than they are today, though fundamental improvements in our theoretical understanding of this interaction are likely to be further off in time.

Continuing changes in both the kinds of education and training required for natural resource management and the nature of the work itself will be occurring, with even less of managers' time spent in primary data gathering and field work and proportionately more time spent in working with information in various digested forms, especially new and richer GIS graphic forms.

Decision makers and policy makers will begin to have a third generation GIS-based decision support environment available to them. A generation of senior managers which has always known computers will be accustomed to their omnipresence; the simpler, more graphic, more transparent, and considerably more reliable support programs will be much more widely accepted and used. While the paperless office will not have arrived, displays of spatially referenced data will be so easy to create and so fast to produce that the use of ephemeral electronic displays will be routine aids to thinking about every kind of natural resource management problem. True three-dimensional map displays, with 'overflight' and zoom capabilities, with draped information, time sequenced displays, richer displays of thematic data over imagery, and similar kinds of capabilities will be widely available. These will be so effective that managers will have to be continuously conscious of the fact that the displays are not the reality, lest they be misled by their information resources.

Because the ability to transmit enormous amounts of data over long distances will have so markedly improved, much greater integration of international production, marketing, and trade information will be the norm. Correspondingly, more people and more governmental and private organizations will have some real insight into more aspects of the activities of all kinds of both government and private resource management organizations. This will likely sharpen some kinds of conflicts, although greatly increased sharing of data resources may head off other kinds of disagreements and instead favor more rational discussion and debate.

Expert systems and artificial intelligence will be more widely applied, with probably a few really critical successes already indicating that much more radical changes in natural resource management are to come as the century goes on.

On the international scene, in the absence of major wars or unforeseeable political developments, and if funding is wisely provided, there will be much greater sharing of natural resource data throughout the world. In particular, the countries of the former eastern bloc will be working with technological help from the rest of the world to plan the cleanup of the environmental problems which have accumulated there over the last hundred years or so. Their efforts, supported by the technologically advanced countries, will be a model which many less developed countries will find attractive and will attempt to follow. Fortunately, the cost to acquire GIS technology will have continued to fall so rapidly that virtually every natural resource agency which would find GIS useful will be able to afford it.

In the many cases around the world where habitat rehabilitation is needed, and where projects are just beginning, GISs will play an especially important role in informing people of what former habitats were like. They will also be used to estimate the possible success of such projects, to plan them, and then to monitor their success.

Throughout the world, some 50 years after the birth of GIS technology, the technology will be so widely accepted and so commonly used in natural resource management that it will have become, to a considerable extent, not just transparent to its users but, to a considerable extent, invisible to them. And meetings of the kind we are having today will be mostly memories of the past.

Conclusions

This is an exciting time to be working in the GIS field. We are in the rare position of being able to look simultaneously back to the beginning of GIS technology and to look forward to the time when it will be quite mature and used by tens of millions of people throughout the world.

While no one can predict the future, fairly reasonable extrapolations suggest that the use of GIS technology in natural resource management will expand rapidly in the years just ahead and that within two decades, the use of the technology will be a fundamental part of the daily and even hourly work of most natural resource managers throughout the world.

More to the point, there is evidence that GIS use will be helping to solve the real problems such managers face today and are going to face in the future.

Thank you all for allowing those of us who are developing that technology to be a growing part of your own increasingly critical work.

Glossary of GIS Terms

By Bruce L. Kessler

This glossary presents many of the words and phrases that a geographic information system (GIS) user may encounter. Some terms have been simplified to limit the overwhelming feeling that many people get when first presented with a GIS. Also, an effort was made to eliminate bias toward any GIS software package. If there is some residual slant, the author does not intend to imply that one GIS package is better or worse than another. Numbers in parentheses refer to the reference list at the end of the glossary.

Absolute map accuracy

The accuracy of a map in relationship to the earth's geoid. The accuracy of locations on a map that are defined relative to the earth's geoid are considered absolute because their positions are global in nature and accurately fix a location that can be referenced to all other locations on the earth. Contrast absolute map accuracy with relative map accuracy. (3)

Acceptance test

A set of particular activities performed to evaluate a hardware or software system's performance and conformity to specifications.

Accuracy

1. If applied to paper maps or map databases, degree of conformity with a standard or accepted value. Accuracy relates to the quality of a result and is distinguished from precision. (5)
2. If applied to data collection devices such as digitizers, degree of obtaining the correct value.

Address matching

A mechanism for relating two files using address as the key item. Geographic coordinates and attributes subsequently can be transferred from one address to the other. (2)

Algorithm

A step-by-step procedure for solving a mathematical problem. For instance, the conversion of data in one map projection to another map projection requires that the data be processed through an algorithm of precisely defined rules or mathematical equations.

Aliasing

The occurrence of jagged lines on a raster-scan display image when the detail exceeds the resolution on the screen. (1)

American National Standards Institute (ANSI)

An institute that specifies computer system standards. The abbreviation is often used as an adjective to computer systems that conform to these standards.

AM/FM

See automated mapping/facilities management.

Analog map

Any directly viewable map on which graphic symbols portray features and values; contrast with digital map. (4)

Annotation

Text on a drawing or map associated with identifying or explaining graphic entities shown. (5)

Application

A program or specially defined procedure, generally in addition to the standard set of basic software functions supplied by a GIS. Historically, an application was developed by the vendor or by a third party and purchased separately. Developed to perform a series of steps, these applications may create specialized reports or complex map products, or lead an operator through a decision process. Some of the more common applications are now becoming part of the basic software functions.

Arc

See line.

Arc-node structure

The coordinate and topological data structure used by some GISs. Arcs represent lines that can define linear features or the boundary of areas or polygons. In arc-node structures, there is an implied direction to the line so that it may have a left and right side. In this way, the area bounded by the arc can also be described, and it is not necessary to double-store coordinates for arcs that define a boundary between two areas.

Architecture

In computers, the architecture determines how the computer is seen by someone who understands its internal commands and instructions and the design of its interface hardware. (5)

Area

A closed figure (polygon) bounded by one or more lines enclosing a homogeneous area and usually represented only in two dimensions. Examples are states, lakes, census tracts, aquifers, and smoke plumes.

ASCII

American Standard Code for Information Interchange, ASCII is a set of codes for representing alphanumeric information (e.g., a byte with a value of 77 represents a capital M). Text files, such as those created with a computer system's text editor, are often referred to as ASCII files. (2)

Aspect

A position facing a particular direction. Usually referred to in compass directions such as degrees or as cardinal directions.

Attribute

1. A numeric, text, or image data field in a relational database table that describes a spatial feature such as a point, line, node, area, or cell. (2)
2. A characteristic of a geographic feature described by numbers or characters, typically stored in tabular format, and linked to the feature by an identifier. For example, attributes of a well (represented by a point) might include depth, pump type, location, and gallons per minute.

Automated mapping/facilities management (AM/FM)

A GIS technology focused on the specific segment of the market concerned with specialized infrastructure and geographic facility information applications and management, such as roads, pipes, and wires.

Reprinted by permission of the publisher, The Society of American Foresters from *The Journal of Forestry*, December 1992, Vol. 90, No. 11.

Axis
A reference line in a coordinate system. (5)

Band
One layer of a multispectral image representing data values for a specific range of the electromagnetic spectrum of reflected light or heat. Also, other user-specified values derived by manipulation of original image bands. A standard color display of multispectral image displays three bands, one each for red, green, and blue. Satellite imagery such as Landsat TM and SPOT provide multispectral images of the earth, some containing seven or more bands. (2)

Base map
A map showing planimetric, topographic, geological, political, and/or cadastral information that may appear in many different types of maps. The base map information is drawn with other types of changing thematic information. Base map information may be as simple as major political boundaries, major hydrographic data, or major roads. The changing thematic information may be bus routes, population distribution, or caribou migration routes.

Benchmark tests
Various standard tests, easily duplicated, for assisting in measurement of product performance under typical conditions of use. (5)

Binary large object (BLOB)
The data type of a column in a relational database management system (RDBMS) table storing large images or text files as attributes.

Bit
The smallest unit of information that can be stored and processed in a computer. A bit has two possible values, 0 or 1, which can be interpreted as YES/NO, TRUE/FALSE, or ON/OFF. (2)

BLOB
See Binary Large Object.

Boolean expression
1. A type of expression based upon, or reducible to, a true or false condition. A boolean operator is a keyword that specifies how to combine simple logical expressions into complex expressions. Boolean operators negate a predicate (NOT), specify a combination of predicates (AND), or specify a list of alternative predicates (OR). For example, the use of AND in "DEPTH > 100 and GPM > 500."
2. Loosely, but erroneously, used to refer to logical expressions such as "DEPTH greater than 100." (2)

Breakline
A line that defines and controls the surface behavior of a triangulated irregular network (TIN) in terms of smoothness and continuity. Physical examples of breaklines are ridge lines, streams, and lake shorelines.

Buffer
A zone of a given distance around a physical entity such as a point, line, or polygon.

Bundled
Refers to the way software is sold. In the early days of computers, software products were sold integrated with hardware, that is, they were "bundled." See unbundled. (5)

Byte
A group of contiguous bits, usually eight, that is a memory and data storage unit. For example, file sizes are measured in bytes or megabytes (1 million bytes). Bytes contain values of 0 to 255 and are most often used to represent integers or ASCII characters (e.g., a byte with an ASCII value of 77 represents a capital M). A collection of bytes (often 4 or 8 bytes) is used to represent real numbers and integers larger than 255. (2)

CAD
See computer-aided design or drafting.

Cadastre
A record of interests in land, encompassing both the nature and extent of interests. Generally, this means maps and other descriptions of land parcels as well as the identification of who owns certain legal rights to the land (such as ownership, liens, easements, mortgages, and other legal interests). Cadastral information often includes other descriptive information about land parcels. (3)

CAE
See computer-aided engineering.

CAM
See computer-aided mapping.

Cardinal
Refers to one of the four cardinal directions—north, south, east, or west.

Cartesian coordinate system
A concept from French philosopher and mathematician Rene Descartes (1596–1650). A system of two or three mutually perpendicular axes along which any point can be precisely located with reference to any other point; often referred to as x, y, and z coordinates. (5) Relative measures of distance, area, and direction are constant throughout the system.

Cell
The basic element of spatial information in a grid data set. Cells are always square. A group of cells forms a grid.

Centroid
The "center of gravity" or mathematically exact center of a irregular-shaped polygon; often given as an x,y coordinate of a parcel of land. (5)

Chain
See line.

Character
1. A letter, number, or special graphic symbol (*, @, -) treated as a single unit of data.
2. A data type referring to text columns in an attribute table (such as NAME). (2)

Clip
The spatial extraction of physical entities from a GIS file that reside within the boundary of a polygon. The bounding polygon then works much like a cookie cutter.

Cluster
A spatial grouping of geographic entities on a map. When these are clustered on a map, there is usually some phenomenon causing a relationship among them (such as incidents of disease, crime, pollution, etc.).

COGO
See coordinate geometry.

Column
A vertical field in a relational database management system data file. It may store one to many bytes of descriptive information.

Command
An instruction, usually one word or concatenated words or letters, that performs an action using the software. A command may also have extra options or parameters that define more specific applications of the action.

Computer-aided design or drafting (CAD)
A group of computer software packages for creating graphic documents.

Computer-aided engineering (CAE)

The integration of computer graphics with engineering techniques to facilitate and optimize the analysis, design, construction, nondestructive testing, operation, and maintenance of physical systems. (5)

Computer-aided mapping (CAM)

The application of computer technology to automate the map compilation and drafting process. Not to be confused with the older usage, computer-aided manufacturing; usually associated with CAD, as in CAD/CAM. (5)

Configuration

The physical arrangement and connections of a computer and its related peripheral devices. This can also pertain to many computers and peripherals.

Conflation

A set of functions and procedures that aligns the arcs of one GIS file with those of another and then transfers the attributes of one to the other. Alignment precedes the transfer of attributes and is most commonly performed by rubber-sheeting operations. (2)

Conformality

Small areas on a map are represented in their true shape and angles are preserved—a characteristic of a map projection.

Connectivity

1. The ability to find a path or "trace" through a network from a source to a given point. For example, connectivity is necessary to find the path along a network of streets to find the shortest or best route from a fire station to a fire.
2. A topological construct.

Contiguity

The topological identification of adjacent polygons by recording the left and right polygons of each arc.

Continuous data

Usually referenced to grid or raster data representing surface data such as elevation. In this instance, the data can be any value, positive or negative. Sometimes referred to as real data. In contrast, see discrete data.

Contour

A line connecting points of equal value. Often in reference to a horizontal datum such as mean sea level.

Conversion

1. The translation of data from one format to another (e.g., TIGER to DXF; a map to digital files).
2. Data conversion when transferring data from one system to another (e.g., SUN to IBM).
3. See data automation.

Coordinate

The position of a point in space with respect to a Cartesian coordinate system (x, y, and/or z values). In GIS, a coordinate often represents locations on the earth's surface relative to other locations.

Coordinate geometry (COGO)

A computerized surveying-plotting calculation methodology created at MIT in the 1950s. (5)

Coordinate system

The system used to measure horizontal and vertical distances on a planimetric map. In a GIS, it is the system whose units and characteristics are defined by a map projection. A common coordinate system is used to spatially register geographic data for the same area. See map projection.

Coterminous

Having the same or coincident boundaries. Two adjacent polygons are coterminous when they share the same boundary (such as a street centerline dividing two blocks). (3)

Curve fitting

An automated mapping function that converts a series of short, connected straight lines into smooth curves to represent entities that do not have precise mathematical definitions (such as rivers, shorelines, and contour lines). (3)

Dangling arc

An arc having the same polygon on both its left and right sides and having at least one node that does not connect to any other arc. (2)

Data

A general term used to denote any or all facts, numbers, letters, and symbols that refer to or describe an object, idea, condition, situation, or other factors. May be line graphics, imagery, and/or alphanumerics. It connotes basic elements of information that can be processed, stored, or produced by a computer. (5)

Data automation

Generally the same as digitizing, but can also mean using electronic scanning for data collection.

Data dictionary

A coded catalog of all data types, or a list of items giving data names and structures. May be on-line (referred to as an automated data dictionary), in which case the codes for the data types are carried in the database. Also referred to as DD/D for data dictionary/directory. (2)

Data integration

The combination of databases or data files from different functional units of an organization or from different organizations that collect information about the same entities (such as properties, census tracts, street segments). In combining the data, added intelligence is derived.

Data model

1. A generalized, user-defined view of the data related to applications.
2. A formal method for arranging data to mimic the behavior of the real-world entities they represent. Fully developed data models describe data types, integrity rules for the data types, and operations on the data types. Some data models are triangulated irregular networks, images, and georelational or relational models for tabular data. (2)

Database

Usually a computerized file or series of files of information, maps, diagrams, listings, location records, abstracts, or references on a particular subject or subjects organized by data sets and governed by a scheme of organization. "Hierarchical" and "relational" define two popular structural schemes in use in a GIS. (5) For example, a GIS database includes data about the spatial location and shape of geographic entities as well as their attributes.

Database management system (DBMS)

1. The software for managing and manipulating the whole GIS including the graphic and tabular data.
2. Often used to describe the software for managing (e.g., input, verify, store, retrieve, query, and manipulate) the tabular information. Many GISs use a DBMS made by another software vendor, and the GIS interfaces with that software.

Datum

A set of parameters and control points used to accurately define the three-dimensional shape of the earth (e.g., as a spheroid). The corresponding datum is the basis for a planar coordinate system. For example, the North American datum for 1983 (NAD83) is the datum for map

projections and coordinates within the United States and throughout North America.

DBMS
See database management system.

DEM
See digital elevation model.

Densify
A process of adding vertices to arcs at a given distance without altering the arc's shape. See spline for a different method for adding vertices.

Digital
Usually refers to data that is in computer-readable format.

Digital elevation model (DEM)
1. A raster storage method developed by the US Geological Survey (USGS) for elevation data.
2. The format of the USGS elevation data sets.

Digital exchange format (DXF)
1. ASCII text files defined by Autodesk, Inc. (Sausalito, California) at first for CAD, now showing up in third-party GIS software. (5)
2. An intermediate file format for exchanging data from one software package to another, neither of which has a direct translation for the other but where both can read and convert DXF data files into their format. This often saves time and preserves accuracy of the data by not reautomating the original.

Digital line graph (DLG)
1. In reference to data, the geographic and tabular data files obtained from the USGS that may include base categories such as transportation, hydrography, contours, and public land survey boundaries.
2. In reference to data format, the formal standards developed and published by the USGS for exchange of cartographic and associated tabular data files. Many non-DLG data may be formatted in DLG format.

Digital map
A machine-readable representation of a geographic phenomenon stored for display or analysis by a digital computer; contrast with analog map. (4)

Digital terrain model (DTM)
A computer graphics software technique for converting point elevation data into a terrain model displayed as a contour map, sometimes as a three-dimensional "hill and valley" grid view of the ground surface. (5)

Digitize
A means of converting or encoding map data that are represented in analog form into digital information of x and y coordinates.

Digitizer
1. A device used to capture planar coordinate data, usually as x and y coordinates, from existing analog maps for digital use within a computerized program such as a GIS. Also called a digitizing table.
2. A person who digitizes.

DIME
See geographic base file/dual independent map encoding.

Dirichlet tesselation
See Thiessen polygons.

Discrete data
Categorical data such as types of vegetation, or class data such as speed zones. In geographic terms, discrete data can be represented by polygons. Sometimes referred to as integer data. In contrast, see continuous data.

Distributed processing
Where computer resources are dispersed or distributed in one or more locations. The individual computers in a distributed processing environment can be linked by a communications network to each other and/or to a host or supervisory computer.

DLG
See digital line graph.

Dots per inch (DPI)
Often referred to in printing/plotting processes, it relates to how sharply an image may be represented. More dots per inch implies that edges of images will be more precisely represented.

Double-precision
Refers to a level of coordinate accuracy based on the possible number of significant digits that can be stored for each coordinate. Whereas single-precision coverages can store up to 7 significant digits for each coordinate and thus retain a precision of 1 meter in an extent of 1,000,000 meters, double-precision coverages can store up to 15 significant digits per coordinate (typically 13–14 significant digits) and therefore retain the accuracy of much less than 1 meter at a global extent. (2)

DPI
See dots per inch.

DTM
See digital terrain model.

DXF
See digital exchange format.

Eastings
The x-coordinates in a plane-coordinate system; see northings.

Edge match
An editing procedure to ensure that all features crossing adjacent map sheets have the same edge locations, attribute descriptions, and feature classes.

Feature
A representation of a geographic entity, such as a point, line, or polygon.

File
A single set of related information in a computer that can be accessed by a unique name (e.g., a text file created with a text editor, a data file, a DLG file). Files are the logical units managed on disk by the computer's operating system. Files may be stored on tapes or disks. (2)

Flat file
A structure for storing data in a computer system in which each record in the file has the same data items, or fields. Usually, one field is designated as a "key" that is used by computer programs for locating a particular record or set of records or for sorting the entire file in a particular order. (3)

Font
A logical set of related patterns representing text characters or point symbology (e.g., A,B,C). A font pattern is the basic building block for markers and text symbols. (2)

Foreign key
In relational database management system terms, the item or column of data that is used to relate one file to another.

Format
1. The pattern in which data are systematically arranged for use on a computer.
2. A file format is the specific design of how information is organized in the file. For example, DLG, DEM, and TIGER are geographic data

sets in particular formats that are available for many parts of the United States.

Fourier analysis
A method of dissociating time series or spatial data into sets of sine and cosine waves. (1)

Fractal
An object having a fractional dimension; one that has variation that is self-similar at all scales, in which the final level of detail is never reached and never can be reached by increasing the scale at which observations are made. (1)

Gap
The distance between two objects that should be connected. Often occurs during the digitizing process or in the edge-matching process.

GBF/DIME
See geographic base file/dual independent map encoding.

Generalize
1. Reduce the number of points, or vertices, used to represent a line.
2. Increase the cell size and resample data in a raster format GIS.

Geocode
The process of identifying a location as one or more x,y coordinates from another location description such as an address. For example, an address for a student can be matched against a TIGER street network to locate the student's home. (2)

Geographic base file/dual independent map encoding (GBF/DIME)
A data exchange format developed by the US Census Bureau to convey information about block-face/street address ranges related to 1980 census tracts. These files provide a schematic map of a city's streets, address ranges, and geostatistical codes relating to the Census Bureau's tabular statistical data. See also TIGER, created for the 1990 census.

Geographic data
The composite locations and descriptions of geographic entities.

Geographic database
Efficiently stored and organized spatial data and possibly related descriptive data.

Geographic information retrieval and analysis (GIRAS)
Data files from the US Geological Survey. GIRAS files contain information for areas in the continental United States, including attributes for land use, land cover, political units, hydrologic units, census and county subdivisions, federal landownership, and state landownership. These data sets are available to the public in both analog and digital form.

Geographic information system (GIS)
An organized collection of computer hardware, software, geographic data, and personnel designed to efficiently capture, store, update, manipulate, analyze, and display all forms of geographically referenced information. Certain complex spatial operations are possible with a GIS that would be very difficult, time-consuming, or impractical otherwise. (2)

Geographic object
A user-defined geographic phenomenon that can be modeled or represented using geographic data sets. Examples include streets, sewer lines, manhole covers, accidents, lot lines, and parcels. (2)

Geographical Resource Analysis Support System (GRASS)
1. A public-domain raster GIS modeling product of the US Army Corps of Engineers Construction Engineering Research Laboratory.
2. A raster data format that can be used as an exchange format between two GISs.

Georeference
To establish the relationship between page coordinates on a paper map or manuscript and known real-world coordinates. (2)

GIRAS
See geographic information retrieval and analysis.

Graduated circle
A circular symbol whose area, or some other dimension, represents a quantity.

Graphical user interface (GUI)
A graphical method used to control how a user interacts with a computer to perform various tasks. Instead of issuing commands at a prompt, the user is presented with a "dashboard" of graphical buttons and other functions in the form of icons and objects on the display screen. The user interacts with the system using a mouse to point-and-click. For example, press an icon button and the function is performed. Other GUI tools are more dynamic and involve things like moving an object on the screen, which invokes a function; for example, a slider bar is moved back and forth to determine a value associated with a parameter of a particular operation (e.g., setting the scale of a map). (2)

GRASS
See Geographical Resource Analysis Support System.

Graticule
A grid of parallels and meridians on a map. (4)

Grid data
1. One of many data structures commonly used to represent geographic entities. A raster-based data structure composed of square cells of equal size arranged in columns and rows. The value of each cell, or group of cells, represents the entity value.
2. A set of regularly spaced reference lines on the earth's surface, a display screen, a map, or any other object.
3. A distribution system for electricity and telephones.

GUI
See graphical user interface.

Hardware
Components of a computer system, such as the CPU, terminals, plotters, digitizers, printers.

Hierarchical
This type of data storage refers to data linked together in a tree-like fashion, similar to the concept of family lines, where data relations can be traced through particular arms of the hierarchy. Knowledge about these data is dependent on the data structure.

Hierarchy
Refers to information that has order and priority.

IGES
See initial graphics exchange specification.

Image
A graphic representation or description of an object that is typically produced by an optical or electronic device. Common examples include remotely sensed data such as satellite data, scanned data, and photographs. An image is stored as a raster data set of binary or integer values representing the intensity of reflected light, heat, or another range of values on the electromagnetic spectrum. Remotely sensed images are digital representations of the earth. (2)

Impedance
The amount of resistance (or cost) required to traverse through a portion of a network such as a line, or through one cell in a grid system. Resis-

tance may be any number of factors defined by the user such as travel distance, time, speed of travel times the length, slope, or cost.

Index
A specialized lookup table or structure within a database and used by an RDBMS or GIS to speed searches for tabular or geographic data.

Infrastructure
The fabric of human improvements to natural settings that permits a community, neighborhood, town, city, metropolis, region, state, etc., to function.

Initial graphics exchange specification (IGES)
An interim standard format for exchanging graphics data among computer systems. (1)

Integer
A number without a decimal. Integer values can be less than, equal to, or greater than zero.

Integrated terrain unit mapping (ITUM)
The process of adjusting terrain unit boundaries so that there is increased coincidence between the boundaries of interdependent terrain variables such as hydrography, geology, physiography, soils, and vegetation units. Often, when this is performed, one layer or unit of geographical/descriptive information will contain more than one central theme.

Intelligent infrastructure
The result of automating infrastructure information management using modern computer image and graphics technology integrated with advanced database management systems; used for spatially linked and networked facilities and land records systems. In addition, intelligent infrastructure systems manage work processes that deal with design, construction, operation, and maintenance of infrastructure elements. (5)

Item
A field or column of information within an RDBMS.

ITUM
See integrated terrain unit mapping.

Jaggies
A jargon term for curved lines that have a stepped or saw-tooth appearance on a display device. (1)

Join
To connect two or more separate geographic data sets.

Key
An item or column within an RDBMS that contains a unique value for each record in the database.

Kriging
An interpolation technique based on the premise that spatial variation continues with the same pattern.

LAN
See local area network.

Layer
A logical set of thematic data, usually organized by subject matter.

Library
A collection of repeatedly used items such as a symbol library—often-used graphic objects shown on a map—or often-used program subroutines. (5)

Line
1. A set of ordered coordinates that represents the shape of a geographic entity too narrow to be displayed as an area (e.g., contours, street centerlines, and streams). A line begins and ends with a node.
2. A line on a map (e.g., a neatline).

Local area network (LAN)
Computer data communications technology that connects computers at the same site. Computers and terminals on a LAN can freely share data and peripheral devices, such as printers and plotters. LANs are composed of cabling and special data communications hardware and software. (2)

Macro
A set of instructions used by a computer program or programs. Macros are usually stored in a text file and invoked from a program that reads the text files as if the commands were typed interactively.

Many-to-one relate
A relate in which many records can be related to a single record. A typical goal in relational database design is to use many-to-one relates to reduce data storage and redundancy. (2)

Map projection
A mathematical model for converting locations on the earth's surface from spherical to planar coordinates, allowing flat maps to depict three-dimensional features. Some map projections preserve the integrity of shape; others preserve accuracy of area, distance, or direction. (2)

Map units
The coordinate units in which the geographic data are stored, such as inches, feet, or meters or degrees, minutes, and seconds.

Meridian
A line running vertically from the north pole to the south pole along which all locations have the same longitude. The prime meridian (0°) runs through Greenwich, England. Moving left or right of the prime meridian, measures of longitude are negative to the west and positive to the east up to 180° halfway around the globe. (2)

Metropolitan statistical area (MSA)
A single county or group of contiguous counties that defines a metropolitan region, usually with a central city with at least 50,000 inhabitants; in the past these have been called standard metropolitan statistical areas (SMSA) and standard metropolitan areas (SMA); the precise definitions and changes therein are established by the US Office of Management and Budget. (4)

Minimum bounding rectangle
The rectangle defined by the map extent of a geographic data set and specified by two coordinates: xmin,ymin and xmax,ymax. (2)

Minor civil division (MCD)
The primary political or administrative subdivision of a county. (4)

Model
1. An abstraction of reality. Models can include a combination of logical expressions, mathematical equations, and criteria that are applied for the purpose of simulating a process, predicting an outcome, or characterizing a phenomenon. The terms modeling and analysis are often used interchangeably, although the former is more limited in scope.
2. Data representation of reality (e.g., spatial data models include the arc-node, georelational model, rasters or grids, and TINs).

Neatline
A border line commonly drawn around the extent of a map to enclose the map, legend, scale, title, and other information, keeping all the information pertaining to that map in one "neat" box.

Network
1. A system of interconnected elements through which resources can be passed or transmitted—for example, a street network with cars as the

resource, or electric network with power as the resource.

2. In computer operations, the means by which computers connect and communicate with each other or with peripherals.

Network analysis
The technique utilized in calculating and determining relationships and locations arranged in networks, such as in transportation, water, and electrical distribution facilities. (5)

Node
1. The beginning or ending location of a line.
2. The location where lines connect.
3. In graph theory, the location at which three or more lines connect.
4. In computers, the point at which one computer attaches to a communication network.

Northings
The y-coordinates in a plane-coordinate system; see eastings. (4)

Operating system (OS)
Computer software designed to allow communication between the computer and the user. For larger computers, it is usually supplied by the manufacturer. The operating system controls the flow of data, the interpretation of other programs, the organization and management of files, and the display of information. Commonly known operating systems are VMS, VM/IS, UNIX, DOS, and OS/2.

Output
The results of processing data.

Overshoot
That portion of a line digitized past its intersection with another line. Sometimes referred to as a dangling line.

Pan
To move the spatial view of data to a different view without changing the scale.

Parallel
1. A property of two or more lines that are separated at all points by the same distance.
2. A horizontal line encircling the earth at a constant latitude. The equator is a parallel whose latitude is 0°. Measures of latitude are positive up to 90° above the equator and negative below. (2)

Pathname
The direction(s) to a file or directory location on a disk. Pathnames are always specific to the computer operating system. Computer operating systems use directories and files to organize data. Directories are organized in a tree structure; each branch on the tree represents a subdirectory or file. Pathnames indicate locations in this hierarchy. (2)

Peripheral
A component such as a digitizer, plotter, or printer that is not part of the central computer but is attached through communication cables.

Pixel
One picture element of a uniform raster or grid file. Often used synonymously with cell.

Plane-coordinate system
A system for determining location in which two groups of straight lines intersect at right angles and have as a point of origin a selected perpendicular intersection. (4)

Planimetric map
A large-scale map with all features projected perpendicularly onto a horizontal datum plane so that horizontal distances can be measured on the map with accuracy. (4)

PLSS
See public land survey system.

Point
1. A single x,y coordinate that represents a geographic feature too small to be displayed as a line or area—for example, the location of a mountain peak or a building location on a small-scale map. (2)
2. Some GIS systems also use a point to identify the interior of a polygon.

Polygon
A vector representation of an enclosed region, described by a sequential list of vertices or mathematical functions.

Precision
1. If applied to paper maps or map databases, it means exactness and accuracy of definition and correctness of arrangement. (5)
2. If applied to data collection devices such as digitizers, it is the exactness of the determined value (i.e., the number 134.98988 is more precise than the number 134.9).
3. The number of significant digits used to store numbers.

Primary key
The central item or column within an RDBMS that contains a unique value for each record in the database, such as the unique number assigned to each parcel within a county.

Projection
See map projection.

Public land survey system (PLSS)
A rectangular survey system that utilizes 6-mile-square townships as its basic survey unit. The location of townships is controlled by baselines and meridians running parallel to latitude and longitude lines. Townships are defined by range lines running parallel (north-south) to meridians and township lines running parallel (east-west) to baselines. The PLSS was established in the United States by the Land Ordinance of 1785. (3)

Quadrangle
A four-sided region, usually bounded by a pair of meridians and a pair of parallels. (4)

Quadtree
A spatial index that breaks a spatial dataset into homogeneous cells of regularly decreasing size. Each decrement in size is 1/4th the area of the previous cell. The quadtree segmentation process continues until the entire map is partitioned. Quadtrees are often used for storing raster data.

Raster data
Machine-readable data that represent values usually stored for maps or images and organized sequentially by rows and columns. Each "cell" must be rectangular but not necessarily square, as with grid data.

RDBMS
See relational database management system.

Record
In an attribute table, a single "row" of thematic descriptors.

Rectify
The process by which an image or grid is converted from image coordinates to real-world coordinates. Rectification typically involves rotation and scaling of grid cells, and thus requires resampling of values. (2)

Relate
An operation establishing a connection between corresponding records in two tables using an item common to both. Each record in one table is connected to one or more records in the other table that share the same value for a common item.

Relational database management system (RDBMS)

A database management system with the ability to access data organized in tabular files that may be related together by a common field (item). An RDBMS has the capability to recombine the data items from different files, thus providing powerful tools for data usage. (2)

Relational join

The process of connecting two tables of descriptive data by relating them by a key item, then merging the corresponding data. The common key item is not duplicated in this process.

Resolution

1. The accuracy at which the location and shape of map features can be depicted for a given map scale. For example, at a map scale of 1:63,360 (1 inch = 1 mile), it is difficult to represent areas smaller than 1/10 of a mile wide or 1/10 of a mile in length because they are only 1/10-inch wide or long on the map. In a larger scale map, there is less reduction, so feature resolution more closely matches real-world features. As map scale decreases, resolution also diminishes because feature boundaries must be smoothed, simplified, or not shown at all.
2. The size of the smallest feature that can be represented in a surface.
3. The number of points in x and y in a grid (e.g., the resolution of a USGS one-degree DEM is 1,201 x 1,201 mesh points). (2)

Route

A process that establishes connections through a network or grid from a source to a destination. A network example would be to establish a route through a network of streets from a fire station to the fire. A grid example would be to move soil particles from a ridgetop to a stream based on equations developed by soil scientists. The determination of these routes usually take into consideration impedances.

Row

1. A record in an attribute table.
2. A horizontal group of cells in a grid or pixels in an image.

Rubber-sheet

A procedure to adjust the entities of a geographic data set in a non-uniform manner. From- and to-coordinates are used to define the adjustment.

Scale

The relationship between a distance on a map and the corresponding distance on the earth. Often used in the form 1:24,000, which means that one unit of measurement on the map equals 24,000 of the same units on the earth's surface.

Scanning

Also referred to as automated digitizing or scan digitizing. A process by which information originally in hard copy format (paper print, mylar transparencies, microfilm aperture cards) can be rapidly converted to digital raster form (pixels) using optical readers. (5)

Single-precision

A lower level of coordinate accuracy based on the possible number of significant digits that can be stored for each coordinate. Single-precision numbers can store up to seven significant digits for each coordinate and thus retain a precision of five meters in an extent of 1,000,000 meters. Double-precision numbers can store up to 15 significant digits (typically 13–14 significant digits) and therefore retain the accuracy of much less than one meter at a global extent. (2)

Sliver polygon

A relatively narrow feature commonly occurring along the borders of polygons following the overlay of two or more geographic data sets. Also occurs along map borders when two maps are joined, as a result of inaccuracies of the coordinates in either or both maps.

Smooth

A process to generalize data and remove smaller variations.

Software

A program that provides the instructions necessary for the hardware to operate correctly and to perform the desired functions. Some kinds of software are operating system, utility, and applications. (5)

Soundex

A phonetic spelling (up to six characters) of a street name, used for address matching. Each of the 26 letters in the English alphabet is replaced with a letter in the soundex equivalent:

English: A B C D E F G H I J K L M N O P Q R S T U V W X Y Z
Soundex: A B C D A B C H A C C L M M A B C R C D A B W C A C

Where possible, geocoding uses a soundex equivalent of street names for faster processing. During geocoding, initial candidate street names are found using soundex, then real names are compared and verified. (2)

Spatial index

A means of accelerating the drawing, spatial selection, and entity identification by generating geographic-based indexes. Usually based on an internal sequential numbering system.

Spatial model

Analytical procedures applied with a GIS. There are three categories of spatial modeling functions that can be applied to geographic data objects within a GIS: (1) geometric models (such as calculation of Euclidian distance between objects, buffer generation, area, and perimeter calculation); (2) coincidence models (such as polygon overlay); and (3) adjacency models (pathfinding, redistricting, and allocation). All three model categories support operations on geographic data objects such as points, lines, polygons, TINs, and grids. Functions are organized in a sequence of steps to derive the desired information for analysis. (2)

Spike

1. An overshoot line created erroneously by a scanner and its raster software.
2. An anomalous data point that protrudes above or below an interpolated surface representing the distribution of the value of an attribute over an area. (2)

Spline

A method to mathematically smooth spatial variation by adding vertices along a line. See densify for a slightly different method for adding vertices.

SQL

See structured query language.

String

See line.

Structured query language (SQL)

A syntax for defining and manipulating data from a relational database. Developed by IBM in the 1970s, it has since become an industry standard for query languages in most RDBMSs. (2)

Surface

A representation of geographic information as a set of continuous data in which the map features are not spatially discrete; that is, there is an infinite set of values between any two locations. There are no clear or well-defined breaks between possible values of the geographic feature. Surfaces can be represented by models built from regularly or irregularly spaced sample points on the surface. (2)

Surface model

Digital abstraction or approximation of a surface. Because a surface contains an infinite number of points, some subset of points must be used to represent the surface. Each model contains a formalized data

structure, rules, and x,y,z point measurements that can be used to represent a surface. (2)

Syntax
A set of rules governing the way statements can be used in a computer language. (1)

Table
1. Usually referred to as a relational table. The data file in which the relational data reside.
2. A file that contains ASCII or other data.

Template
1. A geographic data set containing boundaries, such as land-water boundaries, for use as a starting place in automating other geographic data sets. Templates save time and increase the precision of spatial overlays.
2. A map containing neatlines, north arrow, logos, and similar map elements for a common map series, but lacking the central information that makes one map unique from another.
3. An empty tabular data file containing only item definitions.

Thematic map
A map that illustrates one subject or topic either quantitatively or qualitatively. (4)

Theme
A collection of logically organized geographic objects defined by the user. Examples include streets, wells, soils, and streams.

Thiessen polygons
Polygons whose boundaries define the area that is closest to each point relative to all other points. Thiessen polygons are generated from a set of points. They are mathematically defined by the perpendicular bisectors of the lines between all points. A triangulated irregular network structure is used to create Thiessen polygons. (2)

TIGER
See Topologically Integrated Geographic Encoding and Referencing data.

Tile
A part of the database in a GIS representing a discrete part of the earth's surface. By splitting a study area into tiles, considerable savings in access times and improvements in system performance can be achieved. (1)

TIN
See triangulated irregular network.

Topographic map
A map of land-source features including drainage lines, roads, landmarks, and usually relief, or elevation. (4)

Topologically Integrated Geographic Encoding and Referencing data (TIGER)
A format used by the US Census Bureau to support census programs and surveys. It is being used for the 1990 census. TIGER files contain street address ranges along lines and census tract/block boundaries. These descriptive data can be used to associate address information and census/demographic data to coverage features. (2)

Topology
The spatial relationships between connecting or adjacent coverage features (e.g., arcs, nodes, polygons, and points). For example, the topology of an arc includes its from- and to-nodes and its left and right polygons. Topological relationships are built from simple elements into complex elements: points (simplest elements), arcs (sets of connected points), areas (sets of connected arcs), and routes (sets of sections that are arcs or portions of arcs). Redundant data (coordinates) are eliminated because an arc may represent a linear feature, part of the boundary of an area feature, or both. Topology is useful in GIS because many spatial modeling operations don't require coordinates, only topological information. For example, to find an optimal path between two points requires a list of which arcs connect to each other and the cost of traversing along each arc in each direction. Coordinates are only necessary to draw the path after it is calculated. (2)

Transformation
The process of converting data from one coordinate system to another through translation, rotation, and scaling.

Triangulated irregular network (TIN)
A representation of a surface derived from irregularly spaced sample points and breakline features. The TIN data set includes topological relationships between points and their proximal triangles. Each sample point has an x,y coordinate and a surface or z value. These points are connected by edges to form a set of nonoverlapping triangles that can be used to represent the surface. TINs are also called irregular triangular mesh or irregular triangular surface models. (2)

Tuple
Synonym of record.

Unbundled
Refers to software sold separately from hardware. See bundled.

Undershoot
A digitized line that does not quite reach a line that it should intersect. As with an overshoot, this is also sometimes referred to as a dangling line.

Vector data
A coordinate-based data structure commonly used to represent map features. Each linear feature is represented as a list of ordered x,y coordinates. Attributes are associated with the feature (as opposed to a raster data structure, which associates attributes with a grid cell). Traditional vector data structures include double-digitized polygons and arc-node models. (2)

Vertex
One point along a line.

Z-value
The elevation value of a surface at a particular x,y location. Often referred to as a spot value or spot elevation. (2)

Zoom
To display a smaller or larger region instead of the present spatial data set extent in order to show greater or lesser detail.

References

1. BURROUGH, P.A. 1990. Principles of geographical information systems for land resources assessment. Butler & Tanner Ltd., Fromme, Somerset, Great Britain.
2. ENVIRONMENTAL SYSTEMS RESEARCH INSTITUTE, INC. 1991. ARC/INFO data model, concepts, and key terms. Environ. Syst. Res. Inst., Redlands, CA.
3. HUXHOLD, W. 1991. An introduction to urban geographic information systems. Oxford Univ. Press, New York, NY.
4. MONMONIER, M., and G.A. SCHNELL. 1988. Map appreciation. Prentice Hall, Englewood Cliffs, NJ.
5. MONTGOMERY, G., and G. JUHL. 1990. Intelligent infrastructure workbook. A-E-C Automation Newsletter, Fountain Hills, AZ.

Bruce L. Kessler is applications specialist, Environmental Systems Research Institute, Inc., Boulder, Colorado.

SECTION 2

Environmental Modelling & Assessment

Overview

This section begins with a commentary by Wheeler on linkages between statistical and modelling programs with GIS. Opportunities for understanding global and other large scale patterns and processes from AVHRR data sets are discussed by Loveland et al. and Brown et al. in the second and third papers. The final two papers discuss applications of regional models. Ferris and Congalton estimate Colorado River Basin snowmelt while Burke et al. describe the use of an ecosystem simulation model for climate change scenarios in the Great Plains.

Suggested Additional Reading

Davis, F. W., D. A. Quattrochi, M. K. Ridd, N. Lam, S. Walsh, J. C. Michaelsen, J. Franklin, D. A. Stow, C. J. Johannsen, and C. A. Johnston, 1991. Environmental Analysis Using Integrated GIS and Remotely Sensed Data: Some Research Needs and Priorities. Photogrammetric Enginering and Remote Sensing. 57(6):689-697.

Goodchild, M. F., B. O. Parks., and L. T. Steyaert. (ed.). 1993. Environmental Modeling with GIS. Oxford University Press, New York.

Hastings, D. A., J. J. Kineman, and D. M. Clark, 1991. Development and Application of Global Databases: Considerable Progress, but more Collaboration Needed. International Journal of Geographical Information Systems. 5(1): 137-146.

Jensen, J. R., E. W. Ramsey III, J. M. Holmes, J. E. Michel, B. Savitsky, and B. A. Davis, 1990. Environmental Sensitivity Index (ESI) Mapping for Oil Spills Using Remote Sensing and Geographic Information System Technology. International Journal of Geographical Information Systems. 4(2):181-201.

Lowell, K. E., 1991. Utilizing Discriminant Function Analysis with a Geographic Information System to Model Ecological Succession Spatially. International Journal of Geographical Information Systems. 5(2):175-192.

Rhind, D., 1991. Geograhical Information Systems and Environmental Problems. International Social Science Journal. 43:649-668.

Commentary: Linking Environmental Models with Geographic Information Systems for Global Change Research

Abstract

To effectively analyze the spatial variation inherent in Earth systems, it is essential to integrate the spatial database structures of GIS into the environmental modeling process. This coupling has been attempted using process models in climate, hydrology, biogeochemical, and ecosystem dynamics, but there are a number of technical and theoretical obstacles to overcome before this integration can be fully effective in global change research. This commentary identifies key areas of research involving this integration, and obstacles which limit its success, including data sources, data formats and compatibility, costs, GIS functionality, computing speed, and the level of communication between the modeling and GIS communities. Recommendations for short-term solutions to these problems emphasize improving the transferability of data between existing systems. Long-term solutions suggest changing the way models are designed and how GISs store and process their data.

Introduction

Social and technological activities throughout the world contribute to rapid and potentially stressful changes in the environment. These changes profoundly affect generations to come. Human land-use practices in agriculture, forestry, industry, transportation, and residential development have significantly altered our terrestrial and marine ecosystems. Over the past few decades humans have witnessed a proliferation of pollution and waste, acid precipitation, loss of tropical forests, degradation of soils, and loss of species diversity in both plants and animals. Human activities have also contributed to increasing concentrations of greenhouse gases in the atmosphere and to stratospheric ozone depletion, which may alter our climate.

Global environmental change is an issue of international concern, especially as it affects human habitability. Many less developed nations, where the local environment is severely stressed, are most affected. World organizations, such as the International Geosphere-Biosphere Programme (IGBP) and the World Climate Research Programme (WCRP), were established to support interdisciplinary research on global environmental issues. In cooperation with the IGBP, WCRP, and other international forums, the U. S. Global Change Research Program (USGCRP) was established by Public Law 101-606 in 1990 (U.S. Congress, 1990). This interagency committee is charged with developing national and international policies related to global and regional environmental issues. The USGCRP addresses this task with four streams of research activities: Earth observation and information management, process research, integrated modeling and prediction, and assessment.

GIS technology is integrated into each of the four USGCRP activities. To effectively analyze the spatial variation inherent in Earth systems, the environmental modeling community is using spatial databases in existing GIS programs. However, this is not a simple operation. The integration of modeling and GIS technology requires transdisciplinary skills, and few organizations have sufficient expertise in both complex process modeling and GIS technology (Nyerges, 1993). Inexperience in coupling process models with GISs could potentially lead to misuse of the technology (Moore *et al.*, 1993). GIS technology provides valuable tools for global change modeling. The spatial overlay capability of a GIS makes it possible to integrate varied sources of data within a single system. These spatially referenced data sets may be manipulated and queried to produce new information that was not previously entered into the system. Resulting data may be displayed in hard copy or soft copy as maps, statistics, or text.

Unfortunately, there are still a number of technical and theoretical obstacles to overcome before the coupling of GIS technology with environmental process models can be considered fully effective in global change research.

U.S. Global Change Research Priorities

The major share of global change research taking place in the United States is funded under the direction of the USGCRP, which budgeted 1.372 billion dollars for these activities in fiscal year 1993 (CEES, 1992a). The USGCRP addresses significant uncertainties in knowledge concerning the natural and human-induced changes occurring in the Earth's life-sustaining environment. To fulfill this goal, the USGCRP focuses on four interconnected scientific objectives:

- *Documenting global change (observations and data and information management)* through the establishment of an integrated, comprehensive, and long-term program of observing and analyzing Earth system change on global scales, including data and information management;
- *Understanding of key processes (process research)* through a program of focused studies to improve knowledge of the physical, chemical, biological, geological, and social processes that influence and govern Earth system behavior and the effects of global changes on natural systems and human health and activities;
- *Predicting global and regional environmental change (integrated modeling and prediction)* through the development and application of integrated conceptual and predictive Earth system models; and

Photogrammetric Engineering & Remote Sensing,
Vol. 59, No. 10, October 1993, pp. 1497–1501.

0099-1112/93/5910–1497$03.00/0

Douglas J. Wheeler
U.S. Geological Survey,
521 National Center, Reston, VA 22092.

- *Assessing and synthesizing the state of scientific, technical, and economic knowledge and implications of global change (assessment)* to support national and international policy-making activities that cover the broad spectrum of global and regional environmental issues and to provide guidance for determining research priorities of the USGCRP (CEES, 1992b).

Within these guidelines, seven interdisciplinary science elements provide a framework for proposal reviews and research projects. These elements in order of priority are (1) climate and hydrologic systems, (2) biogeochemical dynamics, (3) ecological systems and dynamics, (4) Earth system history, (5) human interactions, (6) solid Earth processes, and (7) solar influences (CEES, 1992a). Nearly half of the 1993 global change budget was allocated to the first science element (climate and hydrologic systems), which was identified by the international global change community as having the highest priority. Approximately 90 percent of the global change appropriation was divided among the three highest priority elements: climate and hydrologic systems, biogeochemical dynamics, and ecological systems and dynamics.

Another area of the USGCRP relating to the advancement of GIS technology is the development of data and information management systems to support the wide range of data from space and ground-based observations. The USGCRP has a continuing commitment to producing and preserving high-quality, long-term global or regional data sets and data exchange standards; to making data accessible; and to maintaining low cost data for research purposes (CEES, 1992b).

Environmental Process Modeling Activities

Understanding the physical processes that shape our Earth system can help slow the negative effect humans have had on the environment in recent decades. Predictive modeling helps to incorporate descriptions of key processes that modulate the Earth system's behavior with varying degrees of sophistication (Moore *et al.*, 1993). A modeling framework can also provide a basis for evaluating predictive scenarios. This section offers a brief sample of process models relating to the USGCRP's highest priority science elements—climate and hydrologic systems, biogeochemical dynamics, and ecological systems and dynamics. Many of these models were examined at the "First International Conference/Workshop on Integrating GIS and Environmental Models," held in Boulder, Colorado, 15-18 September 1991. Steyaert (1992; 1993) offers a brief overview of the objectives and activities of this conference, and also reviews many environmental simulation modeling activities in progress.

Atmospheric models range from general circulation models, which simulate global climate changes, to small-scale boundary models representing near surface conditions over very small areas. Most atmospheric models consist of a set of differential equations that describe external forcing and the response of the atmosphere to that forcing (Lee *et al.*, 1993). To solve these equations, both initial and boundary conditions must be provided. Accurate characterization of the land surface (albedo, canopy structure, roughness, evapotranspiration, and soil hydrologic properties) is important for correctly initializing these models. Currently, there is no comprehensive global data set providing that land characterization at the required level of detail. Remotely sensed data and interpolated field site data could be incorporated into a GIS to enhance some atmospheric models. The Simple Biosphere model, which simulates the exchange of sensible and latent heat, demonstrates this interaction between vegetation and the atmosphere (Sellers *et al.*, 1986; Xue *et al.*, 1991). This model uses a list of physical and biophysical properties of land cover (bare ground, shrub dominated, grassland, savanna, and forest) that must be described spatially (Schimel, 1993). These models demonstrate that human induced spatial or temporal modifications to the landscape can have a major affect on local climate variations (Lee *et al.*, 1993).

Hydrologic models are defined as mathematical representations of water flow on some part of the land surface or subsurface environment (Maidment, 1993). Because a GIS can provide a representation of the land surface, there is an obvious connection between the two technologies. Hydrologic modeling techniques, however, have developed quite independently of GIS technology, primarily because of the spatially explicit nature of these models. Only recently have attempts been made to integrate GIS data manipulation capabilities into hydrologic models. Previously, a GIS was used mostly as a retrieval system for topographic data. Maidment (1993) presents an excellent review of hydrologic models and the possibility of coupling them with GISs.

Biogeochemical models are often coupled with atmospheric and hydrologic models. An example is the Forest-BGC (biogeochemical cycling) model (Running *et al.*, 1987). The Forest-BGC model uses a leaf area index and, when in mountainous terrain, can incorporate 30-metre digital elevation model data. Models of the Forest-BGC class generally require daily weather data with a low temporal resolution but a high spatial resolution. Another biogeochemical model, named CENTURY, is used in determining net primary production and in tracing carbon and nitrogen cycles while drawing information from a GIS (Schimel, 1993).

Not all ecological models are suitable for GIS applications. Many ecological models are only concerned with the temporal aspects (processes that are independent of adjacent landscape units) of ecological processes (Hunsaker *et al.*, 1993). With the technological tools now available to ecologists, there is an increase in the coupling of terrestrial plant models and freshwater and marine models with GIS technology. Baker (1989) and Hunsaker *et al.* (1993) discuss various ecological models with the potential of incorporating spatial landscape components.

Examples of Linking GIS Technology with Process Modeling

Dangermond (1993) states that, while GIS technology has been used extensively in both the environmental field and in modeling, it has not been used very often for modeling in the environmental field. This is not meant to infer that the many environmental applications that use a GIS cannot be considered as modeling. There are other typologies on the nature of GIS models (Peuquet, 1984; Wheeler, 1988; Tomlin, 1990). Dangermond refers to the direct linking of GIS technology with existing atmospheric or terrestrial process models.

Burrough *et al.* (1988) indicates that, to successfully link models and GIS's for quantitative land resources assessment, the following points need to be considered:

For the Models:
- What are the basic assumptions and methods?
- At what scale or organizational level is the model designed to work?
- What data are needed for control parameters?
- What data are needed to feed the model?
- Under what conditions are certain control parameters or input data more important than others?
- How are errors propagated through the model?

For the GISs:
- Are the right data available at the correct spatial scale and level of generalization?

- Are there sufficient good data to create a finite element substrate when required?
- Are data available for calibrating and validating the model?
- If data are not available, could surrogates be used instead? How should they be transformed?
- How should a user be made aware of the intrinsic quality of the results of modeling?
- Is information available on data quality and errors?
- If the results are not good enough, should the GIS suggest alternative data or alternative models to the user?

One recent effort to integrate GIS technology and hydrologic process modeling links the SWRRB simulation model with a decision support system (Arnold and Sammons, 1989). A library of georeferenced hydrologic, soil, and weather related parameters provides data to fuel the SWRRB model, which simulates water resources of rural catchment basins. Hession *et al.* (1987) and Sharnholtz *et al.* (1990) were successful in linking the FESHM model with digital terrain data using commercial GIS packages. Panuska *et al.* (1991) also were able to integrate terrain data into an agricultural nonpoint source pollution model (AGNPS) at a local scale.

The most widely known example of a regional scale model for assessing vulnerability to ground water pollution is DRASTIC (Aller, 1985), the Environmental Protection Agency's risk assessment and planning tool. The DRASTIC model performs a weighted and summed index of factors influencing ground water contamination, including depth to ground water (D), net recharge rate (R), the aquifer media (A), soil characteristics (S), topography (T), impact of the vadose zone (I), and hydraulic conductivity of the aquifer (C). The simplicity of these weighted parameters makes the DRASTIC model particularly well suited to GIS use, yet its relationships are not based on any explicit physical laws, as is the case with most environmental process models.

Beller *et al.* (1991) and Stutheit (1991) introduced a prototype for a temporal GIS, developed with the cooperation of IBM and Colorado State University, which couples a commercial GIS package with ecological and atmospheric models. This prototype is being used to incorporate multitemporal AVHRR normalized difference vegetation index data from the U.S. Geological Survey's land-cover characteristics database (Loveland *et al.*, 1991; Sturdevant *et al.*, 1991) with existing parameters to determine the strength of relationships between climate and the year-to-year variability of net primary production in grassland areas.

Barriers to Integrating GISs and Process Modeling

GISs were originally designed as a tool to support decision making for land-use planning. The dramatic growth of the GIS industry has generally been spurred by demands for information management capabilities rather than spatial analysis and modeling functions (Goodchild, 1991). The major success of GIS technology is because of its capability for mapping the Earth's surface and for supporting simple queries. Commercial development of GIS software and hardware must, because of financial necessity, support the demands of its majority of users (Dangermond, 1993).

Because of the complex nature of geographic data, GISs rely on more elaborate configurations than do most other information systems or statistical programs. A GIS must support varied graphics oriented hardware peripherals (digitizers, scanners, and plotters) and have a database structure sophisticated enough to handle large volumes of data (including imagery) while referencing each data record to a specific geographic location. Coincidentally, the design and programming of efficient algorithms to perform geographic operations

have added to the complexity of GIS programs (Goodchild, 1991). There are many things that a GIS is designed to do — but it cannot do every task at the same level of efficiency as specialized "reduced task" programs (statistical and simulation modeling packages). No current GIS package has both the structural flexibility for handling spatial and temporal data and the algorithmic flexibility to build and test process models internally (Nyerges, 1993).

There are several obstacles that continue to hinder the coupling of GIS technology with environmental process models. These obstacles are in the categories of (1) data sources and formats, (2) GIS functions, and (3) modeling methods.

Data Sources and Formats

- *Accuracy* (locational, categorical, and sampling) of data. The quality of many data sets is unknown, leading to the inability to assess or define uncertainty in models.
- *Availability* of pertinent data. Multitemporal modeling needs time-series data layers (land cover, soils, and field data), which could be nonexistent, costly to produce, or not technically feasible to produce at prescribed levels of detail. There is a lack of coordination for archived digital data, especially at global scales.
- *Scale or resolution* of data. Data are often collected or stored at levels of detail that are inadequate for use as parameters for environmental models.
- *Transferability* of data between programs or systems.

GIS Functions

- *Multitemporal analysis.* Very little has been done to incorporate the dimension of time (an integral part of process modeling) into GIS data structures or operations.
- *Three-dimensional analysis and visualization.* GIS's incorporate point, line, and area cartographic primitives and allow Z-values as attributes (2.5-dimensional), but do not have sufficient volumetric operations to model three-dimensional Earth processes.
- *Interpolation and extrapolation algorithms.* There is a need for greater variety, accuracy, and efficiency in spatial algorithms used in interpolating point samples, especially when many data layers are used in a single model.
- *Mathematical and statistical functions.* GIS programs do not excel at statistical analyses or complex mathematical relations required by most environmental process models.
- *Import and export capabilities.* The spatial data transfer tools found in many GIS packages are inadequate for linking a GIS with analytical and modeling software or other database systems.
- *Speed of computing.* Because of the program overhead required for manipulating data in its spatial form, GISs are slow compared with other statistical or modeling systems. The time needed for running complex models may be prohibitive.
- *User interface.* Modelers are often faced with learning and tolerating an unfamiliar (and potentially unfriendly) system to process their models.

Modeling Methods

- *Failure to incorporate the spatial context* of the natural environment into models, or neglecting the influence of adjacent landscape units upon natural processes.
- *Inadequate calibration* of models or misinterpreting the degree of influence some parameters (especially spatial) might have on model results.
- *Lack of understanding of GIS technology* and its components, its capabilities, and its limitations.
- *Shortage of adequate data* that can be structured into an acceptable format to be processed in a GIS.
- *Resistance to changing* methods to include new technology

or redesign the parameters or functions of the model to match the processing medium.

Recommendations

Integrating GIS technology with process modeling requires finding the common ground between those who believe GIS technology solves all problems and process modelers who view GIS technology as merely a toy. Scientists must be willing to cooperate across disciplinary boundaries to understand the Earth's global environment. Berry (1993) observes that "the GIS community must become familiar with the process modeler's requirements and incorporate more mathematical functionality in their GIS products. On the other front, the modeling community must ... become familiar with the conditions, considerations and capabilities of the technology."

The following suggestions are addressed to those who have a role in "bridging the gaps" between GIS technology and process modeling of the Earth's environment:

For modelers:

- Recognize the spatial pattern of Earth surface phenomena as an important function of process.
- Develop ecological models that incorporate the influence of adjacent landscape units.
- Refine techniques of performing field studies regarding the spatial and temporal variability of landscape processes. Evaluate if existing models produce valid results.
- Investigate ways to scale up from localized process models to more actively use remotely sensed satellite data or other digital data sets already available.
- Increase development of multiresolution or "nested" models to more effectively capture the influence of human-induced spatial and temporal variability on global processes.
- Communicate with GIS vendors to make them aware of modeling needs.

For GIS developers:

- Improve data structures to more efficiently handle multitemporal data, not as simply multiple snapshots of time, but as a seamless transition or trend.
- Improve three-dimensional capabilities with algorithms designed to depict volume (as opposed to 2.5-dimensional surfaces).
- Incorporate faster processing technologies into hardware and software, reducing turnaround time for model results.
- Support realtime interactive manipulation of model data to see how the alteration of model parameters may affect the results.
- Display dynmic modeling with continuous animation.
- Improve methods and algorithms for data interpolation and extrapolation from point samples, image rectification, scale changes, vector-raster conversions, and data transformations.
- Develop natural language expert shell interfaces to assist modelers in using GISs.
- Improve links between different database models (spatial relational and object-oriented).
- Develop easier and more efficient data import and export capabilities by implementing spatial data transfer standards and incorporating expert systems technology, facilitating data input and allowing seamless transfer of data to and from analytical and modeling packages.
- Provide the means for defining accuracy or uncertainty of individual data elements; then make an "audit trail" of those figures through subsequent GIS operations or transformations.
- Improve algorithms for geometrical operations (area calculation, perimeter, shape, and volume) and develop methods for computing relationships between objects based on their geometry.
- Develop data structures with stronger relational associations.

Assign new attributes to objects based on both existing attributes and complex mathematical rules (models often use differential equations or other mathematical functions to measure the strength of relationships).
- Support and promote less expensive GIS alternatives (public domain software or CD data storage).

For data producers:

- Implement accepted standards in spatial data format, accuracy, and transferability.
- Improve spatial accuracy of field data by incorporating global positioning satellite technology.
- Provide a statement regarding data accuracy and uncertainty and methods of data collection and compilation with every data set distributed.
- Support various data archives and a directory system to access information about available data sets (i.e., meta data).
- Improve automated methods for converting remotely sensed data into digital land-use and land-cover information.
- Test and enhance existing land characteristic databases.

This is an ambitious list of suggestions for the long-term integration of GIS technology with environmental process models. Some of these goals may appear to be dreams, with little likelihood of reaching fruition. GIS technology may not be able to surmount these technical obstacles within the next few years. However, GIS technology is already capable of performing many functions (storing and retrieving spatially referenced data, doing layer comparisons and neighborhood operations, and supporting simple queries). The strength of simulation modeling programs is their ability to process mathematical functions in an efficient manner. For a short-term solution, it may be appropriate to emphasize the relative strengths of these systems and place the highest priority on developing import and export "hooks" or links to transfer data between components (Goodchild, 1991; Nyerges, 1993). This coupling of GIS with statistical and modeling programs would benefit global change research and encourage the development of further links.

References

Aller, L., 1985. *DRASTIC: A Standard System for Evaluating Ground Water Pollution Potential Using Hydrogeologic Settings*, Report No. EPA/600/2-85/018, U.S. Environmental Protection Agency, Robert S. Kerr Environmental Research Lab, Ada, Oklahoma.

Arnold, J.G., and N.B. Sammons, 1989. Decision Support System for Selecting Inputs to a Basin Scale Model, *Water Resource Bulletin*, 24(4).

Baker, W.L., 1989. A Review of Models of Landscape Change, *Landscape Ecology*, 2:111-133.

Beller, A., T. Giblin, K.V. Le, S. Litz, T.G.F. Kittel, and D.S. Schimel, 1991. A Temporal GIS Prototype for Global Change Research, *GIS/LIS '91 Proceedings*, Atlanta, Georgia, pp. 752-765.

Berry, J.K., 1993. Seminar on GIS for Modelers, Part II: Treating Maps as Spatial Data and the Analytical Capabilities of GIS, *Environmental Modeling with Geographic Information Systems* (M. Goodchild, B. Parks, and L. Steyaert, editors), Oxford University Press (in press).

Burrough, P.A., W. van Deursen, and G. Heuvelink, 1988. Linking Spatial Process Models and GIS: A Marriage of Convenience or a Blossoming Partnership?, *GIS/LIS '88 Proceedings*, San Antonio, Texas, pp. 598-607.

Committee on Earth and Environmental Sciences, 1992a. *Our Changing Planet: The FY 1993 U. S. Global Change Research Program*, CEES, Washington, D.C., 79 p.

———, 1992b. *The U.S. Global Change Data and Information Management Program Plan*, CEES, Washington, D.C., 94 p.

Dangermond, J., 1993. The Role of Software Vendors in Integrating

GIS and Environmental Modeling, *Environmental Modeling with Geographic Information Systems* (M. Goodchild, B. Parks, and L. Steyaert, editors), Oxford University Press (in press).

Goodchild, M.F., 1991. Integrating GIS and Environmental Modeling at Global Scales, *GIS/LIS '91 Proceedings*, Atlanta, Georgia, pp. 117-127.

Hession, W.C., V.O. Shanholtz, S. Mostaghimi, and T.A. Dillaha, 1987. *Extensive Evaluation of the Finite Element Storm Hydrograph Model*, ASAE Paper No. 87-2570, American Society of Agricultural Engineers, St Joseph, Michigan, 34 p.

Hunsaker, C.T., R.A. Nisbet, D. Lam, J.A. Browder, M.G. Turner, W.L. Baker, and D.B. Botkin, 1993. Spatial Models of Ecological Systems and Processes: The Role of GIS, *Environmental Modeling with Geographic Information Systems* (M. Goodchild, B. Parks, and L. Steyaert, editors), Oxford University Press (in press).

Lee, T.J., R.A. Pielke, T.G.F. Kittel, and J.F. Weaver, 1993. Atmospheric Modeling and its Spatial Representation of Land Surface Characteristics, *Environmental Modeling with Geographic Information Systems* (M. Goodchild, B. Parks, and L. Steyaert, editors), Oxford University Press, (in press).

Loveland, T.R., J.W. Merchant, D.O. Ohlen, and J.F. Brown, 1991. Development of a Land-Cover Characteristics Database for the Coterminous U.S., *Photogrammetric Engineering & Remote Sensing*, 57(11):1453-1463.

Maidment, D.R., 1993. GIS and Hydrologic Modeling, *Environmental Modeling with Geographic Information Systems* (M. Goodchild, B. Parks, and L. Steyaert, editors), Oxford University Press (in press).

Moore, I.D., A.K. Turner, J.P. Wilson, S.K. Jenson, and L.E. Band, 1993. GIS and Land Surface-Subsurface Process Modeling, *Environmental Modeling with Geographic Information Systems* (M. Goodchild, B. Parks, and L. Steyaert, editors), Oxford University Press (in press).

Nyerges, T.L., 1993. GIS for Environmental Modelers: An Overview, *Environmental Modeling with Geographic Information Systems* (M. Goodchild, B. Parks, and L. Steyaert, editors), Oxford University Press, (in press).

Panuska, J.C., I.D. Moore, and L.A. Kramer, 1991. Terrain Analysis: Integration into the Agricultural Nonpoint Source (AGNPS) Pollution Model, *Journal of Soil and Water Conservation*, 46(1):59-64.

Peuquet, D.J., 1984. A Conceptual Framework and Comparison of Spatial Data Models, *Cartographica*, 21:66-113.

Running, S.W., R. Nemani, and R.D. Hungerford, 1987. Extrapolation of Synoptic Meteorological Data in Mountainous Terrain and Its Use for Simulating Forest Evapotranspiration and Photosynthesis, *Canadian Journal of Forest Research*, 17:472-483.

Schimel, D.S., 1993. Spatial Interactive Models of Atmosphere-Ecosystem Coupling, *Environmental Modeling with Geographic Information Systems* (M. Goodchild, B. Parks, and L. Steyaert, editors), Oxford University Press, (in press).

Sellers, P.J., Y. Mintz, Y.C. Sud, and A. Dalcher, 1986. A Simple Biosphere Model (SiB) for Use Within General Circulation Models, *Journal of Atmospheric Science*, 43:505-531.

Sharnholtz, V.O., C.J. Deai, N. Zhang, J.W. Kleene, C.D. Metz, and J.M. Flagg, 1990. *Hydrologic/Water Quality Modeling in a GIS Environment*, ASAE Paper No. 90-3033, American Society of Agricultural Engineers, St Joseph, Michigan, 17 p.

Steyaert, L.T., 1992. Integrating Geographic Information Systems and Environmental Simulation Models, *Technical Papers, ASPRS/ACSM/RT 92 Fall Convention*, Washington, D.C., August, 1:233-243.

———, 1993. A Perspective on the State of Environmental Simulation Modeling, *Environmental Modeling with Geographic Information Systems* (M. Goodchild, B. Parks, and L. Steyaert, Oxford University Press (in press).

Sturdevant, J.A., J.C. Eidenshink, and T.R. Loveland, 1991. Organizations Challenged by Global Data base Development, *GIS World*, 4(9):73-79.

Stutheit, J., 1991. Temporal GIS Investigates Global Change, *GIS World*, 4(9):68-72.

Tomlin, C.D., 1990. *Geographic Information Systems and Cartographic Modeling*, Prentice-Hall, Englewood Cliffs, N.J., 249 p.

U.S. Congress, 1990. *Global Change Research Act of 1990*, Public Law 101-606: 101st Congress, Nov. 16, 1990, 104 STAT. 3096-3104.

Wheeler, D.J., 1988. A Look At Model Building with Geographic Information Systems, *GIS/LIS '88 Proceedings*, San Antonio, Texas, pp. 580-589.

Xue, Y., P.J. Sellers, J.L. Kinter, and J. Shukla, 1991. A Simplified Biosphere Model for Global Climate Studies, *Journal of Climate*, 4:345-364.

Development of a Land-Cover Characteristics Database for the Conterminous U. S.

Thomas R. Loveland
USGS EROS Data Center, Sioux Falls, SD 57198

James W. Merchant
Center for Advanced Land Management Information Technologies, Conservation and Survey Division, Institute of Agriculture and Natural Resources, University of Nebraska-Lincoln, Lincoln, NE 68588-0517

Donald O. Ohlen
TGS Technology, Inc., USGS EROS Data Center, Sioux Falls, SD 57198

Jesslyn F. Brown*
Center for Advanced Land Management Information Technologies, Conservation and Survey Division, Institute of Agriculture and Natural Resources, University of Nebraska-Lincoln, Lincoln, NE 68588-0517

ABSTRACT: Information regarding the characteristics and spatial distribution of the Earth's land cover is critical to global environmental research. A prototype land-cover database for the conterminous United States designed for use in a variety of global modeling, monitoring, mapping, and analytical endeavors has been created. Database development has involved (1) a stratification of vegetated and barren land, (2) an unsupervised classification of multitemporal "greenness" data derived from Advanced Very High Resolution Radiometer (AVHRR) imagery collected from March through October 1990, and (3) post-classification stratification of classes into homogeneous land-cover regions using ancillary data. Ancillary data sets included elevation, climate, ecoregions, and land resource areas. The resultant database contains multiple layers, including the source AVHRR data, the ancillary data layers, the land-cover regions defined by the research, and translation tables linking the regions to other land classification schema (for example, UNESCO, USGS Anderson System). The land-cover characteristics database can be analyzed, transformed, or aggregated by users to meet a broad spectrum of requirements. Future research plans include examination of impacts of interannual change, landscape and sensor interaction, development of improved analytical tools and methods, and appropriate modes for verification.

INTRODUCTION

INFORMATION REGARDING THE CHARACTERISTICS and spatial distribution of the Earth's land cover is critical to global change research. Capabilities to inventory and map land-cover conditions and to monitor change are required for, among other things, modeling the global carbon and hydrologic cycles, studying land surface-climate interactions, and establishing rates of tropical deforestation (Risser, 1985; Dale, 1990; International Geosphere-Biosphere Programme, 1990; Pinker, 1990; Pielke and Avissar, 1990; Dorman and Sellers, 1989). Global land process research heretofore has had to rely upon simple interpretations of gross land cover and surface properties, such as biomass, albedo, surface roughness, and canopy resistance, at low spatial resolution (Henderson-Sellers *et al.*, 1986). The Matthews land cover and natural vegetation (Matthews, 1983; 1984) and the Olson and Watts major world ecosystems (Olson and Watts, 1982) global databases are the most common sources of land-cover and surface parameter data. These data bases have, respectively, 1° by 1° and 0.5° by 0.5° spatial resolution. Higher resolution data with greater precision for classification are clearly required (International Geosphere-Biosphere Programme, 1990).

During the last decade, substantial progress has been made in using National Oceanic and Atmospheric Administration (NOAA) Advanced Very High Resolution Radiometer (AVHRR) data for land cover characterization (for example, Goward et al., 1985; Tucker *et al.*, 1985; Roller and Colwell, 1986; Townshend *et al.*, 1987; and Lloyd, 1990). AVHRR data have only moderate spatial resolution (1 km) when compared, for example, to Landsat's 80 m for multispectral scanner (MSS) and 30 m for thematic mapper (TM) or SPOT's 20 m for multispectral and 10 m for panchromatic data. AVHRR data are, however, collected

more frequently, with virtually the entire globe imaged twice each day. The high frequency of coverage enhances the likelihood that cloud-free observations can be obtained for specific temporal windows, and makes it possible to monitor change in land cover conditions over short periods, such as a growing season (Miller *et al.*, 1988; Tappan and Moore, 1989; Justice *et al.*, 1985; Goward *et al.*, 1985). Moreover, the moderate resolution of the data makes it feasible to collect, store, and process continental or global data sets.

Research on applications of AVHRR data for land-cover inventory and monitoring has focused on analysis of vegetation "greenness." Greenness is most often measured using a vegetation index, commonly the Normalized Difference Vegetation Index (NDVI) (Goward *et al.*, 1985). A number of investigators have shown that changes in greenness during a growing season can be observed and often correlated with the spatial distribution of major biomes (Townshend *et al.*, 1987; Tucker *et al.*, 1985; Lloyd, 1990). Because of limitations in AVHRR data availability, almost all regional, continental, and global-scale analyses have used data that have been resampled to either 4- or 16-km pixels (Global Area Coverage [GAC] or Global Vegetation Index [GVI] data). Only recently have spatially extensive data sets at the highest nominal resolution (1.1 km) started to become available on a continuing basis for major land areas. (Note: 1-km AVHRR data are referred to as high resolution picture transmission [HRPT] for data collected directly by ground receiving stations, and as local area coverage [LAC] for data gathered using on-board satellite tape recorders.)

The U.S. Geological Survey, National Mapping Division's (USGS NMD) EROS Data Center (EDC) has a program to produce 1-km resolution AVHRR time series data sets for the conterminous U. S., Alaska, and Eurasia as products for applied research (Eidenshink *et al.*, 1991; Kelly and Hood, 1991; Sadowski, 1990). The EDC has direct reception capabilities for NOAA's TIROS

---

*Visiting scientist at the EROS Data Center.

PHOTOGRAMMETRIC ENGINEERING & REMOTE SENSING,
Vol. 57, No. 11, November 1991, pp. 1453–1463.

0099-1112/91/5711–1453$03.00/0
©1991 American Society for Photogrammetry and Remote Sensing

series of polar-orbiting satellites (AVHRR HRPT data) covering most of North America. The EDC also operates a Domestic Communications Satellite System (DOMSAT) downlink that facilitates near-real-time access to virtually all of the AVHRR LAC data collected globally. AVHRR data reception activities are integrated with georegistration, product generation (such as greenness maps and land-cover classifications) and archiving systems developed to insure that high quality data will be available to researchers and land managers.

Because spatially extensive 1-km data sets possessing high temporal resolution have been unavailable, capabilities to use such data for regional land-cover characterization have not been well explored. The initial results of research being conducted by the EDC with the Center for Advanced Land Management Information Technologies (CALMIT) of the University of Nebraska at Lincoln (UNL) focus on the design and evaluation of strategies for detailed land-cover characterization over continental-size areas. Central to the research is the conviction that there is synergism in the integration of data derived by remote sensing with Earth science data acquired from other sources.

RESEARCH OBJECTIVES

The principal objective of the research has been to define and evaluate the potential for using AVHRR 1-km digital imagery and multisource data (such as broad-scale climate, terrain, ecoregions) in concert to characterize global land cover. The investigation included numerous questions involving methodology, data, and product requirements. Initial work focused on development of a prototype 1-km resolution land characteristics database for the conterminous U. S. that is designed for scientists dealing with global and mesoscale climate modeling, land surface change, and biosphere-atmosphere-hydrosphere interactions.

SCIENTIFIC HERITAGE OF THIS RESEARCH

Attempts to characterize land cover over large areas (subcontinental, continental, or global) using AVHRR data extend back at least 15 years. Most studies have focused upon GAC (4-km) or GVI (16-km) data rather than on full-resolution 1-km imagery. Typically, data are transformed to a vegetation index, such as the NDVI, for analysis. Tucker et al., (1985), for example, used NDVI derived from GAC data to map major biomes and observe phenological change over the African continent for a 19-month period in 1982 and 1983. Three-week maximum vegetation index composites and principal components analysis were used to define major ecosystems. The authors observed qualitative agreement between their results and published maps, but argued for further development of analytical techniques and examination of multiple years to determine effects of short-term climatic variations.

Townshend et al., (1987) employed GAC and GVI data in examining three approaches to classification of land cover in South America. They compared a principal-components transformation of 13 dates, a multidate greenness curve-matching methodology, and a maximum-likelihood classification approach. The last method yielded the best outcome. The optimal result was achieved when 13 dates of coverage (rather than fewer) were used. Available ground reference material allowed only qualitative judgment that the outcome of their classification was successful.

Goward et al., (1985) examined GVI data for North America. They analyzed three-week composite maximum greenness (NDVI) images from April through November 1982 to map regions of net primary productivity. They showed that seasonal NDVI patterns could be associated with major land-cover regions, and that multidate greenness images could be used to observe patterns of vegetation growth and senecence. The authors rec-

ommended research on interannual change and further technique development. In later work Goward et al. (1987) compared the vegetation characteristics of North and South American biomes by analyzing GVI data using methods developed in Goward's 1985 research. They found that the differential timing and longer duration of the South American growing season was well captured. Biome distributions appeared, qualitatively, well-associated with published maps. Lloyd (1990) used a supervised binary decision tree classification approach to map world biomes with multidate GVI data. Although the spatial distributions appeared reasonable, no quantitative verification was possible. Gallo and Brown (1990) used biweekly GVI composites to examine global phytoclimatological conditions. They concluded that biweekly histograms of greenness change could be used to indicate general climatic conditions and associated vegetation distributions.

One-kilometre AVHRR data have been used less often than GAC or GVI data because they have not been generally available. Tucker et al., (1984), however, employed 1-km data to monitor vegetation conditions in the Nile delta. No attempt was made to classify land cover, but changes in greenness conditions from May to October 1981 were observed to correspond to known phenological circumstances and agricultural practices. Gervin et al. (1985) compared 1-km data acquired over the Washington, D. C. area to Landsat MSS data. They performed unsupervised classification of single-date images collected in July 1981 to identify Anderson Level I land cover and land use. The first four channels of the AVHRR were used rather than a vegetation index. Accuracies of classification were similar for predominant land-use and land-cover classes, but the MSS classification had higher accuracy on classes that were spatially heterogeneous or of limited spatial extent. Overall accuracy was 71.9 percent for the AVHRR and 76.8 percent for the MSS. The authors concluded that additional work on AVHRR data classification was warranted.

DESIGN CONSIDERATIONS

Discussions of land-cover mapping often lead to debate over classification schemes, assignment of class descriptors and labels, and product specifications. Most classification schemes are designed to be useful for a rather narrow range of applications; conversely, no single classification scheme can satisfy all, or even most, applications. The International Geosphere-Biosphere Programme (IGBP), following a year-long discussion of appropriate land-cover products for global change applications, concluded that "...the varied requirements for the IGBP cannot be satisfied by a single map of one set of attributes..." (International Geosphere-Biosphere Programme, 1990).

A number of studies have indicated that it is possible to produce databases of land characteristics that can satisfy a wide range of applications assuming proper methodological design (Loveland, 1984; Fitzpatrick-Lins et al., 1987). This study is directed to the matter of appropriate design. Five major principles were established to guide the land characterization research (Loveland and Ohlen, 1991). Data analysis strategies and methods developed had to be

- Applicable and repeatable over continental and larger areas;
- Capable of discerning significant seasonal, ecological, and cultural variations in land cover;
- Applicable to very large data sets;
- Able to deal with data varying in quality; and,
- Capable of producing results applicable to various studies.

In keeping with these principles, the initial conceptual strategy, through the use of geographic information system (GIS)-based tools, allows examination of relationships between spatial data sets to characterize land cover, yet relies upon relatively simple methods for image segmentation (Figure 1).

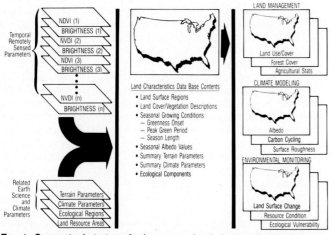

FIG. 1. Conceptual strategy for large-area land characterization includes use of remote sensing and multisource data to create a spatial database that includes seasonally distinct land-cover regions and associated attributes that can be tailored to a number of disparate applications.

Very large data sets present unique image analysis problems. Continental areas typically exhibit greater variations in climate, terrain, and vegetation than are encountered in analyses of single scenes. In addition, data set sizes tend to be extraordinarily large, posing computational and data handling difficulties.

Such problems can be dealt with in two ways. First, the study area can be partitioned into smaller data sets based on, for example, climatic or ecological regions. This would serve to limit the environmental diversity, but would likely create significant post-classification mosaicking and interregional class correlation problems. An alternative solution would be to treat the data set as a single unit. The latter approach was used in this research.

Previous studies suggest that multitemporal, multisource image classification techniques are required for large-area land-cover characterization. Single-date analyses, especially using AVHRR data, are frequently inadequate for discriminating land-cover types because disparate cover types can share spectral reflectance characteristics. The problems are compounded when one deals with large areas exhibiting great climatic, topographic, and ecological diversity. Classification of multitemporal AVHRR-NDVI data should have advantages over single-date observations, though some cover parameters required for global analyses are still likely to be imperfectly characterized. Ancillary data, such as elevation, climate variables, ecological regions are, therefore, considered critical in land cover description.

The prototype land characteristics database has several components:

- "Seasonally distinct" land-cover regions defined employing analysis of AVHRR and ancillary data. These regions exhibit unique phenological characteristics, such as time of onset, magnitude of peak, and seasonal duration of greenness, and possess relatively homogeneous vegetative associations.
- Attributes (or spreadsheets) that describe the characteristics of the landscape regions. Attributes contained in the U.S. prototype are (1) descriptions of vegetation composition and physiognomy; (2) quantitative seasonal characteristics including mean monthly NDVI (March–October 1990) and seasonal parameters (time of onset, magnitude of peak, duration of greenness, and total greenness); (3) site characteristics including, for every pixel, elevation, climate, and ecoregion and Major Land Resources Area (MLRA) membership; (4) translation tables linking the regions to common land-cover classification schemes such as UNESCO, USGS Anderson System, and the vegetation types used in the Simple Biosphere Model and the Biosphere Atmospheric Transfer Scheme (Dickinson et al., 1986); and (5) summary data on climate, terrain, land

use and land cover derived from publications describing U.S. ecological regions and MLRA's, and from sampled digital USGS land-use and land-cover data. The strategy of this approach is to give researchers a capability to compute new parameters, derive new classifications and aggregations of the data to suit specific needs, and develop custom products. This provides the flexibility that may allow the land characteristics database to be used in many models without extensive modification of inputs.

- All source data used to produce the first two components are also included to provide further customization.

As research evolves, other attributes will be added to the land characteristics data base. For example, measurements of surface albedo, primary production estimates, and other surface properties associated with canopy resistance may be added as concensus methods for their calculations are established.

DATA SOURCES

AVHRR DATA

Daily observations of NOAA-11 1-km data were calibrated to reflectance measurements, scaled to byte data, and georegistered to a Lambert Azimuthal Equal Area map projection (Kelly and Hood, 1991; Holben, 1986). The resulting data set dimensions are 2889 rows by 4587 columns.

Seventeen biweekly maximum NDVI composites were generated for the period of March through October 1990. This process involved the creation of a composite image in which the pixel having the maximum NDVI for each composite period was retained (Eidenshink et al., 1991). By selecting for maximum NDVI, nearly cloud-free data sets usually result. An image-to-image registration process was used to assure accuracy within a root-mean-square error of 1 pixel (Kelly and Hood, 1991).

Initial experiments using 1989 biweekly NDVI composites of the western United States suggested that the use of monthly composites would both minimize data volume problems and computational demands without unduly affecting results. Consequently, the 1990 biweekly composites were reduced to eight monthly composites of maximum NDVI. The original biweekly data were, however, retained for use in region characterization. Data quality was improved by the monthly compositing through the elimination of much of the remnant atmospheric, cloud, and off-nadir contamination in the biweekly composites. Although previous studies by other investigators with GAC or GVI data have documented improved classification results as more frequent observations are used (Townshend et al., 1987), practical considerations argue for dimensionality reduction in continental studies using 1-km data.

TERRAIN DATA

Digital elevation data incorporated in the database were originally derived by the Defense Mapping Agency from 1- by 2-degree topographic maps, and were later refined by the National Telecommunications and Information Administration. These data are now distributed by the NOAA National Geophysical Data Center in Boulder, Colorado. The elevation values are rounded estimates to the nearest 20 feet for every 30 seconds of latitude and longitude.

CLIMATE DATA

Climate data layers, including length-of-frost-free-period, average annual precipitation, average monthly precipitation, and monthly mean temperature, were digitized from climate atlas maps (NOAA, 1979). All of the maps were based on long-term means of temperature and precipitation (for example, monthly precipitation from 1931 to 1960). The scales of these maps varied from approximately 1:7,000,000 to 1:18,000,000. Digitized isoline data were subsequently interpolated to a gridded surface. Because of the generalized nature of the source maps, these data

44

relate to continental climate conditions and do not represent local or microclimate conditions.

ECOREGIONS

Ecoregion maps from the U.S. Environmental Protection Agency (Omernik, 1987; Omernik and Gallant, 1990) were digitized and attributes of the regions (land surface form, major soils, land use and potential natural vegetation) were summarized for use in characterization.

MAJOR LAND RESOURCE AREAS

Major land resource area (MLRA) regional boundaries were digitized from a 1:7,500,000-scale map published by the USDA Soil Conservation Service (USDA SCS, 1981). MLRA region attributes include soils, terrain, climate, potential natural vegetation, and land use.

LAND-USE AND LAND-COVER DATA

Land-use and land-cover (LULC) data were sampled from digital land-use and land-cover files obtained from the USGS (U.S. Geological Survey, 1986). These data, classified at Anderson Level II (Anderson et al., 1976), have been developed by the USGS over the past 20 years from visual analyses of aerial photography. The data are keyed to 1:250,000-scale USGS 1- by 2-degree quadrangles. Fifty-one quadrangle-based data sets were converted to a 1-km grid for use in the research. The quads, selected to sample major ecosystems, cover approximately 12 percent of the U.S.

POLITICAL BOUNDARIES

State and county political boundaries from the USGS 1:2,000,000-scale digital line graph national data base were used as reference during the investigation (U.S. Geological Survey, 1990).

WATER MASK

Surface water bodies were separated using Channel 2 data from daily AVHRR scenes. Cloud-free scenes were selected through a visual quality assessment of imagery. After a threshold between land and water values was identified, a binary mask was computed and the water bodies data set was added to a land characteristics database. Approximately 50 AVHRR scenes were used to create the mask.

OTHER DATA

Many other supporting materials, including state, regional and national land use and land cover maps, vegetation maps, atlases, agricultural statistics, and crop calendars, were used.

ANALYTIC METHODS

The strategy developed to characterize U.S. land cover employed both AVHRR and ancillary data in a carefully structured manner (Figure 2). Analytic procedures involved overlaying, exploring, and interrelating the disparate spatial data and attributes.

PRELIMINARY EXPERIMENTS

The image analysis methodology used in the development of the 1990 conterminous U.S. land characteristics database evolved from a series of classification experiments conducted using 1989 AVHRR NDVI data covering the western U.S. These tests indicated that (1) an initial vegetated/barren land stratification would be required, (2) a minimum of 50 spectral-temporal classes would be required to define important land cover types, (3) unsupervised classification was suitable, and (4) the use of monthly rather than biweekly NDVI composites would yield acceptable results.

The vegetated/barren land stratification was used to ensure

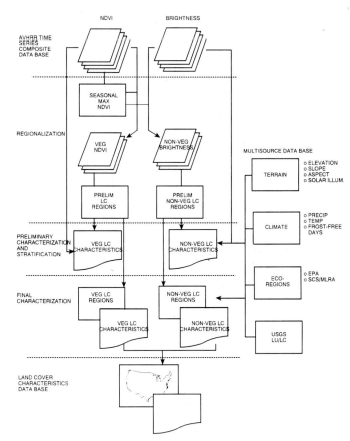

FIG. 2. Processing flow for the development of the prototype land characteristics database. Note that the analysis of brightness data is planned but not yet completed.

that classes exhibiting high intraclass variance, such as, water, bare soil, clouds, and snow/ice, would not dominate the clustering process. Masking of these classes optimizes the spectral discrimination of the classes directly associated with vegetation. Separation and characterization of non-vegetated areas is not, in any case, reliable with NDVI data because of insensitivity of this transformation to low-biomass conditions. Plans call for the characterization of non-vegetated areas using a brightness measure.

IMAGE CLASSIFICATION

Vegetated and non-vegetated land were stratified by analyzing a maximum NDVI composite spanning the March to October 1990 period. Through visual interpretation, an NDVI threshold of 0.09 was selected to separate vegetated and non-vegetated lands. The threshold was determined by comparison of the strata to available maps and imagery, and published data on NDVI-land cover relationships.

An unsupervised clustering algorithm (ISOCLASS) and minimum-distance-to-mean classification methodology was used to define 70 spectral-temporal ("seasonally distinct") classes within the vegetated stratum (Plate 1). A 20 percent systematic sample of the eight monthly composites was employed to derive cluster statistics.

LAND-COVER CHARACTERIZATION

Initial evaluation, labeling, and characterization of the 70 classes was based on a combination of graphic, statistical, and visual tools and techniques. For example, graphs portraying the variation of mean NDVI over the 8-month analysis period yielded a profile of the phenology of each class (Figure 3). The shapes of NDVI multitemporal curves often could be used to identify land cover, and comparisons between curves helped in identifying related classes when analyzed in concert with a display of the spatial distribution of each class. Maps, atlases, agricultural statistics, and Landsat image maps were also used in interpretation of classification results.

Graphical summaries of elevation and frost-free period statistics for each cluster (Figure 4) enabled association of the spatial distribution of each class with site characteristics. Ecoregion and MLRA boundaries were overlaid on the 70-class data set; spatial interrelationships between the data sets were computed; and tables depicting the associations were constructed (Tables 1 and 2). Similar summaries were developed showing the association among the 70 classes and sampled USGS data (Table 3).

The tables indicate the percentage of each of the 70 "seasonally distinct" AVHRR-derived classes falling within MLRA and ecoregion classes, and associated data. Attributes of the ecoregion, MLRA, and LULC data were not considered "ground truth," but were used as aids in understanding site factors, describing land cover, and identifying instances of confusion in the classification. They also provided an opportunity for comparison of alternative methods of landscape regionalization and characterization.

Finally, interpretive maps were developed to portray, respectively, (1) the month in which the NDVI first rose above a threshold value (onset of greenness), (2) the month in which maximum NDVI occurred (peak of greenness), (3) the number of days when the NDVI reached or exceeded a threshold value (duration of greenness), and (4) the cumulative value of the NDVI (total NDVI) for March through October (Plate 2). These maps were derived through analysis of individual class NDVI statistics produced from the original 17 biweekly NDVI composites. Interpretation of temporal NDVI means led to the identification of the four interpretive maps (Figure 5). The four factors are strongly related to the phenologic cycle of vegetation. The month in which the NDVI increases dramatically corresponds to the time of emergence of green vegetation at the beginning of the growing season. The month of maximum NDVI reflects the time of maximum photosynthetic activity (Lloyd, 1990). The time that the NDVI exceeds a certain threshold value is similar to the length of the growing season (Lloyd, 1990; Brown, 1990). The cumulative NDVI through the growing season generally reflects total photosynthetic activity or net primary productivity (Goward *et al.*, 1987; Brown, 1990).

POSTCLASSIFICATION REFINEMENT

As expected, a number of instances of classification confusion were observed. These were instances in which the 70 classes were not uniquely associated with a single cover type. They provided considerable insight about phenological patterns of the U.S. through the process of observing the types and distri-

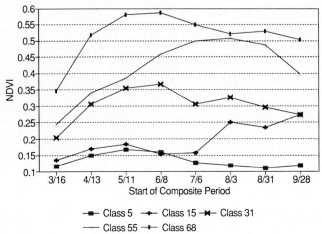

FIG. 3. Example of cluster class NDVI mean values for selected classes.

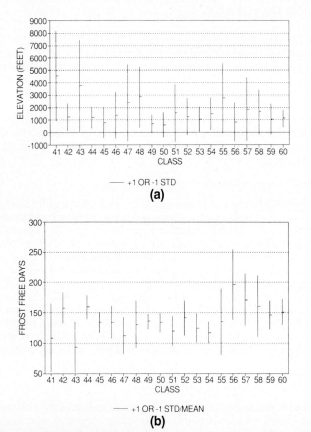

FIG. 4. Statistical relationships between vegetation greenness classes and (a) elevation and (b) frost-free period.

TABLE 1. ECOLOGICAL REGIONS AND THEIR CHARACTERISTICS THAT CORRESPOND TO CLASS 53

Class: 53 Percent: 75.4	Name	Northern lakes and forest
	Landform	Smooth to irregular plains, plains with hills
	PNV	Great Lakes Spruce/Fir, Pine/Northern hardwood
	Landuse	Forest and woodland mostly ungrazed
	Soils	Podzolic
Class: 53 Percent: 5.2	Name	North central hardwood forest
	Landform	Irregular plains
	PNV	Maple/Basswood, Northern hardwoods
	Landuse	Cropland with pasture, woodland, and forests
	Soils	Podzolic
Class: 53 Percent: 4.3	Name	Northeastern highlands
	Landform	Low mountains, open low mountains
	PNV	Northern hardwoods/Spruce
	Landuse	Forest and woodland mostly ungrazed
	Soils	Spodosols

PRELIMINARY VEGETATION GREENNESS CLASSES 1990

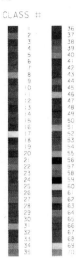

CLASS #

PLATE 1. Preliminary 1990 vegetation greenness classes derived from unsupervised classification of March-October monthly AVHRR NDVI composites.

See page 367 for color plate of Plate 1.

TABLE 2. MAJOR LAND RESOURCE AREAS AND THEIR CHARACTERISTICS THAT CORRESPOND TO CLASS 53

Class	53	Name	Superior Stony and Rocky Loamy Plains
Percent	25.9	Landuse	Forest (80%); crops/pasture (10%); cranberries
		Elev.	300-600M
		Topo.	Undulating to rolling glacial drift plains
		AAP	750mm; majority during growing season
		AAT	2-6 degrees C
		AFFP	80-140 days
		Soils	Orthods
		PNV	Northern hardwood/Pine; Spruce/Larch/Sphagnum Bogs
Class	53	Name	Central Wisconsin and Minnesota Thin Loess and Till
Percent	14.4	Landuse	Forage/feed grains (25%); pasture (15%); forests (60%)
		Elev.	300-500m
		Topo.	Level to rolling till plains mantled with Loess
		AAP	625-750mm; majority in growing season
		AAT	4-7 degrees C
		AFFP	120-140 days
		Soils	Boralfs
		PNV	Mixed northern hardwoods (Oak/Maple/Ash/Elm/Basswood)
Class	53	Name	North Michigan and Wisconsin Sandy Drift
Percent	9.5	Landuse	Forest/lumber; forage/feed crops; cranberries
		Elev.	200-500m
		Topo.	Morainic hills and glacial drift plains
		AAP	675-850mm; minimum in winter
		AAT	4-7 degrees C
		AFFP	120-140 days
		Sojls	Orthods or Saprists
		PNV	Decid (Sugar Maple/Birch/Beech/Hemlock)/Jack/Red Pine
Class	53	Name	Northern Minnesota Gray Drift
Percent	6.8	Landuse	forest/timber (50%); forage/feed grains (50%)
		Elev.	300-500m
		Topo.	Rolling glacial Moraine and outwash
		AAP	525-675mm; majority during growing season
		AAT	3-6 degrees C
		AFFP	100-120 days
		Soils	Boralfs, Aqualfs, Fibrists
		PNV	Forest (Aspen, Northern hardwoods, White Spruce, Blackberry)

butions of confusion. Such information will be useful in future attempts to refine and improve the classification strategy.

Examples of confused land cover are warm season desert grasslands and alpine meadows (class 9). The late "greenup," moderate peak greenness, and short duration of greenness exhibited by grasslands in arid regions receiving limited mid-summer precipitation mimics the phenology of alpine meadows occuring at high elevations. In these instances, elevation and frost-free period data were used for stratification.

In another instance, classes were observed to occur both in areas of the southern Great Plains dominated by winter wheat, and in coastal California where they were associated with cool season grasslands (class 35). Consideration of regional variables led to explanation of this confusion. In the southern Plains,

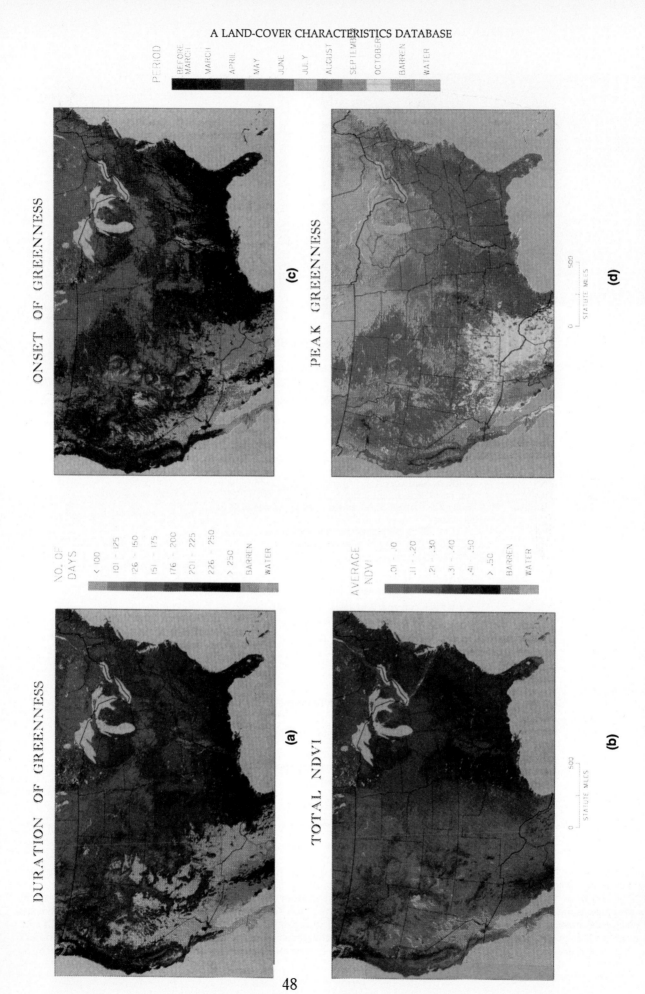

PLATE 2. Seasonal parameters calculated for preliminary vegetation greenness classes include (a) onset of greenness, (b) period of peak greenness, (c) duration of green period, and (d) total NDVI.

See page 368 for color plate of Plate 2.

48

TABLE 3. USGS LAND-USE AND LAND-COVER CATEGORIES AND PROPORTIONS FOUND IN CLASS 53

Class	Anderson Code	Percent	Level II Category
53	43	46.43	Mixed forest land
53	41	21.78	Deciduous forest land
53	61	14.93	Forested wetlands
53	21	6.55	Cropland and pasture

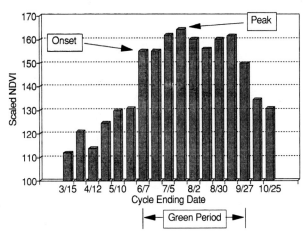

FIG. 5. Example of relationship between NDVI class temporal means (class 53) and selected seasonal parameters.

winter wheat fields "greenup" quickly in April and May, senesce, and are harvested in June. On the west coast, the unique timing of precipitation – winter maximum – influences a similar phenologic pattern in grasses, a type of vegetation similar to wheat in physiognomy and biomass. In this case, the unique ecological characteristics of the two cover types led to the use of ecoregions for resolving confusion.

The postclassification refinement criteria were developed using interactive spatial and graphical comparison techniques. The methodology involved spatial display of each of the 70 classes with histograms of class relationships to ancillary variables such as elevation, ecosystem, and frost-free period. Through interactive selection of minimum and maximum threshold values of the ancillary data, the affected pixels within each class display would be alarmed. Thus, the pixels displayed in specific classes were highlighted in real time, reflecting the effects of selecting a particular threshold value.

Through analytical processes such as those set forth above, 75 percent of the original 70 preliminary vegetation greenness classes were subdivided into 171 seasonally distinct land-cover regions. The final characterization of the 171 classes was then completed, with the development of the descriptive and quantitative attributes of each region.

VERIFICATION

Classification accuracy is a complex issue. The coarse resolution of AVHRR data leads to the development of classes based commonly on land cover mosaics rather than on homogenous landscape regions. The accessibility of consistent site data for verification is also a limitation. An additional complication is the fact that the land characteristics data base is not based on well-defined categories. As a result, verification was limited to comparisons with other data sets such as ecoregions, MLRA's, and LULC.

LINKAGES TO OTHER CLASSIFICATION SYSTEMS

The final step in the prototype effort was to link the AVHRR-based classification and data to other commonly used classification systems (Table 4). Efforts are underway to develop relationships with the USGS (Anderson, 1976), the UNESCO vegetation classification system, and the vegetation types used in the Simple Biosphere Model (SiB) and the Biosphere Atmosphere Transfer Scheme (BATS).

RESULTS AND DISCUSSION

In general, homogeneous land-cover regions were well identified if they comprised relatively large, regular landscape patches. In spatially complex areas, such as the eastern U.S., seasonally distinct land-cover regions were more often correlated with mosaics of land cover having variable physiognomic and vegetative characteristics.

Rangeland classes tended to have seasonal minimum NDVI values of approximately 0.10, and seasonal maxima near 0.30, usually not exceeding 0.40. These regions have low percentage cover and low standing biomass. Many rangeland or grassland classes displayed a dispersed non-contiguous pattern in locations adjacent to and interspersed with forest land cover such as subalpine zones, or agricultural classes. For example, Class 4 has extensive coverage west of the Rocky Mountains, including some contiguous regions, especially in southwestern Wyoming and northeastern Arizona. There are also, however, widespread areas of scattered small occurrences throughout Nevada. These appear to correspond to sagebrush steppe cover in basins between forest-covered mountains.

This biome tends to be confused with eastern urban areas and coastal mixed pixels. In the Southwest, some confusion occurs with mid-elevation open stands of pinyon/juniper woodland having a grass understory. Two differing grassland phenologies, cool season and warm season, contribute to some confusion. For example, Class 14 encompasses both cool-season grasses in California and winter wheat in both Oklahoma and Oregon (Figure 6). Alpine meadows tend to be grouped with other warm-season rangeland.

Regionally distinct patterns representing forest lands were well identified in the classification. Class 54, for example, represents mixed forest land cover (maple/birch/beech with spruce/fir species) of the northeastern mountains and foothills. Class 53 is also primarily northern forests, but, in this case, corresponds to Great Lakes deciduous hardwoods (maple/birch). Class 61 represents a deciduous forest cover of oak/hickory within the Ozark-Boston Mountains and southern Appalachians. The unique hemlock/Douglas fir forests of the northwestern United States are represented by class 70. Figure 7 provides monthly NDVI characteristics for these classes.

Major agricultural regions are clearly identifiable, and NDVI profiles for agricultural classes reveal much about phenology and crop types (Figure 8). For example, winter wheat regions (class 35) in the southern Great Plains are clearly distinguished from spring wheat (class 30) in the northern Great Plains by the different period of greenness onset. Class 44 corresponds to the corn and soybeans regions of the Midwest (Iowa, Illinois, Indiana). Class 43 also is distributed throughout the Midwest, but represents a more mixed landscape with oats, woodlands, and pasture land cover interspersed with corn and soybeans. The NDVI curves for these two classes differ slightly, with class 43 displaying a lower peak green level. It also displays a less rapid greenup rate, which is likely caused by the earlier green-up of the non-corn and soybean elements of the landscape.

The preliminary evaluation indicates that the procedures used are, for the most, part acceptable. However, the research has illuminated many issues that remain to be addressed. For example, the outcome of the NDVI-based classification was clearly

TABLE 4. RELATIONSHIP BETWEEN SELECTED SEASONALLY DISTINCT LAND-COVER REGIONS AND OTHER CLASSIFICATION LEGENDS. PRELIMINARY CLASSIFICATION — CONTERMINOUS U.S.

Class	Typical Vegetation	Anderson Level II	UNESCO Vegetation
3	Saltbrush, Great Basin Sage, Greasewood	32 Shrub and Brush Rangeland	Extremely Xeromorphic Shrubland
6	Grama/Galleta, Bur Sage, Greasewoods	32 Shrub and Brush Rangeland	Mainly Deciduous Scrub
10	Saltbrush, Great Basin Sage, Greasewoods	32 Shrub and Brush Rangeland	Mainly Deciduous Scrub
15	Grama/Buffalo Grass	33 Mixed Rangeland	Short Grassland
16	Pinyon-Juniper, Blackbrush	42 Evergreen Forest Land	Mainly Evergreen Woodland
22	Subalpine Spruce/Fir, Alpine Meadows	42 Evergreen Forest Land	Mainly Evergreen Scrub
26	Wheatgrass/Needlegrass	31 Herbaceous Rangeland	Medium Tall Grassland
37	Ponderosa Pine, Pinyon-Juniper	42 Evergreen Forest Land	Mainly Evergreen Woodland
41	Cedar/Hemlock/Spruce/Fir/Pine	42 Evergreen Forest Land	Mainly Evergreen Forest
53	Maple, Beech, Birch	41 Deciduous Forest Land	Mainly Deciduous Forest
54	Aspen	41 Deciduous Forest Land	Mainly Deciduous Forest
63	Ponderosa Pine	42 Evergreen Forest Land	Mainly Evergreen Forest

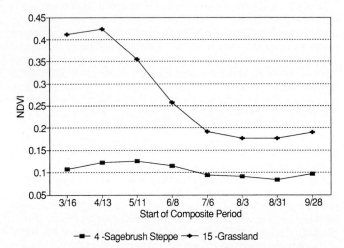

FIG. 6. Monthly NDVI means for selected rangeland categories.

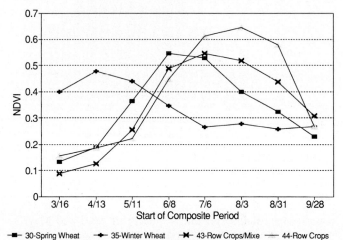

FIG. 8. Monthly NDVI means for selected agricultural categories.

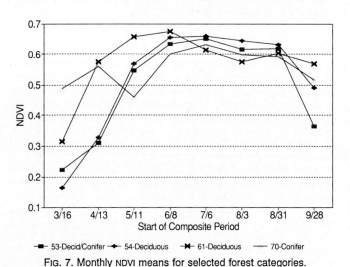

FIG. 7. Monthly NDVI means for selected forest categories.

influenced by the weather during 1990. The preliminary work carried out using the 1989 western United States data set resulted in classes corresponding to drought conditions in the Great Plains during that year. California experienced similar conditions during 1990, which undoubtedly has affected the 1990 classification. The specific effects of climatic anomalies on classification of land cover are, however, uncertain and remain to be investigated.

It is also likely that the classification was affected by the availability of AVHRR data for 1990. The fact that there were no seasonal observations from late-November to March very likely reduced the ability to discern some important cover types in the southeastern United States. The addition of winter composites must be part of future work. It is also not clear whether eight monthly observations are required to characterize land cover. Similar results may be derived from analysis of fewer composites selected at phenologically critical times.

Some cover types cannot be adequately identified using NDVI data. Barren lands, snow and ice, and water bodies have similar NDVI characteristics because of the absence of photosynthetically active plant material. The coarse resolution of AVHRR data in relation to the typically small landscape patches that comprise cover types of limited areal extents, such as wetlands, was limiting. Urban areas could not be uniquely identified because of the complex mixtures of surface conditions within 1-km urban pixels.

The strategy to employ ancillary data in postclassification stratification of the 70 preliminary vegetation greenness classes served to identify some important problems in working with data sets covering large areas. One such problem is exemplified by the case of warm-season desert grassland and alpine cover confusion discussed earlier. Although the initial supposition was that stratification was possible using elevation thresholds, in practice this worked only in local circumstances. Because of the related effects of altitude and latitude on vegetation phenology, the elevation threshold needed to split these classes had to be continually lowered, moving north to south, to achieve

50

acceptable results. In other words, the elevation threshold actually proved to be very difficult to apply. Instead, climate variables such as length of frost-free period, were found to be more effective in postclassification refinement.

Verification of classification results has also presented problems, though these are not unique to this research. In fact, little has been reported on quantitative accuracy assessment of land-cover products derived from analysis of AVHRR data. Tucker *et al.* (1985) note that such work is hampered by the dearth of suitable "ground truth" and lack of agreement between the few extant land cover maps covering the continents. Townshend *et al.* (1987) assert that because existing maps of land cover and land use have been developed differently from AVHRR land-cover databases, they may not even be acceptable standards of reference where available.

Land characteristics databases derived from classification of AVHRR data may produce unconventional regional definitions that do not match classifications used in existing maps, but may be useful. Experience from this study suggests that often the spatial resolution, and probably also the classification precision, of the AVHRR-derived data are higher than those of existing maps. Adequate methods to verify 1-km resolution land-cover classifications conducted over continental-sized areas do not exist. Standards of reference, when they exist at appropriate resolution, are frequently old or have incompatible classifications or other problems (Matthews, 1983). Research is necessary to re-examine conventional image classification accuracy assessment. To employ methods such as those reported, accuracy requirements for global land-cover inventory and monitoring must be established along with a definition of procedures for gauging the quality of land-cover data from coarse-resolution satellite data.

FUTURE RESEARCH DIRECTIONS

The research results reported here are preliminary. Although these findings represent milestones, problems that limit current efforts to characterize continental land cover using multitemporal AVHRR 1-km imagery and ancillary data require work. Some of the important areas in which research is needed include

- Assessment of the effects of seasonal and annual variations on identification and characterization of land-cover regions; year-to-year effects of weather and climate on the development of seasonally distinct land-cover regions, and single-year variation of vegetation and its impacts on determination of the appropriate sample period (biweekly, monthly, or seasonal) for temporally-based classification.
- Identification of influences of landscape-sensor interaction on the definition and characterization of land-cover regions.
- Refinement of data analysis methods, including integration of data from other sensors, use of brightness measures in characterizing unvegetated areas, and potential use of AVHRR thermal channels in land-cover classification.
- Development of verification strategies appropriate for continental-scale land-cover data.

The research suggests that 1-km resolution multitemporal AVHRR/NDVI data employed in concert with ancillary data can be used to characterize land cover over very large areas. Successful land-cover characterization and database development alone, however, are insufficient. The databases must be useful to the global change community and others. Therefore, an important component of future work must be to address specific needs for products.

ACKNOWLEDGMENTS

Most financial support for the participation of Dr. Merchant and Ms. Brown in this research was provided by the Conservation and Survey Division (CSD), University of Nebraska-Lincoln. Special thanks are extended to Dr. Perry B. Wigley, CSD Director. A portion of Dr. Merchant's and Ms. Brown's participation was supported by a U.S. Environmental Protection Agency (EPA) grant-number X007526-01.

REFERENCES

Anderson, J. R., E. E. Hardy, J. T. Roach, and R. E. Witmer, 1976. *A Land Use and Land Cover Classification System for Use with Remote Sensor Data*: U.S. Geological Survey Professional Paper 964, 28 p.

Brown, J., 1990. *Vegetation Discrimination Using AVHRR Global Vegetation Index Data*: M.A. Thesis, University of Nebraska-Lincoln.

Dale, V. H., 1990. *Report of a Workshop on Using Remote Sensing to Estimate Land Use Change*: ORNL Environmental Sciences Division Publication No. 3397, Oak Ridge National Laboratory, Oak Ridge, Tennessee.

Dickinson, R. E., A. Henderson-Sellers, P. J. Kennedy, and M. F. Wilson, 1986. *Biosphere-Atmosphere Transfer Scheme (BATS) for the NCAR Community Climate Model*: NCAR Technical Note 275+STR, National Center for Atmospheric Research, Boulder, Colorado.

Dorman, J. L. and P. J. Sellers, 1989. A Global Climatology of Albedo, Roughness Length and Stomatal Resistance for Atmospheric General Circulation Models as Represented by the Simple Biosphere Model (SiB): *Journal of Applied Meteorology*, Vol. 28, pp. 833–855.

Eidenshink, J. C., R. E. Burgan, and R. H. Haas, 1991. Monitoring Fire Fuels Conditions by Using Time-Series Composites of Advanced Very High Resolution Radiometer Data, *Proceedings, Resource Technology International Symposium on Advanced Technology in Natural Resource Management*, Second, Washington, D.C., November 1990, pp. 68–82.

Fitzpatrick-Lins, K., E. F. Doughty, M. B. Shasby, T. R. Loveland, and S. Benjamin, 1987. Producing Alaska Interim Land Cover Maps from Landsat Digital and Ancillary Data, *Proceedings, Pecora XI Symposium, Satellite Land Remote Sensing: Current Problems and a Look to the Future*, Sioux Falls, South Dakota, pp. 339–347.

Gallo, K. P. and J. F. Brown, 1990. Satellite-Derived Indices for Monitoring Global Phytoclimatology, *Proceedings of the International Geoscience and Remote Sensing Symposium*, Piscataway, New Jersey, pp. 261–264.

Gervin, J. C., A. G. Kerber, R. G. Witt, Y. C. Lu, and R. Sekhon, 1985. Comparison of Level 1 Land Cover Classification Accuracy for MSS and AVHRR Data: *International Journal of Remote Sensing*, Vol. 6, No. 1, pp. 47–57.

Goward, S. N., D. G. Dye, A. Kerber, and V. Kalb, 1987. Comparison of North and South American Biomes from AVHRR Observations: *Geocarto International*, Vol. 1, pp. 27–39.

Goward, S. N., C. J. Tucker, and D. G. Dye, 1985. North American Vegetation Patterns Observed with the NOAA-7 Advanced Very High Resolution Radiometer: *Vegetatio*, Vol. 64, pp. 3–14.

Henderson-Sellers, A., M. F. Wilson, G. Thomas, and R. E. Dickinson, 1986. *Current Global Land-Surface Data Sets for Use in Climate-Related Studies*: NCAR Technical Note 272+STR, Boulder, Colorado, 110 p.

Holben, B., 1986, Characteristics of Maximum Value Composite Images from Temporal AVHRR Data, *International Journal of Remote Sensing*, Vol. 7, pp. 1417–1434.

International Geosphere-Biosphere Programme, 1990. *Global Change*: Report No. 12, Stockholm, Sweden.

Justice, C. O., J. R. G. Townshend, B. N. Holben, and C. J. Tucker, 1985. Analysis of the Phenology of Global Vegetation using Meteorological Satellite Data: *International Journal of Remote Sensing*, Vol. 6, pp. 1271–1318.

Kelly, G., and J. Hood, 1991. AVHRR Conterminous United States Reference Data Set: *Vol. 3, Technical Papers, ACSM-ASPRS Annual Convention*, Baltimore, Maryland, pp. 232–239.

Lloyd, D., 1991. A Phenological Classification of Terrestrial Vegetation Using Shortwave Vegetation Index Imagery: *International Journal of Remote Sensing*, Vol. 11, No. 12, pp. 2269–2279.

Loveland, T. R., 1984. *Copper River, Alaska Terrain and Land Cover Project — Final Report*: EROS Data Center Technical Report, Sioux Falls, South Dakota, 110 p.

Loveland, T. R., and D. O. Ohlen, 1991. A Strategy for Large-Area Land Characterization - the Conterminous U.S. Example, *Proceedings, U.S. Geological Survey Global Change Research Forum*, Reston, Virginia (in press).

Matthews, E., 1983. Global Vegetation and Land Use: New High Resolution Data Bases for Limited Studies: *Journal of Climatology and Applied Meteorology*, Vol. 22, pp. 474–487.

———, 1985. *Atlas of Archived Vegetation, Land Use and Seasonal Albedo Data Sets*: NASA Technical Memorandum 86199, Washington, D.C.

Miller, W. A., S. M. Howard, and D. G. Moore, 1988. Use of AVHRR Data in an Information System for Fire Management in the Western United States, *Proceedings, International Symposium on Remote Sensing of Environment*, 20th, Nairobi, Kenya, December 1986, Vol. 1, pp. 67–79.

National Oceanic and Atmospheric Service, 1979. *Climatic Atlas of the United States*: U.S. Dept. of Commerce, National Oceanic and Atmospheric Administration, Environmental Data Services, Ashville, North Carolina, 80 p.

Olson, J. S., and J. A. Watts, 1982. *Major World Ecosystem Complexes Map, Scale=1:30,000,000*: Oak Ridge National Laboratory, Oak Ridge, Tennessee.

Omernik, J.M., 1987. Ecoregions of the Conterminous United States: *Annals of the Association of American Geographers*, Vol. 77, No. 1, pp. 118–125.

Omernik, J. M., and A. L. Gallant, 1990. Defining Regions for Evaluating Environmental Resources, *Proceedings of the Global Natural Resources Monitoring and Assessment Symposium*, Bethesda, Maryland, pp. 936–947.

Pielke, R. A., and R. Avissar, 1990. Influence of Landscape Structure on Local and Regional Climate, *Landscape Ecology*, Vol. 4, No. 2-3, pp. 133–155.

Pinker, R. T., 1990. Satellites and Our Understanding of the Surface Energy Balance: *Paleogeography, Paleoclimatology and Paleoecology (Global and Planetary Change Section)*, Vol. 82, pp. 321–342.

Risser, P. G., 1985. *Spatial and Temporal Variability of Biospheric and Geospheric Processes: Research Needed to Determine Interactions with Global Change*: International Council of Scientific Unions, Paris.

Roller, N. E. G., and J. E. Colwell, 1986. Coarse-Resolution Satellite Data for Ecological Surveys, *BioScience*, Vol. 36, No. 7, pp. 468–475.

Sadowski, F. G., 1990. Prototype Land Data Sets for Studies of Global Change, *Proceedings, International Geoscience and Remote Sensing Symposium*, 10th, Washington, D.C., May 1990, Vol. 2, p. 1235.

Tappan, G., and Moore, D.G., 1989. Seasonal Vegetation Monitoring with AVHRR Data for Grasshopper and Locust Control in West Africa, *Proceedings, International Symposium on Remote Sensing of Environment*, 22nd, Abidjan, Cote D'Ivoire, October 1988, Vol. 1, pp. 221–234.

Townshend, J. R. G., and C. J. Tucker, 1984. Objective Assessment of Advanced Very High Resolution Radiometer Data for Land Cover Mapping: *International Journal of Remote Sensing*, Vol. 5, No. 2, pp. 497–504.

Townshend, J. R. G. and C. O. Justice, 1988. Selecting the Spatial Resolution of Satellite Sensors Required for Global Monitoring of Land Transformations: *International Journal of Remote Sensing*, Vol. 9, No. 2, pp. 187–236.

Townshend, J. R. G., C. O. Justice, and V. Kalb, 1987. Characterization and Classification of South American Land Cover Types: *International Journal of Remote Sensing*, Vol. 8, No. 8, pp. 1189–1207.

Tucker, C. J., J. A. Gatlin, and S. R. Schneider, 1984. Monitoring Vegetation in the Nile Delta with NOAA-6 and NOAA-7 AVHRR Imagery: *Photogrammetric Engineering & Remote Sensing*, Vol. 50, No. 1, pp. 53–61.

Tucker, C. J., J. R. G. Townshend, and T. E. Goff, 1985. African Land-Cover Classification Using Satellite Data: *Science*, Vol. 227, No. 4685, pp. 369–375.

U.S. Department of Agriculture, Soil Conservation Service, 1981. *Land Resource Regions and Major Land Resource Areas of the United States*, Agriculture Handbook 296, Washington, D.C.

U.S. Geological Survey, 1986. *Land Use and Land Cover Digital Data from 1:250,000- and 1,100,000-Scale Maps*, U.S. Geological Survey Data User's Guide No. 4, Reston Virginia.

———, 1990. *Digital Line Graphs from 1:2,000,000-scale maps*, U.S. Geological Survey Data User's Guide No. 3, Reston Virginia.

Using Multisource Data in Global Land-Cover Characterization: Concepts, Requirements, and Methods

Abstract

Global land-cover data are needed as baseline information for global change research. Multisource data, both coarse-resolution satellite data and ancillary data, were used to produce a land-cover characteristics database for the conterqinous United States. Ancillary data, including elevation and ecological region data sets, were critical to the development, refinement, and information content of each class in the database. They contributed essential evidence for labeling and refining land-cover classes where differing types were represented by single spectral-temporal signatures. The characterization process can be expanded to a global effort depending on (1) the availability of global satellite coverage, (2) the quality and availability of ancillary data, and (3) the evolution of more sophisticated data visualization and analysis techniques.

Introduction

The global change research community has a critical need for current and comprehensive information on the Earth's land cover (Townshend *et al.*, 1991; IGBP, 1992). Both the National Research Council and the International Geosphere-Biosphere Programme (IGBP) have declared that global land-cover data are foremost priorities (U.S. National Academy of Science, 1990; IGBP, 1990). Traditionally, land-cover data have been used for extrapolation of site-specific field data into a global spatial context. More recently, land-cover data were used in the development of process-level models at individual sites and then were applied to the parameterization of algorithms for global analyses. Land cover is viewed as an essential element in biophysical remote sensing methods in which landscapes are stratified into enumeration units so that inversion techniques can be used to estimate regional biophysical parameters (i.e., leaf area index, evapotranspiration, and net primary production).

Investigators have explored methods for generating land-cover information from Advanced Very High Resolution Radiometer (AVHRR) data aboard the National Oceanic and Atmospheric Administration's (NOAA) TIROS series of satellites (Goward *et al.*, 1985; Townshend *et al.*, 1991; Loveland *et al.*, 1991; IGBP, 1992). Although the AVHRR sensor has restricted spectral and spatial resolution compared with the sensors on board the Landsat and SPOT satellites, it possesses temporal resolution advantageous for analyses of global land cover. A location on the Earth's surface is observed twice daily by the AVHRR sensor (once during daylight). The relatively coarse (1 km) spatial resolution of AVHRR data yields a smaller, manageable volume of data for global analyses. For land observations, AVHRR channels 1 and 2 are commonly used to compute a greenness index such as the normalized difference vegetation index (NDVI) (Goward, 1989). Composite images showing the maximum value of the NDVI for each pixel during a multiple-day period (usually 10 or 14 days) result in frequent clear observations of the Earth's surface (Holben, 1986; Eidenshink, 1992).

AVHRR "greenness data" such as the NDVI are useful for depicting change in vegetative activity over time (Goward *et al.*, 1985; Townshend *et al.*, 1987). Land-cover classification and characterization with AVHRR data is often based on associations between land-cover types and variations in periodic observations of greenness through one or more growing cycles (Lloyd, 1990). However, problems exist in discriminating between land-cover types exhibiting similar phenologies (Townshend *et al.*, 1991).

Research, conducted jointly by the U.S. Geological Survey's EROS Data Center and the Center for Advanced Land Management Information Technologies, recently demonstrated that multitemporal AVHRR data, supplemented by ancillary data and analyzed in a structured manner, can be used effectively to characterize land cover (Loveland *et al.*, 1991). A set of 28-day maximum NDVI composite images covering the conterminous United States were clustered into 70 spectral-temporal classes and subsequently stratified, refined, and labeled using ancillary data. The result was a 159-class land-cover characteristics database.

The U.S. study has illuminated many issues that must be addressed in large-area land-cover characterization founded on analysis of coarse-resolution satellite image data. Such efforts require the use of "multisource data." Multisource data include digital images obtained through satellite remote sensing and data from ancillary sources, including terrain, soils, ecoregion, meteorological, and climatic data sets. The U.S. prototype efforts define and illustrate concepts and methods central to land-cover classification at continental and global scales.

The principal objectives of this research are to

Photogrammetric Engineering & Remote Sensing, Vol. 59, No. 6, June 1993, pp. 977–987.

0099-1112/93/5906–977$03.00/0

Jesslyn F. Brown
Center for Advanced Land Management Information Technologies, Conservation and Survey Division, University of Nebraska-Lincoln, Lincoln, NE 68588-0517.
Thomas R. Loveland
U. S. Geological Survey, EROS Data Center, Sioux Falls, SD 57198
James W. Merchant
Center for Advanced Land Management Information Technologies, Conservation and Survey Division, University of Nebraska-Lincoln, Lincoln, NE 68588-0517.
Bradley C. Reed
Donald O. Ohlen
Hughes STX Corporation, EROS Data Center, Sioux Falls, SD 57198.

- establish the conceptual basis and requirements for using multisource data in global land-cover characterization,
- detail multisource data analysis methods used in the prototype effort to characterize land cover for the conterminous United States,
- evaluate the potential for employing such methods in global land-cover characterization, and
- identify needs for future research and data set development.

Background

Remote sensing specialists have long recognized the important role of ancillary data in image interpretation (Campbell, 1978; Townshend and Justice, 1981; Estes *et al.*, 1983). During the last two decades, significant advances have been made in developing techniques and strategies for using ancillary data to improve the results of satellite image analysis. Most efforts have focused on Landsat digital image classification for land-cover mapping (Hutchinson, 1982). The vast majority of research using ancillary data for improving digital image classification has dealt with applications of digital terrain data in classification refinement. Commonly, terrain data are used either to adjust image brightness values for changes in radiance due to rugged relief (Jones *et al.*, 1988), or to sort and (or) subdivide spectrally derived classes to reduce confusion and error induced by the spectral inseparability of certain land-cover types. The latter application is of more concern here.

In one of the first demonstrations of classification improvement with ancillary data, Fleming and Hoffer (1979) used models of observed relationships between land cover, slope, aspect, and elevation to significantly improve a forest-cover map of an area in the southern Rocky Mountains derived from Landsat multispectral scanner (MSS) data. Miller and Shasby (1982) tested both subjective and quantitative techniques for deriving terrain-related decision criteria to enhance Landsat MSS-based maps of vegetation and forest fuels in Arizona and Montana. They reported significant increases in classification precision and a 20 percent improvement in classification accuracy when terrain data were used in post-classification data analysis.

Investigators have made efforts to employ other types of ancillary data in satellite image analysis. Pettinger (1982) used agricultural, upland and lowland environmental strata, and decision rules based on field research to adjust a Landsat MSS land-cover classification in Idaho. He showed that the stratification improved both the detail and the accuracy of the map. Cibula and Nyquist (1987) used terrain data and climatological data (precipitation and climate regimes) in a Landsat MSS classification of Olympic National Park, Washington. The ancillary data and decision logic were used to increase the number of unique land-cover classes from 9 to 21, resulting in an overall accuracy of 91.7 percent. Franklin (1989) used Landsat thematic mapper (TM) data, aeromagnetic, and geologic data in developing maps of geologic structure in central Newfoundland. He also described the joint use of terrain data (elevation, slope, aspect, and upslope and downslope convexity) and land systems (ecoregion) data in a Landsat MSS classification of Gros Morne National Park, Canada. He reported that classification accuracy improved from 40 to 85 percent when ancillary data were used.

As geographic information system (GIS) technology has developed, and integrated GIS-image analysis software has become more common, opportunities for using ancillary data and remotely sensed data in concert have expanded (Trotter, 1991). Innovations in data analysis based on expert systems and related techniques facilitate implementation of complex multisource data analysis strategies (Mason *et al.*, 1988; Sri-

nivasan and Richards, 1990; Wang and Civco, 1992). Bolstad and Lillesand (1992), for example, demonstrated that such approaches improved Landsat TM classification of northern Wisconsin land cover by about 15 percent. Although improved software and analysis methods are now available, progress in using multisource data for land-cover classification has been slow. In most respects, researchers have only begun to realize the potential for combining remotely sensed and ancillary data in such efforts (Trotter, 1991).

Rationale for Using Multisource Data

Our contention is that land cover characterization employing AVHRR data, because of their coarse spatial resolution and constrained spectral resolution, requires the use of ancillary data. Limitations of the sensor are compounded by the fact that AVHRR satellite data are usually employed for observing very large areas such as continents. These large land masses possess enormous variation in terrain, climate, land use, and ecosystems. Even classifications based on multitemporal satellite data are insufficient because phenologic similarities between disparate cover types are common at continental scales.

Virtually all previous research on the use of ancillary data in land-cover classification has focused on relatively small areal domains (e.g., one satellite scene or a relatively small geographic region). A new and different set of problems are encountered in land classification when the objective is to map a continent where environmental complexity and diversity can be much greater than that dealt with in typical satellite remote sensing studies. A multisource approach is essential for land-cover characterization over such vast areas.

In addition, ancillary data can contribute more stable information to characterization, in contrast to satellite data, which fluctuate with the changing seasonal patterns of vegetation. Although the multitemporal NDVI data provide a useful measure of photosynthetic activity through time, allowing aggregation and regionalization of the land surface, additional (nonsatellite) information is needed to describe and refine land-cover units. A multisource approach, including both satellite and ancillary data, is crucial to the development, refinement, explanation, and information content of each land-cover class under analysis.

Campbell (1978) classified image interpretation procedures into five broad strategies. Four of these, he asserted, depend on the use of ancillary data for success. Most analyses of AVHRR data fall within Campbell's class of "probabilistic interpretations." He noted that, "because of the importance of non-image information ... in the application of a probabilistic interpretation process, relationships defined ... are valid only for a particular region" (Campbell, 1978, p. 267). Research in the conterminous United States supports this contention. When dealing with areas encompassing large latitudinal, elevational, climatic, and anthropogenic variation, continual adjustments of models, rules, and assumptions about relationships among image, landscape, and environment must be made (or, in other words, between image and ancillary data).

Experiences from the Conterminous U. S. Database

Creation of the prototype conterminous U.S. land-cover database included (Figure 1)

- processing and classifying AVHRR data,
- labeling and postclassification stratification of pixel clusters using ancillary data, and
- compiling the final land-cover characteristics database. Al-

TABLE 1. ANCILLARY DATA SETS, SOURCES, UNITS OF MEASUREMENT, AND USE OF THE DATA.

Data Set	Source	Units	Use
Elevation	DMA[1]	feet (20-ft resolution)	L[2]/S[3]
Climate	NOAA[4]	frost-free days	L/S
Ecoregions	USEPA[5]	Ecoregions attributes	L/S
MLRA[6]	SCS[7]	MLRA attributes	L
LULC[8]	USGS[9]	LULC attributes	L

[1]Defense Mapping Agency (1986)
[2]Labeling
[3]Stratification
[4]National Oceanic and Atmospheric Service (1979)
[5]U.S. Environmental Protection Agency (Omernik, 1987; Omernik and Gallant, 1990)
[6]Major land resource areas
[7]Soil Conservation Service (USDA SCS, 1981)
[8]Land use and land cover
[9]U.S. Geological Survey (USGS, 1986; Anderson et al., 1976)

TABLE 2. ATTRIBUTES ACCOMPANYING ECOREGION AND MAJOR LAND RESOURCE AREA (MLRA) DATA SETS.

Data set	Attributes
Ecoregions	Name
	Landform
	Potential natural vegetation
	Land use
	Soils
MLRA	Name
	Land use
	Elevation
	Topography
	Average annual precipitation
	Average annual temperature
	Average frost-free period
	Potential natural vegetation

though this paper is mainly concerned with the second step, an overview of the first step is necessary. A more detailed summary of processing and classifying AVHRR data is found in Loveland *et al.* (1991).

Processing and Classifying AVHRR Data

Daily 1-km AVHRR data from NOAA 11 were calibrated to reflectance, scaled to byte range, and georeferenced to the Lambert Azimuthal Equal Area map projection. Eight 28-day composites acquired from March to October 1990, based on maximum NDVI decision rules, were used as input to clustering and classification. A masking procedure ensured that classes exhibiting high intraclass variance, such as water, bare soil, clouds, snow, and ice, did not dominate the clustering process. An unsupervised clustering algorithm (Isoclass) and minimum-distance-to-mean classification were used to define 70 spectral-temporal (seasonally distinct) clusters. A 20 percent systematic sample of each of the eight composites was employed to derive initial cluster statistics. In all but ten cases, the clusters were not associated with a single cover type. Confusion occurred where several different land-cover types (i.e., agriculture and deciduous forest) were classified into one cluster. Ancillary data were then used to identify within-cluster confusion and to stratify clusters into distinct land-cover types.

Introduction of Ancillary Data

Ancillary data in a variety of forms, including discrete, thematic, and continuous, were used to augment database development, labeling, and postclassification stratification. The ancillary data included elevation, frost-free period, ecoregions, major land resource areas (MLRA), and land-use and land-cover data. These data sets, described in more detail by Loveland *et al.* (1991), are summarized in Table 1. The ecoregions and MLRA data contain associated attributes (Table 2), which were especially useful in the database development.

Application of Ancillary Data

In the conterminous U.S. research, ancillary data were found to contribute to classification and characterization of land cover in two ways: (1) for iterative labeling and describing clusters and classes, and (2) for postclassification refinement of spectral-temporal classes by spatial subdivision and merging (see Figure 1).

Preliminary labeling involved comparison of regional patterns exhibited by individual spectral-temporal classes with a wide variety of maps, images, and published data. Both traditional visual-subjective methods and less traditional digital-objective methods were used. Postclassification refinement involved "deterministic modeling" (Franklin, 1989). Visualization software was used to develop decision rules utilizing a combination of field experience and analysis of digital ancillary data similar to that used by Miller and Shasby (1982).

LABELING WITH ANCILLARY DATA.

Each of the original 70 clusters was evaluated in terms of its spatial distribution, phenology (as portrayed graphically by plotting the NDVI against time), and association with the ancillary data. In this way, descriptions for the initial 70 clusters identified clusters with confusion which required subdivision and indicated which types of ancillary data might provide useful separation criteria.

Information was extracted from the ancillary data layers for labeling using GIS overlay procedures. Each spectral-temporal cluster was intersected with the ancillary data layers, and counts or proportions for each association were compiled. For example, Figure 2 shows the distribution of cluster 35. Descriptive (tabular) attributes of the ancillary data (i.e., elevation, MLRA, and ecoregion) are attached as characteristics of the spectral-temporal cluster (Tables 3 to 7). These data provided the basis for class labeling and description (Table 8).

Label refinement occurred at several stages following the clustering of the multitemporal NDVI data. The intersection of each class with each ancillary data set provided additional information about each land-cover region, contributing to a convergence-of-evidence methodology. Graphic visualization of the data contributed to improved understanding of the classes as they were labeled and stratified.

POSTCLASSIFICATION REFINEMENT WITH ANCILLARY DATA.

After preliminary labeling, each cluster was evaluated visually to identify separation criteria. Using visualization techniques developed at the EROS Data Center, each cluster was observed with the associated distribution (histogram) of the elevation, ecoregions, and frost-free data. Subdivisions were made to avoid separating spatially contiguous pixels. Of the 59 spectral-temporal clusters that were subject to postclassification stratification, 27 were divided into two classes, 14

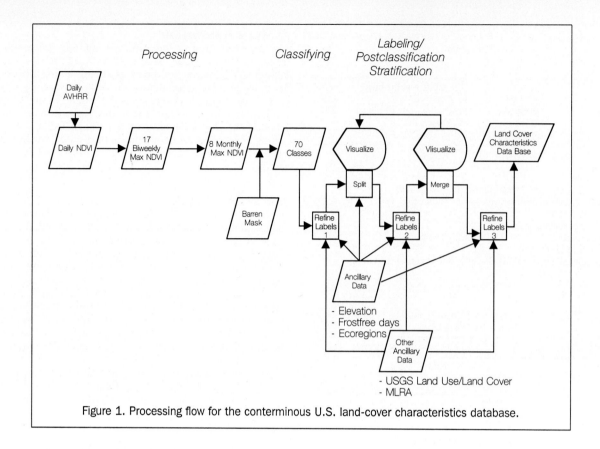

Figure 1. Processing flow for the conterminous U.S. land-cover characteristics database.

were split into three, and 18 were subdivided into four to six classes, resulting in 189 initially stratified classes.

The ecoregions data were used as the most frequently applied stratifier. These data provided separation rules for clusters 86 times as the sole separation criteria and 59 times in conjunction with either frost-free period or elevation criteria. The ecoregions data were especially useful in situations where a single spectral-temporal cluster represented several different land-cover types that were spatially separate. Elevation data were used 31 times as the sole separation criteria and 47 times in combination with the other two ancillary layers. Elevation data helped in situations where disparate land-cover types were in close proximity to each other. The continuous nature of the elevation data allowed interactive adjustment of the separation criteria. Altogether, elevation and ecoregions data were used, either alone or in combination, to solve 127 occurrences, or 67 percent, of cluster confusion during the conterminous U.S. data base construction.

Combining small (<1,000 pixels) land-cover classes was determined by spatial association and similar phenology as depicted in the NDVI multitemporal characteristics. Using these criteria, 70 cluster segments from different parent clusters were merged into 28 classes in the final database.

Land-Cover Issues and the Multisource Data Approach

It was apparent early in the U.S. land-cover work that common approaches for applying ancillary data in labeling and postclassification would not perform well. Within small geographic regions, elevation data can often be used to sort and (or) subdivide spectrally similar classes based on models of terrain-vegetation relationships. However, because of the large latitudinal range of the United States, a single elevation threshold could not be used to divide disparate land-cover

types that had similar phenologies defined by their NDVI greenness curves and belonged to the same spectral-temporal class. As one moved northward, a given elevation threshold had to be adjusted "downslope" to compensate for the diminishing length of the growing season, making establishment of "global" models difficult and impractical. In many instances, the frost-free period was a more effective ancillary data source; however, it may be more difficult to obtain in global coverage than elevation data.

Experiences from the conterminous U.S. land characterization study suggest that classification confusion was most often related to climatic and anthropogenic factors. Climatic influences include the simple latitudinal and elevational limits on the growth of vegetation. Land-cover types that were often found to have similar spectral-temporal NDVI signatures included irrigated agriculture and forest, coastal wetlands and desert shrubland, and tundra and desert shrubland.

Four types of confusion were encountered: (1) those between natural landscapes, (2) those between natural and anthropogenic landscapes, (3) those between anthropogenic landscapes, and (4) undistinguished outliers. These types of problems probably will occur in any continental or global land-cover classification effort.

NATURAL LANDSCAPE CONFUSION.
Confusion between natural land-cover types is frequently influenced by climatic factors. Many of these problems are related to topography and are easily solved using digital elevation data, when available at the appropriate resolution. However, for mountain ranges that cover large latitudinal distances (e.g., the Rocky Mountains of North America or the Andes of South America), elevation influences vary. The

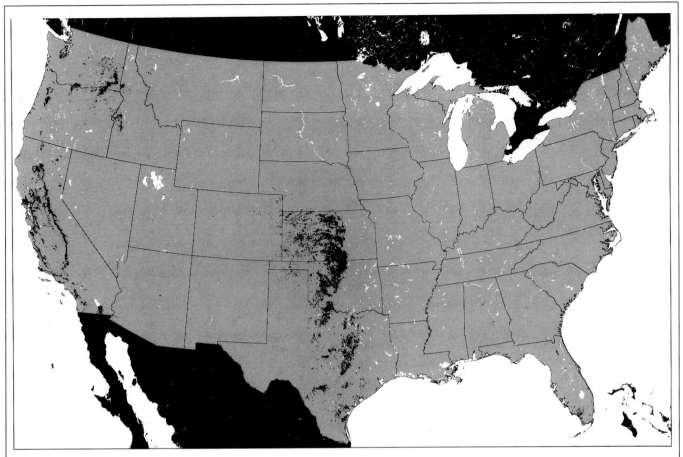

Figure 2. Spatial distribution of cluster 35.

TABLE 3. PERCENT CO-OCCURRENCE OF CLUSTER 35 WITHIN SELECTED ECOREGIONS.

Attribute	Attribute Value
Percent	46.6
Name	Central Great Plains
Landform	Irregular plains
PNV*	Bluestem/grama prairie, bluestem prairie
Land Use	Cropland, cropland with grazing
Soils	Dry mollisols
Percent	11.5
Name	Southern and central California plains and hills
Landform	Irregular plains, tablelands, low mountains
PNV*	California oakwoods, chaparral, California steppe
Land Use	Open woodland, grazing
Soils	Light colored soils of subhumid regions
Percent	7.5
Name	Texas Blackland Prairies
Landform	Irregular plains
PNV*	Bluestem, needlegrass, buffalo grass
Land Use	Cropland
Soils	Vertisols

* potential natural vegetation

frost-free period was found to represent adequately the influence of latitude on elevation zonation of vegetation in the conterminous U.S. study, and is likely to be useful in other regions of the world. Elevation data, used in combination with ecoregions, are a suitable substitute for the frost-free period. Common natural landscape confusion encountered included areas with low seasonal NDVI values such as tundra, desert shrubland, and coastal wetlands.

NATURAL-ANTHROPOGENIC LANDSCAPE CONFUSION.
Similarity between natural and human-influenced landscapes (i.e., wildland forests and grasslands versus agricultural land) was the most common landscape confusion in the U.S. database. It takes many forms and can be addressed using several ancillary variables. A common problem is agricultural vegetation sharing the same spectral-temporal profiles as natural vegetation. In some cases, altitude is a factor, while other cases are influenced by the spatial patterns of rainfall or soil temperatures. Altitude-related problems can be solved with digital elevation data. The others may be corrected with either climate variables or ecoregions.

ANTHROPOGENIC LANDSCAPE CONFUSION.
Land management and settlement practices cause complex problems in landscape confusion. If the confusion is interspersed, correcting it is nearly impossible. When the confusion is spatially separated, ecoregions are the most logical ancillary variable for postclassification stratification.

UNDISTINGUISHED OUTLIER CONFUSION.
A certain amount of confusion is caused by image artifacts, mixed pixels, and atmospheric contamination. There are rarely good strategies to solve these types of problems.

TABLE 4. PERCENT CO-OCCURRENCE OF CLUSTER 35 WITH LAND-USE AND LAND-COVER (LULC) DATA BY ANDERSON LEVEL II CATEGORIES.

Percent	Category
78.00	Cropland
5.42	Evergreen forest land
5.18	Shrub and brush rangeland

Methods for Solving Land-Cover Confusion in the Conterminous United States

The following three examples illustrate working solutions for landscape confusion encountered in characterization of the conterminous United States. Original cluster 35, an example of natural-anthropogenic landscape confusion, was described as mostly winter wheat in the central United States and Pacific Northwest, but also included a significant area of cool season grasslands in the California hills. Labeling was based on ancillary data (see Tables 3 to 7) and the class multitem-

TABLE 5. PERCENT CO-OCCURRENCE OF CLUSTER 35 WITHIN SELECTED MAJOR LAND RESOURCE AREAS.

Attribute	Attribute Value
Percent	17.8
Name	Central Rolling Red Prairies
Land Use	Range/grazing (40%); crop/w.wheat (20%); woodland/urban/pasture (20%)
Elevation	300–500m
Topography	Dissected plain, undulating to gently rolling hills
AAP[1]	625–900mm; maximum in spring
AAT[2]	14–18°C
AFFP[3]	190–230 days
PNV[4]	Mixed prairie (indiangrass, bluestem); trees/shrubs
Percent	9.9
Name	Central Rolling Red Plains
Land Use	Range/grazing (60%); crop/w.wheat/sorg. (35%); irrig. (5%)
Elevation	500–900m
Topography	Dissected plains
AAP[1]	500–750mm; maximum in spring
AAT[2]	14–18°C
AFFP[3]	185–230 days
PNV[4]	Mid/tall grasses (bluestem, sand sagebrush, gramas)
Percent	6.7
Name	Texas Blackland Prairie
Land use	Crops/cotton/sorghum (40%); pasture (45%)
Elevation	100–200m
Topography	Level to gently rolling dissected plain
AAP[1]	750–1150mm; maximum in spring and fall
AAT[2]	17–21°C
AFFP[3]	230–280 days
PNV[4]	Prairie (bluestem) with oak/elm savanna along river
Percent	5.2
Name	Sierra Nevada foothills
Land use	Grassland (75%); dryland ag. (5%); brush/open forest (20%)
Elevation	200–500m with peaks to 1200m
Topography	Rolling to steep dissected hills and low mts.
AAP[1]	350–900mm; dry hot summers, cool moist winters
AAT[2]	13–18°C
AFFP[3]	200–320 days
PNV[4]	Annual grasses, shrubs (chamise, manzanita), trees (oak/pine)

[1]average annual precipitation
[2]average annual temperature
[3]average frost-free period
[4]potential natural vegetation

TABLE 6. FROST-FREE PERIOD STATISTICS FOR CLUSTER 35.

Statistic	Days
Mean	209
Std. Dev.	44
Maximum	338
Minimum	48
Mode	180
Median	202

poral NDVI curve (Figure 3). The distribution of the cluster within several ecoregions with similar attributes indicated a suitable separation criteria. Pixels within five ecoregions (Plate 1), all located along the Pacific coast and containing open woodland or chaparral land cover, were separated by an overlay procedure to form new class 150, and the remaining pixels became new class 13. Class 150 was subsequently labeled as containing annual grasses, manzanita, oak, and white pine; class 13 was described as winter wheat.

In another example of natural-anthropogenic confusion, cluster 57 was identified initially as agricultural land cover

TABLE 7. ELEVATION STATISTICS FOR CLUSTER 35.

Statistic	Feet
Mean	1,469
Std. Dev.	897
Maximum	7,068
Minimum	1
Mode	200
Median	1,361

TABLE 8. DESCRIPTION OF ORIGINAL CLUSTER 35.

35.0 Class 35
    35.1 General—main area is in Kansas and Oklahoma. Some in Washington, Oregon, and California.
    35.2 Groups
        35.2.1 Kansas/Oklahoma—winter wheat with some rangeland.
        35.2.2 Oregon/Washington—eastern parts of States near Columbia River. Winter wheat in east. Also found in Willamette Valley.
        35.2.3 California—cool season grasses.

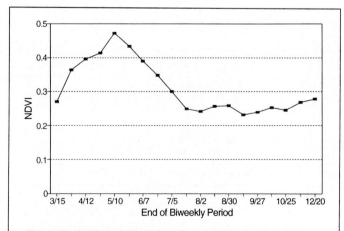

Figure 3. Multitemporal normalized difference vegetation index plot for cluster 35.

in the Midwest, but mostly coniferous forest elsewhere. The distribution of elevation for original cluster 57 (Plate 2) was positively skewed toward low elevations (less than 1,500 ft). Interactive visualization of the data permitted examination of possible subdivision thresholds and their resulting spatial distributions. Accordingly, spatial context was considered along with the ancillary data for each stratification decision. Cluster 57 was subsequently subdivided using a 3,000 ft elevation threshold and divided into two new classes: class 156, which contains lodgepole pine, Douglas fir, and aspen, and class 34, containing wheat, soybeans, corn, and pasture (see Plate 2).

Figure 4 shows an example of multistage stratification using ancillary data applied to a more complicated form of cluster confusion. Original cluster 58 presented a challenge to label and stratify successfully because it contained several kinds of landscape confusion. The cluster had portions of natural, anthropogenic, and mosaic landscapes, as well as undistinguished outliers. Using a three-step process, cluster 58 was subdivided into six classes in the final data base (Table 9). First, class 55 was subdivided using the ecoregions data (see Figure 4, e); pixels within four ecoregions located in the southeastern plains and mid-Atlantic and Gulf coastal plains were included in this class. Class 55 was labeled a cropland/woodland mosaic, with predominant vegetation including oak, pine, soybeans, corn, cotton, and peanuts (see Table 9). The rest of the pixels of cluster 58 were stratified in two stages (see Figure 4), first into two areas and second into smaller regions, some of which were merged with parts of other clusters to form the final class structure.

Classes 47, 117, and 93 were stratified using both ecoregions and elevation (see Figure 4, de). As a group, they were either within the ecoregions of the Northwest coastal mountains or between 5,500 and 12,000 ft in elevation in remaining ecoregions (except within those defining class 55). Class 47 was further stratified by the ecoregions of the central and northeastern plains. This cropland/woodland class was dominated by corn, soybeans, sorghum, and mixed woodlots (see Table 9). Class 93 was further divided by the ecoregions of the Appalachian Mountains and northeastern upland regions. This class was labeled southeast deciduous forest, consisting mostly of oak, hickory, and some mixed cropland. Class 93 was small and was subsequently merged with portions of two other parent clusters. Class 117, western coniferous forest, consisted of all the pixels from cluster 58 within the Northwest coastal range ecoregions above 5,500 ft in elevation, mostly in the Rocky Mountains. This coniferous forest class was dominated by ponderosa pine, lodgepole pine, western white pine, and Douglas fir (see Table 9).

The remaining two classes, 36 and 136, were initially stratified together using elevation (less than 5,500 ft) and ecoregions other than the Northwest coast and the southeastern plains (see Figure 4, de). Class 136 was subdivided by the ecoregions in the northwest Great Lakes and northeast highlands regions. This class merged with another cluster segment and is a mixed forest composed mostly of oak, maple, ash, jack pine, and red pine. The final cluster segment, class 36 (cropland and pasture), consisted mainly of corn, soybeans, and hay pasture (see Table 9) and was contained within the northwest Great Lakes ecoregions.

The above procedures demonstrate flexible and interactive approaches to land-cover regionalization combining clustering procedures with postclassification stratification and merging. The process developed for the conterminous U.S. land database provides a methodology that can be ap-

plied to global land characterization, given the availability of appropriate satellite and ancillary data.

Data Requirements and Sources for Global Land-Cover Characterization

The global change research community is increasingly organized in their call for the development of global land-cover databases. The IGBP, for example, has identified land-cover data as a top research priority (IGBP, 1990). The IGBP has further clarified this requirement by specifying that 1-km AVHRR data are the logical basis for global land-cover data sets (IGBP, 1992). An initiative is underway to organize the multitemporal 1-km AVHRR data needed for a global land-cover mapping effort. However, a parallel effort is needed to organize the multisource data required to permit accurate global land-cover characterization.

Class labeling requires data that support the identification of land cover, vegetation, and other environmental characteristics of individual land-cover regions. For this purpose, consistent, detailed, and spatially comprehensive vegetation, land-cover, and soils maps are especially useful. However, such data with continental coverage are rare. Although not ideal, local or regional maps are valuable, particularly if applied to visual interpretation rather than automated class labeling. Because methods of visual interpretation for class labeling are more flexible and adaptive, data requirements are less rigid. However, additional data may be needed for the more rigorous postclassification refinement application.

Postclassification refinement requires more control and consistency in ancillary data. These data must (1) span the entire continent; (2) serve as surrogates for the climatic, ecological, or anthropogenic factors that create spectral or multitemporal class confusion; (3) contain the qualitative or quantitative information that correlates to the sources of confusion; and (4) have compatible geographic scale and locational accuracy.

Global Data Requirements

The minimum set of ancillary variables needed for postclassification refinement contains digital elevation data and ecoregions. Both data types are likely to be available for continental mapping. Climate variables, particularly the frost-free period and monthly precipitation, are also desirable but are less likely to be available in a suitable form.

DIGITAL ELEVATION DATA.
A global digital elevation data set, ETOPO5, is currently available from NOAA's National Geophysical Data Center. However, because of its approximate resolution of 10 km (based on a cell size of 5 arc minutes), it is inadequate for representing vegetation patterns related to elevation zonation in irregular terrain. Several organizations have programs underway to develop 1-km global digital elevation models (DEM). The U.S. Geological Survey, with the National Aeronautic and Space Administration, is investigating several options for generating a global DEM. The Committee on Earth Observation Satellites is also promoting an multiagency effort to prepare a global DEM. It is likely that appropriate elevation data soon will be available for a global land-cover mapping effort.

ECOREGIONS.
There are several global ecoregion frameworks that can be used for land-cover characterization. The U.S. Forest Service has developed ecoregions based on climate, climax vegetation, and soils (Bailey, 1989; Bailey and Cushwa, 1981). Researchers at Moscow State University have mapped two

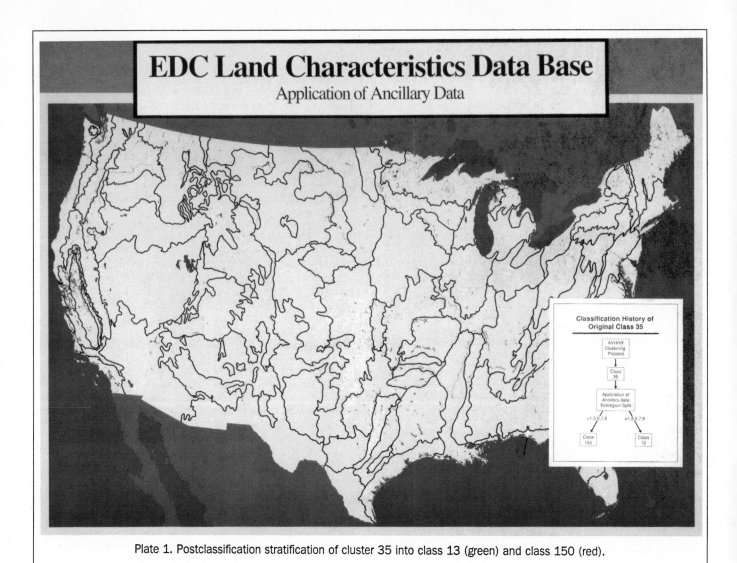

EDC Land Characteristics Data Base
Application of Ancillary Data

Classification History of
Original Class 35

AVHRR
Clustering
Process

Class
35

Application of
Ancillary data
Ecoregion Split-

<1,5,6,7,8   ≠1,5,6,7,8

Class
150

Class
13

Plate 1. Postclassification stratification of cluster 35 into class 13 (green) and class 150 (red).

ecoregion frameworks for the globe. One is based on climate, soils, and potential natural vegetation, and the other includes those plus current land use (Alekseyev *et al.*, 1988). A drawback of these products is that their minimum mapping unit (map scale 1:15,000,000) is more coarse than 1-km AVHRR data. Small-scale data, however, may be the best available sources. Although there are excellent national ecoregion interpretations, it is unlikely that they can be combined to form consistent continental coverage. However, these data can contribute effective labeling information.

CLIMATE VARIABLES.
To use climate data for postclassification stratification, it is necessary to spatially interpolate surfaces for each variable. Adequate representation of precipitation, temperature, or frost-free period require enough stations so that major regional patterns are depicted. Global monthly temperature, precipitation, and atmospheric pressure climatic data are available (Vose *et al.*, 1992); however, the spatial distribution of available stations may not be adequate for postclassification analyses at a 1-km resolution.

Global Data Sources
The United Nations Environment Programme Global Resource Information Database is one source for global and national data sets (UNEP, 1990). Many countries—including Australia, Canada, and the former Soviet Union—have thematic data sets equivalent to the ecoregions data used in this research (Omernik, 1987). Ancillary data sets are available, both in global coverages (Matthews, 1985) and national coverages (for example, Canada (Wiken, 1986; Ecoregions Working Group, Canada Committee on Land Classification, 1989) and Australia (Walker *et al.*, 1985)).

Summary and Conclusions
Ancillary data provide information crucial to the success of large-area land-cover characterization based on NOAA AVHRR data. They contribute essential evidence for labeling and refining land-cover classes where differing types are represented by a single spectral-temporal signature. The attributes of ancillary data, used in conjunction with the spatial distribution of a spectral-temporal region, are the basis

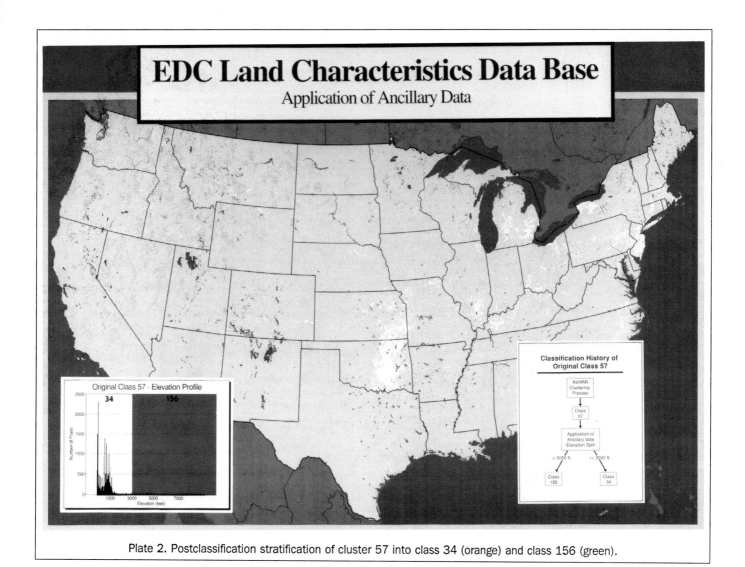

Plate 2. Postclassification stratification of cluster 57 into class 34 (orange) and class 156 (green).

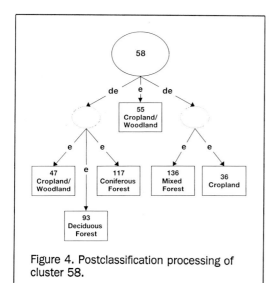

Figure 4. Postclassification processing of cluster 58.

for selecting the appropriate ancillary variable(s), choosing the most reasonable threshold(s), and making a division.

The challenge of characterizing the land surface at global scales is to analyze larger areas while extracting essential information from multisource data. Processing of global data sets presents new computational and interpretational challenges. Large areas possess great variation in climate, terrain,

TABLE 9. FINAL CLASS DESCRIPTIONS FOR CLUSTER 58 SEGMENTS.

Class No.	Cover type	Primary vegetation types
36	Cropland/pasture	Corn, soybeans, pasture/hay
47	Cropland/woodlots	Corn, soybeans, sorghum, mixed-woodlots
55	Woodland/cropland	Mixed-oak, pine, soybeans, corn, cotton, peanuts
93	Mixed-forest/crop	Oak, hickory, mixed-pine, mixed-crops
117	Western-conifer	Western white, ponderosa, lodgepole, douglas fir
136	Northern-forest	Oak, maple, ash, jack-pine, red-pine

61

and vegetation, compounding spectral-temporal confusion among disparate land-cover types. Because a global effort to characterize land cover will probably incorporate a continental strategy, continents crossing the equator (i.e., Africa and South America) may pose more complex problems. Similar vegetation mosaics affected by different growing seasons in the Southern and Northern Hemispheres may exhibit significantly different spectral-temporal signatures; however, the basic types of landscape confusion discussed in this paper are expected.

As larger areas are studied, more advanced methods will be necessary to understand satellite and ancillary data relationships. New techniques in data exploration and visualization will permit analysis of ancillary data and may reveal complex relationships in the data that are vital in explaining land-cover characteristics. Although automated techniques may afford simpler, more efficient methods for doing such work, the interaction of the analyst remains the key to the process of postclassification stratification of large areas because of the complexity of the decision process and the requirement for expert knowledge and reasoning. Therefore, methods should be developed that assist rather than replace the analyst.

The success of global land-cover analysis, central to future global change research, will depend on (1) the availability of global satellite coverage, (2) the quality and level of information within available ancillary data to solve areas of confusion, and (3) the evolution of improved techniques for extracting information from both types of data.

Acknowledgments

The first author, Jesslyn F. Brown, performed this work under U. S. Environmental Protection Agency grant (X0075626-01) while a Visiting Scientist at EROS Data Center. The Hughes STX Corporation performed this work under U. S. Geological Survey contract 1434-92-C-40004.

References

Alekseyev, B., A. Vasilyeva, Y. Golubchikov, L. Kurakova, Y. Lukashova, Y. Milanova, L. Mikhailova, E. Romanova, A. Ryabchikov, N. Sen'kovshaya, V. Uledov, and L. Frolova, 1988. *Geographic Belts and Zonal Types of Landscapes of the World* (translated by A. Kushlin): U.S.S.R. Main Administration for Geodesy and Cartography and Moscow State University, Moscow, map scale 1:15,000,000.

Anderson, J.F., E.E. Hardy, J.T. Roach, and R.E. Witmer, 1976. *A Land Use and Land Cover Classification System for Use with Remote Sensor Data:* U.S. Geological Survey Professional Paper 964, 28 p.

Bailey, R.G., 1989. Explanatory Supplement to Ecoregions Map of the Continents: *Environmental Conservation*, Vol. 16, No. 4, pp. 302–309.

Bailey, R.G., and C.T. Cushwa, 1981. *Ecoregions of North America:* Map. U.S. Fish and Wildlife Service, Office of Biological Services, Eastern Energy and Land Use Team, map scale 1:12,000,000.

Bolstad, P.V., and T. M. Lillesand, 1992. Rule-Based Classification Models: Flexible Integration of Satellite Imagery and Thematic Spatial Data: *Photogrammetric Engineering & Remote Sensing*, Vol. 58, No. 7, pp. 965–971.

Campbell, J.B., 1978. A Geographical Analysis of Image Interpretation Methods: *The Professional Geographer*, Vol. 30, No. 3, pp. 264–269.

Cibula, W.G., and M.O. Nyquist, 1987. Use of Topographic and Climatological Models in a Geographical Data Base to Improve Landsat MSS Classification for Olympic National Park: *Photo-*

grammetric Engineering & Remote Sensing, Vol. 53, No. 1, pp. 67–75.

Defense Mapping Agency, 1986. *Defense Mapping Agency Product Specifications for Digital Terrain Elevation Data (DTED)*, (2d ed.): April, 1986.

Ecoregions Working Group, Canada Committee on Land Classification, 1989. *Ecoclimatic Regions of Canada:* Ecological Land Classification Series No. 23, Environment Canada, Ottawa, Ontario.

Eidenshink, J., 1992. The 1990 Conterminous U.S. AVHRR Data Set: *Photogrammetric Engineering & Remote Sensing*, Vol. 58, pp. 809–813.

Estes, J.E., E.J. Hajic, and L.R. Tinney, 1983. Fundamentals of Image Analysis - Analysis of Visible and Thermal Infrared Data, *The Manual of Remote Sensing* (R.N. Colwell, editor), Falls Church, Virginia, American Society of Photogrammetry and Remote Sensing, Vol. 1, pp. 987–1124.

Fleming, M.D., and R.M. Hoffer, 1979. Machine Processing of Landsat MSS Data and DMA Topographic Data for Forest Cover Type Mapping: *Proceedings of the 1979 Machine Processing of Remotely Sensed Data Symposium*, West Lafayette, Indiana, Purdue University/LARS, pp. 377–390.

Franklin, S.E., 1989. Ancillary Data Input to Satellite Remote Sensing of Complex Terrain Phenomena: *Computers and Geosciences*, Vol. 15, No. 5, pp. 799–808.

Goward, S.N., 1989. Satellite Bioclimatology: *Journal of Climate*, Vol. 2, pp. 710–720.

Goward, S.N., C.J. Tucker, and D.G. Dye, 1985. North American Vegetation Patterns Observed with the NOAA-7 Advanced Very High Resolution Radiometer: *Vegetatio*, Vol 64, pp. 3–14.

Holben, B., 1986. Characteristics of Maximum Value Composite Images from Temporal AVHRR Data: *International Journal of Remote Sensing*, Vol. 7, pp. 1417–1434.

Hutchinson, C., 1982. Techniques for Combining Landsat and Ancillary Data for Digital Classification Improvement: *Photogrammetric Engineering & Remote Sensing*, Vol. 48, No. 1, pp. 123–130.

International Geosphere-Biosphere Programme, 1990. *Global Change:* Report No. 12. Stockholm, Sweden: IGBP Secretariat.

———, 1992. *Improved Global Data for Land Applications:* IGBP Report No. 20. Stockholm, Sweden: IGBP Secretariat.

Jones, A.R., J.J. Settle, and B.K. Wyatt, 1988. Use of Digital Terrain Data in the Interpretation of SPOT-1 HRV Multispectral Imagery: *International Journal of Remote Sensing*, Vol. 9, No. 4, pp. 669–682.

Lloyd, D., 1990. A Phenological Classification of Terrestrial Vegetation Cover using Shortwave Vegetation Index Imagery: *International Journal of Remote Sensing*, Vol. 11, No. 12, pp. 2269–2279.

Loveland, T.R., J.W. Merchant, D.O. Ohlen, J.F. Brown, 1991. Development of a Land-Cover Characteristics Database for the Conterminous U.S.: *Photogrammetric Engineering & Remote Sensing*, Vol. 57, pp. 1453–1463.

Mason, D.C., D.G. Corr, A. Cross, D.C. Hogg, D.H. Lawrence, M. Petrou, and A.M. Tailor, 1988. The Use of Digital Map Data in the Segmentation and Classification of Remotely-Sensed Images: *International Journal of Geographical Information Systems*, Vol. 2, No. 3, pp. 195–215.

Matthews, E., 1985. *Atlas of Archived Vegetation, Land Use and Seasonal Albedo Data Sets:* NASA Technical Memorandum 86199, Washington, D.C.

Miller, W.A., and M.B. Shasby, 1982. Refining Landsat Classification Results Using Digital Terrain Data: *Journal of Applied Photographic Engineering*, Vol. 8, No. 1, pp. 35–40.

National Oceanic and Atmospheric Service, 1979. *Climatic Atlas of the United States:* U.S. Department of Commerce, National Oceanic and Atmospheric Administration, Environmental Data Services, Asheville, North Carolina, 80 p.

Omernik, J.M., 1987. Ecoregions of the Conterminous United States:

Annals of the Association of American Geographers, Vol. 77, No. 1, pp. 118–125.

Omernik, J.M., and A.L. Gallant, 1990. Defining Regions for Evaluating Environmental Resources: *Proceedings of the Global Natural Resources Monitoring and Assessment Symposium*, Bethesda, Maryland, pp. 936–947.

Pettinger, L.R., 1982. *Digital Classification of Landsat Data for Vegetation and Land-Cover Mapping in the Blackfoot River Watershed, Southeastern Idaho:* U.S. Geological Survey Professional Paper 1219, 33 p.

Srinivasan, A., and J.A. Richards, 1990. Knowledge-Based Techniques for Multi-Source Classification: *International Journal of Remote Sensing*, Vol. 11, No. 3, pp. 505–525.

Townshend, J.R.G., and C.O. Justice, 1981. Information Extraction from Remotely Sensed Data - A User View: International Journal of Remote Sensing, Vol. 2, No. 4, pp. 313–329.

Townshend, J.R.G., C.O. Justice, and V. Kalb, 1987. Characterization and Classification of South American Land Cover Types: *International Journal of Remote Sensing*, Vol. 8. No. 8, pp. 1189–1207.

Townshend, J.R.G., C.O. Justice, W. Li, C. Gurney, and J. McManus, 1991. Global Land Cover Classification by Remote Sensing: Present Capabilities and Future Possibilities: *Remote Sensing of Environment*, Vol. 35, pp. 243–255.

Trotter, C.M., 1991. Remotely-sensed Data as an Information Source for Geographical Information Systems in Natural Resources Management - A Review: *International Journal of Geographical Information Systems*, Vol. 5, No. 2, pp. 225–239.

United Nations Environment Programme, 1990. *GRID: Global Resource Information Database:* Nairobi, Kenya, 16 p.

U.S. Department of Agriculture, Soil Conservation Service, 1981. *Land Resource Regions and Major Land Resource Areas of the United States:* Agriculture Handbook 296, Washington, D.C.

U.S. Geological Survey, 1986. *Land Use and Land Cover Digital Data from 1:250,000- and 1,100,000-Scale Maps:* U.S. Geological Survey Data Users Guide No. 4, Reston, Virginia.

U.S. National Academy of Sciences, 1990. *Research Strategies for the U.S. Global Change Research Program:* National Academy of Sciences National Research Council, National Academy Press, Washington, D.C., 219 p.

Vose, R. S., R. Heim, R.L. Schmoyer, T.R. Karl, P.M. Steurer, J.K. Eischeid, and T.C. Peterson, 1992. *The Global Historical Climatology Network: Long-Term Monthly Temperature, Precipitation, Sea Level Pressure, and Station Pressure Data:* Oak Ridge National Laboratory, Environmental Sciences Division, Publication No. 3912, p. 315.

Walker, P., K. Cocks, and M. Young, 1985. Regionalizing Continental Data Sets: *Cartography*, Vol. 14, No. 1, pp. 66–73.

Wang, Y., and D.L. Civco, 1992. Post-Classification of Misclassified Pixels by Evidential Reasoning - A GIS Approach for Improving Classification Accuracy of Remote Sensing Data: *Technical Papers of ASPRS/ACSM/RT 92*, Vol. 4, Bethesda, Maryland, pp. 160–170.

Wiken, E., 1986. *Terrestrial Ecozones of Canada:* Ecological Land Classification Series No. 19. Environment Canada, Ottawa, Ontario.

(Received 4 December 1992; accepted 21 January 1993)

Jesslyn F. Brown

Jesslyn F. Brown is a Research Associate in the Conservation and Survey Division, Institute of Agriculture and Natural Resources, University of Nebraska-Lincoln. Since completing her Masters program in Geography in 1990, she has been a Visiting Scientist at the EROS Data Center in South Dakota. Her current research includes the development and validation of large-area land-cover characteristics data sets using satellite and ancillary data.

Thomas R. Loveland

Tom Loveland heads the Land Sciences research program of the U.S. Geological Survey's EROS Data Center. He is responsible for research projects dealing with the relationship of satellite imagery to land surface properties. His personal research deals with the use of coarse resolution satellite imagery for regional land characterization for land process modeling. Prior to joining the USGS, he worked in land-cover mapping and GIS programs with state governments in South Dakota and Arizona. Mr. Loveland received a B.S. and M.S. in Geography from South Dakota State University, Brookings, South Dakota.

James W. Merchant

James W. Merchant is Associate Professor in the Conservation and Survey Division, Institute of Agriculture and Natural Resources, University of Nebraska-Lincoln where he is Associate Director of the Center for Advanced Land Management Information Technologies (CALMIT). His current research interests include (1) land-cover characterization and landscape regionalization using AVHRR and ancillary data, (2) landscape edge representation in digital satellite imagery, and (3) applications of visualization in GIS and digital image analysis.

Bradley C. Reed

Bradley C. Reed received his Ph.D. in Geography from the University of Kansas in 1990. He was Assistant Professor of Geography at New Mexico State University before taking his present position as Senior Scientist for Hughes STX Corporation at EROS Data Center. His current research involves analyzing interannual variability of vegetation and developing tools for data exploration and visualization.

Donald O. Ohlen

Donald O. Ohlen received a B.S. in Geography from South Dakota State University in 1976. He is currently a Senior Scientist with Hughes STX Corporation at the EROS Data Center, where he has been for 15 years. His research interests include image analysis and database development for spatial environmental analysis of global land processes.

Satellite and Geographic Information System Estimates of Colorado River Basin Snowpack

James S. Ferris and *Russell G. Congalton*
Department of Forestry and Resource Management, University of California, Berkeley, CA 94720

ABSTRACT: Mountain snowmelt accounts for the majority of streamflow in many areas of the world. The timing and volume of this critical resource can be economically forecast for optimal use from satellite observations of spring snowpack. A geographic information system (GIS) was created for the Colorado River watershed to estimate snowpack water volume from topographic and satellite (AVHRR) data. Digital PC-based cloud removal techniques, a regression model, and the program SNOWPAC were developed to facilitate pixel-by-pixel snow water equivalent (SWE) estimates. The model, regressed on 312 satellite observations, predicts SNOTEL ground measured SWE with a correlation of 0.70. Given SWE prediction error averaging and complete two-dimensional basin-wide coverage at over 50,000 data locations, the satellite and GIS estimates point to improved snowmelt streamflow forecasting accuracy over conventional methods.

INTRODUCTION

SNOWMELT ACCOUNTS FOR 50 to 80 percent of the annual streamflow in many mountainous areas of the world including the Sierra Nevada, Rocky Mountains, Alps, and Himalayan Mountains. In the western United States, the annual value of snowmelt water for hydropower and irrigation is $6.60 billion (Castruccio *et al.*, 1980).

The area of interest in this project is the Colorado River Basin, a 644,000 km² watershed of major importance to the southwestern United States (Figure 1). The Colorado's average yearly flow of 15.0 million acre-feet (MAF) is fully allocated and consumed among the seven basin states and Mexico. Accurate forecasts of snowmelt streamflow are critical because of the importance of the Colorado River as a water resource and because its annual flow is so variable — ranging from 5.8 MAF to 24.5 MAF in the last 12 years alone.

Current forecast techniques for the Colorado River Basin rely heavily on 182 snow course point measurements taken monthly from January through June (Tom Perkens, personal communication, July 1987). However, snow survey measurements are highly site-specific and not subject to extrapolation. In addition, there is no simple relationship or model to classify the unique and dynamic characteristics of mountain snowpack (Smith and Berg, 1982).

Daily satellite coverage can be a valuable input variable for synoptic mapping of recent storm activity or changes in melting patterns. The use of satellite imagery provides two-dimensional data which can only be inferred from ground-based measurements (Shafer *et al.*, 1984).

In recent research, the snowpack parameter most frequently estimated using remote sensing is the amount of snow covered area (SCA) expressed as percent of a basin under snow cover (Rango and Peterson, 1980; Makhdoom and Solomon, 1986). A more important parameter for estimating snowpack water volume is snow density or snow water equivalent (SWE). SWE is the vertical depth of water which would be obtained by melting a column of snowpack. For example, if a site had 200 cm of snow depth with a density of 0.40 or 40 percent, the SWE at this site would be 80 cm. Because the visible and near infrared portions of the electromagnetic spectrum do not penetrate snow, but rather measure surface reflectance, it is not possible to directly estimate SWE using these wavelengths. The microwave wavelengths are sensitive to the presence of water and can remotely sense SWE. However, microwave remote sensing cannot currently be used for operational snowpack water volume estimation due to inadequate resolution and difficulty in data

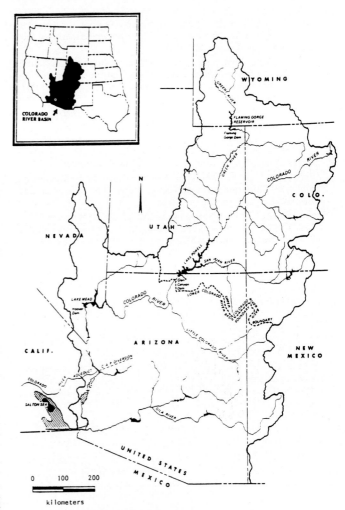

FIG. 1. The Colorado River Basin. Note upper and lower basin boundary. (from Erlenkotter and Scherer, 1977).

interpretation, particularly over mountainous terrain and forested areas where the microwave emission from forest cover tends to override that of snow (Hall *et al.*, 1985).

The objective of this study was to utilize topographic data and remotely sensed digital satellite data in a geographic infor-

PHOTOGRAMMETRIC ENGINEERING AND REMOTE SENSING,
Vol. 55, No. 11, November 1989, pp. 1629–1635.

0099-1112/89/5511–1629$02.25/0
©1989 American Society for Photogrammetry
and Remote Sensing

mation system (GIS) to produce low-cost and improved estimates of Colorado River Basin snowpack water volume. This was attempted through indirect measurement of SWE for each snow covered pixel. Techniques were developed in consultation with river forecasting agencies to be compatible with, but not repetitive of, current forecast procedures. Snowpack water volume estimates derived from methods set forth in this study can be input into existing hydrological and forecast models.

The use of remotely sensed satellite data is advantageous in providing low-cost, repetitive, multispectral, synoptic, and uniform observations over large areas. Recent advances in satellite, microcomputer, and GIS technology make this research undertaking possible. The development of methods taking advantage of this new technology is critical because a mere 1.5 percent increase in Colorado River forecast accuracy would result in a net economic benefit of $5.1 million (Castruccio et al., 1980).

GIS DATA BASE

A raster data base containing 36 informational layers, precision registered in a 900- by 618-pixel grid, was created (Table 1). Because a pixel is represented by a digital number (DN) of 0 to 255 and is stored in one byte, the disk space requirement for the GIS is $900 \times 618 \times 36 = 20.03$ megabytes. Decision Images commercial software was utilized for analysis, supplemented by a FORTRAN program (SNOWPAC) written to compute snowpack water volume. The authors of this paper developed SNOWPAC for automatic cloud recognition and pixel-by-pixel SWE estimates based on the optimal regression model. Although this program was developed for the Colorado River Basin GIS database, it could be modified for use on other watersheds.

SATELLITE DATA

One kilometre Advanced Very High Resolution Radiometer (AVHRR) imagery is utilized in this study (Figures 2 and 3). The use of this imagery is preferred over other remote sensing satellites for a number of reasons: (1) imagery is collected over the western United States twice daily and is available for distribution on computer tape the following day; (2) the resolution of AVHRR Local Area Coverage (LAC) 1 km imagery is appropriate for snowmelt streamflow forecasting on a basin of this size because it is not of such high resolution as to create excessive data handling problems; and (3) the cost of each scene covering the entire basin is only $100. Neither the Landsat nor SPOT satellite systems provide any of these benefits. Another available data product, GOES satellite imagery, has poor spectral coverage, resolution, and viewing geometry.

AVHRR satellite imagery over the Colorado River Basin was previewed from photographic archives at the NOAA Weather Service Forecast Office and receiving station in Redwood City, California. Six high quality scenes, 98 to 100 percent cloud free, were selected. These scenes cover the entire Upper Colorado River Basin (Figure 1) where about 75 percent of the river's flow originates from snowpack (U.S. Department of Interior, 1970).

(The common measurement point for Colorado River flow is near Lake Powell; for the rest of the river's course [lower basin], the minimal additional inflow is balanced by evaporation from the river and its reservoirs.) Each scene covers 35 to 44°N and 105 to 113°W at a pixel resolution of 1.11 km on a side; this creates an image of 900 rows by 618 columns. (1.11 km resolution AVHRR data are typically referred to as simply 1 km data.) Spectral channels 3 and 5 were not used; channel 3 is subject to excessive noise, and the spectral range of channel 5 is similar to channel 4.

To allow for quicker and more flexible GIS manipulation, the ten-bit AVHRR data were geometrically corrected and scaled to eight bits by the Sea Space lab in San Diego. This was a straight linear rescaling accomplished by converting the ten-bit DN to percent reflectance using NOAA pre-launch calibration as per the NOAA Polar Orbiter Data Users Guide (Kidwell, 1986). Because raw ten-bit DN never exceeded an equivalent 64 percent reflectance, the generated eight-bit data were assigned the value (reflectance × 4). This allowed for 0.25 percent reflectance resolution in the eight-bit data as opposed to 0.10 percent resolution in the original ten-bit data. Raw ten-bit DN thermal infrared reflectance was within a range of 64°C, so likewise it was converted to eight bits with 0.25°C resolution (Robert Bernstein, personal communication, August 1988).

The six scenes were loaded onto the Decision Images image processing software system and displayed on a 1024 by 1024 monitor. Near infrared images displayed on different color guns were overlayed and registered to each other by shifting some images one row or one column. Lake shores and steep mountain valleys delineated on channel 2 were used for precise pixel registration.

The Normalized Difference Vegetation Index (NDVI), described by Goward et al. (1987), was included as a GIS data layer in an attempt to account for the vegetation response. In simple terms, NDVI is a ratio of two satellite channels: (near infrared - visible) / (near infrared + visible). If vegetation response could be quantified or separated from snow cover response, perhaps better estimates of pixel SWE might be developed. The elevation and aspect variables also indirectly account for vegetation because these topographic features characterize vegetation type. Because of the size of the Upper Colorado River Basin and the incompatible scale of existing vegetation maps, the vegetation indices were used instead of actual vegetation information.

TOPOGRAPHIC DATA

An elevation database of the study area was compiled at the EROS Data Center by degrading 1:250,000-scale digital elevation data to populate a 960 by 960 array over the Upper Colorado River Basin. Although this elevation model covered the same land area as the satellite scenes, each elevation pixel did not represent a square area on the ground. Therefore, the elevation model was resampled, using a nearest neighbor algorithm, to register with the 900- by 618-pixel satellite scenes. Elevations are digital values ranging from 53 to 207 which, when multiplied by 20, give elevation in metres. Decision Images software was used to generate slope and aspect data layers from the elevation data. Slope is reported in degrees and aspect is coded from 0 to 8: 0 is flat, 1 is north, 2 is northeast, 5 is south, and so on.

A mask of the Upper Colorado River Basin had to be digitized to exclude snowpack outside the watershed. Because the basin covers 875 km north to south, and each pixel covers a square area on the ground, the satellite image is wider in the north and narrower in the south than standard conic projection maps. In addition to this correction, a watershed mask covering this large an area would have to be digitized in segments from large scale maps to be accurately represented. Accuracy at this point was critical because it is the basin boundary pixels, at the highest elevations, that often contain the most snow and water volume

---

TABLE 1. GIS DATA LAYERS.

Visible Reflectance (six dates)
Near Infrared Reflectance (six dates)
Thermal Infrared Reflectance (six dates)
Normalized Difference Vegetation Index (six dates)
Elevation
Slope
Aspect
Aspect Factor
Shade (six dates)
Sub-Basin
SNOTEL Ground Site Locations

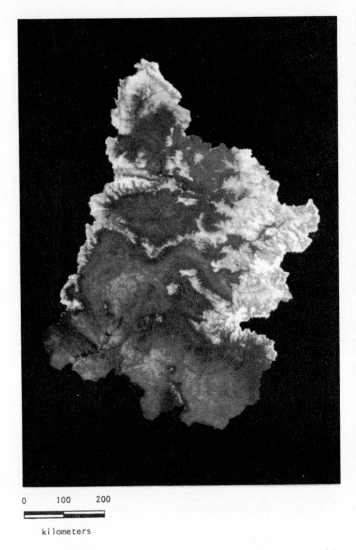

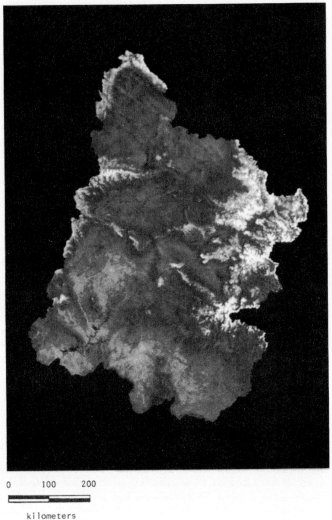

FIG. 2. 14 April 1984 AVHRR channel 2 near infrared satellite image of the Upper Colorado River Basin.

FIG. 3. 12 April 1988 AVHRR channel 2 near infrared satellite image of the Upper Colorado River Basin.

(Figures 2 and 3). An alternative approach was developed. The elevation model was displayed, enlarged, and enhanced to pinpoint mountain crests at the watershed boundaries. From each enlarged area the Upper Colorado River Basin was digitized on the monitor to mask off areas outside the watershed. This method worked quite well — each reiteration indicated the watershed was indeed masked along the highest pixel (mountain crest).

The aspect factor GIS data layer is a modification of the aspect data. The aspect number assignments are arbitrary: for example, aspect 8 (northwest) lies next to aspect 1 (north). In order to use aspect as an independent variable in regression modeling, an aspect factor was developed after Beers *et al*. (1966). Initially, assumptions about the effect of aspect had to be hypothesized. Visible and near infrared satellite response for the 312 observations at SNOTEL sites were high in the southeast and low in the northwest. SNOTEL sites, at 2,360 to 3,740 metres, are largely in forest zones of the Upper Colorado River Basin. Given the semiarid climate, hot southern exposures, and rain shadows on eastern slopes, ground and forest cover may be greatest on the west to north aspects (Paul Zinke, personal communication, October 1988). This assumption was supported by aerial photograph observations. Not only might vegetation cover reduce the response of snow in the north, but southern

sun exposures might enhance response in the south. The aspect factor we used is equal to $\text{Cos}(\text{Amax} - \text{A}) + 1$ where Amax is 315° (northwest) and A is the arbitrary aspect number to be converted (Beers *et al*., 1966). This conversion gives the following aspect factor coefficients:

$$
\begin{array}{ccc}
 & 1.7 & \\
2.0 & \mid & 1.0 \\
 & \text{N} & \\
 & \mid & \\
1.7 - \text{W} - & & - \text{E} - 0.3 \\
 & \mid & \\
 & \text{S} & \\
1.0 & \mid & 0.0 \\
 & 0.3 & \\
\end{array}
$$

These values were eventually multiplied by ten to make all of the variables and coefficients in the regression equation the same order of magnitude.

The shade GIS data layer was developed using formulas given by Kaufmann and Weatherred (1982) for determination of potential direct beam solar irradiance. By taking the sun's position at the time of the satellite overpass, and the pixel's slope and aspect, the percent of potential reflectance was determined. This coefficient in the regression equation is designed to subtract out

66

the effect of varying sun reflectance based on time of day, date, and pixel and satellite orientation. One step beyond this would be to include the effect of shadows caused by topographic relief. Such a transformation, generated from elevation data and sun position, is often called a shade image. Unfortunately, this image processing feature was not available for this study.

The sub-basin GIS data layer divides SNOTEL sites into clusters based on mountain range to minimize weather variation over the 282,000 km² Upper Colorado River Basin. The six sub-basin areas are Wyoming, Uinta, Wasatch, North Colorado, Central Colorado, and San Juan.

GROUND TRUTH DATA

Ground-based SNOwpack TELemetry (SNOTEL) SWE readings taken the same day as each satellite overpass were available for 63 sites in the upper basin. From the latitude and longitude of each site, and with the aid of elevation information, SWE measurement sites were matched with the proper pixel in the 900 by 618 array. These sites represent not only a wide geographic distribution, but also a variety of elevations, slopes, and aspects. For this study there are 315 simultaneous ground measurements of SWE taken at the 63 SNOTEL sites on five image dates. The sixth image date, from 1988, was not part of the modeling but was used to test the model.

Snow/Cloud Discrimination

Several dates had a maximum of 2 percent cloud cover. Cloud cover was visually discriminated from snow by color, shape, and shadows. The color difference in the thermal infrared reflectance proved to be due to colder cloud temperatures registered on channel 4.

Image processing enhancement techniques showed that clouds can be automatically distinguished from snow on the AVHRR scenes. The weather regime in the Upper Colorado River Basin on each image date produced colder brightness temperatures for clouds than for any ground features — including snow. However, occasionally warmer cloud edges and extremely thin cloud cover gave an overlapping DN response with the peak elevations in the basin. Both the snow and cloud temperatures depended on time of day and the time of year of the satellite overpass and the weather.

By using density slicing and color coding of thermal imagery, the coldest scene temperatures produced highlighting of only clouds. The temperature was increased until maximum cloud cover was flagged without picking up the coldest ground response pixels over mountain peaks. In this manner a threshold temperature, between −20 and 0°C, was determined for each scene date for automatic computer discrimination and removal of nearly all pixels with cloud cover.

Regression Modeling

The next step was to estimate SWE for each snow covered pixel so snowpack water volume could be summed over the entire basin. To establish a relationship between SWE and the GIS data layers, information from the 315 ground truth sites was entered into a LOTUS 1-2-3 spreadsheet. Automatic cloud discrimination and visual varification indicated three data points had cloud cover; therefore, regression modeling was done using a data set with 312 observations.

Regression analysis and residual plots were run on all the GIS test parameters to find the best correlation with SWE ground truth sites. The optimal regression equation allows SWE and consequent snowpack water volume, in acre-feet, to be estimated for each snow covered pixel.

The regression equation was written into a FORTRAN computer program called SNOWPAC. SNOWPAC queries the user for the satellite image date to be analyzed and the scene snow/cloud

discriminating temperature. The program accesses the appropriate GIS data layers and computes output information based on over one-half million pixels. Percent cloud cover and percent snow cover is reported for each thousand-foot (305-metre) elevation zone in the snow accumulation zone of 8,000 feet (2,438 metres) and greater. The elevation zone of 7,000 to 8,000 feet (2,134 to 2,438 metres) was not included because the regression model was developed from SNOTEL data which had site elevations of 2,360 to 3,740 metres. Extrapolation could not be justified; in addition, Weisbecker (1974) indicates that the snow accumulation zone may be as high as 9,000 feet (2,743 metres). The selected regression equation (i.e., model) is used by the FORTRAN program SNOWPAC to calculate water volume in million acre-feet (MAF) by elevation zone. The total estimated volume of water for the basin snowpack can then be used by river forecasting agencies in hydrological models to estimate actual river flows for the remainder of the snowmelt season.

RESULTS

Results of the regression and residual plot analysis reveal near infrared reflectance, thermal infrared reflectance, and the aspect factor to be the significant variables for remotely sensed estimates of snow water equivalent. One-km resolution AVHRR pixels and aspect factor could predict ground-based SNOTEL SWE with a correlation of 0.70.

A correlation matrix was produced to analyze the relationship among each of the ten GIS variables and the actual and predicted SWE (Table 2). The single most important predictor was AVHRR channel 2 — the near infrared band. The percent near infrared reflectance gave a correlation of 0.62 with SWE. AVHRR channel 1, the visible band, was nearly as useful a predictor but, because its correlation with the near infrared band is 0.98, it provided no additional information. AVHRR channel 4, the thermal infrared band, and the aspect factor contributed about equally in bringing the correlation from 0.62 to 0.70. Although aspect gave a higher correlation than aspect factor, the former was not used in modeling because coefficients assigned to each aspect could not be explained in terms of the data; this is why the aspect factor was developed.

Vegetation response or density could not be ascertained from the Normalized Difference Vegetation Index. NDVI had a correlation of −0.48 with SWE because it is derived from the highly correlated visible and near infrared reflectance variables.

The elevation data had a weak correlation (0.24) with SWE. The inclusion of the elevation variable in the model did not improve overall correlation because the information it contained

TABLE 2. CORRELATION MATRIX.

	%VIS	%IR	TEMP	NDVI	ELEV	SLOPE	ASPCT	ASFAC	SHADE	BASIN	SWE	PRED
%VIS	1											
%IR	.98	1										
TEMP	−.17	−.09	1									
NDVI	−.74	−.61	.49	1								
ELEV	.21	.22	−.26	−.21	1							
SLOPE	−.09	−.06	−.01	.09	.22	1						
ASPCT	.28	.22	.10	.38	.21	.48	1					
ASFAC	.04	.05	−.06	−.03	.04	.14	.98	1				
SHADE	−.32	−.40	−.48	−.05	−.01	.04	.22	.12	1			
BASIN	.13	.11	.16	.21	.58	.37	*	.32	.06	1		
SWE	.61	.62	−.33	−.48	.24	−.10	.27	.20	−.06	.20	1	
PRED	.90	.89	−.45	−.71	.29	−.01	.36	.31	−.14	.20	.70	1

* both row and column have multiple independent variables (indicator variables) and a correlation is not feasible.

was accounted for by the thermal infrared variable; the elevation verses thermal infrared correlation was −0.26.

Slope was not directly helpful in predicting SWE. It seemed logical that slope, along with aspect as a factor in pixel orientation, might affect the intensity of solar reflectance based on sun and satellite position. This hypothesis led to the shade algorithm. However, the addition of this algorithm did not improve the correlation.

Using indicator variables for the six sub-basins did not significantly improve the ability to predict SWE. What small benefit this approach provided was offset by requiring an additional GIS data layer, increased computer run time, and loss of six degrees of freedom.

The three useful parameters of near infrared reflectance, thermal infrared reflectance, and aspect factor were then tested in a series of non-linear regressions. No significant improvement was found.

The final regression model is the linear equation

$$\text{SWE} = 0.959R - 0.372T + 0.310A$$

SWE is the predicted snow water equivalent in inches, R is the percent near infrared reflectance from AVHRR channel 2, T is the thermal infrared brightness temperature in °C from AVHRR channel 4, and A is the aspect factor. SWE divided by 12 (inches/foot) times the 305-acre (123 hectare) pixel size gives the estimated water volume per pixel in acre-feet.

Table 3 shows the output summary data for SNOWPAC computer runs on each of the six image dates. Percent cloud cover, percent snow covered area (SCA), and snowpack water volume in million acre-feet (MAF) is estimated by elevation zone. Snow zone cloud cover and SCA are presented as weighted average totals along with total estimated basin-wide snowpack water volume.

Cloud cover is not a problem; the number of pixels removed in the snow zone due to cloud cover is at most 1.8 percent. The removed pixels tend to be from higher elevations where clouds form around mountain peaks (Table 3). Estimates of water volume include estimation of water volume by elevation zone for pixels with cloud cover. For example, an elevation zone with 1.2 percent cloud cover has its water volume, as calculated from cloud free pixels, increased 1.2 percent. High interbasin correlation found by Shafer and Leaf (1980) allows estimates of snow cover in adjacent topographically similar areas to be used for characterizing pixels under cloud cover. The final figures for basin-wide snowpack water volume represent the goal of this study. These figures cannot be readily compared for accuracy against actual subsequent snowmelt streamflow volumes. Hydrologic models must be employed to account for loss due to soil retention, upper basin withdrawals, and evaporation, or for additional flow due to subsequent precipitation.

Although four of the five image dates used in regression equation development had exceedingly high water volumes, the equation still did an excellent job of estimating water volume on the sixth image date used to test the model-drought year 1988. The results in Table 3 for 14 April 1984 (one of the wettest years on record) and 12 April 1988 can be compared with Figures 2 and 3.

DISCUSSION

The factors contributing to 1-km pixel response over the Colorado River Basin are complex and highly variable. Topographically, a single pixel can include elevation changes of 500 metres, several slopes and aspects, and shadowing problems. Cover type can span dense forest, scrub, water, and bare rock. Snow cover can be spotty, drifted, windswept from exposed rock, weathered, or freshly fallen and laden on trees. In spite of this variability, snowpack reflectance remotely sensed over a 123 hectare area as a single response enabled a correlation of 0.70 with SWE to be achieved.

As discussed earlier, the near infrared and thermal infrared wavelengths cannot penetrate snow. However, several researchers found a decreased near infrared response for snow undergoing melt due to increased water content and grain size

TABLE 3. SNOWMELT WATER VOLUME ANALYSIS.

FEET ELEVATION	4 APRIL 1984			30 APRIL 1986		
	%CLOUD	%SCA	MAF WATER	%CLOUD	%SCA	MAF WATER
8-9000	0.1	48.7	7.94	1.1	25.1	3.71
9-10000	0.1	34.3	3.23	2.5	55.5	5.07
10-11000	0.2	33.8	2.16	1.8	79.0	5.40
11-12000	0.9	65.7	2.41	1.9	92.2	3.83
>12000	0.5	96.5	1.40	4.0	93.8	1.56
TOTAL	0.2	45.3	17.15	1.8	50.3	19.56
FEET ELEVATION	14 APRIL 1984			7 MAY 1987		
	% CLOUD	%SCA	MAF WATER	%CLOUD	%SCA	MAF WATER
8-9000	0.0	73.9	11.05	0.0	0.5	0.06
9-10000	0.0	78.2	6.88	0.1	5.1	0.36
10-11000	0.0	86.0	5.24	0.1	24.3	1.27
11-12000	0.0	97.8	3.73	0.2	54.0	1.69
>12000	0.1	99.8	1.63	0.3	75.8	0.93
TOTAL	0.0	80.0	28.51	0.1	12.8	4.31
FEET ELEVATION	8 MAY 1984			12 APRIL 1988		
	%CLOUD	%SCA	MAF WATER	%CLOUD	%SCA	MAF WATER
8-9000	1.2	46.5	6.08	0.0	8.0	1.00
9-10000	1.1	74.3	6.05	0.0	11.4	0.85
10-11000	2.1	87.9	5.25	0.1	21.4	1.15
11-12000	3.0	95.7	3.61	0.4	47.7	1.45
>12000	1.9	97.9	1.52	0.2	76.4	0.85
TOTAL	1.5	66.8	22.51	0.1	16.8	5.30

(Rango, 1983; Hall and Martinec, 1985). A decreased response is thought to be associated with increasing SWE. Results of the research presented here indicate exactly the opposite: increasing near infrared response is in a positive linear correlation with increasing SWE. The most likely conclusion is that the dominating factor in near infrared response is the proportion of an individual pixel covered with snow.

A pixel's reflectance value is the weighted average of the reflectance of all the elements in the pixel's field of view. Deeper highly reflective snowpack, sometimes up to five metres deep, means more low reflectance soil, rock, and vegetation is covered. Although ground cover is extremely variable, local relief on the order of 0 to 5 vertical metres seems to be a key in remotely sensed estimates of SWE on a 1-km scale. This is due to a decrease in horizontal cross sectional area of terrain and vegetation features as snowpack depth increases. For example, assume a site near timberline has a stand of four metre fir trees with 40 percent crown closure. The AVHRR channel 2 near infrared reflectance for fir is about 20 percent and for snowpack it may be 55 percent. If the snowpack is two metres deep at the site, and all snow has melted from the tree crowns, remotely sensed pixel reflectance would be 0.4 (proportion trees) × 0.20 (tree reflectance) + 0.6 (proportion snow) × 0.55 (snow reflectance) or 41 percent. With a deeper snowpack of four or more metres, the pixel reflectance would be 1.0 × 0.55 or 55 percent. The role of the trees — or any ground relief less than the depth of maximum snowpack — is like that of a snow course measurement marker. Thousands of such markers are simultaneously measured and averaged in each snow covered pixel of the entire watershed.

The vegetation index variable NDVI did not improve correlation, but vegetation cover was indirectly accounted for in the aspect factor variable. The model would be improved with the incorporation of a detailed vegetation data layer in the GIS. Full hydrological modeling would also require a soils GIS data layer with information on water infiltration capacity.

The correlation between actual SWE and SWE predicted from the model at 312 data points (pixels) is 0.70. An even higher basin-wide correlation can be expected because summing individual pixel SWE estimates over the entire basin tends to average out individual pixel SWE underprediction and overprediction errors. The average residual SWE (error) for the 312 data points is near zero.

Satellite imagery is valuable for providing weekly forecast updates. Imagery can be analyzed in a few hours using the models developed here and a geographic information system in the personal computer (PC) environment. Several researchers have stressed the importance of monitoring short-term weather variation in SWE during the April through June period when snowmelt patterns can drastically alter the magnitude and timing of runoff (Shafer and Leaf, 1980; Kattelmann et al., 1985).

For example, on 1 April 1984 the Colorado Basin River Forecast Center estimated the 1 April — 31 July seasonal runoff for the Colorado River Basin at 11.5 MAF. The 4 April 1984 estimate of basinwide snowpack water volume, based on AVHRR imagery interpreted in the FORTRAN program SNOWPAC, was 17.2 MAF. These two estimates measure different entities; yet reasonable agreement exists when compensating for evaporation, withdrawals, and other sources of loss. Satellite imagery taken just ten days later (Figure 2) and analyzed by SNOWPAC indicated basinwide snowpack water volume had jumped to 28.5 MAF. At this point a mid-month forecast update could have been made to revise significantly upward the 11.5 MAF 1 April - 31 July seasonal runoff estimate. In fact, the actual runoff for this period reached a near record 15.3 MAF. In this historical case, if the methods described in this paper had been employed, the major 1984 runoff event could have been predicted sooner and more accurately.

CONCLUSION

This study reveals the potential of low-cost, synoptic, and daily AVHRR 1-km satellite imagery in a GIS for snowpack water volume estimation. Ground-based estimates are difficult because of vast and inaccessible terrain, and because SWE is so site-specific that relationships do not hold along contour or by elevation zone. AVHRR satellite imagery samples over 50,000 data points in the snow zone of the Upper Colorado River Basin, accounts for a large amount of the SWE variability, and provides two-dimensional information which can only otherwise be inferred from the ground.

Although cloud cover can be a problem in a basin the size of the Upper Colorado spanning five states, methods have been set forth to computer detect and remove cloud cover.

The dominant factor for remotely sensed estimates of SWE is the proportion of snow — verses other ground features — sensed in an individual pixel. The DN response contribution from local terrain and vegetation relief on the order of 0 to 5 vertical metres is related to snowpack depth. In essence, every such relief feature acts as an aerial snow course measurement marker.

The objective of this research was met in demonstrating the potential of digital AVHRR 1-km data in a GIS for pixel SWE and basin-wide snowpack water volume estimation. The GIS includes satellite and topographic data layers accessed by the FORTRAN program SNOWPAC for automated analysis in the PC environment. The methodology described here could be smoothly and economically integrated into current snowmelt streamflow forecasts for improved Colorado River forecast accuracy. The result could be a GIS providing multi-million dollar savings in water resources management due to increased efficiency and conservation in reservoir storage, flood control, hydroelectric power generation, irrigation, wildlife and fisheries management, water quality, and water supply planning.

ACKNOWLEDGMENTS

Funding for this research was provided by the California Water Resources Center, project W-704.

REFERENCES

Beers, T. W., P. E. Dress, and L. C. Wensel, 1966. Aspect Transformation in Site Productivity Research. *Journal of Forestry*, Vol. 64, pp. 691–692.

Castruccio, P. A., H. L. Loats, Jr., D. Lloyd, and P. A. B. Newman, 1980. Cost/Benefit Analysis for the Operational Applications of Satellite Snowcover Observations. *Operational Applications of Satellite Snowcover Observations*, NASA CP-2116, pp. 185–200.

Erlenkotter, D., and C. R. Scherer, 1977. *An Economic Analysis of Optimal Investment Scheduling for Salinity Control in the Colorado River.* University of California, Water Resources Center Project No. UCAL-WRC-W-474, 267 p.

Goward, S. N., D. Dye, A. Kerber, and V. Kalb, 1987. Comparison of North and South American Biomes from AVHRR Observations. *Geocarto International*, Vol. 2, pp. 27–40.

Hall, D. K., and J. Martinec, 1985. *Remote Sensing of Ice and Snow.* Chapman and Hall Ltd., New York, 189 p.

Hall, D. K., J. L. Foster, and A. T. C. Chang, 1985. Microwave Remote Sensing of Snow Cover in Forested and Non-Forested Areas. *Pecora 10 Proceedings*, pp. 262–271.

Kattelmann, R. C., N. H. Berg, and M. K. Pack, 1985. Estimating Regional Snow Water Equivalent with a Simple Simulation Model. *Water Resources Bulletin*, Vol. 21, No. 2, pp. 273–280

Kaufmann, M. R., and J. D. Weatherred, 1982. *Determination of Potential*

Direct Beam Solar Irradiance. USDA Forest Service Research Paper RM-242, 23 p.

Kidwell, K. B. 1986. *NOAA Polar Orbiter Data Users Guide*. NOAA; National Environmental Satellite, Data, and Information Service; National Climatic Data Center; Satellite Data Services Division. 184 p.

Makhdoom, M.T.A., and S. I. Solomon, 1986. Attempting Flow Forecasts of the Indus River, Pakistan Using Remotely Sensed Snow Cover Data. *Nordic Hydrology*, Vol. 17, No. 3, pp. 171–184.

Rango, A., 1983. A Survey of Progress in Remote Sensing of Snow and Ice. *Hydrological Applications of Remote Sensing and Remote Data Transmission*, IAHS Publ. No. 145, pp. 347–359.

Rango, A., and R. Peterson, Eds., 1980. *Operational Applications of Satellite Snowcover Observations*. NASA CP-2116, 301 p.

Shafer, B. A., and C. F. Leaf, 1980. Landsat Derived Snowcover as an Input Variable for Snowmelt Runoff Forecasting in South Central Colorado. *Operational Applications of Satellite Snowcover Observations*, NASA CP-2116, pp. 151–169.

Shafer, B. A., D. T. Jensen, and K. C. Jones, 1984. Analysis of 1983 Snowmelt Runoff Production in the Upper Colorado River Basin. *Proceedings of the 52nd Annual Western Snow Conference*, pp. 1–11.

Smith, J. L., and N. H. Berg, 1982. Historical Snowpack Characteristics at the Central Sierra Snow Laboratory, a Representative Sierra Nevada Location. *The Sierra Ecology Project*, Volume 3, Office of Atmospheric Resources Research, 44 p.

U. S. Department of Interior, 1970. *Project Skywater*. Bureau of Reclamation, Atmospheric Water Resources Program, 16 p.

Weisbecker, L. W., 1974. *The Impacts of Snow Enhancement, Technology Assessment of Winter Orographic Snowpack Augmentation in the Upper Colorado River Basin*. Stanford Research Institute, 624 pp.

Regional Analysis of the Central Great Plains

Sensitivity to climate variability

I. C. Burke, T. G. F. Kittel, W. K. Lauenroth, P. Snook, C. M. Yonker, and W. J. Parton

Global-scale impacts of human activities are changing the way many ecologists define research problems. The new definitions entail a shift of focus from sites and site-specific experiments to regions and regional analyses. It is at the regional scale that interactions and impacts of large-scale processes, such as global warming, can be assessed and understood (Pastor and Post 1986, Rosswall et al. 1988). Furthermore, regions represent socioeconomic and political units whose behavior will both influence, and in turn be influenced by, global change.

This shift in focus to the regional scale is accompanied by a new set of challenges that will require new research questions and methods. Most current knowledge about ecosystems has been generated from studies in

---

I. C. Burke is an assistant professor in the Department of Forest Sciences and a research associate in the Natural Resource Ecology Laboratory, T. G. F. Kittel is a research associate in the Natural Resource Ecology Laboratory and Cooperative Institute for Research in the Atmosphere, W. K. Lauenroth is a professor in the Department of Range Science and the Natural Resource Ecology Laboratory, P. Snook is a research associate in the Natural Resource Ecology Laboratory, C. M. Yonker is a research associate in the Natural Resource Ecology Laboratory and Department of Agronomy, and W. J. Parton is a research associate in the Department of Range Science and the Natural Resource Ecology Laboratory at Colorado State University, Fort Collins, CO 80523. © 1991 American Institute of Biological Sciences.

> **Decisions about land management may be more important than climate change in affecting near-future carbon balance**

small areas (less than 1 km^2), represented by even smaller plots (1–30 m^2). To a large extent, this past work assumed constant climate, and the experiments were designed to minimize the importance of spatial variability. The notable exception is the large-scale watershed studies (e.g., Bormann et al. 1974).

Current concerns about climatic change and two-way interactions between the biosphere and the atmosphere are changing the kind and spatial scale of the information needed to understand the response of ecosystems in these interactions. However, the spatial heterogeneity in biotic and abiotic variables across regions makes it difficult to use the small numbers of traditional site-level ecological studies to assess broad-scale effects. Ecologists are thus beginning to combine studies using large numbers of spatially dispersed sites (Burke et al. 1989, Sala et al. 1988) with tools, such as remote sensing and geographic information systems (GIS), that permit the analysis and management of spatial data.

In this article, we use such tools to determine the potential effects of

short-term climate variation and long-term directional climate change on net primary production and carbon balance of grassland ecosystems in the central Great Plains and adjacent Central Lowlands of the United States. We also ask how changes associated with climate variation compare with the effects of land management on regional carbon storage.

The Great Plains of North America comprise a mosaic of native grasslands and croplands adjacent to the eastern face of the Rocky Mountain chain. It is now important to carefully evaluate this region for several reasons. First, the Great Plains contain the major wheat-producing areas for the continent, in addition to important grazing lands for livestock. Second, ecological and socioeconomic systems in the region are vulnerable to extremes of climate variability, as documented in past droughts (Weaver and Albertson 1944). Third, current global atmospheric circulation models suggest that climatic change resulting from increased levels of greenhouse gases will be large here relative to most other parts of temperate North America (Mitchell et al. 1990).

We have developed a three-step approach for extrapolating site-level information to regions (Burke et al. 1990, Schimel et al. 1990). First, process-level research at one or many field sites is conducted to identify the major driving variables for ecosystem structure and function. Experimental manipulations as well as natural time-series observations are necessary for elucidating interactions among these

Reprinted by permission of the publisher, American Institute of Biological Sciences, *BioScience*, 1994, 1 (10): p.685-692.

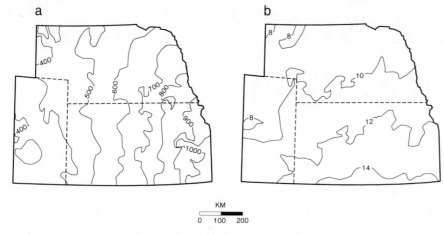

Figure 1. (a) Average annual precipitation in millimeters per year and (b) average annual temperature in degrees Celsius for the central Great Plains and adjacent Central Lowlands. Contours were interpolated from data from more than 400 weather stations within the region.

key driving variables and ecosystem processes. In the central Great Plains, a wealth of data available from USDA and state agricultural experiment stations are used to determine controls over net primary production and soil organic-matter dynamics in grasslands and croplands (e.g., Burke et al. 1989, Sala et al. 1988).

Second, simulation models that represent these relationships are developed and tested across a range of sites. Simulation models are the key tool for extrapolating current knowledge of relationships to new sites, with new combinations of driving variables, and for extrapolating to long time-scales. We have already developed and tested simulation models of ecosystem structure and function for the central Great Plains, for example, CENTURY (Parton et al. 1987) and STEPPE (Coffin and Lauenroth 1990).

Finally, information is collected on the spatial and temporal distribution of driving variables across the region. These data are then used as input to simulation models to represent regional patterns and dynamics (Burke et al. 1990).

Challenges associated with regional analysis of ecosystems have both conceptual and technological components. Today, the key conceptual problem is the lack of rules to guide extrapolation from plot-scale information to increasingly larger spatial units (Rosswall et al. 1988). Our solution to this problem is to stratify the region into a set of spatial units that capture significant variation in driving variables and to run the simulation model for each unit. Technological challenges include the creation of spatial databases of driving variables, integration of these databases into a GIS, and linkage of the GIS databases to ecological simulation models.

Variables controlling the grasslands

Ecosystem structure and function in the central Great Plains and adjacent Central Lowlands (Colorado, Kansas, and Nebraska) are closely associated with regional climatic gradients. Average annual aboveground net primary production ranges from approximately 100 g/m^2 in the west to more than 500 g/m^2 in the east (Lauenroth 1979, Sala et al. 1988). Precipitation is the most important climatic variable. From the west to east, the region consists of shortgrass steppe with annual precipitation of 300–400 mm/yr; mixed-grass prairie with 400–600 mm/yr, and tallgrass prairie with 600–1000 mm/yr. The precipitation gradient is smooth, with a change of approximately 0.7 mm · yr^{-1} · km^{-1} (Figure 1a). Temperature increases from northwest to southeast across the region (8°–14° C; Figure 1b), but it does not account for much of the ecosystem variability (Sala et al. 1988).

Although water availability appears to be most important, there are significant interactions with other controlling factors. In the east, the effects of water are most apparent in drought years. In normal or wet years, other variables, most often nitrogen, are the proximal controlling factors (Knapp and Seastedt 1986). Between the semi-arid west and subhumid east, production and composition of grasslands are controlled by the joint availability of these resources.

The CENTURY model

The CENTURY model was developed to simulate the temporal dynamics of soil organic matter and plant production in grazed grasslands and agroecosystems (Parton et al. 1987, 1988). The dynamics of carbon and nitrogen in the soil-plant system are represented by monthly time steps. Important parameters and driving variables include surface-soil physical properties, monthly precipitation and temperature, plant nitrogen and lignin contents, and land use.

In the CENTURY model, soil organic matter is divided into an active fraction consisting of live microbes and microbial products with a 1- to 2-year turnover time; a fraction that is resistant to decomposition (20- to 40-year turnover time); and a fraction that is physically or chemically protected from decomposition (800- to 1200-year turnover time). As a function of its lignin-to-nitrogen ratio, plant residue is divided into structural (2–5-year turnover time) and metabolic (0.1–1-year turnover time). Decomposition is calculated by multiplying the decay rate for each state variable by the combined effect of soil moisture and soil temperature on decomposition. The decay rate of the structural material is also a function of its lignin content. The active soil-organic-matter decay rate changes as a function of silt and clay content. The model also includes a plant production submodel that simulate monthly dynamics of carbon and nitrogen in live and dead above- and belowground plant material. Maximal potential plant growth is estimated as a function of annual precipitation and is reduced if sufficient nitrogen is not available.

Spatial patterns: steady-state conditions

We developed a spatial database for the central Great Plains and adjacent areas of the Central Lowlands that is stored and accessed in a GIS (ARC/INFO, ESRI, Redlands, CA). The spatial extent of the database is the plains regions of Kansas, Nebraska, and Colorado (Figure 1). This region was chosen because it spans the climatic and vegetation range of the central Great Plains, extending from the semiarid shortgrass steppe to the subhumid tallgrass prairie, and it includes two Long-Term Ecological Research (LTER) sites: the Central Plains Experimental Range (CPER) and the Konza Prairie Research Natural Area (Konza; Franklin et al. 1990).

We obtained long-term climate data for more than 400 weather stations within the region from the CLIMATEDATA database (CLIMATEDATA 1988). Data recorded included monthly mean minimal and maximal temperatures and mean monthly precipitation. These point data were entered into the GIS. To generalize the data both spatially and temporally for input into the CENTURY model, we contoured mean annual precipitation and mean annual temperature (Figure 1) using a triangulated irregular network algorithm and overlaid the two maps. For each polygon created by the overlay, we generated representative monthly temperature and precipitation means by averaging across the stations in each polygon. This averaging approach assumes that precipitation seasonality within any particular annual precipitation band is consistent within the band, an assumption that is justified in this region (Borchert 1950).

Soils data for model input were obtained from the USDA Soil Conservation Service STATSGO soils database (USDA Soil Conservation Service 1989), an association-level database (Figure 2). We decreased the resolution of the soil classifications to soil-texture classes based on surface sand content (the complement of silt plus clay) to match the level of resolution represented in the CENTURY model. Highest sand contents are located in areas of late Holocene aeolian deposition (e.g., the Sand Hills of Nebraska; Muhs 1985). The eastern portion of the region, extending into the Central Lowlands, has the highest proportion of fine-textured soils.

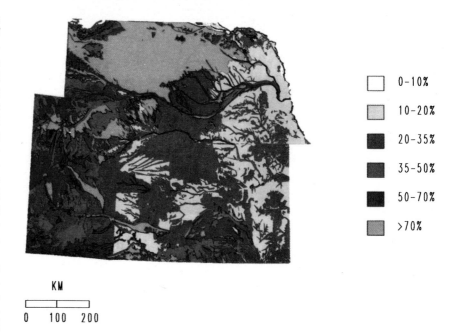

0-10%

10-20%

20-35%

35-50%

50-70%

>70%

KM

0　100　200

Figure 2. Sand classes (based on percent sand) for soil associations within the central Great Plains and adjacent Central Lowlands. Maps and original data are from USDA Soil Conservation Service (1989) STATSGO database. Data for the eastern edge of Kansas were not available.

The climate and soils maps were overlaid in the GIS to produce a polygon map of input variables. The CENTURY model was run under constant climate until steady-state conditions were achieved for all of the state variables (10,000-year runs) for each combination of driving variables on the input map. For these runs, we assumed moderate grazing (less than half of aboveground net primary production removed each season) of native grassland across the entire region, an assumption that would be reasonable if the entire region was well-managed rangelands. Model output was then mapped to the appropriate polygons for analysis.

Sensitivity to short-term climate variation

We are interested in the behavior of these grasslands through time. We devised two sensitivity analyses to judge the response of the region to climatic variation, one addressing short-term (interannual) variation and the other addressing long-term (50-year) response to projected climate change. To test for sensitivity to short-term climate variation, we simulated annual

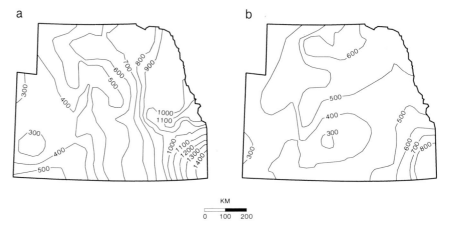

Figure 3. Contoured annual precipitation for the central Great Plains and adjacent Central Lowlands for (a) 1986 and (b) 1988.

73

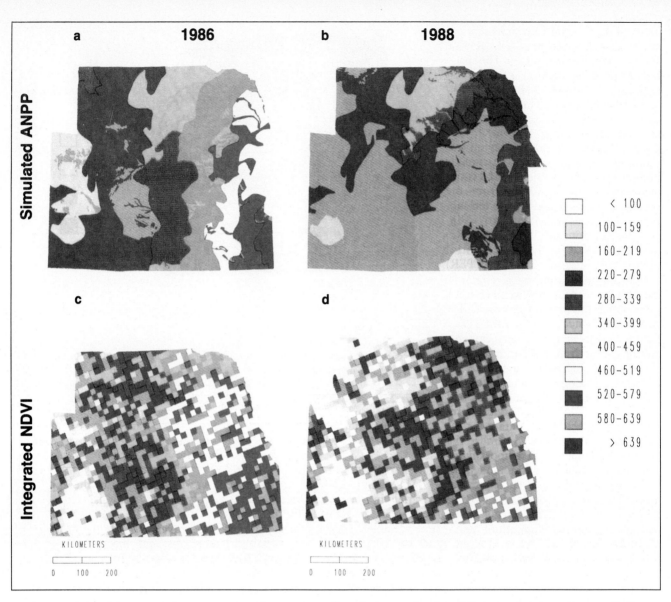

Figure 4. Simulated aboveground net primary production $(g \cdot m^{-2} \cdot y^{-1})$ for grasslands within the central Great Plains and adjacent Central Lowlands for (**a**) 1986 and (**b**) 1988. Annual integral of the normalized difference vegetation index (NDVI) for (**c**) 1986 and (**d**) 1988. Colors correspond to regression values of simulated ANPP, using the following equations. 1986: NDVI (in NDVI day) = 28.1 + 11/modeled ANPP (in g biomass $\cdot m^{-2}$); 1988: NDVI = 42.4 + 9.2/modeled ANPP. Both regressions were highly significant $(p < 0.0001)$.

See page 369 for color plate of Figure 4.

ecosystem dynamics of each polygon for a near-normal precipitation year—1986—and a drought year—1988. We used output from the steady-state simulations as initial conditions and ran the model for one year for each case.

We obtained 1986 and 1988 climate data for 200 weather stations across the study region (CLIMATE-DATA 1988). The extent of the 1988 drought is evident in eastern and central Kansas and Nebraska, which experienced as little as 60% of its long-term average annual precipitation (Figure 3). In the western part of the region, 1988 precipitation was near 1986 levels or higher. Temperature across the region showed little difference between 1986 and 1988.

Net aboveground primary production (ANPP) is one of the most appropriate ecosystem response variables for analysis of sensitivity to short-term climate variation, because it varies at temporal scales of months to years. This scale of variation is well-represented by the CENTURY model. Our simulations showed substantial reductions in ANPP for 1988 across much of the region (Figure 4a,b). ANPP was especially reduced in the south-central portion of the region, with less than 300 g/m² in locations with steady-state production of 500 g/m². In the model, ANPP is primarily controlled by precipitation (influencing both potential plant productivity and nitrogen availability). Thus these

temporal and spatial patterns in ANPP are necessarily a function of precipitation.

Evaluation of the results of regional simulation is difficult. Although progress is being made in multiscalar estimation of ecosystem structure and function (Rosswall et al. 1988), there are currently no methods that provide adequate evaluation. We tested the short-term regional simulations by comparing model output with independent estimates of ANPP at two different spatial scales.

We compared field estimates and our simulated estimates of ANPP for 1986 and 1988 at the CPER and Konza LTER sites. The comparisons showed that the model responded to climatic variations in the same direction as did field-estimated ANPP at both sites (Table 1).

In the 1986 data, the correspondence of model and field data is much greater at Konza than at CPER, because values for monthly precipitation in the polygon containing the Konza site more closely represented precipitation at Konza than did the corresponding polygon for the CPER. A general problem with discrete versus continuous spatial data is that the number associated with each polygon does not represent each point within the polygon but rather, at best, a weighted mean of all possible points within the polygon.

The model overestimated the effects of the 1988 drought for the Konza site. This overestimation is likely the result of the model representing ANPP as a function of current annual precipitation, not soil water. There is evidence from Konza[1] that water stored from previous years' inputs can have a large effect on ANPP. The model is currently being modified to include previous-year effects on soil water storage and ANPP.

Regional estimates of ANPP may be more appropriately compared with continuous rather than with point data. Satellite imagery has been used in regional analyses as a source of spatial data for input into ecological and surface climate simulation models (Running et al. 1989). We were interested in using satellite data as an independent model of regional patterns in ANPP for 1986 and 1988. We used normalized difference vegetation index (NDVI) data derived from the NOAA-9 advanced very high resolution radiometer. NDVI data have been shown to reflect the strong spatial and temporal variation in green biomass or leaf area index at regional and continental scales (Goward et al. 1985, Justice et al. 1985, Running et al. 1989). The growing season integral of NDVI is strongly correlated to annual biomass production across North American vegetation types (Goward et al. 1985). The spatial pattern of mean annual integral NDVI across the entire US Central Grasslands region strongly reflects the pattern of CENTURY-simulated steady-state ANPP (Schimel

[1]T. R. Seastedt, 1990, personal communication. Kansas State University, Manhattan.

Windmill at the Central Plains Experimental Range Long Term Ecological Research Site. Photo: D. Coffin.

et al. in press). We calculated 1986 and 1988 annual integrals of NDVI across the study area at a spatial resolution of approximately 20 km × 20 km. The integrals were based on NOAA's weekly composite global vegetation index product, which we composited to months in an attempt to minimize the effect of clouds.

Comparison of simulated ANPP with integral NDVI for the two years (Figure 4) showed that both indices of aboveground production responded to the 1988 drought with substantial reductions, particularly in central Kansas. Simulated ANPP and NDVI for 1986 shared 71% of their variance (r = 0.84; p < 0.0001), and 35% (r = 0.59; p < 0.0001) for 1988. The apparent limited sensitivity of NDVI to drought conditions may be due at least in part to the spatial compositing procedure, which biases the spectral signature toward the high end. In addi-

Table 1. Comparison of field-estimated and simulated aboveground net primary production at long-term ecological research sites. Values are in g biomass/m² biomass; standard errors are in parentheses.

Year	Source of data	Central Plains Experimental Range	Konza Prairie
1986	Field	54 (24)	392 (21)
	Simulation	127	462
1988	Field	82 (29)	357 (23)
	Simulation	138	263
Change (1988–1986)	Field	+28	−20
	Simulation	+11	−199

Mixed-grass prairie near the Pawnee Buttes, Pawnee National Grassland, eastern Colorado. Photo by D. Coffin.

tion, our coupled GIS-simulation model assumed native grassland and did not account for spatial patterns in croplands; thus our simulation analysis most likely underestimated production for the drought-stricken area. Finally, the comparison between 1988 field data from Konza and simulation results for the region suggest that the model underestimated production for the drought year because it does not incorporate lag effects.

Sensitivity to long-term, directional climate change

We evaluated potential responses to a climate-change scenario using output from the Goddard Institute for Space Studies (GISS) general circulation model (GCM; Hansen et al. 1984) for climate simulations with twice ambient carbon dioxide concentrations. We chose to look at only one of several available carbon dioxide–induced climate change scenarios (e.g., Manabe and Wetherald 1987, Washington and Meehl 1984), because our objective was to evaluate the sensitivity of regional simulations to the magnitudes of change predicted by GCMs.

GCMs are designed to represent global-scale dynamics, and application at the regional scale has limitations with respect to specific values for climatic conditions. Furthermore, confidence intervals around current GCM predictions of climate change are wide (Mitchell et al. 1990). The entire region is encompassed by two 7.8° latitude × 10° longitude GCM grid cells.

Rather than spatially interpolate the GCM changes in mean monthly climate data, we created an overlay of the two grid cells and transferred climatic changes in monthly mean temperature and precipitation to the underlying polygons. The GISS GCM scenario represents a 5° C increase in mean annual temperature across the central Great Plains region and changes in precipitation that range from a 50-millimeter increase in the southern portion to a 50-millimeter decrease in the north.

To evaluate the effects of climate change, CENTURY model runs were initialized with the steady-state regional simulation based on current climate. We then applied the climate change in a single step and evaluated ecosystem changes after 50 model years.

We considered soil organic carbon to be the most important output variable to assess for this analysis. Soil organic carbon is the best single indicator of ecosystem status in grassland/agricultural systems, both as a long-term integrator of productivity and decomposition and as an index of soil fertility (Burke et al. 1989). Soil organic carbon is an appropriate response variable for analysis at a scale of 50 years, because it has considerable variation at that scale but not at scales below a decade. Finally, carbon storage has important continental and global implications for biospheric feedbacks to climate change via carbon dioxide source/sink relationships with the atmosphere.

Simulations of 50 years of climate change resulted in losses of soil organic carbon across the entire region (Figure 5), the result of increased decomposition rates in response to increased temperature. Total losses of up to 350 g/m^2, or approximately 3% of the total soil pool, were predicted for some polygons. Areas with the highest precipitation, and consequently the highest initial soil organic matter, suffered the largest simulated losses in carbon. Soil texture modified the climate change response, with

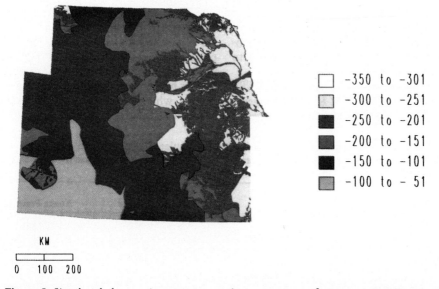

	−350 to −301
	−300 to −251
	−250 to −201
	−200 to −151
	−150 to −101
	−100 to − 51

KM

0   100   200

Figure 5. Simulated changes in ecosystem carbon storage (g/m^2) for grasslands within the central Great Plains and adjacent Central Lowlands in response to 50 years of global climate change. **See page 369 for color plate of Figure 5.**

sandier soils having smaller absolute soil carbon losses than fine soils, but higher losses relative to the total. Slight increases in ANPP (less than 10%) during the 50-year period were also predicted; these increases were a response to increased decomposition and nitrogen mineralization that enhanced nutrient availability (Schimel et al. 1990).

We were interested in assessing the importance of these simulated losses to long-term soil fertility and regional carbon-storage capacity. We compared the climate-change simulation results with a historical analysis of field data from cultivated and rangeland soils (Burke et al. 1989). The historical analysis indicated losses of 800–2000 g C/m² as a result of cultivation since settlement of the plains by Euro-American farmers. Such losses in soil organic carbon are thought to be the result of increased decomposition and erosion due to tillage (Haas et al. 1957, Russel 1929, Tiessen et al. 1982). The simulated losses from climate change over a 50-year period are relatively small compared with calculated losses from cultivation over a comparable period.

Similarly, we estimated total carbon dioxide fluxes that would result from changes in carbon storage across the region and compared these fluxes with an estimate of historical carbon fluxes from cultivation during a recent 50-year period and with recent estimates of increases in global atmospheric carbon ($3.0 \cdot 10^{15}$ g C/yr; Tans et al. 1990). On a regional basis, the simulated potential net loss of carbon dioxide to the atmosphere as a result of climate change is small ($0.0014 \cdot 10^{15}$ g C/yr) relative to historical cultivation effects ($0.018 \cdot 10^{15}$ g C/yr). However, this estimate of potential carbon dioxide flux due to climate change is only preliminary; the magnitude of this estimate is likely to vary under different scenarios. Results also suggesting important land-use influences on global carbon dioxide have been reported by Houghton et al. (1987), Post et al. (1990), and Schlesinger (1990).

Regional analysis in ecology

Although atmospheric scientists have long been working in the area of global- or regional-scale dynamics, ecologists have only recently begun applying knowledge of local-scale ecological phenomena to regional scales. Several investigators have used available survey data to statistically analyze geographic distribution of ecological phenomena (Sharp 1975). Sala et al. (1988) and Burke et al. (1989), for example, used distributed point data on production and soil carbon across the Central Grasslands to test ideas about regional environmental control over ecosystem structure and function. Recently, ecologists have also used distributed geographic point data as input to simulation models. Parton et al. (1987) and Schimel et al. (1990, in press) applied the CENTURY model to individual points having average climatic characteristics and hypothetically uniform soils across the Central Grasslands to simulate sensitivity to spatial variance in climate; results were interpolated across the region from the point data. Pastor and Post (1988) used a similar approach in northeastern forested systems, using a linked forest productivity–soil process model to simulate a set of geographically distributed points that varied in both climate and soils.

Remote sensing has been an especially useful tool for regional analysis of ecosystems, particularly for monitoring changes in land surface characteristics (e.g., Hall et al. 1991, Tucker et al. 1985) and for mapping surface properties such as plant physiological status (e.g., Rock et al. 1986, Waring et al. 1986) or soil biogeochemistry and trace gas flux (e.g., Matson et al. 1989, Reiners et al. 1989). Recently, this approach has been extended to include additional geographic data sources and simulation modeling. For example, in coniferous forest systems of Montana, Running et al. (1988, 1989) used soils, climate, topographic, and satellite imagery data organized in a GIS as input to simulate evapotranspiration and net photosynthesis and found good correspondence with field data.

The approach we used to represent spatial and temporal variation across a large region is only one of many possible methods. We suggest that it may be a particularly powerful approach because it allows multiple important driving variables to have both spatial and temporal heterogeneity, a condition that is true for ecological systems at landscape and larger scales (Pastor and Post 1986). Simulation analysis, rather than correlational mapping, allows a much larger number of combinations of driving variables to occur than we can estimate in the field and provides for extrapolation to future conditions. Such simulations may be a critical source of information for predicting large-scale consequences of ecological processes, such as trace gas flux (Burke et al. 1990) or long-term effects of land use or climate change.

Conclusions

We conducted an analysis of the response of the central Great Plains to climate variability over short and long temporal scales. Our application of an ecosystem simulation model to a multivariate, regional database predicted that the region is susceptible to significant reductions in primary production in response to short-term variation in climate, a result consistent with other data (Table 1, Figure 4). Fifty-year simulations of a climate-change scenario predicted reductions in carbon storage. However, comparisons to historical field data suggested that direct human influences on the region, via decisions about land management, have the potential at human time scales to be important controls over regional carbon balance. The critical next step is to incorporate historical and present-day land-use data into the analysis to represent more accurately current conditions and potential initial conditions for climate change.

Acknowledgments

The authors wish to acknowledge the assistance of D. Hall for development of the graphics, M. Galvin for simulation runs, M. Fowler for NDVI data processing, the US Geologic Survey National Mapping Division for production of the color figures, D. Rind for providing GISS GCM output, and J. Briggs and T. Seastedt (and the Konza Prairie Long-Term Ecological Research Station; NSF BSR #8514327) for Konza ANPP data. D. P. Coffin, D. G. Milchunas, T. Seastedt, J. Aber, J. Pastor, and S. Running provided excellent reviews. This research was funded by the National Science Foundation Central Plains Experimental Range LTER project (BSR #8612105). Additional support was provided by NSF (BSR #8605191), NASA (#NAG-5–910), and the Environmental Systems Research Institute in Redlands, California.

References cited

Borchert, J. R. 1950. The climate of the central North American grasslands. *Annals of the Association of American Geographers* 40: 1–39.

Bormann, R. H., G. E. Likens, T. G. Siccama, R. S. Pierce, and J. S. Eaton. 1974. The export of nutrients and recovery of stable conditions following deforestation at Hubbard Brook. *Ecol. Monogr.* 44: 255–277.

Burke, I. C., D. S. Schimel, W. J. Parton, C. M. Yonker, L. A. Joyce, and W. K. Lauenroth. 1990. Regional modeling of grassland biogeochemistry using GIS. *Landscape Ecol.* 4: 45–54.

Burke, I. C., C. M. Yonker, W. J. Parton, C. V. Cole, K. Flach, and D. S. Schimel. 1989. Texture, climate, and cultivation effects on soil organic matter content in U.S. grassland soils. *Soil Sci. Soc. Am. J.* 53: 800–805.

CLIMATEDATA. 1988. U.S. West Optical Publishing, Denver, CO.

Coffin, D. P., and W. K. Lauenroth. 1990. A gap dynamics simulation model of succession in a semiarid grassland. *Ecol. Modell.* 49: 229–266.

Franklin, J. F., C. S. Bledsoe, and J. T. Callahan. 1990. Contributions of the Long-Term Ecological Research program. *BioScience* 40: 509–523.

Goward, S. N., C. J. Tucker, and D. G. Dye. 1985. North American vegetation patterns observed with the NOAA-7 advanced very high resolution radiometer. *Vegetatio* 64: 3–14.

Haas, H. J., C. E. Evans, and E. R. Miles. 1957. Nitrogen and carbon changes in soils as influenced by cropping and soil treatments. USDA Technical Bulletin 1164, US Government Printing Office, Washington, DC.

Hall, F. G., D. B. Botkin, D. E. Strebel, K. D. Woods, and S. J. Goetz. 1991. Large-scale patterns of forest succession as determined by remote sensing. *Ecology* 72: 628–640.

Hansen, J., A. Lacis, D. Rind, G. Russell, P. Stone, I. Fung, R. Ruedy and J. Lerner. 1984. Climate sensitivity: analysis of feedback mechanisms. Pages 130–163 in J. E. Hansen and T. Takahashi, eds. *Climate Processes and Climate Sensitivity*. American Geophysical Union, Washington, DC.

Houghton, R. A., R. D. Boone, J. R. Fruci, J. E. Hobbie, J. M. Melillo, C. A. Palm, B. J. Peterson, F. R. Shaver, and G. M. Woodwell. 1987. The flux of carbon from terrestrial ecosystems to the atmosphere in 1980 due to changes in land use: geographic distribution of the global flux. *Tellus* 39B: 122–139.

Justice, C. O., J. R. G. Townshend, B. N. Holben, and C. J. Tucker. 1985. Analysis of the phenology of global vegetation using meteorological satellite data. *Int. J. Remote Sens.* 6: 1271–1318.

Knapp, A. K., and T. R. Seastedt. 1986. Detritus accumulation limits productivity of tallgrass prairie. *BioScience* 36: 662–668.

Lauenroth, W. K. 1979. Grassland primary production: North American grasslands in perspective. Pages 3–24 in N. R. French, ed. *Perspectives in Grassland Ecology*. Springer-Verlag, New York.

Manabe, S., and R. T. Wetherald. 1987. Large-scale changes of soil wetness induced by an increase in atmospheric carbon dioxide. *J. Atmos. Sci.* 44: 1211–1235.

Matson, P. A., P. M. Vitousek, and D. S. Schimel. 1989. Regional extrapolation of trace gas flux based on soils and ecosystems. Pages 97–108 in M. O. Andreae and D. S. Schimel, eds. *Exchange of Trace Gases between Terrestrial Ecosystems and the Atmosphere*. John Wiley & Sons, New York.

Mitchell, J. F. B., S. Manabe, V. Meleshko, and T. Tokioka. 1990. Equilibrium climate change and its implications for the future. Pages 131–174 in J. T. Houghton, G. J. Jenkins, and J. J. Ephraums, eds. *Climate Change: The IPCC Scientific Assessment*. Cambridge University Press, New York.

Muhs, D. R. 1985. Age and paleoclimatic significance of Holocene sand dunes in northeastern Colorado. *Annals of the Association of American Geographers* 75: 566–582.

Parton, W. J., D. S. Schimel, C. V. Cole, and D. S. Ojima. 1987. Analysis of factors controlling soil organic matter levels in Great Plains grasslands. *Soil Sci. Soc. Am. J.* 51: 1173–1179.

Parton, W. J., J. W. B. Stewart, and C. V. Cole. 1988. Dynamics of C, N, P and S in grassland soils: a model. *Biogeochemistry* 5: 109–131.

Pastor, J., and W. M. Post. 1986. Influence of climate, soil moisture, and succession on forest carbon and nitrogen cycles. *Biogeochemistry* 2: 3–27.

———. 1988. Response of northern forests to CO_2-induced climate change. *Nature* 334: 55–58.

Post, W. M., T. Peng, W. R. Emanuel, A. W. King, V. H. Dale, and D. L. DeAngelis. 1990. The global carbon cycle. *Am. Sci.* 78: 310–326.

Reiners, W. A., L. L. Strong, P. A. Matson, I. C. Burke, and D. S. Ojima. 1989. Estimating biogeochemical fluxes across sagebrush-steppe landscapes with thematic mapper imagery. *Remote Sens. Environ.* 28: 121–129.

Rock, B. N., J. E. Vogelmann, D. L. Williams, A. F. Vogelmann, and T. Hoshizaki. 1986. Remote detection of forest damage. *BioScience* 36: 439–445.

Rosswall, T., R. G. Woodmansee, and P. G. Risser, eds. 1988. *Scales and Global Change*. John Wiley & Sons, New York.

Running, S. W., and J. C. Coughlan. 1988. A general model of forest ecosystem processes for regional applications. I. Hydrologic balance, canopy gas exchange, and primary production processes. *Ecol. Modell.* 42: 125–144.

Running, S. W., R. R. Nemani, D. L. Peterson, L. E. Band, D. F. Potts, L. L. Pierce, and M. A. Spanner. 1989. Mapping regional forest evapotranspiration and photosynthesis by coupling satellite data with ecosystem simulation. *Ecology* 70: 1090–1101.

Russel, J. C. 1929. Organic matter problems under dry-farming conditions. *Agron. J.* 21: 960–969.

Sala, O. E., W. J. Parton, L. A. Joyce, and W. K. Lauenroth. 1988. Primary production of the central grassland region of the United States: spatial pattern and major controls. *Ecology* 69: 40–45.

Schimel, D. S., T. G. F. Kittel, and W. J. Parton. In press. Terrestrial biogeochemical cycles: global interactions with the atmosphere and hydrology. *Tellus*.

Schimel, D. S., W. J. Parton, T. G. F. Kittel, D. S. Ojima, and C. V. Cole. 1990. Grassland biogeochemistry: links to atmospheric processes. *Clim. Change* 17: 13–25.

Schlesinger, W. H. 1990. Evidence from chronosequence studies for a low carbon-storage potential of soils. *Nature* 348: 232–234.

Sharp, D. M. 1975. Methods of assessing the primary production of regions. Pages 147–166 in H. Lieth and R. Whittaker, eds. *Primary Productivity of the Biosphere*. Springer-Verlag, New York.

Tans, P. P., I. Y. Fung, and T. Takahashi. 1990. Observational constraints on the global atmospheric CO_2 budget. *Science* 247: 1431–1438.

Tiessen, H., J. W. B. Stewart, and J. R. Bettany. 1982. Cultivation effects on the amounts and concentration of carbon, nitrogen, and phosphorus in grassland soils. *Agron. J.* 74: 831–835.

Tucker, C. J., J. R. G. Townsend, and T. E. Goff. 1985. African land cover classification using satellite data. *Science* 227: 369–374.

USDA Soil Conservation Service. 1989. STATSGO soil maps. National Cartographic Center, Fort Worth, TX.

Waring, R. H., J. D. Aber, J. M. Melillo, and B. Moore III. 1986. Precursors of change in terrestrial ecosystems. *BioScience* 36: 433–438.

Washington, W. M., and G. A. Meehl. 1984. Seasonal cycle experiment on the climate sensitivity due to a doubling of CO_2 with an atmospheric general circulation model coupled to a simple mixed-layer ocean model. *J. Geophys. Res.* 89: 9475–9503.

Weaver, J. E., and F. W. Albertson. 1944. Nature and degree of recovery of grassland from the great drought of 1933 to 1940. *Ecol. Monogr.* 14: 393–479.

SECTION 3

Soils

Overview

This section features articles on the national soils database, erosion modelling, and soil-landscape mapping. In the first article, Bliss and Reybold describe the nationwide coverage of the State Soil Geographic (STATSGO) database. The purpose of this article is to give a basic description of STATSGO to readers that have not yet used this important national coverage. The second paper by Bocco et al. describes the use of GIS to model gully erosion in Mexico. In the last paper, Skidmore et al. discuss an expert system approach to mapping soils using a digital elevation model and a forest stand map.

Suggested Additional Reading

Fisher, P. F., 1991. Modelling Soil Map-Unit Inclusions by Monte Carlo Simulation. International Journal of Geographical Information Systems. 5(2): 193-208.

Karneili, A., 1991. Stepwise Overlay Approach for Utilizing a GIS with a Soil Moisture Accounting Model. ITC Journal. 1991(1):11-18.

Zhou, H. J., K. B. MacDonald, and A. Moore, 1991. Some Cautions of the Use of GIS Technology to Integrate Soil Site and Area Data. Canadian Journal of Soil Science. 71:389-394.

Small-scale digital soil maps for interpreting natural resources

The Chesapeake Bay watershed serves as the pilot area for testing a new soil geographic data base that will ultimately have nationwide application for state and regional planning

By Norman B. Bliss and William U. Reybold

THE Chesapeake Bay and its watershed contain natural resources of nationwide significance. Numerous federal, state, local, and private organizations are involved in monitoring and cleaning up pollution problems in the bay area.

Nonpoint-source pollution from agricultural land is a particularly important consideration in the bay area, and information on soils is necessary to target adequately critical areas for pollution control. While resource managers require detailed soil maps for planning at the county level, smaller scale maps are appropriate for planning on regional, state, or multistate levels.

To meet such needs, the Soil Conservation Service (SCS) is developing the State Soil Geographic (STATSGO) data base (4). Nationwide coverage is scheduled for completion in mid-1989. This represents a new series of general soil maps, compiled at a scale of 1:250,000.

Using such a geographic information system, it will be possible to make interpretive maps for a variety of specific soil properties and interpretations. Data can be combined with other maps and used as input for hydrologic, erosion, or other models.

A new approach

There are several problems with using soil maps over large areas. Detailed soil surveys, often published on a county basis at scales from 1:15,840 to 1:31,680, have too much detail and require too many map sheets to compile information effectively for an area as large as the Chesapeake Bay watershed. Such maps often contain the information needed for regional analysis. Because of the high cost of digitizing, however, it may be

Norman B. Bliss is a senior applications scientist, TGS Technology, Inc., EROS Data Center, Sioux Falls, South Dakota 57198 (Work performed under U.S. Geological Survey contract 14-08-0001-22521). William U. Reybold is the national leader for soil geography, Soil Conservation Service, U.S. Department of Agriculture, Washington, D.C. 20013. Publication authorized by the Director, U.S. Geological Survey.

years before the data will be in a form suitable for computer analysis using a geographic information system. The data may have been compiled over many years, and there may have been changes in the definitions of the mapping units. The map sheets may not match across county and state boundaries due to changes in mapping concepts, geometric inaccuracies, or both.

Many county soil surveys contain a general soil map as a color fold-out at a scale of about 1:250,000. The general soil map units often are defined in terms of two or three dominant soil series. It is not possible to relate a general soil map unit accurately to the detailed properties of the soils. Thus, it is not possible to produce accurate interpretive maps based on those properties.

Recognizing the value of small-scale maps for regional and national analysis, SCS has undertaken a national program to produce the STATSGO data base. This data base will overcome many of the problems associated with previous methods of mapping soils over large areas. The maps are being compiled at a consistent scale (1:250,000) and according to national standards (6). The map sheets will join along edges. The percentage composition of the phases of soil series that occur in the general map unit are recorded, and a linkage is made to the national Soil Interpretations Record data base that provides detailed information on the properties and interpretations for each soil.

The U.S. Geological Survey (USGS) is cooperating with SCS to investigate how the data can be used in a geographic information system and to explore potential mechanisms for archiving and distributing the data. The Chesapeake Bay watershed serves as a pilot study area for testing the procedures.

Uses of STATSGO data

STATSGO data will be useful for many types of regional, statewide, and national studies. The data provide a synoptic view in visual form by plotting large areas on maps at scales smaller than 1:250,000. A synoptic view is also possible in statistical form because the attribute data can be expressed in terms of the area (acres or square kilometers) meeting criteria specified by a user.

Small-scale soil maps can be used as screening tools for locating either desirable areas for activity location or undesirable areas for hazard avoidance. An investigator with a set of soil property or interpretations criteria can query the data base and plot interpretive maps showing the areas where those properties occur. Once the areas are identified on the small-scale soil maps, detailed soil maps in the selected areas can be consulted for additional information.

Components representing phases of soil series are stored for each of the STATSGO soil map units. The percentage composition of each map unit thus is available for any desired property. This information can be used to characterize the soils of a region in more detail than is apparent in the graphics displayed at the 1:250,000 scale. Much of the information in the detailed soil mapping at scales from 1:15,840 to 1:31,680 is retained in the quantitative analysis of the STATSGO attribute data.

Presently, the only other digital soil map available on a nationwide basis is related to the major land resource area (MLRA) 1:7,500,000-scale map (5).

SCS is evaluating the use of the attribute data available in the 1982 National Resources Inventory (3) to provide interpretations of the MLRA map. Digital map data at this scale are referred to as the National Soil Geographic (NATSGO) data base (4).

STATSGO map units

The STATSGO maps are compiled by generalizing more detailed soil survey maps that are available for about 75 percent of the United States. Map unit delineations are drawn on the basis of physiography; these delineations are composed of soils associated on the landscape. Soils in a map unit

Reprinted by permission of the publisher, Soil and Water Conservation Society, *Journal of Soil and Water Conservation*, 1989, 44 (1): 30-34.

generally are formed in similar kinds of material and have a similar repeating pattern of landforms. The associated soils generally are dissimilar in one or more characteristics. When more detailed soil maps are not available, data about the geology, topography, vegetation, and climate are assembled, together with Landsat images. Soils of analogous areas are studied and a determination of the probable classification and extent of the soils is made.

Phases of soil series are components of the STATSGO map units. Phases are used because they can be interpreted precisely for a wide range of uses. The percentage of each soil phase in each STATSGO map unit is determined by transecting or sampling areas on more detailed soil maps and expanding the data statistically to characterize the whole map unit. The proportion of the area of the map unit delineation that each soil phase occupies is recorded as the "percent composition." Recording this composition enables the user to extract more quantitative interpretations from the soil map than would be expected from the scale of the map. The percentage composition of the components can be used to get reasonably accurate estimates of the total land area that meets a specific criteria. Interpretive maps are designed to reflect the percentage of the map unit having the characteristics queried for.

Integrating soils and other data

The STATSGO soil data have been integrated with USGS land use and land cover data. When the soil data are overlayed with the land use data, statistics on the co-occur-

A STATSGO slope map of Fairfax County is plotted with a shaded relief background derived from a Digital Elevation Model. The polygons with lighter tones have steeper slopes, with more than 50 percent of the area in the polygon having a slope greater than 7 percent.

rence of the land use data with the soil data must be interpreted carefully. The composition of the STATSGO map unit can be characterized independently for both the land use and for the soil component, but there are no data on their joint occurrence at a more detailed level.

Analysis of the overlayed data should be on a map polygon basis. It would be incorrect to assign land use attributes to the soil components by multiplying the proportions of soil components by the proportions of land uses.

Additional boundaries may be intersected with the soil data. These might include maps of political jurisdictions or watershed boundaries. Although the composition of each political or watershed unit may be described in terms of the STATSGO map units, information is not available to assign the components of the map units (the soil phases) to the boundary units with full accuracy. As with the land use categories, the analysis should be restricted to the classified map units rather than to classified components.

Visual orientation can be provided by using additional data files. For STATSGO interpretive maps and many natural resource purposes, a shaded relief background can provide visual reference of the topography in an easily understandable fashion. An example is the shaded relief background image from USGS Digital Elevation Model data, which is formatted in 1:250,000-scale quadrangles (2).

Other data types, such as USGS Digital Line Graph data for transportation or

hydrography, can be used to help orient a reader to a map (7). If road or stream data need to be incorporated into an analysis, it may be desirable to create a buffer zone around the linear feature and then use an overlay operation to intersect the resulting corridor area with the interpreted soil map.

Complex models can be constructed using the soil attribute data in conjunction with other data sources. The model output can be displayed in map form using a geographic information system. Examples include soil erosion models, soil suitability for specific pesticides, crop productivity models, or suitability for urban development. Calculations typically are made on the basis of each component soil phase. For example, in an erosion model, the slope and erodibility (K-factor) are extracted for each soil phase. The results of the calculation for each component then can be displayed in map form using the percentage composition techniques discussed earlier.

Interpretive maps

On a simple soil map, such as most county soil survey maps, each polygon represents a single soil phase. An interpretive map is formed by classifying each polygon according to some soil property. The legend for a simple slope map reports a slope range for each polygon.

On a STATSGO map, in contrast, each polygon contains several components for

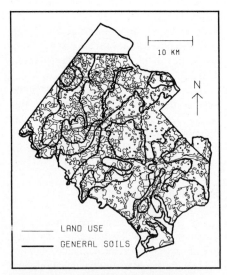

An overlay of STATSGO soil map units with USGS land use and land cover data allows calculation of the percentage composition of land use within each soil polygon. Area shown is Fairfax County, Virginia.

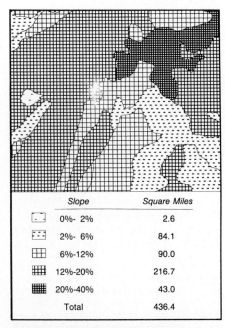

	Slope	Square Miles
	0%- 2%	2.6
	2%- 6%	84.1
	6%-12%	90.0
	12%-20%	216.7
	20%-40%	43.0
	Total	436.4

An interpretive map for slope from a detailed survey, with one soil phase per map unit, has categories in terms of percent slope. STATSGO maps, in contrast, must show the percentage of a map unit meeting a criterion.

which there are attribute data, but there is no distinction visible in the map as to the location of these components within the polygon. Thus, to present information on an attribute, a simple map is not sufficient for the STATSGO data. A series of maps must be used to portray the more complex set of available information.

We have mapped a portion of a series of slope maps using STATSGO data for Fairfax County, Virginia (see map). The criterion for each map is defined in terms of the high end of the slope range being less than or equal to some number. For the first map, the number is set at 2 percent. Only a small portion of the mapped area (5 square miles) is flat enough so that at least 80 percent of a map unit has soils of less than 2 percent slope; 125 square miles of the mapped area have between 21 percent and 40 percent of the map unit with slopes in the 0- to 2-percent range.

The second map shows soils with slopes less than or equal to 7 percent. The map units in which most of the soils are steeper than the criterion continue to be represented by light tones. For example, 127 square miles of the area have at least 80 percent of

the map units with a high end of the slope range greater than 7 percent slope. The dark tones represent flat areas. The map units that have at least 80 percent of the area in slopes less than or equal to 7 percent occupy 44 square miles.

The third map shows soils with slopes less than or equal to 15 percent. The series could be continued with higher limits, such as slope (high) less than or equal to 45 percent and 75 percent. For these data, a criterion of less than 75 percent slope would be met by all components of all map units.

The entire map (399 square miles) would be classified in the 81- to 100-percent category, representing an extreme case at the high end of the series.

Care must be used in evaluating the statistics presented in the legend. These statistics represent the areas of the STATSGO map units in each class, but they do not represent the areas of the soil components that satisfy the criterion. A separate table shows the areas of the second map (slopes less than or equal to 7 percent) in which the area meeting the criterion is separated from the area not meeting the criterion. The area of each map unit component is recorded in the

data base and can be used to produce this table, although the components cannot be displayed directly on the map. Thus, the actual area for which the high end of the slope range is less than or equal to 7 percent is 169 square miles.

Although a series of maps is needed to display all of the information contained in the attribute data, if one map must be used a map with a fairly uniform distribution of percentage ranges is preferred. Thus, in the case of the series of slope maps, the map of slopes less than or equal to 7 percent contains more information about the overall slope conditions than the map of slopes less than or equal to 2 percent.

The soil data contain information on some properties as a function of depth in the soil profile. One such property is the available water capacity. An investigator can narrow

STATSGO data have map unit delineations (polygons) that incorporate several component soil phases. Detailed properties, such as slope, are available for the components. To display all of the information requires a series of maps. Part of a series is shown here, portraying slopes less than or equal to 2 percent, 7 percent, and 15 percent.

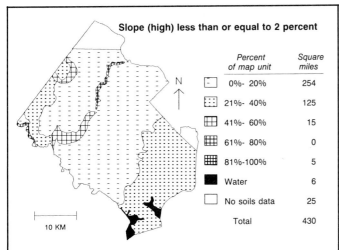

Slope (high) less than or equal to 2 percent

	Percent of map unit	Square miles
	0%- 20%	254
	21%- 40%	125
	41%- 60%	15
	61%- 80%	0
	81%-100%	5
	Water	6
	No soils data	25
	Total	430

10 KM

Slope (high) less than or equal to 15 percent

	Percent of map unit	Square miles
	0%- 20%	0
	21%- 40%	0
	41%- 60%	44
	61%- 80%	277
	81%-100%	78
	Water	6
	No soils data	25
	Total	430

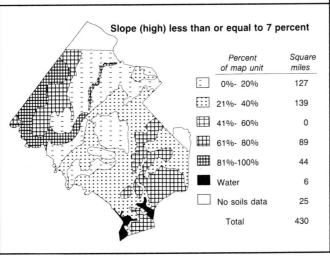

Slope (high) less than or equal to 7 percent

	Percent of map unit	Square miles
	0%- 20%	127
	21%- 40%	139
	41%- 60%	0
	61%- 80%	89
	81%-100%	44
	Water	6
	No soils data	25
	Total	430

Areas within each legend category that have slopes less than or equal to 7 percent

Legend Category (percent of map unit)	Area With Slopes Less Than or Equal to 7%	Area With Slopes Greater Than 7%	Total Area	Percent Slopes Less Than or Equal to 7%
	square miles			
0- 20%	19	108	127	15
21- 40%	50	88	139	36
41- 60%	0	0	0	0
61- 80%	60	29	89	67
81-100%	40	5	44	90
Water	0	6	6	0
No soils data	0	25	25	0
Total	169	261	430	39

the analysis to a specific depth range, such as the surface 30 inches, and analyze the available water capacity within that range.

Data preparation

A reformatting process is used to prepare the attribute data (soil properties) for use within a geographic information system. Each map unit delineation (polygon) on a STATSGO map is labeled with a map unit identifier representing a physiographic area of soils. Each map unit can be defined using multiple components. The components are generally phases of soil series for which the most precise interpretations can be made. The Map Unit Use File links the map unit identifier to information on the components of the map unit. Each component is defined in terms of the soil interpretations record number, percentage of the map unit area, surface texture and texture modifier, slope range (low, high), flooding category (none, rare, occasional, frequent), and other attributes needed to define the soil phase.

This set of data is used to match each map unit component to the appropriate information from the Soil Interpretations Record (Soil-5) data base. The Soil-5 data base contains more than 150 attributes for each soil series in the United States. By matching the records between the Map Unit Use File and the Soil-5 data base, these 150 attributes can be related to each component of the soil polygons. The result of this match is called the single-phase interpretation format. A FORTRAN program is used to further reformat the single-phase format into a set of 12 relational tables for use in the relational data base management system of a geographic information system (1).

The 12 tables accomodate all of the information available in the Soil Interpretations Record, including one for texture, two for engineering properties, and five for biological interpretations.

The remaining four tables are illustrated here as: PAT, MAPUNIT, COMP, and LAYER. They are introduced in the order in which they are related to the map polygon (an analysis typically proceeds in the reverse order, from LAYER to COMP to MAPUNIT to PAT).

Each polygon on the STATSGO map is coded with a unique numeric identifier (POLYGON#). A Polygon Attribute Table (PAT) is used to relate the POLYGON# to the area calculated by the geographic information system software (AREA) and to the map unit identifier (MUID) assigned by the SCS map compiler, such as 'VA038'. An extra variable, identified as PAT@, is added to the table to store the results of analysis generated from the other tables. Each code

An overview of the process for linking soil attributes to soil maps in the pilot study. In an operational system, data users should be able to order data in a relational table form directly usable by a geographic information system.

Soil Map
   Contains a map unit identifier for each polygon

Key: Map unit identifier

Map Unit Use File (Soil-6)
   Defines component phases of soil series for each soil map unit

Soil Interpretation Record (Soil-5)
   Contains more than 150 soil properties and interpretations for all phases in a soil series

The following data items are used as keys for matching SOIL-5 and SOIL-6:
   Soil interpretations record number,
   Slope (low), slope (high), surface texture, flooding, and "other"

Single Phase Interpretation Format
   A full (150 variable) set of attributes for each component of each map unit

Reformatting program splits each single-phase record into a set of 12 relational tables

Set of Relational Tables
   Format appropriate for query in a geographic information system with a data base management system

can be assigned a color for shading the output map.

The MAPUNIT table can be used to store information on soil properties that are characteristic of the map unit. In the STATSGO data, there are no soil properties or interpretations stored in the MAPUNIT table. The table is still useful, however, for storing the results of the analysis. Because a STATSGO map unit may occur as several delineations in various places on a map, the area of the map unit can be aggregated from the polygon attribute table and stored as a property of the map unit (AREAMU). As soil properties are interpreted using the component table, a criterion can be tested, and the cumulative percentage composition meeting that criterion will become a property of the map unit, identified as PERCENT@. These percentage composition numbers can be classified into a limited number of groups. The result of this classification is stored in a field for the model result (MAPUNIT@). There is a many-to-one relationship between records in the PAT and MAPUNIT tables.

The component table (COMP) is used to relate the map units to the components. In the COMP table, VA038 has six components. The COMP table uses the map unit identifier field (MUID) to relate to the

MAPUNIT table. A unique component number field (COMPNUM) identifies each component. The component percentage field (COMPPCT) is needed to synthesize the detailed information about the components (soil phases) to make an interpretation for each STATSGO map unit. The Soil Interpretations Record Number (S5NUM) shows which record in the Soil-5 data base was the source of the properties and interpretations. The intermediate results of an analysis can be stored in the AVE@ and COMP@ fields, as explained below.

The layer table (LAYER) contains information on variables that are described for each layer in the soil profile. Three fields are required to identify the record uniquely: the map unit identifier (MUID), the component number (COMPNUM), and the layer number (LAYNUM). Two fields, LAYDEPL and LAYDEPH, describe the depth of the layer, measured in inches from the surface. The available water capacity range is illustrated using AWCL and AWCH. The results of analysis are stored in the LAYER@ field.

Analytic procedure

Available water capacity is the capacity of a soil to hold water in a form available to

Complex criteria can be used for extracting information from the attribute data base. This interpretive map shows percentages of the map unit where the average available water capacity is less than or equal to 0.14 inches of water per inch of soil. The weighted average accounts for the thickness of each soil horizon layer, with calculations limited to the surface 30 inches of the soil.

plants, expressed in inches of water per inch of soil depth. An example of an analysis of available water capacity starts in the LAYER table, where the low and high ends of the available water capacity range are averaged and the result is stored in the LAYER@ field. The result for each layer is then weighted by the thickness of that layer, and

the average value for each component is stored in the AVE@ field of the COMP table. The components are then classified as to whether the criterion of "average available water capacity is less than or equal to 0.14 inch of water per inch of soil" is met or not met. If the criterion is met, then "YES" is entered in the COMP@ result field, otherwise "NO" is entered. The YES component percentages are accumulated and the result is stored in the PERCENT@ field of the MAPUNIT table. The PERCENT@ result is classified into five percentage ranges, and the result is stored in the MAPUNIT@ field. This result is then copied to the PAT@ field in the PAT table using the map unit identifier (MUID) to relate the tables. Shading or colors can be assigned to each code, and an interpretive map can be produced.

Conclusions

Geographic information systems that enable automated manipulation of map data are changing and improving the way state and federal agencies evaluate information. Users of such systems agree that soil information is one of the more important data layers for natural resource analysis. STATSGO provides consistent spatial soil information at a scale practical for automated manipulation in regional, state, and multicounty applications. It differs from general soil maps published for many U.S. states and counties in that the components (phases of soil series) of each STATSGO map unit are determined accurately and linked to the Soil Interpretations Record computer data base. This provides information with a degree of validity not available for most general soil maps.

The STATSGO data represent a valuable new data source for computerized analysis of natural resources. Soil information is provided to users in nationally uniform formats that take advantage of modern technology.

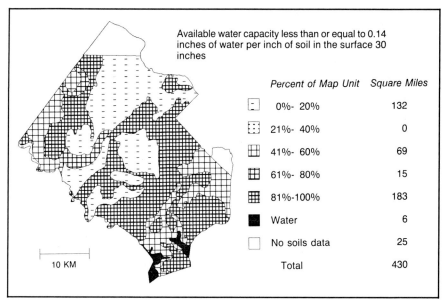

Available water capacity less than or equal to 0.14 inches of water per inch of soil in the surface 30 inches

	Percent of Map Unit	Square Miles
⊡	0%- 20%	132
⊞	21%- 40%	0
⊞	41%- 60%	69
⊞	61%- 80%	15
⊞	81%-100%	183
■	Water	6
☐	No soils data	25
	Total	430

10 KM

Selected portions of the relational tables for soil attributes illustrate the calculations for an interpretive map of available water capacity

Map

1 red
2 yellow
3 red

Polygon attribute table (PAT)

Polygon Identifier Polygon#	Polygon Area (square miles)	Map Unit Identifier MUID	Model Result PAT@
1	20	VA037	5 (red)
2	14	VA038	4 (yellow)
3	33	VA037	5 (red)

Map unit table (MAPUNIT)

Map Unit Identifier MUID	Map Unit AREAMU (square miles)	Percentage Meeting Criterion PERCENT@	Model Result MAPUNIT@
VA037	53	95	5
VA038	14	71	4

Component table (COMP)

Map Unit Identifier MUID	Component Number COMPNUM	Component Percentage COMPPCT	SIRNO S5NUM	Analysis Value AVE@	Satisfies Criterion COMP@
VA038	1	65	SC0022	0.04	Yes
VA038	2	15	VA0199	0.16	No
VA038	3	12	NC0044	0.16	No
VA038	4	2	AL0033	0.16	No
VA038	5	4	VA0145	0.10	Yes
VA038	6	2	VA0032	0.12	Yes

Layer Table (LAYER)

Map Unit Identifier MUID	Component Number COMPNUM	Layer Number LAYERNUM	Depth (Low) LAYDEPL	Depth (High) LAYDEPH	Available Water Capacty AWCL	Available Water Capacty AWCH	Model Result LAYER@
VA038	1	1	0	10	0.02	0.06	0.04
VA038	1	2	10	49	0.02	0.06	0.04
VA038	1	3	49	80			0.00
VA038	2	1	0	5	0.14	0.22	0.18
VA038	2	2	5	43	0.10	0.22	0.16
VA038	2	3	43	60			0.00

REFERENCES CITED
1. Bliss, N. B. 1987. *Structuring the soils-5 data into a relational data base.* In ESRI User's Conference Proceedings. Environ. Systems Res. Inst., Redlands, Calif.
2. Elassal, A. A. and V. M. Caruso. 1983. *Digital elevaton models.* Circ. 895-B. U.S. Geol. Surv., Reston, Va.
3. National Research Council. 1986. *Soil conservation: Assessing the national resources inventory.* Nat. Acad. Press, Washington, D.C.
4. Reybold, W. U., and G. W. TeSelle. 1986. *Soil geographic data bases.* J. Soil and Water Cons. 44(1): 28-29.
5. Soil Conservation Service. 1981. *Land resource regions and major land resource areas of the United States.* Agr. Handbk. 296. U.S. Dept. Agr., Washington, D.C.
6. Soil Conservation Service. 1984. *State general soil map geographic data base.* Nat. Instruction No. 430-302. U.S. Dept. Agr., Washington, D.C.
7. U.S. Geological Survey. 1987. *Digital line graphs from 1:2,000,000-scale maps.* Data Users Guide 3. Reston, Va. □

Gully erosion modelling using GIS and geomorphologic knowledge

Gerardo Bocco,[*] Jose Palacio[*] and Carlos R Valenzuela[**]

ABSTRACT

Gully erosion dynamics in a Quaternary volcanic terrain were modelled in a GIS using both remote sensing data and field observations. Of the actual gullied areas, 75 percent occur on gently sloping (< 15 percent gradient) accumulative terrains under rainfed agriculture or grassland. Areas with severe gully erosion risk can be predicted. The model was successfully applied to a different area of the same physiographic province. The approach is suggested for determining conservation priorities.

An environmental inventory is an essential component in the assessment of such phenomena as gully erosion. It provides quantitative data of natural and anthropogenic processes and their interrelationships. These data can be transformed into usable information through manipulation of the datasets generated during mapping and field work using spatial and attribute databases and GIS procedures.

Gully eroded areas, which are clearly depicted on enhanced SPOT stereo photographic images, can be mapped using standard photo interpretation techniques [3]. Simple GIS procedures make it possible to georeference and quantify these features. The stereoscopic images also allow the mapping of geomorphically-defined landscape units, such as terrain mapping units (TMUs) [9]. Further, the spectral resolution contained in the colour composite aids in land cover and land use mapping. When required, additional detailed data can be gained if aerial photographs at larger scales are available. Existing maps can also be incorporated in the GIS database. A topographic map, for example, permits the construction of digital elevation

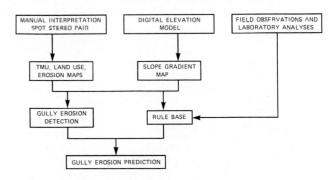

FIGURE 2 Method flow chart

models (DEM) and the derivation of slope gradient maps. The corresponding terrain mapping unit, land use or slope gradient of the eroded area can be quickly determined by combining the appropriate maps.

The explanation of a given landscape feature, such as a gully, in terms of selected landscape variables introduces the possibility of predicting the probable future occurrence of similar features if a specific set of conditions—derived from the analysis—also occurs. In other words, an inventory can provide the basic data required for spatial modelling.

In this article, we report on the use of GIS and remote sensing techniques as means for modelling gully erosion dynamics in Quaternary volcanic terrains. The approach was tested in two areas in the Mexican Volcanic Belt (Tlalpujahua and Huasca, Figure 1), a large, densely populated physiographic province. The climate is temperate subhumid with contrasting dry winters and rainy summers. The main land use on gentle terrain is rainfed agriculture and grazing. Steeper slopes are usually under oak-pine forest. In both study areas, research on badland and gully erosion development is continuing [7, 2].

MATERIALS AND METHOD

Materials for the study included:
- two enhanced false colour SPOT (stereo) images of October 1987 (end of the wet season), enlarged to 1:100 000 scale
- aerial photographs, panchromatic black-and-white, approximate scales 1:50 000 and 1:25 000
- photogrammetric topographic maps at 1:50 000 scale, with a contour interval of 10 m [5].

The analysis was carried out using ILWIS [8]. The method is summarized in Figure 2.

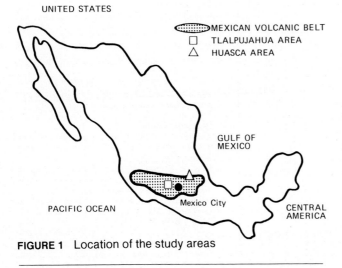

UNITED STATES

MEXICAN VOLCANIC BELT
☐ TLALPUJAHUA AREA
△ HUASCA AREA

GULF OF MEXICO

PACIFIC OCEAN

Mexico City

CENTRAL AMERICA

FIGURE 1 Location of the study areas

* Institute of Geography, University of Mexico, 04510 Mexico DF
** Department of land resource surveys and rural development, ITC

Reprinted by permission of the publisher, International Institute for Aerospace Survey and Earth Sciences, *ITC Journal*, 1990, 3: p. 253-261.

DATABASE DESIGN

The following input data were digitized into the GIS:

(1) A TMU map (Figure 3) derived from the SPOT stereopair (for a thorough description of the TMU approach, see [6]. TMUs are based largely on genesis and lithology. Analysis of variance of morphometric attributes in the study area indicated that slope gradient was the most critical variable explaining their differentiation [1].

(2) A map of gullied terrain (Figure 4) derived from the same image. Gullied terrain consists basically of relatively shallow (usually less than 5 m deep) valley-side gullies. Gullied terrain can be conveniently interpreted on the basis of tone, shape and pattern. Gullies have high reflectance in all bands, are irregularly shaped and represent recent geomorphic features on depositional areas.

(3) A land use map (Figure 5) derived from the same image. Land use interpretation was based mostly on cover data provided by the infrared band of the colour composite.

(4) A slope gradient map (Figure 6) based on elevation data digitized from the topographic map. In mountainous and hilly terrains, contours were digitized at 50 m intervals. In areas with low relief amplitude,

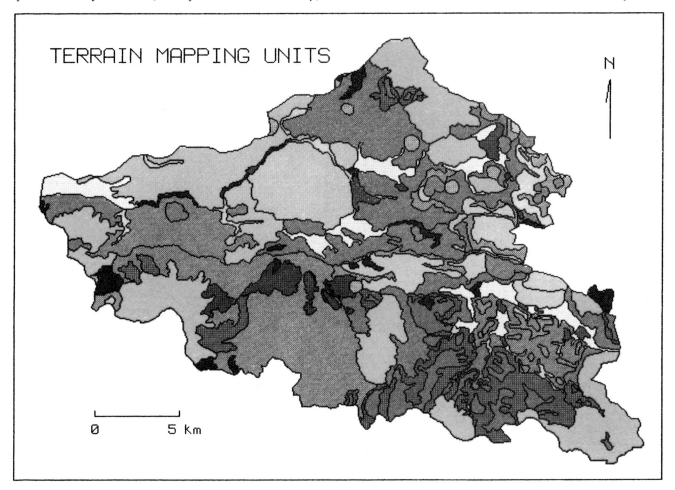

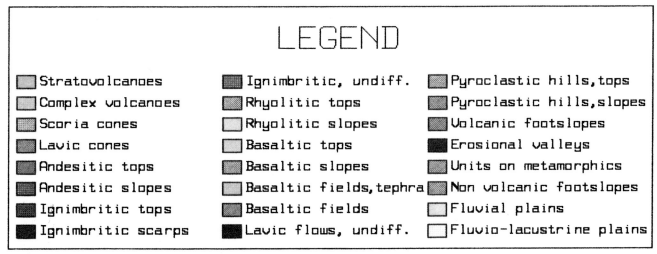

FIGURE 3   Terrain mapping units

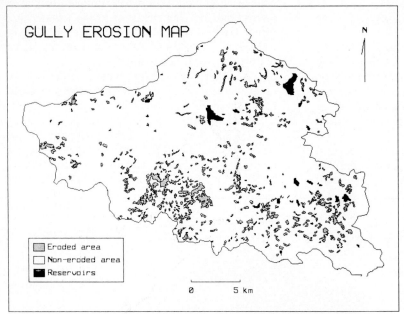

FIGURE 4 Map of gullied terrain

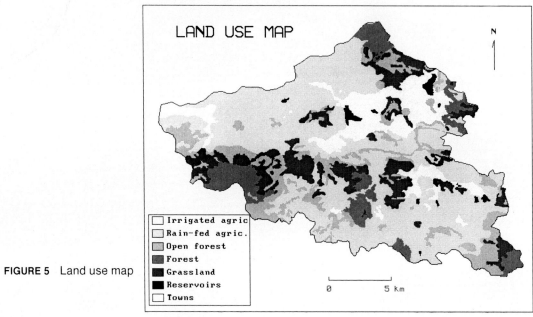

FIGURE 5 Land use map

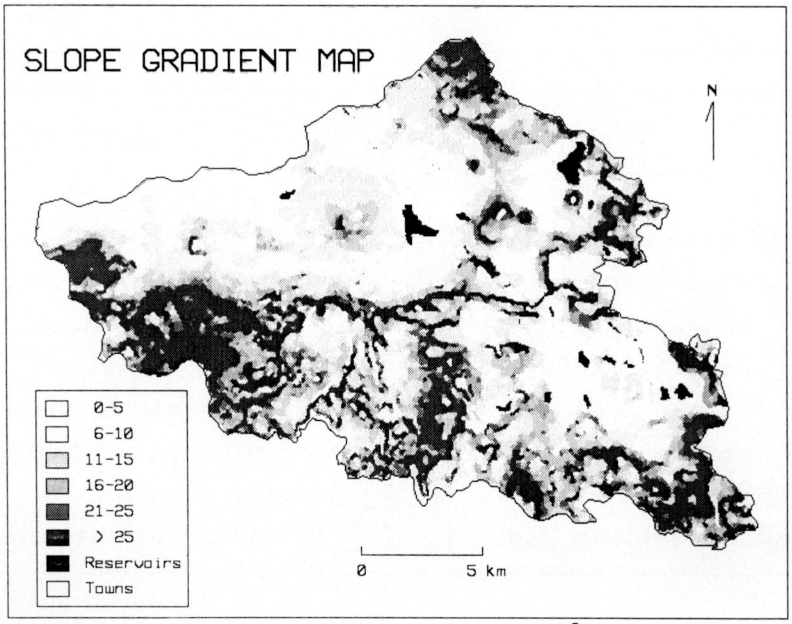

FIGURE 6 Slope gradient map

all contour lines were digitized. The slope map was constructed using standard directional filter techniques and GIS operations in raster format.

The terrain mapping units were defined by segmenting the entire area into relatively homogeneous landscape areas; they were used as the basic information units. The TMU map was combined with the other input maps to quantify the occurrence of gully erosion, slope and land use classes per terrain mapping unit. In addition, the classified slope map was combined with the land use map and the erosion map so that the relationships between natural and man-made features of the landscape were established. Map overlaying never involved more than two maps to avoid large error propagation.

ACCURACY OF THE DATASETS

An accuracy threshold should always be established to indicate the confidence of the procedures. According to Walsh *et al* [10], there are two main sources of error: inherent and operational. Inherent error is present in the source documents. Operational error is produced through data capture and manipulation functions of a GIS. Both types of error can be further categorized as "location" (positional) and "identification" (labelling).

Boundaries of natural bodies (such as landscape units) are usually not precise lines on the ground but transitional areas where changes occur. In this sense, more emphasis should be given to identification than to location errors. When the input data are derived from remotely sensed products, the operational error is usu-

ally smaller than the inherent (identification) error introduced in the mapping units because of (1) generalizations during photo interpretation (both within units and along boundaries), (2) scale limitations of the source documents and (3) the intrinsic accuracy of the image.

The maps drawn from the SPOT photographic images were transformed to Universal Transverse Mercator (UTM) coordinates using 30 control points, with an accuracy (rms) of 0.5 the cell size. All data were digitized and rasterized to a 50 m cell size (this cell size was selected bearing in mind the scale of the SPOT stereopair). Because 0.5 mm on the image corresponds to 50 m on the ground, it was accepted that the accuracy would not be better than 0.25 ha.

The resolution of the SPOT enlargement at 1:100 000 allows the visual detection of features which are smaller than the threshold given by the combined effect of thickness of the drawing pen and the inaccuracies resulting from digitizing and vector-to-raster conversion. All maps were visually scrutinized and information errors were minimized.

The accuracy of the maps derived from the image, however, is mainly a function of the image scale. The accuracy will not be better than that of maps manually drawn using aerial photos and plotted using simple photogrammetric equipment. If more than one input scale is used, the final accuracy will be that of the smallest scale [4]. In other words, the use of a GIS does not imply an improvement in terms of the total accuracy but in terms of the ease with which the accuracy is attained. Further, a GIS better pre-

TABLE 1 Terrain mapping units, dominant slopes and land use classes

Terrain Mapping Units	Area		Predom Slope %	Predominant Land Use Class
	ha	%		
VOLCANIC ORIGIN				
VOLCANOES				
1 Stratovolcanoes	7479	15.20	> 25	Forest
2 Complex volcanoes	2480	5.00	7–8	Rainfed agricul
3 Scoria cones	341	0.70	> 25	Open forest
4 Lavic cones	859	1.80	> 25	Open forest
VOLCANIC FLOWS				
5 Andesitic tops	2042	4.20	5–6	Rainfed agricul
6 Andesitic slopes	3545	7.20	> 25	Rainfed agricul
7 Ignimbritic tops	954	1.90	5–6	Grasses
8 Ignimbritic scarps	52	0.10	> 25	Open forest
9 Ignimbritic, undifferent	188	0.40	> 25	Grasses
10 Rhyolitic tops	303	0.60	7–8	Grasses
11 Rhyolitic slopes	504	1.00	> 25	Forest
12 Basaltic tops	2320	4.70	3–4	Rainfed agricul
13 Basaltic slopes	1130	2.30	> 25	Open forest
14 Basaltic fields, tephra	4077	8.30	3–4	Rainfed agricul
15 Basaltic fields	586	1.20	3–4	Rainfed agricul
16 Lavic flows, undifferent	712	1.40	7–8	Rainfed agricul
VOLCANIC DENUDATIONAL ORIGIN				
17 Pyroclastic hills, tops	370	0.70	3–4	Rainfed agricul
18 Pyroclastic hills, slopes	1356	2.80	3–4	Rainfed agricul
19 Volcanic footslopes	8227	16.80	5–6	Rainfed agricul
20 Erosional valleys	381	0.80	9–10	Open forest
DENUDATIONAL ORIGIN				
21 Units on metamorphic rocks	5630	11.50	> 25	Rainfed agricul
22 Non-volcanic footslopes	1827	3.70	5–6	Rainfed agricul
FLUVIAL AND LACUSTRINE ORIGIN				
23 Fluvial plains	694	1.40	0–2	Irrigated agricul
24 Fluvio-lacustrine plains	2518	5.10	0–2	Irrigated agricul
Reservoirs	554	1.10		
TOTAL	49126	100.00		

suitable for the analysis. Terrain mapping subunits were defined particularly according to slope gradient (Table 1). The slope map was reclassified into nine classes of slope gradient in which gentler slopes were finely discriminated (Table 2). Land use was divided into seven categories (Table 3).

TABLE 2 Eroded terrain per slope class

Slope Class (%)	Area ha	%	Eroded Area ha	%class	%tot area	Cum%
0-2	6339	13.1	218	3.4	7.6	7.6
3-4	6610	13.7	339	5.1	11.8	19.4
5-6	6379	13.2	359	5.6	12.4	31.8
7-8	4713	9.8	276	5.9	9.5	41.3
9-10	3149	6.5	203	6.4	7.0	48.3
11-15	5749	11.9	557	9.8	19.2	67.5
16-20	4143	8.6	392	9.5	13.5	81.0
21-25	3167	6.6	234	7.4	8.1	89.1
> 25	8062	16.6	317	3.9	10.9	100.0
Total		100.0	2895			
Reservoirs	554					
Towns	262					

TABLE 3 Eroded terrain per land use class

Land Use Class	Area ha	%	Eroded Area ha	%class	%total
1 Irrigated agriculture	5954	12.1	111	1.9	3.8
2 Rainfed agriculture	24490	49.9	2084	8.5	72.0
3 Open forest	7122	14.5	163	2.3	5.6
4 Forest	4283	8.7	30	0.7	1.0
5 Grasses	6464	13.2	507	7.8	17.5
6 Reservoirs	554	1.1			
7 Towns	262	0.5			
Total	49129	100.0	2895		100.0

serves the accuracy.

Data were generalized to levels of aggregation

RESULTS AND DISCUSSION

The results of the map calculations are attribute databases that can be retrieved and updated at will. Table 1 indicates the size, dominant slope class and land use per terrain mapping unit. The table was constructed by aggregating the results of the overlays of the TMU map with the slope and land use maps. The consistency of decision rules used during photo interpretation can be verified, and a quantitative characterization of the homogeneity of TMUs in terms of slope gradient classes and land use types is obtained. Slope frequencies can also be analyzed per mapping unit. This is an excellent guide for detecting information errors per unit and, if coupled with geologic and other morphometric data, the possibility of computer-assisted geomorphic mapping is introduced.

Table 4 and Figure 7 show the relationship between TMU and gully erosion. The eroded area per terrain mapping unit is expressed as an absolute value in hectares, as a percentage of each mapping unit, and as a percentage of the entire eroded area.

The most eroded units are the denudational ones on metamorphics, the gently sloping pyroclastic hills, the tops of ignimbritic flows and the andesitic flows. Including the volcanic footslopes, 75 percent of total gully erosion occurs on these units. Except for the metamorphics and the andesitic slopes, most gully erosion occurs on gentle to almost flat, accumulative

TABLE 4 Eroded area per terrain mapping unit

Terrain Mapping Units	Unit Area (ha)	ha	Eroded %TMU	Area %tot erod
1 Stratovolcanoes	7479	159	2.1	5.5
2 Complex volcanoes	2480	65	2.6	2.2
3 Scoria cones	341	21	6.1	0.7
4 Lavic cones	859	20	2.4	0.7
5 Andesitic tops	2042	171	8.4	5.9
6 Andesitic slopes	3545	288	8.1	10.0
7 Ignimbritic tops	954	108	11.3	3.7
8 Ignimbritic scarps	52	0	0.0	0.0
9 Ignimbritic, undiffer	188	17	8.9	0.6
10 Rhyolitic tops	303	14	4.5	0.5
11 Rhyolitic slopes	504	5	0.9	0.2
12 Basaltic tops	2320	117	5.0	4.0
13 Basaltic slopes	1130	50	4.4	1.7
14 Basaltic fields, tephra	4077	133	3.3	4.6
15 Basaltic fields	586	31	5.3	1.1
16 Lavic flows, undiffer	712	22	3.2	0.8
17 Pyroc hills, tops	370	30	8.2	1.1
18 Pyroc hills, slopes	1356	173	12.7	6.0
19 Volcanic footslopes	8227	463	5.6	16.0
20 Erosional valleys	381	3	0.8	0.1
21 Denud units (metam)	5630	942	16.7	32.5
22 Non-volc footslopes	1827	43	2.3	1.5
23 Fluvial plains	694	10	1.5	0.3
24 Fluvio-lac plains	2518	10	0.4	0.3
Reservoirs	554	0	0.0	0.0
Total	49129	2895		100.0

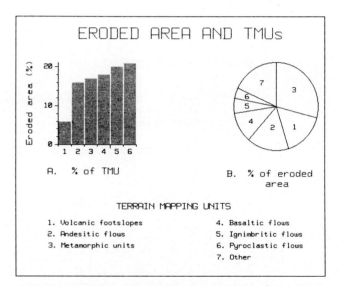

FIGURE 7 Gully erosion per terrain mapping unit

terrains. These volcanic terrain units are characterized by the occurrence of relatively shallow, hydraulic impeding layers [1].

The relationship between slope gradient and gully erosion is shown in Table 2 and Figure 8. Nearly 70 percent of the total erosion occurs on slopes of less than 15 percent (8° to 9°), a critical major break of slope between depositional units (such as volcanic footslopes) and hilly to mountainous terrains (such as volcanoes or other steep lavic slopes). Further, nearly 50 percent of erosion occurs on slopes of less than 10 percent (6°, Table 2), a range which includes most of the tops of lavic flows (including basaltic fields) and the slopes of the pyroclastic hills (Table 1). The mode (nearly 30 percent of the total eroded area) occurs on slopes ranging between 5 and 10 percent (3°

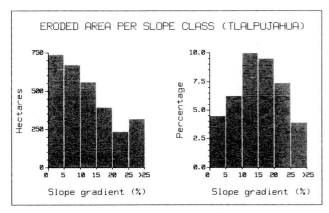

FIGURE 8 Gully erosion and slope gradient

to 6°). In these slope classes, 18 percent of the total area is eroded. This range of slope (5 to 10 percent) seems to be critical for gully erosion processes on the volcanic terrains.

Slope gradient is a relevant factor because it controls slope hydrology and the accumulation of slope materials susceptible to slope processes and gullying. The dominance of eroded terrain on relatively gentle slopes agrees with results obtained in the analysis of gully initiation on ignimbritic tops and pyroclastic slopes [2].

When erosion is analyzed per land use class (Table 3, Figure 9), it becomes apparent that rainfed agriculture and grassland are the most eroded; together they account for approximately 90 percent of the total erosion. Nearly 7 percent of the total area with those land uses is eroded. There is little gully erosion in irrigated areas; these areas, however, deserve special attention because, with flat or nearly flat gradients, they are the best agricultural terrains of the entire basin.

The results for the rainfed agricultural lands were as expected, since most of the cropping area is devoted to maize, a row crop providing a relatively poor cover. Other factors, such as agricultural practices (*eg*, drainage of parcels, types of plowing), may also be important for explaining the particular relationship between agriculture and gully erosion in the study area. Field observations indicate that abandonment of lands following migration to urban areas (Mexico City

can be reached from the study area by public transport in two hours) has contributed to the development of erosion. This fact highlights the importance of social and economic factors in the actual development of erosion in central Mexico.

Grass-covered areas, however, should provide good protection against rainfall erosivity. The eroded areas on originally grassed terrains can be explained by the dominance of subsurficial hydrologic and erosion processes, including mass movements. Table 5 indicates that 75 percent of the erosion on originally grass-covered terrain occurs on slopes of less than 20 percent (11°). Most of the remaining 25 percent (on slopes steeper than 20 percent) occurs on the denudational slopes on metamorphic rocks.

The analysis helped to clarify a particular pattern regarding land use and erosion in the denudational

TABLE 5 Gully erosion on grassland, per slope range

Slope Class %		Eroded Area	
	ha	%	Cum%
0-2	7	1.4	1.4
3-4	29	5.7	7.1
5-6	59	11.7	18.8
7-8	50	10.0	28.8
9-10	42	8.4	37.2
11-15	117	23.0	60.2
16-20	76	15.1	75.3
21-25	40	7.9	83.2
> 25	85	16.8	100.0
Total	505	100.0	

units on the metamorphic rocks and also on the slopes of andesitic flows close to mining areas. In these instances, erosion occurs on relatively steeper slopes compared with the rest of the basin. Relatively steep slopes (> 20 percent) on metamorphics have been deforested since colonial times to satisfy wood requirements for mining, and severe erosion processes have been triggered on formerly forested surfaces. The exhumed regolith (weathered schists and slates) is highly erodible and has been incised by gullies more than 5 m deep. This pattern of erosion development is different from that of the volcanic terrains where the regolith operates as a hydrologic and erosional base level.

Field observations indicate that relatively gentle (foot)slopes in the metamorphic units are overlain by fluvially reworked tephra, intermingled with other slope deposits in very complex stratigraphic profiles. In these places, seepage flow and gullying develop as in the volcanic terrains [1].

In the case of the andesitic flows, despite the fact that predominant slopes exceed 25 percent (14°), 83 percent of gully erosion in areas of rainfed agriculture occurs on slopes of less than 15 percent (8° to 9°) and nearly 50 percent between 5 and 10 percent (Table 6).

SPATIAL MODEL FORMULATION

An earlier analysis of gully initiation indicated that gully development in Quaternary volcanic terrains under seasonal climates could be explained by particular subsurface hydrologic processes operating above

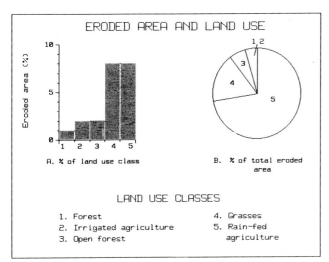

FIGURE 9 Gully erosion and land use

TABLE 6 Gully erosion on andesitic slopes

Slope Class %	ha	Eroded Area %	Cum%
0–2	2	1.2	1.2
3–4	14	8.2	9.4
5–6	40	23.2	32.6
7–8	24	13.9	46.5
9–10	17	9.9	56.4
11–15	46	27.0	83.4
16–20	18	10.4	93.8
21–25	5	3.1	96.9
> 25	5	3.1	100.0
Total	171	100.0	

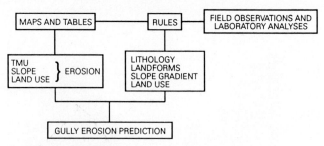

FIGURE 10 Model flow diagram

hydraulic impeding layers on gentle volcanic slopes [2]. These findings allow a thorough interpretation of the results obtained using GIS procedures. In other words, the degree of uncertainty in the relationship obtained by these means is reduced substantially.

Extrapolation to the entire study area becomes feasible and areas of severe gully erosion risk can be predicted. The extrapolation assumes homogeneous climatic patterns and homogeneity in slope gradient and slope materials per terrain mapping unit. Gully erosion development can be explained by land use, slope materials and slope hydrology; all these factors are partially controlled by slope gradient and were taken into account in the design of the terrain mapping units.

A spatial model (Figure 10) based on frequencies of gully erosion occurrence and describing critical conditions for gully erosion initiation can be formulated on the basis of the following rule:

> If temperate seasonal climate and Quaternary volcanic terrains, and hydrologic impeding layer, and slope gradient > 2 percent and < 15 percent and land use is agriculture or grassland, then predict area under gully erosion risk.

The percentage of total gully erosion predicted is 75 (1864 of 2486 ha of gullied terrain). An area of 103 km² satisfies those conditions and can be considered as the area with more severe gully erosion risk (Figure 11). This area should receive high priority

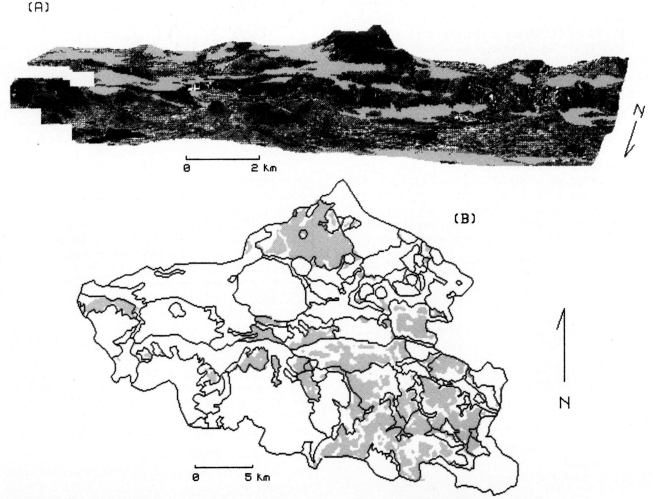

FIGURE 11 Three- and two-dimensional representations of areas with more severe gully erosion risk (in orange)

92

during conservation planning.

TESTING THE RESULTS

Results obtained in the study area were tested in Huasca de Ocampo, a 300 km² volcanic area, selected at random, and located some 200 km east of the Tlalpujahua river basin, within the same physiographic province and with similar climatic and land use conditions (Figure 1). Similar patterns of shallow mass-movement and gully erosion were observed in the field.

Land use, landforms and gullies were mapped from panchromatic black-and-white aerial photographs at a 1:50000 scale and plotted on the topographic map using simple photogrammetric equipment. The slope gradient map was derived using the same procedure

and input data as the Tlalpujahua case.

The main characteristics of the TMUs are shown in Table 7 and the relationship with gully erosion is indicated in Table 8. The most eroded are the volcanic footslopes and basaltic flows, both gently sloping units. The scoria cones represent less than 2 percent of the total erosion (Table 8).

The relationships between erosion and slope and land use are given, respectively, in Tables 9 and 10. The eroded terrain on slopes steeper than 15 percent represents less than 10 percent of the total eroded area (Figure 12); nearly 40 percent of the area with slopes less than 10 percent is eroded (Table 9). Nearly 85 percent of the total eroded area is agricultural land and/or grassland (Table 10). Most

TABLE 7 Terrain mapping units of Huasca test site

Terrain Mapping Units	Area		Predominant	
	ha	%	Slope %	Land Use Class
1 Lavic cones	216	0.7	21–30	Forest
2 Scoria cones	170	0.6	21–30	Forest
3 Basaltic flows, tops	11134	36.5	3–4	Agriculture
4 Basaltic flows, slopes	421	1.4	4–5	Grasses/bare
5 Rhyolitic flows, slopes	4152	13.6	21–30	Open forest
6 Trachytic flows, slopes	1901	6.2	11–15	Forest
7. Lahar slopes	984	3.2	11–15	Forest
8 Erosional valleys	5702	18.7	> 50	Shrubs
9 Volcanic footslopes	4151	13.6	3–4	Rainfed agricul
10 Denudational slopes	693	2.3	11–15	Shrubs
11 Fluvial plains	817	2.7	0–2	Agriculture
Reservoirs	162	0.5		
Total	30506	100.0		

TABLE 8 Relationship of TMUs and gully erosion (Huasca)

Terrain Mapping Units	Eroded Area		
	ha	%TMU	%total
1 Lavic cones	0	0.0	0.0
2 Scoria cones	26	15.1	1.7
3 Basaltic lows, tops	613	5.5	40.1
4 Basaltic flows, slopes	43	10.3	2.8
5 Rhyolitic flows, slopes	3	0.1	0.2
6 Trachytic flows, slopes	53	2.8	3.5
7 Lahar slopes	111	11.3	7.3
8 Erosional valleys	29	1.1	1.9
9 Volcanic footslopes	636	15.3	41.6
10 Denudational slopes	10	1.5	0.7
11 Fluvial plains	2	0.7	0.1
Total	1526		100.0

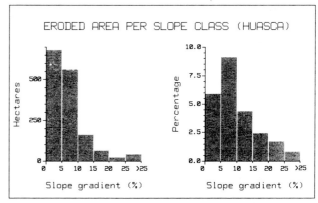

FIGURE 12 Slope gradient and gully erosion in Huasca

TABLE 9 Slope distribution and eroded area (Huasca)

Slope %	Area			Eroded Area			
	ha	%	Cum%	ha	%class	%total	Cum%
0–2	4157	13.6	13.6	131	3.2	8.6	8.6
3–4	5150	16.8	30.4	296	5.6	19.4	28.0
5–6	4359	14.2	44.6	411	9.4	26.9	54.9
7–8	2359	7.7	52.3	271	11.5	17.7	72.6
9–10	1625	5.3	57.6	127	7.8	8.3	80.9
11–15	3700	12.1	69.7	162	4.4	10.6	91.5
16–20	2534	8.2	77.9	62	2.4	4.1	95.6
21–30	2690	8.8	86.7	46	1.7	3.0	98.6
31–50	1875	6.1	92.8	13	0.7	0.9	99.5
> 50	2208	7.2	100.0	8	0.4	0.5	100.0

TABLE 10 Land use and eroded area (Huasca)

Land Use Class	Area		Eroded Area		
	ha	%	ha	%class	%total
1 Irrigated agricul	2292	7.5	40	1.7	2.6
2 Rainfed agricul	7305	23.9	384	5.1	25.2
3 Forest	7671	25.1	97	1.3	6.4
4 Open forest	558	1.8	1	0.2	0.1
5 Grassland	2506	8.2	153	5.7	10.0
6 Grass/agricul	3025	9.9	748	24.1	49.0
7 Grass/bare rock	419	1.4	42	10.0	2.7
8 Shrubs	6631	21.7	61	0.9	4.0
9 Reservoirs	153	0.5			
Total	30559	100.0	1526		100.0

of the grassland and/or agricultural land is located on slopes gentler than 6 percent gradient.

The results agree with those obtained in the Tlalpujahua river basin. The critical slope gradient for gully erosion occurrence, as described for Tlalpujahua, is particularly relevant—on the one hand, because it supports the importance of subsurface (erosion) processes in gully erosion initiation, and on the other hand because the digital elevation model and the slope map derived from it are both quantitative documents that largely eliminate any possibility of biased interpretation, as may occur with the TMU or land use map.

The model proposed for Tlalpujahua was applied to Huasca. Eroded areas on agricultural and/or grassland with slope steepness less than 15 percent represent 75 percent of the total eroded area (1152 of 1526 ha), which agrees with results obtained for the research area. Nearly 90 percent of the eroded area explained occurs on the tops of basaltic flows (44 percent) and on volcanic footslopes (43 percent)—both depositional, gently sloping units (Table 9). The 25 percent of the erosion not explained by this model occurs on originally forested areas and shrubland, and on steep lands under rainfed agriculture. A partial explanation for this may include agricultural practices, such as ill-defined parcel ditches that allow runoff concentration.

CONCLUSIONS

Simple spatial modelling can be based on the explanation of the occurrence of gully-eroded areas in terms of landscape variables interpreted from remote sensing products or measured from topographic maps and using GIS techniques. In this approach to gully erosion modelling, different scales of analysis and different techniques are combined using GIS procedures. Areas of probable gully initiation can be predicted to guide conservation efforts.

ACKNOWLEDGEMENTS

Reserch was carried out at ITC and at the Institute of Geography, University of Mexico, with fundings from both institutions. Comments on an earlier version of the manuscript by H Th Verstappen and J A Zinck are gratefully acknowledged.

REFERENCES

1 Bocco, G. 1986. Aspects of the Anthropic Erosion in the Tlalpujahua River Basin. An Applied Geomorphological Approach. Unpub MSc thesis, ITC, Enschede.

2 Bocco, G. 1990. Gully Erosion Analysis using Remote Sensing and GIS. PhD diss, University of Amsterdam.

3 Bocco, G, J L Palacio and C R Valenzuela. 1989. Geomorphological mapping using SPOT for gully erosion assessment. Proc 11th geomorphological cong, Frankfurt.

4 Burrough, P A. 1986. Principles of Geographical Information Systems for Land Resources Assessment. Clarendon Press, Oxford.

5 Direccion General de Geografia. 1977. Carta topografica "El Oro de Hidalgo". INEGI, SPP, Mexico.

6 Meijerink, A M. 1988. Data acquisition and data capture through terrain mapping units. ITC Journal 1988-1, pp 23-44.

7 Palacio, J L. 1989. Evaluating gully erosion using ILWIS; an example in central Mexico. Int rep ITC, Enschede.

8 Valenzuela, C R. 1988. ILWIS overview. ITC Journal 1988-1, pp 4-14.

9 Verstappen, H Th. 1989. Satellite remote sensing, geomorphological survey and natural hazard zoning. Some new developments at ITC, The Netherlands. Suppl Geogr Fis Dinam Quat 2, pp 103-109.

10 Walsh, S J, D R Lightfoot and D R Butler. 1987. Recognition and assessment of error in geographic information systems. Photogr Eng and Rem Sens 53 (10), pp 1423-1430.

RESUME

Des dynamiques de ravinement dans un terrain volcanique du Quaternaire ont été modelées dans un GIS, à l'aide de données de télédétection et d'observations de terrain. De l'actuelle zone de ravinement, 75 pourcent se produisent sur des terrains accumulatifs de pente douce (< 15 pourcent) dans des zones agricoles ou de pâturages gorgées d'eau. On peut prévoir des zones à risques sévères de ravinement. Le modèle a été appliqué avec succès à différentes zones de la même province physiographique. Cette approche est proposée afin de déterminer les priorités de conservation.

RESUMEN

Se propone un modelamiento de la dinamica de carcavas en terrenos volcanicos Cuaternarios, utilizando percepcion remota y observaciones de campo en el contexto de un SIG. De las zonas erosionadas, un 75 porciento occurre en terrenos acumulativos, suavemente ondulados (pendientes < porciento), bajo agricultura de temporal o pastizal. Las areas bajo severo riesgo a la erosion pueden predecirse sobre esta base. El modelo fue aplicado en forma satisfactoria a otra zona de la misma provincia fisiografica. Este enfoque se sugiere para definir prioridades de conservacion.

INT. J. GEOGRAPHICAL INFORMATION SYSTEMS, 1991, VOL. 5, NO. 4, 431–445

Use of an expert system to map forest soils from a geographical information system

ANDREW K. SKIDMORE

School of Geography, University of New South Wales,
P.O. Box 1, Kensington, N.S.W. 2033, Australia

PHILIP J. RYAN

Wood Technology and Forest Research Division,
Forestry Commission of N.S.W., P.O. Box 100,
Beecroft, N.S.W. 2119, Australia

WARWICK DAWES, DAVID SHORT and
EMMETT O'LOUGHLIN

Division of Water Research, CSIRO, Black Mountain,
Canberra, A.C.T. 2601, Australia

Abstract.   Mapping forest soils using conventional methods is time consuming and expensive. An expert system is described and applied to the mapping of five forest soil–landscape units formed on a single granitoid parent material. Three thematic maps were considered important in influencing the distribution of soils. The first showed the distribution of nine classes of native eucalypt forests, and the second and third were derived from a digital elevation model and represented slope gradient and a soil wetness index combined with topographical position. These layers were input to a raster based geographical information system (GIS) and then geometrically co-registered to a regular 30 m grid. From a knowledge of soil distributions, the relationships between the soil–landscape units and the three data layers were quantified by an experienced soil scientist and used as rules in a rule based expert system. The thematic layers accessed from the GIS provided data for the expert system to infer the forest soil–landscape unit most likely to occur at any given pixel. The soil–landscape map output by the expert system compared favourably with a conventional soil–landscape map generated using interpretation of aerial photographs.

1. Introduction

Maps of forest soils have traditionally been made by the interpretation of aerial photographs supported by ground surveys. Attempts to improve the efficiency of this process by the analysis of digital remotely sensed imagery have been disappointing owing to vegetation cover obscuring the soil response (Tucker and Miller 1977, Siegel and Goetz 1977, Westin and Lemme 1978). Forest soils were correctly mapped only where they were correlated with species in the overstorey (Thompson *et al.* 1981).

Where vegetation is sparse or absent (as a result of cultivation or drought), soil types have been visually delineated on remotely sensed imagery (Lewis *et al.* 1975, Westin and Frazee 1976), although attempts to map soils using conventional techniques of computer pattern recognition have had limited success at the level of soil units (Kornblau and Cipra 1983, Thompson and Henderson 1984). In addition to vegetation cover, spectral reflectance over soils is confounded by varying levels of soil moisture, especially in the infrared, thermal and microwave regions (Orbukhov and Orlov 1964, Slater and Jackson 1982, Huete *et al.* 1985, Fung and Ulaby 1983, Owe and

Chang 1988), atmospheric effects (Huete and Jackson 1988, Cipra *et al.* 1980), physical soil characteristics (Myers 1983) and observation conditions (for example, intensity and direction of illumination). Thus mapping forest soils directly from remotely sensed data is difficult because of the complexity of environmental factors contributing to the spectral reflectance measured by a sensor.

Image processing uses the spectral (and occasionally spatial) attributes of the remotely sensed imagery. Additional data may be available over an area, such as elevation, derived terrain variables, geology and climatic parameters. This information, together with experience and knowledge, may be used by a soil scientist for interpreting the soil units. Expert systems have been proposed, and tested, as a method of integrating data from various sources (Lee *et al.* 1987, Ripple and Ulshoefer 1987, Robinson and Frank 1987, Skidmore 1989 a). Decision tree analysis has also been developed as a method of integrating diverse spatial data (Moore *et al.* 1990).

The objective of this study was to develop an expert system for mapping forest soil–landscape units underneath a complex native eucalypt forest in south–east Australia, using available information, which included Landsat Thematic Mapper (TM) digital data, a digital terrain model and an experienced soil scientist with knowledge about the position of soil types in the forest environment. The soil–landscape map derived by the expert system should be similar to that produced by an experienced soil scientist after considering the physical and biological characteristics of an area.

2. Description of the study area

A major experiment by the Forestry Commission of New South Wales to study the effects of fire and logging on a eucalypt forest provided much of the ground plot data and colour aerial photographs. A study area of 3 × 3 km, situated approximately 40 km west of the coastal township of Eden in south–east Australia, was taken from this larger Forestry Commission experimental area. The forest cover is mostly dry schlerophyll forest (Anon 1989), with the overstorey tree canopy being totally dominated by *Eucalyptus* spp. Some wet schlerophyll forest appears in gullies (Anon 1989). The parent material was described by Beams (1980) as a coarse grained, felsic adamellite–granite and it is an integral part of the larger Devonian Bega Batholith. The parent material is essentially homogeneous within the study area. The topography is moderate, ranging in elevation from 150 to 600 m.

3. Conventional soil mapping

Within the Forestry Commission of New South Wales experimental forest area, 48 soil profiles were sampled using a stratified random design. There were 21 of these profiles located within the 9 km^2 block used in this study. The profiles were described using the terminology of McDonald *et al.* (1984) and classified using the great soil groups of Australia (Stace *et al.* 1968) and *A Factual Key* (Northcote 1979).

Soil development on the Wallagaraugh Adamellite has been studied in detail at the Yambulla research catchments, 15 km to the south of the study area. A soil–geomorphological model based on the terminology of Paton (1978) was devised to explain the variation in this coarse grained granitic material. The following five soil–landscape units were recognized by Ryan (1991).

Residual crests and interfluves (RC). These are stable, flat and well drained soils with little erosional or depositional activity. Movement of soil water is limited to vertical infiltration. Soil classifications include yellow to red podzolic great soil groups (Stace *et al.* 1968) or sandy mottled yellow duplex soils (Dy5.41, Dy5.81) (Northcote 1979). An increase in the clay content and structure of the B horizons compared with the other soil–landscape units is seen.

Degraded mid to upper slopes (DS1). These soils are found on ridges and hill slopes where they are affected by transportational geomorphological processes. That is, these soils are continually being stripped of surface material and are therefore geomorphically unstable or degraded (Paton 1978). Slopes are steep, so the surface and subsurface lateral soil water flows play an important role in soil formation. The morphology of these soils is that of shallow, coarse sandy loams to sandy clay loams with limited horizon and structural development, although deeper profiles can occur in colluvium dammed behind adamellite tors. Lithosols and brown and yellow earths are the most common great soil groups, whereas the primary profile forms range from uniform coarse (Uc) through gradational (Gn) to duplex (Dy). Adamellite tors and surface rock outcrops are common features of this soil–landscape type.

Degraded lower slopes (DS2). When the gradient decreases, the transportational processes are not as severe. These soils tend to be deeper than DS1 soils, with the development of distinctly coloured B2 horizons and often evidence of the colluvial origin of the surface horizons. Surface and subsurface water flows are still the dominant geomorphological agents. Yellow earths and a few yellow podzols are the common great soil groups and the principal profile forms include Gn2.21, Gn3.01 and Dy4.81.

Aggraded well drained slopes (AS1). Thick layers of coarse sandy alluvium can accumulate on the lower slopes. If these aggraded areas are well drained and relatively stable, then a podzol morphology can develop. These soils display a thick humic A1 horizon, a bleached A2 horizon and an illuviated humic–sesquioxide B2 horizon which is often cemented. The soil textures are clayey coarse sand to coarse sandy loams, reaching a depth of at least 1 m. These podzol soils (Uc2.31) are uncommon because the aggraded layers usually occur in drainage lines which have semi-permanent water tables.

Aggraded slopes with restricted drainage (AS2). The presence of fluctuating water tables in these thick layers of sandy colluvium limits the development of podzol soil morphology and produces more hydromorphic features. Thick humic A1 horizons and bleached A2 horizons still occur, but the B2 horizons tend to be yellow mottled with pale or gleyed colours. These soils often display evidence of more than one depositional episode. Humic gleyed and gleyed podzolic great soil groups (Gn1.84, Uc4.24, Uc2.23) are the common classifications within this soil–landscape unit.

The relative position of these five soil–landscape units is shown in figure 1.

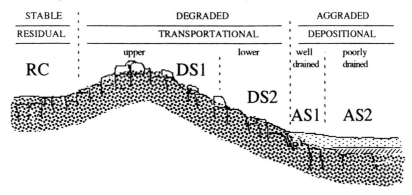

Figure 1.   Geomorphological model showing the five soil units recognized in this study (after Ryan 1991).

Over 50 per cent of the profiles located in the study area are on DS1 sites. The DS1 sites are usually associated with silvertop ash (*Eucalyptus sieberi*) and the stringybarks. The next most important soil–landscape type is AS2 (25 per cent of the profiles), which is associated with thick *Melaleuca–Hakea–Leptospermum* swamps that carry few eucalypts. Vegetation associations on DS2 sites are similar to those on the DS1 soil–landscape units, although there can be a greater abundance of *Eucalyptus agglomerata*, *Eucalyptus consideniana* and *Eucalyptus cypellocarpa*, reflecting the deeper soils and better availability of water. Few distinguishing vegetation associations separate RC from DS1 sites, with *Eucalyptus sieberi* dominating both. The AS1 soil–landscape unit was the least common (5 per cent of the study area), so few definitive statements can be made other than association with *Eucalyptus obliqua*, *Eucalyptus consideniana* and *Eucalyptus cypellocarpa*.

The study area was conventionally mapped by the interpretation of 1 : 10 000 scale colour aerial photographs. The aerial photograph interpretation used the relationships of the soil–landscape model, plus the observed vegetation associations. This information, in addition to the known areal extent of each soil–landscape unit, was used by the expert system to infer soil–landscape unit classes.

4. Developing data layers for the GIS

A raster database was constructed using the SPIRAL GIS (Myers 1986). The database was geometrically corrected to a UTM projection using a standard map base and resampled to a regular 30 m grid. The parameters considered important for determining the distribution of forest soils over the study area included forest overstorey, gradient, topographical position and a soil wetness index. These data sets were input, and stored, as separate layers in the GIS. In addition, a set of rules relating the database layers to forest soil distributions was generated from field work and the knowledge of an experienced soil scientist. The GIS data layers and rules are now described.

4.1. *Forest overstorey*

A vegetation map showing the forest overstorey of the study area was prepared from digital elevation data and remotely sensed data using an expert system approach as described by Skidmore (1989 a). Alternatively, the map of the forest overstorey may have been conventionally interpreted from aerial photographs, followed by digitization and input to the GIS.

4.2. *Digital elevation model*

Topographic variables can be readily generated in digital form and merged with other digital data, such as remotely sensed data. Streamlines and high points were digitized from the 1 : 25 000 Mount Imlay map sheet. Within the study area, 346 spot heights and 322 points along stream lines were selected. An interpolation program developed by Hutchinson (1989) was used to calculate the elevation values to 1 m contours on a regular 30 m grid. The method for generating the regular digital elevation grid used in this study has been described in detail by Skidmore (1989 b).

4.3. *Digital terrain models*

Digital terrain variables were modelled from the regular grid of digital elevation data using a third-order finite difference method to calculate the gradient (Skidmore 1989 c). This method has been shown by Skidmore (1989 b) to be the most accurate and efficient for calculating gradients. An algorithm, developed by Skidmore (1990), was used to calculate the terrain position (i.e. ridge, upper midslope, midslope, lower midslope and valley) of each cell in the regular grid. This algorithm locates ridges and stream lines from geographical principles and then interpolates midslopes using a modified Euclidean distance measure.

4.4. *Soil wetness index*

The digital elevation model (DEM) used to produce estimates of gradient and topographical position at each 30 m grid cell was also used to calculate a soil wetness index. The soil wetness index was used to test for conditions of local soil waterlogging, in addition to showing relative levels of wetness through the area under study. The algorithm used here was described fully by O'Loughlin (1986).

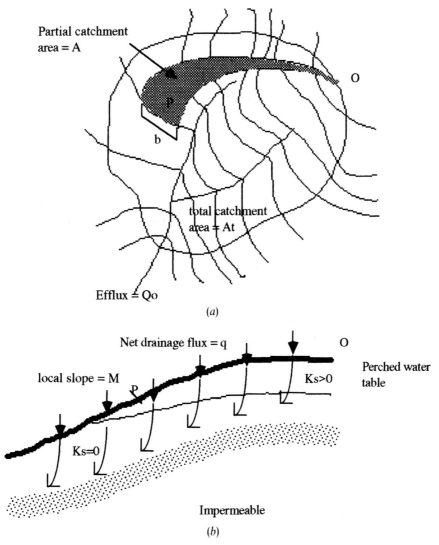

Figure 2. Schematic diagram for identifying the notation used by O'Loughlin (1986). (*a*) Plan; (*b*) section through O–P.

The O'Loughlin (1986) model is based on contours calculated from the DEM. Partial catchment areas (A) are calculated upslope from contour segments (of length b), allowing the catchment area contributing to a point (P) in the catchment to be estimated (see figure 2, taken from O'Loughlin 1986). The net drainage flux (q) at point (P) equals the net efflux Q_0, so over the whole catchment area (A_t) generating the outflow Q_0, the relationship between q and Q_0 is

$$\int_{A_t} q \, dA = Q_0. \tag{1}$$

Local saturation will occur when the drainage flux is greater than the efflux at a point (x, y). That is, the product of the upslope partial catchment area A and drainage flux q is greater or equal to the local soil transmissivity T and the local surface gradient M

$$\frac{1}{b} \int q(x, y) \, dA \geqslant TM. \tag{2}$$

As the local drainage flux is difficult to measure, q is assumed to have a uniform distribution with an average value q. In addition, the mean catchment transmissivity T is estimated. If the soil transmissivity and drainage flux are uniform everywhere, then soil wetness at a point can be estimated from a topographic map alone. Normalizing equation (2) for mean transmissivity and mean drainage flux, the following estimate of wetness $w(x, y)$ at a point in the catchment is obtained

$$w(x, y) = \frac{1}{MbL} \left[\frac{\bar{T}}{T} \right] \int \left[\frac{q}{\bar{q}} \right] dA \geqslant \frac{\bar{T} A_t}{Q_0 L}. \tag{3}$$

The study area was located over a Devonian granite parent material and was considered to have a uniform transmissivity. Detailed hydrological experiments had been conducted in a similar catchment area to the south of the study area (Moore *et al.* 1986), so these results could be used to estimate the transmissivity and drainage flux.

The soil wetness model as currently implemented operates on only one catchment at a time. The study area was covered by 13 catchments (or parts thereof), so the soil wetness index was calculated for each individual catchment and then concatenated into one map showing soil wetness for the whole study area. For the soil wetness to be derived, the whole catchment area must be available for the soil wetness model. The Wallagaraugh River flows through the south–west quadrant of the study area, although the watershed of this river does not occur within the study area. No accurate information on soil wetness was therefore available for this portion of the study area.

The soil wetness index data were derived from the DEM, so they were geometrically corrected to the remotely sensed and the topographic data (i.e. gradient and topographical position).

4.5. *Combining soil wetness and topographical position*

Combining soil wetness and topographical position allows the importance of the topographical feature in the landscape to be inferred. For example, a gully with a low soil wetness index will be found high in a catchment (i.e. it is a high order stream), whereas a gully with a high soil wetness index will have more catchment contributing to its flow and will therefore be a lower order stream. In a similar way, the importance of ridges and midslopes in the landscape may be ascertained from their soil wetness. A dry ridge will represent a watershed, whereas a wetter ridge indicates that the ridge occurs within a catchment area. A dry midslope will occur relatively high in the catchment, whereas a wet midslope will occur nearer the outflow.

Table 1. Soil wetness–topographical position strata and abbreviations.

Topographical position	Wetness index			
	Very dry	Dry	Moist	Wet
Gully	GVD	GD	GM	GW
Lower midslope	LVD	LD	LM	LW
Midslope	MVD	MD	MM	MW
Upper midslope	UVD	UD	UM	UW
Ridge	RVD	RD	RM	RW

Four soil wetness states (very dry, dry, moist and wet) were overlain on the map showing the five topographical positions (ridge, upper midslope, midslope, lower midslope and gully) using the GIS. Thus 20 soil wetness–topographical position strata were created, as shown in table 1. The abbreviations used for these strata are also shown in table 1.

The soil wetness–topographical position strata increased the amount of expert knowledge that could be recorded for each soil–landscape unit, thereby allowing a better discrimination of the soil–landscape units by the expert system.

⋅ More generally, the soil wetness–topographical position strata offer a mechanism for automatically ranking the importance of the topographical features in the environment. For example, overlaying the streams with soil wetness allows a relative stream order to be inferred. The combination of topographical position and soil wetness index may also indicate processes of soil formation (weathering and leaching) within a landscape.

5. Expert system rules

The link between the described GIS database layers and the knowledge of the experienced soil scientist is provided by rules. The rules were constructed by relating the GIS data layers to the soil–landscape units. In this instance the rules were expressed as the probability of an item of evidence occurring (e.g. gradient is less than 5°) given a particular hypothesis (e.g. that forest soil–landscape unit is DS1).

The rules are the most subjective aspect of an expert system (Forsyth 1984). In an ideal situation the rules may be derived statistically, although this is often not possible. Thus a rule is a heuristic, estimated from the 'feeling' or 'knowledge' of experts.

Rules concerning environmental relationships cannot normally be expressed with absolute certainty (i.e. true or false). In other words, a rule lies in a continuum between true (probability of unity) and false (probability of zero), depending on how sure we are that the rule is true (or false). In this study, the rules were estimated by interviewing an experienced soil scientist (P.J.R.) and from consideration of the results from the soil pits. The rules and their associated probabilities are detailed in table 2. For example, the probability that there is a very dry gully (GVD) given that the residual crest (RC) soil–landscape unit occurs is 0·4.

The usefulness of combining soil wetness indices with topographical position can also be observed in table 2. For example, the DS2 type was considered to have a low probability of occurring on moist sites ($p = 0.3$) and a low probability of occurring on midslope sites ($p = 0.3$). In other words, given that any of the topographical positions (i.e., ridge, upper midslope, midslope, lower midslope and gully) were moist, the chance that the soil–landscape unit was DS2 would be low. However, it was observed that sites occurring on moist midslopes had a moderate probability of being DS2. Such specific knowledge could be captured using the soil wetness–topographical position strata.

6. Definition of the expert system

The expert system approach used here was described in detail by Skidmore (1989 a) and the same terminology is used. In this instance the research question to be answered by the expert system is 'what soil–landscape unit occurs at a given location in the forest?'. The expert system infers the most probable soil–landscape unit that would occur at a given grid cell, using information from the GIS database layers.

Table 2. Expert system rules.

Environmental variable	Soil–landscape unit				
	RC	DS1	DS2	AS1	AS2
GVD	0·4	0·6	0·2	0·2	0·3
GD	0·3	0·5	0·5	0·4	0·5
GM	0·2	0·4	0·6	0·5	0·7
GW	0·1	0·4	0·5	0·4	0·8
LVD	0·3	0·6	0·5	0·4	0·2
LD	0·3	0·5	0·6	0·6	0·3
LM	0·2	0·4	0·7	0·6	0·4
LW	0·1	0·3	0·6	0·5	0·6
MVD	0·4	0·7	0·5	0·4	0·2
MD	0·3	0·6	0·6	0·6	0·3
MM	0·2	0·5	0·7	0·6	0·4
MW	0·1	0·3	0·6	0·4	0·6
UVD	0·5	0·7	0·4	0·3	0·2
UD	0·5	0·7	0·4	0·3	0·2
UM	0·4	0·5	0·7	0·5	0·4
UW	0·3	0·4	0·6	0·3	0·6
RVD	0·6	0·5	0·2	0·1	0·1
RD	0·6	0·5	0·3	0·1	0·1
RM	0·5	0·5	0·5	0·2	0·3
RW	0·4	0·4	0·6	0·3	0·4
<5	0·7	0·2	0·4	0·5	0·5
6–10	0·3	0·6	0·5	0·4	0·4
11–20	0·4	0·6	0·3	0·3	0·3
>21	0·3	0·6	0·4	0·3	0·2
Q/R	0·4	0·5	0·3	0·1	0·1
Y	0·2	0·3	0·5	0·5	0·5
TT	0·1	0·1	0·2	0·2	0·8
S/MG	0·4	0·6	0·3	0·3	0·2
BLS	0·4	0·5	0·4	0·3	0·2
STA	0·5	0·5	0·4	0·3	0·1
REG	0·4	0·4	0·3	0·2	0·2
MG/STA	0·2	0·3	0·5	0·6	0·2

See table 1 for soil wetness–topographical position abbreviations.

Abbreviations: <5 = less than 5° slope; 6–10 = 6 to 10° slope; 11–20 = 11 to 20° slope; >21 = greater than 21° slope; Q/R = quarry/road; Y = yertchuk; TT = tea tree; S/MG = stringybark/monkey gum tree; BLS = blue leaved stringybark tree; STA = silvertop ash tree; REG = regenerating forest; and MG/STA = monkey gum/silvertop ash trees.

6.1. *Formal statement of the expert algorithm*

In this instance, let S_a be the forest soil–landscape unit class (for $a = 1, \ldots, n$ classes) occurring at location $X_{i,j}$, that is at the ith row and jth column of the GIS raster database. Let E_b be an item of evidence (for $b = 1, \ldots, k$ items of evidence) known at location $X_{i,j}$. Set up a hypothesis (H_a) that class S_a occurs at location $X_{i,j}$. A rule may be defined as $E_b \Rightarrow H_a$, that is, given a piece of evidence E_b, then infer H_a. The expert system then infers the most probable soil–landscape unit at a given cell using Bayes' theorem to update the probability of the rule that the hypothesis (H_a) occurs at location (i, j) given a piece of evidence (E_b), i.e. $P(H_a|E_b) = [P(E_b|H_a)P(H_a)]/P(E_b)$.

As explained in Skidmore (1989 a), $P(E_b|H_a)$ is the *a priori* conditional probability that there is a piece of evidence E_b (e.g. a slope of less than 5°) given a hypothesis H_a (e.g. a residual crest soil–landscape unit) that class S_a occurs at location (i, j) (also known as the class-conditional probability—see Duda and Hart 1973). In other words, $P(E_b|H_a)$ is a rule expressed in table 2. $P(H_a)$ is the probability for the hypothesis (H_a) that class S_a occurs at location (i, j) and is estimated by the experienced soil scientist on the expected extent of each soil–landscape unit in the area. On iterating with the $b = 2, \ldots, k$ items of evidence from the GIS database, $P(H_a|E_b; b = 1)$ (i.e. the posterior probability of H_a given E_b, for $b = 1$) replaces $P(H_a)$. $P(E_b)$ is the 'classical marginal probability' and is the probability of the evidence alone, or, the probability that any cell has an item of evidence $\{E_b\}$, such as a southerly aspect. Bayes' theorem provides a formula to calculate $P(E_b)$

$$P(E_b) = \sum_{a=1}^{n} P(E_b|H_a)P(H_a),$$

thereby allowing $P(E_b)$ to be continually updated at run time as $P(H_a)$ is updated. The expert system developed for this study used forward chaining with a complete enumeration of the data (i.e. a blind search terminated by the running out of evidence).

The evidence $\{E_b\}$ at $X_{i,j}$ should be independent, otherwise $P(E_b)$ would become larger or smaller, and perhaps cause the posterior probabilities to be incorrect. In this instance the evidence $\{E_b b = 1, \ldots, k\}$ was assumed to be independent. However, Bayes' theorem appears fairly robust with respect to this problem, as it is usually the relative magnitude of the probabilities which are of interest (Naylor 1989). In addition, the same number of items of evidence was used to calculate each hypothesis in this study, ensuring that the relative order of errors is the same (Naylor 1989). The soil–landscape unit assigned to each cell by the expert system is that which has the highest posterior probability $\{\max P(H_a)|a = 1, \ldots, n\}$ at location (i, j).

This expert system algorithm was programmed using Fortran-77 and executed on a DEC VAX computer. The thematic maps output from the various classification strategies were plotted on Tektronix hardware using Uniras software (European Software Contractors 1982) and the Map Analysis Package (MAP) software (Tomlin 1987).

7. Results

The geometrical correction of the cell locations of the forest overstorey layer were less than ±0·6 of a cell from the true map values. The root mean square planimetric error ($RMSE_x$ and $RMSE_y$) values were ±13 and ±15 m, respectively. Results for the geometrical correction of the DEM data were better, with the maximum error being less than ±0·4 of a pixel and the $RMSE_{xy}$ values being ±10 and ±11 m, respectively.

The GIS data layers accessed by the expert system were soil wetness (figure 3), gradient (figure 4), topographical position (figure 5) and overstorey vegetation

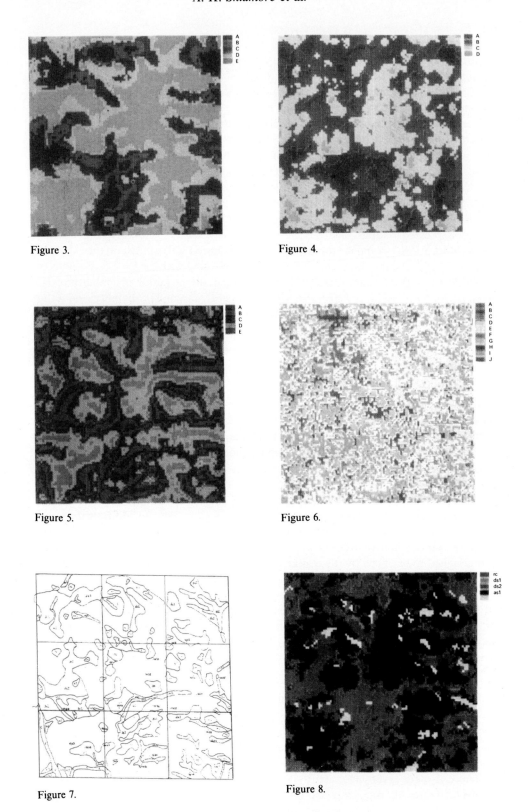

Figure 3.

Figure 4.

Figure 5.

Figure 6.

Figure 7.

Figure 8.

See page 370 for color plate of Figures 1 thru 8.

(figure 6). A map of the soil–landscape unit boundaries derived using conventional methods is given in figure 7. A thematic soil–landscape map generated by the expert system is given in figure 8. Note that the DS1 soil–landscape unit is white on figure 7 and black on figure 8. In addition, note that a soil wetness index of greater than or equal to 10 on figure 3 represents waterlogged conditions.

The soil–landscape map produced by the expert system (figure 8) was qualitatively compared with the conventional map (figure 7). In addition, the soil types associated with the 21 soil pits were checked against the classes predicted on the soil–landscape map produced by the expert system and 14 were found to be correctly classified.

8. Discussion

Visual inspection of the maps of the soil–landscape units generated by conventional methods and the expert system showed that they compared well (figures 7 and 8). Some differences between the two maps were obvious and were generally caused by inaccuracies in the GIS data layers. For example, in the centre of the south–west quadrant of the study area, there is a large area of DS2 delineated on figure 7 that does not appear on the expert system derived map (figure 8). This was due to the soil underneath the Wallagaraugh River being modelled as dry (owing to the catchment not occurring within the study area) (figure 3), when in fact it should be wet. Another example of a discrepancy between the two maps occurred at the border between the south–west and west quadrants on figure 7. The DS2 and AS2 were mapped using conventional methods, whereas RC was predicted by the expert system. This was caused by an error in the DEM resulting in a ridge being incorrectly located in figure 5. Errors in the GIS data layers will reduce the mapping accuracy of the thematic images derived by the expert system. The extent to which errors are accumulated from the GIS data layers to the final derived thematic image is uncertain, and requires further theoretical and empirical evaluation.

There was some disagreement in the location of the AS2 soil–landscape unit on the conventional and expert system maps, because a critical factor in the identification of this soil–landscape unit was the presence of *Melaleuca–Hakea–Leptospermum* swamp. In places this swamp vegetation had a width of much less than the 30 m resolution of the Landsat TM imagery, and consequently was not delineated on the vegetation layer in the GIS accessed by the expert system, whereas swamp vegetation of less than approximately 5 m width could be delineated on the aerial photographs. As the narrow strips of swamp vegetation could not be defined from the Landsat TM imagery, the AS2 soil–landscape type could not be mapped by the expert system.

Figure 3.   Variation of soil wetness over the study area. (A) Very wet; (B) wet; (C) moist; (D) dry; (E) very dry.

Figure 4.   Variation of gradient over the study area. (A) $\leqslant 5°$; (B) 6–10°; (C) 11–20°; (D) $\geqslant 21°$.

Figure 5.   Topographical position over the study area. (A) Gully; (B) lower midslope; (C) midslope; (D) upper midslope; (E) ridge.

Figure 6.   Overstory vegetation (derived in Chapter 8). (A) *Allocasuarina* spp.; (B) monkey gum/silvertop ash; (C) regenerating forest; (D) silvertop ash (shadow); (E) silvertop ash (sunlit); (F) blue-leaved stringybark; (G) yellow stringybark/monkey gum; (H) teatree; (I) yertchuk; (J) quarry/road.

Figure 7.   Soil map interpreted by conventional methods. (RC) Residual crest; (DS1) degraded upper slope; (DS2) degraded lower slope; (AS1) aggraded lower slope; (AS2) aggraded lower slope (hydromorphic).

Figure 8.   Soil map derived by the expert system.

Another source of error in the expert system map resulted from the ambiguity or incompleteness of the expert system rules and data layers. None of the environmental variables which may affect the distribution of soil–landscape units were included in the model. For example, the RC soil–landscape unit occurred on wide and flat areas. However, there was no data layer in the GIS indicating the areal extent of the flat regions, although such a data layer would be useful for improving the mapping accuracy of the RC soil–landscape unit.

The 21 soil pits indicated a mapping accuracy for the expert system map of 66·7 per cent (i.e. 14/21), although it should be emphasized that the small sample ($n = 21$) has a very wide confidence interval around the accuracy estimate. For example, applying a method proposed by Thomas and Allcock (1984) to the small sample obtained in this study, it is concluded that only 34 per cent of the pixels are correctly mapped with a 95 per cent confidence level. To assess the error of the conventional and expert map in a statistically significant manner, an adequate number of soil pits has to be sampled. At least 30 soil pit samples per stratum are recommended (Van Genderen *et al.* 1978), with a preference for over 50 (Hay 1979); in other words a sample of 150–250 soil pits is required. The conventional and expert system maps still need to be checked further in the field, to test the techniques adequately and to be able to narrow the confidence limits around the estimated map accuracy. Although the number of sample points was low, it was concluded that the soil–landscape map generated by the expert system was qualitatively similar to the map drawn by conventional methods.

The descriptions of the soil–landscape units are rather vague, which poses difficulties for accurate soil–landscape mapping by both the conventional and expert system methods. Soil is actually a continuum of different types (see figure 1) which are artificially split into units. The uncertainty in defining soil–landscape units is reflected in the probabilities assigned to the expert system rules (table 2). When mapping by conventional methods, the position of the soil–landscape unit boundaries are difficult to identify, because soils are hidden entities, which makes them difficult to assess even on aerial photographs or in the field (Webster and Beckett 1968). In fact, the conventional mapping was inconsistent and was revised on the basis of the expert system results.

The soil–landscape map produced by the expert system may be further improved by using additional data layers. Environmental variables such as parent material, elevation, latitude and longitude, climate and overstorey vegetation may dominate soil type (Jenny 1941), and effective extrapolation of the expert system approach requires that the principal environmental factors affecting forest soil distribution are re-cognized. The use of an expert system may be one of the most effective ways of quantitatively applying Jenny's (1941) state factor model of soil formation to an actual soil survey. Conventional soil survey mapping can only simulate this via the qualitative skill of the surveyor.

The choice of auxiliary data sets to use for forest soil mapping is determined primarily by the availability of such data. Topographical information is readily available for most areas and remains relatively constant over a time scale of hundreds of years. Similarly, parent material is another data type that is reasonably constant, although substantial field work by expert geologists is often needed to successfully map geological boundaries. In contrast, other data layers such as remotely sensed imagery may vary in less than a year due to changes in features such as vegetation and land use.

The speed, objectivity and cost effectiveness of the expert system approach means that soil maps are not affected by individual bias and that larger areas could be systematically mapped, compared with using conventional methods. The costly and labour intensive manual interpolation of forest soil maps can be effectively automated, provided good ground truth knowledge is available that allows relationships to be developed between the readily available digital spatial data and the soil types. The inclusion of additional data layers and more sophisticated rules will further improve mapping accuracy.

9. Conclusions

A forest soil–landscape map has been successfully generated using an expert system to integrate readily available digital spatial data, including Landsat TM and a DEM. From the DEM, three data layers important for determining soil–landscape units were calculated i.e. topographical position, gradient and soil wetness (note that the model used to calculate soil wetness required additional information including average transmissivity and drainage flux). A map detailing the overstorey vegetation was constructed from remotely sensed data and the DEM.

Knowledge about the relationship of soil–landscape units to environmental variables was encapsulated as rules using a matrix of prior probabilities. These rules were used by the expert system to link the digital terrain data layers (gradient and topographical position), the soil wetness index and the overstorey vegetation to create a map showing the distribution of soil–landscape units in the study area.

References

ANON, 1989, Forest types in New South Wales. *Forestry Commission of N.S.W. Research Note* No. 17, 2nd edn. (Sydney: Forestry Commission of N.S.W.).

BEAMS, S. D., 1980, Magnetic Evolution of the Southwest Lachlan Fold Belt, South Eastern Australia. *Unpublished PhD Thesis*, La Trobe University, Melbourne, Victoria, Australia.

CIPRA, J. E., FRANZMEIER, D. P., BAUER, M. E., and BOYD, R. K., 1980, Comparison of multispectral measurements from some nonvegetated soils using Landsat digital data and a spectrometer. *Soil Science Society of America Journal*, **44**, 80–84.

DUDA, R. O., and HART, P. E., 1973, *Pattern Classification and Scene Analysis* (New York: Wiley).

EUROPEAN SOFTWARE CONTRACTORS, 1982, *Uniras User Manuals for GEOPAK, RASPAK, GIMAGE and KRIGPAK* (Gentofte, Denmark: European Software Contractors).

FORSYTH, R., 1984, *Expert Systems: Principles and Case Studies* (London: Chapman and Hall).

FUNG, A. K., and ULABY, F. T., 1983, Matter-energy interaction in the microwave region. In *Manual of Remote Sensing* Vol. 1, edited by R. N. Colwell (Falls Church, VA: American Society of Photogrammetry), Ch. 4.

HAY, A. M., 1979, Sampling design to test land-use map accuracy. *Photogrammetric Engineering and Remote Sensing*, **45**, 529–533.

HUETE, A. R., JACKSON, R. D., and POST, K. F., 1985, Spectral response of a plant canopy with different soil background. *Remote Sensing of the Environment*, **17**, 35–53.

HUETE, A. R., and JACKSON, R. D., 1988, Soil and atmosphere influences on the spectra of partial canopies. *Remote Sensing of the Environment*, **25**, 89–105.

HUTCHINSON, M. F., 1989, A new procedure for gridding elevation and stream line data with automatic removal of spurious pits. *Journal of Hydrology*, **106**, 211–232.

JENNY, H., 1941, *Factors of Soil Formation* (New York: McGraw-Hill).

KALENSKY, Z., and SCHERK, L. R., 1975, Accuracy of forest mapping from Landsat CCT's. *Proceedings of the 10th International Symposium on Remote Sensing of the Environment*, Vol. 2, pp. 1159–1163.

KORNBLAU, M. L., and CIPRA, J. E., 1983, Investigation of digital Landsat data for mapping soils under range conditions. *Remote Sensing of the Environment*, **13**, 103–112.

LEE, T., RICHARDS, J. A., and SWAIN, P. H., 1987, Probabilistic and evidential approaches for multisource data analysis. *IEEE Transactions on Geoscience and Remote Sensing*, **GE–25**, 283–293.

LEWIS, D. T., SEEVERS, P. M., and DREW, J. V., 1975, Use of satellite imagery to delineate soil associations in the sand hills region of Nebraska. *Soil Science Society of America Journal,* **39,** 330–335.

MCDONALD, R. C., ISBELL, R. F., SPEIGHT, J. G., WALKER, J., and HOPKINS, M. S., 1984, *Australian Soil and Land Survey Handbook* (Melbourne: Inkata Press).

MOORE, D. M., LEES, B. G., and DAVEY, S. M., 1991, A new method for predicting vegetation distributions using decision tree analysis in a geographic information system. *Environmental Management,* **15,** 59–71.

MOORE, I. D., MACKAY, S. M., WALLBRINK, P. J., BURCH, G. J., and O'LOUGHLIN, E. M., 1986, Hydrological characteristics and modelling of a small forested catchment in southeastern New South Wales. Pre-logging condition. *Journal of Hydrology,* **83,** 307–335.

MYERS, V. I., 1983, Remote sensing applications in agriculture. *Manual of Remote Sensing,* Vol. 2, edited by R. N. Colwell (Falls Church, VA: American Society of Photogrammetry), Ch. 33.

MYERS, W. L., 1986, SPIRAL steps and system structure, Publ. No. LW8607, Office of Remote Sensing of Earth Resources, Pennsylvania State University, University Park, PA, U.S.A.

NAYLOR, C., 1989, How to build an inferencing engine. In *Expert Systems: Principles and Case Studies,* 2nd edn, edited by R. Forsyth (London: Chapman & Hall).

NORTHCOTE, K. H., 1979, *A Factual Key for the Recognition of Australian Soils* (Glenside, South Australia: Rellim).

O'LOUGHLIN, E. M., 1986, Prediction of surface saturation zones in natural catchments by topographic analysis. *Water Resources Research,* **22,** 794–804.

ORBUKHOV, A. I., and ORLOV, D. C., 1964, Spectral reflectivity of the major soil groups and possibility of using diffuse reflectance in soil investigations. Pochvovedeniye No. 2. Reported in Myers, V. I., 1983, Remote sensing applications in agriculture. In *Manual of Remote Sensing,* Vol. 2, edited by R. N. Colwell (Falls Church, VA: American Society of Photogrammetry), Ch. 33.

OWE, M., and CHANG, A., 1988, Estimating surface soil moisture from satellite microwave measurements and a satellite derived vegetation index. *Remote Sensing of the Environment,* **24,** 331–345.

PATON, T. R., 1978, *The Formation of Soil Material* (London: Allen and Unwin).

RIPPLE, W. J., and ULSHOEFER, V. S., 1987, Expert systems and spatial data models for efficient geographic data handling. *Photogrammetric Engineering and Remote Sensing,* **53,** 1431–1433.

ROBINSON, V. B., and FRANK, A. U., 1987, Expert systems for geographic information systems. *Photogrammetric Engineering and Remote Sensing,* **48,** 1435–1441.

RYAN, P. J., 1991, Soil formation in the Wallagaraugh Adamellite, southeastern N.S.W., Australia. *Catena,* in press.

SIEGEL, B. S., and GOETZ, A. F. H., 1977, Effect of vegetation on rock and soil type discrimination. *Photogrammetric Engineering and Remote Sensing,* **43,** 191–196.

SKIDMORE, A. K., 1989 a, An expert system classifies eucalypt forest types using Landsat Thematic Mapper data and a digital terrain model. *Photogrammetric Engineering and Remote Sensing,* **55,** 1449–1464.

SKIDMORE, A. K., 1989 b, A comparison of techniques for calculating gradient and aspect from a gridded digital elevation model. *International Journal of Geographical Information Systems,* **3,** 323–334.

SKIDMORE, A. K., 1990, Terrain position as mapped from a gridded digital elevation model. *International Journal of Geographical Information Systems,* **4,** 33–49.

SLATER, P. N., and JACKSON, R. D., 1982, Atmospheric effect on radiation reflected from soil and vegetation as measured by orbiting sensors using various scanning directions. *Applied Optics,* **21,** 3923–3931.

STACE, H. C. T., HUBBLE, G. D., BREWER, R., NORTHCOTE, K. D., SLEEMAN, J. R., MULCAHY, M. J., and HALLSWORTH, E. G., 1968, *A Handbook of Australian Soils* (Adelaide: Rellim).

THOMAS, I. L., and ALLCOCK, G. M., 1984, Determining the confidence interval for a classification. *Photogrammetric Engineering and Remote Sensing,* **50,** 1491–1496.

THOMPSON, D. R., HAAS, R. H., and MILFORD, M. H., 1981, Evaluation of Landsat multispectral scanner data for mapping vegetated soil landscapes. *Soil Science Society of America Journal,* **45,** 91–95.

THOMPSON, D. R., and HENDERSON, K. E., 1984, Detecting soils under cultural vegetation using digital Landsat Thematic Mapper data. *Soil Science Society of America Journal,* **48,** 1316–1319.

Tomlin, C. D., 1987, *Introduction to Geographic Information Systems: M.A.P. Manual* (New Haven, CT: Yale School of Forestry and Environmental Studies).

Tucker, C. J., and Miller, L. D., 1977, Soil spectra contributions to grass canopy spectral reflectance. *Photogrammetric Engineering and Remote Sensing*, **43**, 721–726.

Van Genderen, J. L., Lock, B. F., and Vass, P. A., 1978, Remote sensing: statistical testing of thematic map accuracy. *Remote Sensing of the Environment*, **7**, 3–14.

Webster, R., and Beckett, P. H. T., 1968, Quantity and usefulness of soil maps. *Nature (London)*, **219**, 680–682.

Westin, F. C., and Frazee, C. J., 1976, Landsat data, its use in a soil survey program. *Soil Science Society of America Journal*, **40**, 137–142.

Westin, F. C., and Lemme, G. D., 1978, Landsat spectral signatures: studies with soil associations and vegetation. *Photogrammetric Engineering and Remote Sensing*, **44**, 315–325.

SECTION 4

Water Resources

Overview

GIS is making a significant contribution in identifying pollution problems for both ground and surface water conditions. In the first two articles, Evans and Meyers. and Rundquist et al. describe the DRASTIC GIS model for assessing ground water pollution. The third article, by See et al., describes using a spatial regression model to identify sources of stream pollution from irrigation sources. In the last article, Jensen et al. describe a technique to predict macrophyte distribution on a lake using boolean logic with the variables of water depth, slope, exposure, soil type, and temperature.

Suggested Additional Reading

Baker, C. P., and E. C. Panciera, 1990. A Geographic Information System for Groundwater Protection Planning. Journal of Soil and Water Conservation. 45(2):246-248.

Lo, C. P., and W. T. Hutchinson, 1991. Determination of Turbidity Patterns of the Zhujiang Estuarine Region, South China, Using Satellite Images and a GIS Approach. Geocarto International. 6(3):27-38.

Oliver, J. J., 1990. Selecting a GIS for a National Water Management Authority. Photogrammetric Engineering and Remote Sensing. 56(11):1471-1475.

Shih, S. F., 1990. Satellite Data and Geographic Information System for Rainfall Estimation. Journal of Irrigation and Drainage Engineering. 116:319-331.

Siverton, A., L. E. Reinelt, and R. Castensson, 1988. A GIS Method to Aid in Non-point Source Critical Area Analysis. International Journal of Geographical Information Systems. 2(4):365-378.

A GIS-based approach to evaluating regional groundwater pollution potential with DRASTIC

By Barry M. Evans and Wayne L. Myers

THE potential for groundwater contamination to occur at any given geographic location depends upon a wide range of physical and environmental variables, including soil type, depth to groundwater, and aquifer size. While many sophisticated computer models have been developed for assessing potential groundwater impacts on a site-by-site basis, most models are far too complex to use for impact assessment on a regional or statewide basis (6). More simple, computer-based approaches, however, can be used for regional assessment of pollution's potential effect on important groundwater resources.

One such approach involves the use of a geographic information system (GIS). In general, a GIS is designed to store, process, retrieve, and display spatially referenced data. In situations where complex environmental relationships exist, it has been found that data concerning different aspects of the physical environment can be used more effectively in combination than separately. One of the primary functions of a GIS is the combination and evaluation of disparate data layers for the purpose of providing "new" information.

In one recent study, a GIS-based approach to regional groundwater pollution modeling was developed. Most groundwater pollution potential modeling techniques developed to date (1, 2, 3, 4, 7) rely upon the use of site-specific data for local evaluations. This methodology, however, relies on the use of commonly available large-area groundwater-related data for evaluating groundwater pollution potential in regional areas larger than 50 square miles.

This study consisted of two primary components:

► The creation of a multilayered geographic data base for a 100-square-mile area

Barry M. Evans is president of Geo Decisions, Inc., P.O. Box 1028, Lemont, Pennsylvania 16851. Wayne L. Myers is co-director of the Office for Remote Sensing of Earth Resources, Pennsylvania State University, University Park, 16802. Work on which the paper is based was supported by the Delaware Department of Natural Resources and Environmental Control.

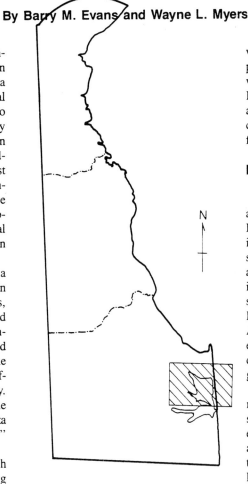

in southeastern Delaware.

► Predictive modeling that resulted in the creation of groundwater pollution "risk" and "hazard" assessment maps for the study area.

In the study, efforts were restricted to evaluating potential pollution impacts on the unconfined upper aquifer (Columbia) from which most drinking water in this part of the state is withdrawn. The hydrogeologic setting of this area is characterized by moderately low relief and gently dipping, interbedded, unconsolidated and semiconsolidated deposits that consist primarily of sand, silt, and clay. The Columbia aquifer consists of shallow surficial deposits that serve as a local source of water and provide recharge for deeper regional aquifers.

The ultimate goal of the study was to define the specifications of an inexpensive, easy-to-use computer-based system that would assist state regulatory and planning personnel in evaluating potential groundwater pollution problems anywhere within Delaware. This system would use as input an integrated data base created from data currently available in one form or another from various state and federal agencies.

Data base creation

A geographic data base was created for a preselected area around Rehoboth Beach, Delaware, that contained various data layers, including land use/cover, soil permeability, septic system density, depth to groundwater, and hydraulic conductivity. The geographic information system software used in this study was the ERDAS package developed by Earth Resources Data Analysis Systems in Atlanta. ERDAS was used to overlay and evaluate these layers of spatially oriented data to determine the potential for negative groundwater impacts within the study area.

The various types of groundwater impact-related information initially collected for the study site included data on transmissivity, elevation of the base of the unconfined aquifer, water table (top of the aquifer) elevation, surface elevation, soil permeability, land use/cover, and sewer system service areas. Each item of information had to be in map form to be entered into the computer for subsequent spatial analysis. Although most of the required data were already in this form, several new maps had to be prepared. The soil permeability map was created by aggregating soil mapping units having similar soil permeability rates (measured in inches per hour), as represented on Soil Conservation Service soil survey maps of the area. In addition, several new intermediate maps or data layers were created using various digital techniques.

Once maps for the study area had been prepared, information was entered into the computer by "digitizing" the data. This was accomplished by using a manually operated line digitizer. The specific x, y coordinates for each feature on a given map were recorded and stored in a digital file. This process

Reprinted by permission of the publisher, Soil and Water Conservation Society, *Journal of Soil and Water Conservation*, 1990, 45 (2): 242-245.

allowed for accurate positioning of map features, maintaining of spatial relationships between adjacent map features, and referencing of map features to a common geographic coordinate system, in this case, universal transverse mercator.

Although grid-cell data sets were created for surface elevation, groundwater elevation, aquifer transmissivity, and elevation of the base of the aquifer, the actual data layers needed for this study were depth to groundwater, hydraulic conductivity, and land surface slope. Because these types of data were not available for the study area, it was necessary to derive the data sets from other existing data. This was achieved by using the multiple-grid operation facilities of ERDAS that allow element-by-element arithmetic operations (such as multiplication and division) to be performed on one or two data layers for the purpose of creating a new map layer. Using this approach, each element in the groundwater elevation matrix was subtracted from its corresponding element in the surface elevation matrix to produce a matrix that represented variations in depth to groundwater. Similarly, the hydraulic conductivity matrix was created via manipulation of the groundwater elevation, elevation of the base of the aquifer, and aquifer transmissivity data sets. The slope data set was produced by applying a slope calculation routine to the surface elevation data. For this study, the cell size was set arbitrarily at one acre.

Predictive modeling

Predictive modeling, in the context of this study, involved manipulating appropriate data in various ways to provide qualitative assessments of the potential for negative groundwater impacts for any given parcel of land, or cell, in the study area. For any given cell, this assessment took the form of a numeric value derived by evaluating the cell's respective value for each data layer used; weighting each value in terms of its importance in affecting groundwater quality; and integrating all of the values into a single index value that denotes the groundwater pollution potential for that particular location. For example, parcels of land that exhibit such characteristics as highly permeable soil, a shallow depth to groundwater, and high septic system density would be designated as highly susceptible to groundwater contamination. On the other hand, a forested parcel of land situated in highly impermeable soil would be designated as much less susceptible to groundwater contamination. This method of predictive modeling involves a combination of subjective ranking and "additive-overlay" processes.

The additive-overlay process is relatively straightforward. Corresponding data layer values for a particular cell are multiplied by an importance coefficient to produce a composite score. This, of course, is also done for every other cell in the matrix. Alternatively, the cell values for each layer actually may be "recoded³" to reflect importance and then summed to produce a composite score layer. With this latter approach, the actual cell values for each layer could be recoded in terms of relative rankings and subsequently summed to produce a composite "sensitivity" map.

Critical to performing the second type of additive overlaying is having a computer program that can handle "conditional" overlay commands. Such a program affords the opportunity to conduct "Boolean-type" operations that may take the form "if cell a in data layer x has a value of n, change that cell value to b in data layer y." In this manner, actual cell values can be changed arbitrarily to meet the requirements of a specific type of analysis or overlay operation.

Based upon the characteristics of the six hydrogeologic variables included in the final geographic database (soil permeability, depth to groundwater, hydraulic conduc-

Conceptual illustration of additive overlay process.

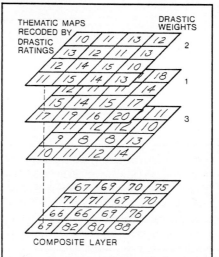

Assigned weights for DRASTIC features

Feature	Weight
Depth to water table	5
Net recharge	4
Aquifer media	3
Soil media	2
Topography	2
Impact of the vadose zone	5
Hydraulic conductivity of the aquifer	3

tivity, slope, land use/cover, and septic system density), subjective numeric values or "weights" were assigned to each datum according to its relative importance in affecting groundwater quality. The relative rankings assigned to the variables were then summed cell-by-cell to produce composite scores that indicated the groundwater impact potential for each one-acre cell in the study area.

The empirical model used in this study to evaluate regional groundwater pollution potential is based upon a recent methodology developed by the National Water Well Association under a cooperative agreement with the U.S. Environmental Protection Agency (5). This methodology was designed to permit systematic evaluation of the pollution potential in any hydrogeologic setting anywhere in the United States. The system has two major components: (1) the designation of mappable units, termed hydrogeologic settings, and (2) the superposition of a relative rating system having the acronym DRASTIC.

Inherent in each hydrogeologic setting are the physical characteristics that affect groundwater pollution potential. In the development of the DRASTIC system, a wide range of technical viewpoints was considered regarding the relative importance of the many physical characteristics that affect pollution potential. The availability of mappable data was also considered. As a result of this evaluation, the most important mappable factors that control groundwater pollution potential were determined to be depth to water (D), net recharge (R), aquifer media (A), soil media (S), topography (slope) (S), impact of the vadose zone (I), and conductivity (hydraulic) of the aquifer (C).

These factors were arranged to form the acronym DRASTIC for ease of reference. While this list is not all inclusive, these factors, in combination, were determined to include the basic requirements needed to assess the general pollution potential of each hydrogeologic setting. The DRASTIC factors represent measurable parameters for which data generally are available from a variety of sources.

With the DRASTIC system, a numerical ranking scheme is used to assess groundwater pollution potential in varying hydrogeologic settings. The system contains three significant parts: weights, ranges, and ratings. In developing the scheme, each DRASTIC factor was evaluated with respect to the others to determine the relative importance of each factor. The most significant factors have a weight of 5, the least significant a weight of 2.

Each DRASTIC factor also was divided into either ranges or significant media types that have an impact on pollution potential. Similarly, each range for each DRASTIC feature was evaluated with respect to the others to determine the relative significance of each range with regard to pollution potential. The factors of D, R, S, T, and C were assigned one value per range. A and I were assigned both a "typical" rating and a variable rating. The variable rating permits the user to choose either a typical value or to adjust the value based on more specific knowledge.

This system allows the user to determine a numerical value for any hydrogeologic setting by using an additive model. The equation for determining the DRASTIC index is as follows:

$$\text{Pollution potential} = D_r D_w + R_r R_w + A_r A_w + S_r S_w + T_r T_w + I_r I_w + C_r C_w$$

where r is the rating and w is the weight.

Once a DRASTIC index has been computed, it is possible to identify areas that are more likely to be susceptible to groundwater contamination relative to one another. The higher the DRASTIC index, the greater the groundwater pollution potential. However, the DRASTIC index provides only a relative evaluation tool and is not designed to provide absolute answers.

In this particular study, a modified DRASTIC approach was used to evaluate groundwater pollution potential. Actually, two different types of groundwater evaluations were made. With one type, an evaluation of pollution potential (or "risk") was made based upon the DRASTIC factors of depth to water, hydraulic conductivity, slope, and soil media (a reflection of soil permeability). In this case, the aquifer media (A), net recharge (R), and impact of vadose zone (I) factors were not used because the DRASTIC "ranges" and "ratings" for these factors did not vary appreciably in the study area. In other words, the aquifer media (sand and gravel), net recharge, and vadose zone material (sand and gravel) are essentially uniform across this area.

With the other type of pollution evaluation, a qualitative determination was made of the "probability" of groundwater pollution occurring at a given location based upon its pollution potential or risk index (as determined above) in combination with other such factors, such as land use/cover and septic system density. Underlying this type of "hazard assessment" is the assumption that the probability of pollution occurring at a given location is a function not only of its hydrogeologic setting but also of society's "pollution contribution" to that area.

Aside from some additional factors, the equation used in this model to predict groundwater pollution risk or hazard for this

DRASTIC ranges and ratings for depth to water	
Range (feet)	Rating
0-5	10
5-15	9
15-30	7
30-50	5
50-75	3
75-100	2
100 +	1

DRASTIC ranges and ratings for aquifer media		
Range	Rating	Typical Rating
Massive shale	1-3	2
Metamorphic/ igneous	2-5	3
Weathered metamorphic/ igneous	3-5	4
Thin bedded sandstone, limestone shale sequences	5-9	6
Massive sandstone	4-9	6
Massive limestone	4-9	6
Sand and gravel	6-9	8
Basalt	2-10	9
Karst limestone	9-10	10

Modified DRASTIC ranges and ratings for land use/cover	
Range	Rating
Landfill/dump	10
Industrial waste disposal	10
Agricultural land	9
Auto junkyard/salvage	9
Quarries/gravel pits	6
Other surface mining	6
Wastewater spray irrigation	6
Confined feedlots	6
Unconfined feedlots	5
Miscellaneous urban	5
Golf course	3
High-Density residential	3
Medium-Density residential	2
Seasonal Trailer park	2
Low-Density residential	1
Wastewater Treatment plant	1
All other	0

Modified DRASTIC ranges and ratings for septic system density	
Range	Rating
0-2 systems/acre	1
2-4 systems/acre	3
More than 4 systems/acre	6

study was the same as that used in the DRASTIC system. The specific weights, ranges, and ratings used for the DRASTIC factors were used as recommended.

System outputs

One of the primary goals of this study was to develop map products from the geographic data base using ERDAS software in conjunction with the DRASTIC groundwater evaluation system. The main purpose of producing various computer-generated maps was to demonstrate the types of products or analyses that could be accomplished using a GIS-based methodology for assessing regional groundwater pollution potential. In this study, two basic types of digital maps were produced. During the development of the geographic data base, assorted intermediate polygon and isopleth maps were produced from individual data layers or two-layer combinations. While these types may be valuable for specific applications, the most important maps produced in terms of the focus of this study were the ones that depicted regional groundwater pollution potential.

As described earlier, two different types of groundwater evaluations were made. With the first type, an evaluation of the pollution potential for any given location, or cell, was made based on local depth to groundwater, hydraulic conductivity of the aquifer, land surface slope, and soil permeability. The results of this analysis were displayed on a "risk assessment" map. With the other type of pollution evaluation, a qualitative determination was made of the probability of groundwater pollution occurring at a given location, based upon its pollution potential or risk index (as reflected by the risk assessment map) in combination with human-related factors, such as land use/cover and septic system density. This particular analysis resulted in a "hazard assessment" map.

In terms of areal extent, 10 percent of the land area was determined to be in a "low-risk" category; 30 percent was determined to be in a "medium-risk" category; and 60 percent was determined to be in a "high-risk" category. When land use/cover and septic system density were also considered, 17 percent of the land area was considered to have a low hazard potential, and 34 percent and 49 percent of the land area were considered to have a medium and high hazard potential, respectively. It is interesting to note that more than 50 percent of the areal extent of two land use/cover types known to be associated with groundwater problems—agriculture and waste disposal—occurs in areas predicted by DRASTIC to

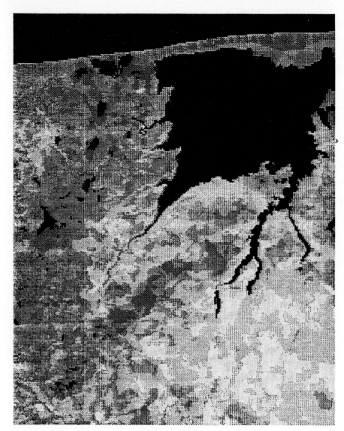

Groundwater pollution risk assessment map based on depth to groundwater, hydraulic conductivity, slope, and soil permeability. Lighter tones indicate a greater risk index value. North is to the left in both illustrations.

Groundwater pollution hazard assessment map based on depth to groundwater, hydraulic conductivity, slope, soil permeability, land use/cover, and septic system density. Lighter tones indicate a greater hazard index value.

be "high risk" areas. Conversely, only two percent of another critical land use/cover type—mixed urban—appeared to coincide with high risk areas.

Preliminary findings suggest that this approach can generate groundwater-related information for large geographic areas that is sufficiently detailed for use by government agencies involved in protecting groundwater resources. The regional perspective and parcel-size data resolution afforded by a GIS appear to be compatible with information requirements of various planning and regulatory activities conducted by such agencies. In the case of Delaware, the Department of Natural Resources and Environmental Control plans to use the results of GIS-based risk and hazard assessments to develop strategies to safeguard groundwater resources presently endangered by proliferating commercial and residential development in sensitive coastal zone areas.

Although this GIS was initially designed for assessing regional groundwater quality, the geographic data base can be expanded easily to encompass other applications ranging from urban planning and land appraisal to soil erosion and nonpoint pollution source evaluation.

REFERENCES CITED

1. Bagio, J. V., and D. B. Meade. 1986. *Spatial data processing for groundwater modeling using a geographic information system.* In Proc., East. Region Groundwater Conf. Nat. Water Well Assoc., Dublin, Ohio pp. 169-180.
2. Fleischer, E. J., R. R. Noss, P. T. Kostecki, and E. J. Calabrese. 1986. *Evaluating the subsurface fate of organic chemicls of concern using the SESOIL environmental fate model.* In Proc., East. Region Groundwater Conf. Nat. Water Well Assoc., Dublin, Ohio pp. 357-370.
3. Rojas, K. W., C. S. Hebson, and D. G. Decoursey. 1988. *Modeling agricultural management subject to subsurface water quality constraints.* In *Modeling Agricultural, Forest, and Rangeland Hydrology.* Am. Soc. Agr. Eng., St. Joseph, Mich. pp. 108-116.
4. Rouhani, S., and T. Hall. 1987. *Geostatistical schemes for groundwater monitoring in southwest Georgia.* In Khanbilvardi and Filos [eds.] *Pollution, Risk Assessment, and Redemediation in Groundwater systems.* Scientific Publ. Co., Washington, D.C. 452 pp.
5. U. S. Environmental Protection Agency. 1985. *DRASTIC: A standardized system for evaluating groundwater pollution potential using hydrogeologic settings.* EPA/600/2-85/018. Robert S. Kerr Environ. Res. Lab., Ada, Oklahoma. 163 pp.
6. Walton, W. C. 1984. *Practical aspects of groundwater modeling.* Nat. Water Well Assoc., Dublin, Ohio. 587 pp.
7. Ward, A. D., C. A. Alexander, N. R. Fausey, and J. D. Dorsey. 1988. *The ADAPT agricultural drainage and pesticide transport model.* In *Modeling Agricultural, Forest, and Rangeland Hydrology,* Am. Soc. Agr. Eng., St. Joseph, Mich. pp. 129-141.

Land use/cover areal summary and cross-tabulation of land use/cover by risk category

Land Use/Cover Type	Areal Extent (%)	Risk Category (%)		
		Low	Medium	High
Agriculture	29.1	13	33	54
Quarries/mining	<1	5	50	45
Waste disposal	<1	7	23	70
Animal feedlots	1.0	26	49	25
Wooded areas	25.7	4	21	75
Low-density residential	3.0	12	33	55
Medium-density residential	2.0	22	38	40
High-density residential	2.8	38	32	30
Open land	2.4	10	49	41
Mixed urban	1.0	44	54	2
Wetlands	8.5	5	30	65
Beach areas	1.0	5	67	33
Water	23.5			

Remote Sensing and GIS

Editor: Stan Aronoff
WDL Consultants
P.O. Box 585
Station B, Ottawa, Ontario

Statewide Groundwater-Vulnerability Assessment in Nebraska Using the DRASTIC/GIS Model

Donald C. Rundquist
Center for Advanced Land Management Information
Technologies
Conservation and Survey Division
Institute of Agriculture and Natural Resources
University of Nebraska-Lincoln
Lincoln, Nebraska 68588-0517, U.S.A.

Donn A. Rodekohr
ERDAS, Inc.
Atlanta, Georgia 30329, U.S.A.

Albert J. Peters
Department of Earth Sciences
New Mexico State University
Las Cruces, New Mexico 88003, U.S.A.

Richard L. Ehrman
Nebraska Department of Environmental Control
Lincoln, Nebraska 68509-8922, U.S.A.

Liping Di
Center for Advanced Land Management Information
Technologies
Conservation and Survey Division
Institute of Agriculture and Natural Resources
University of Nebraska-Lincoln
Lincoln, Nebraska 68588-0517, U.S.A.

Gene Murray
Delta Environmental Consultants, Inc.
St. Paul, MN 55112, U.S.A.

Abstract

The paper summarizes a technique for implementing the "DRASTIC" groundwater-vulnerability model within the context of an automated raster-based geographic information system. Discussion focuses on a methodological development and a statewide project completed recently in Nebraska. The final products, a comprehensive flow chart illustrating procedures and a map of calculated potential pollution hazard, are presented. The methodology can be executed successfully with minimal training and experience. Areas of Nebraska considered vulnerable to groundwater pollution are identified.

Introduction

The saturated zone of the terrestrial subsurface constitutes 21 percent of the world's total fresh water and 97 percent of the world's unfrozen fresh water (Dunne and Leopold, 1978). Such an important natural resource must be protected to insure the health and well-being of the human species.

Problem

Issues of groundwater quality in Nebraska are similar to those being addressed by planners and resource managers in many central and western states (Engberg, 1984). Vast areas of intensive irrigated-cropland agriculture, with associated fertilizer and pesticide applications, combine with the usual problems of feedlot run-

Reprinted from *Geocarto International* published by Geocarto International Centre, G.P.O. Box 4122, Hong Kong.
Geocarto International (2) 1991

off, landfills, and various non-agricultural sources of pollution to pose a threat to Nebraska's extensive and precious groundwater reserve. Therefore, resource managers have deemed it necessary to identify geographic areas of the state where the groundwater supply may be vulnerable to pollution originating at the terrestrial surface. Thus, we were faced with a problem of integrating several environmental variables within a spatially organized framework, and doing so in automated fashion.

Purpose

The purpose of our paper is to summarize a methodology which evolved at the Center for Advanced Land Management Information Technologies (CALMIT), University of Nebraska-Lincoln, for using the "DRASTIC" methodology (Aller *et al.*, 1987) in conjunction with a commercially available raster-based geographic information system (GIS) to produce maps of groundwater vulnerability. Methodological development, occurring over the previous three years, culminated in a statewide project carried out in conjunction with the Nebraska Department of Environmental Control (DEC). That project serves as the focal point of our paper in that the methodological development is highlighted.

"DRASTIC"

One of the tools created for the purpose of groundwater protection in the United States is a methodology referred to as "DRASTIC," developed as the result of a cooperative agreement between the National Water Well Association (NWWA) and the U.S. Environmental Protection Agency (EPA). The procedure was designed to provide for systematic evaluation of groundwater-pollution potential in any hydrogeologic setting.

DRASTIC consists of several components, the first of which is the designation of mappable hydrogeologic parameters (Aller *et al.*, 1987). The seven variables from which the name of the model is derived, include Depth to water, Recharge, Aquifer media, Soil media, Topography, Impact of the vadose zone, and Conductivity (hydraulic). These mappable parameters are generally available for all of the U.S. or can be derived from various sources.

The numerical ranking system, another DRASTIC component, is used to assess the groundwater-pollution potential for each hydrogeologic variable. The system contains three parts: 1) weights; 2) ranges; and 3) ratings (Aller *et al.*, 1987). Each DRASTIC parameter has been assigned a relative weight between 1 and 5, with 5 being considered most significant in regard to contamination potential and 1 being considered least significant (Table 1). In turn, each of the variables is "subdivided" into either numerical ranges (e.g., depth to

water in feet) or media types (e.g., materials making up a soil) which impact pollution potential. Table 2 illustrates the ranges and ratings for soil media. Finally, the ratings are used to quantify the ranges/media with regard to likelihood of groundwater pollution.

The final result for each hydrogeologic setting (i.e., geographic area) is a numerical value obtained using the following simple equation:

DRASTIC INDEX =
$$D_R D_w + R_R R_w + A_R A_w + S_R S_w + T_R T_w + I_R I_w + C_R C_w \qquad (1)$$
Where: $\quad$ R = rating
$\quad\quad\quad\quad$ W = weight

A high numerical index resulting from Equation (1) is assumed to be indicative of a geographic area that is likely to be susceptible to groundwater pollution. But, as Aller *et al.* (1987) warn, "the DRASTIC Index provides only a relative evaluation tool and is not designed

Table 1
Assigned weights for hydrogeologic settings

SETTING	WEIGHT
Depth to Water	5
Net Recharge	4
Aquifer Media	3
Soil Media	2
Topography	1
Impact of the Vadose Zone Media	5
Hydraulic Conductivity of the Aquifer	3

Source: Aller *et al.*, 1987

Table 2
Ranges and ratings for soil media

RANGE	RATING
Thin or Absent	10
Gravel	10
Sand	9
Peat	8
Shrinking and/or Aggregated Clay	7
Sandy Loam	4
Loam	5
Silty Loam	4
Clay Loam	3
Muck	2
Nonshrinking and Nonaggregated Clay	1

Source: Aller *et al.*, 1987

to provide absolute answers." Thus, one must understand that DRASTIC was intended as a reconnaissance tool, but it has proven its value as an indicator of areas deserving a detailed hydrogeologic evaluation.

Placed within a spatial context, the methodology is based upon a series of seven maps, one for each hydrogeologic parameter (Figure 1). While the DRASTIC methodology can be implemented manually by means of visual map comparison and overlay, the time requirements and error potential associated with printed maps at different scales and plotted on various map projections are well known by resource managers (e.g., Marble, 1987). Therefore the DRASTIC model was automated within the framework of a digital geographic information system. Such an approach is consistent with the notion that modelling is an important key to furthering research in GIS (Smith, 1988) and that approaches which improve the process of spatial inquiry are useful for resource evaluation.

Related Research

Several researchers have used GIS concepts to address issues related groundwater contamination. Hendrix and Buckley (1986) used the technology in three Vermont study sites to examine water supplies affected by naturally occurring radon contamination in a dolomite aquifer, aquifers with a high potential for contamination from surface activities, and areas suited for land application of waste water. Kaplan *et al.* (1986) developed a GIS aimed at ground-water management for Nassau and Suffolk counties on Long Island, New York. The research demonstrated applications in mapping of aquifer surfaces, identification and mapping of contaminated areas within aquifers, and identification of possible contaminant sources. Broten *et al.* (1987), while developing a prototype GIS for managing hazardous waste and groundwater contamination problems, interfaced their GIS with a numerical groundwater-flowpath model which allowed delineation of potential contaminant source areas for points of known contamination in the San Gabriel Basin of California. Barringer *et al.* (1987) de-

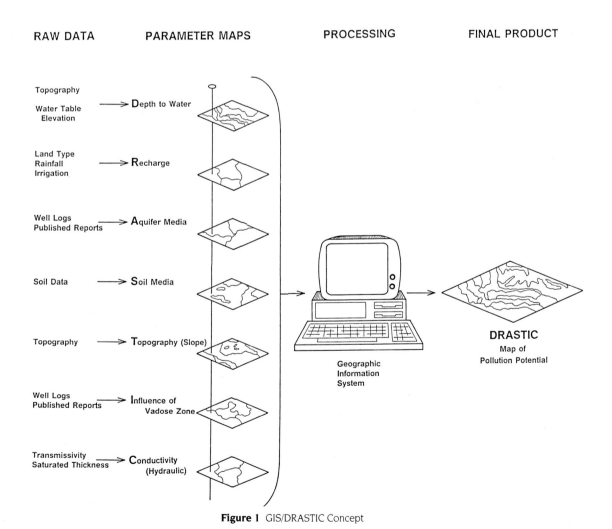

Figure 1 GIS/DRASTIC Concept

119

scribed methods for mapping areas of corrosive groundwater in New Jersey along with the hydrogeologic variables that exerted control on groundwater chemistry. A GIS was used to determine the relationship between the corrosive groundwater and the hydrogeologic features. Kittleson and Kruska (1987) used a microcomputer-based groundwater-management system in conjunction with a GIS to map the occurrence of nitrates in the groundwater of Kalamazoo County, Michigan.

The first project involving the partial automation of DRASTIC using GIS concepts occurred at the University of Kansas where Whittemore *et al.* (1987) and Merchant *et al.* (1987) applied the commercially available "Erdas"* (Earth Resources Data Analysis System) GIS software package to data compiled for Harvey Country, Kansas. The KU investigators extended the DRASTIC methodology by generating time-related capture zones for pumping wells in a well field. Later, Griner (1989) digitized the seven DRASTIC layers for the Southwest Florida Water Management District into an INTERGRAPH* system, but did the overlay analysis using ARC/INFO. Mullen (1991) used MapInfo* software and the DRASTIC model to produce county-level scores for Nebraska. The latter study, which was completed subsequent to the project described in this paper, focused on the threat of atrazine contamination.Our work serves as a refinement and extension of the earlier work completed at Kansas.

In Nebraska, two feasibility projects were preliminary to our statewide activity. The first, funded by the Nebraska Department of Health (DOH), focused on an area of six 7-1/2 minute U.S. geological Survey (USGS) quadrangles around the city of Cozad, Nebraska (Murray, 1987). The activity, which depended heavily on assistance from the KU researchers cited above: 1) served to raise the level of visibility of GIS and related technologies in Nebraska; 2) allowed Nebraska researchers to automate, on an Erdas-resident workstation, portions of the DRASTIC/GIS procedure; 3) attracted a considerable amount of attention on the part of Nebraska resource managers to the prospect of using a partially automated DRASTIC model in Nebraska and 4) highlighted a potential solution to the problem of identifying geographic areas which may be vulnerable to groundwater pollution. The success and visibility given in Nebraska to the DOH project led to a larger cooperative activity between CALMIT and the Nebraska Department of Environmental Control (DEC), the second of the two feasibility studies. The objective of the DEC project was to utilize automated DRASTIC/GIS procedures in preparing groundwater-vulnerability maps for 28 sites in Nebraska, ranging in size from a few 7-1/2 minute quadrangles to an entire county. Each site was selected by DEC because it corresponded to an area where contamination of groundwater had been detected in municipal wells. These areas were under consideration for designation as Special Groundwater Quality Protection Areas (SPAs). The DEC activity led to both further development of our methodology and improved techniques for an automated DRASTIC model.

STATEWIDE IMPLEMENTATION

CALMIT and DEC undertook a cooperative project in 1988 aimed at production of DRASTIC maps at 1:250,000 for all of Nebraska. The procedures employed in the statewide project, which were again based upon use of the Erdas-GIS software, are summarized below.

Preprocessing Steps

Prior to dealing with each of the seven layers in the model, certain "housekeeping" or preprocessing steps were executed. Most importantly, we identified and recorded the corner coordinates of each 1:250,000 scale USGS quadrangle map comprising the study site. For our statewide product, we processed data on the basis of those maps, with the spatial extent of each expressed in UTM (Universal Transverse Mercator) coordinates. These were later concatenated to provide statewide coverage.

Parameter #1: Depth to Water

Depth to water was computed using two datasets: 1) land-surface topography, available on magnetic tape from the USGS as Digital Elevation Models (DEM) at 1:250,000 and 2) water-table-surface topography, available from the state geological survey. The water-table contours were digitized and georeferenced (using map corner coordinates) to the appropriate USGS quadrangle map. This map was then rasterized and smoothed (using a low-pass filter) to produce a digital file that was in the same format as the DEM used to describe the land surface. Water-table elevations were simply subtracted from land-surface elevations on a pixel-by-pixel basis to compute depth to water.

Paramteres #2, 3, and 6: Recharge, Aquifer Media, and Impact of the Vadose Zone

Since neither digital datasets nor paper maps existed for recharge, aquifer media, and impact of the vadose zone, the first step was to employ a hydrogeologist to map these three parameters using well-long data, climatic maps, and topographic-regions maps. Aller *et al.* (1987) provide detail on the computation of such parameters. Each prepared map was then digitized and registered to the appropriate quadrangle coordinates. The data were rasterized and converted into a format consistent with the depth-to-water map produced in the previous step, and DRASTIC indices assigned.

Soils

Digitized "STATSGO" soil-association data for Nebraska were acquired from the Soil Conservation Service. STATSGO information is produced at 1:250,000, and available on magnetic tape. The digital soils data were rectified, rasterized, and classified into the appropriate DRASTIC index values (Aller *et al.*, 1987).

Topography

Percent slope of the land surface was calculated using the USGS DEM's. The Erdas software allowed for (%) slope computation and recoding to a DRASTIC index value. The topography variable was the easiest and most straightforward of the seven DRASTIC variables to calculate.

Hydraulic Conductivity

Maps of hydraulic conductivity for specific areas of Nebraska are generally not available; however, maps of the two components of conductivity — transmissivity and saturated thickness — are more frequently available or can be generated by a hydrogeologist from well logs. Our procedure involved digitizing contour lines of transmissivity and saturated thickness as derived from hydrogeologic interpretation, creating a "DEM-like" surface image of each, and then dividing transmissivities

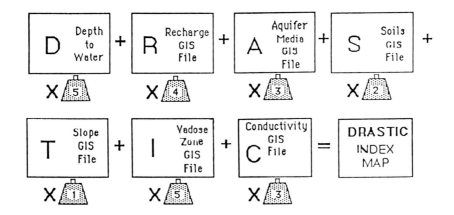

Figure 2 Procedure for calculation of final index map

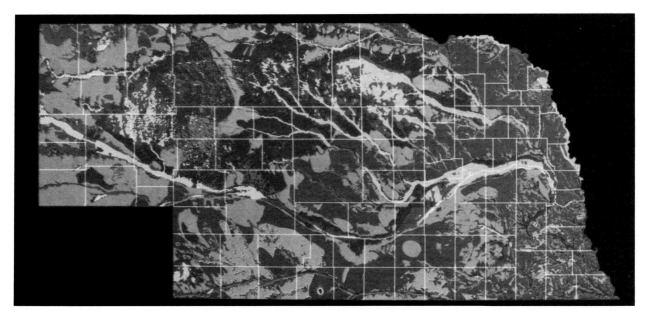

Figure 3 Statewide map of potential groundwater vulnerability

See page 371 for color plate of Figure 3.

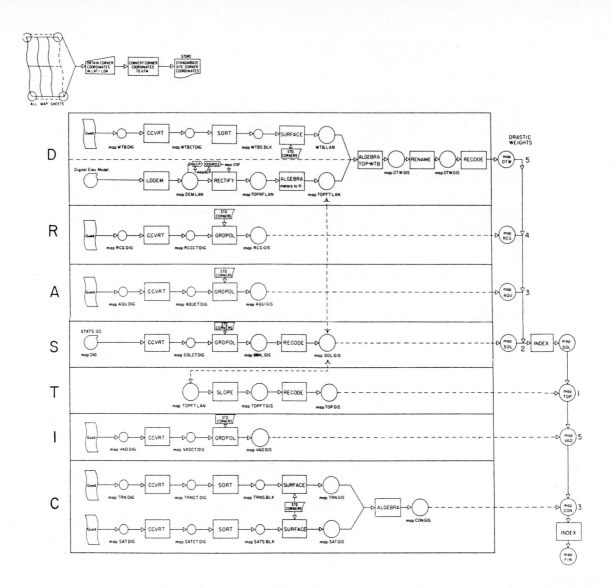

Figure 4 Composite flowchart for implementing DRASTIC on Erdas

by saturated thicknesses on a pixel-by-pixel basis. The result was a map of hydraulic conductivity which was then classified into DRASTIC index values according to Aller *et al.* (1987).

Generation of a Final Product

When each of the seven data layers were completed, the final index map was generated. As noted earlier, each parameter carried a specific weighting factor based upon its relative importance in permitting a pollutant to reach the groundwater. Therefore, equation (1) was implemented using the Erdas INDEX function (Figure 2).

The procedure described in the preceding paragraphs was executed 13 times, once for every 1:250,000-scale USGS quadrangel in Nebraska. Then, all 13 of the resulting datasets ware concatenated to produce the final product, a map of Nebraska showing pollution potential (Figure 3). This map shows the final DRASTIC values for the state of Nebraska. In general, the cool colors (gray, blue) indicate low DRASTIC indices while the warm colors (yellow, red) represent high values. Surficial features such as the Platte River valley (central portion of map extending west to east) and other drainages, and the Sand Hills (north-central and western portions of map) can be readily identified by the predominantly high values mapped in those areas. This is understandable given the shallow depths to water, high net recharge, and coarse surface and subsurface materials

122

common in those parts of Nebraska. In contrast, large portions of southern and eastern Nebraska are characterized by low indices generated by the occurrence of significant depths to water, low net recharge, and fine surface and subsurface materials.

Care must be used when interpreting DRASTIC maps to not read more into them than the method is designed to produce. This is especially true with regard to the spatial resolution, which by the nature of the model, is extremely coarse.

Comprehensive Flow Chart

One of the most useful results from our work involving the implementation of DRASTIC on an Erdas system was a comprehensive flow chart illustrating each step in the process (Figure 4). Notice that the flow chart uses, in every case, the specific names of Erdas programs. Our intention here is to provide a mechanism for others with similar hardware/software configurations to implement DRASTIC.

The steps shown in Figure 4 can be executed with minimal training and experience. Once the flow chart was developed and operationalized, we encountered few problems in project completion. Potential users should be aware, however, that a study for a large state such as Nebraska, being done at 1:250,000, requires substantial disk space (on the order of 300 mgb) for executing the various steps shown by the flow chart.

Summary

Our paper provides an overview of the methods which we used for implementing the DRASTIC groundwater-vulnerability model on a statewide basis using Erdas-GIS software. The culmination of our effort was a map depicting groundwater-pollution potential over the entire state. The statewide project, which began in October of 1988 and ended in September of 1989, was completed almost entirely by student employees for a total cost of approximately $66,000, or a mere $710 per county. Hopefully, the procedures summarized in our paper will be of use to other groups embarking on similar projects.

Current CALMIT research, being done to strengthen the method, involves the addition of a land-cover layer to the seven DRASTIC layers. Landsat Thematic Mapper data are being used to map crop type, a variable which is important in estimating both the kind and quantity of farm chemicals applied.

References Cited

Aller, L., T. Bennet, J. H. Lehr, and R. J. Petty, 1987. DRASTIC: A standardized system for evaluating groundwater pollution potential using hydrogeologic settings. USEPA Document #EPA/600/2-85-018.

Barringer, J. L., R. L. Ulery, and G. R. Kish, 1987. A methodology for relating regions of corrosive ground water to hydrogeologic variables in the New Jersey coastal plain. Proceedings, International Geographic Information Systems (IGIS) Symposium, Vol. 3, 73-86.

Broten, M., L. Fenstermaker, and J. Shafer, 1987. An automated GIS for ground water contaminated investigation. Proceedings of the Conference on Solving Ground Water Problems with Models, Denver, CO: National Water Well Association, 3-19.

Dunne, T. and L. B. Leopold, 1978. Water in environmental planning. San Francisco: W. H. Freeman and Co.

Engberg, R. A., 1984. Appraisal of data for groundwater quality in Nebraska. U.S. Geological Water-Supply Paper 2245.

Griner, A. J., 1989. The automation of DRASTIC — a regional model for mapping susceptibility of groundwater contamination. Proceedings, GIS/LIS'89, Vol. 2, Falls Church, VA: American Society for Photogrammetry and Remote Sensing, 679-684.

Hendrix, W. G. and D. J. A. Buckley, 1986. Geographic information system technology as a tool for ground water management. Proceedings, ACSM-ASPRS Annual Convention, Vol. 3, Falls Church, VA: American Society for Photogrammetry and Remote Sensing, 230-239.

Kaplan, E., A. Meinhold, J. Naidu, and M. Hauptmann, 1986. Use of a geographic information system in ground water management. In Opitz, B. K. (ed), Geographic Information Systems in Government, Vol. 1, Hampton, VA: A. Deepak Publishing Co., 329-343.

Kittleson, K. and R. Kruska, 1987. Groundwater resource management: a geographic information system approach. Spectrum, East Lansing, MI: Center for Remote Sensing, Michigan State University, 1-2.

Marble, D. F. Geographic information systems: an overview. In Ripple, W. J. (ed.), GIS for resource management: a compendium. Falls Church, VA: American Society of Photogrammetry and Remote Sensing, 2-8.

Merchant, J. W., D. O. Whittemore, J. L. Whistler, C. D. McElwee, and J. J. Woods, 1987. Groundwater pollution hazard assessment: A GIS approach. Proceedings, International Geographic Information Systems (IGIS) Symposium, Vol. 3, 103-115.

Mullen, M.P., 1991. A GIS technology for ground water assessments. Technical Papers, ACSM/ASPRS annual convention, Vol.2, 243-252.

Murray, G. A standardized evaluation of ground water pollution potential for Cozad, Nebraska using DRASTIC. Technical Memorandum #87-02. Center for Advanced Land Management Information Technologies, University of Nebraska-Lincoln.

Smith, T. R., 1988. Emerging software/GIS capabilities. Plenary address, GIS symposium on intergrating technology and geoscience applications, Denver, Colorado, September 29.

Whittemore, D. O., J. W. Merchant, J. L. Whistler, C. D. McElwee, and J. J. Woods, 1987. Ground water protection planning using the ERDAS geographic informatin system: automation of DRASTIC and time-related capture zones. Paper presented at the National Water Well Association FOCUS Conference, 15 pp.

Acknowledgements

The authors wish to express their sincere appreciation to numerous individuals who have contributed significantly to our project involving the automation of the DRASTIC model including James W. Merchant (University of Nebraska), Craig Savage and Paul Brookner (Delta Environmental Consultants, Inc.), Lee H. Pulsifer, (TGS), Dave Jensen (Idaho Department of Health), John W. Jones and John Eno (U.S. Geological Survey), Scott A. Samson (University of Alabama), Alan Loy (National Park Service), and Jack Daniel (Nebraska Department of Health), and Mingqing Yang (University of Nebraska). The constructive criticism of Stephen J. Walsh (University of North Carolina) was most helpful in improving the manuscript.

WATER RESOURCES BULLETIN
AMERICAN WATER RESOURCES ASSOCIATION

VOL. 28, NO. 2   APRIL 1992

GIS-ASSISTED REGRESSION ANALYSIS TO IDENTIFY
SOURCES OF SELENIUM IN STREAMS[1]

Randolph B. See, David L. Naftz, and Charles L. Qualls[2]

ABSTRACT: Using a geographic information system, a regression model has been developed to identify and to assess potential sources of selenium in the Kendrick Reclamation Project Area, Wyoming. A variety of spatially distributed factors was examined to determine which factors are most likely to affect selenium discharge in tributaries to the North Platte River. Areas of Upper Cretaceous Cody Shale and Quaternary alluvial deposits and irrigated land, length of irrigation canals, and boundaries of hydrologic subbasins of the major tributaries to the North Platte River were digitized and stored in a geographic information system. Selenium concentrations in samples of soil, plant material, ground water, and surface water were determined and evaluated. The location of all sampling sites was digitized and stored in the geographic information system, together with the selenium concentrations in samples. A regression model was developed using stepwise multiple regression of median selenium discharges on the physical and chemical characteristics of hydrologic subbasins. Results indicate that the intensity of irrigation in a hydrologic subbasin, as determined by area of irrigated land and length of irrigation delivery canals, accounts for the largest variation in median selenium discharges among subbasins. Tributaries draining hydrologic subbasins with greater intensity of irrigation result in greater selenium discharges to the North Platte River than do tributaries draining subbasins with lesser intensity of irrigation.
(KEY TERMS: selenium; irrigation drainage; geographic information system.)

INTRODUCTION

The irrigation of arid lands might lead to undesirable effects as excessive salt accumulations develop in soil, biota, and water resources. Selenium has been identified as a contaminant in irrigation drainage water, and has affected fish and waterfowl adversely at the Kesterson National Wildlife Refuge in the San Joaquin Valley in California (National Research Council, 1989). In 1985, as a result of the problems at the Kesterson National Wildlife Refuge, the U.S. Department of Interior established the National

Irrigation Water Quality Program to identify other areas in the West where irrigation-induced water-quality problems might arise.

As part of the National Irrigation Water Quality Program, the Kendrick Reclamation Project Area (KRPA) in Wyoming was selected for a reconnaissance investigation during 1986-87 (Peterson *et al.*, 1988) and subsequently for a detailed investigation starting in 1988 (See *et al.*, 1992). The reconnaissance investigation was directed toward determining whether irrigation drainage has (1) caused harmful effects on human health, fish, and wildlife; or (2) affected adversely the suitability of water for beneficial uses. Results of the reconnaissance investigation at the KRPA indicated elevated concentrations of selenium in the water, bottom sediment, and biological samples (Peterson *et al.*, 1988). The objectives of the detailed study were to determine the extent, magnitude, and effects of contaminants associated with irrigation drainage; and, where effects are documented, to determine the sources and exposure pathways that cause contamination. The findings and conclusions of the detailed study will be the basis for decisions regarding the need for and type of corrective actions.

Streams in the study area (Figure 1) flow into the North Platte River upstream from several municipalities that obtain water supplies from the river and from wells completed in the alluvium along the river (Crist, 1974). Soil on land used for agriculture in the KRPA is derived almost entirely from geologic materials containing large concentrations of selenium (Erdman *et al.*, 1989). Although the irrigation water delivered to the KRPA contains little or no selenium, selenium is leached from the soil when irrigation water is applied.

The purpose of this article is to describe the use of a geographic information system (GIS) as an

[1]Paper No. 91123 of the *Water Resources Bulletin*. **Discussions are open until December 1, 1992.**

[2]Hydrologists, U.S. Geological Survey, 2617 E. Lincolnway, Suite B. Cheyenne, Wyoming 82001.

analytical tool to assist in the development of a regression model that will help to identify and to assess those areas that might have the greatest potential to contribute selenium to water resources in the study area. The GIS was used as an analytical tool to produce and display a variety of maps and tables used to evaluate spatially distributed data. GIS techniques were used to determine values of independent variables for use in a stepwise multiple regression analysis. ARC/INFO was the GIS software used for this study. (Use of brand, firm, or trade names in this article is for descriptive purposes only and does not constitute endorsement by the U.S. Geological Survey.)

The development of a regression model to identify and to assess potential selenium contamination areas could assist in the evaluation of factors contributing to selenium loads in the study area. GIS techniques were used to assist in the analysis of information, and to provide an effective means of displaying the data gathered during the detailed study. The GIS was used to determine and display the spatial relations in the study area, and to tabulate information based on the relations which would have been difficult to obtain with other techniques. The GIS analysis produced a set of independent variables for the physical and chemical characteristics of the study area.

Several other studies have linked land use to water quality. Hren *et al.* (1984) and Duckson (1989) used statistical approaches to evaluate large data sets and correlate the effects of land-use activities on water quality in coal-mining areas. Gilliland and Baxter-Potter (1987) used a GIS to predict water-quality problems associated with nonpoint-source agricultural pollution.

STUDY AREA DESCRIPTION

The study area of this investigation, shown in Figure 1, includes about 193,000 ha in Natrona County, central Wyoming. The boundary of the study area of the investigation is an arbitrary line drawn about 5 miles outside the approximate boundaries of the KRPA. Crist (1974) used this boundary in a report on selenium in waters of the study area. Most surface water and up to 97 percent of the selenium discharge originates from within the KRPA.

Water is delivered from Alcova Reservoir to the Casper Canal on demand. Irrigation water within the project is supplied primarily by the Casper Canal and then through lateral canals to irrigated fields. A network of drainage canals collects drain water and returns the drain water to the North Platte River via major tributaries. Water-quality sampling was con-

centrated in the area bounded by the North Platte River and Casper Creek on the east and the Casper Canal on the west, the approximate boundaries of the KRPA.

Soils in the study area have developed on outcrops of 14 formations of Cretaceous through Quaternary age. The nonirrigated, native soils have developed on several Cretaceous formations containing carbonaceous shales and coals, and several Tertiary formations containing bentonite, claystone, shale, and sandstone or siltstone. Ninety-five percent of the irrigated soils is developed on the Cody Shale of Late Cretaceous age (35 percent) and unconsolidated alluvial deposits of Quaternary age (60 percent). The alluvium is derived mainly from weathering and erosion of the Cody Shale. The areal extent of the Cody Shale, alluvium, and irrigated land is shown in Figure 2. Crist (1974) presented a geologic map and Lageson (1980) prepared a detailed lithologic description of geologic units in the study area. Because the limited areal extent of irrigated soils developed on formations other than Cody Shale, other pre-Cretaceous rocks have not been considered.

The KRPA includes about 10,120 irrigated ha of which about 8,090 ha are harvested annually. Forage crops are the most important crop type in the project area because the high elevation and short growing season make it difficult to grow most other crops. Alfalfa hay is grown on about 55 percent of the irrigated land. The rest of the irrigated land is used as follows: (1) other hay, pasture, and corn – 35 percent; (2) cereal crops – 5 percent; and (3) other miscellaneous uses – 5 percent (Peterson *et al.*, 1988).

METHODS

A large variety of information was available for examining factors that might contribute to selenium contamination of water resources in the study area. Map features were digitized and physical and chemical attributes associated with the map features were stored with the digitized data in the GIS. The base map was from U.S. Geological Survey digital line graphs digitized from 1:100,000-scale quadrangle series (U.S. Geological Survey, 1985). Geology (Figure 2) was digitized from a 1:62,500-scale map from Crist (1974, plate 1). Irrigated areas (Figure 2) were digitized from 1:24,000-scale maps revised in 1982 by the Casper-Alcova Irrigation District for an application for amended appropriations for water rights. Locations of Cody Shale, alluvium, and irrigated areas in the study area are shown in Figure 2. The relative distribution of Cody Shale, alluvium, and irrigated area (Figure 3) was calculated from digitized

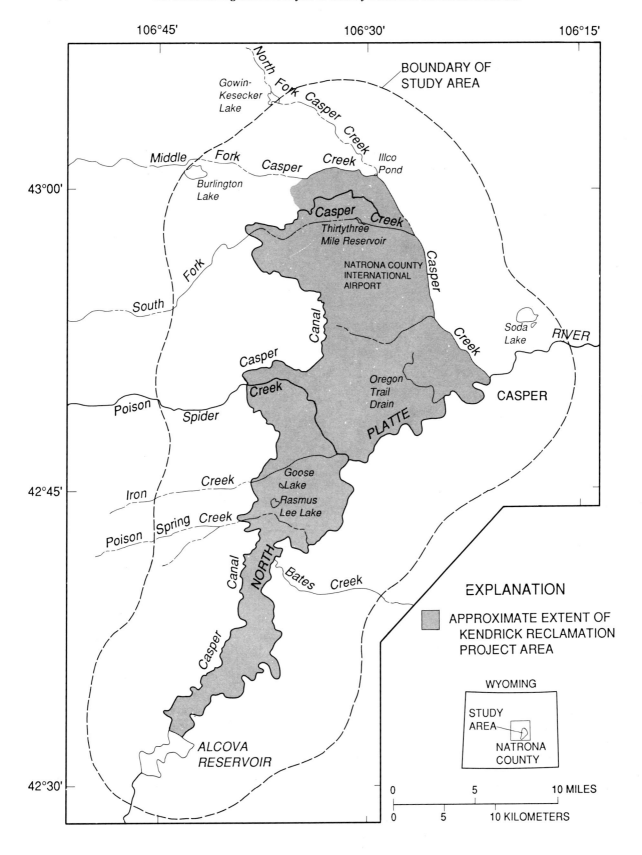

Figure 1. Map Showing Location of the Kendrick Reclamation Project Area and the Study Area.

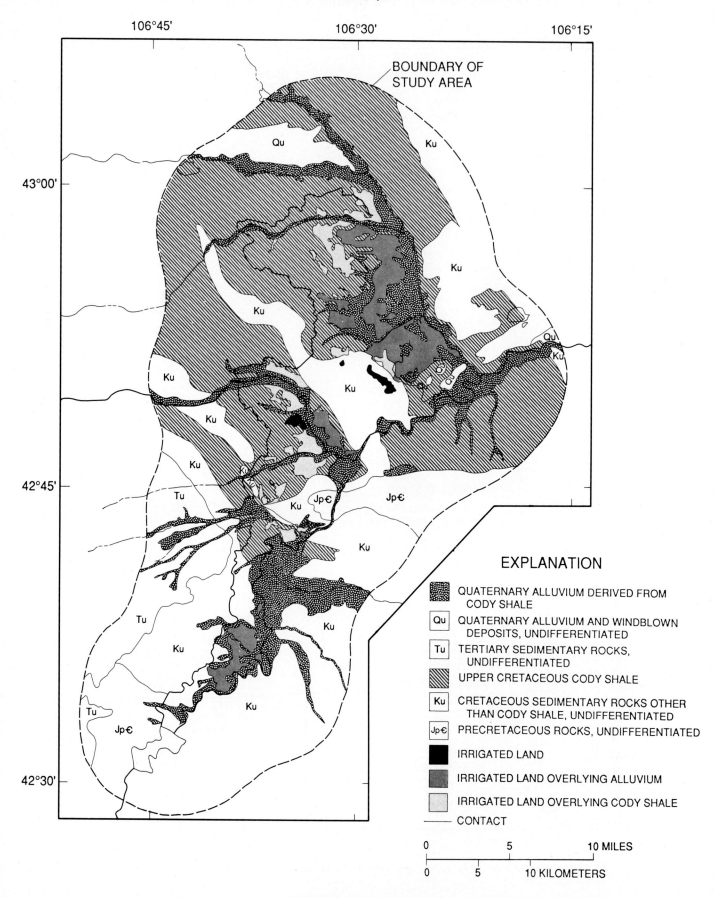

Figure 2. Map Showing Generalized Geologic Map and Irrigated Land in the
Kendrick Reclamation Project Study Area.

128

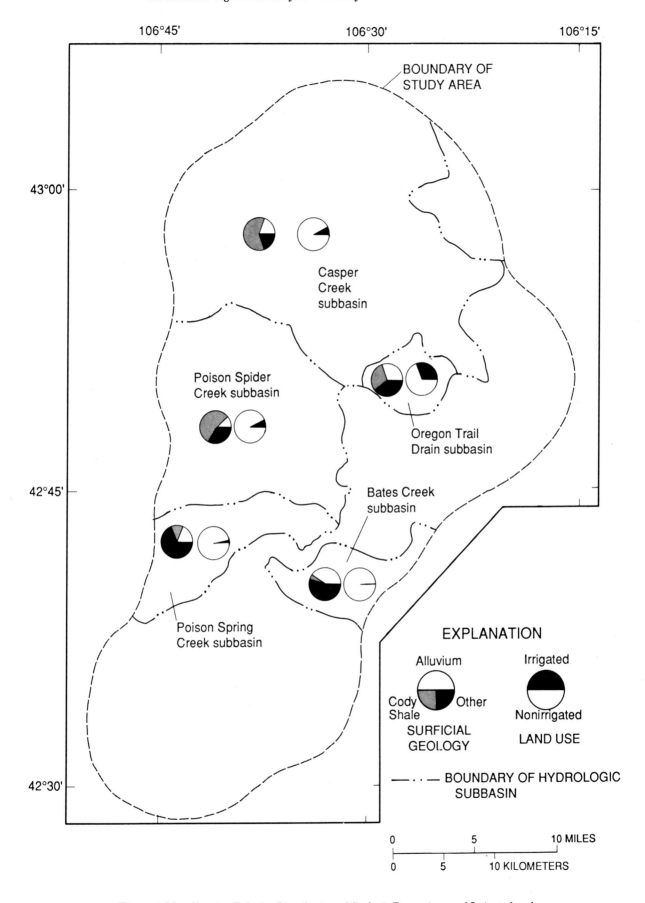

Figure 3. Map Showing Relative Distribution of Geologic Formations and Irrigated and Nonirrigated Lands for Selected Hydrologic Subbasins.

areas in Figure 2 using GIS techniques. Boundaries of selected hydrologic subbasins (Figure 3) for the five major tributaries to the North Platte River were determined using U.S. Geological Survey 1:100,000 scale topographic maps of the area. Irrigation delivery canals (Figure 7) were digitized from 1:48,000-scale engineering maps provided by the U.S. Bureau of Reclamation.

The GIS was used to store map features such as areas, lines, and points, along with physical and chemical attributes of the study area. Attributes of spatial features such as areas of irrigated land or length of streams were computed and stored in the GIS. Selenium concentrations at the sampling sites were stored in the GIS.

A series of overlaying, merging, and extracting procedures were used to complete spatial analyses of the physical and chemical attributes of the study area. Areas of spatial features, lengths of linear features, and point data for specific areas were extracted for selected hydrologic subbasins and analyzed in a tabular format using stepwise multiple regression techniques.

Some irrigated land has been reported in the Bates Creek subbasin. However, most of the water rights for irrigated fields in the Bates Creek subbasin are junior rights, and, during most years, only limited irrigation water is available. When irrigation water is available, it is generally for only short periods during the early part of the season (George Davis, U.S. Soil Conservation Service, oral commun., 1990; Randy Toolis, Wyoming State Engineer's Office, oral commun., 1991). For the purposes of this study, area of irrigated land in the Bates Creek subbasin has been estimated at 0 ha.

Data on selenium in soils and plants from nonirrigated native soils and irrigated soils in the study area were obtained from published reports: Erdman *et al.*, 1989; Severson *et al.*, 1989a; Severson *et al.*, 1989b. The location of soil and plant sampling sites and ranges of total selenium concentrations are shown in Figures 4 and 5. These locations were generated digitally using latitudes and longitudes provided by the sampling personnel. The total selenium concentrations in samples from each site also were stored in the GIS. The selenium concentrations then were linked to the site locations using a relational data base management system. INFO was the data-base system used.

Separate sampling designs were used for nonirrigated native rangelands and irrigated lands. The purpose of the sampling design on nonirrigated native soils was to identify the geologic formations that were possible sources of selenium. For nonirrigated native soils, successive land sections (2.59 ha) were selected randomly in each of 12 randomly selected townships

until all surficial geologic units in the township had been sampled twice (Erdman *et al.*, 1989). A total of 120 nonirrigated native soil samples was collected (Figure 4). The purpose of the sampling design on irrigated soils was to use the results of soil analyses to produce maps showing lines of equal selenium concentrations (Erdman *et al.*, 1989). Irrigated soils were sampled on an approximate grid interval of 1.6 km. A total of 109 irrigated soil samples was collected (Figure 4).

Big sagebrush (*Artemisia tridenta Nutt.*) and alfalfa (*Medicago sativa L.*) were sampled as potential indicators of selenium availability. The use of plants as indicators of available selenium has been discussed in numerous earlier reports (Combs and Combs, 1986; Erdman *et al.*, 1989; and Kubota *et al.*, 1967). At 101 nonirrigated native soil sampling sites (Figure 5), a sample of the previous year's growth of big sagebrush was clipped from plants in a circular area with a 10-meter radius from a soil-auger hole. At 105 irrigated soil sampling sites (Figure 5), a sample of alfalfa was collected in the 10-percent bloom stage (Erdman *et al.*, 1989).

During 1968-70, water samples were collected from 126 wells in the study area and analyzed for selenium (Crist, 1974). During 1988, water samples were collected from an additional 48 domestic wells in the study area by the U.S. Geological Survey in cooperation with the Natrona County Health Department. The sampling locations and range of selenium concentration in ground-water samples are shown in Figure 6. Because data from the ground-water samples were used to display ranges of selenium concentrations, and not individual concentrations, the two data sets were combined for analysis in this study. Mean values were used when two samples were obtained from the same well and analyzed; median values were used when three or more samples were obtained from the same well and analyzed.

During 1988-89, surface-water samples were collected monthly at sites along the five major tributaries to the North Platte River in the study area. Samples were collected concurrently at upstream and downstream sites on the four creeks and one drain in order to determine total selenium discharge from individual subbasins (Figure 7).

The selenium discharge was calculated by subtracting the selenium concentration at the upstream site from the selenium concentration at the downstream site and multiplying the difference by the streamflow, determined at the time of sampling.

Irrigation drain-water samples from constructed irrigation drains and channels draining irrigated fields were collected at 50 sites during June and August 1988. The sampling-site locations and range of selenium concentrations in irrigation drain-water

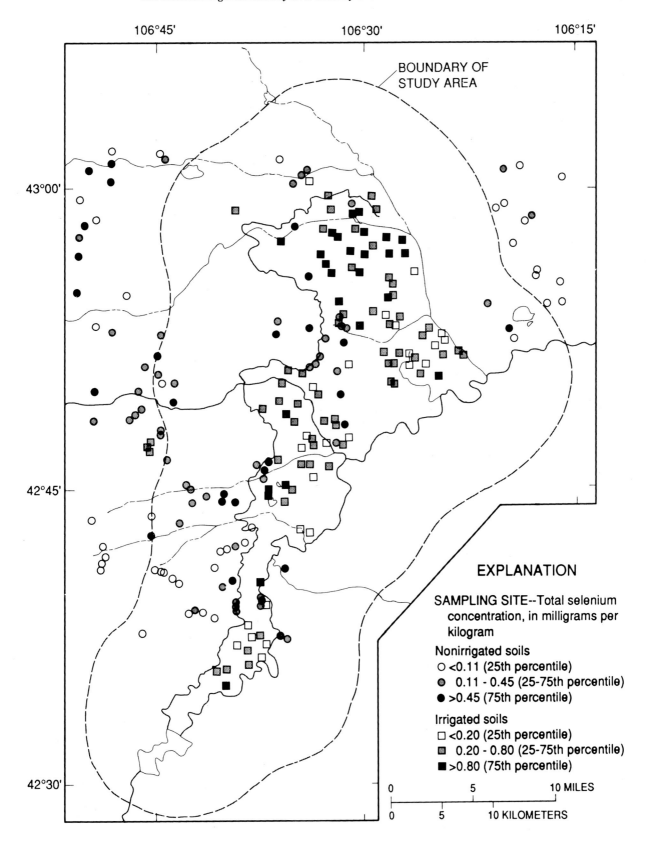

Figure 4. Map Showing Location of Sampling Sites and Range of Total
Selenium Concentrations in Soil Samples.

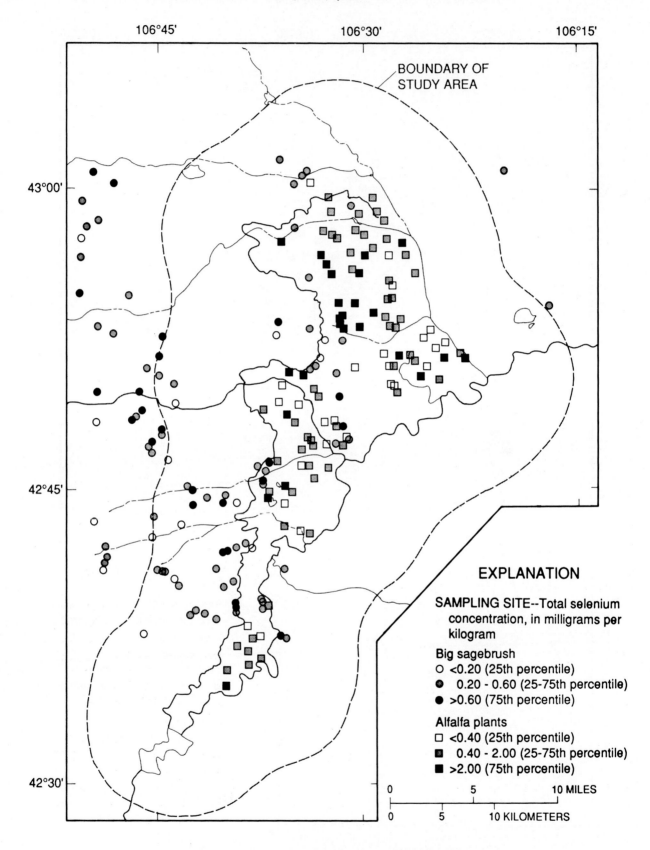

Figure 5. Map Showing Location of Sampling Sites and Range of Total Selenium
Concentrations in Big Sagebrush and Alfalfa Samples.

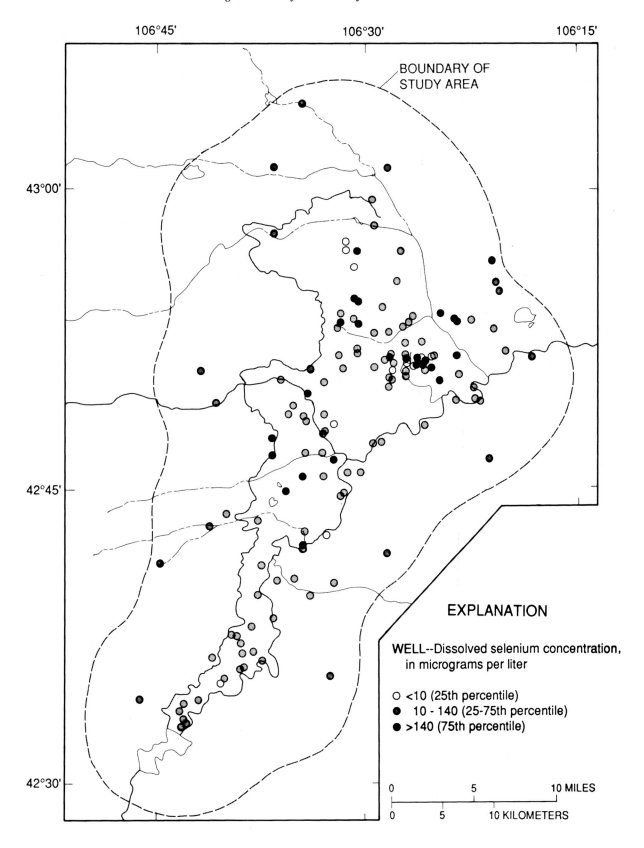

Figure 6. Map Showing Location of Wells and Range of Dissolved Selenium
Concentrations in Ground-Water Samples.

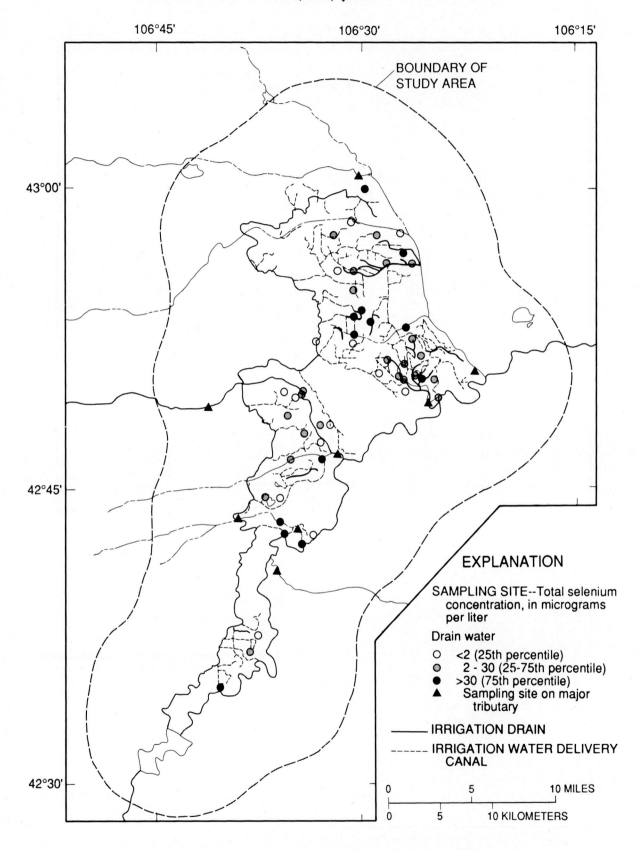

Figure 7. Map Showing Location of Sampling Sites for Water Samples from Major Tributaries
to the North Platte River and Irrigation Drains, and Range of Dissolved
Selenium Concentrations in Water Samples from Irrigation Drains.

134

samples, which were stored in the GIS, are shown in Figure 7.

Selenium discharge, surface areas of irrigated soils overlying Cody Shale and alluvium derived from Cody Shale, length of streams and irrigation-water delivery canals, and other measured variables were aggregated using the GIS. This was accomplished by digitally overlaying the sample sites with the boundaries of the five subbasins (Figure 3). During this operation, the GIS automatically annotates the sampling-sites attribute data with the identity of the subbasin in which each site is located and, thus, allows aggregation of the data. Tabular data files then were generated by the GIS. These data were analyzed using PSTAT statistical software, and summary statistics were calculated for measured variables in each of the subbasins (Table 1).

Median selenium discharges based on approximately monthly sampling during 1988 were selected as the dependent variable for regression analysis. Tributaries draining the study area pick up nearly all of their selenium within the KRPA. For example, eight samples from Poison Spring Creek upstream from the KRPA contained selenium concentrations less than the detection limit of 1 μg/L, compared to a median selenium concentration of 91.5 μg/L in Poison Spring Creek at the confluence with the North Platte River. A similar increase in concentrations was noted in Poison Spider Creek; approximately 97 percent of the selenium discharge in Poison Spider Creek originated within the KRPA. Casper Creek has three forks near the upstream edge of the KRPA, but South Fork Casper Creek and North Fork Casper Creek did not flow and were not sampled. The Middle Fork Casper Creek was sampled four times, but only one sample contained detectable selenium concentrations. The selenium discharge associated with that sample was 0.003 kg/d, much less than the median selenium discharge of 2.61 kg/d in Casper Creek at the confluence with the North Platte River.

DISCUSSION

GIS techniques were used to tabulate physical and chemical attributes of the study area. To calculate percentages of land area, GIS techniques were used to overlay digitally the irrigated-lands areal-boundary polygons on the surficial geology areal-boundary polygons. During this operation, the GIS calculated the digital union of the overlaying and overlayed polygons, transferred the identities of contributing polygons to the new polygons being formed, calculated the areas of the new polygons, and stored the results as attribute data for each new polygon. After completing

TABLE 1. Summary Statistics for Selected Hydrologic Subbasins in the Study Area, 1988-89.

Subbasin (see Figure 3 for location)	Median Selenium Discharge (kg/day)	Irrigated Area (ha)	Total Area (ha)	Area of Cody Shale (ha)	Area of Alluvial Deposits (ha)	Length of Irrigation Canals (km)	Length of Perennial Streams (km)	Median Total Selenium Concentration (μg/g)				Median Total Selenium Concentrations (μg/L)	
								Non-Irrigated Soil	Irrigated Soil	Big Sagebrush	Alfalfa	Ground Water	Drain Water
Casper Creek	2.61	4,980	59,410	35,940	11,990	193.9	148.7	0.37 (14)*	0.60 (51)	0.20 (13)	1.20 (50)	25.5 (36)	13.50 (18)
Oregon Trail Drain	0.85	1,280	4,140	1,200	1,300	28.5	11.9	–	0.20 (12)	–	0.70 (12)	17.5 (40)	7.25 (12)
Poison Spider Creek	1.96	2,270	28,760	15,960	3,370	80.5	61.0	0.30 (20)	0.30 (26)	0.40 (19)	0.71 (26)	50.0 (25)	4.25 (12)
Poison Spring Creek	0.36	236	10,600	1,250	2,070	22.5	30.2	0.10 (14)	0.45 (6)	0.35 (13)	1.60 (6)	10.0 (6)	8.00 (5)
Bates Creek	0.14	0	6,400	314	2,600	0.0	28.8	0.60 (1)	–	0.40 (1)	–	20.0 (4)	–

*Numbers in parentheses represent number of values.

these calculations, the percentage of irrigated lands overlaying Cody Shale or alluvium derived from Cody Shale was calculated using the stored attributes for each new polygon. The largest concentrations of total selenium in soils were detected in samples of the irrigated soils. Ninety-five percent of the irrigated soils in the study area are located on Cody Shale or on unconsolidated alluvial deposits derived from Cody Shale. Erdman *et al.* (1989, p. 13) determined that the Cody Shale and unconsolidated alluvial deposits derived from Cody Shale have the largest median concentrations of total selenium of any of the geologic formations exposed in the study area. A large number of the irrigated soil samples collected by Erdman *et al.* (1989) from the area south of South Fork Casper Creek contained total selenium concentrations larger than 0.80 µg/g (75th percentile) (Figure 4). Except for two samples, the concentrations of total selenium in nonirrigated and irrigated soil samples collected in the study area were less than 3.3 µg/g norm established for soils from the northern Great Plains (Severson and Tidball, 1979).

Alfalfa samples from a cluster of sampling sites in the area south of South Fork Casper Creek have total selenium concentrations larger than 2.00 µg/g (75th percentile) (Figure 5). This cluster of alfalfa sampling sites is in approximately the same area where many irrigated-soil samples also had total selenium concentrations larger than 0.80 µg/g (75th percentile).

Erdman *et al.* (1989) determined low statistical correlation in comparisons of total selenium concentrations in nonirrigated soil samples with concentrations in big sagebrush samples or of total selenium concentrations in irrigated soil samples with concentrations in alfalfa samples. The largest geometric mean concentrations of total selenium, however, were calculated for both nonirrigated soil samples and big sagebrush samples collected from sampling sites where soil was on Cody Shale.

Ground-water samples with dissolved selenium concentrations larger than 140 µg/L (75th percentile) are from wells scattered throughout the KRPA. Water samples containing concentrations of dissolved selenium larger than 140 µg/L (75th percentile) were collected from a cluster of wells in an area west of the confluence of Casper Creek and the North Platte River. However, also in this area are several wells for which water samples contained dissolved selenium concentrations less than 10 µg/L (25th percentile). The largest median dissolved selenium concentration (50.0 µg/L) in ground-water samples was from wells in the Poison Spider Creek subbasin (Table 1).

The geologic formation in which the well is completed and the depth interval in which the well is open to the formation might have a large effect on the quality of water sampled. Crist (1974) also observed

large seasonal fluctuations of the concentrations of selenium in ground-water samples. Changes in selenium concentrations in water samples in some wells indicated that irrigation water dilutes the concentration of selenium in the ground water during certain times of the year.

Dissolved selenium concentrations ranged from 30 to 2,100 µg/L in 25 percent of the irrigation drain-water samples. Drain-water samples with total selenium concentrations larger than 30 µg/L (75th percentile) were collected at sampling sites in several areas throughout the KRPA (Figure 7). The largest median concentration of dissolved selenium in irrigation drain water was from the Casper Creek subbasin.

A regression model was developed using median selenium discharges from each subbasin as a dependent variable regressed on measured physical and chemical characteristics of the hydrologic subbasins as the independent variables. The physical characteristics consisted of areas of Cody Shale and alluvium derived from Cody Shale, lengths of streams, lengths of irrigation-water delivery canals, and areas of irrigated land, among others. The calculation of these characteristics was accomplished using the GIS as previously discussed. Several relations were evident between median selenium discharge in streams and the independent variables. Median selenium discharges in streams from subbasins in the study area increase as the area of irrigated land in the subbasin increases (Figure 8). In addition, median selenium discharges in streams from the subbasins increase as the lengths of irrigation-water delivery canals increase (Figure 9).

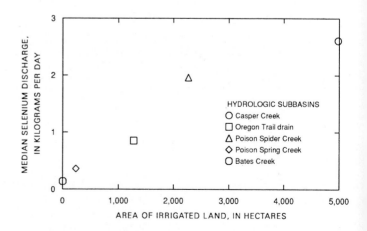

Figure 8. Graph Showing Median Selenium Discharge as a Function of Area of Irrigated Land.

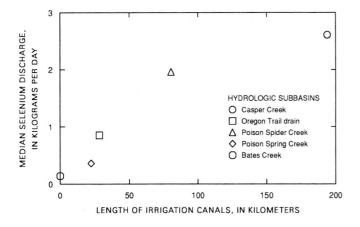

Figure 9. Graph Showing Median Selenium Discharge as a
Function of Length of Irrigation Canals.

Median selenium discharge is correlated highly
with several other measured variables, including area
of Cody Shale or alluvium and total subbasin area.
However, natural removal of selenium by leaching is
unimportant, because the precipitation in the study
area is insufficient to produce effective percolation
through the soil (Larsen, 1951). When the irrigated
land is considered as a percentage of total subbasin
area (Figure 10), median selenium discharges per
hectare of subbasin area increase with increasing percentage of irrigated area, indicating that irrigation,
not total area of the subbasin, controls selenium discharges. A plot of median selenium discharge as a
function of median total soil selenium concentration is
shown in Figure 11. Poison Spring Creek and Bates
Creek subbasins have the smallest irrigated area of
the subbasins examined (Table 1). Although soil samples from Poison Spring Creek (irrigated soil) and
Bates Creek (nonirrigated soil) subbasins, compared
to other subbasins, had relatively large median total
selenium concentrations (Table 1), the median selenium discharges from these subbasins are relatively
small. Increasing irrigation in Poison Spider and
Bates Creeks subbasins might cause a large increase
in median selenium discharges.

Constraints existed on the number of variables
that could be included in the model because of the
small number of subbasins for which median selenium discharges in streams could be estimated.
Because the total number of independent variables
was larger than the number of median selenium discharges, the statistical software available for regression analysis could not perform all possible
regressions; stepwise regression was used as an alternative. Each of the measured independent variables
(Table 1) was evaluated using a stepwise multiple
regression analysis. The largest amount of variability

($R^2 = 0.97$) in median selenium discharges was
explained by the following model:

Log_{10} median selenium discharge = 0.68 Log_{10}
(area of irrigated land, in hectares) + 0.35 Log_{10}
(length of irrigation canals, in kilometers) – 0.08.

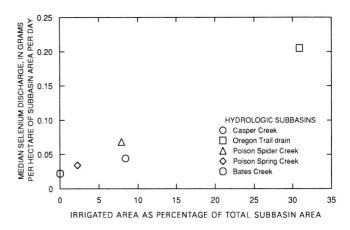

Figure 10. Graph Showing Median Selenium Discharge
Per Hectare of Subbasin Area as a Function of
Percentage of Irrigated Land in a Subbasin.

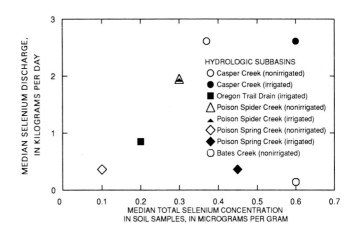

Figure 11. Graph Showing Median Selenium Discharge
as a Function of Median Total Selenium
Concentration in Soil Samples.

Spurious correlation can exist between the area of
irrigated land and length of irrigation canals in a subbasin because irrigated land is associated with irrigation canals. However, investigations of the
geochemical processes that control selenium concentrations in the study area indicate that evaporation
and dissolution processes are important in controlling
selenium concentrations in water resources of the

137

study area. Because evaporation and leaching processes associated with canals could increase selenium discharges from a subbasin, length of irrigation canals has been retained as a significant variable in the regression model.

Using this regression model, predicted selenium yield was calculated for each land section (259 ha) in the study area. The predicted selenium discharge for each section was divided by 259 to obtain selenium yield in grams per day per hectare. The sections that have potential for contributing selenium to tributaries of the North Platte River are shown in Figure 12.

The regression results indicate that the irrigation intensity, as measured by area of irrigated land and length of irrigation-water delivery canals in a subbasin, is responsible for a large part of the selenium discharge from subbasins. The range of total selenium concentration in soil from the study area is typical of total selenium concentration in soils in the northern Great Plains; however, irrigation appears to increase dissolution of minerals containing selenium and to leach selenium from the soil. Seasonal changes in soil moisture, related to irrigation create changing reduction/oxidation conditions within the soil profile. These changing soil conditions affect the solubility and transport.

The use of the GIS has assisted in the integration of data into an estimate of selenium discharge contributions to tributaries of the North Platte River. The use of the GIS assisted in calculating areas of spatial features, such as geologic formations and irrigated land. Point data could be located in specific subbasins by the GIS so that statistical relations could be tested. Finally, the use of GIS provided a means for displaying all data in a standard format, but retained a flexibility that assisted in analytical interpretations.

Improvements in this model could be made with more detailed selenium discharge determinations for a larger number of smaller hydrologic subbasins in the area. For example, discharge could be determined on each of the tributaries to Casper Creek. Such an increase in the number of subbasins for which selenium discharges were determined might increase the number of significant variables in the model.

Use of the model derived from GIS analyses, combined with an understanding of the geochemical processes controlling selenium in the study area, should provide a basis for planning measures to control selenium concentrations in the water resources of the KRPA. The model suggests that by decreasing the irrigated area, the volume of soil from which selenium could be leached would be decreased, thus decreasing the selenium discharges in tributaries to the North Platte River. Although soil and plant data did not explain a large amount of the variation in selenium

discharge, these data were useful for locating areas of large selenium concentrations.

SUMMARY

A geographic information system (GIS) provided information for a regression analysis that was used to help identify areas of potential sources of selenium in the Kendrick Reclamation Project area, Wyoming. The physical and chemical characteristics of selected hydrologic subbasins were used as independent variables in the regression analysis. The analysis was used to evaluate which characteristics contributed to selenium discharges in tributaries to the North Platte River.

The physical characteristics of the study area were determined using GIS techniques, and chemical characteristics were determined from samples of soil, plants, and water. Physical and chemical characteristics were used to evaluate which factors contributed to selenium discharges in tributaries to the North Platte River. Physical characteristics included areas of the Cody Shale and the alluvium, area of irrigated land, length of irrigation-water delivery canals, length of perennial streams, and boundaries of hydrologic subbasins of the major tributaries to the North Platte River. Chemical characteristics included concentrations of selenium in samples of soil, plant material, ground water, and surface water.

Each of the measured independent variables was evaluated, using a stepwise multiple regression analysis. The area of irrigated land and length of irrigation canals within each subbasin are the most important factors in explaining the variability of median selenium loads. The net effect of greater area of irrigated land and length of irrigation-water delivery canals is to increase the volume of soil, and to provide the source of water from which selenium is leached while increasing the selenium discharge in tributaries to the North Platte River.

The results indicate that soils with typical total selenium concentrations can supply large selenium discharges to tributary streams if irrigation intensity, as measured by area of irrigated land and length of irrigation canals, is large. While the approach does not yield estimates of selenium discharges as accurate as those obtained by direct monitoring, the use of GIS-generated information for a regression model provides a method that generally defines areas that might constitute sources of selenium in streams.

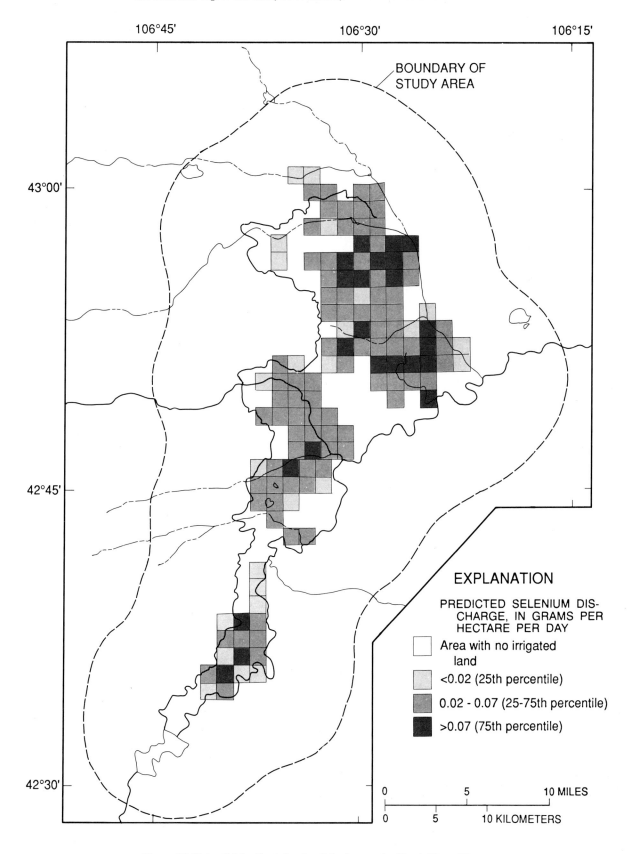

Figure 12. Potential for Contributing Selenium to the North Platte River
from Land Sections in the Study Area.

ACKNOWLEDGMENTS

Funding for this study was provided by the U.S. Department of Interior and the Wyoming Department of Environmental Quality.

LITERATURE CITED

Combs, G. E. and S. B. Combs, 1986. The Role of Selenium in Nutrition. Academic Press, New York, New York.

Crist, M. A., 1974. Selenium in Waters in and Adjacent to the Kendrick Project, Natrona County, Wyoming. U.S. Geological Survey Water-Supply Paper 2023.

Duckson, D. W., Jr., 1989. Land-Use and Water-Quality Relationships in the Georges Creek Basin, Maryland. Water Resources Bulletin 25(4):801-807.

Erdman, J. A., R. C. Severson, J. G. Crock, T. F. Harms, and H. F. Mayland, 1989. Selenium in Soils and Plants from Native and Irrigated Lands at the Kendrick Reclamation Project Area, Wyoming. U.S. Geological Survey Open-File Report 89-628, 28 pp.

Gilliland, M. W. and W. Baxter-Potter, 1987. A Geographic Information System to Predict Nonpoint Source Pollution Potential. Water Resources Bulletin 23(2):281-291.

Hren, Janet, K. S. Wilson, and D. R. Helsel, 1984. A Statistical Approach to Evaluate the Relation of Coal Mining, Land Reclamation, and Surface-Water Quality in Ohio. U.S. Geological Survey Water-Resources Investigations Report 84-4117, 325 pp.

Kubota, J., W. H. Allaway, D. L. Carter, E. E. Cary, and V. A. Lazar, 1967. Selenium in Crops in the United States in Relation to Selenium-Responsive Diseases of Animals. Journal of Agricultural and Food Chemistry 15(3):448-453.

Lageson, D. R., 1980. Geology, in Natrona County, Wyoming. The Geological Survey of Wyoming County Resource Series No. 6.

Larsen, J. H., 1951. Ground Water Conditions of a Part of the Kendrick Project, Natrona County, Wyoming. University of Wyoming, Unpublished Masters Thesis, 56 pp.

National Research Council, 1989. Irrigation-Induced Water Quality Problems. National Academy Press, Washington, D.C.

Peterson, D. A., W. E. Jones, and A. G. Morton, 1988. Reconnaissance Investigation of Water Quality, Bottom Sediment, and Biota Associated with Irrigation Drainage in the Kendrick Reclamation Project Area, Wyoming, 1986-87. U.S. Geological Survey Water-Resources Investigations Report 87-4255, 57 pp.

See, R. B., D. L. Naftz, D. A. Peterson, J. G. Crock, J. A. Erdman, R. C. Severson, Pedro Ramirez, and J. A. Armstrong, 1992. Detailed Study of Selenium in Soil, Representative Plants, Water, Bottom Sediment, and Biota in the Kendrick Reclamation Project Area, Wyoming, 1988-90. U.S. Geological Survey Water-Resources Investigations Report 91-4131, 142 pp.

Severson, R. C., J. G. Crock, and J. A. Erdman, 1989a. Lateral and Depth Variability in Chemical Composition of Soil at the Kendrick Reclamation Project Area, Wyoming. U.S. Geological Survey Open-File Report 89-470, 27 pp.

Severson, R. C., J. A. Erdman, J. G. Crock, and T. F. Harms, 1989b. Listing of Geochemical Data, and Assessment of Variability for Plants and Soils at the Kendrick Reclamation Project Area, Wyoming. U.S. Geological Survey Open-File Report 89-652, 65 pp.

Severson, R. C. and R. R. Tidball, 1979. Spatial Variation in Total Element Concentration in Soil Within the Northern Great Plains Coal Region. U.S. Geological Survey Professional Paper 1134-A, 18 pp.

U.S. Geological Survey, 1985. Digital Line Graphs from 1:100,000-scale Maps. U.S. Geological Survey Data Users Guide 2, 74 pp.

Predictive Modeling of Cattail and Waterlily Distribution in a South Carolina Reservoir Using GIS

John R. Jensen, Sunil Narumalani, Oliver Weatherbee, and *Keith S. Morris, Jr.*
Department of Geography, University of South Carolina, Columbia, SC 29208
Halkard E. Mackey, Jr.
Savannah River Laboratory, Westinghouse Savannah River Company, Aiken, SC 29802

ABSTRACT: Par Pond and L Lake are cooling reservoirs located on the Savannah River Site in South Carolina. Large beds of aquatic macrophytes (primarily cattail and waterlilies) exist in Par Pond and are now beginning to develop in L Lake. Biophysical knowledge about Par Pond was used to develop "environmental constraint criteria" to predict the future spatial distribution of aquatic macrophytes in L Lake. The L Lake biophysical data were placed in a 5- by 5-m raster geographic information system (GIS) and analyzed using Boolean logic. Areas in L Lake which were ≤ 4 m in depth, ≤ 10 percent slope, had a fetch of ≤ 500 m, were on suitable soil, and had water temperatures ≤ 33°C were identified. The final GIS model isolated 26.94 ha that meet all five environmental constraint criteria and are thus suitable aquatic macrophyte habitat (8.76 ha are suitable for cattails, 18.18 ha for waterlilies). Information on the future spatial distribution of aquatic macrophytes in L Lake is valuable when developing lake management plans.

INTRODUCTION

IN THE LAST FEW DECADES, society has begun to recognize that wetlands play a key role in pollution assimilation and flood and sediment control, serve as breeding and nursery grounds for many species of fish and wildlife, and help maintain ground water supplies and water quality (Patrick, 1976; Mitsch and Gosselink, 1986; Dahl, 1990). Unfortunately, recent proposed changes in the definition of "wetland" appear to place freshwater wetlands at increased risk (Lemonick, 1991). Aquatic macrophytes (non-woody plants larger than microscopic size that grow in water) such as cattails and waterlilies have an important influence on the physical and chemical processes in these freshwater ecosystems (Carpenter and Lodge, 1986; Frodge *et al.*, 1990). It is imperative that they be inventoried, studied, and managed wisely (Odum, 1989; Kiraly *et al.*, 1990).

Modern remote sensing techniques, including the use of aerial photography (Wilen, 1990; Patterson and Davis, 1991), aircraft multispectral scanner data (Jensen *et al.*, 1987), and satellite imagery (Gao and Coleman, 1990; Jensen *et al.*, 1991), may be used to accurately inventory freshwater wetlands. Using such technology, it is possible to measure the actual aquatic macrophyte distribution for individual dates of remotely sensed data and then identify growth by performing change detection analysis (Jensen *et al.*, 1991). However, what is even more important for wetland management in certain instances is the ability to predict the future distribution of aquatic macrophytes. Unfortunately, most *predictive* ecology studies simply identify the species composition that should be present with no indication of their future geographic distribution (e.g., Smith and Kadlec, 1985; Van der Valk *et al.*, 1989). Only a few predictive ecological studies have attempted to retain the spatial information [e.g., Liebowitz *et al.* (1989) modeled the loss of marsh in Louisiana; Costanza *et al.* (1990) predicted future wetland landscapes in the Atchafalaya delta; and Davis *et al.* (1990) identified biotic communities and species in need of preservation management (gap analysis)]. Therefore, it is not surprising that modern ecologists feel it is imperative that their models begin to incorporate more spatially distributed biophysical information (Ustin *et al.*, 1991).

To date, no ecological study has attempted to predict the future spatial distribution of cattails and waterlilies in a freshwater lake using spatially distributed biophysical information and geographic information system (GIS) technology. In order to perform such predictive modeling, it is necessary to

- obtain spatially registered biophysical information,
- store the data using the appropriate GIS architecture, and
- specify and apply "environmental constraint criteria" rules.

This paper describes the application of such a system for predictive modeling of the dominant freshwater macrophytes in L Lake in South Carolina.

THE NATURE OF AQUATIC MACROPHYTES IN LAKES AND RESERVOIRS ON THE SAVANNAH RIVER SITE

The Savannah River Site (SRS) is a 777 km² Department of Energy facility located 21 km south of Aiken, South Carolina along the Savannah River (Figure 1). Par Pond (1,000 ha) and L Lake (400 ha) are cooling ponds which have received thermal effluent from nuclear reactor operations. Par Pond has developed extensive beds of persistent and non-persistent aquatic macrophytes since its construction in 1958. Cattail beds (*Typha latifolia*) tend to dominate the areas adjacent to the shore and persist from year to year. Conversely, waterlilies (*Nymphaea odorata*) and lotus (*Nelumbo lutea*) are the dominant surface macrophytes found in deeper water habitats at the outer edge of the cattail beds. These deeper water macrophytes do not persist through the winter. The aquatic macrophytes in Par Pond have been studied for more than 30 years, resulting in detailed knowledge about their growth characteristics and spatial distribution (e.g., Polisini and Boyd, 1972; Gladden *et al.*, 1985; Workman and McLeod, 1990).

Ideally, the knowledge gained about the aquatic macrophyte distribution in Par Pond can be used to predict the growth and spatial distribution of aquatic macrophytes in similar cooling lakes. For example, L Lake (approximately 7000 m long with an average width of 600 m) was built on the SRS in 1985 to receive thermal effluent from L Reactor (Figure 1). It is operated in approximately the same manner as Par Pond. Aquatic macrophytes are now beginning to appear in L Lake through natural invasion and some planting (Workman and McLeod, 1990). This study demonstrates how biophysical aquatic macrophyte knowledge from Par Pond can be used to develop a predictive model of the likely spatial distribution of aquatic macrophytes

PHOTOGRAMMETRIC ENGINEERING & REMOTE SENSING,
Vol. 58, No. 11, November 1992, pp. 1561–1568.

0099-1112/92/5811–1561$03.00/0
©1992 American Society for Photogrammetry
and Remote Sensing

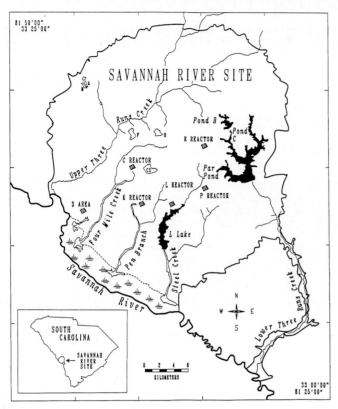

FIG. 1. A map of the Savannah River Site (SRS) in South Carolina. Par Pond and L Lake are cooling reservoirs. Aquatic macrophytes are prevalent in Par Pond which was built in 1958 and are beginning to invade L Lake which was built in 1985.

in L Lake. A geographic information system (GIS) was used to (1) store the important spatial information, (2) query the database using "environmental constraint criteria" rules (Jensen and Christensen, 1986), and (3) employ Boolean logic to predict the type and spatial distribution of aquatic macrophyte habitat in L Lake.

L LAKE AQUATIC MACROPHYTE "ENVIRONMENTAL CONSTRAINT CRITERIA" AND DESCRIPTION OF THE BOOLEAN LOGIC MODEL

Several biophysical factors are believed to have a major influence on the growth and distribution of aquatic macrophytes in Par Pond (Pearsall, 1920; Rorslett, 1984; Harvey *et al.*, 1989; Sand-Jensen, 1989), including

- water depth (D),
- percent slope (%S),
- exposure (fetch) (E),
- soil types (substrate composition) (S),
- water temperature (T),
- wave action, and
- suspended sediment.

Obtaining spatially distributed information on all of these factors is difficult. Nevertheless, it was possible to obtain spatial information for the first five (5) variables. Wave action and suspended sediment distribution in L Lake change rapidly; thus, it was judged impossible to measure and include these variables in the analysis at this time.

The basic assumption was that aquatic macrophytes (A) should be present in a digital map of L Lake if all the "environmental constraint criteria" for depth (D), percent slope (%S), exposure (E), soils (S), and water temperature (T°) were met for each picture element (i.e., pixel) in a raster (matrix) database. The

constraints may be stated in Boolean logic notation as a series of "and" intersections, i.e.,

$$A = D \cap \%S \cap E \cap S \cap T°$$

The logic can also be displayed as a Boolean algebra logic gate (Davies and Hicks, 1975), e.g.,

Application of this algorithm will yield a final map surface, depicting the presence or absence of aquatic macrophytes (A) on a pixel by pixel basis. Figure 2 summarizes the general "environmental constraint criteria" for each variable which can be measured empirically to model the spatial distribution of aquatic macrophytes in L Lake. The following sections describe the nature of these variables and the detailed constraint criteria used in a Boolean algebra predictive model.

WATER DEPTH

Generally, the greater the depth, the less the amount of light available for photosynthesis by aquatic plants (Barko *et al.*, 1982). The clarity of the water is influenced greatly by the amount of suspended sediment and/or organic matter in the water column (Ramsey and Jensen, 1990). Therefore, the ideal situation would be to map the amount of light available at various depths throughout the lake. Because such a map is very difficult to create, water depth was used as a surrogate for the amount of light present in the photic zone. Empirical evidence from 48 transects in Par Pond has shown that cattails usually grow in water up to a depth of approximately 1 metre whereas waterlilies and lotus are primarily observed between depths of 1.1 to 4 metres (Jensen *et al.*, 1991).

Depth was derived from a digital elevation model (DEM) of the region. Initially, four U.S. Geological Survey DEMs centered on L Lake were acquired and edge-matched. Unfortunately, the contour edgematch was poor; therefore, these data were not used. Instead, large scale (1:1,200) engineering drawings with 1-foot contour intervals depicting the topography of the L Lake area prior to its flooding were used as the main data source. Areas where construction had altered the original topography (the dam and discharge canal) were updated using "as-built" 1:1,200-scale engineering drawings. The 1-foot contour lines were digitized, converted into a triangulated irregular network (TIN) model, and finally resampled to a 5- by 5-m Universal Transverse Mercator (UTM) grid of the study area. L Lake is maintained at an almost constant 190-foot water level (± 0.1 foot). A shaded-relief portrayal of the terrain with lighting from the northwest and the 190-foot contour superimposed is shown in Figure 3. The suitability of aquatic macrophyte development in L Lake using 0 to 1-m (cattail) and 1.1- to 4-m (waterlily) depth criteria is shown in Figure 4.

SLOPE

Generally, the less the slope, the greater the probability of aquatic macrophyte development in shallow water (Mackey, 1990). Therefore, a percent slope surface was derived from the digital elevation model using standardized techniques (Muehrcke, 1986; Burrough, 1987). The conversion from a degree to a percentage slope simply involves a tangent function; i.e., tangent (degree) = percentage (Brown *et al.*, 1991). Thus, tan 0° = 0 (0 percent) and tan 45° = 1 (100 percent). Slopes between 45° and 90° are expressed as percentages between 100 percent and in-

Predictive Model of L Lake Aquatic Macrophyte Growth

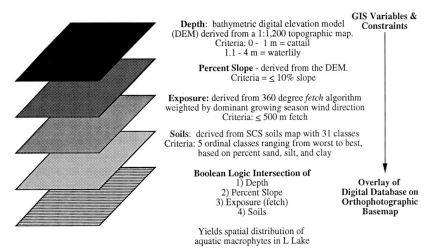

Depth: bathymetric digital elevation model (DEM) derived from a 1:1,200 topographic map.
Criteria: 0 - 1 m = cattail
1.1 - 4 m = waterlily

Percent Slope - derived from the DEM.
Criteria = ≤ 10% slope

Exposure: derived from 360 degree *fetch* algorithm weighted by dominant growing season wind direction
Criteria: ≤ 500 m fetch

Soils: derived from SCS soils map with 31 classes
Criteria: 5 ordinal classes ranging from worst to best, based on percent sand, silt, and clay

GIS Variables & Constraints

Boolean Logic Intersection of
1) Depth
2) Percent Slope
3) Exposure (fetch)
4) Soils

Overlay of Digital Database on Orthophotographic Basemap

Yields spatial distribution of aquatic macrophytes in L Lake

FIG. 2. The Boolean logic and environmental constraint criteria used to develop a predictive model of L Lake aquatic macrophyte growth. All files were geo-referenced to an orthophotographic basemap in a Universal Transverse Mercator (UTM) projection.

L Lake
Shaded Relief
190' Contour

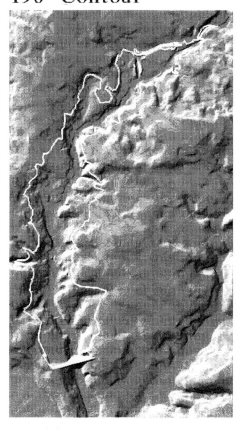

FIG. 3. A shaded relief representation of the L Lake digital elevation model with sunlight from the northwest. The 190-ft contour of L Lake is superimposed. Water goes over the spillway at 190.1 feet.

L Lake
Depth Suitability

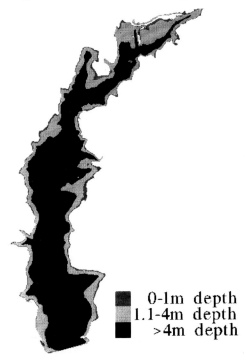

0-1m depth
1.1-4m depth
>4m depth

FIG. 4. The suitability of aquatic macrophyte development in L Lake using 0 to 1 m (cattail) and 1.1 to 4 m (waterlily) depth criteria. All depth information were derived from the digital elevation model.

finity (e.g., a slope of 63.435° is a 200 percent slope; tan 63.435° = 2.0).

Previous *in situ* research on the 48 transects in Par Pond revealed that macrophyte growth occurs predominantly on slopes of ≤ 10 percent (Jensen *et al.*, 1991). Application of this constraint criteria to the digital terrain model (Figure 5) revealed

L Lake
Percent Slope Suitability

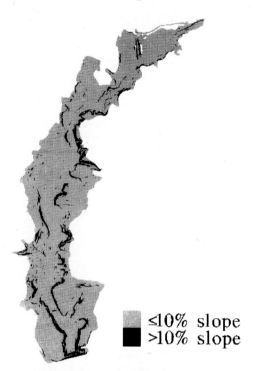

☐ ≤10% slope
■ >10% slope

Fig. 5. Areas in L Lake suitable for the growth of aquatic macrophytes based on percent slope criteria. Pixels with slopes > 10 percent were not suitable.

TABLE 1. RESULTS OF APPLYING BOOLEAN LOGIC OPERATORS TO PREDICT AQUATIC MACROPHYTE DISTRIBUTION IN L LAKE

Boolean Logic Operation	Predicted Distribution (hectares)
Depth (0-1m) cattails	27.33
Depth (1.1-4m) waterlilies	112.45
Depth (0-1m) + Slope (≤10%)	26.99
Depth (1.1-4m) + Slope (≤10%)	103.34
Depth (0-1m) + Slope (≤10%) + Fetch (≤500m)	23.01
Depth (1.1-4m) + Slope (≤10%) + Fetch (≤500m)	59.13
Depth (0-1m) + Slope (≤10%) + Fetch (≤500m) + Soils (good & best)	12.29
Depth (1.1-4m) + Slope (≤10%) + Fetch (≤500m) + Soils (good & best)	25.01
Depth (0-1m) + Slope (≤10%) + Fetch (≤500m) + Soils (good & best) + Temp (≤33°C)	8.76
Depth (1.1-4m) + Slope (≤10%) + Fetch (≤500m) + Soils (good & best) + Temp (≤33°C)	18.18

that slopes > 10 percent occur mainly along the former Steel Creek channel and the northeastern portion of L Lake. When both the depth and slope criteria are used in the predictive model, 26.99 ha of cattail and 103.34 ha of waterlilies should be present in L Lake (Table 1). Slopes > 10 percent have their greatest impact on waterlilies (a loss of 9.11 ha of potential habitat) and only minimal effect on cattails (a loss of 0.34 ha of potential habitat).

EXPOSURE (FETCH)

Fetch may be defined as the unobstructed distance that wind can blow over water in a specified direction (Kinsman, 1984). Generally, the greater the fetch (wind exposure) of a specific site, the higher the probability of larger waves or stronger currents developing and the lower the probability of aquatic macrophyte development (Keddy, 1982). Sculthorpe (1967) and Harvey *et al.* (1989) found that sheltered areas along lake shorelines tend to support more dense communities of aquatic macrophytes because they offer protection from wind and wave action.

As demonstrated by Harvey *et al.* (1989), fetch is often calculated at *in situ* sample locations by averaging the distance in eight specific directions (north, south, east, west, and the nearest point in each quadrant) as shown in Figure 6a. Unfortunately, the L Lake problem is much more complex. In this research it was necessary to compute the fetch for *all* points along the shoreline and within the interior of L Lake. The digital terrain model of the lake was used to identify all the areas interior (recoded as pixels with a value of 0) and exterior (recoded as pixels with a value of 2) to the 190-foot contour (recoded as pixels with a value of 1). Then, a new algorithm was developed

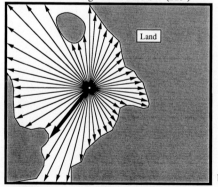

Fig. 6. (a) A traditional method of computing fetch for a specific *in situ* measurement site is to compute the mean of the eight measurements shown (north, south, east, west, and the closest point in each quadrant). (b) The improved fetch algorithm computes the mean from all 360 directions for the pixel in question and weights more heavily the vector associated with the dominant wind direction. In this example the southwest vector (225°) was weighted more heavily in the final fetch computation for the pixel under investigation. It is up to the investigator to determine how heavily to weight the dominant wind direction vector (e.g., 2×, 5×, 10×).

which computed the mean distance in 360° directions for each pixel with a value of 0 or 1 in the database (Figure 6b). This is a much more robust fetch measurement. Furthermore, it is possible to weight the fetch factor by increasing the weight of the vector which is aligned with the dominant wind direction during the growing season of April through October. In this case it was from the southwest; i.e., 225° (determined from Bush Field Airport meteorological records). The equation used to compute fetch at pixel location *i,j* was

$$\text{Fetch}_{ij} = \left[\left(\sum_{a=1}^{360} V_{ija} \right) + w \, (V_{ijd}) \right] / 360$$

where V_{ija} = the distance from the pixel *i,j* to the shore at a specific angle, *a*, which can range from 0 to 360°; V_{ijd} = the distance from the pixel *i,j* to the shore in the direction of dominant wind, *d*; and w = a weight to be applied to the dominant wind direction vector. Because the dominant wind vector was already counted once in the 360° computation, a desired weight of *n* would mean that $w = n - 1$. The application of a 2× weight for the 225° dominant wind direction vector resulted in the creation of an L Lake fetch surface (Plate 1a) ranging from 0 to 800 m.

As expected, pixels in the center of the lake have the greatest fetch (exposure) while those in sheltered coves have much lower exposure. The maximum fetch distance which can be tolerated by macrophytes is dependent on the size and shape of the water body. For example, Welch *et al.* (1988) found that aquatic macrophytes do not grow in areas where average fetch exceeds 850 m in Lake Marion, South Carolina. Fetch data from Par Pond revealed that aquatic macrophytes grow best when ex-

posed to a fetch ≤ 500 m. Plate 1b depicts this ≤ 500 m constraint applied to the original fetch file and reveals that the northern arm of L Lake and several large coves are still suitable for aquatic macrophyte growth. When depth, percent slope, and fetch criteria are used in the predictive model, there should be 23.01 ha of cattail and 59.13 ha of waterlilies in L Lake (Table 1). Fetch ≥ 500 m reduced the distribution of cattails from the preceding predictive model by 3.98 ha while dramatically decreasing the distribution of waterlilies by 44.21 ha.

SOIL TYPE

Spence (1982) suggested that soils play an important role in macrophyte growth. Organic soils generally provide better substrate conditions for the growth of aquatic plants compared to sandy substrate (Wetzel, 1975). Unfortunately, soils in the SRS area are predominantly sandy, with a low percentage of clay and silt. The sand content of the soils in the L Lake region ranged from 50 percent to 99 percent (Soil Conservation Service, 1990). In order to acquire data on soils within the L Lake area, the Soil Conservation Service (SCS) maps of the SRS were digitized.

The SCS description of each of the 31 soil types was used to establish soil texture characteristics. Each soil was then plotted on the soil texture diagram described by Brady (1984). The 31 soil types found in the L Lake area were then ordinally ranked and reclassified into just five categories: worst, poor, moderate, good, and best. These data were then converted from vector to raster format and summarized in the environmental constraint criteria shown in Figure 7. The "good" and "best" soils were considered suitable for macrophyte growth.

If depth, percent slope, fetch, and soils criteria are used in

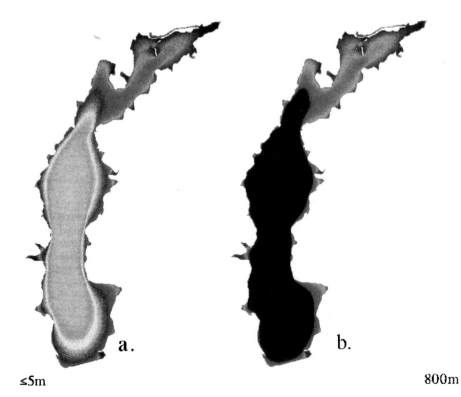

≤5m   800m   ▓ Cattails ░ Waterlilies

PLATE 1. (a) A map of fetch in L Lake computed for each pixel in 360 directions. The vector associated with the dominant wind direction (southwest 225°) was weighted by a factor of 2. The range of fetch in L Lake was from 0 to 800 metres. (b) A map showing those areas in L Lake which have a fetch of ≤ 500 m.

PLATE 2. The suitability of aquatic macrophyte growth in L Lake based on depth, percent slope, exposure (fetch), soils, and water temperature characteristics. If all these criteria are met L Lake should have 8.76 ha of cattails and 18.18 ha of waterlilies in the locations shown.

L Lake
Soil Suitability

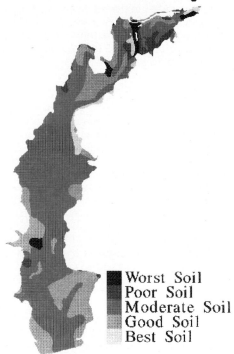

Worst Soil
Poor Soil
Moderate Soil
Good Soil
Best Soil

FIG. 7. A raster version of the soils map recoded into five (5) ordinal classes of soil suitability.

L Lake
Temperature Suitability

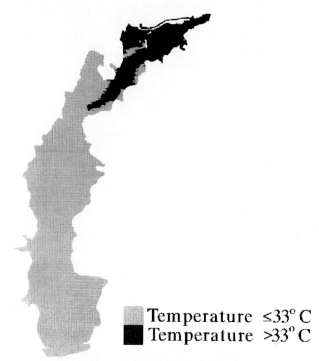

Temperature ≤33° C
Temperature >33° C

FIG. 8. A binary map of the temperature characteristics of L Lake on 18 May 1988, derived through analysis of pre-dawn thermal infrared imagery with the reactor at 50 percent power. Water temperature <33°C negatively impacts aquatic macrophyte growth.

the predictive model, there should be 12.29 ha of cattail and 25.01 ha of waterlilies in L Lake (Table 1). Unsuitable soils reduced the distribution of cattails from the preceding model by 10.72 ha while decreasing the distribution of waterlilies by 34.12 ha. Soil is one of the most important factors affecting the future spatial distribution of aquatic macrophytes in L Lake. As a reservoir ages, the inundated soils change from a terrestrial to an aquatic ecosystem (Gunnison *et al.*, 1985; Kimmel and Groeger, 1986). Additional research is required which documents the rate of change in soil composition as the reservoir ages.

TEMPERATURE

Barko *et al.* (1982), Westbury (1989), and Pip (1989) describe the importance of water temperature on aquatic macrophyte growth. In some instances, warmer temperatures help maintain high productivity levels in parts of the lake, irrespective of the season. Conversely, water that is too warm can inhibit growth. According to Wilde and Tilly (1985), the addition of heated water in Par Pond creates a thermal gradient which may be responsible for spatial variations in macrophyte standing crop. Water temperature > 33°C may inhibit aquatic macrophyte growth.

Daedalus DS-1268 aircraft multispectral imagery acquired on 18 May 1988 were used to map the thermal characteristics of L Lake when the reactor was operating at 50 percent power (the norm). The thermal channel (8 to 14 μm) of the data was rectified to a 5- by 5-m spatial resolution using a nearest neighbor resampling algorithm (Jensen, 1986). The data were calibrated to be within ±0.2° C of the apparent temperature of the terrain. Temperatures in the lake were found to range from 28.5°C to 39.3°C, and were classified into 11 classes (not shown). Portions of L Lake with temperatures > 33°C were judged less suitable for macrophyte growth (Figure 8). When depth, percent slope,

fetch, soils, and water temperature criteria are used in the predictive model, there should be 8.76 ha of cattail and 18.18 ha of waterlilies in L Lake (Plate 2; Table 1). Basically, with the reactor running at half power, much of the upper portion of L Lake would have reduced aquatic cattail and waterlily habitat.

ANALYSIS

The L Lake aquatic macrophyte environmental constraint criteria discussed were applied to the GIS database using the Boolean algebra logic shown diagrammatically in Figure 2. If all areas of L Lake were ≤ 4 m in depth, ≤ 10 percent slope, completely sheltered with a fetch of ≤ 500 m, on good soil, and had a water temperature ≤ 33°C, then aquatic macrophytes would theoretically occupy the entire lake. This is not the case, however, as each of the aforementioned variables reduces the amount of aquatic macrophytes which may be present in L Lake. Plate 2 identifies the areas in L Lake which meet the depth, percent slope, exposure (fetch), soil, and water temperature environmental constraint criteria.

Table 1 summarizes the cumulative effect on the aquatic macrophytes as each constraint is applied. Depth was used to depict all possible areas of macrophyte occurrence based on Par Pond species distribution. Cattails found in 0 to 1 m of water would occupy 27.33 ha while waterlilies in 1.1 to 4 m of water would occupy 112.45 ha. Subtracting areas with > 10 percent slope removed very little cattail area (now 26.99 ha) and only 8 percent of the waterlilies (now 103.34 ha). Fetch > 500 m reduced cattail area by 15 percent (down to 23.01 ha) and waterlilies by 43 percent (down to 59.13 ha). Soils that did not fall in the "good" and "best" categories had the greatest impact on the total hectares of probable macrophyte habitat. Areas of probable cattail habitat declined to 12.29 ha (reduction of 47 percent), while waterlilies dropped to 25.01 ha (reduction of 58 percent). The water temperature criteria caused a further reduction of areal coverage of each macrophyte species — cattails declined to just 8.76 ha and waterlilies to 18.18 ha. Plate 2 reveals that, if all the environmental constraint criteria were met, an area 26.94 ha (cattails = 8.76 ha; waterlilies = 18.18 ha) would be suitable for aquatic macrophyte growth. This represents a conservative estimate of the areal extent of aquatic macrophytes which may grow in L Lake. Most of these areas occur in sheltered regions of L Lake. The variable that had the greatest effect on the predicted macrophyte distribution was soils. If the moderate soil suitability category were included and all the other constraints were held constant, there would be 71.75 ha of aquatic macrophytes possible in L Lake (a 166 percent increase).

CONCLUSION

This research placed *spatially* distributed *biophysical* information in a GIS and queried it using Boolean logic to predict the type and spatial distribution of aquatic macrophytes in a cooling reservoir. In this example, all environmental constraints were assumed to be equally weighted. Additional biophysical *in situ* measurement is required to obtain information on the relative importance of these constraints so that weights can be applied in the Boolean logic. Research is underway to develop a logistic multiple regression model (e.g., Pereira and Itami, 1991) of Par Pond using the same biophysical variables discussed. When this is completed, it should be possible to extract coefficients (weights) for each of the variables used which should refine the L Lake predictive model. It is important to note that aquatic macrophytes are developing in many of the areas identified by the model (Plate 2). Aerial photography of L Lake is acquired frequently and can be used to quantitatively document the accuracy of the predictions. Monitoring has also revealed that, as the model predicted, the best aquatic macrophyte growth to date has been in protected coves and along the southeastern shoreline of L Lake. The GIS modeling techniques described here can be of value when predicting where freshwater aquatic macrophytes could occur in the future. Additional environmental constraint criteria can be included in the Boolean logic model to identify those aquatic macrophyte resources at risk due to the new wetland definition. Finally, if a "no net loss of wetlands" policy remains in effect (National Wetlands Policy Forum, 1988), the predictive techniques can be used to identify potential sites for new wetlands development projects (i.e., mitigation).

ACKNOWLEDGMENTS

The information contained in this report was developed under Contract No. DE-AC09-89SR18035 with the U.S. Department of Energy. Steven Riley and Joel Griffin of the SRS/WSRC assisted in the field data collection. All digital image processing and GIS analyses were performed using ERDAS and/or ARC-Info software.

REFERENCES

Barko, J. W., D. G. Hardin, and M. S. Matthews, 1982. Growth and Morphology of Submersed Freshwater Macrophytes in Relation to Light and Temperature, *Canadian Journal of Botany*, 60(6):877-887.

Brady, N. C., 1984. *The Nature and Properties of Soils*, Macmillan Co., N.Y., 750 p.

Brown, N., C. Smith, and S. Strater, 1991. *Field Guide*, ERDAS, Inc., Atlanta, Georgia, pp. 169–182.

Burrough, P. A., 1987. *Principles of Geographical Information Systems for Land Resources Assessment*. Clarendon Press, Oxford, pp. 49–52.

Carpenter, S. R., and D. M. Lodge, 1986. Effects of Submersed Macrophytes on Ecosystem Processes, *Aquatic Botany*, 26:341–370.

Costanza, R., F. H. Sklar, and M. L. White, 1990. Modeling Coastal Landscape Dynamics, *BioScience*, 40(2):91–107.

Dahl, T. E., 1990. *Wetlands Losses in the United States 1780's to 1980's.* U.S. Department of Interior, U.S. Fish & Wildlife Service, Washington, D.C., 21 p.

Davies, H. G., and G. A. Hicks, 1975. *Mathematics for Scientific and Technical Students*, Longman, N.Y., pp. 388–401.

Davis, F. W., D. M. Stoms, J. E. Estes, J. Scepan, and J. M. Scott, 1990. An Information Systems Approach to the Preservation of Biological Diversity, *International Journal of Geographical Information Systems*, 4(1):55–78.

Frodge, J. D., G. L. Thomas, and G. B. Pauley, 1990. Effects of Canopy Formation by Floating and Submergent Aquatic Macrophytes on the Water Quality of Two Shallow Pacific Northwest Lakes, *Aquatic Botany*, 38:231–248.

Gao, T., and T. L. Coleman, 1990. Use of Satellite Spectral Data for Mapping Aquatic Macrophytes and Nutrient Levels in Lakes, *International Geoscience & Remote Sensing Symposium (IGARSS)*, Washington, D.C., pp. 109–116.

Gladden, J. B., M. W. Lower, H. E. Mackey, W. L. Specht, and E. W. Wilde, 1985. *Comprehensive Cooling Water Study, Volume XI: Ecology of Par Pond, Savannah River Plant.* Savannah River Lab, E. I. DuPont de Nemours & Co., (#DP-1697-11), Aiken, S.C., 289 p.

Gunnison, D., R. M. Engler, and W. H. Patrick, 1985. Chemistry and Microbiology of Newly Flooded Soils: Relationship to Reservoir Water Quality, *Microbial Processes in Reservoirs* (D. Gunnison, editor), W. Junk Publishers, Boston, Mass.

Harvey, R. M., J. R. Pickett, and R. D. Bates, 1989. Environmental Factors Controlling the Growth and Distribution of Submersed Aquatic Macrophytes in Two South Carolina Reservoirs, *Lake and Reservoir Management*, 3:243–255.

Jensen, J. R., 1986. *Introductory Digital Image Processing: A Remote Sensing Perspective*, Prentice Hall, Inc., Englewood Cliffs, N.J., 278 p.

Jensen, J. R., and E. J. Christensen, 1986. Solid and Hazardous Waste Disposal Site Selection Using Digital Geographic Information System Technologies, *Science of the Total Environment*, 56(1986):265–276.

Jensen, J. R., S. Narumalani, O. Weatherbee, and H. E. Mackey, 1991. Remote Sensing Offers An Alternative for Mapping Wetlands, *GeoInfo Systems*, October, pp. 46–53.

Jensen, J. R., E. W. Ramsey, H. E. Mackey, E. J. Christensen, and R. R. Sharitz, 1987. Inland Wetland Change Detection Using Aircraft MSS Data, *Photogrammetric Engineering & Remote Sensing*, 53(5):521–529.

Keddy, P. A., 1982. Quantifying Within-Lake Gradients of Wave Energy: Interrelationships of Wave Energy, Substrate Particle Size and Shoreline Plants in Axe Lake, Ontario, *Aquatic Botany*, 14:41–58.

Kimmel, B. L., and A. W. Groeger, 1986. Limnological and Ecological Changes Associated with Reservoir Aging, *Reservoir Fisheries Management: Strategies for the 80's* (G. E. Hall and M. J. Van Den Avyle, editors), Southern Div. American Fisheries Society, Bethesda, Maryland, pp. 103–109.

Kinsman, B., 1984. *Wind Waves: Their Generation and Propagation on the Ocean Surface*, Dover Publications, N.Y., 676 p.

Kiraly, S., F. H. Cross, and J. D. Buffington, 1990. Overview and Recommendations, *Federal Coastal Wetland Mapping Programs*, U.S. Fish & Wildlife, Biology Report #90, Washington, D.C., (18), pp. 1–9.

Leibowitz, S. G., F. H. Sklar, and R. Costanza, 1989. Perspectives on Louisiana Land Loss Modeling, *Freshwater Wetlands and Wildlife*, (R. R. Sharitz and J. W. Gibbons, editors), U. S. Dept. of Energy, Report #8603101, Washington, D.C., pp. 729–753.

Lemonick, M. D., 1991. War Over the Wetlands, *Time*, 27 August 1991, p. 53.

Mackey, H. E., 1990. Monitoring Seasonal and Annual Wetland Changes in a Freshwater Marsh with SPOT HRV Data, *Technical Papers, ACSM-ASPRS Convention*, pp. 283–292.

Mitsch, W. J., and J. G. Gosselink, 1986. *Wetlands*, Van Nostrand Reinhold, N.Y., 537 p.

Muehrcke, P. C., 1986. *Map Use: Reading, Analysis & Interpretation.* J. P. Publications, Madison, Wisconsin, pp. 255–256.

National Wetlands Policy Forum, 1988. *Protecting America's Wetlands: An Action Agenda.* The Conservation Foundation, Washington, D.C.

Odum, E. P., 1989. Wetland Values in Retrospect, *Freshwater Wetlands and Wildlife* (R. R. Sharitz and J. W. Gibbons, editors), U.S. Dept.of Energy, Report #8603101, Washington, D.C., pp. 1–8.

Patrick, R., 1976. The Role of Aquatic Plants in Aquatic Ecosystems, *Biological Control of Water Pollution* (J. Tourbier and R. W. Pierson, Jr., editors), University of Pennsylvania Press, Philadelphia, pp. 53–59.

Patterson, G. G., and B. A. Davis, 1991. *Distribution of Aquatic Macrophytes in 15 Lakes and Streams in South Carolina.* U.S. Geological Survey Publication #89-4132, Washington, D.C., 58 p.

Pearsall, W. H., 1920. The Aquatic Vegetation of the English Lakes, *Journal of Ecology,* 8(3):163–201.

Pereira, J., and R. M. Itami, 1991. GIS-Based Habitat Modeling Using Logistic Multiple Regression: A Study of the Mt. Graham Red Squirrel, *Photogrammetric Engineering & Remote Sensing,* 57(11):1475–1486.

Pip, E., 1989. Water Temperature and Freshwater Macrophyte Distribution, *Aquatic Botany,* 34:367–373.

Polisini, J. M., and C. E. Boyd, 1972. Relationships Between Cell-wall Fractions, Nitrogen, and Standing Crop in Aquatic Macrophytes, *Ecology* (53):484–488.

Ramsey, E., and John R. Jensen, 1990. The Derivation of Water Volume Reflectances from Airborne MSS Data Using *In situ* Water Volume Reflectances, and a Combined Optimization Technique and Radiative Transfer Model, *International Journal of Remote Sensing,* 11(6):979–998.

Rorslett, B., 1984. Environmental Factors and Aquatic Macrophyte Response in Regulated Lakes — A Statistical Approach, *Aquatic Botany,* 19:199–220.

Sand-Jensen, K., 1989. Environmental Variables and Their Effect on Photosynthesis of Aquatic Plant Communities, *Aquatic Botany,* 34:5–25.

Sculthorpe, C. D., 1967. *The Biology of Aquatic Vascular Plants,* Edward Arnold, London, 610 p.

Smith, L. M., and J. H. Kadlec, 1985. Predications of Vegetation Change Following Fire in a Great Salt Lake Marsh, *Aquatic Botany,* 21:43–51.

Soil Conservation Service, 1990. *Soil Survey of Savannah River Plant Area and Parts of Aiken, Barnwell, and Allendale Counties, South Carolina,* U.S. Dept. of Agriculture, Washington, D.C., 127 p.

Spence, D. H. N., 1982. The Zonation of Plants in Freshwater Lakes, *Advances in Ecological Research* (A Macfadyen and E. D. Ford, editors), 12:37–125.

Ustin, S. L., C. A. Wessman, B. Curtiss, E. Kasischke, J. Way, and V. C. Vanderbilt, 1991. Opportunities for Using the EOS Imaging Spectrometers and Synthetic Aperture Radar in Ecological Models, *Ecology,* 72(6):1934–1945.

Van der Valk, A. G., C. H. Welling, and R. L. Pedersen, 1989. Vegetation Change in a Freshwater Wetland: A Test of a priori Predictions, *Freshwater Wetlands and Wildlife* (R. R. Sharitz and J. W. Gibbons, editors), U. S. Dept. of Energy, Report #8603101, Washington, D.C., pp. 207–217.

Welch, R. A., M. M. Remillard, and R. B. Slack, 1988. Remote Sensing and Geographic Information System Techniques for Aquatic Resource Evaluation, *Photogrammetric Engineering & Remote Sensing,* 54(2):177–185.

Westbury, M., 1989. *L-Lake Habitat Formers: L-Lake/Steel Creek Biological Monitoring Program Jan. 1986 - Dec. 1988,* for E. I. du Pont de Nemours & Company by Normandeau Associates Inc, Report #NAI-SR-77, 110 p.

Wetzel, R. G., 1975. *Limnology,* Saunders College Publishers, Philadelphia, 743 p.

Wilde, E. W., and L. J. Tilly, 1985. *Influence of P-Reactor Operation on the Aquatic Ecology of Par Pond: A Literature Review,* U.S. Dept. of Energy, Savannah River Lab, Washington, D.C., 127 p.

Wilen, B. O., 1990. U.S. Fish & Wildlife Service's National Wetlands Inventory, *Federal Coastal Wetland Mapping Programs,* U.S. Fish & Wildlife, Biology Report #90, Washington, D.C., (18), 9–20.

Workman, S. W., and K. W. McLeod, 1990. *Vegetation of the Savannah River Site: Major Community Types.* Savannah River Ecology Laboratory, Aiken, S.C., 137 p.

SECTION 5

Forestry

Overview

Articles selected for this section are on three important topics in forestry including forest cover change, timber supply, and forest management planning. In the first article, Maclean et al. present a case study on how to use GIS to quantify forest cover change over time. The second article, written by Baskent and Jordan, illustrates the use of a spatial wood supply model which uses both wildlife habitat values and extraction economics. Susilawati and Wier describe, in the last article, GIS applications in forest land allocation, forest monitoring, and road design.

Suggested Additional Reading

Chuvieco, E., and R. G. Congalton, 1989. Application of Remote Sensing and Geographic Information Systems to Forest Fire Hazard Mapping. Remote Sensing of the Environment. 29(2):147-159.

Mohie el Deen, F. A., 1991. The Use of GIS, GPS, and Satellite Remote Sensing to Map Woody Vegetation in Kazgail Area, Sudan. ITC Journal. 1991(1):11-18.

Shelstad, D., L. Queen, and D. French, 1991. Describing the Spread of Oak Wilt Using a Geographic Information System. Journal of Arboriculture. 17:192-199.

Using GIS to Estimate Forest Resource Changes

A case study in northern Michigan

By Ann L. Maclean, David D. Reed, Glenn D. Mroz, Gary W. Lyon, and Thomas Edison

Forest managers as well as the general public have had a continuing interest in the level and quality of forest management on small nonindustrial private forestlands. Those in forest industries have been mostly concerned about future supplies of wood fiber, but the nation as a whole is concerned about the effects that healthy forest stands have on such things as air quality, esthetic quality, wildlife habitat, and water quality. Timely regeneration following harvesting is obviously key to the concerns of both groups. Use of remotely sensed data, computer-assisted image processing, and geographic information systems (GIS) technology allows quick and efficient evaluation of the resource base. This article presents a case study illustrating the application of these technologies.

Huron Pines Project

In the late 1980s, resource professionals within the 11-county Huron Pines Resource Conservation and Development District (HPRCDD) in the northern Lower Peninsula of Michigan (*fig. 1*) were concerned that there had been an increase in harvesting activity, particularly on privately held land. An expansion of traditional wood manufacturing and wood-burning electrical power generation in the late 1980s led to increased demand for wood fiber in the region. Historical inventory information indicated a surplus (i.e., greater growth than removals) of both jack and red pine within the Huron Pines area, which was undoubtedly a reason for the industrial expansion. However, field professionals became concerned that the increased demand was accelerating harvesting activity on private lands without giving adequate attention to regeneration.

A project was undertaken to assemble existing regional forest inventory information and to assess changes in the resource base since 1986, particularly on privately held forestlands. The analysis was facilitated through computer-assisted interpretation of Landsat Thematic Mapper imagery and the use of GIS technology. The classified imagery was registered with ownership maps from county tax records in 1986 and 1989 to quantify harvesting rates of jack and red pine during that time.

Existing Inventory Information

In 1980, the USDA Forest Service published information on the timber resources of the northern Lower Peninsula of Michigan (Jakes 1982). This inventory was updated in 1987 using the STEMS growth model (Belcher 1981) and records of pulpwood (Blyth and Smith 1985), sawlog (Blyth et al. 1981), and veneer (Raile and Smith 1983) removals along with removal rates indicated in the 1980 survey (Smith and Hahn 1986). The baseline analysis information came from the 1980 survey and the 1987 update. Michigan is currently being resurveyed—fieldwork is scheduled for completion in 1992, with publication of results scheduled in 1994.

The 11-county HPRCDD covers 4.1 million acres, with 3.0 million acres classified as commercial forestland (i.e., land capable of producing 20 cubic feet per acre per year of annual growth under management and not withdrawn from timber use). Of this total, 40,300 acres are under the control of forest industry; 500,000 acres are owned by farmers (defined as operators of 10 or more acres from which the sale of agricultural products is greater than $50 annually); 236,500 acres are owned by miscellaneous private corporations; and 867,800 acres are owned by other private individuals. The remainder is held by federal, state, or county governments.

The two cover types of concern are jack pine (*Pinus banksiana*) and red pine (*Pinus resinosa*). There are approximately 354,300 acres of jack pine stands within the 11-county region. The net annual growth of growing stock on these stands is 10,140,000 cubic feet, with an estimated rate of removals in 1980 of 5,846,000 cubic feet. Between 1980 and 1987 the area of jack pine expanded by an estimated 6,000 acres, with a corresponding increase in growing stock of 43,929,000 cubic feet.

Red pine covers approximately 176,200 acres in the 11-county area, with a net annual growth of 11,617,000 cubic feet and an estimated removal rate of 793,000 cubic feet per year in 1980. Growing stock of red pine probably increased from 199,064,000 to 311,300,000 cubic feet from 1980 to 1987, partially due to an

Reprinted by permission of the publisher from *The Journal of Forestry*, December 1992, Vol. 90, No. 12., "Using GIS to Estimate Forest Resource Changes", Ann L. Maclean, David D. Reed, Glenn D. Mroz, Gary W. Lyon, and Thomas Edison.

estimated increase of 2,000 acres in the red pine cover type.

In addition to increased acreage for both species, volume rose because growth exceeded harvest in the 1980–87 period. An estimated 42% of the jack pine and 93% of the red pine growth was retained in the stands and not lost to removals or natural mortality.

Changing Resource Utilization

With the projected increases in jack pine and red pine acreages, and with the low level of removals (especially red pine), this region was recognized as having a resource base that could sustain expansion of forest products manufacturing. As a result, several wood products companies in the region expanded their operations. Also, other companies recognized that low-quality wood could be used as fuel for electrical generation. LFC Power Systems Corporation established a biomass power generation plant at Hillman, Michigan, and Central Michigan University in Mt. Pleasant converted to biomass power generation.

As demand for wood fiber in the region increased, soil conservation districts reported no increase in requests for seedlings by private landowners. If private lands were being replanted, an increase in seedling orders would have been expected. This led field professionals to suspect that regeneration activity might be seriously lagging behind harvesting, especially on privately held lands.

Current Harvesting

To quantify the harvest rate for the area, Landsat Thematic Mapper (TM) scenes were acquired for June 8, 1986, and July 2, 1989. A 100 x 100 kilometer (3,861 square mile) subset of each scene, the center of the 11-county district, was interpreted. Although this provided information for the entire area, the HPRCDD requested that analyses be concentrated on two selected townships within each county (to minimize interpretation and analysis time). By sampling townships within counties, ownership information from county plat books could be used to identify areas of public and private ownership. Presque Isle County was not included in the analysis because the purchased TM scenes did not include a sufficient area of that county, and budget

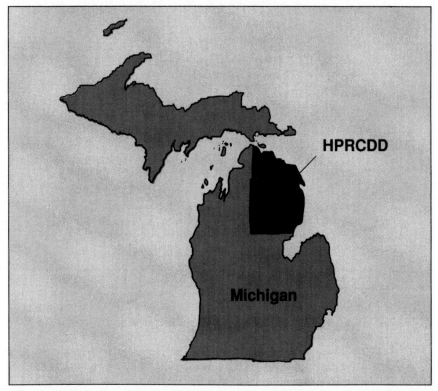

Figure 1. **The Huron Pines Resource Conservation and Development District (HPRCDD), Lower Peninsula, Michigan.**

constraints prohibited acquiring additional imagery.

Within the 20 sampled townships, areas were classified according to cover type in 1986 and 1989. Although the same cover type scheme developed by the Forest Service inventory was used in the image classification, classes derived from the imagery do not correspond exactly with those used in the inventory. The Forest Service classifies forest stands into fixed timber types (jack pine, red pine, white pine, white spruce, etc.) as indicated by the dominant species. However, it is not possible to assign clear classifications to mixed stands from the TM scenes. Stands that were predominantly jack or red pine were identified with high accuracy, but stands that contained a mixture of both species, or that included large white pine or hardwood components, were classified as mixed pine.

Prior to classification, the imagery was georeferenced to the Universal

Table 1. GIS cross-tabulation for a sample township in Crawford County, Michigan (diagonal numbers represent areas of no change; off-diagonal elements indicate change in land cover from 1986 to 1989).

1986 classification	1989 classification (acres)					
	Water	Red pine	Hardwoods	Nonforested	Jack pine	Mixed pine
Water	60					
Red pine		1,470		1,366		
Hardwoods			8,492			
Nonforested				3,230	1,024	227
Jack pine				702	5,425	
Mixed pine						1,044

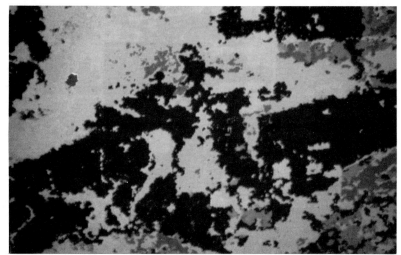

Figure 2. **Forest cover map from 1986 Thematic Mapper imagery for a sample township in Crawford County, Michigan (cyan = water, yellow = nonforested land, orange = jack pine, red = red pine, brown = mixed conifers, green = hardwoods).**

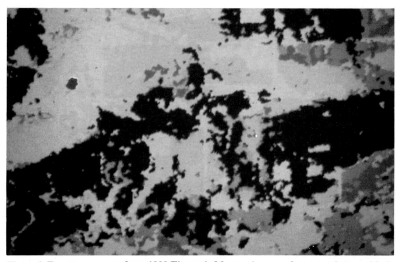

Figure 3. **Forest cover map from 1989 Thematic Mapper imagery for a sample township in Crawford County, Michigan (cyan = water, yellow = nonforested land, orange = jack pine, red = red pine, brown = mixed conifers, green = hardwoods).**

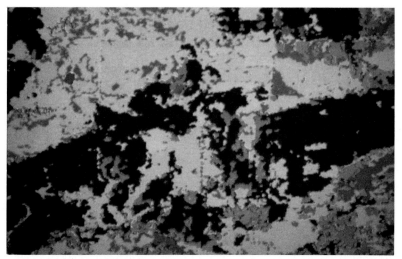

Figure 4. **Pictorial representation of GIS cross-tabulation for a sample township in Crawford County, Michigan. Turquoise indicates removals of jack and red pine. Light green indicates areas replanted to jack or red pine. Cyan = water, yellow = nonforested, orange = jack pine, red = red pine, brown = mixed conifers, and green = hardwoods.**

Transverse Mercator (UTM) coordinate system to permit overlaying the classified imagery with ownership boundaries. The imagery was then transformed using a feature-oriented principal components technique. This transformation (Maclean 1987) permits the cover types of interest (i.e., jack and red pine) to be highlighted. A supervised classification, using a maximum likelihood classification algorithm, divided the imagery into jack pine, red pine, mixed pine, hardwood, nonforested, wetlands, and agriculture. The results were field-checked, and an accuracy assessment was performed as outlined by Congalton et al. (1983).

The resulting classifications (*figs. 2, 3*) were then overlaid with ownership boundaries to identify private and public ownerships. The boundaries were digitized from US Geological Survey 7-1/2-minute quadrangle sheets. Using ERDAS GIS software, the 1986 and 1989 forest type classifications for the townships were then cross-tabulated, which permits two GIS files of the same area to be rapidly and accurately compared to determine areas where land cover class has changed (i.e., jack pine to nonforested). This information can be presented in pictorial form (*fig. 4*) or tabular form (*table 1*).

Of the 4.1 million acres within the 11-county area, the 20 sampled townships covered 431,700 acres, a little more than 10% of the total. The Forest Service inventory, by contrast, actually sampled less than 1% of the area. Within counties, the proportion of land area included ranged from 7% to almost 15%. In each county, the proportion of the timber resource included in the sampled townships varied considerably. In Alpena County, 13% of the sampled area accounted for 61% of the jack pine area reported by the Forest Service. Eight percent of the total land area in Oscoda County was sampled, but it represented only 3% of the total jack pine area.

Overall, the sampled townships contained 16% of the total jack pine resource (57,300 acres) in the HPRCDD, 11% of the red pine resource (19,100 acres), and 53,300 acres of mixed pine stands. Of the 57,300 acres of jack pine, 11,500 acres (20.1%) were in private ownership. For red pine, 3,200 acres or 17% were on private land while 26,200 (49%) of the mixed pine stands were privately owned.

Cover type changes were investigated by comparing TM images from the summers of 1986 and 1989. Of particular interest were 1986 stands in jack, red, or mixed pine that were nonforested (open) by 1989. Such areas had been harvested, burned, or otherwise disturbed to remove the overstory within those three years. By knowing the percentages of red and jack pine stands included in the 20 townships and their total area, the area within each county that had been converted from pine forest to nonforest was estimated using cluster sampling (Cochran 1977).

Results indicated that 77,163 acres within the 10 sampled counties were converted from jack, red, or mixed pine forest in 1986 to a nonforested condition in 1989. This is 15% of the total jack pine and red pine acreages in the 10 counties as estimated by the Forest Service: 28,000 acres (36%) in private ownership and 49,163 acres in public ownership.

While removal of 15% of the jack pine and red pine cover types in a three-year period is certainly a warning flag, some mitigating circumstances must be considered. In 1980, the Forest Service estimated than 75,400 acres of jack pine (approximately 20% of the total) were more than 60 years of age. Height growth of jack pine can be expected to slow after age 50, and stand breakup begins at age 60 on poorer sites (Burns and Honkala 1990). In addition, 18,400 acres of jack pine (of a total of 30,900 acres removed on public land) were estimated to be in Crawford County, most of it as part of the Kirtland warbler recovery program (pers. commun., S. Tayler, Michigan Department of Natural Resources, 1991).

Replanting Efforts

While the condition of the resource and associated management activity are each partly responsible for the high removal rate in jack and red pine stands between 1986 and 1989, the real questions concern the number of acres being replanted to conifer cover types, and whether this indicates a long-term reduction of the resource base in this region. While the harsh site conditions in this region do not guarantee the success of regeneration programs, state and federal management practices dictate that harvested stands be naturally or artificially

regenerated. Success is monitored, and further silvicultural efforts are undertaken if stand establishment does not occur. However, few private owners would undertake such extensive replanting efforts, probably decreasing regeneration success.

A harvest of 28,000 acres over the three-year period averages out to 9,300 acres per year on private land that should be regenerated to maintain the forest resource base. For some sites it is possible to rely on natural regeneration, but the largest proportion of sites—particularly those currently in jack pine—are so harsh that natural regeneration is difficult, and some sort of artificial regeneration will probably be needed to ensure success. To

---

The long-term resource base in this region may be in jeopardy

---

replant the entire 9,300 acres at common spacings would require 6–11 million seedlings per year. The soil conservation districts (SCD) in the 11-county area, the primary source for seedlings by private owners, are distributing around 2 million seedlings per year. This is far short of the number required to replant the total harvested area. Area resource managers also indicate that much of the SCD seedlings are used to regenerate abandoned fields, not the cutover sites identified here. Thus it appears that there is a decrease in the conifer land base of the region.

It is not clear what the future resource base in this region will be. The results of this study indicate a need to explore policy options designed to encourage replanting jack pine or red pine following harvesting on privately owned lands. The current forest survey of Michigan will provide more information concerning regeneration efforts and current resource age structure when results are available in 1994.

Conclusion

In recent years, forest utilization has greatly increased throughout the 11-county HPRCDD. Regionwide forest in-

ventory information is available from the Forest Service, but it is several years old (1980) and updated information will not be available for another 2–3 years. Remotely sensed cover type imagery supplied inexpensive information for a specific time period with which to evaluate changes in forest removal rates. A geographic information system provided rapid processing of this information and a link between satellite imagery and landowner information from tax records. This investigation of removal patterns on both public and private lands confirmed the beliefs of resource professionals that the long-term resource base in this region may be in jeopardy. ■

Literature Cited

BELCHER, D.W. 1981. The user's guide to STEMS: the stand and tree evaluation and modeling system. USDA For. Serv. Gen. Tech. Rep. NC-70. 49 p.

BLYTH, J.E., and W.B. SMITH. 1985. Pulpwood production in the north central region by county, 1983. USDA For. Serv. Resour. Bull. NC-85. 25 p.

BLYTH, J.E., J. ZOLLNER, and W.B. SMITH. 1981. Primary forest products industry and timber use, Michigan, 1977. USDA For. Serv. Resour. Bull. NC-55. 54 p.

BURNS, R.M., and B.H. HONKALA. 1990. Silvics of North America: 1. Conifers. USDA For. Serv. Agric. Handb. 654. 675 p.

COCHRAN, W.G. 1977. Sampling techniques. Ed. 3. John Wiley & Sons, New York. 428 p.

CONGALTON, R.G., R.G. ODERWALD, and R.A. MEAD. 1983. Assessing Landsat classification accuracy using discrete multivariate analysis statistical techniques. Photogramm. Eng. & Remote Sens. 49:1671–78.

JAKES, P.J. 1982. Timber resource of Michigan's northern Lower Peninsula, 1980. USDA For. Serv. Resour. Bull. NC-62. 120 p.

MACLEAN, A.L. 1987. Evaluation of Thematic Mapper imagery for forest type mapping and its use in a computerized hazard-rating system. PhD thesis, Univ. Wisc., Madison. 172 p.

RAILE, G.K., and W.B. SMITH. 1983. Michigan forest statistics, 1980. USDA For. Serv. Resour. Bull. NC-67. 101 p.

SMITH, W.B., and J.T. HAHN. 1986. Michigan's forest statistics, 1987: an inventory update. USDA For. Serv. Gen. Tech. Rep. NC-112. 44 p.

Ann L. Maclean is assistant professor, and David D. Reed and Glenn D. Mroz are professors, School of Forestry and Wood Products, Michigan Technological University, Houghton; Gary W. Lyon is resource operations manager, Connor Forest Industries, Ironwood, Michigan; and Thomas Edison is resource specialist, Montmorency Soil and Water Conservation District, Atlanta, Michigan.

Spatial wood supply simulation modelling

by E.Z. Baskent[1] and G.A. Jordan[2]

Abstract

Conventional wood supply simulation models have been found inadequate in both calculating true assessments of wood supply and in translating management strategies into on-the-ground management design. These models treat forests as aspatial entities and are unable to include economic and wildlife considerations in management design and calculation of wood supply. This paper presents and discusses the design and construction of a GIS-based (geographic information system) spatial wood supply model. The model uses geographic distribution of stand development types and stages and their change over time to control harvesting and calculate wood supply based on extraction economics ($/m^3) and wildlife habitat values (opening size and green-up). The paper points out that: a spatial model is capable of producing harvest schedules and forest performance indicators that reflect geographic context as well as condition of stands; a GIS database is more important in spatial modelling than GIS technology; harvest blocks are the basic geographic element in spatial modelling; a spatial model provides a truer assessment of wood supply; and stand topology makes it relatively easy to integrate wildlife and timber management.

Key words: Timber, wildlife, forest management, GIS, simulation model, wood supply

Résumé

Les modèles courants de simulation des approvisionnements en bois se révelent inadéquats à la fois pour calculer les évaluations précises d'approvisionnement en matière ligneuse et pour transposer les stratégies d'aménagement en conception réelle sur le terrain. Ces modèles traitent la forêt en tant qu'entités spatiales et ne peuvent inclure les considérations économiques et fauniques dans la conception de l'aménagement et le calcul de l'approvisionnement en bois. Cet exposé présente et discute de la conception et de l'élaboration d'un modèle spatial d'approvisionnement en bois à partir d'un SIRS (systèmes informatisé de références spatiales). Le modèle utilise la distribution géographique des peuplements en fonction de leur type et de leur stade de développement ainsi que de leurs modifications en fonction du temps pour contrôler la récolte et calculer l'approvisionnement en bois à partir des coûts d'extraction ($/m^3) et des valeurs de l'habitat faunique (superficie des coupes et zones de protection). Cet exposé souligne: qu'on modèle spatial peut produire des cédules de récolte et des indices de la performance de la forêt qui reflètent aussi bien le contexte géographique que les conditions du peuplement; qu'une banque de données SIRS est plus importante pour la modélisation spatiale que la technologie SIRS; que les blocs exploités constituent l'élément géographique de base en modélisation spatiale; qu'un modèle spatial procure une évaluation plus juste de l'approvisionnement en bois; et que la topologie du peuplement est relativement facile à intégrer dans l'aménagement pour la faune et le matière ligneuse.

Introduction

The focus of forest management for wood supply is the creation and maintenance of a timber inventory that will, over the long term, sustain a harvest level that satisfies wood demand. Creating and maintaining a long-term wood supply requires the design and implementation of intervention plans. Given an initial timber inventory, these plans specify methods, amounts, timings and locations of interventions, in the form of harvest and silviculture schedules, that will control forest change in a calculated fashion and create and maintain a timber inventory capable of supporting a desired wood supply. Harvest schedules are designed to extract wood from a forest in a predictable, economic and timely fashion but, in combination with silviculture schedules, are also designed to control forest change. Control is possible, since harvesting, like silviculture, alters stand development patterns and timing of development. For example, clearcutting an overmature stand recycles the area to a new regenerating stand sooner than if the stand were left to develop naturally. Havesting, depending upon amount, timing and locations,

will have long-lasting effects on composition of stand development types and stages in a forest. Assuming every stand clearcut in a forest would react in a predictable fashion with respect to timing and pattern of development, the potential for controlling forest composition over time exists. Since timber inventory at any point in a forest's development is a direct function of mixture of stand development types and stages, clearcut harvesting, like silviculture, is a powerful tool in forest management for wood supply.

However, wood supply in a forest is a fraction of total timber inventory, determined by both numerical and geographic distribution of stand development types and stages and their change over time. The change over time in numerical distribution of stand development types and stages (number of hectares of each) has a direct effect on wood supply in terms of available merchantable and economically harvestable quantities. For example, in Eastern Canada the available supply of softwood sawlogs in a forest over time would be determined by the pattern of change in number of hectares of spruce and fir stands in mature to overmatter development stages. Many hectares of pure mature spruce stands would provide large economic harvests. Many hectares of overmature spruce would contain lesser quantities and larger harvesting costs. Many hectares of mature fir-spruce stands would provide limited quantities at very high harvesting costs. Like numerical distribution, the change over time in geographic distribution of stand development types and stages, both in terms of absolute and relative locations,

[1]Research Assistant in the Faculty of Forestry, Karadeniz Technical University, Trabzon, Turkey. Currently a graduate student at the University of New Brunswick, Fredericton, NB.
[2]Associate Professor in the Faculty of Forestry, University of New Brunswick, BSN 44555, Fredericton, New Brunswick E3B 6C2.
This paper presents an elaboration of the concept and implementation of spatial modelling as introduced at GIS'91.

Reprinted by permission of the publisher, The Canadian Institute of Forestry, from *The Forestry Chronicle*, December 1991, Vol. 67, No. 6.

also has a direct effect on wood supply. Simply, how merchantable and economically harvestable wood quantities are geographically located and positioned relative to one another determines their cost of extraction (roadside to mill). Widely distributed amounts will be more expensive (road cost per cubic metre) than those that are geographically concentrated. All said, wood supply is limited to those merchantable timber quantities that are also economically extractable. A true assessment of a forest's sustainable wood supply, therefore, must consider geographic as well as numerical distribution of stand development types and stages and their change over time. Spatial distribution of timber inventory is fundamental information in wood supply analysis.

Unfortunately, contemporary wood supply simulation models are characterizied by a strictly aspatial approach which limits their usefulness in management design. Recall that wood supply is limited to those merchantable timber quantities that are economically harvestable and extractable. Simulation models such as FORMAN (Wang 1982) used in Eastern Canada, forecast a forest's timber growing stock based on numerical distribution of its stand development types and stages. FORMAN is an improvement of WOSFOP (Wood Supply and Forest Productivity Model) developed by Hall (1977), and accommodates multiple stand development types, but forecasts are based on forest strata[3], as opposed to individual stands. Thus, FORMAN does not permit geographic control of harvest and silviculture schedules, nor the incorporation of wood supply economics based upon geographic distribution of stand development types and stages. Later simulation models, for example TSAM (Timber Supply Assessment Model) by Rose et al. (1984) and TREES (Timber Resources Economic Estimation System), attempted to model the forest in a more spatial manner but were severely constrained by a lack of spatial data.

While contemporary wood supply simulation models provide ample opportunity to design and test harvest and silviculture schedules involving consideration of stand development types and stages, they commonly lack any ability to include geographic control of schedules. This lack of geographic control adds to the distortion of forecast wood supply. For the most part, comtemporary wood supply simulation models are unable to use geographic distribution in computing wood supply or in controlling the design of harvest and silviculture scehdules. While they are sufficient for defining and developing management design strategies, today's wood supply simulation models are insufficient for on-the-ground management design on a practical scale.

While the state of wood supply modelling was explained by the state of timber industry databases when models were first programmed, an inventory constraint no longer exists. Timber inventories of the time were characterized by a computer-based numerical component and a map-based geographic component. The lack of geographic information in digital form precluded its use in wood supply modelling. Today, digital timber inventories with both numerical and geographic components are not only feasible, but commonplace. By 1980, software solutions to digital storage and processing of geographic information and hardware advances in data processing and storage capacities made possible the commercialization of geographic information system (GIS) technology (Lee and Zhang 1989). For example, using a commercial GIS, the Province of New Brunswick completed in 1987 a province-wide inventory begun in 1982.

Geographic information systems, while sharing much in common with contemporary database management system (DBMS) technology, are better suited to the problem of forest management design. Their ability to store, process and display numerical and geographic information, i.e. spatial data, in a unified fashion distinguish them from other database technologies. From a forest management design perspective, these spatial database management systems are significant in two ways. First, a GIS maintains a timber inventory database containing geographic location of stand development types and stages. Secondly, the relative geographic positions of stand development types and stages are available via the topological relationships among stands, i.e. what's next to what, stored in a timber inventory database. Since, as already discussed, change over time in numerical and geographic distribution of stand development types and stages has a direct effect on wood supply in terms of merchantable quantities economically harvestable and extractable, GIS is a significant technology in wood supply modelling.

As Jordan and Erdle (1989) noted, forest management, and spatial wood supply modelling in particular, requires data that describe both the present and future forest resource in terms of conditions and geographic distribution. These spatial data are formed of two components: locational attributes describing the absolute and relative positions(topology) of stands, and thematic attributes describing the conditions of these stands (Fig. 1). In the widely used Universal Transverse Mercator (UTM) coordinate system, location is represented by one or more x, y coordinate pairs. Topological relationships define the relative positions of stands and are expressed in terms of connectivity, adjacency and enclosure (Masry and Lee 1988; Aronoff 1989). Thematic data refer to non-spatial attributes that identify stand development types and stages and other stand conditions. Because GIS offers the unique capability of accommodating spatial data, it is prerequisite technology for assembling and processing a forest inventory suitable for economically meaningful wood supply modelling.

Until the 1980's and the commercialization of GIS technology, the spatial aspect of wood supply modelling received little attention. Wood supply models employing a GIS, i.e., spatial models, are very sparse. Even with the state of GIS technology and the proliferation of GIS-based timber inventories, GIS is rarely used as a decision-making tool in management design. Jordan and Erdle (1989) noted that in New Brunswick a wood supply simulation model had been linked to a GIS database, but the approach only served to map harvest schedule results. Lougheed (1988), on the other hand, developed a road network design model with the TimberRAM model using a GIS. The model found the minimum haul cost ($/m^3) with respect to minimum relative distance from each stand to a given mill based on user generated road networks for five, five-year periods. The model, however, did not consider the effect of relative geographic position of individual stands in calculating haul costs and economic wood supply, nor can model results be easily

---

[3]A stratum is an aggregate of forest stands which have at least age, current condition (e.g., volume, species mix) and pattern of future development in common. Stands of a stratum do not have to be geograpically contiguous.

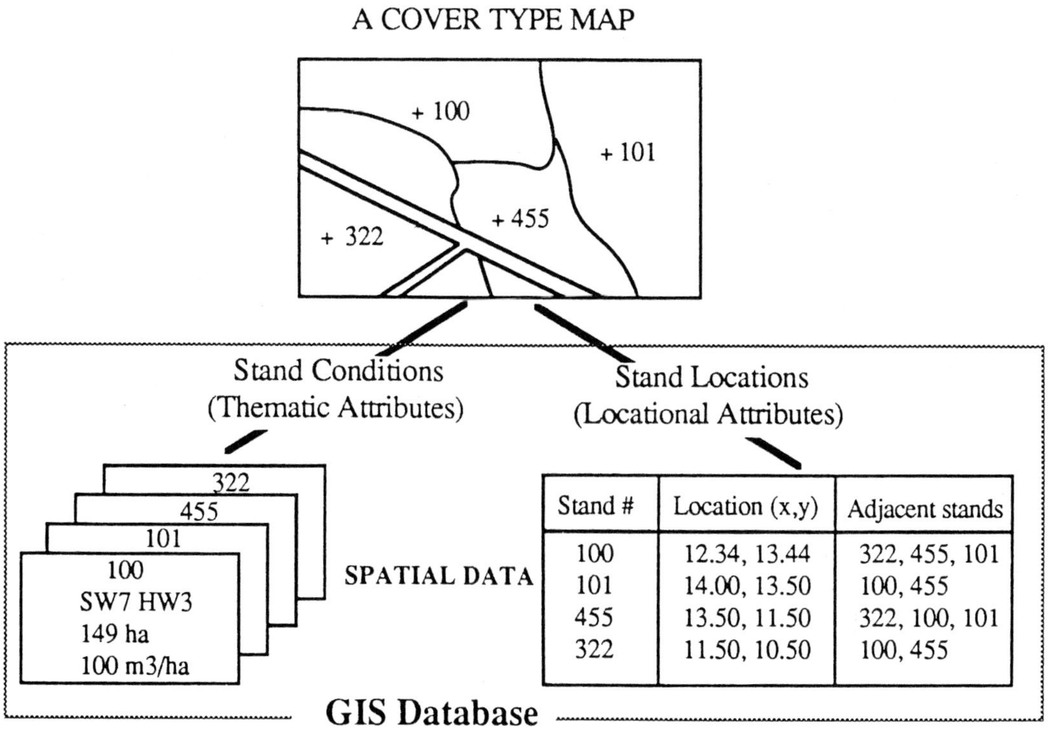

A COVER TYPE MAP

Figure 1. Spatial data describing both conditions and locations (absolute and relative) of stands (adapted from Jordan and Erdle (1989)).

translated into on-the-ground actions because of stand aggregation. A more recent model, the Harvest Schedule Generator (HSG) wood supply model developed by Moore (1989), models a forest on an individual stand basis. While the model uses a GIS database for data input and display, it offers no control over geographic distribution of harvest. Similarly, other GIS-based wood supply modelling efforts have concentrated on simply mapping forest schedules or have failed to use the geographic distribution of stand development types and stages in controlling the harvest and in calculating wood supply.

This paper describes a GIS-based spatial wood supply simulation model that calculates 'wood supply' based on extraction economics and wildlife habitat values by controlling the geographic distribution of harvest.

A Spatial Wood Supply Model Design

A spatial model differs from aspatial models in two important respects. First, a spatial model would incorporate and consider the geographic location of each forest stand as opposed to aggregating stands into stand classes. Second, a spatial model would incorporate relative positions of stands in controlling geographic distribution of harvest. Both features would be incorporated using the stand-by-stand attributes, geographic locations and relative positions maintained in a GIS database. These features are crucial in management design for wood supply. It is important to identify the geographic position of stands so that harvest schedules can be translated into on-the-ground management design, while relative stand positions are important in controlling the geographic distribution of harvest with extraction costs and wildlife habitat values in mind. Thus, besides numerical distribution, as in aspatial models, geographic distribution of stand development types and stages may be considered in a spatial model. Inclusion of geographic distribution permits a truer assessment of a forest's sustainable wood supply calculated on the basis of geographic control of harvest, extraction economics and wildlife considerations.

The economics of harvest extraction dictate that operable volume amounts have to be geographically concentrated as a function of relative positions of stand development types and stages. Widely dispersed amounts will be more expensive than those that are geographically concentrated. Traditional North American harvest operations have long recognized this reality and develop harvest schedules consisting of temporally and spatially distributed harvest blocks that group neighbouring stands together for harvest so that operable volume is geographically concentrated around a shared operating road[4]. The approach is used to control operating road cost ($/m^3) — one component of extraction cost — by forming and scheduling for harvest only harvest blocks that have an acceptable operating road cost. Therefore, for a spatial model to control harvesting and calculation of wood supply in the manner just described, it would require that each stand be characterized, not only by its state, but by that of its neighbours as well. In other words, volume that is economically extractable, termed "extractable volume" in this paper, is determined by neighbourhood level factors. This means that the relative positions of a forest's stand development types and stages are used to quantify operating road cost.

A stand's operating road cost at any time can be quantified by defining both the area and the total operable volume of itself and its neighbouring stands. Specifically, the operating

---

[4]Operating road refers to the temporary road network within a harvest block.

road cost associated with a stand can be determined as the total operating road construction cost, plus a portion of the fixed cost to move construction equipment to the stand, divided by the total operable volume of the stand and its neighbours. Therefore:

$$\text{Operating road cost} \atop (\$/m^3) = \frac{(\$/km \times \text{operating road length}) + \text{fixed cost}}{\text{total operable volume } (m^3)} \quad (1)$$

The number and state of operable stands that are present in a neighbourhood at any time influence the size of the neighbourhood, its total operable volume and the length of operating road required. Specifically, the operating road cost in a neighbourhood changes as a function of changes in component stands' development types and stages. As the volume concentration increases in a neighbourhood, its operating road cost decreases and vice versa, provided the size of a neighbourhood remains the same.

A proper assessment of a forest's wood supply will be based upon both operability and extractability. Not all operable forest growing stock is economically extractable. Extractable wood must not exceed a certain maximum $/m^3

operating road cost. In other words, stands have to be both operable and extractable to contribute to wood supply and to be available for harvesting. Figure 2b shows the total operable volume (volume concentration) change of a stand and its neighbours over time and Fig. 2a shows the associated change in operating road cost of harvesting that volume. For example, if the stand and its operable neighbours of 20 ha were harvested when volume totalled 2 000 m^3, $6 of road cost would be borne by each cubic metre harvested. At some point the stand (and its neighbours) would become unavailable for harvesting because of excessive extraction cost, even though a certain operable volume would exist. For example, if the economics of the day indicated that $5 was the maximum acceptable cost of extracting one cubic metre and that harvest had to be concentrated in an area greater than 25 ha then, to be available, a stand (and its neighbours) would have to have 2 500 m^3 operable volume concentration. In this example this state is not reached until the stand is age 55. This means that, while the stand has operable volume from age 45 onwards (Fig. 2c and 2d), this volume is not economically available for harvesting until age 55. Likewise, beyond age 130 the stand (and its neighbours) no longer have the minimum volume concentration of 1600 m^3 although

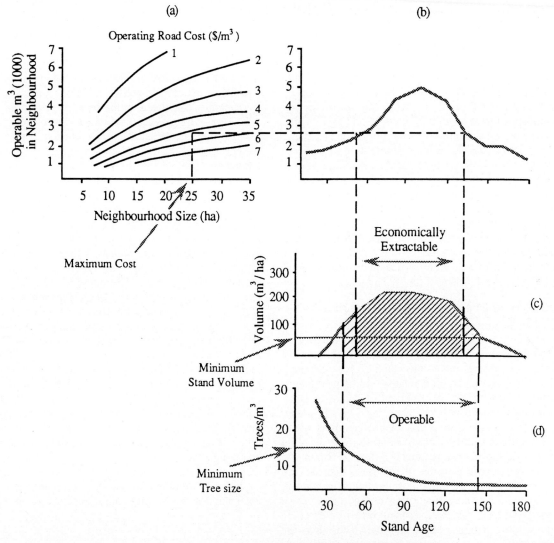

Figure 2. Extractability of a forest stand determined by operable volume concentration and area of its neighbours.

the stand has operable volume. So, in fact, the stand does not contribute to wood supply before age 55 nor after age 130, as opposed to 45 and 145 if extraction economics are ignored. Windows of extractability could be likewise defined for all stands in a forest as a function of change in neighbouring stand development types and stages. At any point in a forest's development, its wood supply, i.e. extractable volume, would be calculated by totalling operable volume of all individual stands falling within their windows of extractability. Obviously, if at some point in a forest's development, the geographic distribution of its stand development types and stages was such that few hectares of stands fell within windows of extractability, wood supply would be low, whereas if many hectares of stands fell within windows of extractability, wood supply would be higher.

To complicate the wood supply issue further, not all extractable volume is available due to wildlife habitat considerations. Habitat considerations limit the size and availability of harvest blocks. In many jurisdictions, harvest block sizes are limited for this reason (in New Brunswick to 125 ha). This means that blocks in a harvest period must not exceed a specified area, nor can adjacent blocks, in consecutive periods, be harvested. These constraints obviously have the potential to reduce further wood supply across a forest at any time since they reduce the number of harvest blocks available for harvest.

Either volume concentration or operating road cost values, calculated for each stand in a forest, as well as maximum opening size and adjacency delay[5] constraints, provide a spatial wood supply modelling basis for controlling the geographic distribution of harvest schedules. Stand queuing strategies (rules along with limits) based upon operating road cost can be used to provide control. For example, stands and their neighbours could be queued for harvest to minimize operating road cost ($/m^3) across a forest for each planning period. With this queuing strategy, stands can become not only operable but also economically extractable before harvest. Harvesting is concentrated in geographic areas where there is more operable volume, i.e. more volume per hectare and thus less operating road cost. Or, stands could be queued to maximize volume concentration (m^3). With this strategy, havesting is concentrated in geographic areas where there is greatest operable volume, regardless of operating road cost. Another strategy might be aimed at capturing volume loss in a fashion analogous to mortality capture strategies common in aspatial models. Here, harvesting is mostly concentrated in geographic areas where the stands are of older development stages. Further, maximum operating road cost, maximum block opening size and adjacency delay limit block availability for harvest and thus effect the geographic distribution of harvest. Since each strategy would result in a different distribution of harvest over time across a forest and a different response, any spatial wood supply model implementing such strategies would provide useful mechanisms for controlling the geographic distribution of harvest schedules and the forest.

The physical implementation of a spatial model would require a forest to be modelled on a neighbourhood-by-neighbourhood basis using stand level information. This is a marked departure from contemporary aspatial models, and reflects the fact that actual harvest schedule decision making in North America is not hectare-based, or stand-based, but harvest block-based. However, FORMAN still provides a reasonable and generally accepted framework for wood supply simulation modelling and was therefore employed here in executing the physical design of a spatial model. The approach taken was to expand its basic design to employ stand attributes and neighbourhood detail to permit geographic control of harvest and calculation of wood supply. While stand attributes would be directly available to the spatial model in a GIS database, neighbourhood detail would not. It is possible, though, to assemble the necessary neighbourhood detail using the stand topology maintained in a GIS database. However, it was felt that the process should be done external to the spatial model, since neighbourhoods are fixed for a given forest and need not be generated for each forecast. A separate program, called CALCADJ.F, was developed to assemble lists of neighbouring stands for all stands in a forest. The model, called GISFORMAN (Geographic Information System linked FORest MANagement), and CALCADJ.F were programmed using the FORTRAN programming language, the ARC/INFO™ GIS, New Brunswick's provincial timber inventory database and the UNIX™ operating system running on a SUN 4/110 workstation. Subsequent sections provide details.

Forming Neighbourhoods

As depicted in Fig. 3, ARC/INFO organizes spatial data into digital maps called coverages consisting of thematic and locational attribute components (ESRI 1989). The thematic attributes are stored and managed by the INFO DBMS in a two-dimensional file where individual features are represented as rows and corresponding feature attributes are represented as columns. Likewise, locational attributes are simply structured with coordinates and topology in two-dimensional tables stored and managed by ARC. Numerical identifiers, e.g. Stand#, are used to relate stand attributes, stand centroids (the center point of a stand), stand topology and arc topology tables. Each arc is defined by its starting and ending nodes and stores the identification of the Stand# on the left and right sides of the arc. For example, in Fig. 3, the thematic attributes of stand 104 are linked to stand and arc topology via the identifies, Stand# and Arc#.

These stand attribute, centroid and topological information are significant since they provide the basis to identify stands that are immediately adjacent (i.e., contiguous) or, alternatively, within proximity of one another (i.e., non-contiguous). For example, immediately adjacent stands can be determined from the stand and arc topology tables via Stand# and corresponding Arc#s. Alternatively, stands whose centroids are within a specified distance of one another also form a neighbourhood. Thus, contiguous stand neighbourhoods may be identified and formed by examining the topology of each forest stand, while non-contiguous neighbourhoods are achieved by moving a window of specified size from stand to stand over the whole forest. The contiguous approach will be illustrated in this paper.

---

[5]An adjacency delay is a wildlife habitat consideration that specifies a time delay between harvest of adjacent areas.

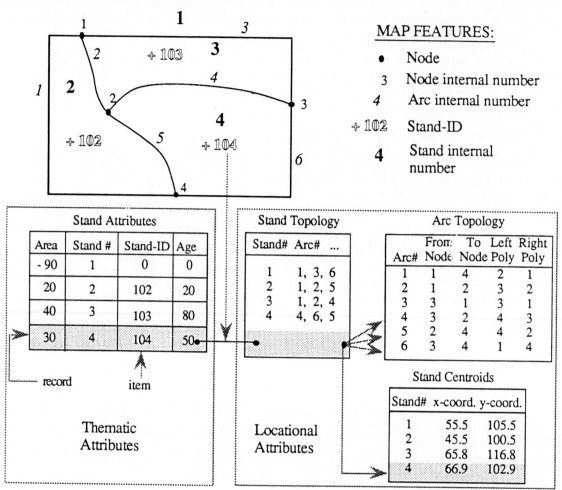

Figure 3. Identifying the relationships among thematic and locational data using the ARC/INFO spatial data model (modified from Aranoff (1989)).

Contiguous Neighbourhood Formation

As already hinted, topology provides the basis for forming stand neighbourhoods in a forest. In a contiguous neighbourhood-forming approach each stand is considered as a target stand at the center of a group of stands. A target stand's immediately adjacent neighbours are determined to form initially a contiguous neighourhood (Fig. 4). If harvest block size constraints, either minimum and/or maximum, are involved, additional contiguous stands are added or existing stands are eliminated from the initial neighbourhood to form the final contiguous neighbourhood. The specific procedure involves looking for a new stand adjacent to the most recently added stands until the minimum area constraint is reached. On the other hand, stands are eliminated from the initial neighbourhood if its size is greater than the given maximum. This is done by choosing the stand that is farthest away from the target stand or sharing the smallest arc length with the target stand. For example, Fig. 4 depicts how a contiguous neighbourhood for stand 103 could be identified given a maximum block size of 85 ha. First, all the adjacent stands (touching) of stand 103 are identified by looking at stand topology. These stands are, including the target stand: 155, 133, 99, 77, 61, and 65. All these stands comprise 135 ha — the initial block size. Next, since this size exceeds the maximum block size of 85 ha, some stands have to be eliminated. Stand 77 is the first candidate to be eliminated and stand 155 is the second since they are farthest away and share shortest arc lengths with stand 103. Eliminating stands 77 and 155 results in a total area of 80 ha, 5 ha less than the maximum. Finally, stands 133, 99, 65, 61, along with the target stand, from a contiguous neighbourhood. In like fashion, contiguous neighbourhoods for all stands in a forest could be formed.

A Neighbourhood Formation Program

Given the approaches developed in the previous section, a computer program, CALCADJ.F, was implemented that creates two stand neighbourhood files using ARC/INFO spatial data files. Both serve as input to the GISFORMAN model. The first, a user-named harvest block configuration file, identifies and forms all stand neighbourhoods in a given forest. Specifically, it stores for each stand in an ARC/INFO covertype coverage the identity (Stand-ID, Stand#) of either the contiguously adjacent stands within minimum and maximum block sizes or the non-contiguous stands within a specified window of search area. The second file, named ADJ$FWO, stores only the identity of immediately adjacent stands of each stand in an ARC/INFO covertype coverage. GISFORMAN uses the block configuration file to calculate volume concentration (m³), operating road length (km),

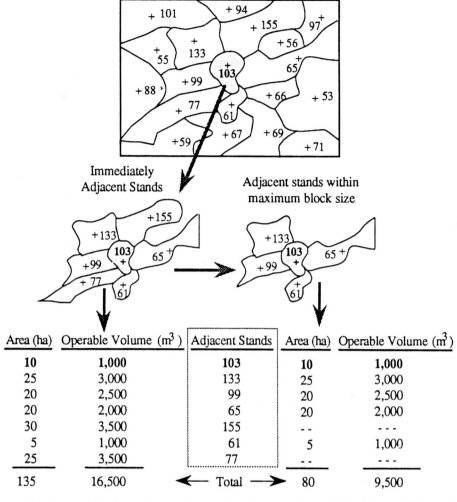

A COVER TYPE MAP

Area (ha)	Operable Volume (m³)	Adjacent Stands	Area (ha)	Operable Volume (m³)
10	**1,000**	**103**	**10**	**1,000**
25	3,000	133	25	3,000
20	2,500	99	20	2,500
20	2,000	65	20	2,000
30	3,500	155	--	---
5	1,000	61	5	1,000
25	3,500	77	--	---
135	16,500	← Total →	80	9,500

Figure 4. Characterizing a stand by the operable volume of surrounding stands that form a contiguous block within a neighbourhood of specified size.

block mortality loss and operating road cost ($/m³) associated with each forest stand. On the other hand, the model uses the adjacency file to apply the maximum opening size and adjacency delay constraints.

The GISFORMAN Model

GISFORMAN was programmed as a stand-based, spatial wood supply forecasting model. Like its aspatial counterparts, the model projects forest response to alternative management strategies and calculates and displays forest performance indicators in tabular form. However, since the model is stand-based it can group stands into harvest blocks, apply an operating road cost limit, maximum opening size and adjacency delay constraints and display forecast results in map form. It is these characteristics that make it possible to use the model to generate location specific, geographically controlled harvest schedules and wood supply calculated on the basis of extraction economics. Figure 5 summarizes the GISFORMAN modelling process. The process has four primary stages, data input, harvest control, forecasting, and results output. These are explained in more detail in the following sections.

Data Input

GISFORMAN was developed around two basic data inputs: numerical and geographic. Although the modelling process is stand-by-stand and GIS database-based, numerical input is mostly traditional. It consists of yield curve data and treatment cost data for each stand. However, the model is unique in requiring additional numerical and geographic stand information. The latter includes the harvest block configuration and stand adjacency files discussed earlier, while numerical data files — yield curve, treatment cost and the stand information — are discussed at length in sections that follow. A summary of all input data required by the model is provided (Table 1).

Yield Curve, Silviculture Cost and Stand Information Data Files

The yield curve data file includes sets of curves reflecting the natural and treated yield of stands over time, product percentages and harvest costs. Curves are derived using different estimation procedures according to the requirements of the organization performing the analysis and are outside the scope of this study. A curve set consists of 5 separate

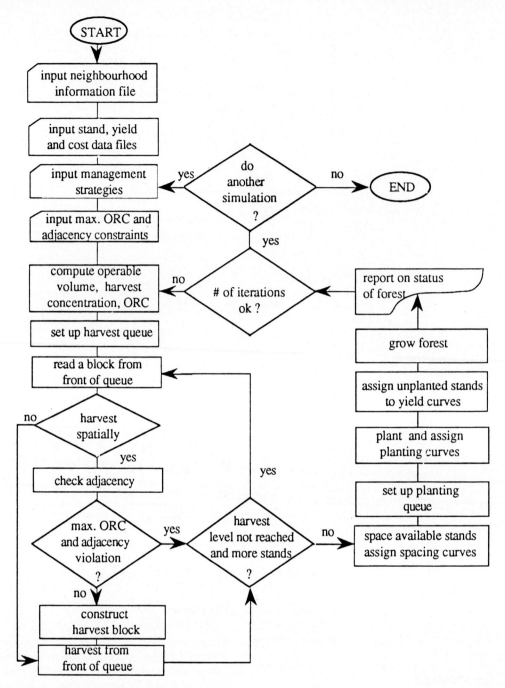

Figure 5. Flowchart of GISFORMAN modelling process.

curves: primary volume (m³/ha) (usually softwood in New Brunswick), secondary volume (m³/ha) (usually hardwood), product % (e.g., sawlogs), harvest cost ($/m³), and other (e.g., a partial cutting response yield curve). One yield curve set is required for each development type to which stands will be assigned. Each yield curve is a record in the yield curve file and assigned a yield curve set ID and number of vertices (volume-at-age points). Additionally, a spacing response yield curve and operability limits are assigned to each primary volume curve.

The Silviculture cost data file includes treatment costs ($/ha) associated with converting a stand from any present pattern of development to any future pattern of development.

These costs can include those associated with basic silviculture treatments designed to improve primary volume production, such as planting and precommercial thinning, as well as maintenance level treatments employed to maintain precut productivity levels.

The stand information data file stores thematic data associated with each forest stand. Each stand is considered as a record and its associated attributes are considered as items. Items of area, perimeter, internal number, and the user ID of each stand are derived from the PAT (Polygon Attribute Table) file existing in an ARC/INFO covertype coverage. Stand identifiers (Stand#, Stand-ID) will ultimately be used as relate items to associate the stand information file with

Table 1. Summary of GISFORMAN model data requirements.

Data	Format	Descriptions
COVER TYPE(*)	map coverage	One map of all wood supply areas containing polygon topology and associated attribute files
STAND	attribute file	A data file including stand development patterns, some locational attributes
YIELD	attribute file	A data file including forest development characteristics, yield curve sets
COST	attribute file	A data file containing treatment costs
NEIGHBOURHOOD	attribute file	A random access, variable record length file containing harvest block information
MIN. BLOCK SIZE[1]	number	The minimum harvest block size (ha)
MAX. BLOCK SIZE[1]	number	The maximum harvest block size (ha)
RADIUS[1]	number	Radius of a circular search area
MAXIMUM OPERATING ROAD COST	number	Maximum cost of extracting one m^3 volume from a harvest block in terms of operating road construction cost plus a partial fixed cost to access that block for each period ($/m^3$)
ACCESS AREA	number	Hectares accessed by one kilometre of road
HARVEST RULES	number	Harvesting strategies upon which the stands will be ordered for harvesting for each iteration
HARVEST LEVEL	number	The amount of harvest per year for each period (m^3/ha)
PLANTING LEVEL	number	The amount of area desired for planting for each period (m^3/ha)
SPACING LEVEL	number	The amount of area desired for spacing for each period (m^3/ha)
SPACING WINDOW	number	The upper-lower ages of stands for spacing

[1]These data are specifically needed for establishing a harvest configuration file.

either the PAT, the harvest block configuration or adjacency files to calculate harvest blocks. The remaining items such as stand age, yield curve IDs, operating road cost, volume and treatment periods represent additional stand characteristics.

The stand information file, just described, is significant in implementing a spatial wood supply model in a number of respects. First, the file holds stand-by-stand information. This is important since all stand-related information can be linked to geographic locations via stand identifiers. Second, the file is changed dynamically throughout a simulation. As a result, it is unnecessary to store all forest information in the computer's memory as arrays and there is no limitation on the number of forest stands that can be simulated — as long as the computer has sufficient mass storage. Last, any additional stand attributes can be added to this file as an item and be used by the model to improve the forecasting and management design capabilities.

Harvest Control With Harvest Queuing Rules

Before forecasting forest development over time, it is necessary to define management strategies to be tested. In FORMAN terms, a harvest strategy consists of a set of rules for queuing stands for harvest and a set of levels at which these activities will be conducted. The rules, along with maximum operating road cost limit, maximum block opening size and adjacency delay are used to control numerical and geographic distribution of harvest schedules. Harvest rules can be combined to control harvest by both stand condition and geographic arrangement, i.e., on the basis of both numerical and geographic distribution of development types and stages. Specific new harvesting rules available in GISFORMAN, in addition to seven old FORMAN rules, are:
(i) Rule 8 — Minimize operating road cost ($/m^3$),
(ii) Rule 9 — Maximize volume concentration (m^3) and

(iii) Rule 10 — Minimize unharvested primary volume loss (i.e., mortality loss) on a harvest block basis.

The minimize operating road cost rule is used for queuing harvest blocks across a forest in each period based on their operating road cost per cubic metre ($/m^3$). The more primary operable volume per kilometre of operating road associated with a harvest block, the closer it will be to the front of the harvesting queue. The rule concentrates harvesting in geographic areas where there is more operable volume, i.e., more volume per hectare and thus less operating road cost. The maximize volume concentration rule, by contrast, queues blocks based on volume concentration, regardless of their size and therefore cost. The larger its volume concentration, the closer a block will be to the front of the harvesting queue. Like the minimize operating road cost rule, harvesting is concentrated in geographic areas where there is greatest operable volume, but operating road cost is ignored. The minimize block mortality loss rule, on the other hand, is aimed at capturing volume loss on a harvest block basis, in a fashion analogous to mortality capture strategies common in aspatial models. Blocks are assigned harvest priority by their expected total primary volume loss over the next period. The harvest block with the highest mortality will be harvested first. Here, harvesting is mostly concentrated in geographic areas where stands are of older development stages. Any of the queuing rules just described, combined with maximum operating road cost limit, maximum block opening size and adjacency delay, control harvesting geographically by concentrating it into harvest blocks based on numerical and geographic distribution of stand development types and stages.

One or two combinations of harvest rules may be set up for queuing blocks for harvest in first, second, and third order priorities. A lower priority rule will be invoked where a higher priority rule results in two or more blocks having the same value upon which the ordering takes place. In this regard the application of harvesting rules in GISFORMAN is similar to that in FORMAN.

Simulation Process

Similar to other wood supply simulation models, GISFORMAN forecasts forest development over time in response to a management strategy. Forest response to harvesting and silviculture of specific amounts, times and geographic locations, as controlled by queuing rules, is forecast on an iteration-by-iteration basis. There is no attempt to 'optimize' the strategy over the entire simulation time horizon, since GISFORMAN is not an optimization model. The following sections detail how, in GISFORMAN, harvest block attributes are calculated, how they are used in harvest queuing and how associated forest performance indicators are calculated.

Queuing Blocks for Harvest

Before GISFORMAN queues blocks for harvest it calculates several stand parameters and writes them under their associated item names in the stand information file. First, volumes (primary and secondary) of each stand are determined at the beginning of each period. Operable volumes are calculated for each stand by multiplying stand area by the volume per hectare indicated by the curve set along which a stand is presently tracking. Following the calculation of operable volume of each stand, volume concentration of each operable stand that forms, along with its operable neighbours, a possible harvest block is determined as well. Volume concentration is calculated for each operable stand by summing up the operable volumes of it and its neighbours. Then, operating road length of each possible harvest block is calculated. Operating road length can be calculated in two ways. One approach divides the total operable area of a harvest block by the hectares specified as accessible by 1 kilometre of road. The second approach bounds the total operable area of a harvest block with a circle, and uses its diameter as the operating road length. However, in both cases, while the number of stands in a block are fixed at the start of the simulation, the operating road length is still calculated for each iteration since the number of operable stands in a block changes as stands develop over time. Finally, having determined volume concentration and operating road length of each possible harvest block, the model calculates their operating road costs. The model does not account for the situation where a block (or one or more of its constituent stands) has been previously harvested and, as a result, has an operating road network in place. This is not unreasonable given that: (i) the model does not attempt to retain 'old' harvest block identities and is likely to requeue few with their original stand compositions intact, and (ii) the temporary nature of operating roads would likely mean, after a lapse of one rotation, a 'renewal' cost close to original construction cost in any event.

Once the harvest block parameters are determined, the model then queues all blocks in descending order of priority specified in the first combination of harvesting rules. Starting at the front of the queue, those blocks satisfying the operating road cost limit, maximum opening size and adjacency delay constraints (if specified) are then harvested. Harvesting stops when the 5-year harvest level is reached or the harvest queue

is empty. If a portion of the harvest is to be taken using the second combination of harvesting rules, the unharvested blocks are requeued and harvested accordingly.

It is important to note that GISFORMAN does not consider a major road network in queuing blocks for harvest. As a result, control of geographic distribution of harvest blocks is impossible.

Determining the Availability of Queued Blocks for Harvest

Depending on the mix of harvest rules and operating road cost limit, maximum opening size and adjacency delay constraints, the model harvests queued blocks with two different approaches. One approach harvests blocks without any spatial considerations, namely each stand is assumed as a harvest block and all operable stands are considered available for harvesting. When the harvesting rules are not 8, 9 or 10, stands are harvested with this approach. No harvest block information is generated. The second harvesting approach harvests on a block basis subject to maximum operating road cost limit, maximum block opening size and adjacency delay. With this approach, the harvesting assumption is that if any stand is to be harvested then those stands within its harvest block, i.e. neighbourhood, that are operable are also harvested. Obviously, not all operable stands would be available for harvesting if operating road cost limit, maximum opening size and adjacency delay constraints are involved.

GISFORMAN determines block availability in the following order. Since each block's volume is already, at the start of simulation, calculated based upon component stand's operability limits, a block's operability is easily determined by the model. As explained earlier, operating road cost is the key in determining whether an operable block is economically extractable. Simply, if a maximum operating road cost ($/m^3) constraint is given then the model considers those blocks whose operating road costs are less than the given maximum, economically extractable and not the rest. Finally, once a block is determined as extractable, the model ensures that component stands do not violate the maximum opening size and adjacency delay constraints. Adjacency is checked by the model using the adjacency file, ADJ$FWO, and the item in the stand information file that stores the period of stand harvest for each stand along with its neighbours. If an adjacency conflict is not found then the block is considered available for harvest in the period. Once a block is available, the target stand's operable volume is added to the forest's effective growing stock — operable, extractable and constraint-free growing stock. Then the block is harvested and the period number assigned to all its stands.

Planting and Spacing

Following harvesting, if a planting level has been specified, stands are queued in descending order of planting priority. Harvested stands having planting priority are considered eligible for planting. Starting at the front of the queue, stands are planted until the specified periodic level is reached or all the eligible stands have been planted. Any remaining unplanted harvested stands are assigned to their appropriate natural response curve. Stands planted are assigned the planted time period.

Following planting, if a spacing level has been specified, stands are queued in describing order of age. Those stands tracking on a curve with a non-zero spacing response curve and having an age falling within the spacing window are considered candidates for spacing. Starting at the front of the queue, spacing then proceeds until the specified periodic level is reached or all the eligible stands have been spaced. Spacing is simulated by reassigning a stand from its present curve set to its spacing response curve. Stands spaced are assigned the spaced time period.

Aging

When harvesting, planting and spacing are completed in a period, the forest is simulated by aging all its stands one period. Harvested stands are reassigned to the first age class and new development types for treated stands take over in the next iteration. Stands that are not harvested and move beyond operability are reassigned to the first age class after breakup and are assumed to follow their predecessor yield curve. The cycle of harvesting, planting and thinning is repeated until the desired time horizon is reached or the available growing stock is exhausted. If the harvest level cannot be sustained, the model stops the simulation and reduces the desired harvest level by a specified percentage before starting the simulation from the beginning again.

Results Output

Three forms of output can be produced in each period during one simulation run: screen, ASCII file and database. Screen output provides 'run time' information. It simply reports the status of a set of forest performance indicators as well as forest and harvest block statistics for every period. The ASCII file stores much more information such as harvest block information, age class distribution, and operating road cost distribution over the whole forest for each period. New performance indicators, effective growing stock, growing stock cost and average operating road cost are provided in this file. Further, this file stores number of blocks harvested, average number of stands per block and average block size for each period. The database on the other hand contains individual stand information necessary for examining and mapping harvest, planting and thinning schedules or forest condition at each period of simulation.

In addition to the three types of outputs described above, GISFORMAN can display information generated during the simulation in map form using ARC/INFO's ARCPLOT display subsystem capabilities. For example, treatment periods for havested, planted and spaced stands can be mapped for the entire simulation or for any period. With this, the geographic location and distribution of actual harvest blocks over the forest is evident.

Performance

GISFORMAN has been tested on a forest of 111 296 ha (72 526 ha productive) in the Canaan area of Eastern New Brunswick. The inventory database consisted of 9 640 productive stands. Results show that the model takes half an hour to complete an 80-year forecast of this forest using a 7 MIPS Sun 4/110 workstation computer. However, since model performance is mostly dependent upon the speed of disk I/O, results will vary greatly depending upon memory buffering capacity and disk drive throughput characteristics. Further, since the model does not use computer memory to store stand information, the size of forest, in terms of number

of stands, is only limited by mass storage capacity. Typical Canadian forests should be easily accommodated with 0.5 to 1 Gigabyte.

Conclusions

A spatial model is capable of producing harvest schedules that reflect geographic context as well as condition of stands. Unlike most current aspatial wood supply models, the spatial model described in this paper can incorporate extraction economics, as determined by geographic distribution of harvest, throughout wood supply forecasting process: starting inventory, harvest strategy and forecast results. As starting inventory, forest conditions and locations are kept on an individual stand-by-stand basis as opposed to aspatial stand aggregates. Harvest strategies that consider the conditions of stands and their relative positions are used. Forecast results are provided as mapped harvest block schedules and associated forest response indicators.

Surprisingly, a GIS database is more important in spatial modelling than GIS technology. Simply stated, one doesn't need a GIS to build a spatial model, but needs a spatial database. There is a good reason for this. Topology, maintained in a GIS database, is a crucial component in starting forest inventory. It provides the basis from which stand neighbourhood lists and harvest blocks may subsequently be formed and queued for harvest based on extraction economics and wildlife habitat values. Topology provides the wherewithal to develop a spatial wood supply model capable of dealing with the geographic distribution of stand development types and stages.

Topology, besides absolute stand locations, makes it relatively easy to integrate wildlife timber management. Since habitat supply is evaluated in much the same manner as timber, but spatial consideration is made of the proximity and juxtaposition of vegetation types that are critical factors of habitat supply (Jordan et al. 1990), it is apparent that they share much in common. Thus topology provides great opportunities to deal with habitat supply simultaneously with timber supply in a management planning model. Both are characterized by geographic distribution of stand development types and stages. For example, the spatial model described in this paper included two important wildlife habitat supply considerations: maximum block size and adjacency delay. Stand adjacency detail and stand neighbourhood information, derived from topology in a spatial database, provided adjacency check and block size limiting capability. It is obvious that wildlife considerations, like timber extraction economics, affect growing stock available for harvest, i.e., effective growing stock. Their inclusion as limits in harvest strategy formation and testing permit integration of wildlife and timber is assessing wood supply.

Spatial modelling has potential to improve management design for wood supply. First, a spatial model determines a truer assessment of wood supply since it is determined as a function of both geographic and numerical distribution of stand development types and stages. Second, since a spatial model employs the stand-by-stand data maintained in a GIS database, strategies are easily translated into on-the-ground management designs/schedules. Third, since a spatial model produces harves schedules in the form of harvest blocks, the way that harvesting occurs in actual practice is mimicked. Fourth, with production of new spatially-oriented performance indicators,

GIS applications in forest land management in Indonesia
Siti Susilawati* and Michael J C Weir**

ABSTRACT

Indonesia's forests are one of its most important natural re-sources. Managing this resource effectively requires reliable infor-mation. ILWIS's potential use to support typical forest manage-ment problems in Indonesia was assessed using a number of case studies in different parts of the country. This article describes applications in the fields of forest land allocation, forest monitoring and the design of logging roads.

Forests and forest land are an important natural re-source in many parts of the world and provide the raw material for a wide range of wood-based indus-tries. In some countries, timber and timber products are major export commodities and forestry is among the main sectors of the national economy. In addition to its formal role, the forest can also provide the local population with a variety of products, most notably fuelwood. Forests and forest land are also important for regulating water supply, controlling erosion, pro-tecting wildlife and as areas for outdoor recreation.

Although the demand for timber, pulpwood and other forest products continues to grow, the resource base that supplies these commodities is under pres-sure. In many developing countries, forests are seen as potential areas for agricultural production. In re-cent years, the clearing of tropical forests for shifting cultivation, to provide land for agricultural resettle-ment schemes and for livestock ranching has become a matter of international concern.

Forest management is concerned with ensuring a sustainable supply of timber and other forest products, while at the same time keeping ecologic considerations and other uses of the forest land in mind. Not only is this a complex task, but forest management agencies must also be aware that the consequences of current operations may be apparent only decades later. Eco-nomically viable and ecologically sound forest manage-ment can therefore be achieved only by careful plan-ning.

The preparation, control and execution of a forest management plan requires a wide range of information, much of which is spatially referenced. Forest invento-ry data and maps showing the current state of the forest land are important inputs for the preparation of forest management plans. It is therefore not surpris-ing that forest management agencies are also looking to the technology of geographic information systems (GIS) to help them in their work. This article de-scribes the application of the ILWIS geographic infor-mation system to some typical forest management problems in Indonesia.

GIS IN FOREST MANAGEMENT

The management of forest land requires a wide variety of spatial information. This information con-cerns not only the forest vegetation, but also a wide range of natural and artificial features which must be considered in planning and executing forestry opera-tions (see Table 1). Consequently, forest management agencies are among the most important organizations responsible for resource mapping. Since the forest is continually changing as a result of human activities (such as timber harvesting and planting) and natural occurrences (such as forest fires), forest management agencies must regularly update their maps and other management information to take account of changing conditions and policies (Figure 1). Aerial photographs and, more recently, satellite images are important data sources for this task.

During the last decade, there has been consider-able interest in the potential use of geographic infor-mation systems to support forest management. This trend has been most noticeable in Canada and the United States, where every major forest management agency has acquired, or has plans to acquire, GIS capability [11].

The potential uses of GISs to support forest management are considerable. The production and revision of maps and the accurate determination of area data are important tasks in forest manage-ment. Traditionally, the acquisition of these data has been tedious and time consuming. Using GIS, forest managers are, in principle, able to easily and quickly store, update and manipulate the wide range of spatial information needed for their work. The main advan-tage of a GIS in forestry lies, however, in its ability to perform complex spatial analysis and modelling opera-tions in support of forest management planning. For-est management agencies in North America and other developed regions are now using GIS to assist in tasks

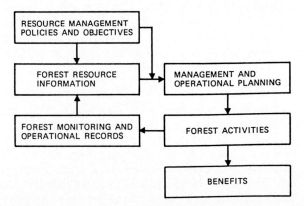

FIGURE 1 The forest management information cycle (from [4])

* Agency for Forestry Research and Development, Ministry of Forestry, Jakarta, Indonesia
** Department of land resource surveys, ITC

TABLE 1 Typical spatial information requirements for forest management

Information category	Purpose
Administrative boundaries - cadastral boundaries - forest administration boundaries - compartments and sub-compartments - timber concession boundaries	General administration, management and planning
Terrain features - elevation - slope - aspect - drainage	Planning of timber harvesting (*eg*, road construction); site assessment (*eg*, susceptibility to windthrow)
Infrastructure - roads, tracks, etc - power lines, pipelines, etc - buildings and other structures	Planning and management of forest operations
Soil and understory vegetation	Site assessment and silvicultural treatment
Forest stand characteristics - species composition - age - yield class - density	Planning and management of forest operations (thinning, harvesting, etc)
Management activities - realized and planned silvicultural treatment (thinning, harvesting, etc) - land use zoning (*eg*, nature protection) - fire control - damage control (*eg*, insects, wind)	

such as forest monitoring [6], the design of forest roads [9], management of timber harvesting operations [3] and the preparation of measures to combat forest damage caused by fire and insect attack [8].

More recently, forest management agencies in many developing countries, particularly the major timber producing nations of Southeast Asia (Indonesia, Malaysia and Thailand), have started to make use of GIS technology.

FOREST MANAGEMENT IN INDONESIA

With approximately 75 percent of the total land area, or 144 million ha, covered by forest, Indonesia ranks as the most richly forested nation in Southeast Asia. Approximately 110 million ha are under prima-

ry forest which has been designated for either "protection" or timber "production" under a system of selective cutting. With an export revenue of US$ 2.88 billion in 1988, timber and timber-based products play a vital role, second only to oil and gas, in the Indonesian economy.

Recognizing the importance of the country's forests, the Indonesian government in 1981 drew up the so-called "consensus on forest land use", or TGHK (Tata Guna Hutan Kesepakatan). TGHK is a policy which aims at organizing forest planning within each province through a general agreement among all involved agencies [1]. The TGHK allocates the forest land according to its planned function (see Table 2). This allocation is based on both physical conditions and economic and social considerations.

TABLE 2 Forest land use in Indonesia

Type of Forest	Code	Area (ha)	Purpose	Forest exploitation
Park and nature reserve	PPA	18 725 215	Conservation	None
Protection forest	HL	30 316 100	Watershed protection	None
Limited production forest	HPT	30 525 300	Erosion control	Selection felling
Normal production forest	HBP	33 866 600	Timber production	Selection or clear felling
Conversion forest	HPK	30 537 400	Conversion to agriculture	Clear felling
Total		144 010 615		

TABLE 3 Slope, soil and rainfall classes for calculation of the TGHK erosion index (from [1])

No	Slope classes Slope %	Points	No	Soil classes* Erodibility	Points	No	Rainfall intensity classes** Intensity	Points
1	0–8	20	1	None	15	1	13.6	10
2	9–15	40	2	Low	30	2	13.6–20.7	20
3	16–25	60	3	Medium	45	3	20.8–27.7	30
4	26–45	80	4	High	60	4	27.8–34.8	40
5	45	100	5	Very high	75	5	> 34.8	50

*Soil classes
1   Alluvial, gley, Planosol, blue grey hydromorphic, groundwater laterite
2   Latosol
3   Brown forest soil, Mediterranean
4   Andosol, laterite, Gumosol, Podzols, Podzolic
5   Regosol, Litosol, Organosol, Rendizinas
**Rainfall intensity = mean annual rainfall (mm) divided by mean annual rain days (a rain day being one in which rainfall is 1.0 mm or more)

The TGHK site index for the area in question is calculated using a system of points for the physical conditions of slope, soil type and rainfall intensity (see Table 3), all of which are critical factors in determining soil erosion. The site index is obtained by summing the points for each of these three criteria to give a forest management class as follows:
- a site index less than 125 indicates normal production forest (HPB) or conversion forest (HPK)
- a site index between 125 and 174 indicates limited production forest (HPT)
- a site index of 175 or more indicates protection forest (HL)

Even if the site index is less than 175, land will be classified as protection forest if any of the following conditions apply:
- the slope exceeds 45 percent
- the soil type is in class 5 and the slope is greater than 15 percent
- the area is within 200 m of a spring
- the elevation is 2000 m or more
- the Ministry of Forestry so determines

Since it incorporates a variety of physical land attributes, in addition to economic and other non-physical considerations, the TGHK system is well suited to a computer-assisted approach using map overlays in a GIS. The Indonesian Ministry of Forestry is already taking steps to introduce GIS in support of its forest management tasks. Effective forest management is not, however, simply a matter of appropriate land allocation. Within a designated forest area, it is necessary to determine appropriate management options, monitor the state of the forest and plan and assess the outcome of forest operations.

SCOPE

This article is based on research into the organizational and operational aspects of GIS for planning and monitoring forest management activities in Indonesia [10]. The aims of this research were (1) to examine general user requirements for geographic information to support forest management in Indonesia; (2) by means of a number of case studies, to examine in detail the information required for three particular types of forest management as applied in three selected study areas; and (3) to use these case studies to assess ILWIS's potential use in supporting forest management in Indonesia. Our principal concerns here are the last two objectives.

The case studies included:

(1) comparison of forest land allocation according to TGHK with the actual forest land use in the Kali Konto region, east Java. This case study was extended to determine the most appropriate locations for establishing fuelwood plantations

(2) monitoring changes in forest land use with satellite images (Landsat MSS) of the Cepu region, central Java

(3) planning logging roads for timber extraction

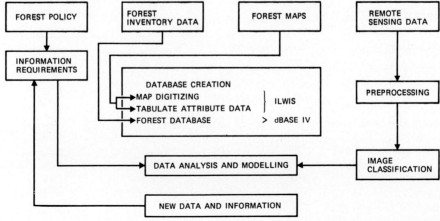

FIGURE 2 Research method

in two forest concession blocks in east Kalimantan.

ILWIS APPLICATION

All three case studies were carried out with ILWIS (version 1.1), using locally available maps and other data. Certain non-spatial database operations were undertaken with dBASE IV. The general procedure of data analysis and modelling for forest land management used in this research is shown in Figure 2.

Forestry agencies are becoming increasingly aware of the advantages of using custom-designed or commerical database management systems (dbms) to handle the large amounts of data required in planning and executing forest operations. Since many forest operations are carried out on fixed spatial units (*eg*, compartments or forest stands), each of which is uniquely identified on a forest management map, a dbms provides an efficient means for maintaining records relating to these units.

The combination of a dbms for handling attribute data and a GIS to store and manipulate map and remote sensing data is potentially a very flexible tool for forest management. Complex spatial modelling operations—such as those required in harvest planning—become possible with a GIS, while tasks such as updating stand or compartment records after silvicultural treatment can be carried out in the dbms without resorting to more cumbersome map analysis operations.

CASE STUDY 1: FOREST LAND ALLOCATION, KALI KONTO, EAST JAVA

The Kali Konto watershed is a sub-catchment of the Brantas river basin. Watershed management and forestry for rural development are priority issues in the development of the area. Of the 23573 ha in the area, some 66 percent is forest land under jurisdiction of the State Forest Corporation, Perum Perhutani (see Table 4).

The shrub land has no commercial forestry value, but is used by the local population as a source of fuelwood and fodder. The main objective of the management of the forest land is not only to ensure

TABLE 4 Forest types and other land use/cover, Kali Konto project area

Type	Area (ha)	(%)
Natural forest	6 081.00	25.80
Protection forest	5 828.00	24.72
3 Commerical species	1 834.50	7.78
4 Non-commerical species	1 585.75	6.73
5 Scrub	178.50	0.76
6 Special/other use	58.25	0.25
7 Village land	7 690.75	32.63
8 Selorejo lake	316.50	1.34
Total	23, 573.25	100.00

Source: Perum Perhutani, inventory data 1982 and forest management map 1986

profitable timber production, but also to support the development of the local population and protect the environment. A careful allocation of forest land use is therefore important.

In order to classify the Kali Konto area according to TGHK criteria, three maps—a slope map, a soil map and a rainfall intensity map—were required. The slope map was derived by filtering a digital elevation model (DEM) consisting of a regular grid of elevation values for the area. This DEM was itself derived from digitized contours using the interpolation facility of ILWIS. Data on rainfall intensity are rather sparse in the area. Two rainfall intensity classes were determined by relating available meteorologic data to elevation. The soil type information was obtained from recently published soil maps.

The three maps were assigned codes, as indicated in Table 3, and subsequently overlaid, the summation of the three codes giving a preliminary TGHK score for each pixel. It was then necessary to reclassify as protection forest all pixels with a site index of less than 175 for which limiting conditions applied. The resulting TGHK map (Figure 3) was compared with a map of the actual forest land use obtained by digitizing the

legend :

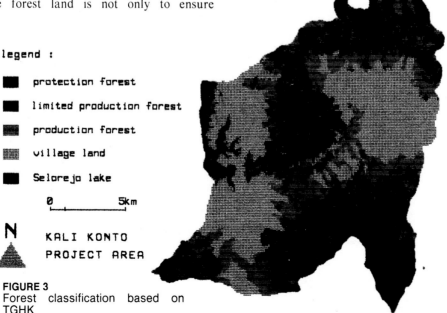

- protection forest
- limited production forest
- production forest
- village land
- Selorejo lake

0   5km

N   KALI KONTO
    PROJECT AREA

FIGURE 3
Forest classification based on TGHK

169   See page 371 for color plate of Figure 3.

TABLE 5 Kali Konto: actual forest types compared with TGHK classification (ha)

Actual forest type	Protection	TGHK Classification Limited production	Production
Natural forest	3 251.25	2 097.50	730.50
Protection forest	704.25	2 823.00	2 300.75
Production forest			
- Commerical species	82.25	787.00	965.25
- Non-commerical species	79.75	708.50	797.25
Scrub land	3.72	109.50	57.25
Other	0.25	10.50	47.50

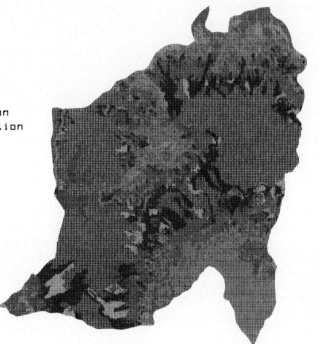

legend :

■ suitable for fuelwood plantation

▦ commercial production forest

▦ non-commercial production forest

▦ limited production forest

▦ protection forest

▦ village land

■ Selorejo lake

0 ⊢——⊣ 5km

N▲ KALI KONTO PROJECT AREA

FIGURE 4A
Physical suitability for fuelwood plantation

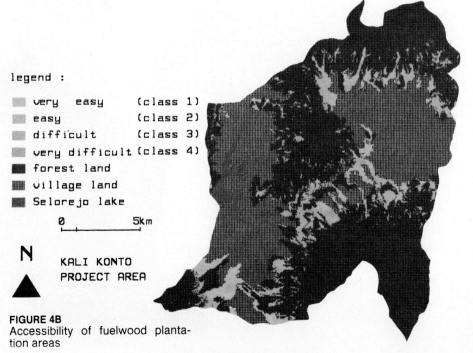

legend :

▦ very easy (class 1)

▦ easy (class 2)

▦ difficult (class 3)

▦ very difficult (class 4)

■ forest land

▦ village land

■ Selorejo lake

0 ⊢——⊣ 5km

N▲ KALI KONTO PROJECT AREA

FIGURE 4B
Accessibility of fuelwood plantation areas

See page 372 for color plate of Figure 4A, and 4B.

forest management map of Perum Perhutani. The results of this comparison are shown in Table 5.

An examination of Table 5 shows that 730.5 ha and 2097.5 ha of natural forest can be used for production or limited timber production, respectively. Similarly, 2300.75 ha and 2823 ha of protection forest can be converted to production or limited production forest, respectively. The areas suitable for limited production can be considered as a reserve which can be exploited if there is a timber shortage. According to the TGHK classification, 162 ha of production forest should in fact be designated as protection forest and 1495 ha of production forest should be retained for only limited production. These figures refer to a reallocation based on only physical criteria.

Application of the TGHK scale using only physical criteria is not sufficient. The determined land use allocations may have to be altered to cater for economic or other forest management considerations, such as minimum manageable area. An example in which a reallocation would be necesssary is where pockets of production forest are found within protection forest. Although more complex modelling procedures can help in solving some of these problems, they are not a substitute for the knowledge of an experienced forest manager.

In view of the importance of managing the forest land in the Kali Konto area for the benefit of the local population, an attempt was made to determine areas suitable for the establishment of fuelwood plantations. The criteria used in this analyis were:
- the area should not fall within protection or limited production forest
- natural forest or production forest of commercial species should not be converted to fuelwood plantation
- selected areas should be within reasonable walking distance, in this instance 3 km, of a village

Using these criteria, the sub-compartments of the forest land which are suitable for fuelwood plantation were determined (Figure 4).

CASE STUDY 2: FOREST MONITORING WITH SATELLITE IMAGES

Traditionally, aerial photographs have been an important source of data for forest resource assessment and the production and revision of forest maps [5, 13]. More recently, remotely sensed images from the Landsat (MSS and TM) and SPOT resource satellites have proved an invaluable source of additional data to assist forest managers in monitoring the state of the land under their jurisdiction [7]. In countries like

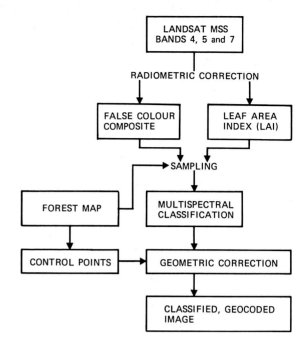

FIGURE 5 Satellite image processing

Indonesia, which have extensive forest resources, satellite images may be the only feasible means of obtaining reliable and timely data for forest resource assessment.

The aim of this case study was to assess ILWIS's potential for processing and analyzing satellite images for the purpose of forest monitoring. Tests were carried out using Landsat MSS images of the forest district of Cepu in central Java, the main centre of teak production in Indonesia. The area selected was the 4703 ha sub-district of Blungun. The area is intensively managed, with forest inventories and forest map revision carried out every 10 years. In general, the rotation age for teak in the area is 60 years. The maximum cutting regime is set at 2 percent of the total forest area per annum. The most common method of harvesting is clear cutting, although selective cutting is used on steep slopes and other critical areas.

Forest changes over a 15-year period were analyzed by comparing Landsat MSS images of 1972 and 1987. For both sets of images, a multispectral classification was used, based on maximum likelihood using bands 4, 5 and 7 together with LAI (leaf area index). The images were geocoded to match the digitized forest management maps. The processing steps are shown in Figure 5.

Comparison of the two images (see Table 6)

TABLE 6 Comparison of classified Landsat MSS images November 1972 and November 1987 (ha)

Classified image of 02/11/72	Forest class 1	Forest class 2	Classified Image of 01/11/87 Bare land	Shadow	Cloud	Total
Forest class 1	1,474	1,012	215	5	17	2,723
Forest class 2	313	855	293	1	-	1,462
Bare land	128	172	149	4	-	453
Shadow	55	22	6	-	-	83
Cloud	42	17	10	-	-	69
Total	2,012	2,078	673	10	17	4,790

shows that between 1972 and 1987, 1 227 ha (25.6 percent) of the area had changed from forest class 1 (dense or high vegetation cover) to forest class 2 (open or low vegetation cover) or to bare land. A further 293 ha had changed from forest class 2 to bare land. These figures indicate that a total of 1 520 ha, or 31.7 percent of the area, had been effected by forest clearing or thinning. On the other hand, only 613 ha, or 12.8 percent of the area, had changed from forest class 2 to class 1 or from bare land to forest class 1 or 2.

On the basis of these results, it can be concluded that timber felling is proceeding faster than the forest is being re-established through planting and natural growth. Since the images were geocoded, it is possible to determine which compartments are effected by change and to examine the compartment records to see whether changes were the result of forest management operations or some other cause (Figure 6).

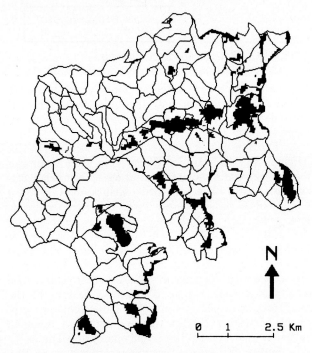

FIGURE 6 Harvested areas 1972-1987, Cepu forest district, Blungun sub-district

CASE STUDY 3: FOREST ROAD PLANNING

In forest areas which are managed for timber production, good access is essential to extract the harvested logs. Intensively managed forests, like those on Java described in the preceding two case studies, generally have a well established network of all-weather roads from which temporary logging roads can be laid out to the harvest area. Such an established infrastructure is not generally present in areas of less intensive management.

The province of east Kalimantan is one of the principal timber producing regions of Indonesia. Areas of primary forest which have been classified as production forest, limited production forest or conversion forest (forest land to be cleared for resettlement projects) are allocated to logging companies under a concession system. The forests of the region are dominated by species of the family *Diptero-*

carpaceae, many of which, for example the merantis, are of high commercial value.

A concession area will generally not have any established road network within or even near it. Logs are generally transported by river to sawmills in Samarinda and other centres. To transport the felled logs to a convenient river, it is necessary to construct a system of logging roads suitable for large timber trucks and other machinery. Since road construction in a jungle environment is a costly undertaking, it is essential to plan the most economical route.

Like any road construction project, the design of a new logging road is based on a number of variables such as limiting gradient and curvature, maximum load, and costs for land clearing, earthworks (cut and fill), bridge construction, etc. For logging roads, which are usually only temporary, it is essential that the construction cost be kept within limits defined by the value of the timber to be transported over the road. Furthermore, forest road construction has to take into consideration not only the total construction cost but also the cost of transportation from the logging area to the offloading point, the question of favourable and unfavourable gradients in relation to vehicle performance (timber trucks generally enter the forest empty but leave fully loaded), curvature limits imposed by the maxiumum log length and the need to avoid traversing areas, such as protection forest, which should not be disturbed.

A route selection program (see [2]) was applied to two timber cutting blocks between Balikpapan and Samarinda. This program selects the most direct route and the cheapest route using cost data for each cell of a raster-based GIS (in this instance ILWIS). The original program uses specified origin and destination points. For logging roads in east Kali-

TABLE 7 Cost factors (in rupiah per meter) used in logging road design[1] (US$ 1 = ± Rp 1800)

Land clearing per land use		
Forest	15 000 (less timber value 12 000)	3 000
Swamp forest	15 000 (less timber value 12 000; plus earthworks 350 000)[3]	353 000
Scrub	15 000	15 000
Agriculture	15 000 (plus land price 10 000)	25 000

Slope (%)	
0	0
1–5	12 500
6–10	37 500
11–15	62 500
> 15	200 000

Soil compaction per soil type	
Podsol	0
Podsol complex	0
Alluvial	0
Organo–clay	350 000

Bridge construction per river width	
0–7.5 m	375 000
7.5–25 m	1 250 000

Notes
1 based on a road width of 5 m
2 based on an average timber volume of 188 m³ ha and a timber price of Rp 145 000 per m³
3 construction of embankments

172

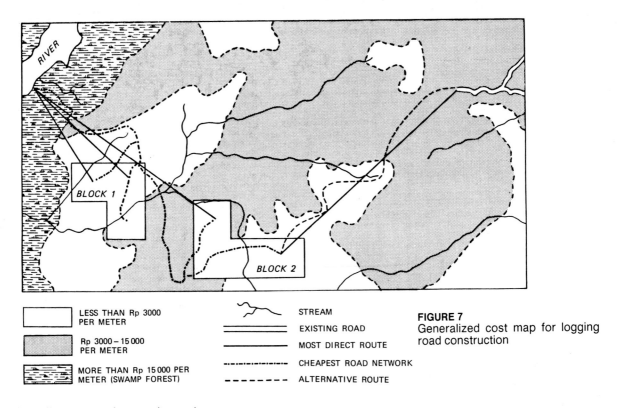

LESS THAN Rp 3000
PER METER

Rp 3000 – 15000
PER METER

MORE THAN Rp 15000 PER
METER (SWAMP FOREST)

STREAM

EXISTING ROAD

MOST DIRECT ROUTE

CHEAPEST ROAD NETWORK

ALTERNATIVE ROUTE

FIGURE 7
Generalized cost map for logging
road construction

mantan and similar areas, the starting points are selected at convenient locations within the cutting block. The destination, however, is rarely predetermined. Logs are usually transported to the most convenient offloading point on the nearest river or existing road, *ie*, to a line. The program was therefore adapted to meet this particular requirement. The cost data used, calculated on a per metre basis, are shown in Table 7. These data are "best estimates" based on the limited information available. Before using this approach under operational conditions, it will be necessary to obtain more reliable figures. Some of the costs used are peculiar to the forestry conditions in the area. Thus land clearance costs in cells classified as production forest include a "profit" element based on the commerical value of the cleared timber. Areas such as protection forest, which should not be disturbed by road construction, are avoided by assigning a very high value to the land.

Figure 7 shows the most direct routes from selected points within the blocks to a nearby river and an existing road. From the point of view of efficiency, it is necessary to design a network of logging roads which will allow timber to be extracted from various points within the blocks, while keeping construction costs to a minimum. This network is also shown in Figure 7, and the cost diagram for part of it is shown in Figure 8.

In this particular study, it was not possible to consider all aspects of logging road design. In particular, the relatively large cell size (100 m) made it impossible to consider the question of limiting curvature. It would also be useful to adapt the program to cater for the question of favourable and unfavourable gradients. Ultimately, it may be possible to use the general approach of the program to cater for other methods of timber extraction, including the design of cable logging systems.

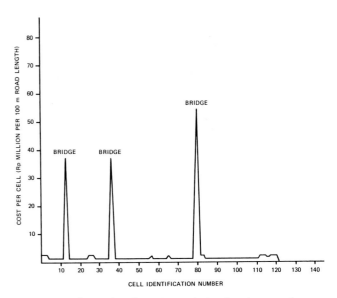

FIGURE 8 Example of cost graph for logging road construction

CONCLUSIONS

These case studies suggest that ILWIS is able to perform many of the spatial analysis and modelling operations required to provide information for forest management in Indonesia. As with all raster-based systems, however, information is lost when converting the original map data from vector to raster format. In a previous study [12], it was shown that in forestry, where reliable area data and accurate locational information are essential, this loss of information can be serious (Table 8). In intensively managed forests, linear features—such as property, forest compartment and stand boundaries—are important elements on forest management maps. In Europe, for example, such maps are generally produced at a scale of 1:10 000 and typically have an accuracy (root mean square error) tolerance of $\pm$ 1 mm. Since this can be achieved only with a raster-based system by selecting a very small cell size (5 m or less), thus creating very high volumes of data to be stored and processed, a GIS for forestry should normally include capabilities for handling vector data.

TABLE 8 Loss of information caused by converting 1:10 000 scale forest stand map to raster format (from [12])

	Original forest map	Raster maps (grid size) 25 m	50 m	100 m
Number of map units (forest stands)	71	74	68	36
% reduction in perimeter	-	17.1	31.9	67.5

In the ILWIS version (1.1) used in this research, the digitizing software was able to handle only a limited number of coordinate pairs, line segments and polygons. Difficulties were therefore encountered in two of the larger study areas. It should be noted, however, that these areas are—in forest management terms—relatively small. A large forest management unit may comprise several thousand individual areal units in the form of compartments and timber stands. In ILWIS version 1.2, these constraints on data volume appear to have been solved, while facilities for raster-to-vector conversion and data exchange––with Arc/Info and other vector-based systems commonly used by forest management agencies—provide greater flexibility.

As noted above, one of the aims of this research was to examine user requirements for geographic information to support forest management in Indonesia. Although this particular aspect has not been discussed here, it does have an important bearing on the conclusions presented above. The Indonesian Ministry of Forestry is a large organization with a wide range (both literally and figuratively) of tasks and responsibilities. Although it has been identified as a potentially valuable tool to assist Indonesian forest managers in their work, GIS technology is only now entering into operational forest management. Research, such as the work described here, can provide a useful indication of the potential of GIS technology. Successful *application* of this technology depends also on well trained staff and an appropriate operational environment.

ACKNOWLEDGEMENT

Our thanks to Martin Ellis of ITC's computer department for his assistance with the route selection program for the logging road design.

REFERENCES

1 Abell, T M B. 1988. The application of land systems mapping to the management of Indonesian forests. J World Forest Resource Management, Vol 3, pp 111-127.

2 Akinyede, J O. 1990. A geotechnical cost model for highway route planning. ITC Journal 1990-3.

3 Dunningham, A and S Thompson. 1989. Use of geographic information systems in New Zealand forestry applications. Commonwealth Forestry Rev, 68(3), pp 203-213.

4 Gillis, M D and J A Edwards. 1988. Volume compilation procedures in forest management inventories. Inform Report PI-X-79, Petawawa Nat Forestry Inst, Canada, 20 pp.

5 Grainger, A. 1984. Quantifying changes in forest cover in the humid tropics: overcoming current limitations. J World Forest Resource Management, Vol 1(1), pp 3-63.

6 Heygi, F and P Sallaway. 1986. The integrated three-dimensional forest land information system of BC, Canada. Proc 18th IUFRO world congress, Ljubljana, Study Group 6.05, 7 pp.

7 Jano, A P. 1988. Remote sensing as applied to forest inventory and forest cover monitoring in Canada. In: Satellite imageries for forest inventory and monitoring: experiences, methods and perspectives. Univ of Helsinki, Dept of Forest Mensuration and Management, Research notes No 21, pp 17-30.

8 Jordan, G and L Vietinghoff. 1987. Fighting spruce budworm with a GIS. Proc AutoCarto 8, pp 492-499.

9 Martin, F C. 1985. Using a geographical information system for forest land mapping and management. Photogram Eng and Rem Sens, Vol 51, No 11, pp 1753-1759.

10 Susilawati, S. 1990. Organizational and operational aspects of geographical information systems for planning and monitoring forest management activities in Indonesia. Unpub MSc thesis, ITC, Enschede, 130 pp.

11 Tomlinson, R F. 1987. Current and potential uses of geographical information systems - the North American experience. Int J of Geographical Information Systems, Vol 1(3), pp 203-218.

12 Weir, M J C. 1988. Assessing the influence of cell size and sampling technique on forest resource data in a raster-based GIS. Proc 9th Asian conference on remote sensing, Bangkok, November 23-29, 8 pp.

13 Weir, M J C and M Sumaryono. 1990. Kartenrevision in der Forstwirtschaft. Centralblatt für das Gesamte Forstwesen, 107(2), pp 101-112.

RESUME

Les forêts représentent une des principales ressources naturelles de l'Indonésie. Gérer cette ressource efficacement exige des informations sûres. Le potentiel d'ILWIS utilisé pour assister les problèmes typiques de gestion de forêt en Indonésie a été évalué en utilisant un certain nombre d'études de cas dans différentes parties du pays. Cet article décrit ses utilisations dans les champs de répartition de terre, de gestion et exploitation forestières ainsi que des projets de chemins d'exploitation forestière.

RESUMEN

Los bosques de Indonesia son uno de sus recursos naturales mas importantes. Manejar este recurso en forma eficiente requiere de informacion confiable. El uso potencial de ILWIS como un apoyo para problemas tipicos de manejo de los bosques en Indonesia fue evaluado utilizando una serie de estudios de caso en diferentes partes del pais. Este articulo describe aplicaciones en los campos de adjudicacion de terreno, monitoreo de bosque y diseno de caminos para la explotacion forestal.

SECTION 6

Landscape Ecology

Overview

Johnson begins this section with a preview article and extensive bibliography on ecological applications with GIS. The next two articles focus on analyzing forest landscape patterns in Oregon (Ripple et al.) and Michigan (Pastor and Broschart). This is followed by Davis and Goetz, who overlaid environmental variables to predict the distribution of coast live oak. The potential of using GIS and landscape metrics for understanding ecological patterns and processes is explored by Turner in the last article.

Suggested Additional Reading

Johnston, C. A., and J. Bonde, 1989. Quantitative Analysis of Ecotones Using a Geographic Information System. Photogrammetric Engineering and Remote Sensing. 55(11):1643-1647.

LaGro, J., 1991. Assessing Patch Shape in Landscape Mosaics. Photogrammetric Engineering and Remote Sensing. 57:285-293.

Lowell, K. E., and J. H. Astroth, Jr., 1989. Vegetative Succession and Controlled Fire in a Glades Ecosystem. A Geographical Information System Approach. International Journal of Geographical Information Systems. 3(1):69-81.

Moore, D. M., 1991. A New Method for Predicting Vegetation Distribution Using Decision Tree Analysis in a GIS. Environmental Management. 15(1):59-72.

Landscape Ecology vol. 4 no. 1 pp 31-43 (1990)
SPB Academic Publishing bv, The Hague

Analyzing spatial and temporal phenomena using geographical information systems
A Review of Ecological Applications

Lucinda B. Johnson
Natural Resources Research Institute, University of Minnesota, Duluth

Keywords: GIS, geographical information system, natural resources, spatial, temporal, applications

Abstract

In ecological studies the recent emphasis on larger study areas over longer time spans has coincided with the development of geographical information systems (GIS). GISs are a set of computer hardware and software for analyzing and displaying spatially referenced features (*i.e.*, points, lines, polygons) with non-geographic attributes (*i.e.*, species, age). In the fields of natural resources management and ecology the GIS has been used most frequently for 1) derivation of area or length measures, 2) spatial intersection functions such as file merging, analysis of spatial coincidence and detection of temporal change, 3) proximity analyses, and 4) derivation of data for input in simulation or growth models or calculation of specific metrics. Several current applications of GISs in ecology and natural resources are reviewed.

1. Introduction

Many ecologists in the past have simplified spatial interactions by assuming that the environment is homogeneous, or by assuming that what occurs at one point is independent of what occurs at others. The fluxes of energy, organisms and materials between adjacent systems, however, affect and are affected by spatial and temporal heterogeneity. This spatial and temporal heterogeneity of ecological systems makes it difficult to extrapolate from data collected at points to larger regional or global scales. A number of current issues (*i.e.*, global climate change, desertification, forest dieback, deforestation, acid precipitation) have caused ecologists to consider a global perspective (*c.f.*, Minshall 1988); this has resulted in a call for acquisition and funding of long-term data sets over larger regions by programs such as Man and the Biosphere (di Castri *et al.* 1988), the International Geosphere-

Biosphere Program (Dyer *et al.* 1988), and the National Science Foundation Long Term Ecological Research (Gosz 1986). While the fields of patch dynamics (Pickett and White 1985), hierarchy theory (Allen and Starr 1982; Urban *et al.* 1987), and landscape ecology (Forman and Godron 1981, 1986; Naveh and Lieberman 1984) are all addressing the issues of spatial and temporal heterogeneity, until recently the tools for addressing this issue have not been available. Recent advances in computer software and hardware have led to the development of geographical information systems, which now permit the quantitative assessment of the consequences of heterogeneity in ecological systems over a broad range of spatial and temporal scales.

Geographical information systems (GISs) are computer-based systems for the manipulation and analysis of spatially-distributed data. The GIS can be used to 1) analyze temporal change, 2) determine spatial coincidence of physical and biological fea-

First published in *Landscape Ecology*, Vol. 4 (1): 31-47, 1990. "Analyzing Spatial and Temporal Phenomena using Geographic Information Systems: A Review of Ecological Applications," Lucinda B.Johnson.

tures, 3) determine spatial characteristics such as proximity, contiguity, and patch size and shape, 4) analyze the direction and magnitude of fluxes of energy, organisms or materials, 5) produce graphic output, and 6) interface with simulation models to generate new spatial data. Whereas computer aided design (CAD) and computer graphics systems are heavily oriented towards display and manipulation of a graphic product, the GIS emphasizes complex analyses of geographically referenced data, with emphasis on spatial and non-spatial attributes (Burrough 1986).

The power and utility of the GIS has, in the past five years, gained wide-spread recognition in the fields of urban and regional planning, natural resource planning and management, and landscape architecture. Land use planning departments now link the GIS with their primary databases for accounting and planning purposes (Wear and Eschweiler 1986; Raymond 1986; Chang 1986). Foresters and other natural resource planners use the GIS for inventories and management (Johnston 1987; Ripple 1987). These applications primarily make use of a GIS's map creation, update and overlay capabilities.

Ecologists have been slower to recognize the utility of this tool for research applications. This is not surprising, given that early GISs were hardware-specific, lacked sufficient documentation, were difficult to learn and operate, and did not include the analysis capabilities required for some research applications. Now that GISs are more widely available and easier to operate, their value for examining spatial and temporal ecological relationships has just begun to be exploited.

The objectives of this paper are to 1) present a brief review of the existing uses of GIS in natural resources, 2) to describe the use of GIS in ecological research applications, and 3) point out some potential uses of GISs for ecological applications. It is impossible to cover all GIS applications in the area of natural resources; however I have made an effort to describe how the GIS has been used to improve upon old methods or to develop new methods. I hope to illustrate that the GIS is a powerful analytical tool that is available for an array of ecological applications.

2. Background

Geographical data describe features as points, lines, areas, or volumes in terms of their location in a known coordinate system, their physical or biological characteristics (*e.g.*, soil type, species) and their spatial relationship with respect to other features in the map (topology). This ability to generate topology is a key component of a GIS that distinguishes it from other types of computer graphics (Burrough 1986). A functional definition of the GIS includes two additional components: the ability to automatically synthesize data layers and to update a spatial database (Cowen 1987).

Geographical information system programs store and manipulate data as rasters (cells, pixels) or vectors (lines, polygons) (Table 1). Raster systems assign individual data values to each cell either by gridding existing maps which have been electronically traced (digitized), or by using remote sensors which assign data to individual picture elements (pixels). The raster format was used by early GISs, such as SYMAP, GRID, IMGRID, and GEOMAP. The major advantages of raster-based GISs are the computational simplicity of spatial analyses, such as overlays and Boolean operations (Maffini 1987), their compatibility with remotely sensed and automated data capture technologies (Faust 1987) as well as many types of simulation models. Disadvantages of raster data are that linear and areal measurements performed with raster data can be inaccurate if the cell size is large relative to the feature being represented, and raster data are stored inefficiently in comparison to vector data (Burrough 1986). Raster data are most appropriately used to represent data with 'fuzzy' boundaries, such as soils or wildlife ranges.

Vector data depict homogeneous areas as polygons delimited by curvilinear boundaries rather than cells. This data format is used extensively by cartographers for map production, because it simulates the linework on a conventional map. Polygon data are widely used for analysis of linear features, such as flow patterns and perimeter lengths. The advantages of the polygon data structure include a compact storage format, and accurate representation of graphics (Burrough 1986). Topological

Table 1. Characteristics of different data structures used by geographical information systems.

Raster	Vector	Quadtree
Data generalized by array of grid cells all equal in size	Data represented by strings of exact coordinates	Data generalized by array of grid cells of different sizes
Best for depicting areas with inexact boundaries (*e.g.*, natural features)	Accurately represent points and linear features, areas with exact boundaries (*e.g.*, man-made features)	Best for depicting large, homogenous areas with inexact boundaries
Best for overlay analysis functions, Boolean operations	Best for network analysis*	Best for analysis of regional characteristics
Requires large amounts of disk storage for complex maps; light usage of 'CPU' for analyses	Requires large amounts of memory for spatial analyses; heavy usage of 'CPU' for analyses	Best for systems with limited disk storage; moderate usage of 'CPU' for analyses
Measures spatial variability within polygons	Attributes apply uniformly to entire polygon	As in raster data

* Network analysis involves examination of the linkages of a series of interconnected arcs to determine distance relationships between two points along an arc. Subsequent analyses can focus on the flow and allocation or distribution of resources along the network.

structure, used for describing areal extent, connectivity, and contiguity, is also easily derived from vector data (Maffini 1987). The disadvantages of the vector data format include large central processing unit (CPU) requirements for processing, difficulty in interfacing with simulation models (Burrough 1986), and limitation to representation of planar surfaces as opposed to volumes or solids. Vector data are most appropriately used to represent data that have fixed boundaries, *e.g.*, property boundaries.

The quadtree is a subset of the raster data structure that attempts to reduce the redundancy of data by dividing data sets into sequentially smaller quads until either a homogeneous area or the minimum pixel size is encountered. Coverages with large, homogeneous polygons are most appropriate for storage and analysis of this data structure. Quadtree data has been used to describe geometric properties (Samet and Tamminen 1985), and is suggested as the data structure most amenable for integration with expert systems, based on current technology (Robinson and Frank 1987). Research efforts are currently being focused on use of the quadtree structure to store vector data (Ibbs and Stevens 1988).

A major deterrent to the use of GIS in ecological research has been the lack of suitable digital data at an appropriate resolution. While data sets at resolutions ranging from 10 m (*i.e.*, panchromatic SPOT satellite imagery) to greater than 1 km (*i.e.*, NOAA AVHRR series) are now available from satellite imagery (Jensen 1986), most fine-resolution data sets must be generated by manual digitization or automated scanning of analogue maps. These are time consuming and (relatively) expensive processes. If suitable maps do not exist, they can be generated from 1) field measurements, 2) radio telemetry, or 3) analysis of air photos or other images. Alternatively, output generated from a simulation model can be in a mapped format. Fortunately, the availability of ecologically-relevant data is increasing as state, federal, and international agencies increase their use of GISs.

3. Use of the GIS in natural resources and ecology

The use of the GIS by natural resource managers and ecologists has concentrated on, but not been limited to three types of operations: 1) characterization and measurement of linear and areal features, 2) intersection of spatially referenced data, and 3) proximity analyses.

3.1. Characterization and measurement of areas

GIS and/or database operations frequently are used to derive or reclassify attributes of polygons or areas. Attributes may be derived or modified based on the properties of points that overlap with polygons. This can be accomplished most simply by assigning the attribute(s) of the points to the polygon with which it coincides. More quantitative methods for assigning attributes involve interpolation between points in order to achieve a continuous spatial change. Interpolation techniques such as trend surface analyses, Fourier series, spline functions, moving average methods, and kriging are frequently used (Burrough 1986).

Once assigned, properties of areas can be reclassified using Boolean functions (*i.e.*, and, or, not, xor). Johnston and Naiman (1990), for example, originally classified beaver impoundments into 38 wetland categories, and then reclassified these into 15 categories for analysis. This characteristic of the GIS permits efficient use of large, expensive data bases for multiple purposes.

Areal measurements are standard output in any type of GIS; they are calculated automatically in most systems and are stored for ad hoc queries. When coupled with attribute data such as cover type, areal measurements form the basis of natural resource inventories. Forest managers in both the public and private sector now routinely use the inventory capabilities of the GIS at the federal (Chambers 1986; Hart *et al.* 1985; Root 1986; Steffenson 1987), state (Tosta and Davis 1986;

Anonymous 1987) and local levels (Wakeley 1987). Inventory data are primarily obtained from field observations and aerial photography, although satellite image analysis has shown promise as a forest mapping tool (Fox *et al.* 1985; Hopkins *et al.* 1988).

Unlike printed maps, which remain static once published, GIS digital maps can be updated as frequently as necessary (Cowen 1987). This capability is essential for maintaining timely inventories of forests as they are harvested. Comparing chronologically sequenced coverages can provide data on the location and density of harvested patches over time. Management practice histories such as planting, thinning, and fertilization data can be incorporated with tree stand data to evaluate their effectiveness or predict future stand characteristics (Herrington and Koten 1988).

Areal measurements are also an essential component of an ecological database. The size of ecological patches within a landscape are easily obtained from GIS data in both the raster and vector format. The number, type, and diversity of patches can also be determined when coupled with suitable attribute data. Many landscape studies have used these GIS capabilities (Iverson 1988; Iverson and Risser 1987; Johnston and Naiman 1990; Pastor and Broschart 1990; Robinove 1986; Turner 1987, 1990; Turner and Ruscher 1988). Areal data can be expressed in either their original units or as a proportion of the total landscape, and can be analyzed statistically within the GIS or exported to statistical programs for further analysis.

Areal measurements can also be performed on subsets of data layers by buffering a class or classes of features (*e.g.*, rivers, urban areas), or by extracting a region using a template as a 'cookie cutter'. For example, buffers were established around rivers in order to determine the effects of landuse on water quality (Johnston *et al.* 1988; Osborne and Wiley 1987). Buffers were also used to test for bias in General Land Office Survey Records in a study of landuse changes in Illinois (Iverson and Risser 1987). Extraction of a spatial subset by use of a template is a common operation, since many automated data sets are regional in extent and must be subdivided for analysis.

Thematic subsets can also be derived from digital data sets; for example, forested land or hydrology can be extracted from a general landuse/land cover map (*e.g.*, USGS GIRAS data from the National Digital Cartographic Database). As high quality, automated global and regional data sets become increasingly available, extraction of thematic and spatial subsets will become an increasingly common operation (Dangermond 1988).

Areal measurements and data derived from simple statistical procedures are also used during the development of land classification systems (Davis and Dozier 1990). As the emphasis of many ecological studies shifts to regional or global phenomenon, classification systems are increasingly sought to extrapolate data from small areas to entire regions. Coupled with data from satellite imagery, the GIS is proving to be a powerful tool for development of both general and specialized classification systems (Clark *et al.* 1986).

Several theories, models and analytical techniques that use area, length, or frequency measures derived from a GIS are being employed in spatial studies. These include 1) percolation theory, for analysis of diffusion of energy, organisms, or materials across landscape (O'Neill *et al.* 1988), 2) neutral models, which permit simulation of landscape patterns in the absence of processes (*i.e.*, disturbance) that drive them (Gardner *et al.* 1987), 3) mutual information theory, derived from information theory (Shannon and Weaver 1949), for ecological and classification (Davis and Dozier 1990), 4) numerical taxonomy techniques, also for land classification (Gordon 1985) and 5) kriging, for estimation of spatial distributions from point-sampled data (Burrough 1986).

3.2. Spatial coincidence

One of the most powerful operations that can be performed by the GIS is the vertical intersection, or overlay, of spatially distributed data. Overlay operations can be performed for the purpose of merging separate spatial data bases, (*e.g.*, hydrology layer with a soil layer), for analyzing spatial intersections between data layers, or for analyzing temporal

change. Previously, this operation was performed using transparent overlays; however this was a time-consuming process and the results were generally inaccurate. The development of automated procedures for accomplishing this operation has been a contributing factor in the commercial success of the GIS (Burrough 1986).

3.2.1. Spatial intersection

Natural resource managers and researchers commonly use spatial intersection operations to create habitat suitability models for identifying or managing wildlife habitats. GISs and satellite imagery, and/or radio telemetry have been linked successfully on a number of occasions to predict the occurrence of populations based on coincidence of required environmental or biotic factors (Hodgson *et al.* 1987, 1988; Mead *et al.* 1988; Scepan *et al.* 1987; Stenback *et al.* 1987) or conversely, to describe the habitat requirements based on experimental evidence or field observations (Shaw and Atkinson 1988; Young *et al.* 1987). Habitat characteristics such as land cover and general vegetation type of large regions can be identified from satellite imagery (*e.g.*, Palmeirim 1988). Using GIS overlay operations, essential habitat components such as soils and topography can then be intersected with land cover data. Polygon attributes can be weighted to reflect their relative importance (*e.g.*, vegetation type A versus vegetation type B; standing water and low elevation gradients versus running water and steep gradients). Finally, scores or indices reflecting the overall characteristics of each polygon are derived. By selectively weighting habitat properties and describing spatial variables such as patch size, shape, and arrangement (with respect to other patches) both the quality and the quantity of the habitat can be estimated (Davis and DeLain 1984; Donovan *et al.* 1987; Hodgson *et al.* 1987, 1988; Scepan *et al.* 1987; Stenback *et al.* 1987; Young *et al.* 1987). These models are known as weighting or ordinal models.

Behavioral studies are also enhanced by the use of the GIS coupled with satellite imagery and radio telemetry. Characteristics and size of the spotted owl's home range were described using these tools (Young *et al.* 1987), as were the foraging and nesting site preferences of the Indiana bat (Elizabeth Cook and Eugene Gardner pers. comm.). Both studies used preference tests to detect non-random associations with specific habitat types.

Whereas climate data such as wind speed, temperature and relative humidity have been used in GIS fire management models (Salazar and Power 1988), and for improvement of satellite image classification of vegetation and landcover (Cibula and Nyquist 1987), habitat suitability studies seldom incorporate climate variables. An exception is a study that examined the temporal changes in the wood stork's foraging cover through a 'wet' and 'dry' year (Hodgson et al. 1988). The next step in improving habitat suitability models would be to link them with models predicting the outcome of stochastic events such as fire, storms, etc.. This would increase the predictive power of the model over time for a broader range of environmental conditions.

While spatially explicit habitat suitability models are being used with some regularity, these models are static. Linking habitat suitability models with forest growth models and other management tools would result in a fully integrated management system. Another linkage that would greatly benefit ecologists and wildlife biologists is the coupling of models predicting species abundance from habitat data. To my knowledge, neither of these models have been coupled with a GIS to date.

In addition to habitat suitability models, overlay operations also are used in ordinal or weighting models for generating land suitability (Hendrix and Price 1986; Lyle and Stutz 1983), and hazard rating indices (DeMars 1986) for forests and croplands, and critical area indices for identifying regions subject to non-point source pollution (Sivertun et al. 1988). Hazard ratings also can be used to predict the establishment and spread of disturbance. For example, the Nicolet National Forest hazard rating index calculates a site potential based on soil and tree type, and uses it with data on vegetation cover and topography to predict the location of future infestations by the gypsy moth and Saratoga spittlebug (Morse 1986). Again, incorporation of data on cyclical (e.g., climate variables) and stochastic (e.g., weather) events would increase the predictive power of these models.

In an ecological context, vertical intersection of spatial data can be used to detect inter- and intraspecific interactions, interactions between boundaries (e.g., ranges of a plant species and an herbivore) and landscapes, or edaphic factors and organisms. For example, the GIS was used to map and analyze the distribution of hemlock and hardwood species in an old-growth forest with respect to soil types, topographic slope and aspect, and landscape features such as bogs and lakes. These relationships were discerned through the use of appropriate statistical techniques on spatial data derived from the GIS; they were not apparent from visual inspection of the covertype map (Pastor and Broschart 1990).

Empirical relationships between organisms and edaphic factors are also used as predictors or classifiers. For example, the distribution and extent of aquatic macrophyte growth is used to predict water quality (Welch et al. 1986; Welch and Remillard 1988). In addition, relationships between vegetation pattern and geology, elevation, slope, aspect, clear-sky insolation and drainage basin position are used to derive an ecological land classification system (Davis and Dozier 1990) and predict environment-vegetation associations (Frank Davis pers. comm.).

Another spatial interaction that can be analyzed by the GIS is the relationship between processes and landscapes. Animals, for example, can have a profound effect on the nature of landscapes. The effect of dam-building behavior on the hydrology of a region (Johnston and Naiman 1990) and the effects of bark beetle herbivory (Coulson et al. 1988) have both been examined using the GIS. The effect of human disturbance on landscapes has also been studied in this manner (Krummel et al. 1987; Iverson 1988). Conversely, the effects of landscape structure on a process, namely, fire behavior were modeled using GISs for data input (Salazar and Power 1988).

Detection of long-term landscape alterations resulting from human or stochastic disturbances can be enhanced by data collection by satellites and analyzed with a GIS. These techniques have been used to detect the location and extent of deforestation in northern Thailand (Hutacharoen 1987), and to estimate forest production in the Smoky Mountains (Cook *et al.* 1989).

3.2.2. Temporal change

One of the most powerful aspects of GISs is the ability to examine spatially referenced objects over time. Temporal analyses can span days or centuries, and are primarily limited by the availability of historical data. Inventories, for example, are updated on a scale of days as plantings and harvests take place. On the other hand, witness trees data from the early !800's were mapped and compared to current U.S. Geological Survey Land Use (LUDA) and Landsat Thematic Mapper data to determine the extent of changes in the vegetation patterns and landuse in Illinois since colonization (Iverson and Risser 1987; Iverson 1988). The GIS was used not only to determine the rate, but also the suitability of landuse conversions from one type to another.

Temporal changes in shapes of landscape patterns have been analyzed with particular emphasis on the effects of anthropogenic and 'natural' processes (Stringer *et al.* 1988; Turner and Ruscher 1988; Turner 1990). Landscape patterns are characterized by the number of landscape types and the amount of edge between them, by patch shape, and indices of dominance, diversity, and contagion (O'Neill *et al.* 1988). Landscape changes have been correlated with physiographic provinces (Turner and Ruscher 1988) and soil associations (Iverson 1988). These studies have taken place in areas where topographic constraints on landscape alterations have not been severe, thereby enabling fairly simple landscapes to evolve in the presence of anthropogenic disturbance. It will be interesting to see these methods being applied in areas with greater topographic relief under natural disturbance regimes.

In the absence of historical aerial photography, several novel approaches have been used to derive historical data. For example, results of historic events such as logging or burning in the same area were compared empirically (Hall *et al.* 1987), and changing vegetation patterns were detected by projecting tree diameters backwards to presettlement times using a forest simulation model (Covington *et al.* 1987).

In a shorter time frame, the effects of impoundment activities of beaver on the hydrology of Voyageurs National Park in Minnesota were examined over a 40 year period. While it would have been feasible to determine the changes in impoundment area over time using manual overlay techniques, the GIS enabled data to be collected for a large study area (250 km^2), and further, permitted analyses of pond shape (C. Johnston, unpublished data) and location relative to other ponds and landscape features (Naiman *et al.* 1988).

Temporal analyses using GISs have been used heavily for detection of landscape or regional phenomena, yet the potential exists for studies at a finer scale. Analysis of circadian rhythms of behavior with respect to environmental gradients of temperature, light, moisture or nutrients would be small scale applications worth investigating.

4. Proximity analyses

Proximity, or neighborhood analyses, are performed to examine spatial interrelationships in a horizontal plane. These relationships can be derived from the results of a buffer operation, or by analysis of the topology of one data layer with respect to another. In the most simplistic type of a proximity analysis, topological relationships are used to produce a map in which the boundaries between classes of features are eliminated. For example, crown maps of individual size classes of a tree species can be overlayed. A composite crown map of all age classes can then be produced by removing the boundaries between individual trees. While these operations are quite powerful, it is the analytical capabilities of neighborhood analyses that are important to ecologists. Proximity analyses have recently been used to quantify inter- and intraspecific relationships by examining the selective juxtaposition of hemlock and hardwood tree species (Pastor and Broschart 1990). Proximity functions also have been used to determine contiguity of landscape patches in order to provide a descriptor for landscape structure (O'Neill *et al.* 1988; Pastor and Broschart 1990; Turner 1987, 1990; Turner and Ruscher 1988), or to predict susceptibility and/or results of disturbance (Gardner *et al.* 1987). Recent discussions on the maintenance of biodiversity have focused on landscape patch dynamics to the extent that patch contiguity variables are now being incorporated in wildlife habitat models and studies (Donovan *et al.* 1987; Hodgson *et al.* 1988).

5. Linear measurements and analyses

Perimeter measurements, which are easily derived in vector, but not raster GISs, are used increasingly in landscape analyses. The fractal dimension, an area-perimeter ratio, is believed to relate patch shape to substrate, disturbance, or other processes. It has been used to describe river networks (Tarboton *et al.* 1988), forest patches (Krummel *et al.* 1987; Pastor and Broschart 1990), landscape patches (Iverson, 1988; O'Neill *et al.* 1988; Turner 1987, 1990; Turner and Ruscher 1988), soil units (Burrough 1983) and cloud shapes (Lovejoy 1982). Further use of the fractal dimension in landscapes subject to natural versus anthropogenic disturbances will be useful to explain some of the discrepancies found between patch shapes measured by Pastor and Broschart (1990) and others (Iverson 1988; Krummel *et al.* 1987; Turner and Ruscher 1988).

Another use for linear distance measures is the network analysis. A network analysis calculates an optimum route along a path (*i.e.*, the shortest distance between two points) and can be constrained by variables such as traffic patterns or physical obstacles such as topography. In addition, resources can be allocated along the path to centers having finite capacities (Lupien *et al.* 1987). A typical network analysis problem would determine the optimal route for transport of timber from stands to processing plants (Berry 1986; Berry and Sailor 1981). The ecological correlate would be a study of the browse pattern of a large herbivore in a patchy landscape.

Limited use has been made of the GIS for predation or foraging studies, except in the cases described above, where the sizes and characteristics of foraging areas were described (*e.g.*, Young *et al.* 1987). In a resource utilization study of several Amerindian populations in Alaska, a network function was employed to allocate the hunting and fishing resources over the landscape. The paths between resource utilization areas served as the arcs of the network (Anthony Burns, pers. comm.). Network analyses alone, or coupled with predation or foraging models, could prove to be powerful tools for ecological studies.

6. Linkage with spatial models

A more advanced application of GISs to resource management and ecology is the use of spatially-linked models. The spatial distribution, coincidence, or proximity of variables (*e.g.*, stand characteristics, soil properties) can be used as input from the GIS to the model. The results of the predictive model can be tested with independent data, or can be reentered into the GIS for spatial analysis or display. In an iterative process, successive model runs can be performed. Models can also use empirical information and analytical techniques to determine the appropriate variables and weights in these analyses (DeMars 1986; Johnston 1987; Morse 1986; Parks *et al.* 1987; Rowland 1986; White 1986). Recently the GIS has been used for input in an air dispersion model (Gould *et al.* 1988), and a groundwater model (Anonymous 1986) as well as a biogeochemical cycling model for the Great Plains (Burke *et al.* 1990). Sensitivity analyses run at different scales in the latter study point towards some of the inherent advantages of using the GIS, namely, the ability of the GIS to rapidly process data at different scales permits an analysis of the sensitivity of model parameters to data base resolution. However, reliance on digital data collected from unknown or unreliable sources can lead to uncontrolled errors (Burke *et al.* 1990). Integration of the GIS with spatial models holds enormous promise for ecosystem, regional, and global modeling efforts and is discussed in some detail by Wheeler (1988) and Burrough *et al.* (1988).

7. Conclusions

As increased emphasis is placed on long-term studies covering larger areas, GISs will play a greater role in data storage and analysis. Commercial development of fast, more user-friendly, accurate, and relatively inexpensive software and hardware is occurring to meet these demands. In addition, research aimed at improving data capture, storage, and analysis procedures, as well as improving the integrity and resolution of the data is underway in several fields (Faust 1987; Greenlee 1987).

While the applications described above seemingly have glorified the GIS as a tool that permits complex spatial analyses over both very large or very small areas, there is a 'down' side to the technology. Concern has focused on lack of standardized data sets, error propagation, and misuse of the technology (Berry 1987). It is apparent, though, that many Federal agencies are now addressing the issues of production of standardized digital data sets (c.f., Gebhard 1987; Kineman 1987). Error propagation in the GIS environment, however, is still a source of concern. Sources of error include: 1) overt errors resulting from use of outdated source material, and inappropriate or incompatible data format, resolution, and scale, 2) manuscript error derived from georeferencing errors, poor or outdated data collection and measurement methods, and natural variation not captured by appropriate interpolation techniques, and 3) processing errors generated by the operator, equipment, or software algorithms (Burrough 1986). The magnitude of the error is compounded with successive overlays (Walsh *et al.* 1987). Increased usage of GISs has brought about a greater awareness of the first two sources of errors listed above, however, the third source is inherent in many of the programs in use today, and is therefore more difficult for the average user to comprehend and correct. As a result, it is incumbent on GIS users to develop an understanding of methods for calculating map variance and uncertainty (c.f., Berry 1987; Walsh 1987) and to incorporate uncertainty and sensitivity analyses in modeling efforts (c.f., Dale *et al.* 1988).

Errors in area calculations in raster data sets are inherent in the data format; however, fuzzy set theory should provide more accurate estimations of area for different classes (Stoms 1987). Fuzzy set theory explains the degree of membership of an element X in set A. In a raster data set, each pixel is assigned a pure classification based on a Boolean function. Thus underestimation of rare cover types, and overestimation of common cover types is the norm, unless a very small pixel size, relative to the areas depicted, is used. Fuzzy theory is believed to be important for the refinement of expert systems (Stoms 1987).

The development of expert system-GIS interfaces offers the greatest prospect of advancement for GISs in the near future. Focus will be concentrated in four areas of GIS capabilities: map design, feature extraction, database management, and decision-making (suitability analyses) (Robinson and Frank 1987). Intelligent GISs in the natural resources and ecological sciences will focus on integrating management models with natural resource models interpreting landscape data, and animal behavior studies (Coulson *et al.* 1987). A review of existing systems can be found in Robinson and Frank (1987). The greatest challenges for development of these systems are posed by the array of data structures used by GISs, and more importantly, by the range of reliability and sources of data (Ripple and Ulshoefer 1987).

While advances in expert systems, data capture, and data storage techniques are forthcoming, it is now incumbent upon the ecologists themselves to explore the capabilities of the GIS. Terrestrial ecologists are realizing its utility for spatial analyses and coupling with growth and simulation models. Aquatic ecologists, however, have yet to recognize the potential of this tool, although they have recently begun using satellite imagery for monitoring purposes (Chase *et al.* 1973; Mortimer 1988; Smith and Blackwell 1980; Vande Castle *et al.* 1988; Welch *et al.* 1986; Welch and Remillard 1988), remote detection of primary production (Mortimer 1988; Perry 1986) and biomass estimates (Gross *et al.* 1987). As in terrestrial systems, GISs should prove to be equally valuable for predation and foraging studies and analysis of spatial relationships in habitats such as the hyporheic zone and the sediment-water interface. The current availability of georeferenced water quality data from Environmental Protection Agency-STORET (Office of Water and Hazardous Materials), and the forthcoming availability of a three-dimensional (volumetric) GIS (*e.g.*, Interactive Volume Modeling from Dynamic Graphics, Inc.) should open up many avenues of research in limnology and aquatic ecology.

Acknowledgements

Grateful acknowledgement is made to Joseph Berry, Carol Johnston, David Mladenoff, Terry Jackson and an anonymous reviewer for critical comments on this manuscript. This is Contribution No: 47 of the Center for Water and the Environment, Natural Resources Research Institute, and Contribution No. 3 of the NRRI Geographic Information System Laboratory.

References

Allen, T.F.H. and Starr, T.B. 1982. Hierarchy. University of Chicago Press, 310 pp., Chicago, IL.

Anonymous, 1986. San Gabriel Basin geographic information system demonstration, Los Angeles County, California. Environmental Protection Agency TS-AMD-85742-0.

Anonymous, 1987. Interview: Larry Sugarbaker. Photogrammetric Engineering and Remote Sensing 53: 1467–1472.

Berry, J.K. and Sailor, J.K. 1981. A spatial analysis of timber supply. Proceedings of the In-Place Resource Inventories: Principles and Practices. University of Maine, pp. 828–833. Orono, ME.

Berry, J.K. 1986. Using a microcomputer system to spatially characterize effective timber accessibility. *In*: Proceedings of the GIS Workshop, pp. 273–283, Atlanta, GA.

Berry, J.K. 1987. Computer-assisted map analysis: potential and pitfalls. Photogrammetric Engineering and Remote Sensing 53: 1405–1410.

Burke, I.C., Schimel, D.S., Yonker, C.M., Parton, W.J. and Joyce, L.A. 1990. Regional modeling of grassland biogeochemistry using GIS. Landscape Ecol. (this issue)

Burrough, P.A. 1983. Multiscale sources of spatial variation in soil. The application of fractal concepts to nested levels of soil variation. J. Soil Sci. 34: 577–597.

Burrough, P.A. 1986. Principles of geographical information systems for land resources assessment. Monograph on Soils and resources Survey No. 12. Oxford Science Publications, 193 pp., Clarendon Press, Oxford, U.K.

Burrough, P.A., van Deursen, W. and Heuvelink, G. 1988. Linking spatial process models and GIS: a marriage of convenience or a blossoming partnership? Proceedings of GIS/LIS '88, 3rd Annual International Conference, pp. 598–607, San Antonio, TX.

Chambers, D. 1986. Development and application of a pilot geographic information system for the U.S. Forest Service: Tongass National Forest. *In*: Proceedings of the Geographic Information Systems Workshop, pp. 162–171, Atlanta, GA.

Chang, K-T. 1986. The development of a geographical information system for regional planning in Taiwan. *In*: Proceedings of the American Society of Photogrametry and Remote Sensing and American Congress on Surveying and Mapping, pp. 126–130, Washington, D.C.

Chase, P.E. and Reed, L. 1973. Utilization of ERTS-1 data to monitor and classify eutrophication of inland lakes. *In*: Proceedings of Symposium on significant results obtained from the Earth Resources Technology Satellite-1 Vol 1(B) pp. 1597–1604.

Cibula, W.G. and Nyquist, M.O. 1987. Use of topographic and climatological models in a geographical data base to improve Landsat MSS classification for Olympic National Park. Photogrammetric Engineering and Remote Sensing 53: 67–75.

Clark, C.A., Cate, R.B., Trenchard, M.H., Boatright, J.A. and Bizzell, R.M. 1986. Mapping and classifying large ecological units. BioScience 36: 476–477.

Cook, E.A., Iverson, L.R. and Graham, R.L. 1989. Estimating forest productivity with Thematic Mapper and biogeographical data. In Press: Remote Sensing of the Environment.

Coulson, R.N., Folse, L.J. and Loh, D.K. 1987. Artificial intelligence and natural resource management. Science 237: 262–267.

Covington, W.W., Moore, M.M. and Andariese, S.W. 1987. Changes in forest patterns and multiresource conditions in an Arizona ponderosa pine forest since European settlement. *In*: Proceedings of GIS'87, 2nd Annual International Conference, Exhibits and Workshops on Geographic Information Systems, pp. 701, San Francisco, CA.

Cowen, D.J. 1987. GIS vs. CAD vs. DBMS: What are the differences? *In*: Proceedings of GIS'87, 2nd Annual International Conference, Exhibits and Workshops on Geographic Information Systems, pp. 46–56, San Francisco, CA.

Dale, V.H., Jager, H.I., Gardner, R.H. and Rosen, A.E. 1988. Using sensitivity and uncertainty analyses to improve predictions of broad-scale forest development. Ecol. Model. 42: 165–178.

Dangermond, J. 1988. A review of digital data commonly available and some of the practical problems of entering them in the GIS. Technical Papers. ACSM-ASPRS Annual Convention, pp. 1–10, St. Louis, MO.

Davis, F.W. and Dozier, J. 1990. Mutual information analysis of a spatial database for ecological land classification. Photogrammetric Engineering and Remote Sensing. In press.

Davis, L.S. and DeLain, L.I. 1984. Linking wildlife-habitat analysis to forest planning with ECOSYM. *In*: Wildlife 2000. Modeling habitat relationships of terrestrial vertebrates, Chapter 51, pp. 361–370. Edited by J. Verner, M.L. Morrison and C.J. Ralph. University of Wisconsin Press, Madison, WI.

DeMars, C. 1986. Applying RID*POLY to rate forest stand hazard for tree mortality. *In*: Proceedings of the Geographic Information Systems Workshop, pp. 284–292, Atlanta, GA.

DiCastri, F., Hansen, A.J. and Holland, M.M. 1988. A new look at ecotones. Special Issue 17, Biology International. International Union of Biological Sciences News Magazines, 163 pp.

Donovan, M.L., Rabe, D.L. and Olson, C.E., Jr. 1987. Use of geographic information systems to develop habitat suitability models. Widl. Soc. Bull. 15: 574–579.

Dyer, M.I. DiCastri, F. and Hansen, A.J. 1988. Geosphere-Biosphere observatories. Their definition and design for studying global change. Biology International Special Issue 16. International Union of Biological Sciences News Magazine, 39 pp.

Faust, N.L. 1987. Automated data capture for geographic information systems: A commentary. Photogrammetric Engineering and Remote Sensing 53: 1389–1390.

Forman, R.T.T. and Godron, M. 1981. Patches and structural components for a landscape. BioScience 31: 733–740.

Forman, R.T.T. and Godron, M. 1986. Landscape Ecology. 619 pp, John Wiley and Sons, New York, N.Y.

Fox, L. III., Brockhaus, J.A. and Tosta, N.D. 1985. Classification of timberland productivity in Northwestern California using Landsat, topographic, and ecological data. Photogrammetric Engineering and Remote Sensing 51: 1745–1752.

Gardner, R.H., Milne, B.T., Turner, M.G. and O'Neill, R.V. 1987. Neutral models for analysis of broad-scale landscape pattern. Landscape Ecol. 1: 19–28.

Gebhard, R.L. 1987. The National Wetlands Inventory. In: Proceedings of GIS'87, 2nd Annual International Conference, Exhibits and Workshops on Geographic Information Systes, Vol. 3, pp. 98–101, San Francisco, CA.

Gordon, S.I. 1985. Computer models in environmental planning. 225 pp, Van Nostrand Reinhold Co., New York, N.Y.

Gosz, J.R. 1986. Biogeochemistry research needs: observations from the Ecosystem Studies Program of the National Science Foundation. Biogeochemistry 2: 101–112.

Gould, M.D., Tatham, J.A. and Savitsky, B. 1988. Applying spatial search techniques to chemical emergency management, pp. 843–851. In: Proceedings of GIS/LIS'88, 3rd Annual International Conference. San Antonio, TX.

Greenlee, D.D. 1987. Raster and vector processing for scanned linework. Photogrammetric Engineering and Remote Sensing 53: 1383–1387.

Gross, M.F., Hardinsky, M.A., Klemas, V. and Wolf, P.L. 1987. Quantification of biomass of the marsh grass *Spartina alterniflora* Loisel using Landsat Thematic imagery. Photogrammetric Engineering and Remote Sensing 53: 1577–1583.

Hall, F.G., Strebel, D.E. and Nickeson, J.E. 1987. Satellite derived temporal profiles of natural vegetation. 2nd Annual Landscape Ecology Symposium, Charlottesville, VA. Abstract.

Hart, J.A., Wherry, D.B. and Bain, S. 1985. An operational GIS for Flathead National Forest. In: Proceedings of the American Society of Photogrammetry and Remote Sensing and American Congress on Surveying and Mapping, pp. 244–253, Washington, D.C.

Hendrix, W. and Price, J. 1986. Application of geographic information systems for assessment of site index and forest management constraints. In: Proceedings of the Geographic Information Systems Workshop, pp. 263–272, Atlanta, GA.

Herrington, L.P. and Koten, D.E. 1988. A GIS based decision support system for forest management. In: Proceedings of GIS/LIS'88, 3rd Annual International Conference, pp. 825–831, San Antonio, TX.

Hodgson, M.E., Jensen, J.R., Mackey, H.E., Jr. and Coulter, M.C. 1987. Remote sensing of wetland habitat: A woodstork example. Photogrammetric Engineering and Remote Sensing 53: 1075–1080.

Hodgson, M.E., Jensen, J.R.,, Mackey, H.E., Jr. and Coulter, M.C. 1988. Monitoring wood stork foraging habitat using remote sensing and geographic information systems. Photogrammetric Engineering and Remote Sensing 54: 1601–1607.

Hopkins, P.F., Maclean, A.L. and Lillesand, T.M. 1988. Assessment of thematic mapper imagery for forestry applications under Lake States conditions. Photogrammetric Engineering and Remote Sensing 54: 61–68.

Hutacharoen, M. 1987. Application of geographic information systems technology to the analysis of deforestation and associated environmental hazards in northern Thailand. In: Proceedings of GIS'87, 2nd Annual International Conference, Exhibits and Workshops on Geographic Information Systems, pp 509–518, San Francisco, CA.

Ibbs, T.J. and Stevens, A. 1988. Quadtree storage of vector data. Int. J. Geographical Information Systems 2: 43–56.

Iverson, L.R. 1988. Land-use changes in Illinois, USA: The influence of landscape attributes on current and historic land use. Landscape Ecol. 2: 45–61.

Iverson, L.R. and Risser, P.G. 1987. Analyzing long-term changes in vegetation with geographic information system and remotely sensed data. Adva. Space Res. 7: 183–194.

Jensen, J.R. 1986. Introductory digital image processing. 379 pp., Prentice Hall, Englewood Cliffs, N.J.

Johnston, C.A., Detenbeck, N.E. and Niemi, G.J. 1988. Geographic information systems for cumulative impact assessment. Photogrammetric Engineering and Remote Sensing 54: 1609–1615.

Johnston, C.A. and Naiman, R.J. 1990. Use of a GIS to analyze long-term landscape alteration by beaver. Landscape Ecol. (this issue)

Johnston, K.M. 1987. Natural resource modeling in the geographic information system environment. Photogrammetric Engineering and Remote Sensing 53: 1411–1415.

Kineman, J.J. 1987. Global databases for the systems science era: a summary of activities at the National Geophysical Data Center. In: Proceedings of GIS'87, 2nd Annual International Conference, Exhibits and Workshops on Geographic Information Systems, Vol. 3, pp. 117–123, San Francisco, CA.

Krummel, J.R., Gardner, R.H., Sugihara, G., O'Neill, R.V. and Coleman, P.R. 1987. Landscape patterns in a disturbed environment. Oikos 48: 321–324.

Lovejoy, S. 1982. Area-perimeter relation for rain and cloud areas. Science 216: 185–187.

187

Lupien, A.E., Moreland, W.H. and Dangermond, J. 1987. Network analysis in geographical information systems. Photogrammetric Engineering and Remote and Sensing 53: 1417–1421.

Lyle, J. and Stutz, F.P. 1983. Computerized land use suitability mapping. Cartography. J. 20: 39–49.

Mead, R.A., Cockerham, L.S., Robinson, C.M. 1988. Mapping gopher tortoise habitat on the Ocala National Forest using a GIS. In: Proceedings of GIS/LIS'88, 3rd Annual International Conference, pp. 395–400, San Antonio, TX.

Minshall, G.W. 1988. Stream ecosystem theory: a global perspective. J. North Amer. Benthol. Soc. 7: 263–288.

Morse, B. 1986. Forecasting forest pest hazard with a geographic information system. In: Proceedings of the Geographic Information Systems Workshop, April 1–4, 1986, pp. 255–262, Atlanta, GA.

Mortimer, C.H. 1988. Discoveries and testable hypotheses arising from Coastal Zone Scanner imagery of southern Lake Michigan. Limnol. Oceanogr. 33: 203–226.

Naiman, R.J., Johnston, C.A. and Kelley, J.C. 1988. Alteration of North American streams by beaver. BioScience 38: 753–762.

Naveh, Z. and Lieberman, A.S. 1984. Landscape Ecology. 356 pp. Springer-Verlag, New York, N.Y.

O'Neill, R.V., Krummel, J.R., Gardner, R.H., Sugihara, G., Jackson, B., DeAngelis, D.L., Milne, B.T., Turner, M.G., Zygmunt, B., Christensen, S.W., Dale, V.H. and Graham, R.L. 1988. Indices of landscape pattern. Landscape Ecol. 1: 153–162.

Osborne, L.L. and Wiley, M.J. 1988. Empirical relationships between land use/cover patterns and stream water quality in an agricultural watershed. J. Env. Manag. 26: 9–27.

Palmeirim, J.M. 1988. Automatic mapping of avian species habitat using satellite imagery. Oikos 52: 59–68.

Parks, B.O., Simmons, G. and Gage, S. 1987. A spatial model and geographic information system for state-wide assessment of risks due to gypsy moth infestation in Michigan. In: Proceedings of GIS'87, 2nd Annual International Conference, Exhibits and Workshops on Geographic Information Systems, pp. 707, San Francisco, CA.

Pastor, J. and Broschart, M. 1990. The spatial pattern of a north conifer-hardwood landscape. Landscape Ecol. (this issue).

Perry, M.J. 1986. Assessing marine primary production from space. BioScience 36: 461–467.

Pickett, S.T.A. and White, P.S. (eds) 1985. The ecology of natural disturbance and patch dynamics. 472 pp., Academic Pres, Inc., Orlando, FL.

Raymond, G. 1986. Land information systems in Canada. In: Proceedings of the American Society of Photogrametry and Remote Sensing and American Congress on Surveying and Mapping, March 16–21, 1986, pp. 100–106, Washington, D.C.

Ripple, W.J. (ed). 1987. Geographic information systems for resource management: A compendium. American Society of Photogrammetry and Remote Sensing and American Con-

gress on Surveying and Mapping, 288 pp., Falls Church, VA.

Ripple, W.J. and Ulshoefer, V.S. 1987. Expert systems and spatial data models for efficient geeographic data handling. Photogrammetric Engineering and Remote Sensing 53: 1431–1433.

Robinove, C.J. 1986. Spatial diversity index mapping of classes in grid cell maps. Photogrammetric Engineering and Remote Sensing 52: 1171–1173.

Robinson, V.B. and Frank, A.U. 1987. Expert systems for geographic information systems. Photogrammetric Engineering and Remote Sensing 53: 1435–1441.

Root, R.R., Stitt, S.C., Nyquist, M.O., Waggoner, G.S. and Agee, J.K. 1986. Vegetation and fire fuel models mapping of North Cascades National Park. In: Proceedings of the American Society of Photogrametry and Remote Sensing and American Congress on Surveying and Mapping. March 16–21, 1986, pp. 78–85, Washington, D.C.

Rowland, E. 1986. Use of a GIS to display establishment and spread of gypsy moth infestation. In: Proceedings of the Geographic Information Systems Workshop, April 1–4, 1986. pp. 249–254, Atlanta, GA.

Salazar, L.A. and Power, J.D. 1988. Three-dimensional representations for fire management planning: A demonstration. Proceedings of GIS/LIS'88, pp. 948–960, San Antonio, TX.

Samet, H. and Tamminen, M. 1985. Computing geometric properties of images represented by linear quadtrees. IEEE Transactions on Pattern Analysis and Machine Intelligence PAMI-7: 229–240.

Scepan, J., Davis, F. and Blum, L.L. 1987. A geographic information system for managing condor habitat. In: Proceedings of GIS'87, 2nd Annual International Conference, Exhibits and Workshops on Geographic Information Systems, pp. 476–486, San Francisco, CA.

Shannon, C.E. and Weaver, W. 1949. The mathematical theory of communication. University of Illinois Press, Urbana, IL.

Shaw, D.M. and Atkinson, S.F. 1988. GIS applications for golden-cheeked warbler habitat description. In: Proceedings of GIS'87, pp. 401–406, San Antonio, TX.

Sivertun, A., Reinelt, L.E. and Castensson, R. 1988. A GIS method to aid in non-point source critical area analysis. Int. J. Geographical Informations Systems 2: 365–378.

Smith, A.Y. and Blackwell, R.J. 1980. Development of an information data base for watershed monitoring. Photogrammetric Engineering and Remote Sensing 46: 1027–1038.

Steffenson, J.R. 1987. Application of a geographic information system to design a vegetation resource inventory. In: Proceedings of GIS'87, 2nd Annual International Conference, Exhibits and Workshops on Geographic Information Systems, pp. 431–439, San Francisco, CA.

Stenback, J.M., Travlos, C.B., Barrett, R.H. and Congalton, R.G. 1987. Application of remotely sensed digital data and a GIS in evaluating deer habitat suitability on the Tehama deer winter range. In: Proceedings of GIS'87, 2nd Annual International Conference, Exhibits and Workshops on Geographic Information Systems, pp. 440–445, San Francisco, CA.

Stoms, D. 1987. Reasoning with uncertainty in intelligent geographic information systems. *In*: Proceedings of GIS'87, 2nd Annual International Conference, Exhibits and Workshops on Geographic Information Systems, pp. 693–700, San Francisco, CA.

Stringer, W.J., Groves, J.E. and Olmsted, C. 1988. Landsat determined geographic change. Photogrammetric Engineering and Remote Sensing 54: 347–351.

Tarboton, D.G., Bras, R.L., Rodriguez-Iture, I. 1988. The fractal nature of river networks. Water Resources Research 24: 1317–1322.

Tosta, N. and Davis, L. 1986. Utilizing a geographic information system for statewide resource assessment: The California case. *In*: Proceedings of GIS'87, 2nd Annual International Conference, Exhibits and Workshops on Geographic Information Systems, pp. 147–154, San Francisco, CA.

Turner, M.G. 1987. Spatial simulation of landscape changes in Georgia: A comparison of 3 transition models. Landscape Ecol. 1: 29–36.

Turner, M.G. 1990. Analyzing landscape data and extrapolating across spatial scales. Landscape Ecol. (this issue).

Turner, M.G. and Ruscher, C.L. 1988. Changes in landscape patterns in Georgia. Landscape Ecol. 1: 241–251.

Urban, D.L., O'Neill, R.V. and Shugart, H.H. 1987. Landscape ecology: a hierarchical perspective. BioScience 37: 119–127.

Vande Castle, J.R., Lathrop, R.G., Jr., Lillesand, T.M. 1988. The significance of GIS and remote sensing technology in Great Lakes monitoring and resource management. *In*: Proceedings on The Great Lakes: Living with North America's Inland Waters. pp. 155–161. Edited by D.H. Hickcox. American Water Resources Association, Bethesda, MD.

Wakeley, R. 1987. GIS and Weyerhaeuser – 20 years experience, pp. 446–457. *In*: Proceedings of GIS'87, 2nd Annual International Conference, Exhibits, and Workshops on Geographical Information Systems, San Francisco, CA.

Walsh, S.J., Lightfoot, D.R. and Butler, D.R. 1987. Recognition and assessment of error in geographic information systems. Photogrammetric Engineering and Remote Sensing 53: 1423–1430.

Wear, S. and Eschweiler, P.Q. 1986. Current applications of geographical information systems in the State of New York. Proceedings of the American Society of Photogrametry and Remote Sensing and American Congress on Surveying and Mapping, pp. 1–11, Washington, D.C.

Welch, R., Remillard, M., Fung, S. and Slack, R. 1986. Monitoring aquatic vegetation and water quality with a geographic information system. *In*: Proceedings of the Geographic Information Systems Workshop, pp. 302–303, Atlanta, GA.

Welch, R. and Remillard, M.M. 1988. Remote sensing and geographic information system techniques for aquatic resource evaluation. Photogrammetric Engineering and Remote Sensing. 54: 177–185.

Wheeler, D.J. 1988. A look at model-building with geographic information systems. Proceedings of GIS/LIS'88, pp. 580–585, San Antonio, TX.

White, W. 1986. Modeling forest pest impacts-aided by a geographic information system in a decision support system framework. *In*: Proceedings of the Geographic Information Systems Workshop, pp. 238–254, Atlanta, GA.

Young, T.N., Eby, J.R., Allen, H.L., Hewitt, M.J., III and Dixon, K.R. 1987. Wildlife habitat analysis using Landsat and radiotelemetry in a GIS with application to spotted owl preference for old growth. *In*: Proceedings of GIS'87, 2nd Annual International Conference, Exhibits and Workshops on Geographic Information Systems, pp. 595–600, San Francisco, CA.

Biological Conservation **57** (1991) 73–88

Measuring Forest Landscape Patterns in the Cascade Range of Oregon, USA

William J. Ripple

Environmental Remote Sensing Applications Laboratory, Department of Forest Resources,
Oregon State University, Corvallis, Oregon 97331, USA

G. A. Bradshaw

Environmental Remote Sensing Applications Laboratory and Department of Forest Science,
Oregon State University, Corvallis, Oregon 97331, USA

&

Thomas A. Spies

USDA Forest Service, Pacific Northwest Research Station and
Oregon State University, Corvallis, Oregon 97331, USA

(Received 24 April 1990; revised version received and accepted 8 October 1990)

ABSTRACT

This paper describes the use of a set of spatial statistics to quantify the landscape pattern caused by the patchwork of clearcuts made over a 15-year period in the western Cascades of Oregon. Fifteen areas were selected at random to represent a diversity of landscape fragmentation patterns. Managed forest stands (patches) were digitized and analysed to produce both tabular and mapped information describing patch size, shape, abundance and spacing, and matrix characteristics of a given area. In addition, a GIS fragmentation index was developed which was found to be sensitive to patch abundance and to the spatial distribution of patches. Use of the GIS-derived index provides an automated method of determining the level of forest fragmentation and can be used to facilitate spatial analysis of the landscape for later coordination with field and remotely sensed data. A comparison of the spatial statistics calculated for the two years indicates an increase in forest fragmentation as characterized by an increase in mean patch abundance and a decrease in interpatch distance, amount of interior natural forest habitat, and

73

the GIS fragmentation index. Such statistics capable of quantifying patch shape and spatial distribution may prove important in the evaluation of the changing character of interior and edge habitats for wildlife.

INTRODUCTION

The Douglas-fir *Pseudotsuga menziesii* (Mirb.) Franco forests of western Oregon have been cut extensively during the past 40 years. In these forests, clearcuts, new plantations, and second-growth stands now exist on the landscape formerly dominated by extensive old-growth forests and younger forests resulting from fire disturbance (Spies & Franklin, 1988). Consequently, the landscape has become more spatially heterogeneous. Some of the effects of this newly created landscape on the forest ecosystem are immediately apparent. For example, the amount of old-growth forest habitat for interior species such as the northern spotted owl *Strix occidentalis caurina* is altered with forest harvesting practices. Less well understood are the long-term and more subtle interactive effects on ecosystem processes (e.g. changes in species diversity and abundance, nutrient cycling and primary forest productivity), which may occur as a result of the changed forest mosaic. It is generally accepted that wildlife ecology and behavior may be strongly dependent on the nature and pattern of landscape elements (Forman & Godron, 1986), but few precise measurements relating these changes to landscape spatial alteration have been made. Properties of forested landscapes such as patch size, the amount of edge, the distance between habitat areas, and the connectedness of habitat patches have a direct influence on the flora and fauna (Thomas, 1979; Harris, 1984; Franklin & Forman, 1987; Ripple & Luther, 1987). For these reasons, models and monitoring schemes are urgently needed for prescribing the location, size, and shape of future harvest units and old-growth habitat patches. With proper design, these forest landscapes should be able to achieve desired habitat values and maintain biological diversity (Noss, 1983; Harris, 1984; Franklin & Forman, 1987).

As a first step to studying forest landscape pattern, the spatial character of the landscape must be quantified to relate ecological processes to landscape configuration. Numerous methods and indices have been proposed for these purposes (e.g. Forman & Godron, 1986; Milne, 1988; O'Neill *et al.*, 1988). Landscape pattern can be quantified using statistics in terms of the landscape unit itself (e.g. patch size, shape, abundance, and spacing) as well as the spatial relationship of the patches and matrix comprising the landscape (e.g. nearest-neighbor distance and amount of contiguous matrix). A selection of these measures can therefore describe the several aspects of fragmentation which occur as the result of forest harvesting practices.

Because spatial analyses are often cumbersome due to large amounts of data, it is desirable that the analysis be automated. Furthermore, it should be amenable for study at various scales in concert with a variety of data types. Automated systems such as geographical information systems (GIS) address such needs (Ripple, 1987, 1989). With the development of GIS, the ability to readily measure spatial characteristics of landscapes in conjunction with field and remotely sensed data has become possible.

The overall goal of the present study was to test the feasibility of measuring forest landscape patterns accurately using a set of spatial statistics and a GIS. Specifically, we set out to apply a set of statistics to a series of forested landscapes in the Cascade Range of western Oregon to (1) assess the sensitivity of these statistics to characterize landscape pattern; (2) develop and test a GIS-derived index to measure fragmentation; and (3) quantify the change and types of forest fragmentation through time in our study area. The results of this pilot study are intended to aid the forester, wildlife biologist, and land manager in assessing change in wildlife habitat and alteration in ecosystem processes as a result of forest fragmentation.

STUDY AREA

The study area consisted of the Blue River and Sweet Home ranger districts of the Willamette National Forest. According to Franklin and Dyrness (1973), these ranger districts lie primarily in the western hemlock *Tsuga heterophylla* and pacific silver fir *Abies amabilis* vegetation zone, with the major forest tree species consisting of Douglas-fir, western hemlock, pacific silver fir, noble fir *Abies procera*, and western redcedar *Thuja plicata*. The climate can be characterized as maritime with wet, mild winters and dry, warm summers. Under natural conditions, Douglas-fir is the seral dominant at elevations below 1000 m, where it typically develops nearly pure, even-aged stands after fire. Large areas are covered by old-growth Douglas-fir/western hemlock forests in which Douglas-firs are over 400 years old. Fires during the past 200 years have created a complex mosaic of relatively even-aged natural stands throughout the study area. Superimposed on this natural mosaic is a second component of pattern complexity resulting from timber harvesting over the last 40 years.

METHODS

Data acquisition

Landscapes were classified in terms of managed and natural elements. Managed forest stands (typically young forest plantations of up to

192

approximately 40 years old established after clearcutting) were defined as internally homogeneous units (or managed patches) embedded in a matrix consisting of natural, uncut forest. This two-phase mosaic is a simplified representation of a more complex system in which many patch and matrix types exist. For the present analysis, however, we chose to classify the elements of the system as either 'managed' or 'natural'. A managed patch consisted of one, or (if adjacent) more than one, unit that was clearcut in the past.

Maps of forest patterns were constructed for the years 1972 and 1987. Managed forest patches for 1972 were mapped using high-altitude infrared images (scale 1:60 000) and were transferred to US Forest Service vegetation maps using a zoom transfer scope. The 1987 data were acquired from vegetation maps produced in 1987 by the Forest Service at a scale of 1:15 840 for the entire Willamette National Forest. Fifteen forested landscapes were chosen at random from the Blue River and Sweet Home ranger districts' vegetation maps for this study. Each sample landscape consisted of a rectangle representing approximately 3·5 × 5·0 km (1750 ha). To qualify for selection, each landscape was required to be forested, lie within US Forest Service land, and contain at least one managed patch by 1972. Other landscapes were rejected during the random selection process. Several of the selected landscapes included roadless areas with much uncut forest land. The locations, sizes, and shapes within the managed forest patches and the natural forest matrix were digitally recorded as polygons for both the 1972 and 1987 data. The total number of digitized patches for 1972 and 1987 were 150 and 298, respectively.

Landscape statistics

The degree of fragmentation sustained by the forest matrix which characterizes a given landscape may be described as a function of the varying size, shape, spatial distribution, and density of clearcut patches (Burgess & Sharpe, 1981). Thus the degree of fragmentation can be measured in a number of ways. Because a single statistic is usually deemed insufficient to capture the entire spatial character of the landscape, a suite of statistics was selected. Five groups of statistics were used to quantify landscape heterogeneity and pattern for each of the fifteen areas for each of the two years: (1) patch size; (2) patch abundance; (3) patch shape; (4) patch spacing; and (5) matrix characteristics. Patch sizes and shapes were only determined for interior patches (i.e. patches that were not truncated by the borders of the landscape study sites).

Patch size for each year and sample area were expressed in terms of the average patch area and average patch perimeter. The area and perimeter of each patch were computed using the digitizing routine mentioned above.

The means of the patch areas and perimeters for each landscape for each year were also calculated. The second set of statistics, 'patch abundance', includes a measure of the patch density (expressed as the number of managed forest patches present per landscape study area) and percent in patches (the percent of the total landscape area occupied by managed patches). Means of these two statistics were calculated for each landscape and year. Because patch shape and patch spacing statistics can involve more than one variable in their calculation, some background discussion of the equations is included.

Patch shape was measured in three different ways: (1) the simple ratio of patch perimeter to patch area; (2) the fractal dimension; and (3) a diversity index. All three indices are a function of the perimeter and area of a given patch. The application of these similar measures on the same data set afforded an opportunity to compare their ability to detect spatial pattern.

The fractal dimension, D, was used to quantify the complexity of the shape of a patch using a perimeter–area relation. Specifically

$$P \approx A^{D/2} \tag{1}$$

where P is the digitized patch perimeter and A is the patch area (Burrough, 1986). The fractal dimension for each sample area and year was estimated by regressing the logarithm of patch area on its corresponding log-transformed perimeter. The appeal of fractal analysis is that it can be applied to spatial features over a wide variety of scales. A fractal dimension greater than 1 indicates a departure from a euclidean geometry, i.e. an increase in shape complexity. As D approaches 2, the patch perimeter becomes 'infilling' (Krummel *et al.*, 1987).

A similar index is the diversity index, DI, which was used to express patch shape as

$$DI = \frac{P}{2\sqrt{\pi A}} \tag{2}$$

where the variables are defined as above in eqn (1) (Patton, 1975). Theoretically, the diversity index increases to 1 as the unit shape approaches a circle, similar to the case of the fractal dimension. However, in contrast, the diversity index increases without limit as patch shape becomes more complex.

Patch spacing was characterized by measures of the mean nearest-neighbor distance and a measure of dispersion. The mean nearest-neighbor distance was calculated manually with a scale by measuring the distance from the centroid of each patch to the centroid of its nearest neighbor and computing the mean distance for the sample landscape. The centroid of each patch was determined through an ocular estimate procedure. Clark and

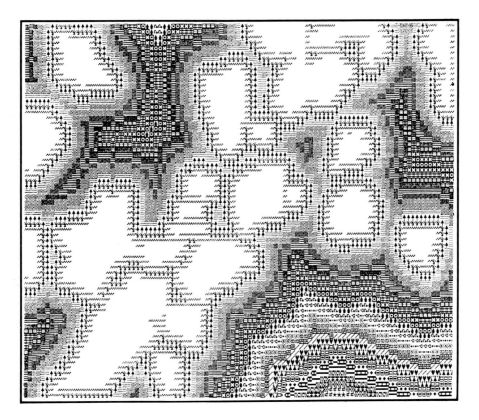

Proximity to Managed Patches
50m Cells

⁀⁀⁀	0.05 Km		0.90 Km
♦♦♦	0.10 Km	▫▫▫	0.95 Km
▲▲▲	0.15 Km	▬▬▬	1.00 Km
≡	0.20 Km	///	1.05 Km
/////	0.25 Km	♥♥♥	1.10 Km
	0.30 Km		1.15 Km
▬▬	0.35 Km	▫▫▫	1.20 Km
≡	0.40 Km	⊖⊖⊖	1.25 Km
▬▬	0.45 Km	▸♦♦◂	1.30 Km
⊞⊞⊞	0.50 Km	⊞⊞	1.35 Km
⊞⊞⊞	0.55 Km	—	1.40 Km
⊞⊞⊞	0.60 Km		1.45 Km
⊙⊙⊙	0.65 Km		1.50 Km
▲▲▲	0.70 Km	⁂⁂⁂	1.55 Km
ᴖᴖᴖ	0.75 Km	⊞⊞⊞	1.60 Km
◁◁◁	0.80 Km	★★★	1.65 Km
▪▪▪▪	0.85 Km		

Fig. 1. An example of a proximity map using the spread function in the pMAP geographic information system. Cell values in the matrix were assigned based on their distance to the nearest managed forest patch (areas shown in white). The GIS fragmentation index (GISfrag) was determined by calculating the mean of all grid cell values on the proximity map.

Evans (1954) developed a measure of dispersion of patches using the equation

$$R = 2\rho^{1/2}\bar{r} \tag{3}$$

where R is dispersion, $\bar{r}$ is the mean nearest-neighbor distance, and ρ is the mean patch density (number of patches per unit area; see also Pielou, 1977, p. 155). Dispersion is a measure of the non-randomness of the patch arrangement. In a random population, $R = 1$; R less than 1 indicates aggregation of the patches, while R greater than 1 indicates that the patch population forms a regular dispersed pattern or spacing.

A fifth group of statistics was calculated which predominantly reflects the character of the matrix (in this case, natural forested land) as opposed to managed patch configuration (clearcut areas): namely, a GIS-derived index (christened *GISfrag*), matrix contiguity, interior habitat, and total patch edge. To determine contiguity, a mylar sheet with an 8×8 grid consisting of 64 cells each with a size of 27 ha was overlaid on the sample landscape maps. The largest contiguous natural forest area (i.e. the largest number of contiguous grid cells) in the sample landscape was recorded. Using this 8×8 grid, the contiguity index could potentially range from 0 (a landscape with no natural forest patches greater than 27 ha, i.e. highly fragmented) to 64 (a landscape with no managed stands, and hence no fragmentation). A 27-ha cell size was chosen because it was considered to be a viable habitat patch size and fits within the structure of the existing landscape.

The GIS fragmentation index (GISfrag) was computed by first producing a proximity map using the SPREAD function in the pMAP GIS software (Spatial Information Systems, 1986). This procedure assigned cell values based on the distance to the managed forest patches (i.e. a distance of one cell away from a managed patch was equal to 50 m, a distance of two cells was equal to 100 m, and so forth; see Fig. 1 for an example of a digital map illustrating all matrix distances to managed patches). A GISfrag was computed as the mean value of all the grid cell values on the proximity map, including the managed patches which were assigned values of zero. Large mean values reflected a low degree of forest fragmentation while maximum fragmentation occurred when the mean values approach zero.

The spread function in pMAP was also used to calculate the amount of interior forest habitat. Interior forest was defined as the amount of natural forest remaining after removing an edge zone of 100 m (approximately two tree heights) into the natural forest matrix (Fig. 2). The mean total edge was simply the average of the total managed patch edges for each landscape. A non-parametric test (Wilcoxon rank sum) for the difference between mean values was performed for each landscape and year for each of the variables listed above to assess the ability of these variables to reflect landscape change.

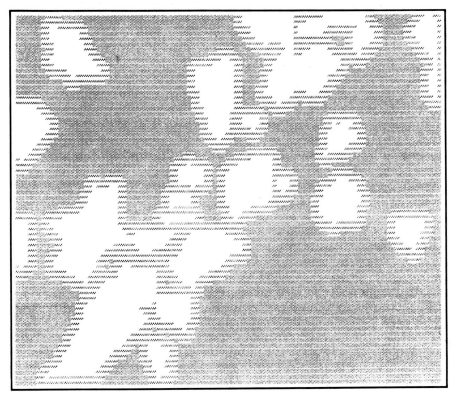

Interior Forest Habitat
50m Cells

Symbol	Label	Percent
	Interior Habitat	57.73
	Edge Effect (100m)	21.87
	Managed Forest	20.40

Fig. 2. An example of an interior forest habitat map generated by pMAP. The interior forest habitat is defined here as the amount of natural forest remaining after removing an edge zone of 100 m into the natural forest.

RESULTS AND DISCUSSION

Landscape structure

The degree of forest fragmentation as measured by the statistics discussed above increased significantly over the 15 years spanning 1972 to 1987 (Table 1 and Fig. 3). Overall, patch area and patch perimeter decreased by 17% and

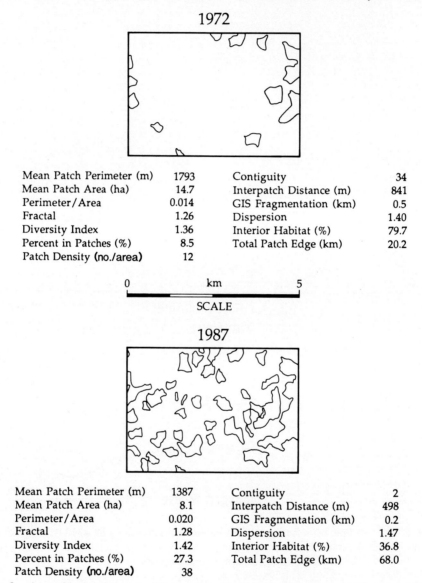

1972

Mean Patch Perimeter (m)	1793	Contiguity	34
Mean Patch Area (ha)	14.7	Interpatch Distance (m)	841
Perimeter/Area	0.014	GIS Fragmentation (km)	0.5
Fractal	1.26	Dispersion	1.40
Diversity Index	1.36	Interior Habitat (%)	79.7
Percent in Patches (%)	8.5	Total Patch Edge (km)	20.2
Patch Density (no./area)	12		

0   km   5

SCALE

1987

Mean Patch Perimeter (m)	1387	Contiguity	2
Mean Patch Area (ha)	8.1	Interpatch Distance (m)	498
Perimeter/Area	0.020	GIS Fragmentation (km)	0.2
Fractal	1.28	Dispersion	1.47
Diversity Index	1.42	Interior Habitat (%)	36.8
Percent in Patches (%)	27.3	Total Patch Edge (km)	68.0
Patch Density (no./area)	38		

Fig. 3. A graphical and statistical illustration of landscape change between the years 1972 and 1987 for one of the landscapes used in the study.

TABLE 1
Descriptive Statistics for 1972 and 1987 Landscapes

Variable	Mean	Standard deviation	Minimum	Maximum	p value
Managed patch size					
Mean patch perimeter (m) 1972	2 075	512	1 599	3 492	
Mean patch perimeter (m) 1987	1 848	452	1 211	2 797	0·096
Mean patch area (ha) 1972	19·5	9·1	1·7	42·7	
Mean patch area (ha) 1987	16·2	8·3	6·6	38·5	0·027
Managed patch shape					
Perimeter/area 1972	0·013	0·0037	0·007	0·022	
Perimeter/area 1987	0·018	0·0053	0·007	0·028	0·027
Fractal 1972	1·26	0·02	1·24	1·28	
Fractal 1987	1·27	0·02	1·24	1·32	0·023
Diversity index 1972	1·38	0·11	1·22	1·53	
Diversity index 1987	1·40	0·09	1·23	1·52	0·027
Managed patch abundance					
Percent in patches 1972	9·5	7·0	1·3	27·3	
Percent in patches 1987	18·2	9·6	1·3	38·1	0·001
Patch density (no./area) 1972	10·3	8·2	2	28	
Patch density (no./area) 1987	19·6	9·7	2	38	0·001
Managed patch spacing					
Nearest-neighbor distance (m) 1972	928	251	589	1 375	
Nearest-neighbor distance (m) 1987	661	247	454	1 375	0·001
Dispersion 1972	1·22	0·27	0·79	1·66	
Dispersion 1987	1·24	0·23	0·79	1·60	1·000
Matrix characteristics					
GIS fragmentation (km) 1972	0·8	0·5	0·1	1·8	
GIS fragmentation (km) 1987	0·5	0·5	0·1	1·8	0·003
Matrix contiguity 1972	36·6	19·9	1	59	
Matrix contiguity 1987	20·6	19·1	1	59	0·003
Interior habitat (%) 1972	78·2	16·1	38·4	96·9	
Interior habitat (%) 1987	60·2	19·7	25·6	96·9	0·001
Total patch edge (km) 1972	19·9	15·6	2·8	59·5	
Total patch edge (km) 1987	38·4	19·8	2·8	71·6	0·001

These statistics were calculated using patch and matrix variables of the fifteen landscapes to investigate the change in forest fragmentation over time. A non-parametric means test (Wilcoxon rank sum) was performed to evaluate the statistical significance of the differences in the means (see p values).

11% or from 19·5 to 16·2 ha and 2075 to 1848 m, respectively. Although some 1972 patches 'grew' by 1987 as a result of the coalescence of two or more managed patches, individual managed patch size on the whole decreased.

The fractal dimension, the perimeter-to-area ratio, and diversity index indicate a statistically significant increase in patch complexity over time. A contributing factor to this increased complexity may be attributed to the linking of several smaller managed patches which often produces an irregularly shaped patch. The fractal dimension and diversity index appear to be fairly robust measures of an 'average' patch shape and may be capable of discerning subtle changes in patch configuration which are difficult to assess by visual inspection alone. In contrast, because it is not scale-invariant, the perimeter-to-area ratio must be interpreted carefully.

Patch density increased over the 15 years by 98%. The percent of the landscape in managed patches nearly doubled in the 15-year period from 9·5% to 18·2%. The mean of the index of contiguity decreased by 44% by 1987, reflecting the increased number of clearcuts made in the area. Not surprisingly, the mean nearest-neighbor distance also decreased significantly from 928 to 661 m. Dispersion, however, did not register the change in spatial distribution of patches over time. There was no difference in dispersion from 1972 to 1987 (1·22 versus 1·24), which represents a regular, dispersed spacing pattern for both dates. Since dispersion is a function of

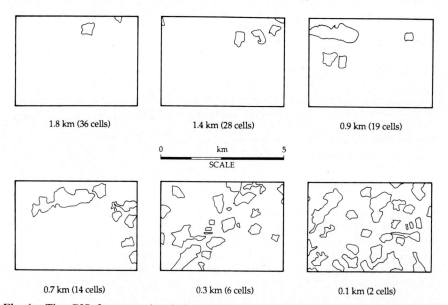

1.8 km (36 cells)   1.4 km (28 cells)   0.9 km (19 cells)

0   km   5
SCALE

0.7 km (14 cells)   0.3 km (6 cells)   0.1 km (2 cells)

Fig. 4. The GIS fragmentation index (GISfrag) for a progression of landscape fragmentation levels. Low levels of GISfrag reflect high amounts of forest fragmentation in terms of number of clearcut patches and amount of patch aggregation. This figure consists of six different landscapes and does not represent the same landscape over time.

both patch density and interpatch distance, we expected it to change because these other variables were statistically different over time. However, the mean change in these two variables was in opposite directions, i.e. patch density *increased* while nearest-neighbor distance *decreased*. We conclude that their combined effects canceled one another. The amount of interior forest habitat decreased from 78·2% in 1972 to 60·2% in 1987. This decrease in interior habitat (18% loss) was approximately twice the areal increase in managed patches (8·7%).

The GISfrag mean decreased by 0·3 km in 1987, indicating an increase in forest fragmentation (Table 1). Figure 4 shows the GISfrag for a progression of landscape fragmentation levels. The GISfrag seems to be sensitive to the abundance of patches and the amount of unfragmented contiguous natural forest. Figure 5 demonstrates the influence of patch spacing and the amount of contiguous natural forest on the GISfrag by showing the GISfrag for a pair of landscapes that had the same patch density but a different level of patch aggregation. It should be noted that the GISfrag is only comparable among study areas that are the same size and shape, because the truncation of the matrix as it intersects the study area boundary may influence the value of this index.

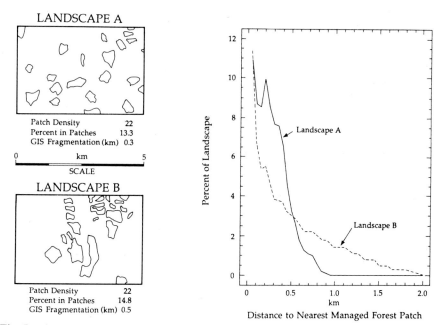

Fig. 5. An example of two landscapes (A and B) having the same patch density (22) but differing level of patch aggregation reflected by correspondingly different GIS fragmentation indices. The accompanying figure to A and B is a graph of percent of each landscape versus distance of each point in the landscape to a clearcut (managed) forest patch. The B profile shows more of the landscape with greater distances to the nearest managed patch than A.

Ecological and management implications

An examination of the results reveals the varying ability of each analysis to describe change in patch and matrix characteristics. The nature and amount of change detected by these different landscape statistics have significance to the ecology and management of forest landscapes. Changes that were evident in patch-level characteristics indicate a trend toward smaller units and a slight trend toward more irregular units. These changes may reflect the increased cutting on steeper, more irregular terrain, more careful 'fitting' of the cutting units as the available cutting area decreased, an effort to optimize big game habitat by increasing the number of cuts, and/or an effort to reduce the visual impact of clearcutting.

The increase in the number of young, managed stand patches and the total amount of edge has implications for habitat potential of the landscapes. Although conclusive information on the effect of edges on vertebrates in western coniferous forest landscapes is not yet available, an increase in edge can benefit some species but prove detrimental to others (Yahner, 1988). For example, it has been observed that big game animals show an affinity for edges (Brown, 1985) and that some bird species occur more frequently on edges than in forest interiors (Rosenberg & Raphael, 1986). The fact that edge density increased in the present study areas over the past 15 years suggests that the habitat potential has increased for such species as elk, which can successfully utilize the edge environment. The increased dispersal of small clearcuts into the matrix of forest cover provides a corresponding increase in the amount of hiding cover close to forage areas used by the elk (Brown, 1985).

Conversely, a number of other vertebrate species, such as the northern spotted owl, Townsend's warbler *Dendroica townsendi*, and *pileated* woodpecker *Dryocopus pileatus*, may avoid edges (Bull, 1975; Brown, 1985; Rosenberg & Raphael, 1986). The increase in edge density indicates that habitat conditions for such species favoring interior forest have probably declined markedly. Specifically, the decrease in the mean distance of matrix to managed patch (as measured by GISfrag) and interior forest area are evidence of the decline in interior species habitat conditions. The manner and degree to which the decline affects interior species populations in the study areas are difficult to assess. Although Rosenberg and Raphael (1986) did not find a strong response of vertebrate communities in northern Californian landscapes which sustained a mean percent clearcut of 18% (roughly the same as the present study), the authors warned that the fragmentation in the region is a relatively recent phenomenon. Long-term vertebrate responses were not yet discernible.

The continued use of dispersed clearcutting increases fragmentation of forest landscapes at a rate more rapid than the rate of cutting on a per area basis. Given that the present cutting patterns are decreasing potential interior habitat at a rapid rate, alternative cutting patterns should be considered to reduce the loss of interior habitat and retain the area of large forested patches. Alternative models which aggregate cutting (Franklin & Forman, 1987) are available and may not require altering current standards and guidelines.

CONCLUSIONS

In an attempt to describe forest fragmentation, five groups of statistics were employed: patch abundance, patch shape, patch size, patch spacing, and matrix characteristics. By comparing two sets of data representing two dates over a 15-year period, we found that patch abundance, patch spacing measures, and matrix characteristics were most useful in capturing the amount of forest fragmentation over time. Patch size and shape statistics contribute information on specific characteristics of the individual patches and may be useful for applications designed to study specific interior and edge habitats or for the prescription of new clearcuts. In addition, a GIS fragmentation index was developed which proved sensitive to both the quantity and spacing of patches. The GIS provides an automated method of quantifying forest fragmentation to aid in forest and wildlife management decisions, and a means by which field and image data may be used in concert.

Current concerns over forest fragmentation are typically related to a landscape condition in which forest islands occur in a matrix of managed forest plantations. This study suggests that on many Forest Service lands in the Cascade Range this condition is not yet realized, in contrast to many privately owned landscapes in the Cascades in which the matrix is the harvested area and the patches are the natural forest. Consequently, in characterizing fragmentation in some landscapes, characteristics of the matrix (the unmanaged forest) may be of more interest than characteristics of the patches (the managed plantations). Where the matrix is of interest, the interior area, the total edge, and the mean distance to the nearest managed patch (GISfrag) will be the useful descriptors of fragmentation. Additional research is needed to document and substantiate the relationship between forest landscape pattern and the subsequent wildlife/ecosystem response.

ACKNOWLEDGEMENTS

This project was funded in part by NASA grant number NAGW-1460. The authors would like to thank Robert Gaglioso for assisting in the patch mapping and digitization, and Miles Hemstrom, E. Charles Meslow and David H. Johnson for providing valuable suggestions on an earlier version of the manuscript.

REFERENCES

Brown, E. R. (1985). *Management of Wildlife and Fish Habitats in Forests of Western Oregon and Washington*. US Forest Service, Pacific Northwest Region, Portland, Oregon.

Bull, E. L. (1975). Habitat utilization of the pileated woodpecker, Blue Mountains, Oregon. MS thesis, Oregon State University.

Burgess, R. L. & Sharpe, D. M. (eds) (1981). *Forest Island Dynamics in Man-dominated Landscapes*. Springer-Verlag, New York.

Burrough, P. A. (1986). Principles of geographic information systems for land resources assessment. *Monographs on Soil and Resources Survey*, No. 12. Oxford University Press, Oxford.

Clark, P. J. & Evans, F. C. (1954). Distance to nearest neighbor as a measure of spatial relationships in populations. *Ecology*, **35**, 445–53.

Forman, R. T. T. & Godron, M. (1986). *Landscape Ecology*. John Wiley, Chichester.

Franklin, J. F. & Dyrness, C. T. (1973). *Natural Vegetation of Oregon and Washington*. Oregon State University Press, Oregon.

Franklin, J. F. & Forman, R. T. T. (1987). Creating landscape patterns by cutting: ecological consequences and principles. *Landscape Ecol.*, **1**, 5–18.

Harris, L. D. (1984). *The Fragmented Forest*. University of Chicago Press, Chicago.

Krummel, J. R., Gardner, R. H., Sugihara, G., O'Neill, R. V. & Coleman, P. R. (1987). Landscape patterns in a disturbed environment. *Oikos*, **48**, 321–4.

Milne, B. T. (1988). Measuring the fractal geometry of landscapes. *Appl. Math. Comput.*, **27**, 67–79.

Noss, R. F. (1983). A regional landscape approach to maintain diversity. *BioScience*, **3**, 700–6.

O'Neill, R. V., Krummel, J. R., Gardner, R. H., Sugihara, G., Jackson, B., DeAngelis, D. L., Milne, B. T., Turner, M. G., Zygmunt, B., Christensen, S. W., Dale, V. H. & Graham, R. L. (1988). Indices of landscape pattern. *Landscape Ecol.*, **1**, 153–62.

Patton, D. R. (1975). A diversity index for quantifying habitat 'edge'. *Wildl. Soc. Bull.*, **3**, 171–3.

Pielou, E. C. (1977). *Mathematical Ecology*. Wiley, New York.

Ripple, W. J. (ed.) (1987). *Geographic Information Systems for Resource Management: A Compendium*. American Society for Photogrammetry and Remote Sensing, Bethesda, Maryland.

Ripple, W. J. (ed.) (1989). *Fundamentals of Geographic Information Systems: A Compendium*. American Society for Photogrammetry and Remote Sensing, Bethesda, Maryland.

Ripple, W. J. & Luther, T. (1987). The Use of Digital Landsat Data for Wildlife Management on the Warm Springs Indian Reservation of Oregon. *Proc. Ann. Convention Amer. Soc. Photogramm. & Remote Sensing, Baltimore, Maryland*, pp. 266–74.

Rosenberg, K. V. & Raphael, M. G. (1986). Effects of forest fragmentation on vertebrates in Douglas-fir forests. In *Wildlife 2000*, ed. J. Verner, M. L. Morrison & C. J. Ralph. University of Wisconsin Press, Madison, Wisconsin, pp. 263–72.

Spatial Information Systems (1986). *pMAP: A Software System for Analysis of Spatial Information*. Omaha, Nebraska.

Spies, T. A. & Franklin, J. F. (1988). Old growth and forest dynamics in the Douglas-fir region of western Oregon and Washington. *Natural Areas Journal*, **8**, 190–201.

Thomas, J. W. (ed.) (1979). Wildlife habitats in managed forests—the Blue Mountains of Oregon and Washington. *USDA For. Serv. Agric. Hdbk*, No. 53. Portland, Oregon.

Yahner, R. H. (1988). Changes in wildlife communities near edges. *Conserv. Biol.*, **2**, 333–9.

Landscape Ecology vol. 4 no. 1 pp 55-68 (1990)
SPB Academic Publishing bv, The Hague

The spatial pattern of a northern conifer-hardwood landscape

John Pastor and Michael Broschart
Natural Resources Research Institute, University of Minnesota, Duluth, MN 55811

Keywords: *Acer saccharum*, fractals, geographic information systems, northern landscapes, old growth, soils, spatial pattern, *Tsuga canadensis*

Abstract

A geographic information system, fractal analyses, and statistical methods were used to examine the spatial distributions of old growth hemlock, northern hardwood, mixed hardwood/hemlock stands and wetlands with respect to each other and also soils and topography. Greater than 80% of the stands of any covertype were less than 20 ha in area. Nearly pure hemlock and northern hardwood stands were associated with soils having a fragipan, while mixed hardwood/hemlock stands were associated with sandier soils. Hemlock stands were distributed independently of hardwood and mixed hardwood/hemlock stands, but hardwood and mixed hardwood/hemlock stands were usually surrounded by hemlock. Bogs and lakes were usually surrounded by hemlock stands and are distributed independently of hardwood stands. The shapes of all stands vary from extremely simple to extremely complex, with a general tendency for hemlock stands to be more convoluted than hardwoods. The analyses suggest segregation across soil types and a disturbance regime favoring the establishment of hardwoods and mixed hardwood/hemlock stands in a hemlock matrix as reasons for the origin of the observed spatial patterns.

Introduction

The different ways that species compete for resources and alter their availabilities cause them to segregate across the landscape. However, the reasons for the origins of these spatial patterns are not always clear. A particular example is the pattern of the forested landscape of the northeastern United States, which is often composed of discrete stands of hemlocks (*Tsuga canadensis*) intermixed with discrete stands of northern hardwoods. Proposed hypotheses to explain this pattern include segregation according to soil type (Oosting and Billings 1939; Milfred *et al.* 1967; Pastor *et al.* 1984; Hix and Barnes 1985), segregation according to topographically-induced differences in microclimate (Oosting and Hess 1956; Adams and Loucks 1971), and establishment of one covertype or the other following disturbance. Of the disturbance-related hypotheses, there is some evidence that hemlock is favored by disturbances such as light ground fires (Maissurow 1941; Cline and Spurr 1942; Hough and Forbes 1943; Miles and Smith 1960; Goff 1967; McIntosh 1972; Spies 1983; Spies and Barnes 1985a, b), but there is also evidence that periodic fire eliminates hemlock from hardwood stands (Spies and Barnes 1985a, b). Furthermore, Spies and Barnes (1985a, b) point out that certain types of disturbances might be associated with certain topographic features, and that disturbance alone may not be a sufficient explanation for the development of all stands of a given type. It is

First published in *Landscape Ecology*, Vol. 4 (1): 55-68, 1990. "*The Spatial Pattern of a Northern Conifer-Hardwood Landscape*," John Paster and Michael Broschart.

entirely possible that there are multiple reasons for stand origins, even within the same region. Finally, it is possible that these different stands arise at random with respect to each other and to the distribution of soils or topographic features, and the origin of any stand is determined by larger scale processes that appear stochastic at this scale, such as the climate during stand development.

These hypotheses have been evaluated largely by gathering data on the structure and processes of individual stands. However, each hypothesis implies a particular, large-scale landscape pattern between one covertype and the other, and between each covertype and the distribution of soils or topographic features. In particular:

1. if hemlock and hardwoods segregate according to soil type or topographic feature, then each should be associated with one soil type, slope or aspect, etc. to a greater or lesser degree than would be expected at random.
2. if hardwoods require disturbances within a hemlock matrix to become established, then they should be surrounded by hemlock to a greater degree than would be expected at random. The converse also applies if hemlock requires disturbances in a hardwood matrix to become established.
3. if there are multiple reasons for the origin of particular covertypes, and in particular if these processes work at different scales, then stands of different covertypes and different sizes should have different shapes (Krummel *et al.* 1987).
4. if the development of each stand is controlled solely by larger scale stochastic processes, then there should be no association between covertype and soil type, slope, aspect, or adjacent stand other than that which would be expected at random.

The development of geographic information systems makes the quantitative analyses of these patterns possible, and therefore provides a new tool with which to test hypotheses about species segregation in the landscape. The objective of this paper is to test the above hypotheses about the segregation of hemlock from northern hardwoods by quantitatively analyzing the spatial distribution of these covertypes with respect to each other and with respect to landscape properties.

Study area

This study was conducted in the Sylvania Recreation Area in the Ottawa National Forest in the western Upper Peninsula of Michigan about 5 km southwest of Watersmeet, MI (46°15′N, 89°15′W). Sylvania is an 8500 ha tract of old growth northern hardwood and conifer forest which has had only minimal timber harvesting limited to selective logging of a few white pines (*Pinus strobus*) near the turn of the century. This is one of the few remaining large, contiguous tracts of old growth timber in the Lake Superior region, and thus affords an opportunity to determine presettlement landscape structure. The upland is dominated by old growth eastern hemlock and sugar maple (*Acer saccharum*) forests with yellow birch (*Betula allegheniensis*) and basswood (*Tilia americana*) present as scattered codominants. Aquatic and wetland patches in the landscape are conifer forested wetlands, marshes, and lakes.

Methods

The covertypes present on Sylvania were delineated on 1:24000 color infrared stereo imagery taken May 1, 1980 before the hardwoods had leafed out. The smallest covertype patch observable on the aerial photographs, which was approximately 0.01 ha (100 m²), was mapped. Field verification of covertypes delineated on aerial photographs was conducted from 5 May to 7 May 1987. A total of 37 sites were visited to relate aerial photograph signature with on-ground upland covertypes and wetland vegetative cover and water regime.

Nine different covertypes were classified. Stands classified as hemlock contained 70–100% hemlock trees. Mixed stands of hardwoods (sugar maple) and hemlock were composed of 30–70% hemlock. Hardwood stands were primarily sugar maple with less than 30% hemlock present. Conifer forested

207

wetlands were dominated by black spruce (*Picea mariana*) or combinations of black spruce, tamarack (*Larix laricina*), and northern white cedar (*Thuja occidentalis*). The substrate of many of the conifer wetlands observed during field reconnaissance was a floating mat of *Sphagnum* spp., though some of the wetland conifer forests may have been rooted in organic soil. Hardwood species such as yellow birch, red maple (*Acer rubrum*) and black ash (*Fraxinus nigra*) were often mixed with conifers in these wetlands. However, the photo signature indicated primarily conifer cover and this was verified in the sample of conifer wetlands observed in the field. Evergreen shrub wetlands were dominated by leatherleaf (*Chamaedaphne calyculata*) and *Sphagnum* spp. with Labrador tea (*Ledum groenlandicum*) often in association. Swales were shallow forested depressions containing both hardwood and conifer species including hemlock, black spruce, northern white cedar, yellow birch, red maple, and black ash. Wetlands included marshes (*Carex* spp.; *Scirpus* spp.; *Typha* spp.; and wetland grasses), alder (*Alnus rugosa*) swamps, flooded dead trees of unknown species, and ponds (open water < 20 ha). Each of these classes had a characteristic photo signature based on color, texture, and topographiic position which was verified on the ground. Due to the coarse classification scheme, many finer distinctions observed in other studies (Spies and Barnes 1985a, b) may have been included in other broader classifications. For example, conifer forested wetlands may have included some hardwood-conifer swamps due to the similarity of photo signature as a result of the presence of conifer cover.

Description of soil types were taken from a soil map of the Sylvania Recreation Area prepared by Jordan (1973). Five soil classes were used in this study to determine associations between covertypes and soils: 1) well-drained to moderately well-drained with coarse-loamy textures and a moderate fragipan, 2) well-drained to moderately well-drained with sandy textures, 3) well-drained with sandy textures, 4) moderately well-drained with coarse silty textures, and 5) very poorly drained organic soils of strongly to slightly acid herbaceous and woody materials.

The mapped units on the aerial photographs and the soil map were transferred to overlays on USGS topographic base maps by using a Bausch and Lomb Zoom Transfer Scope. These map overlays were computer digitized using a microcomputer based ERDAS Geographic Information System (ERDAS, Inc. 1987). Contour lines on USGS topographic maps were also digitized to create a digital map of slope. All digital maps were gridded into 10 × 10 meter cells.

Although the soils were mapped at a coarser level of resolution (0.4 ha) than the vegetation (0.01 ha), this mapping resolution was consistent with the complexity of these features as observed in the field using a soil auger. Therefore, we feel that superimposing these two maps does not confuse soil-cover-type associations. The slope and covertype maps had similar distributions of map unit sizes and the minimum mapping unit size is the same for both maps, being 0.01 ha (Fig. 3).

We analyzed the maps to answer the following questions: 1. what are the shapes of individual stands and how do they vary with covertype and size?; 2. what is the size distribution of stands of each covertype?; 3. how are the covertypes distributed on different soils?; 4. how are the covertypes distributed on different slopes and aspects?; 5. how are the covertypes distributed with respect to one another?

In order to answer the first two questions, it was necessary to differentiate individual stands. Using the CLUMP program of ERDAS, clumps of contiguous pixels with the same class value were numbered sequentially so that each stand or lake had a unique data class value. The size distribution of the individual stands were then analysed using the LOTUS spreadsheet program.

Theory of fractals (Mandelbrot 1977) has made it possible to quantify patch shapes. Lovejoy (1982), Krummel *et al.* (1987), and Turner and Ruscher (1988) used the area-perimeter relation to determine the fractal dimension of various types of planar shapes and how patch shape is related to substrate, disturbance, or other processes. We calculated the fractal dimensions of hemlock, hardwood, hardwood/hemlock stands and lakes by obtaining the area and perimeter measurements from the grid cell data of the digital computer maps.

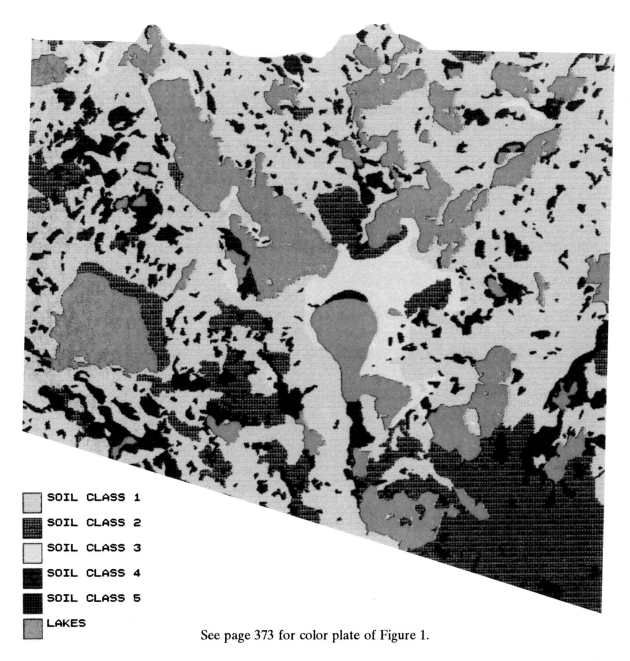

See page 373 for color plate of Figure 1.

Fig. 1. Computer generated map of the soil types represented on the Sylvania Recreation Area, MI., from Jordan (1973). Soil class 1 was well-drained to moderately well-drained with coarse loamy textures and a moderate fragipan; soil class 2 was well-drained to moderately well-drained with sandy textures; soil class 3 was well-drained with sandy textures; soil class 4 was moderately well-drained with coarse silty textures; and soil class 5 was very poorly drained organic soils of strongly to slightly acid herbaceous and woody materials.

Successive linear regressions of log(Perimeter/4) against log(Area) were performed by increments of 20 such that the smallest 20 stands were regressed first and then followed in succession by regressions where the smallest stand is removed and the next largest is added (Lovejoy 1982; Krummel *et al.* 1987). The fractal dimension(D) of a geometric shape was then equal to twice the slope of the regression line (Turner and Ruscher 1988). This regression approach was used because it often reveals trends in the data that others do not (Burrough 1986). For smooth shapes D = 1, the dimension of

209

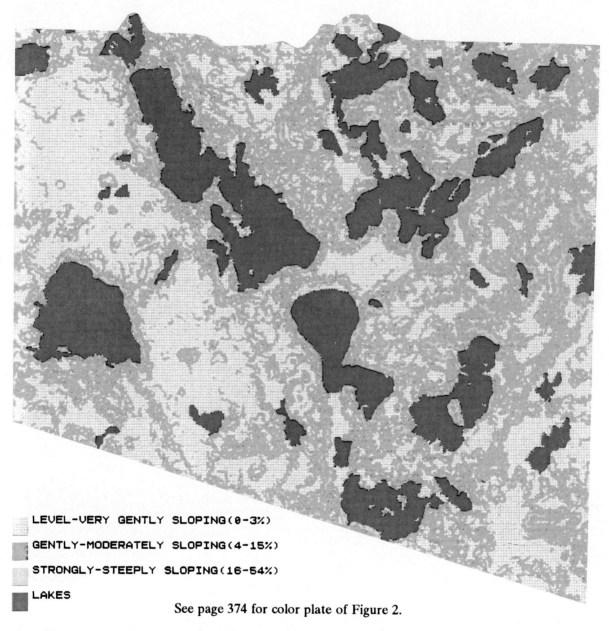

LEVEL-VERY GENTLY SLOPING(0-3%)

GENTLY-MODERATELY SLOPING(4-15%)

STRONGLY-STEEPLY SLOPING(16-54%)

LAKES

See page 374 for color plate of Figure 2.

Fig. 2. Computer generated map of the slope classes present on the Sylvania Recreation Area, MI.

a line, whereas for more complex shapes D approaches the value 2 (Lovejoy 1982). Values of D less than 1.5 indicated simpler shapes than obtained by randomly assigning covertypes to individual pixels, and values of D greater than 1.5 indicated more complex shapes than would be obtained at random (Krummel *et al.* 1987).

Composite maps were created by intersecting pairs of maps using the ERDAS MATRIX program to determine how features coincided spatially. For example, by this method we determined the intersections of vegetation covertypes with soils. The ERDAS BSTATS program was then used to obtain frequency distributions of covertypes with soils and slope classes.

Data for spatial adjacency analyses were obtained using the SEARCH program. The vegetation map was dissected into separate maps for each covertype. Then, a four pixel-wide (40 m) buffer was created around each stand. The resulting map was then overlayed onto the original vegetation map, and the covertypes in the buffer zone were determined using OVERLAY and BSTATS. The result was a map and statistical summary of the distribution of covertypes i within the 40 meter bands adjacent to stands of covertype j.

In order to test the null hypothesis that covertypes were distributed randomly across the landscape, we required a metric to assess the statistical distribution of stands on a given slope class, on a given soil type, or in juxtaposition to each other. The electivity index as proposed by Jacobs (1974) and utilized by Jenkins (1979) was originally used to determine if herbivores prefer or discriminate against a particular plant food given the food's distribution in the community. Here, we used this index to determine whether given stands of a specific covertype were selectively juxtaposed with any other covertype, were selectively found on any slope class, or selectively found on any soil type.

The formula to calculate the electivity indices for each covertype for soil and slope classes was:

$$E_{ij} = \ln[(r_{ij})(1 - p_j)/(p_j)(1 - r_{ij})]$$

For the analyses of cover type distribution by soil type, r_{ij} was the proportion of covertype i on soil type j and p_j was the proportion of the landscape occupied by soil type j. Similarly, for the analyses of covertype distribution by slope class, r_{ij} was the proportion of covertype i on slope j and p_j was the proportion of the landscape occupied by slope class j. For the analyses of spatial adjacency of each covertype relative to all others, the formula becomes:

$$E_{ij} = \ln[(r_{ij})(1 - p_{ij})/(p_{ij})(1 - r_{ij})]$$

where E_{ij} was the electivity index for proximal covertype i adjacent to covertype j, r_{ij} was the proportion of proximal covertype i in an arbitrarily selected 40 m band around covertype j, and p_{ij} was the proportion of proximal covertype in all 40 m wide bands along all boundaries except those of covertype j.

An electivity index greater than 0 indicated a preference by the searched covertype for a given soil, slope class, or proximal covertype and a value less than 0 implied selection against a given soil, slope class, or proximal covertype. The electivity indices were tested against the chi-square distribution according to the formula:

$$\chi^2 = E_{ij}/[1/x_{ij} + 1/(m_j - x_{ij}) + 1/y_i + 1/(n_t - y_i)]$$

where x_{ij} was the area of covertype i on soil type or slope class j or the area of proximal covertype i in the band around searched covertype j, y_i was the area of covertype i in the landscape as a whole for soil and slope class analyses or the area of proximal covertype i in all bands for adjacency analyses, and m_j was the area of all classes on soil type or slope class j or in bands around searched covertype j, and n_t was the area of the entire landscape for soils and slope class analyses or the area of all classes in all bands. The calculated χ^2 was compared with a χ^2 distribution with one degree of freedom at a significance level p = 0.05.

Results

Distribution of physical features

The soils of Sylvania were separated into five general categories with upland soil classes 1−4 comprising 84% of the soil types present (Table 1, Fig. 1). Soil Type 1, a well-drained to moderately well-drained soil with a coarse loamy texture and a moderate fragipan, was most abundant, covering 60% of the land area.

The majority of the Sylvania area was level to gently rolling topography with 0−3% slopes constituting 51% of the area (Table 1, Fig. 2). Moderate slopes (4−15%) were found on 44% of Sylvania while steep slopes (16−54%) were rare and occurred on only 5% of the area.

Distribution of covertypes

Hemlock was the dominant covertype, constituting 37% of the study area (Fig. 3, Table 1). Mixed sugar maple and hemlock stands were second in importance, followed by hardwood stands (mainly sugar maple with basswood and yellow birch). The most common wetland covertype was the conifer

Table 1a. Distribution of soil classes for the Sylvania Recreation Area, Watersmeet, MI.

Soil classes*	Percent
1	60.6%
2	17.1%
3	5.6%
4	0.5%
5	16.3%

*

1 – Well-drained to moderately well-drained, coarse-loamy texture and moderate fragipan.
2 – Well-drained to moderately well-drained soils with sandy textures.
3 – Well-drained soils with sandy texture.
4 – Moderately well-drained soils with coarse-silty textures.
5 – Very poorly drained organic soils, strongly to slightly acid.

Table 1b. Distribution of slope classes for the Sylvania Recreation Area.

Slope class	Percent
Level-very gently sloping: 0–3%	51.0%
Gently-moderately sloping: 4–15%	44.3%
Strongly-steeply sloping: 16–54%	4.7%

Table 1c. Cover type distribution on the Sylvania Recreation Area.

Cover type	Percent
Hemlock	37.%
Hardwoods	11.7%
Hdwd/hemlock mixed	17.1%
Conifer forested wetland	8.0%
Evergreen shrub wetland	2.9%
Wetlands	1.1%
Lakes	20.6%
Swales	1.4%
Upland openings	0.1%

forested wetlands which covered 8% of the area overall and 60% of the wetland area. Combining swales and conifer forested wetlands, over 70% of wetland area was covered by forested wetlands. Spies and Barnes (1985b) similarly found that forested wetland units covered 80% of the wetland area. Lakes constituted 21% of the Sylvania landscape, more than any covertype except hemlock.

Hemlock and hardwood stands were significantly associated with soil class 1 (coarse loamy spodosols with fragipans) but not with any other soil class (Table 2). However, hardwood/hemlock were more strongly associated with soil classes 2 and 3. As expected, all of the wetland classes were found on the very poorly drained organic soils (soil class 5) while no upland forest stands were found on this soil.

There were strong preferences of some covertypes for and against certain slope classes. Although the steeply sloping areas comprised less than 5% of Sylvania and hardwood stands comprised only 18% of the upland forest stands, close to 30% of the steep slopes had hardwood stand cover, resulting in a significant positive association between hardwood stands and steep areas (Table 3). Both hardwood and hardwood/hemlock stands were negatively associated with level areas and were positively associated with moderate slopes. Hardwood/hemlock stands were negatively associated with steep slopes. Hemlock stands, making up 56% of the upland forest, were distributed randomly with respect to slope class. All covertypes were randomly distributed with respect to aspect.

Covertype size distribution

The majority of the forest stands were less than 20 ha in size (Fig. 4). Hemlock stands had the largest mean size of 27.9 ha with a standard deviation of 116 due to a few very large stands. Conifer forested wetlands were the smallest of the four at 2.9 ha (sd = 6.0). Hardwood and hardwood/hemlock stands had an average stand size of 10.8 and 14.5 ha respectively (sd = 16.8 and sd = 33.6 respectively). Over 50% of the hemlock and conifer forested wetland stands less than 20 ha were 2 ha in size or smaller while hardwood and hardwood/hemlock stands less than 20 ha were evenly distributed up to 10 ha in size.

Covertype adjacency analysis

There was a strong positive association between hemlock stands and lakes as well as between evergreen shrub wetlands and lakes (Table 4). This indicated that lakes were distributed in the 40 meter bands around hemlock and evergreen shrub wetlands in greater proportion than lakes were distributed in the landscape. Similarly, hemlock and

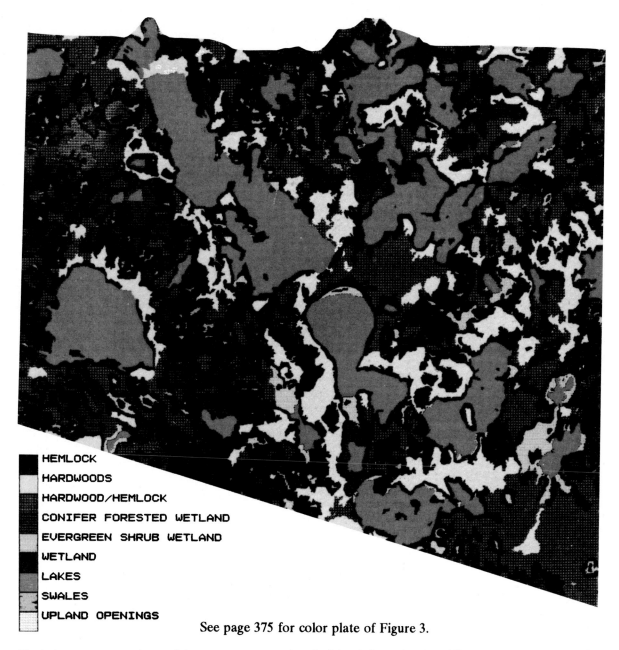

HEMLOCK
HARDWOODS
HARDWOOD/HEMLOCK
CONIFER FORESTED WETLAND
EVERGREEN SHRUB WETLAND
WETLAND
LAKES
SWALES
UPLAND OPENINGS

See page 375 for color plate of Figure 3.

Fig. 3. Computer generated map of the cover types observed on the Sylvania Recreation Area, MI.

evergreen shrub wetlands were found in a greater proportion in the 40 meter bands around lakes than they were distributed over the whole area. Spies and Barnes (1985a) also observed the physiographic juxtaposition of hemlock stands to lake and wetland margins. Hardwood stands, hardwood/hemlock stands, conifer forested wetlands, and evergreen shrub wetlands had hemlock stands adjacent to them in greater proportion than hemlock was found in the landscape. However, the reciprocal association does not hold as these covertypes were found adjacent to all hemlock stands in the proportion they were found in the landscape. In other words, given the presence of a hardwood stand, hardwood/hemlock stand, or a wetland, there was a high probability of finding an adjacent hemlock

213

Table 2. Association of upland cover types with soils on the Sylvania Recreation Area.

Stands	Soil classes			
	Soil 1	Soil 2	Soil 3	Soil 4
HE	+	0	0	0
HD	+	0	0	0
HD/HE	0	+	+	0

(0) – No association
(+) – Significant positive association ($P(\chi^2 > 3.84) = 0.05$)
(−) – Significant negative association ($P(\chi^2 > 3.84) = 0.05$).

Table 3. Association of upland cover types with slope on the Sylvania Recreation Area.

Stands	Scope classes		
	Level (0–3%)	Moderate (4–15%)	Steep (16–54%)
HE	0	0	0
HD	−	+	+
HD/HE	−	+	−

(0) – No association
(+) – Significant positive association ($P(\chi^2 > 3.84) = 0.05$)
(−) – Significant negative association ($P(\chi^2 > 3.84) = 0.05$).

stand, but hardwood and hardwood/hemlock stands and wetlands were not found adjacent to hemlock more than would be expected at random. In contrast, hardwood and hardwood/hemlock stands were significantly dissociated from conifer forested wetlands, evergreen shrub wetlands, and lakes and vice versa.

Fractal analysis

The hemlock stands between 0.25 and 0.65 ha (log A = 3.40 to 3.41 m^2) had a constant fractal value of about 1.00 (Fig. 5). The shape of hemlock stands then gradually became more complex up to a fractal dimension of 2.00 for stands between 2.00 and 3.00 ha (log A = 4.30 to 4.50 m^2). After leveling off at a fractal value of 2.00, the fractals decreased sharply, and stands between 3.00 and 10.00 ha (log A = 4.50 to 5.00 m^2) generally had simpler shapes than expected at random, but fractal dimensions of these

stands were extremely variable with respect to stand size. Boundary complexity then increased and was extremely complex for stands greater than 12.5 ha (log A = 5.10 m^2).

Inspection of the hemlock stands within each fractal class showed that these stands can be categorized into three types according to the relation between area and fractal dimension. Island stands which were small and entirely surrounded by wetlands or lakes had low fractal dimensions. Narrow string-like stands border the edge of lakes or wetlands, and were small to moderate sized but with high fractal dimension. Island stands had a mean area of 1.5 ha (sd = 2.2, range 0.1 – 10.0) and narrow border stands averaged 6.0 ha (sd = 5.7, range 0.8 – 22.4). Generally, island and narrow border stands had very few inclusions or patches in them.

Matrix stands were the background in which internal patches of other upland forests, wetlands, and lakes were embedded. Matrix stands were larger stands with a mean size of 125 ha (sd = 240, range 12 – 1070) and with many internal patches. Matrix stands had a mean of 23 internal patches/stand and a mean area of 86 ha of internal patches/stand. Thus, the area of internal patches in hemlock stands was nearly 70% of the area of the stands themselves exclusive of the patches. Wetlands represented the largest internal patch area in matrix hemlock stands and made up 42% of the patch area. Of these wetland patches, conifer forested wetlands were the most prominent, constituting over 65% of the wetland patch area. Lakes were the second most important patch in hemlock stands at 22% of total patch area followed by hardwood/hemlock stands (20%) and hardwood stands (16%).

The window of extremely variable stand shape between 3 and 10 ha was explainable as a mixture of both island and string stands in this size class. The shapes of these stands were poorly explained by size alone, as the regressions of perimeter against area had insignificant r^2 values in this size range. Within the 3 to 10 ha range for hemlock stands, there were 13 narrow border stands and 11 island stands. For a given area, narrow border stands have greater perimeter lengths and therefore more complex shapes than island stands which have

214

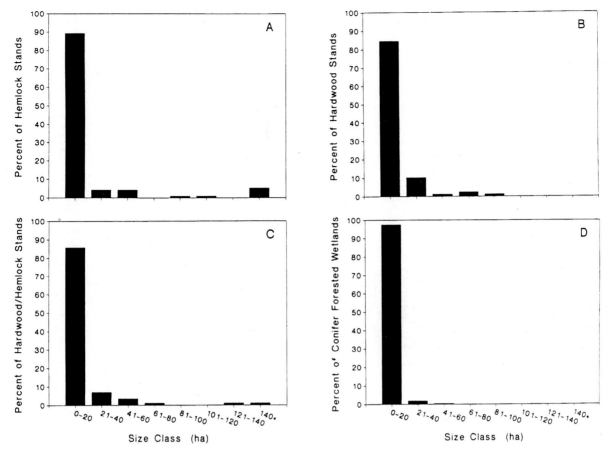

Fig. 4. Frequency distribution of stand size for hemlock, hardwood, hardwood/hemlock, and conifer forested wetland.

shorter perimeters and simpler shapes.

Hardwood and mixed hardwood/hemlock stands did not segregate into different shapes as well as did the hemlock stands. Hardwood stands less than 2.50 ha (log A = 4.40 m^2) had simpler shapes and those greater than 6.55 ha (log A = 4.80 m^2) had more complex shapes than expected at random, with much variation around a randomly expected fractal dimension of 1.5 for stands between 2.50 and 6.55 ha (Fig. 5).

The fractal dimension for hardwood/hemlock stands from 1.53 to 3.00 ha (log A = 4.20 to 4.50 m^2) was between 1.0 and 1.4, indicating stands with simple shapes (Fig. 5). Over the middle range of stand sizes from 3.00 and 10.50 ha (log A = 4.50 to 5.00 m^2), the fractal value fluctuated widely between 1.0 and 2.0. The fractals for stands greater than 10.50 ha ranged between 1.5 and 2.0, indicating stands with complex shapes. Unlike the matrix

hemlock stands, the large hardwood and hardwood/hemlock stands had few inclusions, and were complex because they were amoeboid in shape. The small, simple hardwood and hardwood/hemlock stands were generally surrounded by hemlock. There were few hardwood or hardwood/hemlock stands that could be categorized as string stands.

From the graphs in Fig. 5, it is evident that stands smaller than 3 ha are relatively simple in shape while those greater than 10 ha are extremely complex. In contrast, stands of all three upland cover-types between about 3–10 ha (log A = 4.50 to 5.00 m^2) can be either very simple or extremely complex. This area of noise or unexplained variation may indicate that within this size class, several factors, as yet unknown, are influencing stands shape, whereas above and below this size class shape is governed by fewer factors. In other words, there

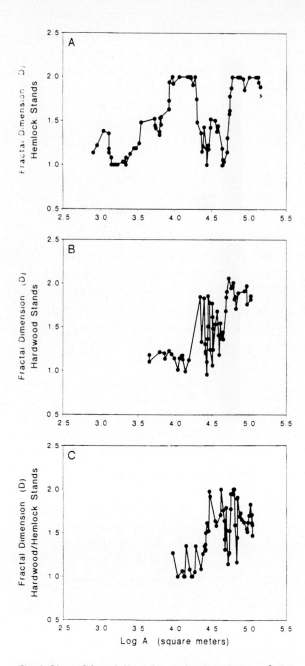

Fig. 5. Plots of fractal dimension against log of area (m²) for hemlock, hardwood, and hardwood/hemlock stands.

may be processes determining stand shape that operate at scales of 3 ha and less and produce simple shapes, and other processes that operate at scales of 10 ha and greater and produce complex shapes. For stands between 3 and 10 ha in size, both sets of factors are operable, yielding extremely variable boundary shapes.

Table 4. Association of cover types on the Sylvania Recreation Area.

Stands searched	Stands in 40M band					
	HE	HD	HD/HE	CFW	EVW	LA
HE	0	0	0	0	0	+
HD	+	0	0	−	−	−
HD/HE	+	0	0	−	−	−
CFW	+	−	−	0	0	−
EVW	+	−	−	0	0	+
LA	+	−	−	−	+	0

(0) − No association
(+) − Significant positive association (P(χ^2>3.84) = 0.05
(−) − Significant negative association (P(χ^2>3.84) = 0.05.

Discussion

The salient findings of this study of vegetation patterns of old growth, northern hardwood-conifer forest are:

1. Most stands of any covertype are small, less than 20 ha;
2. Nearly pure hemlock and nearly pure hardwood stands are associated with soils having a fragipan, while mixed hemlock-hardwood stands are associated with sandier soils;
3. Hemlock stands are distributed independently of hardwood and mixed hemlock-hardwood stands, but hardwood and mixed hemlock-hardwood stands usually are surrounded by hemlock;
4. Bogs and lakes are usually surrounded by hemlock and dissociated with hardwood and mixed hemlock-hardwood stands;
5. The shapes of all types of stands vary from extremely simple to extremely complex, with a general tendency for increasing complexity with size and for hemlock stands to be more convoluted than hardwood or mixed hemlock-hardwood stands.

These characteristics suggest that the Sylvania landscape is a matrix of eastern hemlock forest, based on the criteria of being the landscape element with the greatest relative area and a high degree of connectivity (Forman and Godron 1986), embedded with terrestrial patches of hardwood stands and patches of mixed composition dominated by hardwoods and eastern hemlock. This pattern is not readily apparent by inspection of the vegetation map (Fig. 3), but becomes apparent only after statistical analyses of the sizes, shapes, and distributions of stands using a geographic information system.

Of the four original hypotheses cited for the origin of a hemlock and hardwood mosaic, two, perhaps not mutually exclusive, are supported by these observations:

1. the hardwood stands arise after disturbances in the hemlock matrix and hemlock-hardwood stands are those in various stages of recovery toward pure hemlock stands.
2. mixed hemlock-hardwood stands represent a finer-grained pattern of interspersion of hemlocks and hardwoods on sandier soils, while on soils with fragipans hemlocks and hardwoods are interspersed in a coarse-grained pattern.

Support for the first hypothesis is suggested by the analyses of spatial association among upland cover-types, conifer forested wetlands, and lakes. If disturbances are imposed on a hemlock matrix, then the hardwood stands arising in these disturbances would be surrounded by hemlock stands, and the surrounding hemlock would be a seed source for the formation of mixed hemlock-hardwood stands. Thus, hardwood stands would require a disturbance to the hemlock climax matrix and mixed stands would require a nearby hemlock seed source, but hemlock stands would require neither hardwood nor mixed stands for their origin. Frelich (1986) found that small and frequent disturbances are randomly distributed in this region. A random disturbance regime imposed on a hemlock matrix would result, as shown, in hemlock stands being distributed independently of hardwoods, since many areas of hemlock may remain undisturbed. Such a disturbance regime would also produce the extremely complex shapes and numerous inclusions seen in the larger hemlock stands because the larger stands would, simply by virtue of their area, have a greater chance of 'receiving' more disturbances

within their borders. Finally, the invasion of hardwoods in disturbances within a hemlock matrix explains the amoeboid shape with few inclusions observed in the larger hardwood stands.

Lakes and conifer forested wetlands may be barriers to disturbances such as fires, or in the case of conifer forested wetlands, seed sources for rapid invasion of hemlock into surrounding disturbances on the upland (Spies 1983; Spies and Barnes 1985a). Both roles will cause lakes and conifer forested wetlands to be associated with hemlocks and dissociated with hardwoods, as we have seen and as also noted by Spies and Barnes (1985a).

The question of whether disturbances such as fire favor hemlock or hardwood establishment has beem long debated. Some investigators interpret the even-aged condition of many hemlock stands and the sporadic regeneration of hemlock in hardwood stands as evidence of a requirement of hemlock for disturbance (Maissurow 1941; Cline and Spurr 1942; Hough and Forbes 1943; Miles and Smith 1960; Goff 1967; McIntosh 1972; Hix and Barnes 1984). However, Graham (1941) points out that hemlock regeneration is sporadic because of exacting requirements for moist soil, and that hemlock stands with an apparent even-aged structure may be due to periodic light ground fires that remove saplings without killing the overstory and therefore need not originate after catastrophic fire. Furthermore, if hemlock requires disturbances in a hardwood matrix for stand establishment, then the spatial associations between hemlock, hardwood, and mixed stands would be the opposite of that found here, namely a predominance of hardwoods and mixed stands around hemlock stands, but no preference for hardwoods to be adjacent to hemlock stands. Although some hemlock stands in Sylvania owe their origin to fires (Spies 1983 and Spies and Barnes 1985a, b), it seems unlikely that a strict requirement of hemlock for fire would have produced the observed landscape pattern.

Support for the second hypothesis is suggested by the different soil preferences for mixed hemlock-hardwood stands on the one hand and pure hardwood or hemlock stands on the other. If mixed stands are simply the result of hemlock invading hardwood stands that arise from disturbance, then mixed stands should also have the same preference for soil class 1 that both hemlock and hardwood stands do.

Segregation according to soil type as well as the particular juxtapositions of stands with each other and lakes and wetlands suggests multiple reasons for their origin. Multiple origins of stands is also supported by the fractal analyses. Others (Krummel et al. 1987; Turner and Ruscher 1988) have demonstrated that different processes cause different fractal patterns at different covertype sizes. However, the presettlement landscape of Sylvania is distinguished from these other studies in anthropogenically disturbed areas by the more complex fractal patterns. Although at present both disturbances and soil types appear responsible for the observed spatial patterns, the segregation of pure stands from mixed stands according to soil type can be reconciled with the disturbance hypothesis if mixed stands are a fine-grained version of interspersed hemlock and hardwood stands, and if the size of disturbances on sandy soils correspond to this finer-grained scale.

New and very different studies are needed to resolve these problems. These studies should focus on what happens at the boundaries between different stand types, since it is here that the mechanisms by which one species invades stands composed of others becomes apparent. The spatial pattern of individual tree-by-tree replacements at stand borders may help explain the larger scale spatial pattern in the landscape.

The distributions of covertypes suggest a different model of landscape evolution than that proposed by Turner et al. (1989). They hypothesize that the landscape is a grid with rules for assigning occupancy of grid cells by various covertypes. Their model describes the distribution of vegetation in Georgia (Turner and Ruscher 1988). However, using this model, fractal values never approach 2 for various theoretical spatial patterns, ranging from random to clumped to dispersed. This is at variance with the shapes of stands in this northern forest. This northern forest suggests an alternative model of landscape evolution, which we term the 'Swiss cheese' model. In this model, one covertype forms a matrix (the 'cheese') within which disturbances create holes that then become occupied by other covertypes. In the present example, hemlock is the 'cheese' with 'holes' created by fire or windthrow that are then occupied by hardwoods, or topographic disturbances that are occupied by lakes and wetlands. A quantitative simulation of this landscape therefore requires data on the size, shape, frequency, and spatial patterns of holes within the matrix, and the probability of particular covertypes filling those holes. These probabilities are in turn dependent on the nature of the disturbance, the underlying soil, climate, and competitive interactions with the species forming the matrix. In contrast, the Turner et al. model requires data on the spatial patterning and probability of particular covertypes occupying particular grid cells. Both models may be valid models for different landscapes, but the rules for applying one model over the other remain to be determined.

Acknowledgements

Tom Spies, Carol Johnston, Margaret Davis, and an anonymous reviewer made helpful suggestions to an earlier version of this manuscript. The assistance and advice of Jim Jordan of the U.S. Forest Service is greatly appreciated. This research was supported by a grant from the National Science Foundation's Ecology Program (BSR-8615196) to Davis and Pastor. This is contribution number 5 of the Natural Resources Research Institute GIS Laboratory (NSF DIR-8805437).

Literature cited

Adams, M.S. and Loucks, O.L. 1971. Summer air temperatures as a factor affecting net photosynthesis and distribution of eastern hemlock [Tsuga canadensis L. (Carrierre)] in southwestern Wisconsin. The American Midland Naturalist 85: 1–10.

Burrough, P.A. 1986. Principles of geographic information systems for land resources assessment. Clarendon Press, Oxford.

Cline, A.C. and Spurr, S.H. 1942. The virgin upland forest of New England. Harvard Forestry Bulletin 21.

ERDAD, INC. 1987. Image Processing System User's Guide. ERDAS, INC., Atlanta.

Frelich, L. 1986. Natural disturbance frequencies in the

hemlock-hardwood forests of the Upper Great Lakes Region. Ph.D. Thesis, University of Wisconsin, Madison, Wisconsin.

Forman, R.T.. and Godron, M. 1986. Landscape Ecology. John Wiley and Sons Inc., New York. 619 pp.

Goff, F.G. 1967. Upland vegetation. In: Soil Resources and Forest Ecology of Menominee County, Wisconsin. pp. 60–90. Wisconsin Geological and Natural History Survey Bulletin 85, Soil Series 60, Madison, Wisconsin.

Graham, S.A. 1941. The question of hemlock establishment. Journal of Forestry 39: 567–569.

Hix, D.M. and Barnes, B.V. 1984. Effects of clar-cutting on the vegetation and soil of an eastern hemlock dominated ecosystem, western Upper Michigan. Canadian Journal of Forest Research 14: 914–923.

Hough, A.F. and Forbes, R.D. 1943. The ecology and silvics of forests in the high plateaus of Pennsylvania. Ecological Monographs 13: 299–320.

Jacobs, J. 1974. Quantitative measurement of food selection: a modification of the forage ratio and Ivlev's electivity index. Oecologia 14: 413–417.

Jenkins, S.H. 1979. Seasonal and year-to year differences in food selection by beavers. Oecologia 44: 112–116.

Jordan, J.K. 1973. A soil resource inventory of the Sylvania Recreation Area. USDA Forest Service, Ottawa National Forest, Watersmeet Ranger District.

Krummel, J.R., Gardner, R.H., Sugihara, G., O'Neill, R.V. and Coleman, P.R. 1987. Landscape patterns in a disturbed environment. Oikos 48: 321–324.

Lovejoy, S. 1982. Area-perimeter relation for rain and cloud areas. Science 216: 185–187.

Maissurow, E.E. 1941. The role of fire in the perpetuation of virgin forests in northern Wisconsin. Journal of Forestry 39: 201–207.

Mandelbrot, B.B. 1977. The Fractal Geometry of Nature. W.H. Freeman and Company, New York.

McIntosh, R.P. 1972. Forests of the Catskill Mountains, New York. Ecological Monographs 42: 143–161.

Miles, M.L. and Smith, E.C. 1960. A study of the origin of hemlock forests in southwestern Nova Scotia. Forestry Chronicles 36: 375–390.

Milfred, C.J., Olson, G.W., Hole, F.D., Baxter, F.P., Goff, F.G., Creed, W.A. and Stearns, F. 1967. Soil Resources and Forest Ecology of Menominee County, Wisconsin. Wisconsin Geological and Natural History Survey Bulletin 85, Soil Series 60, Madison, Wisconsin.

Oosting, H.J. and Billings, W..D 1939. Epaho-vegetational relations in Ravenel's Woods. The American Midland Naturalist 22: 333–350.

Oosting, H.J. and Hess, D.W. 1956. Microclimate and a relic stand of Tsuga canadensis in the lower piedmont of North Carolina. Ecology 37: 28–39.

Pastor, J., Aber, J.D., McClaugherty, C.A. and Melillo, J.M. 1984. Aboveground production and N and P cycling along a nitrogen mineralization gradient on Blackhawk Island. Wisconsin. Ecology 65: 256–268.

Spies, T.A. 1983. Classification and analysis of forest ecosystems of the Sylvania Recreation Area, Upper Michigan. Ph.D. Thesis, University of Michigan, Ann Arbor, Michigan.

Spies, T.A. and Barnes, B. 1985a. A multifactor ecological classification of the northern hardwood and conifer ecosystems of Sylvania Recreation Area, Upper Peninsula, Michigan. Can. J. For. Res. 15: 949–960.

Spies, T.A. and Barnes, B. 1985b. Ecological species groups of upland northern hardwood-hemlock forest ecosystems of the Sylvania Recreation Area, Upper Peninsula, Michigan. Can. J. For. Res. 15: 961–972.

Turner, M.G. and Ruscher, C.L. 1988. Changes in landscape patterns in Georgia, U.S.A. Landscape Ecology 1: 241–251.

Turner, M.G., Costanza, R. and Sklar, F.H. 1989. New methods to compare spatial patterns for landscape modeling and analysis. Ecological Modelling (in press).

Landscape Ecology vol. 4 no. 1 pp 69-80 (1990)
SPB Academic Publishing bv, The Hague

Modeling vegetation pattern using digital terrain data

Frank W. Davis[1] and Scott Goetz[2]
[1] Department of Geography, University of California, Santa Barbara, CA 93106; [2] Science Applications
Research, Inc. Greenbelt, MD 20771

Keywords: California, geographic information system, oak forest, patch size, predictive mapping, remote
sensing

Abstract

Using a geographic information system (GIS), digital maps of environmental variables including geology,
topography and calculated clear-sky solar radiation, were weighted and overlaid to predict the distribution
of coast live oak (*Quercus agrifolia*) forest in a 72 km^2 region near Lompoc, California. The predicted distribution of oak forest was overlaid on a map of actual oak forest distribution produced from remotely sensed
data, and residuals were analyzed to distinguish prediction errors due to alteration of the vegetation cover
from those due to defects of the statistical predictive model and due to cartographic errors.

Vegetation pattern in the study area was associated most strongly with geologic substrate. Vegetation pattern was also significantly associated with slope, exposure and calculated monthly solar radiation. The
proportion of observed oak forest occurring on predicted oak forest sites was 40% overall, but varied substantially between substrates and also depended strongly on forest patch size, with a much higher rate of success for larger forest patches. Only 21% of predicted oak forest sites supported oak forest, and proportions
of observed vegetation on predicted oak forest sites varied significantly between substrates. The non-random
patterns of disagreement between maps of predicted and observed forest indicated additional variables that
could be included to improve the predictive model, as well as the possible magnitude of forest loss due to
disturbances in different parts of the landscape.

Introduction

Regional vegetation analyses are conducted routinely by landscape ecologists, geographers and
resource managers in order to describe the distribution of plant species and to relate observed distribution patterns to biotic and abiotic site factors
(Causton 1988). Typically, vegetation and site
measurements from scattered samples are analyzed
to develop empirical equations relating vegetation
composition to measured site variables. Even in
relatively undisturbed areas, such equations or
vegetation 'site models' meet with mixed success in
predicting actual vegetation patterns because of the
complexity and dynamic behavior of plant communities across a range of spatial and temporal scales
(Rowe and Sheard 1981). Ground samples inevitably comprise a very small fraction of the mapped
region, raising the question of how representative
resulting models are for unsampled areas. Samples
are of predetermined area deemed suitable for
describing vegetation stands, fixing somewhat arbitrarily the spatial scale of the analysis (Noy-Meir
and Anderson 1971). Also, samples are usually located subjectively in homogeneous stands selected
to be representative of idealized types (*e.g.*, associa-

tions, wildlife habitat types, etc.), leading to selective sampling of only some components of actual vegetation cover. As a result, a site model may predict a vegetation pattern very different from the actual pattern over the study region. These predictive errors may have practical consequences when site models are used to project the historical extent of vegetation types, for example to locate restoration projects or natural preserves.

A site model can be tested through additional field sampling; however, there are limits to the amount of field data that can be collected. When maps of site model variables (*e.g.*, geology, topography and soils) exist, a predictive vegetation map can be produced by map weighting and overlaying using a Geographic Information System[1] (GIS). Given a map of actual vegetation distribution, one can overlay the maps to compare predicted to observed vegetation patterns to analyze spatial patterns of disagreement (cf. Thomas 1960).

A number of studies have used GIS capabilities of map weighting and overlay for modeling vegetation pattern based on mapped environmental variables (*e.g.*, Box 1981). Most recently, predictive vegetation maps have been used in remote sensing applications to improve land cover classifications based on digital satellite data (*e.g.*, Strahler 1981; Morissey and Strong 1986; Cibula and Niquist 1987). In these studies, predictive models were developed from ground samples and the GIS was used to extrapolate across unsampled areas. Our research approach is similar, except that we are concerned with comparing predicted vegetation patterns to independently derived maps of actual vegetation (*e.g.*, Hill and Kelly 1987).

In principle, the interpretation of residual patterns from a comparison of observed and predicted vegetation maps is extremely complicated, because predictive errors can originate both from errors in maps of site variables and actual vegetation, and from inadequacies of the site model. We have found in practice, however, that residual patterns may be interpretable based on the analysts' knowledge of the data sources and the region under investigation, supplying much information not obtainable from simple goodness-of-fit statistics or additional field sampling. For example, patterns in residuals may reveal model biases, ecological subregions or ecological variables not previously recognized. Furthermore, knowing how a vegetation model performs in different parts of the study region can temper its application to management and planning decisions.

We have used digital maps of site variables (*i.e.*, geology, topography and calculated clear-sky solar radiation) and GIS capabilities to map the predicted distribution of natural vegetation types in coastal California whose actual distributions were mapped using Thematic Mapper Simulator (TMS) data. We compared the actual distribution of one vegetation type, coast live oak (*Quercus agrifolia* Neé) forest, to the distribution predicted by a quantitative site model, to answer the following questions:

- What is the total area and patch size distribution of observed oak forest?
- What is the total area and patch size distribution of predicted oak forest?
- For areas of observed oak forest, what is the amount and patch size distribution of predicted vegetation types?
- For areas of predicted oak forest, what is the amount and patch size distribution of observed vegetation types?
- How are areas where predicted and observed maps disagree distributed with respect to geology and topography?

Our overriding objectives in this paper are to test the power of mapped site variables for predicting the distribution of natural vegetation in coastal California, to demonstrate the utility of high resolution satellite data and GIS capabilities in regional vegetation analyses, and to call attention to some methodological issues of data scale and data quality that must be addressed in applying these technologies to regional vegetation modeling.

---

[1] Burrough (1986, p. 6) defines a GIS as 'a set of tools for collecting, storing, retrieving at will, transforming, and displaying spatial data from the real world for a particular set of purposes.'

Study area

We modeled natural vegetation pattern over a 72 km² area northeast of Lompoc, California (latitude 34°42′N, longitude 120°27′W). The climate here is mediterranean, with relatively cool summers and mild winters. Over 90% of the 36 cm average annual precipitation falls between November and April.

Two distinct physiographic regions occur in the study area; Burton Mesa and the Purisima Hills. Burton Mesa is a marine terrace underlain by marine sedimentary rocks that are covered with Orcutt sandstone, 0.5–40 meters of weakly cemented Quaternary aeolian sands (Diblee 1950). Level upland expanses from 100–120 m above sea level are separated by wide valleys filled with Quaternary alluvium.

Most vegetated areas are covered by maritime chaparral, which is dominated by evergreen shrub species including *Adenostoma fasciculatum, Ceanothus ramulosus, Arctostaphylos rudis* and *A. purisima* (Davis *et al.* 1988). Multi-stemmed coast live oaks 3–6 m in height are interspersed throughout the chaparral, attaining 40–70% crown cover in areas not recently disturbed by burning or clearing. Coastal sage scrub and annual grassland occur on formerly cleared sites and on south-facing slopes. Coast live oak forest is most extensive on steep north-facing slopes and in riparian corridors.

The Purisima Hills are a northwest-southeast trending anticline of marine sedimentary rocks. Elevations range from 225 to 450 m, and topography consists of rolling hills with short steep slopes. Important geologic formations in the study area include the Sisquoc diatomite and shale, the Careaga sandstone and the Paso Robles conglomerate. Predominant vegetation types in the Purisima Hills include coastal sage scrub, chaparral, bishop pine (*Pinus muricata*) forest, coast live oak woodland and coast live oak forest. Vegetation pattern is associated strongly with geology and topography. Cole (1980) documented the association of bishop pine forest with the diatomaceous member of the Sisquoc Formation, coast live oak forest with north facing slopes of the Careaga sandstone and Sisquoc shale, and coastal sage scrub or chaparral with steep south facing slopes of the Purisima Hills.

Natural vegetation in the study area is fragmented by roads, residential areas, agriculture and other developments. Remaining vegetation has experienced a complex disturbance history over the past century or more that includes wildfire, grazing and clearing. These disturbances exert a strong and persistent effect on vegetation composition and weaken the association between actual vegetation and mapped site variables (*e.g.*, Wells 1962; Davis *et al.* 1988). We applied predictive mapping only within areas where actual vegetation was dominated by native shrub or tree species. We excluded annual grasslands, nearly all of which were either actively grazed or recently burned or cultivated (see below).

Although we modeled the distribution of 5 vegetation types (Table 1), we focused on the actual and predicted distribution of coast live oak (*Quercus agrifolia* Neé) forest, which we define as vegetation where the species attains at least 60% canopy cover. Because coast live oak is the only dominant broadleaf evergreen tree in the study area, vegetation containing the species has a distinctive reflectance and can be mapped reliably with high resolution satellite data and aerial photography (Davis 1987). Furthermore, because coast live oak is relatively less adapted to drought than other mediterranean plant species, oak forests are generally restricted to mesic substrates and sites such as steep north-facing slopes and riparian corridors (Wells 1962; Griffin 1973; Cole 1980). The documented association of the species with mapped surficial geology and topography makes it especially suited for testing the potential of GIS-based predictive mapping.

Methods

A vegetation map for the study area was produced using Thematic Mapper simulator data (28 m resampled to 30 m resolution) collected in July 1984 (Davis 1987). Natural vegetation classes were mapped with 89% accuracy overall (accuracy determined following Card (1982); see Davis (1987) for details). All classes were mapped with greater than 85% accuracy except for oak forest, which was

Table 1. Classification system used to map dominant natural vegetation types in the study region. For logistic regression analysis, oak woodland and chaparral were merged into a 'woodland/chaparral' category. Grassland and Willow woodland were excluded from the analysis. Map accuracy for each class is the proportion of samples classified correctly in the TMS-derived vegetation map, based on 141 test sites (see Davis (1987) for details).

Class	% Oak cover	Dominant species	Map accuracy (%)
Coast live oak forest	>60	*Quercus agrifolia* *Toxicodendron diversilobum*	79
Coast live oak woodland	20–60	*Quercus agrifolia*	86
Chaparral	0–20	*Adenostoma fasciculatum* *Arctostaphylos spp.* *Quercus agrifolia* *Adenostoma fasciculatum* *Ceanothus ramulosus* *C. impressus* *Arctostaphylos rudis* *A. purisima*	89
Coastal Scrub	*0–20*	*Salvia mellifera* *Baccharis pilularis* *Ericameria ericoides* *Artemisia californica*	86
Conifer Forest	0–30	*Pinus muricata* *Quercus agrifolia* *Heteromeles arbutifolia*	92
Grassland	0–20	*Bromus spp.* *Vulpia spp.* *Avena barbata* *Brassica spp.*	89
Willow woodland	0–20	*Salix spp.*	100

mapped with 79% accuracy (Table 1). Oak forest was most frequently confused with dense oak woodland. This is not a severe mapping error, given that one class grades into the other.

The vegetation map was co-registered in Universal Transverse Mercator (UTM) projection to a geologic map of the study area (Dibblee 1950) that we digitized using Earth Resources Data Analysis System (ERDAS) software (Fig. 1). Dibblee originally mapped 19 geologic series at 1:50,000 scale. We did not attempt to quantify the accuracy of the map. To simplify the analysis of association between vegetation and geology, recent Quaternary deposits, including terraces, alluvium and Orcutt sandstone, were merged into a single class (Orcutt sand comprised 86% of this class). All three series were characterized by deep sandy soils. We analyzed three other widespread lithologic units, including the Paso Robles conglomerate, Careaga sand-

stone, and Sisquoc diatomaceous shale. Although soil maps exist for the study area, we did not use them because the soil maps for the Purisima Hills were less detailed than the geologic map and had less predictive value.

Topographic variables including elevation, slope angle and slope aspect, clear-sky solar radiation and drainage area were derived from the U.S. Geological Survey 30 m digital elevation model (DEM) for the Lompoc quadrangle using software developed at the UCSB Department of Geography (Frew and Dozier 1986). Unsmoothed elevations possessed 1 m vertical and 30 m horizontal resolution, with a nominal root mean square error of 3.0 m in both vertical and horizontal dimensions. Based on transit surveys of several hillslope profiles on eastern Burton Mesa, there was good agreement between actual and mapped elevations ($r^2 = 0.93$), but only fair agreement between actual and mapped

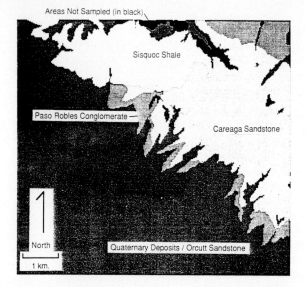

Sisquoc Shale

Paso Robles Conglomerate —

Careaga Sandstone

North

1 km.

Quaternary Deposits / Orcutt Sandstone

Fig. 1. Surficial geology of the study area (simplified from Dibblee 1950).

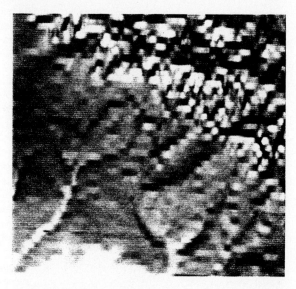

Fig. 2. Distribution of integrated January insolation calculated from digital elevation data. Image brightness is proportional to total insolation. Image orientation and area are the same as in Fig. 1.

slope angle ($r^2 = 0.41$) and slope aspect ($r^2 = 0.38$) (Goetz 1987). This is partly because errors in elevation data were amplified by the local differencing operations used to calculate slopes and exposures. Errors were concentrated in areas of rapidly changing slope and exposure such as ridges and ravines, and included both resolution errors (*i.e.*, undersampling in areas of rapid change) and stereomodel errors (*e.g.*, overestimating surface elevation in riparian corridors filled with tall, continuous tree canopy).

Incident radiation on a slope was calculated using maps of slope angle and slope aspect as well as a horizon file which provided, for each cell in the elevation model, the angle to the local horizon for 8 different azimuth sectors (*i.e.*, north, northeast, ...) (Dozier 1980; Dozier *et al.* 1981). Terms for diffuse irradiance and reflected radiation from surrounding terrain were estimated under specified conditions of atmospheric scattering and transmittance and surface albedo. The range in elevations was small enough that the atmosphere was treated as the same at all locations.

To produce maps of monthly solar radiation for the months of December through June, we calculated instantaneous radiation at hourly intervals for three days in each month, and integrated these

Fig. 3. Distribution of coast live oak forest mapped using July, 1984 TMS data, shaded to indicate predicted vegetation types on observed oak forest. Black areas are non-forested areas. Colored areas are existing oak forest that were predicted by the logit regression model to be oak forest (red), oak woodland (blue), coastal scrub (green) or conifer forest (white). Image orientation and area are as in Fig. 1.

values over the entire month. Because we could only roughly estimate seasonal atmospheric properties, the calculated insolation values were treated as relative and scaled from 0 to 255 (Fig. 2).

Variation in soil moisture related to drainage basin position (*e.g.*, upper slope versus lower slope) was modeled by calculating, for each cell, the number of cells in the basin which were expected to drain through that cell based on maps of slope and exposure (*e.g.*, Band 1986; Marks *et al.* 1984).

The association of vegetation and mapped terrain variables was modeled using polychotomous logit regression analysis (Wrigley 1975). Vegetation samples were located by stratifying the study area into six subregions, and then sampling 40–60 vegetation stands from each subregion that were at least 60 by 60 meters in area on 'uniform' geology and topography (to minimize cartographic error). Sample neighborhood was selected randomly, but sample locations were sometimes adjusted 30–60 m to meet our criteria of uniform vegetation and site conditions. Vegetation type and percent cover by coast live oak in each sample were determined using 1983 1:24,000 color aerial photography (high photointerpretation accuracy was verified during numerous field visits between 1985 and 1987). Geologic substrate and values for topographic variables were taken from the digital database.

The data consisted of 258 samples of four vegetation types, oak forest (n = 60), oak woodland and hard chaparral (n = 116), coastal scrub (n = 62) and conifer forest (n = 20). We excluded willow woodland because it is infrequent and is associated with riparian areas that we could not model successfully using the DEM data. As mentioned above, we also excluded grassland because this type occurs nearly exclusively on recently disturbed sites. Initially, oak woodland and chaparral were analyzed separately, but we observed no difference in the site relations of these two types so these types were combined to increase class sample size for estimating logit model coefficients. Oak cover increases during fire-free intervals on many chaparral-covered sites in the study area, and on these sites chaparral is probably seral to woodland (Wells 1962; Davis *et al.* 1988).

Initial data exploration indicated that site relations of the vegetation classes differed among the substrates, so separate logit regression models were developed for each geologic class. Topographic variables analyzed included elevation, slope, exposure, monthly and seasonal solar radiation and drainage basin position. Regression coefficients were estimated by ordinary least squares. Model performance was evaluated using the RHO-squared goodness-of-fit statistic (Costanzo *et al.* 1982) and by comparison of predicted and observed vegetation patterns (see below).

To generate a map of predicted vegetation pattern, vegetation class probabilities for each cell in the database were calculated from the regression equations, and the cell was assigned to the vegetation class with the highest calculated probability of occurrence using the program PROBCLAS (Maynard and Strahler 1981).

The correspondence between maps can be measured by testing for non-random distribution of map residuals using spatial measures of contiguity or spatial autocorrelation (Cliff and Ord 1981), or using aspatial measures of contingency or correlation (Phipps 1981). Given the large sample size (n = 79,605 cells) we assessed map correspondence using non-spatial analyses of randomly located samples. The use of conventional significance tests of association was problematic because the spatial dependence in mapped variables violated the assumption of sample independence (Fingleton 1986). To avoid this problem we sub-sampled the maps at a sampling density low enough so that sample values were expected to be independent at the average intersample distance. For topographic variables, the sampling distance was determined empirically by semi-variogram analysis (Oliver and Webster 1986) to be around 210 m, corresponding to a 2% sample of the region. Accordingly, the association of observed vegetation pattern with topographic variables was measured for a random sample of 1450 cells (1.8% of the study region) from the database.

Results

Oak forest was mapped over 4.5% of the study area (Fig. 3). The remaining area was mapped as oak woodland and chaparral (19.4%), coastal

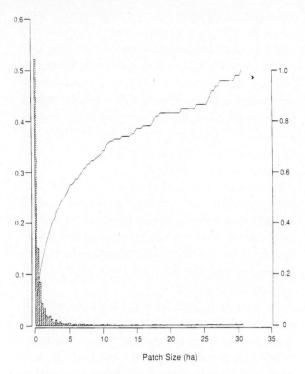

Fig. 4. Patch size distribution of observed oak forest in classified TMS image (bars) and cumulative proportion of forested area as a function of patch size (line).

scrub (20.0%), conifer forest (2.9%), or other (residential, cropland, grassland, willow woodland) (53.2%). Mapped stands of oak forest averaged 0.51 ha, with the size distribution strongly skewed towards the 0.09 ha resolution of the TMS data (Fig. 4). Some of the small patches were local dense clusters of oaks in stands of oak woodland and chaparral (Davis 1987). These occurred primarily on Burton Mesa. Other small patches were forest stands that were highly localized in riparian corridors or mesic coves, or were remnant fragments in areas subjected to historical clearing and burning.

Table 3. Summary of polychotomous logit regression models for four potential natural vegetation classes, Burton Mesa and Purisima Hills. Signs in parentheses indicate the direction of the relationship between the topographic variable and the likelihood of oak forest.

Geologic substrate	Significant variables	RHO-squared
Quarternary deposits	March insolation (−) Slope (−)	0.246
Paso robles conglomerate	March insolation (−)	0.174
Careaga sandstone	March insolation (−) Aspect (+)	0.228
Sisquoc Diatomite	December insolation (−) Elevation (−)	0.192
All substrates		0.338

Overlaying maps of geology and vegetation corroborated the observations by Cole (1980) that conifer forest in the region is essentially restricted to diatomaceous shale of the Sisquoc formation (Table 2). Stratification of the region by geology combined with logit regression models based on topographic variables gave a relatively high RHO-squared of 0.338 (Table 3). The separate logit regression models had only moderate predictive skill, with values for RHO-squared of 0.17−0.25. Calculated March radiation was the topographic variable most strongly associated with the pattern of natural vegetation on all substrates except the Sisquoc diatomite, where December radiation was a better predictor. Differences in the association of vegetation pattern and solar radiation for the months of December through March were slight (correlation of March and December radiation = 0.97).

The RHO-squared statistics indicated how well the model fit the 258 training samples, but a more

Table 2. Frequencies and relative percentages of 4 natural vegetation classes and other land cover types on four geologic substrates in the study area (n = 79,605 cells). Percentages for each substrate sum to 100%.

Geology	Oak forest		Oak woodland/chaparral		Coastal scrub		Conifer forest		Other	
Quaternary deposits	2423	0.05	18824	0.39	8572	0.18	4	0.00	18530	0.38
Paso Robles conglomerate	588	0.12	1335	0.26	1343	0.26	3	0.00	1811	0.36
Careaga sandstone	1927	0.11	6468	0.37	6195	0.36	8	0.00	2848	0.16
Sisquoc shale	939	0.11	5034	0.58	1434	0.16	500	0.06	819	0.09

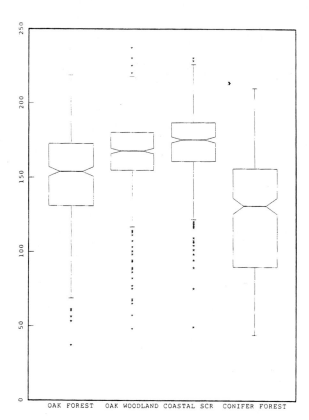

Fig. 5. Boxplots showing the distribution of March insolation for 4 vegetation classes on all geologic substrates, based on a random sample of 1450 cells from the database. Sharp ridges and ravines were excluded from the sample, because of the lower accuracy of DEM data in those areas. Boxes show the upper quartile, median and lower quartile for observations; vertical lines and asterisks show upper and lower extremes and outliers. Non-overlapping of notches indicates difference at a rough 5% significance level (Chambers *et al.* 1983).

general test of model performance was provided by comparing predicted to observed vegetation patterns for the entire study region. The proportion of observed oak forest that occurred on predicted oak forest sites was 40% overall, but varied substantially between substrates (Table 4). For example,

most observed oak forest on Quaternary deposits mapped onto predicted oak woodland sites. Low predictive success of model was the result of: 1) cartographic error due to confusion of dense oak woodland and oak forest in the map of actual vegetation, and 2) ecological error, in the sense that oak forest was not as restricted to low radiation environments as the model predicted. For example, many small patches of oak forest were predicted oak woodland sites on level uplands of Burton Mesa that were not recently burned or cleared.

The proportion of observed oak forest on predicted oak forest sites also depended strongly on patch size (Fig. 6), with a much higher rate of success for larger patches of forest. Excluding patches less than 2 hectares (58% of mapped oak forest), 60% of remaining forest occurred on predicted oak forest sites. The three largest patches of oak forest, all greater than 10 ha in size, fell entirely within predicted oak forest areas. Although we could not account fully for this scale-dependence in model fit, it was due in part to the high error rate for small oak forest patches on Quarternary deposits. Also, larger patches of oak forest tended to occur on larger more homogeneous slopes, which were more accurately depicted by the DEM data. Finally, we observed in the field that many smaller patches of mapped oak forest occurred near seeps, along geologic contacts, in swales and near lower order streams, all environments that were not depicted reliably by the database.

Only 21% of predicted oak forest sites supported oak forest. 55% supported oak woodland and chaparral and 24% supported coastal scrub, conifer forest or other cover types (mainly grassland, cropland and residential) (Fig. 7). Proportions of observed vegetation on predicted oak forest sites varied sharply between substrates (Table

Table 4. Relative proportions of observed oak forest on predicted vegetation types as a function of substrate type (columns sum to 1).

Predicted vegetation	Quaternary deposits	Paso Robles conglomerate	Careaga sandstone	Sisquoc shale
Oak forest	0.24	0.27	0.42	0.50
Oak woodland	0.73	0.37	0.42	0.02
Coastal scrub	0.03	0.36	0.16	0.13
Conifer forest	0.00	0.00	0.0	0.35

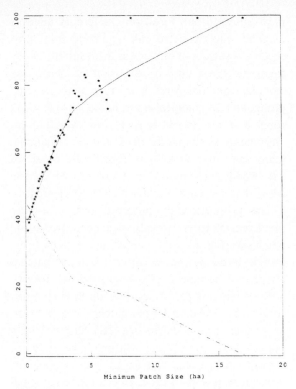

Fig. 6. Percent of observed oak forest occurring on predicted oak forest sites as a function of minimum forest patch size analyzed. Asterisks are actual data values. Solid line was fitted using locally weighted regression (Chambers *et al.* 1983). Broken line shows corresponding percent of observed oak forest on predicted oak woodland sites.

5). For example, most predicted oak forest on Sisquoc shale was observed to be oak woodland and chaparral, whereas on the Paso Robles it was mainly coastal scrub and other. This partly reflected differences in land use and disturbance on these substrates. Fire has been the major form of disturbance on Sisquoc shale, whereas large areas of the Paso Robles conglomerate and Careaga sandstone have been cleared and grazed. On several substrates the residuals were systematically associated with different topographic variables. For example, on the Sisquoc shale, conifer forest and oak woodland/chaparral occurred at significantly higher elevation than oak forest on predicted oak forest sites. We attributed this result to the association of these vegetation types with the diatomaceous member of the Sisquoc Formation, which occupes higher elevations. Thus this model bias could be reduced by including a more detailed geologic classification.

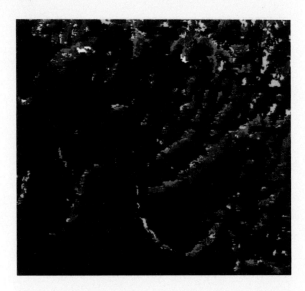

Fig. 7. Predicted distribution of coast live oak forest based on geology, topography and insolation. Black areas are predicted vegetation other than oak forest. Colored areas are predicted oak forest sites on which mapped existing vegetation was oak forest (red), oak woodland (blue), coastal scrub (green), conifer (white) or other land cover types (yellow). Image orientation and area are as in Fig. 1.

See page 376 for color plate of Figure 7.

Discussion

The association between vegetation and calculated monthly radiation was relatively strong for the months of December through March, in spite of the inaccuracies and relatively coarse resolution of the DEM data. Also, vegetation pattern was more strongly associated with calculated radiation than with measures of slope orientation that did not account for shading by local horizons. These results indicate the potential for analyzing plant species distributions in relation to dynamic patterns of solar radiation using high resolution (*e.g.*, 5–10 m) digital elevation data. Previously such analyses were possible only for sample points or localized transects (*e.g.*, Kirkpatrick and Nunez 1980). Using accurate higher resolution data it should also be possible to relate vegetation patterns to topographically-controlled patterns in soil moisture or surface hydrology (*e.g.*, O'Loughlin 1986; Band 1986).

Results of predictive mapping suggest that coast

Table 5. Relative proportions of observed vegetation or land cover types on areas predicted as oak forest sites, as a function of substrate type (columns sum to 1).

Observed vegetation	Quaternary deposits	Paso Robles conglomerate	Careaga sandstone	Sisquoc shale
Oak forest	0.17	0.14	0.18	0.13
Oak woodland	0.54	0.24	0.35	0.65
Coastal scrub	0.14	0.34	0.33	0.05
Conifer forest	0.00	0.00	0.00	0.04
Other	0.14	0.28	0.15	0.13

live oak forest occupies only a small fraction of existing suitable habitat in the region, and that in most areas it has been replaced by oak woodland and chaparral. Wells (1962) blamed anthropogenic fires, cutting and grazing for the conversion of large areas of oak forest to chaparral in this area. Oak forest may require several to many decades to recover from such disturbances (Davis *et al.* 1988), although the rates probably vary between sites and depending on the nature of the disturbance. In this study we observed that much of the observed oak forest occurred only on the lower portion of slopes that were predicted oak forest. This could be a systematic flaw in the predictive site model, an indication of less frequent or less intense disturbance (especially fire) of lower hillslope areas, or more rapid recovery of oak forest from disturbances in these sites. Including maps of recent fire and land use histories should help to resolve some of the discrepancies between observed and predicted vegetation patterns in the region.

Our analyses of coast live oak forest are based on relatively simple GIS operations combining map weighting and overlay, patch size analysis, and spatial sampling. Such GIS-based ecological analyses are useful to the degree that maps derived from a sequence of cartographic operations are of sufficient spatial resolution to describe the ecological processes under investigation, and are of sufficient accuracy so that ecological information is not overwhelmed by cartographic noise. Digital maps contain inaccuracies due both to inherent errors in the original data and operational errors from map digitizing and registration (Burrough 1986; Walsh *et al.* 1987), so that a geographical database is at best a 'fuzzy' representation of the landscape

(Robinson and Strahler 1984). For this reason there is a trade-off between model complexity (*e.g.*, more variables or more complex spatial operations) and model reliability (Burrough 1986). In the analyses reported here, we could readily generate enough samples from the database to outweigh cartographic errors, so that previously documented associations of vegetation pattern with geology and topography were detectable (*e.g.*, Wells 1962; Harrison *et al.* 1971; Cole 1980; Westman 1981).

The results presented above are intended to illustrate how GIS-based cartographic modeling can contribute to the analysis of regional vegetation patterns and the association of vegetation with environmental variables. We are not suggesting that cartographic modeling can substitute for field sampling in developing and testing vegetation site models. However, the types of cartographic analyses conducted here complement traditional field survey methods by measuring associations or testing field results with many more random samples and at larger spatial scales than can practically be collected in the field, facilitating the analysis of large heterogeneous landscapes. Furthermore, we have found that the ability to overlay predicted on observed landscape patterns gives a strong sense of the true predictive skill and bias of quantitative site models, providing useful guidance in terms of model improvement and application.

Acknowledgements

Research support was provided by the California Space Institute. We are grateful to Carol Johnston and two anonymous reviewers for providing helpful comments on the draft manuscript.

229

References

Band, L.E. 1986. Topographic partition of watersheds with digital elevation models. Wat. Resour. Res. 22: 15–23.

Box, E.O. 1981. Macroclimate and plant forms: an introduction to predictive modeling in phytogeography. Dr W. Junk, The Hague.

Burrough, P.A. 1986. Principles of geographic information systems for land resource assessment. Clarendon Press, Oxford.

Card, D.H. 1982. Using known map category marginal frequencies to improve estimates of thematic map accuracy. Photogramm. Engng. and Rem. Sens. 48: 431–439.

Causton, D.R. 1988. Introduction to vegetation analysis. Unwin Hyman, London.

Chambers, J.M., Cleveland, W.B., Kleiner, B. and Tukey, P.A. 1983. Graphical methods for data analysis. Duxbury Press, Boston.

Cibula, W.G. and Nyquist, M.O. 1987. Use of topographic and climatological models in a geographical data base to improve Landsat MSS classification for Olympic National Park. Photogramm. Engng. and Rem. Sens. 53: 67–76.

Cliff, A.D. and Ord, J.K. 1981. Spatial processes. Pion, London.

Cole, K. 1980. Geologic control of vegetation in the Purisima Hills, California. Madrono 27: 79–89.

Costanzo, C.M., Halperin, W.C., Gale, N.D. and Richardson, G.D. 1982. An alternative method for assessing goodness-of-fit for logit models. Environ. and Plann. A 14: 963–971.

Davis, F.W. 1987. Thematic mapper analysis of coast live oak in Santa Barbara County. In: Proceedings of the Symposium on Multiple-use Management of California Hardwood Resources, pp. 317–324. United States Forest Service Pacific Southwest Range Experiment Station Gen. Tech. Rep. PSW-100. Berkeley, California.

Davis, F.W., Hickson, D.E. and Odion, D.C. 1988. Composition of maritime chaparral related to fire history and soil, Burton Mesa, California. Madrono 35: 169–195.

Dibblee, T.W. 1950. Geology of southwestern Santa Barbara County, California Division of Mines. Bulletin 150. Sacramento, California.

Dozier, J. 1980. A clear-sky spectral solar radiation model for snow-covered mountainous terrain. Water Resour. Res. 16: 709–718.

Dozier, J., Bruno, J. and Downey, P. 1981. A faster solution to the horizon problem. Comput. Geosci. 7: 145–151.

Fingleton, B. 1983. Log-linear models with dependent spatial data. Environ. and Plann.A 15: 801–813.

Frew, J. and Dozier, J. 1986. The image processing workbench – portable software for remote sensing instruction and research. In: Proceedings of the 1986 International Geoscience and Remote Sensing Symposium, ESA SP-254. pp. 271–276. European Space Agency, Paris.

Goetz, S. 1987. Predictive mapping of Coast live oak in California using digital terrain data. M.A. Thesis, University of California, Santa Barbara.

Griffin, J.R. 1973. Xylem sap tension in three woodland oaks of central California. Ecology 54: 862–868.

Harrison, A.T., Small, E. and Mooney, H.A. 1971. Drought relationships and distribution of two mediterranean-climate California plant communities. Ecology 52: 869–875.

Hill, G.J.E. and Kelly, G.D.1987. A comparison of existing map products and landsat for land cover mapping. Cartography 16: 51–57.

Kirkpatrick, J.B. and Nunez, M. 1980. Vegetation-radiation relationships in mountainous terrain: eucalypt-dominated vegetation in the Risdon Hills, Tasmania. J. Biogeogr. 7: 197–208.

Marks, D., Dozier, J. and Frew, J. 1984. Automated basin delineation from digital terrain data. Geo-Processing 2: 299–311.

Maynard, P.F. and Strahler, A.H. 1981. The logit classifier: a general maximum likelihood discriminant for remote sensing applications. In: 15th International Symposium on Remote Sensing of the Environment. pp. 1009–1026. Ann Arbor, Michigan.

Morissey, L.A. and Strong, L. 1986. Mapping permafrost in the Boreal Forest with thematic mapper satellite data. Photogramm. Engng. and Rem. Sens. 52: 1513–1520.

Noy-Meir, I. and Anderson, D.J. 1971. Multiple pattern analysis, or multiscale ordination: towards a vegetation hologram? In: Statistical Ecology III: Many Species Populations, Ecosystems and Systems Analysis. pp. 207–231. Edited by G.P. Patil, E.C. Pielou and W.E. Waters. Pennsylvania State University Press, University Park.

Oliver, M.A. and Webster, R. 1986. Semi-variograms for modelling the spatial pattern of landform and soil properties. Earth Surf. Processes Landforms 11: 491–504.

O'Loughlin, E.M. 1986. Prediction of surface saturation zones in natural catchment by topographic analysis. Wat. Resour. Res. 22: 794–804.

Paysen, T.E., Derby, J.E. , Black, H., Jr., Bleich, C. and Mincks, J.W. 1980. A vegetation classification system applied to Southern California. Gen. Tech. Rep. PSW-45. United States Forest Service Pacific Southwest Range Experiment Station. Berkeley, California.

Phipps, M. 1981. Entropy and community pattern analysis. J. Theor. Biol. 93: 253–273.

Robinson, V.B. and Strahler, A.H. 1984. Issues in designing geographic information systems under conditions of inexactness. In: Symposium on Machine Processing of Remotely Sensed Data. pp. 198–204. IEEE, New York.

Rowe, J.S. and Sheard, J.W. 1981. Ecological land classification: a survey approach. Environ. Manage. 5: 451–464.

Strahler, A.H. 1981. Stratification of natural vegetation for forest and rangeland inventory using Landsat digital imagery and collateral data. Int. J. Rem. Sens. 2: 15–41.

Thomas, E.W. 1960. Maps of residuals from regression: their characteristics and uses in geographic research. Department of Geography Publication No. 2, State University of Iowa, Iowa City.

Walsh, S.J., Lightfoot, D.R. and Butler, D.R. 1987. Recognition and assessment of error in geographic information systems. Photogramm. Engng. and Rem. Sens. 53: 1423–1430.

Wells, P.V. 1962. Vegetation in relation to geological substratum and fire in the San Luis Obispo Quadrangle, California. Ecol. Monogr. 32: 79–103.

Westman, W.E. 1981. Diversity relations and succession in California coastal sage scrub. Ecology 62: 170–184.

Wrigley, N. 1975. Analyzing multiple alternative dependent variables. Geogr. Anal. 7: 187–195.

Landscape Ecology vol. 4 no. 1 pp 21-30 (1990)
SPB Academic Publishing bv, The Hague

Spatial and temporal analysis of landscape patterns

Monica G. Turner
Environmental Sciences Division, Oak Ridge National Laboratory, Oak Ridge, TN 37831

Keywords: geographic information systems, GIS, spatial pattern analysis, scale, neutral model, disturbance

Abstract

A variety of ecological questions now require the study of large regions and the understanding of spatial heterogeneity. Methods for spatial-temporal analyses are becoming increasingly important for ecological studies. A grid cell based spatial analysis program (SPAN) is described and results of landscape pattern analysis using SPAN are presented. Several ecological topics in which geographic information systems (GIS) can play an important role (landscape pattern analysis, neutral models of pattern and process, and extrapolation across spatial scales) are reviewed. To study the relationship between observed landscape patterns and ecological processes, a neutral model approach is recommended. For example, the expected pattern (*i.e.*, neutral model) of the spread of disturbance across a landscape can be generated and then tested using actual landscape data that are stored in a GIS. Observed spatial or temporal patterns in ecological data may also be influenced by scale. Creating a spatial data base frequently requires integrating data at different scales. Spatial scale is shown to influence landscape pattern analyses, but extrapolation of data across spatial scales may be possible if the grain and extent of the data are specified. The continued development and testing of new methods for spatial-temporal analysis will contribute to a general understanding of landscape dynamics.

Introduction

A variety of ecological questions now require the study of large regions and the understanding of spatial heterogeneity. Landscape ecology seeks to understand the ecological function of large areas and hypothesizes that the spatial arrangement of ecosystems, habitats, or communities has ecological implications. For example, landscape patterns may influence the spread of disturbance (*e.g.*, Romme and Knight 1982; Franklin and Forman 1987; Turner 1987a), the distribution and persistence of populations (*e.g.*, Van Dorp and Opdam 1987; Fahrig and Paloheimo 1988), large herbivore foraging (*e.g.*, Senft *et al.* 1987), the horizontal flow of

materials such as sediment or nutrients (*e.g.*, Peterjohn and Correll 1984; Ryszkowski and Kedziora 1987), and other ecologically important processes such as net primary production (*e.g.*, Turner 1987b; Sala *et al.* 1988). Landscape-level phenomena are also receiving increasing attention as questions of global change become more prominent. Therefore, methods to analyze and interpret heterogeneity at broad spatial scales are becoming increasingly important for ecological studies.

The need to consider spatial and temporal scale in ecological analyses has often been noted (*e.g.*, Allen and Starr 1982; Delcourt *et al.* 1983; O'Neill *et al.* 1986; Addicott *et al.* 1987; Getis and Franklin 1987; Meentemeyer and Box 1987; Morris 1987;

Urban *et al.* 1987). Given the dramatic expansion of the range of scales at which ecological problems are posed, this need may be greater than ever. Parameters and processes important at one scale are frequently not important or predictive at another scale, and information is often lost as spatial data are considered at coarser scales of resolution (Henderson-Sellers *et al.* 1985; Meentemeyer and Box 1987). Ecological problems may also require the extrapolation of fine-scale measurement for the analysis of broad-scale phenomena. Therefore, the development of methods that will preserve information across scales or quantify the loss of information with changing scales has become a critical task. Such methods are necessary before ecological insights can be extrapolated between spatial and temporal scales.

Geographical information systems (GIS) of varying complexity have emerged as useful tools in addressing landscape-level research questions. Many current ecological problems can be addressed more easily by using some type of GIS. Such questions might include: How has landscape structure changed through time? What factors control landscape patterns? How does landscape pattern affect ecological processes? Can measures of landscape pattern be directly related to ecological function? How does landscape pattern affect the spread of disturbance? Can landscape changes be predicted using simulation models? How does spatial scale influence the analysis of landscape pattern?

The objectives of this paper are to review several topics in which GIS can play an important role and to highlight current research results. In particular, I will focus on the analysis of landscape data, the use of neutral models of pattern and process, and extrapolation across spatial scales.

Landscape pattern analysis

Before the interaction between landscape structure and ecological processes can be understood, landscape patterns must be identified and quantified in meaningful ways. Landscape mosaics are mixtures of natural and human-managed patches that vary in size, shape, and arrangement (*e.g.*, Burgess and

Sharpe 1981; Forman and Godron 1981, 1986; Krummel *et al.* 1987; Turner and Ruscher 1988). Considerable progress has been made in landscape pattern analysis (*e.g.*, Milne 1988; O'Neill *et al.* 1988; Turner and Ruscher 1988). Many studies employ user-generated computer programs to perform the analyses rather than commercially available GIS. User-generated programs allow the inclusion of customized analytical methods and easy linkages to other programs such as spatial simulation models. Such programs generally lack the advanced graphics capabilities of commercially available GIS, but may have the ability to run on almost any computer. I will describe a spatial analysis program that I developed in FORTRAN and briefly review some of its applications.

Spatial analysis program (SPAN)

SPAN is a grid-cell based analysis program that can be applied to any kind of categorical data (note that SPAN is not related to the commercially available geographic information system, SPANS). The program was developed to quantify landscape patterns and their changes in an ecologically meaningful manner (Turner and Ruscher 1988) and to evaluate the predictions of a spatial simulation model (Turner 1987c, 1988). SPAN can be used with any kind of categorical data that can be rasterized at an appropriate level of resolution. The program provides printed output with some summary statistics and computerized output in the form of data files that can be statistically analyzed using SAS.

SPAN incorporates a series of measures of spatial pattern (Table 1). The fraction of the landscape, p, occupied by each type of data (*e.g.*, cover type) is calculated. Nearest neighbor probabilities, q_{ij} are then calculated, representing the probability of cells of land use type i being adjacent to cells of land use type j. The q_{ij} values are calculated by dividing the number of cells of type i that are adjacent to type j by the total number of cells of type i. Nearest neighbor probabilities can be calculated both vertically and horizontally (even diagonally) such that anisotropism, or directionality, in the spatial pattern can be measured. The degree of

Table 1. Measurements of landscape pattern that are calculated in SPAN.

Variable	Description
Pk	Proportion of the landscape occupied by each category
s, l	Size and perimeter of each patch
d	Fractal dimension of patch perimeters
$E_{i,j}$	Edges between each pair of categories
$q_{i,j}$	Probabilities of adjacency (vertical and horizontal) between categories
H	Diversity index
D	Dominance index
C	Contagion index

anisotropism in a landscape may depend upon topographic or other physical constraints and may also vary with the extent of human influence. The differences between the horizontal and vertical probabilities of adjacency can indicate this directional alignment of spatial components.

The amount of edge between each land use is determined by summing the number of interfaces between adjacent cells of different land uses, then multiplying by the length of a cell (*e.g.*, 100 m for 1-ha cells). The amount of edge between all categories is printed, and the edge data files can be statistically analyzed using SAS.

Each patch in the landscape matrix is then identified. A patch is defined as contiguous, adjacent (horizontally or vertically) cells of the same land cover; diagonal cells are not considered to be contiguous. Each patch in the landscape matrix is located, and its size (s) and perimeter (l) are recorded. The number and mean size of patches by any category can then be calculated for each matrix using SAS (SAS Institute 1982). The complexity of patch perimeters is measured using fractal dimensions (Mandelbrot 1983), which can be used to compare the geometry of landscape mosaics (Milne 1988). The fractal is calculated for grid cell data using an edge to area relationship (Burrough 1986; Gardner *et al.* 1987) in which ($l/4$) is the length scale used in measuring the perimeter. To calculate an overall fractal dimension for each or all data categories in a matrix, linear regression analysis of log ($l/4$) against log(s) is done using SAS. The fractal dimen-

sion of the patch perimeters is equal to twice the slope of the regression line. In this analysis, the fractal dimension can theoretically range from 1.0 to 2.0, with 1.0 representing the linear perimeter of a perfect square and 2.0 representing a very complex perimeter encompassing the same area.

Three indices (O'Neill *et al.* 1988) based on information theory (Shannon and Weaver 1962) are also included in SPAN. The first index, H, is a measure of diversity:

$$H = - \sum_{k=1}^{m} (P_k) \log(P_k), \qquad (1)$$

where P_k is the proportion of the landscape in cover type k, and m is the number of land cover types observed. The larger the value of H, the more diverse the landscape.

The second index, D, is a measure of dominance, calculated as the deviation from the maximum possible diversity:

$$D = H_{\max} + \sum_{i=1}^{m} (P_k) \log(P_k), \qquad (2)$$

where m = number of land use types observed on the map, P_k is the proportion of the landscape in land use k, and $H_{\max}$ in Eq. 2 normalizes the index for differences in number of land cover types between different landscapes; the terms in the summation are negative, so Eq. 2 expresses the deviation from the maximum. Large values of D indicate a landscape that is dominated by one or a few land uses, and low values indicate a landscape that has many land uses represented in approximately equal proportions. However, the index is not useful in a completely homogeneous landscape (*i.e.*, $m = 1$) because D then equals zero.

The third index, C, measures contagion, or the adjacency of land cover types. The index is calculated from an adjacency matrix, Q, in which $Q_{i,j}$ is the proportion of cells of type i that are adjacent to cells of type j, such that:

$$C = K_{max} + \sum_{i=1}^{m} \sum_{j=1}^{m} (Q_{i,j}) \log (Q_{i,j}), \quad (3)$$

where $K_{max} = 2$ m $\log(m)$ and is the absolute value of the summation of $(Q_{i,j})\log(Q_{i,j})$ when all possible. The summation term is negative, and Eq. 3 gives the deviation from the maximum possible contagion. K_{max} normalizes landscapes with differing values of m and causes C to be zero when $m = 1$ or all possible adjacencies occur with equal probability. When $m \geq 2$, large values of C will indicate a landscape with a clumped pattern of land cover types.

Landscape pattern analysis using SPAN

SPAN was used by Turner and Ruscher (1988) to determine how landscape patterns in Georgia (southeastern U.S.) had changed during the past 50 years and whether the patterns varied by physiographic region. Historical aerial photography from the 1930's to the 1980's was digitized in grid cell format and analyzed using SPAN.

Changes in the landscape pattern through time were identified. The Georgia landscape has become less fragmented and more connected, as indicated by a general decrease in edges, fractal dimensions, contagion, and dominance. Forests, the natural vegetative cover, became more connected, increasing in aerial extent and in mean patch size. The dominant types of edge changed qualitatively (from transitional-agricultural and transitional-hardwood to agricultural-pine and pine-hardwood), reflecting the successional changes that followed cropland abandonment. The changes observed in the Georgia landscape contrast with the decreased connectively observed in other areas of the U.S. (Burgess and Sharpe 1981; Whitney and Somerlot 1985; Sharpe *et al.* 1987) and many European countries (*e.g.*, Van Dorp and Opdam 1987).

Regional differences in the Georgia landscape were identified. The piedmont and mountain regions were most patchy, whereas the coastal plain had fewer and larger patches. Complex patch perimeters, as indicated by higher fractal dimensions, were observed in the mountains and piedmont; simpler shapes were observed in the coastal plain. The highest diversity and most edges were observed in the mountains, and there was a geographic trend of decreasing diversity and increasing dominance and contagion from the mountains to the lower coastal plain. Thus, broad-scale topographic patterns and physiography may be reflected in the landscape patterns. Other studies (*e.g.*, Swanson *et al.* 1988) have also suggested the importance of landforms in controlling landscape pattern.

Landscape components that were less influenced by humans (*e.g.*, hardwood forests) tended to be more complex in shape than those which received greater human influence (*e.g.*, urban or agricultural lands). Similar results have been reported for other sections of the United States (Krummel *et al.* 1987). The observed complexity of patches of transitional land and lower deciduous forest may reflect topographic or edaphic patterns.

Several of these indices may provide different information at different spatial scales. Using a data set that covers most of the eastern U.S., O'Neill *et al.* (1988) used three indices (dominance, contagion, and fractal) to discriminate among major landscape types such as urban coastal landscapes, mountain forest, and agricultural areas at one point in time. In the Georgia study, Turner and Ruscher (1988) observed significant changes in the diversity and dominance indices through time but not among physiographic regions. In contrast, contagion, which identifies finer-scaled aspects of pattern (O'Neill *et al.* 1988) differed significantly among physiographic regions but not through time. Edges and patch sizes, which describe even finer detail, varied significantly in Georgia both through time and among regions. Thus, broad-scale measures of pattern may be useful to detect large temporal changes but may be less useful to differentiate spatial patterns within a biotic province.

Neutral models of landscape pattern

Once landscape patterns have been quantified, understanding their causes and potential effects on ecological processes is of tremendous interest. Geographic information systems can play an important role in such studies if explanatory variables are included in the spatial data base. However, the relationship between observed landscape patterns and an ecological process can only be rigorously tested if the expected pattern in the absence of the process is known (Gardner *et al.* 1987). This type of expected pattern has been termed a 'neutral model' (Caswell 1976). Neutral models can be used to measure the improvement in predictability which may be achieved by modeling topographic, climatic, and disturbance effects, for which data are frequently contained in a GIS.

The movement of disturbances across landscapes is being studied in a neutral model context by Turner *et al.* (1988, 1989a) using percolation theory (Stauffer 1985; Orbach 1986; Gardner *et al.* 1987). A landscape can be characterized in terms of habitat that is susceptible to a particular disturbance (*e.g.*, pine forests susceptible to bark beetle infestations) and habitat that is not susceptible to the disturbance (*e.g.*, hardwood forests, grasslands, etc.). The spatial arrangement of the disturbance-susceptible habitat can be randomly generated at probability p on an appropriately scaled percolation map, and the propagation of disturbances that spread within the susceptible habitat may then be studied. Turner *et al.* focused on two disturbance characteristics, intensity and frequency, as they interact with landscape pattern. Disturbance frequency is defined as the probability that a new disturbance will be initiated in a unit of susceptible habitat at the beginning of the simulation. Intensity is defined as the probability that the disturbance, once initiated, will spread to adjacent sites of the same habitat. The spread of a disturbance across a landscape is then predicted as a function of (1) the proportion of the landscape occupied by the disturbance-prone cover type, (2) disturbance intensity, and (3) disturbance frequency.

The neutral model of disturbance quantitatively predicted the spread and effects of disturbance on the susceptible habitat and identified a critical threshold in the spatial pattern. Disturbance propagation and effects on landscape pattern were qualitatively different when the proportion (p) of the landscape occupied by disturbance-susceptible habitat was above or below the percolation threshold (p_c) (Fig. 1). (The percolation threshold is the probability at which the largest patch or cluster can span the entire grid and is approximately 0.5928). The distribution and spatial arrangement of the susceptible habitats helps explain these differences. Habitats occupying less than p_c tend to be fragmented, with numerous, small patches, and low connectivity (Gardner *et al.* 1987). The spread of a disturbance was constrained by this fragmented spatial pattern, and the sizes and numbers of clusters were not substantially affected by the intensity (i) of disturbance. Habitats occupying more than p_c tend to be highly connected, forming continuous clusters (Gardner *et al.* 1987). Disturbance could spread through the landscape even when frequency was relatively low.

The neutral model of disturbance propagation can be tested using landscape pattern and disturbance data for actual landscapes. A digitized map of the habitat types in the landscape would be required, and a temporal sequence of landscape patterns before and after disturbances would be particularly useful. Data for landscapes that have different spatial patterns but are susceptible to the same disturbance (*e.g.*, fire or pest outbreak) might also be used. In addition, data on the number of initiations, the rate of spread, and the spatial extent of disturbance would be necessary. Knowledge of a few parameters that describe landscape heterogeneity and the propagation of disturbance may provide useful insights for predicting landscape effects.

The expected patterns of a variety of ecological phenomena (*e.g.*, spatial distribution of species) can also be studied using a neutral model approach. For example, the suitability of a landscape for particular species (*e.g.*, Palmeirim 1988) could be predicted, and boundary phenomena (*e.g.*, Wiens *et al.* 1985; Schonewald-Cox 1988) could be studied. As the use of GIS becomes increasingly widespread, it will become more important to consider expected patterns in the absence of specific processes before the observed patterns can be explained.

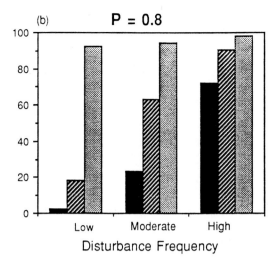

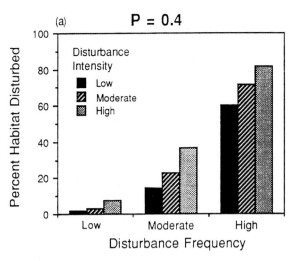

Fig. 1. The percent of susceptible habitat on a random landscape that is affected by disturbances of different frequency and intensity when the proportion of susceptible habitat was (a) below or (b) above the critical threshold ($p_c = 0.5928$). When $p < p_c$, disturbances frequency has a greater influence than intensity, whereas when $p > p_c$, disturbance intensity is very important even when frequency is low. (Adapted from Turner *et al.* 1989a).

(a) Increasing grain size

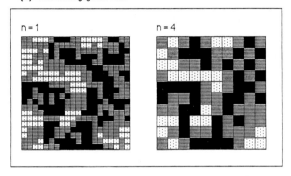

(b) Increasing extent

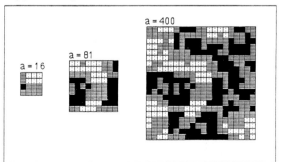

Fig. 2. Illustration of changing two components of spatial scale, grain and extent. (a) Grain size refers to the resolution, *n*, of each data unit. (b) Extent refers to the size of the study area, *a*. Changes in grain and extent affect the measurement of landscape pattern in different ways. (from Turner *et al.* 1989b).

Extrapolation across spatial scales

The patterns observed in ecological data may be influenced by spatial scale. In studies of landscape structure or function, information may be available at a variety of levels of resolution, data must often be compared across large geographic regions, and it may be necessary to extrapolate information from local to regional scales. Applications of GIS also frequently require the integration of data obtained at different spatial scales. It is therefore important to develop an understanding of and ability to predict changes in ecological phenomena with changes in scale.

The spatial scale of ecological data encompasses both grain and extent (Fig. 2). Grain refers to the resolution of the data, *i.e.*, the area represented by each data unit. For example, a fine-grain map might organize information into 1-ha units, whereas a map with an order of magnitude coarser resolution would have information organized into 10-ha units. Extent refers to the overall size of the study area. For example, maps of 100 km^2 and 100,000 km^2 differ in extent by a factor of 1000. The effects of grain and extent are of particular concern, and the responses of ecological parameters measured on the landscape to changes in spatial scale are not known. It has been suggested (Allen *et al.* 1987) that

237

information can be transferred across scales if both grain and extent are specified.

Turner *et al.* (1989b) used an experimental approach to study the effects of spatial scale on landscape pattern. The purpose of the study was to observe the effects of changing the grain (the finest level of spatial resolution possible with a given data set) and extent (the total area of the study) of landscape data on observed spatial patterns and to identify some general rules for comparing measures obtained at different scales. Simple random maps, maps with contagion (*i.e.*, clusters of the same land cover type), and actual landscape data from USGS land use (LUDA) data maps were used in the analyses. Landscape patterns were compared using indices measuring diversity (*H*), dominance (*D*) and contagion (*C*). Rare land cover types were lost as grain became coarser. This loss could be predicted analytically for random maps with two land cover types, and it was observed in actual landscapes as grain was increased experimentally. What was particularly interesting, however, was the manner in which the spatial pattern influenced the rate at wwhich information was lost as grain became coarser. Although less dominant cover types always declined, cover types that were dispersed were lost most rapidly and cover types that were clumped were lost most slowly. The diversity index decreased linearly with increasing grain size, but D and C did not show a linear relationship. The indices *D* and *C* increased with increasing extent, but *H* exhibited a variable response. The indices were sensitive to the number (*m*) of cover types observed in the data set and the fraction of the landscape occupied by each cover type (P_k); both *m* and P_k varied with grain and extent.

The results demonstrated how the spatial scale at which landscape patterns are quantified can influence the result, and that measurements made at different scales may not be comparable. Qualitative and quantitative changes in measurement across spatial scales will differ according to how scale is defined. Therefore, the definition and methods of changing scale must always be explicitly stated. It is important to define the scale of ecological data in terms of both grain, S_g, and extent, S_e. The identification of properties that do not change or

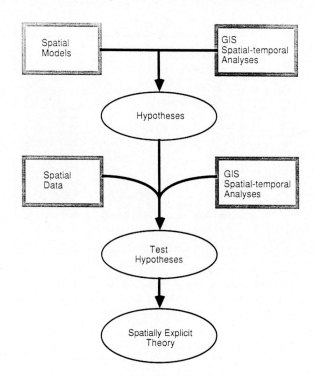

Fig. 3. Illustration of how models, GIS, and data can contribute to the development of theory that addresses the ecological implications of spatial patterns. These methods make it possible to generate and test landscape-level hypotheses.

change predictably across scales would simplify the extrapolation of measurements from fine scales to broad scales. Characterizing the relationships between ecological measurements and the grain and extent of the data may make it possible to predict or correct for the loss of information with changes in spatial scale. More importantly, the ability to predict how ecological variables change with scale may open the door to extrapolating information to larger scales and to comparing data measured in different regions.

Conclusion

Spatial-temporal analysis in ecology promises to provide additional insight into ecological processes at a variety of scales. Hypotheses at the landscape level can now be generated and tested by combining models, spatial-temporal analyses, and spatially explicit data (Fig. 3). Analytical methods are neces-

Table 2. General hypotheses that can now be tested by using models, data, and spatio-temporal analyses.

Measures of landscape pattern can be directly related to ecological processes at different scales.

Landscape patterns can be predicted using a small set of ecological variables.

Predictive variables differ with spatial and temporal scale.

Landscape effects on ecologically important parameters can be detected by comparing expected patterns (*i.e.*, neutral models) and observed patterns.

There are critical thresholds in the spatial patterns in the landscape at which ecological processes will qualitatively change.

The spatial spread of disturbance can be predicted using a few parameters describing landscape heterogeneity and disturbance characteristics.

Information may be extrapolated across spatial scales if the grain, extent, and contagion of the data are known.

sary for changes or differences in spatial patterns to be identified. Therefore, these methods are also necessary for the development of ecological theory that incorporates the implications of spatial arrangement. Models can be constructed to improve our theoretical understanding of spatially influenced phenomena, just as experiments are conducted to improve understanding of an empirical problem (Caswell 1988). Combining spatial-temporal analyses with models permits the development of hypotheses that can then be empirically tested using spatial data.

The selection of particular methods of analysis (*e.g.*, user-generated programs or the many commercial GIS systems) depends upon the objectives of a particular study and the available equipment. The analysis programs described in this paper are relatively simple and were developed to answer specific landscape-level questions. The programs are easy to run and interpret and can be applied to any categorical data that are in raster format. Analysis programs such as SPAN can also be linked with spatial simulation models and used to test the goodness-of-fit between model predictions and landscape data.

The results reviewed in this paper suggest some directions for future research. Simple indices and measures such as those presented here can capture aspects of landscape pattern at different scales. Significant changes in landscape patterns through time and differences across regions can be identified. These analyses could be applied to a variety of data in a GIS to determine how the patterns of different variables were related. The measures also show

promise of relating to ecological processes (*e.g.* disturbance), but more research is required to elucidate the linkage between pattern and process.

Neutral models may be extremely useful in identifying the factors causing landscape patterns or the effects of ecological processes. The disturbance model presented here is one example of a neutral model relating pattern and process; many others could be developed. Data that are in a GIS can be used to test neutral models and determine how the addition of ecological factors improves predictability. The existence of critical thresholds (*e.g.*, p_c beyond which dramatic changes occur could also be tested using a GIS.

Spatial scale influences the analysis of landscape data, and the comparison of data obtained at different scales may not be straightforward. Rules for extrapolating across spatial scales may be possible but scale must be defined and specified in terms of grain and extent. Considerable additional research is required to develop a more complete understanding of the relationship between scale and the patterns and processes observed on the landscape.

With the availability of GIS and other methods of spatial-temporal analysis, hypotheses can now be tested at broad spatial scales. Some general hypotheses that emerge from the research reviewed here are presented in Table 2. These hypotheses could be tested using appropriate ecological processes in actual landscapes. New methods of analysis will continue to be developed and tested as ecological research focuses on broader spatial and temporal scales. The development of robust analytical methods, models, and experiments that provide unique insights into ecological processes will contribute to a general theory of landscape dynamics.

Acknowledgements

I thank V.H. Dale, R.L. Graham, and two anonymous reviewers for comments on this manuscript. This research was supported by the Ecological Research Division, Office of Health and Environmental Research, U.S. Department of Energy, under Contract No. DE-AC05-840R21400 with Martin Marietta Energy Systems, Inc. and through an Alexander P. Hollaender Distinguished Postdoctoral Fellowship, administered by Oak Ridge Associated Universities, to M.G. Turner. This is publication no. 3240 of the Environmental Sciences Division, Oak Ridge National Laboratory.

Literature cited

Addicott, J.F., Aho, J.M., Antolin, M.F., Padilla, D.K., Richardson, J.S. and Soluk, D.A. 1987. Ecological neighborhoods: scaling environmental patterns. Oikos 49: 340–346.

Allen, T.F.H. and Starr, T.B. 1982. Hierarchy. University of Chicago Press, Chicago.

Allen, T.F.H., O'Neill, R.V. and Hoekstra, T.W. 1987. Interlevel relations in ecological research and management: some working principles from hierarchy theory. Journal of Applied Systems Analysis 14: 63–79.

Burgess, R.L. and Sharpe, D.M., eds. 1981. Forest island dynamics in man-dominated landscapes. Springer-Verlag, New York.

Burrough, P.A. 1986. Principles of geographic information systems for land resources assessment. Clarendon Press, Oxford.

Caswell, H. 1976. Community structure: a neutral model analysis. Ecol. Monogr. 46: 327–354.

Caswell, H. 1988. Theory and models in ecology: a different perspective. Bull. Ecol. Soc. Amer. 69: 102–109.

Delcourt, H.R., Delcourt, P.A. and Webb, T., III. 1983. Dynamic plant ecology: The spectrum of vegetation change in space and time. Quaternary Science Review 1: 153–175.

Fahrig, L. and Paloheimo, J. 1988. Effect of spatial arrangement of habitat patches on local population size. Ecology 69: 468–475.

Forman, R.T.T. and Godron, M. 1981. Patches and structural components for a landscape ecology. BioScience 31: 733–740.

Forman, R.T.T. and Godron, M. 1986. Landscape Ecology. John Wiley & Sons, New York.

Franklin, J.F. and Forman, R.T.T. 1987. Creating landscape patterns by forest cutting: ecological consequences and principles. Landscape Ecology 1: 5–18.

Gardner, R.H., Milne, B.T., Turner, M.G. and O'Neill, R.V. 1987. Neutral models for the analysis of broad-scale landscape pattern. Landscape Ecology 1: 19–28.

Getis, A. and Franklin, J. 1987. Second-order neighborhood analysis of mapped point patterns. Ecology

Henderson-Sellers, A., Wilson, M.F. and Thomas, G. 1985. The effect of spatial resolution on archives of land cover type. Climatic Change 7: 391–402.

Krummel, J.R., Gardner, R.H., Sugihara, G., O'Neill, R.V. and Coleman, P.R. 1987. Landscape patterns in a disturbed environment. Oikos 48: 321–324.

Mandelbrot, B.B. 1983. The fractal geometry of nature. W.H. Freeman and Co., San Francisco, CA.

Meentemeyer, V. and Box, E.O. 1987. Scale effects in landscape studies. In: Landscape heterogeneity and disturbance. pp. 15–34. Edited by M.G. Turner. Springer-Verlag, New York.

Milne, B.T. 1988. Measuring the fractal dimension of landscapes. Appl. Math. Comp. 27: 67–79.

Morris, D.W. 1987. Ecological scale and habitat use. Ecology 68: 362–369.

O'Neill, R.V., DeAngelis, D.L., Waide, J.B. and Allen, T.F.H. 1986. A hierarchical concept of ecosystems. Princeton University Press, New Jersey.

O'Neill, R.V., Krummel, J.R., Gardner, R.H., Sugihara, G., Jackson, B., DeAngelis, D.L., Milne, B.T., Turner, M.G., Zygmunt, B., Christensen, S.W., Dale, V.H. and Graham, R.L. 1988. Indices of landscape pattern. Landscape Ecology 1: 153–162.

Orbach, R. 1986. Dynamics of fractal networks. Science 231: 814–819.

Palmeirim, J.M. 1988. Automatic mapping of avian species habitat using satellite imagery. Oikos 52: 59–68.

Peterjohn, W.T. and Correll, D.L. 1984. Nutrient dynamics in an agricultural watershed: observations on the role of a riparian forest. Ecology 65: 1466–1475.

Romme, W. and Knight, D.H. 1982. Landscape diversity: the concept applied to Yellowstone Park. BioScience 32: 664–670.

Ryszkowski, L. and Kedziora, A. 1987. Impact of agricultural landscape structure on energy flow and water cycling. Landscape Ecology 1: 85–94.

Sala, O.E., Parton, W.J., Joyce, L.A. and Lauenroth, W.K. 1988. Primary production of the central grassland region of the United States. Ecology 69: 40–45.

SAS Institute. 1982. User's guide: statistics. SAS Institute, Cary, North Carolina.

Schonewald-Cox, C. 1988. Boundaries in the protection of nature reserves. BioScience 38: 480–486.

Senft, R.L., Coughenour, M.B., Bailey, D.W., Rittenhouse, L.R., Sala, O.E., and Swift, D.M. 1987. Large herbivore foraging and ecological hierarchies. BioScience 37: 789–799.

Shannon, C.E. and Weaver, W. 1962. The mathematical theory of communication. University of Illinois Press, Urbana.

Sharpe, D.M., Guntenspergen, G.R., Dunn, C.P., Leitner,

L.A. and Stearns, F. 1987. Vegetation dynamics in a southern Wisconsin agricultural landscape. *In*: Landscape heterogeneity and disturbance. pp. 139–158. Edited by M.G. Turner. Springer-Verlag, New York.

Stauffer, D. 1985. Introduction to percolation theory. Taylor and Francis, London.

Swanson, F.J., Kratz, T.K., Caine, N. and Woodmansee, R.G. 1988. Landform effects on ecosystem patterns and processes. BioScience 38: 92–98.

Turner, M.G., ed. 1987a. Landscape heterogeneity and disturbance. Springer-Verlag, New York.

Turner, M.G. 1987b. Land use changes and net primary production in the Georgia landscape: 1935 to 1982. Environ. Manage. 11: 237–247.

Turner, M.G. 1987c. Spatial simulation of landscape changes in Georgia: a comparison of 3 transition models. Landscape Ecology 1: 29–36.

Turner, M.G. 1988. A spatial simulation model of land use changes in Georgia. Appl. Math. Comp. 27: 39–51.

Turner, M.G. and Ruscher, C.L. 1988. Changes in the spatial patterns of land use in Georgia. Landscape Ecology 1: 241–251.

Turner, M.G., Gardner, R.H., Dale, V.H. and O'Neill, R.V. 1988. Landscape pattern and the spread of disturbance. *In*: Proc. VIIIth Intl. Symp. Probs. Landsc. Ecol. Res., Vol. 1. pp. 373–382. Edited by M. Ruzicka, T. Hrnciarova, and L. Miklos. Institute of Experimental Biology and Ecology, CBES SAS, Bratislava, Czechoslovakia.

Turner, M.G., Gardner, R.H., Dale, V.H. and O'Neill, R.V. 1989a. Predicting the spread of disturbance in heterogeneous landscapes. Oikos. 55: 121–129.

Turner, M.G., O'Neill, R.V., Gardner, R.H. and Milne, B.T. 1989b. Effects of changing spatial scale on the analysis of landscape pattern. Landscape Ecology 3(3/4): 153–163.

Urban, D.L., O'Neill, R.V. and Shugart, H.H. 1987. Landscape ecology. BioScience 37: 119–127.

Van Dorp, D. and Opdam, P.F.M. 1987. Effects of patch size, isolation and regional abundance on forest bird communities. Landscape Ecology 1: 59–73.

Whitney, G.T. and Somerlot, W.J. 1985. A case study of woodland continuity and change in the American midwest. Biol. Conserv. 31: 265–287.

Wiens, J.A., Crawford, C.S. and Gosz, J.R. 1985. Boundary dynamics: a conceptual framework for studying landscape ecosystems. Oikos 45: 421–427.

SECTION 7

Wildlife

Overview

Agee et al. start this section with a discussion of GIS analysis of landscape types associated with grizzly bears in Washington. In the second article, by Breininger et al., Florida scrub jay habitat is evaluated using proximity analysis. In the following article, Pereira and Itami demonstrate the use of logistic regression for habitat modelling of red squirrels. In the last article by Stoms et al., sensitivity analysis is presented as a way to assess uncertainties in input data and assumptions of habitat models.

Suggested Additional Reading

Johnston, Carol A., and Robert J. Naiman. 1990. The Use of a Geographic Information System to Analyze Longterm Landscape Alteration by Beaver. Landscape Ecology. 4:5-19.

Lehmkuhl, J. F., and M. G. Raphael. 1993. Habitat Pattern Around Northern Spotted Owl Locations on the Olympic Peninsula, Washington. Journal of Wildlife Management. 57(2):302-315.

Spies, T. A., W. J. Ripple, and G. A. Bradshaw. 1994. Dynamics and Pattern of a Managed Coniferous Forest Landscape in Oregon. Ecological Applications. (In Press).

A Geographic Analysis of Historical Grizzly Bear Sightings in the North Cascades

James K. Agee
National Park Service Cooperative Park Studies Unit, College of Forest Resources, University of Washington, Seattle, WA 98195
Susan C. F. Stitt, Maurice Nyquist, and Ralph Root
National Park Service, Geographic Information System Division, P. O. Box 25287-GIS, Denver, CO 80225

ABSTRACT: Historic grizzly bear sightings in the North Cascades area of Washington were analyzed using the GRASS geographic information system (GIS) software. A 22-class land-cover database that was determined to be 85 percent accurate was compared to 91 historic sightings of grizzly bears. The historic sightings were positively associated with the whitebark pine - subalpine larch and subalpine herb cover types. The sighting locations were found to have similar land-cover richness but land-cover interspersion different from the overall landscape within the study area. These data were used to develop new map layers for relative cover type and diversity selection which were then combined into a map of sighting potential for grizzly bears in the North Cascades.

INTRODUCTION

THE GRIZZLY BEAR (*Ursus arctos*) currently occupies less than half of its historic range in North America. Major population declines have occurred south of the Canadian border (Martinka and Kendall, 1986). Efforts to help grizzly bear populations recover were formally initiated in 1975, when the grizzly bear was classified as a "threatened" species under the Endangered Species Act. As part of the recovery effort, six areas have been designated as "grizzly bear ecosystems": four have specific plans for bear recovery and two, including the North Cascades area in Washington, are considered evaluation areas. The North Cascades Working Group, an interagency team, is evaluating the suitability of the North Cascades Grizzly Bear Evaluation Area (Figure 1) to support a viable grizzly bear population. The area contains over 3,000,000 ha of contiguous National Park and National Forest System lands, and is within the historic range of the grizzly bear, but the status of the current population is unknown. If a population is present, it is reclusive and probably small.

The evaluation effort will consider biological and social constraints and opportunities for grizzly bear management. If a recovery plan is approved, boundaries for the grizzly bear ecosystem will be delineated. The five-year evaluation period is complicated because of the apparent low numbers of grizzly bears in the area, making ecosystem-wide animal use studies difficult. The final decision will incorporate information from specific habitat studies (both radio-telemetry data on grizzlies, if available, and seasonal habitat and food identification) and apply them at a landscape (millions of hectares) level. A geographic information system (GIS) database is being built to assist the habitat analysis capability over this large area.

A digital database currently exists for a smaller area encompassing the North Cascades National Park Service Complex (Figure 1; Agee et al., 1985). The objective of this research was to determine if the land-cover characteristics surrounding historic grizzly bear sightings were distributed differently from those in the existing database, and if so, to provide an analysis of areas where grizzly bears are most likely to be sighted.

To null hypotheses were tested for the grizzly bear sighting and land-cover data:

- Historical grizzly bear sightings by cover type have occurred in the same proportions as the availability of the cover types on the landscape.
- Historical grizzly bear sightings have occurred in areas proportional to the cover type diversity (measured by richness and interspersion) in the landscape within the GIS data base.

The objective of testing these hypotheses was to apply the results over the entire GIS database to determine the geographic locations of highest sighting potential. Analyses were based on the assumptions that grizzly bear sightings are a function of cover type and cover type diversity.

In other areas where grizzly habitat has been studied, a variety of vegetation units (habitat type, community type, habitat component, etc.) have been used to define habitat, on the basis that grizzly bears use the resources within these units preferentially (Craighead et al., 1982; Mace, 1986); however, no system appears to be universally accepted. Characterizing diversity is even less standardized than the individual unit of habitat. It is known in the Yellowstone area that grizzly bears prefer forest-nonforest ecotones (Blanchard, 1983; Weaver et al., 1986) but measurement of such diversity is difficult. Our objective differed from these studies in that we attempted to define sighting potential rather than habitat value. Although verification of model predictions are important (Lyon et al., 1987), such verification is nearly impossible when dealing with animals in a part of their range where they are very rare.

METHODS

The existing North Cascades GIS data base includes 22 land-cover classes over a 850,000 ha area: eighteen vegetation classes and four inert classes (water, rock/bareground, snow/ice, and shadow). The raster database has a pixel size of 50 by 50 metres. The cover type classes were developed from 1978 and 1979 Landsat MSS data used in conjunction with Defense Mapping Agency (DMA) 1:250,000 topographic data (aspect, slope, elevation) and digitized precipitation isohyets. The cover type map was determined to be 85 percent accurate (Agee et al., 1985).

In a separate study over a larger area, Sullivan (1983) mapped historic and recent reports of grizzly bear sightings. Such presence data are often used to verify species presence in certain areas or habitats (Jones, 1986). Sightings were identified by year, location, and reliability. Reliability was defined in one of four classes: Class 1, photograph or carcass; Class 2, multiple identification characteristics present: hump, claws, face, tracks, or scat; Class 3, a single characteristic; Class 4, size or color only, or lack of details (Sullivan, 1983). The percentage of observations in each class were Class 1, 5.2 percent; Class 2, 28.7 percent; Class 3, 43.8 percent; and Class 4, 22.3 percent. Within

PHOTOGRAMMETRIC ENGINEERING AND REMOTE SENSING,
Vol. 55, No. 11, November 1989, pp. 1637–1642.

0099-1112/89/5511–1637$02.25/0
©1989 American Society for Photogrammetry and Remote Sensing

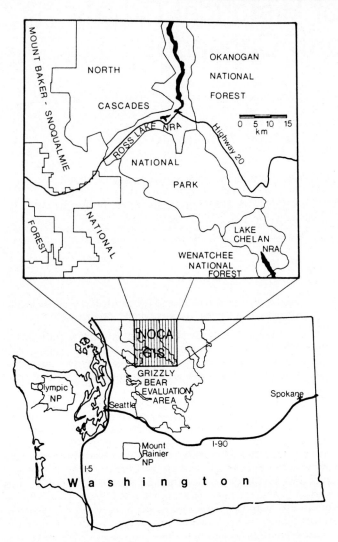

FIG. 1. The North Cascades area is in north-central Washington. The wavy line enclosing the larger area is the approximate boundary for the North Cascades Grizzly Bear Evaluation Area. The smaller box is the area covered by the existing North Cascades GIS, which is shown in more detail.

vations are more probable in open landscapes where sight distances are longer. Such bias must be recognized when interpreting results.

Analyses were performed using the Geographic Resources Analysis Support System (GRASS) developed by the Army Corps of Engineers, Construction Engineering Research Laboratory. Through GRASS, various site descriptive analyses as well as separate map layers can be created and integrated.

A total of 91 grizzly bear sightings within the area of the USGS North Cascades National Park special map were remapped from Sullivan's (1983) 1:250,000 map to the park 1:100,000 map and the UTM coordinates were digitized. All classes of observations were used, as the mapped locations were not identified to a particular sighting reliability class. Another 91 random UTM coordinates were generated from random number tables within that same map area for comparison. These coordinates were entered into the GIS data base through a dBASE III file.

The first hypothesis was tested using the most commonly occurring cover type in variable sized windows around each historic grizzly bear sighting and random locations. Matrices were considered the most appropriate units to analyze, rather than points, due to the inexact locations of the grizzly sightings. The GRASS "sites occurrence" tool was used to compare the cover type distribution of historic sighting locations and randomly chosen locations to the expected number of locations in each cover type based on proportions of each cover type on the landscape.

The Chi-square analyses provided by the computer software have potential bias as some of the expected frequencies were less than five, so further analyses were conducted once an optimum matrix size was determined. A G-statistic based on the log-likelihood ratio (Zar, 1984), which is less sensitive to frequencies less than 5 and proportions less than 0.2, was applied to the same data. Individual cover types with high positive contributions to the G-statistic had critical lower confidence limits computed using the relationship between the F distribution and the binomial distribution (Zar, 1984). This allowed a more objective identification of those cover types where bears were sighted in higher than expected proportions.

The second hypothesis was tested by the GRASS "neighbors-diversity," "interspersion," and "sites-occurrence" tools, which generated two land-cover diversity analyses. Diversity was defined as a combination of cover type richness (number of cover types represented) and interspersion, which can be considered a form of beta diversity (between community or stand). Diversity as characterized by richness was measured as the number of cover types within the 11 by 11 matrices, with the richness being assigned to the center cell for mapping purposes. Richness was calculated for matrices around each historic grizzly bear sighting and for the randomly located points. The mean cover type richness of the two analyses was tested for significant differences by a t-test (Zar 1984). Diversity as characterized by interspersion was calculated by first running a 3 by 3 window through the land-cover file, and assigning the percent difference in cover types between the center and immediate surrounding cells, as a measure of interspersion, to the center cell. Then the distribution of interspersion values within each 11 by 11 matrix around historic grizzly sightings were summarized through "sites-occurrence" and compared to the distribution of interspersion for the landcover file as a whole.

Three final layers in the GIS database were generated from the analyses above, using the GRASS "reclass" tool. For the first layer (cover type preference), each pixel was assigned a value of 0, 2, or 4 based on the lower, average, or higher than expected proportions of historic grizzly bear sightings for the cover type represented in that pixel.

For the second layer (cover type diversity), a similar 0 to 4

the area covered by the existing GIS database, the proportion of observations were similarly distributed (Chi-square = 3.51; critical value$_{0.05,3}$ = 7.81). The locations were mapped at 1:250,000, and 91 of the 233 sightings were in the area of the existing North Cascades GIS database.

There are three significant sources of potential error relevant to the association of cover types with the sighting data. First, large dots were used to identify locations; each dot covered an area > 1 square kilometre. Although the center of each dot can be precisely located, the dot in some cases represents only an approximate sighting location. Second, the sightings occurred over more than a century, introducing error associated with potential cover type change with time. About 10 percent of the sightings recorded occurred before 1920, 34 percent between 1920 and 1950, and 56 percent since 1950. None of the forests at the sighting locations appear to have been logged. Successional change in subalpine portions of the area, particularly after fire (Agee and Smith, 1984; Agee et al., 1986) or climate change (Franklin et al., 1971) have proceeded slowly, so that significant cover type change is unlikely. A third source of concern is the type of data which Sullivan collected. Visual obser-

value was produced from the combination of cover type richness (0 to 2) and interspersion (0 to 2). The cover type richness around historic grizzly bear sightings was compared to the random locations to determine if grizzly sighting locations had a significantly different distribution. If the distributions differed, a value of 2 would be assigned to each pixel with most preferred cover type richness, 1 to those pixels with possibly preferred richness, and 0 for richness levels not well represented in the grizzly sighting matrices. The distribution of cover type interspersion was compared to the distribution of interspersion for the entire landcover file using a G-test (Zar, 1984), and the two groups showing the largest differences between observed and expected (based on p levels) were assigned 2 and 1, respectively, with other groups being assigned a 0.

The third layer was developed under the assumption that cover type and diversity are equally important in grizzly bear sighting potential. The values in the first two layers were added together using GRASS tool "Gmapcalc," to form a possible range of values from 0 to 8, representing low to high potential for the sighting of grizzly bears.

RESULTS

Sightings by Cover Type

Cover type analyses around grizzly bear sightings were made for pixel windows 1 by 1, 3 by 3, 5 by 5, 7 by 7, 9 by 9, 11 by 11, 13 by 13, 15 by 15, and 17 by 17. For the 1 by 1 matrix, subalpine herb was the most common cover type in which grizzly bears were sighted, but the whitebark pine/subalpine larch cover type had the largest proportional difference between actual sightings and the number expected if sightings were proportional to cover type distribution on the landscape. As matrix size increased, subalpine herb remained the most common cover type in which obervations were made; the largest differences between expected and actual cover type distribution of sightings were for the whitebark pine/subalpine larch types (both open and closed canopy), subalpine herb, and open canopy subalpine fir (Table 1).

The Chi-square analyses indicate that cover types on which grizzlies have been sighted differ significantly from that expected based on availability on the landscape. All of the matrix sizes had Chi-square values above the critical level (alpha 0.05,21 = 32.7; Figure 2). Matrices around the randomly chosen points do not significantly differ in cover type distribution from the overall map expected distribution. As matrix size increases, the grizzly sighting Chi-square values peak at the 9 by 9 matrix size and 11 by 11 matrix size, while the random point Chi-square values slowly decline as matrix size increases. The 11 by 11 pixel matrix (30.25 ha) was selected as the optimum size for further analysis.

Because the frequency of many of the expected cover types is less than 5, the Chi-square analysis (Table 1, Figure 2) could be statistically biased. For the 11 by 11 matrix, the calculated G-statistic (G = 39.07; $G_{0.01,21}$ = 38.9) confirmed the results of the Chi-square test. Confidence limits (e.g., Neu et al. (1974)) were calculated for the proportion of total landscape in cover types which had high positive contributions to the G-statistic (Zar, 1984). Critical levels of significance were computed using these limits and expected proportions (Table 2), indicating that the whitebark pine/subalpine larch cover type (open and closed canopy) had the highest sighting potential, followed by the subalpine herb cover type. Characteristics of the whitebark pine/subalpine larch cover type and the subalpine herb cover type are summarized in Table 3, adapted from Agee et al. (1985). Dominant plant species characteristic of these cover types (huckleberries [Vaccinium spp.], whitebark pine, and a wide variety of herbaceous species) are similar to species preferred by

TABLE 1. DISTRIBUTION OF GRIZZLY BEAR SIGHTINGS BY COVER TYPE FOR THE 11 BY 11 MATRIX. TABLE GENERATED BY THE GRASS SITE OCCURRENCE REPORT.

Cover Type*	Percent Cover in GIS**	Expected Sites**	Actual Sites
Douglas-fir (C)	10.1	9.2	7
Subalpine fir (C)	10.2	9.3	10
Whitebark pine/subalpine larch (C)	2.2	2.0	5
Mountain hemlock (C)	3.8	3.5	5
Pacific silver fir (C)	8.4	7.7	4
Western hemlock (C)	10.1	9.2	7
Hardwood forest	1.2	1.1	0
Tall shrub	4.9	4.5	4
Lowland herb	1.6	1.5	1
Subalpine herb	8.5	7.7	12
Heather meadow	0.6	0.5	0
Ponderosa pine (O)	0.2	0.2	0
Douglas-fir (O)	4.5	4.1	3
Subalpine fir (O)	4.5	4.1	7
Whitebark pine/subalpine larch (O)	1.7	1.5	8
Mountain hemlock (O)	2.0	1.8	2
Pacific silver fir (O)	2.5	2.2	2
Western hemlock (O)	5.2	4.7	4
Water	1.1	1.0	0
Snow	3.9	3.5	0
Rock, Inert	12.3	11.2	10
Shadow	0.8	0.7	0
Total	100.0	91.0	91

*(C) and (O) refer to closed canopy and open canopy portions of a forested cover type, defined by Landsat spectral signature. Open canopy denotes significant herbaceous, deciduous, or inert (rock/soil) cover within the type.

**sum of individual values may vary from total due to rounding off.

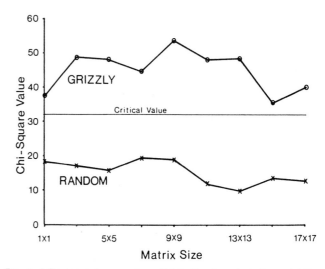

FIG. 2. Differences in cover type distribution for grizzly bear sightings and randomly located points compared to availability of cover types over the North Cascades GIS data base. Separate analyses were done for various sized matrices around each sighting or random point. The straight horizontal line represents the critical Chi-square value for p = 0.05, d.f. = 21. The elements of each matrix are 50 by 50 m pixels.

grizzly bears in the Rocky Mountains (Serveen, 1983; Eggers, 1986; Almack, 1986).

The first null hypothesis was rejected. The grizzly sightings exist in significantly higher than expected proportions in certain cover types.

TABLE 2. CRITICAL VALUES FOR THE PROPORTION OF A SAMPLE IN A SINGLE COVER TYPE COMPARED TO ITS AVAILABILITY ON THE LANDSCAPE. COVER TYPES SHOWN ARE THE SIX LARGEST CONTRIBUTORS TO THE G-STATISTIC, AND MOST LIKELY TO HAVE PROPORTIONS OF TOTAL GRIZZLY BEAR SIGHTINGS SIGNIFICANTLY HIGHER THAN EXPECTED.

Cover Type	p-value*
Whitebark pine/subalpine larch open canopy	<0.001
Whitebark pine/subalpine larch closed canopy	<0.10
Subalpine herb	<0.16
Subalpine fir - open canopy	<0.25
Mountain hemlock - closed canopy	<0.50
Subalpine fir- closed canopy	<0.50

*This is the probability of a cover type proportion exceeding the expected proportion based on availability on the landscape if in fact no real differences occur between the two proportions. A probability >0.50, for example, means that there is more than a 50 percent chance that a proportion for that cover type as large as shown in Table 1 will occur from a similar; sized random sample from the North Cascades GIS data base.

TABLE 3. CHARACTERISTICS OF THE THREE COVER TYPES WITH PREFERENTIAL HISTORIC SIGHTINGS OF GRIZZLY BEARS.

Characteristic	Whitebark pine-subalpine larch open canopy	Subalpine herb	Subalpine fir open canopy
Average elevation (m)	1912	1670	1652
Average slope (percent)	52	42	53
Tree Basal Area (sq. m/ha)			
Subalpine fir	9	0	9
Whitebark pine	4	0	1
Subalpine larch	4	0	0
Other	3	0	11
Tree Cover (percent)	30	T	22
Common Shrub Constancy (percent)			
White heather	25	8	52
Mountain juniper	19	–	–
Partridgefoot	–	20	40
Oregon boxwood	33	–	35
Red heather	71	24	55
Mountain-ash	–	20	40
Blue huckleberry	24	24	45
Big huckleberry	–	–	40
Common Herb Constancy (percent)			
Arnica	–	16	25
Sedge	38	64	25
Daisy	38	36	25
Lupine	38	28	30
Bluegrass	52	32	–
Valerian	19	44	25
False hellebore	–	32	25

COVER TYPE DIVERSITY

The richness of cover types for 11 by 11 matrices around grizzly bear sightings showed higher (5.42) but statistically non-significant (at alpha = 0.05) diversity compared to matrices around randomly chosen locations (5.07). Grizzly bears are not usually sighted in the most fragmented landscapes or the most homogeneous (there was a range of from 1 to 12 different cover types in the surrounding 11 by 11 matrix), but were sighted in essentially the same proportions of cover type richness as contained in the entire database. The first part of the second null hypothesis was therefore accepted: grizzly bears are being seen in landscapes of similar diversity as the landscape in the GIS database.

The second part of the diversity hypothesis was tested by comparing the distribution of land-cover interspersion around grizzly sightings to the entire land-cover file (Figure 3). The distributions were significantly different (G = 19.84, $G_{0.001,4}$ = 18.5). Therefore, the second part of the cover type diversity null hypothesis was rejected. Bears were sighted in areas with different land-cover interspersion than that available for the entire database. Confidence limits for the interspersion levels indicated bears were being sighted preferentially in the 31 to 45 percent interspersion class (p < 0.005) and the 46 to 60 percent class (0.025 < p < 0.05).

AREAS OF HIGH SIGHTING POTENTIAL

The previously described analysis provided input to develop a map identifying areas of high, medium, and low sighting potential based on the characteristics of the historic grizzly bear sightings. Two new files were created using the GRASS "reclass" procedure. The first file was based on the cover type analysis. For the entire GIS data base, those cover types with highest sighting potential (Table 2; p < 0.2) – whitebark pine/subalpine larch (open and closed canopy) and subalpine herb – were assigned a 4, those with 0.25 < p < 0.20 (subalpine fir-open canopy) were assigned a 2, and those with p > 0.25 were assigned a 0.

For the cover type diversity file, land-cover richness of the matrices around grizzly bear sightings did not differ from that available for the landscape as whole. Therefore, no new file was created for land-cover richness as all pixels would have been assigned a 0. For land-cover interspersion, which did show significant differences between grizzly sightings and the overall landscape, a 2 was assigned to each pixel with 31 to 45 percent interspersion, a 1 was assigned to each pixel with 46 to 60 percent interspersion, and a 0 was assigned to pixels with higher or lower interspersion.

The two files were then added together using the GRASS tool "Gmapcalc," producing a file with sighting potential values ranging from 0 to 6. This procedure weights cover type selection more heavily than land-cover diversity, because of the lack of association between grizzly sightings and land-cover richness.

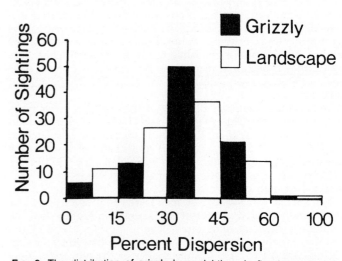

FIG. 3. The distribution of grizzly bear sightings in five interspersion classes, compared to the interspersion distribution for the landscape as a whole. Grizzly bear sightings are skewed to the moderate to high interspersion of 30 to 60 percent, representing relative differences between the land-cover assignment of a pixel and its eight immediately surrounding pixels.

This file was then mapped, and a subset of the entire file is shown in Plate 1 for the western and eastern portion of the study area.

DISCUSSION

The analysis of historical grizzly bear sightings shows generally higher potential for such sightings in the eastern part of the North Cascades GIS (Plate 1). This is where the highest concentration of the whitebark pine/subalpine larch cover type is found. The subalpine herb cover type is also more widespread there, although it is also found in the more maritime western portion of the North Cascades.

The higher potential for sightings in the eastern portion of the study area may reflect areas with both higher potential occurrence and a more open landscape. For example, Agee and Kertis (1987) showed that the North Cascades cover types with an interior climatic influence (ponderosa pine, Douglas-fir, and subalpine fir) have slightly higher proportions of cover in "open canopy" than the corresponding maritime climate forest cover types (western hemlock, Pacific silver fir, and mountain hemlock) and presumably would have longer sight distances. Herbaceous types might also have a higher probability of sightings due to the open nature of the landscape.

Access has historically been easier in the eastern portion of the North Cascades, due to continental instead of alpine glaciation (Franklin and Dyrness, 1973), which produced more moderate topography. The eastern Cascades also have better weather for camping, hiking, fishing, and hunting, so more people have been present to make sightings. However, the data from Table 1 do not support such a hypothesis of observability bias. The sum of expected observations based on availability for closed forest cover types is 40.9, and the actual observations totaled 38. The expected sum for all forest cover types (open plus closed canopy) is 60.6, with actual observations totaling 64. Non-forested sites had expected and actual observations of 30.6 and 27. Had observability bias been evident actual observations should have been much higher in the non-forested cover types and much lower in the forested ones, particularly the closed canopy forest cover types.

Despite the identified biases, including the reliability of the observations and their locations, the analysis does have utility in the evaluation of the North Cascades area for defining suitability of the area to support grizzly bears. First, it indicates, at a landscape level, areas having characteristics similar to those where grizzly bears have historically been sighted. This reduces some of the access bias, but it may still omit other areas where grizzly bears have moderate to high potential of occurring.

For example, closed forest types have often been shown to be used by grizzly bears less than expected based on availability (Servheen, 1983), yet a bear may have chosen a home range because of the presence of forest (McLellan, 1986). Timber adjacent to areas of high sighting potential may be an important element of grizzly bear habitat even if its grizzly bear sighting potential is low. Second, the analysis serves as a model for expanded analysis of the 230+ historic and continuing observations of grizzly bears over a larger geographic area than the current 850,000 ha study area. Third, it serves as a comparative data set for potential analyses of radio telemetry data. The telemetry data, if available, will likely be of limited geographic scope, however, and can suffer from similar difficulties in terms of precise location of observations, particularly in the rough terrain of the North Cascades (Springer, 1979).

It is most probable that several additional types of information, including telemetry and food analyses on actual grizzly bears, will be useful in the definition of suitable habitat for grizzly bears, when coupled with GIS analysis techniques. Such techniques will supplement and strengthen the eventual database that will be used to support critical management decisions relative to grizzly bears in the North Cascades area.

(a)

(b)

PLATE 1. Grizzly bear sighting potential in the western (a) and eastern (b) portions of the North Cascades GIS. The hues of green-yellow-orange-red represent increasing potential for sighting grizzly bears. The eastern portion of the data base has higher sighting potential than the western portion, based on historical grizzly bear observations.

REFERENCES

Agee, J. K., and J. Kertis, 1987. Forest types of the North Cascades National Park Service Complex. *Can. J. Bot.* 65: 1520–1530.

Agee, J. K., and L. Smith, 1984. Subalpine tree reestablishment after fire in the Olympic Mountains, Washington. *Ecology* 65: 810–819.

Agee, J. K, M. Finney, and R. deGouvenain, 1986. *The Fire History of Desolation Peak.* Unpub. Rep., Natl. Park Serv. Coop. Park Studies Unit, College of Forest Resources, Univ. Washington, Seattle, Washington.

Agee, J. K., S. G. Pickford, J. Kertis, M. Finney, R. deGouvenain, S. Quinsey, M. Nyquist, R. Root, S. Stitt, G. Waggoner, and B. Titlow, 1985. *Vegetation and Fuel Mapping of North Cascades National Park Service Complex.* Final Report on NPS Contract CX-9000-3-E029. Pacific Northwest Region, Seattle, Washington.

Almack, J. A., 1986. Grizzly bear habitat use, food habits, and movements in the Selkirk Mountains, northern Idaho. *Proceedings - Grizzly*

Bear Habitat Symposium. USDA For. Serv. Gen. Tech. Rep. INT-207: 150–157.

Blanchard, B. M., 1983. Grizzly bear - elk relationships in Yellowstone National Park. *Int. Conf. Bear Research and Manage.* 5: 118–123.

Craighead, J. J., J. S. Sumner, and G. B. Scaggs, 1982. *A Definitive System for Analysis of Grizzly Bear Habitat and other Wilderness Resources.* West. Wildl. Inst. Monog. 1. Univ. Montana, Missoula, Montana.

Eggers, D. E., 1986. Management of whitebark pine as potential grizzly bear habitat. *Proceedings - Grizzly Bear Habitat Symposium.* USDA. For. Serv. Gen. Tech. Rep. INT-207: 170–175.

Franklin, J. F., and C. T. Dryness, 1973. *Natural Vegetation of Oregon and Washington.* USDA For. Serv. Gen. Tech. Rep. PNW-8.

Franklin, J. F., W. H. Moir, G. W. Douglas, and C. Wiberg, 1971. Invasion of subalpine meadows by trees in the Cascade Range, Washington. *Arctic and Alpine Res.* 3: 215–224.

Jones, K. B., 1986. Data types. *Inventory and Monitoring of Wildlife* (Cooperrider, A.Y., *et al.*, eds.) USDI Bureau of Land Management. pp. 11–18.

Lyon, J. G., J. T. Heinen, R. A. Mead, and N. E. G. Roller, 1987. Spatial data for modeling wildlife habitat. *J. Surveying Engineering* 113: 88–100.

Mace, R. D., 1986. Analysis of grizzly bear habitat in the Bob Marshall Wilderness, Montana. *Proceedings - Grizzly Bear Habitat Symposium.* USDA For. Serv. Gen. Tech. Rep. INT-207: 136–149.

Martinka, C. J., and K. C. Kendall, 1986. Grizzly bear habitat research and Glacier National Park, Montana. *Proceedings - Grizzly Bear Habitat Symposium.* USDA For. Serv. Gen. Tech. Rep. INT-207: 19–23.

McLellan, B. N., 1986. Use-availability analysis and timber selection by grizzly bears. *Proceedings - Grizzly Bear Habitat Symposium.* USDA For. Serv. Gen. Tech. Rep. INT-207: 163–166.

Neu, C. W., C. R. Byers, and J. M. Peek, 1974. A technique for analysis of utilization-availability data. *J. Wildl. Manage.* 38: 541–545.

Servheen, C., 1983. Grizzly bear food habits, movements, and habitat selection in the Mission Mountains, Montana. *J. Wildl. Manage.* 47: 1026–1035.

Springer, J. T., 1979. Some sources of bias and sampling error in radio triangulation. *J. Wildl. Manage.* 43: 926–935.

Sullivan, Paul T., 1983. *A Preliminary Study of Historic and Recent Reports of Grizzly Bears (Ursus arctos), in the North Cascades Area of Washington.* Unpub. Rep., Washington Dept. Game, Olympia, Washington.

Weaver, J., R. Escano, D. Mattson, T. Puchlerz, and D. Despain, 1986. A cumulative effects model for grizzly bear management in the Yellowstone ecosystem. *Proceedings - Grizzly Bear Habitat Symposium.* USDA For. Serv. Gen. Tech. Rep. INT-207: 234–246.

Zar, J. H., 1984. *Biostatistical Analysis.* Prentice-Hall. Englewood Cliffs, New Jersey.

Mapping Florida Scrub Jay Habitat for Purposes of Land-Use Management

David R. Breininger, Mark J. Provancha, and *Rebecca B. Smith*
The Bionetics Corporation, NASA Biomedial Operations and Research Office, John F. Kennedy Space Center, FL 32899

ABSTRACT: Geographical information system (GIS) applications were used to map areas of primary and secondary Florida Scrub Jay habitat on Kennedy Space Center (KSC) using vegetation and soils maps. Data from field studies were used for accuracy assessment and evaluating the importance of mapping classes. Primary habitat accounts for 15 percent of the potential habitat and contained 57 percent of the Florida Scrub Jay population on KSC. Proximity analysis identified potential population centers, which were 44 percent of the potential habitat and contained 86 percent of the population. This study is an example of how remote sensing and GIS applications can provide information for land-use planning, habitat management, and the evaluation of cumulative impacts.

INTRODUCTION

REMOTE SENSING AND GEOGRAPHIC INFORMATION SYSTEM (GIS) applications have been used for mapping habitat of several avian and mammalian species (Barnard *et al.*, 1981; Craighead *et al.*, 1986; Scepan *et al.*, 1987; Young *et al.*, 1987; Shaw and Atkinson, 1990). Many of these studies were an intermediate step in a program to refine habitat maps.

The size of the Florida Scrub Jay (*Aphelocoma coerulescens coerulescens*) population has declined by half in the last century due to habitat destruction and degradation (Cox, 1984). This subspecies has been listed as threatened by the U.S. Fish and Wildlife Service (USFWS). The largest population occurs on the John F. Kennedy Space Center (KSC) (Cox, 1984; Breininger, 1989). Federal agencies with jurisdiction in Florida Scrub Jay habitat are mandated by the Endangered Species Act of 1973, as amended (16 U.S.C. 1531 *et seq.*), to consider effects on the Florida Scrub Jay population from their operations. This requires knowledge of a project site and its significance to the population.

The first objective of this study was to apply remote sensing and GIS techniques to map areas that vary according to their habitat potential for Florida Scrub Jays, recognizing that comprehensive field surveys could not be performed. Field studies revealed much variation in Florida Scrub Jay density across the KSC (Breininger, 1981; Breininger, 1989; Breininger and Smith, 1989; Breininger and Schmalzer, 1990). Animal populations are often maintained by a subset of the total area used by the population, due to differences in habitat suitability across the landscape (Wiens and Rotenberry, 1981; Pulliam, 1988; Pulliam and Danielson, in press). Habitat suitability models can be used in environmental impact studies (Williams, 1988; O'Neil *et al.*, 1988). Relying on models, remote sensing and GIS applications can provide information to evaluate habitat suitability across large areas (Lyon, 1983; Payne and Long, 1986; Ormsby and Lunetta, 1987; Stenback *et al.*, 1987; Agee *et al.*, 1989; Heinen and Lyon, 1989).

There has been a proliferation of habitat suitability models, but most have not been adequately tested (Lancia *et al.*, 1982; Cole and Smith, 1983). Model development or testing is often based on densities or information from sightings or radiotracking; these data are not always accurate indicators of habitat suitability (Van Horne, 1983; Hobbs and Hanley, 1990). Despite problems, habitat modeling shows promise for the management of wildlife diversity (Verner *et al.*, 1986; Davis *et al.*, 1990). Assumptions used for mapping and accuracy assessment must be carefully considered because GIS applications can generate seemingly accurate maps with little knowledge of true spatial relationships (Burrough, 1986; Berry, 1987).

Most accuracy assessments of wildlife habitat maps do not measure actual habitat suitability; long-term study of population dynamics is needed to quantify suitability (Van Horne, 1983; O'Connor, 1986; Hobbs and Hanley, 1990) and is beyond the scope of most mapping applications. Accuracy assessments use indicators of habitat suitability such as vegetation cover type (Miller and Conroy, 1990), sightings (Agee *et al.*, 1989), or measures of animal abundance (Cannon *et al.*, 1982; Lyon, 1983). Additional problems include the feasibility of acquiring enough field samples to test what proportion of sites are classified correctly (Cannon *et al.*, 1982), and the quantification of commission errors (Hodgson *et al.*, 1988), because it can not always be determined whether an animal has never or will never use a site.

The second objective was to use existing data for a preliminary accuracy assessment of Florida Scrub Jay habitat maps. Empirical testing developed from the GIS application could not be done in a timely manner without requiring biological assumptions that were possibly invalid. Instead, long-term reproductive success and survival studies will be used to evaluate the habitat maps. The third objective was to estimate the contribution of mapping class types to the Florida Scrub Jay population and estimate the spatial variability of habitat potential within each mapping class, using existing field data.

BACKGROUND

Florida Scrub Jays live in territories defended year-round by a permanently monogamous breeding pair (Woolfenden and Fitzpatrick, 1984). The Florida Scrub Jay is a disjunct race that differs from the various western subspecies by having helpers. These helpers are usually offspring of previous breeding seasons which remain in their natal territory for at least one year. They participate in nest and territory defense, and in the care of young (Woolfenden and Fitzpatrick, 1984).

Habitat requirements of Florida Scrub Jays include the need for open sandy spaces, a sufficient cover of scrub oaks (*Quercus* spp.), little or no tree cover, and a suitable shrub height (Westcott, 1970; Woolfenden, 1974; Breininger, 1981; Cox, 1984). Densities are highest in scrub and slash pine flatwoods where oak canopy cover exceeds 50 percent; areas with oak cover less than 30 percent have few Florida Scrub Jays (Breininger, 1981; Cox, 1984). Within scrub and slash pine flatwoods on KSC, mean oak cover is 78 percent (optimal) on well drained soils and 22 percent (marginal) on poorly drained soils (Breininger *et al.*, 1988). Densities in coastal strand are low because few scrub oaks occur there (Stout, 1980), but Florida Scrub Jays will use coastal strand where it is adjacent to scrub (Breininger, 1981) or coastal woodlands (Simon, 1986).

PHOTOGRAMMETRIC ENGINEERING & REMOTE SENSING,
Vol. 57, No. 11, November 1991, pp. 1467–1474.

0099-1112/91/5711–1467$03.00/0
©1991 American Society for Photogrammetry
and Remote Sensing

Habitat potential is an important mapping criterion because habitat suitability changes with time since fire (Cox, 1984; Woolfenden and Fitzpatrick, 1984; Breininger et al., 1988). There are unburned areas not occupied by Florida Scrub Jays that would become suitable if they were burned (Westcott, 1970; Cox, 1984; Woolfenden and Fitzpatrick, 1984) because fires usually affect structural features and not scrub oak occurrence (Schmalzer and Hinkle, 1987). Scrub oak cover is the best indicator of a site's potential to be suitable habitat for Florida Scrub Jays (Westcott, 1970; Cox, 1984; Woolfenden and Fitzpatrick, 1984), but we have been unable to reliably map scrub oaks over large areas. The use of vegetation and soils maps provides a method to map potential habitat and population centers of Florida Scrub Jays.

Areas dominated by scrub oaks occur as narrow linear features among marginal habitat. Florida Scrub Jays occupy large territories (Woolfenden and Fitzpatrick, 1984) relative to patches of optimal habitat. Areas that can be managed as population centers need to be identified because this is where industrial development would have the most impact. The structure of optimal habitat allows Florida Scrub Jays to scan their surroundings for long distances (Woolfenden and Fitzpatrick, 1984), which is important for the detection of predators, especially hawks (McGowan and Woolfenden, 1989). Human development within population centers can result in a discontinuous fuel structure that often burns poorly (Breininger and Schmalzer, 1990) and has a tall shrub layer (Breininger et al., 1988) that interferes with the ability to spot hawks. Mortality of adult Florida Scrub Jays has been high and reproductive success has been poor in tall, disturbed areas (Breininger and Smith, unpublished data).

Most of KSC has been subdivided into fire management units (FMUs) that allows specific fire management prescriptions for each unit. The evergreen nature of scrub oaks makes them less prone to burn than adjacent habitats that have a high cover of flammable grasses and forbs (Webber, 1935) or saw palmetto (Schmalzer and Hinkle, 1987; Breininger et al., 1988). Repeated prescribed fires during dry weather patterns could burn habitat dominated by scrub oaks more frequently than is suitable for Florida Scrub Jays (Breininger et al., 1988).

STUDY SITE

Lands and lagoons of KSC comprise 57,000 ha in Brevard and Volusia counties located along the east coast of central Florida. Most of KSC is on northern Merritt Island which forms a barrier island complex with the adjacent Cape Canaveral. Temperate and subtropical plant associations that include closed forests, open woodlands, scrub communities, and marshes dominate the landscape (Sweet et al., 1980). Scrub and slash pine flatwoods, which are similar to scrub but have an open canopy of slash pine, occupy most upland areas. In scrub and slash pine, saw palmetto dominates the wet end of the gradient and scrub oaks dominate the dry end; in most areas dominance is mixed (Schmalzer and Hinkle, 1987; Breininger et al., 1988). Marshes and woodlands are found in low areas that are interspersed throughout the scrub or slash pine.

METHODS

HABITAT MODEL

Primary habitat of Florida Scrub Jays was defined as all scrub and slash pine occurring on well drained soils; secondary habitat was defined as scrub and slash pine occurring on poorly drained soils. Also included in secondary habitat was coastal strand where scrub or coastal woodlands was within 300 m, which is the width of an average territory (Woolfenden and Fitzpatrick, 1984).

Large areas that represent potential population centers were identified as a combination of all primary habitat, secondary habitat within 300 m of primary habitat, and ruderal habitat within 100 m of primary habitat. Primary habitat usually occurs as narrow strips, so that Florida Scrub Jay territories occupying primary habitat often include secondary habitat (Breininger and Smith, 1989). The width of an average territory (300 m) was considered to represent a suitable buffer of secondary habitat surrounding primary habitat. In areas where ruderal and primary habitat coincide, Florida Scrub Jay territories extend into ruderal areas as far as 100 m (Breininger and Smith, 1989). This was assumed to be an adequate distance to identify ruderal areas as being part of potential population centers.

Accuracy assessments of primary and secondary habitat maps were performed using existing data on scrub oak cover. The model of potential habitat suitability is based on average Florida Scrub Jay densities (Breininger 1981) in different scrub oak cover classes (Figure 1). This model is being tested using long-term studies of reproductive success and survival.

REMOTE SENSING AND GIS ANALYSIS

All analyses for defining these habitats were run with ERDAS 7.3 GIS software (ERDAS, 1987) on a Compaq 386 25 MHz computer. Aerial photography provided the necessary resolution to map vegetation types. Vegetation on KSC is frequently represented by narrow, linear polygons because of the ridge and swale topography that is characteristic of the landscape. Season has little influence on the appearance of scrub and slash pine because the shrubs that dominate these habitats are evergreen. Fifty vegetation and land-use types were interpreted from November, 1979 aerial color infrared photography (ACIR) at 1:12,000 scale (Provancha et al., 1986). Scrub and slash pine were distinct with respect to texture and color on aerial photographs. Some areas of saw palmetto scrub had a lighter appearance and more uniform texture than oak scrub, which frequently had a dark red signature. However, most areas had an intermediate appearance and, because mesic shrubs also had a red signature, it was not possible to accurately map oak scrub across large areas. Soils data were taken from USDA Soil Conservation Service soils survey maps (1:20,000 scale) of Brevard (Huckle et al., 1974) and Volusia (Baldwin et al., 1980) counties. Soils and vegetation/land-use themes were gridded into a database with a

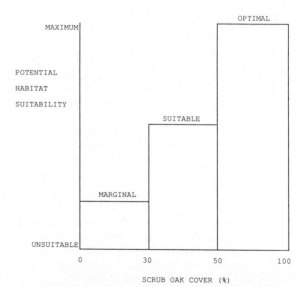

FIG. 1. Potential habitat suitability based on average Florida Scrub Jay densities in different scrub oak cover classes (Breininger, 1981).

252

pixel resolution of 22 m. This pixel size allowed the identification of small, isolated wetlands found within scrub and slash pine. Boundaries of FMUs (Fire Management Plan, Merritt Island National Wildlife Refuge, Titusville, Florida) were transferred to 1:24,000-scale topographic quadrangle maps and digitized using 22-m pixel resolution.

Coastal strand, disturbed scrub, oak/palmetto scrub, and slash pine were recorded as potential habitat from the KSC vegetation map (Figure 2). Hereafter, oak/palmetto scrub and disturbed scrub are referred to as scrub. The following soils types were recoded as well drained soils based on their descriptions (Huckle *et al.*, 1974; Baldwin *et al.*, 1980) : Astatula, Bulow, Canaveral sand, Canaveral urban complex, Cocoa sand, Daytona sand, Orsino, Palm Beach, Paola, Pomello, Quartzipsamments, St Lucie, and Welaka. Remaining soil types were recorded as poorly drained. Coastal strand was separated from the file of potential habitat by a recoding function. The ERDAS routine MATRIX was used to develop a file of primary habitat (slash pine and scrub that coincided with well drained soils) and secondary habitat without coastal strand (slash pine and scrub that coincided with poorly drained soils). A file was developed that included all pixels within 308 m of scrub and coastal woodlands using proximity analysis. A search distance of 308 m was used because it

was the closest possible distance to 300 m, given a pixel size of 22 m. This file was overlaid with the coastal strand file to develop a file of coastal strand classified as secondary habitat. An overlay was then performed to develop a file of all secondary habitat (Figure 2, Step 8).

Proximity analysis was used to generate a map of potential Florida Scrub Jay population centers. All pixels that were within 308 m of primary habitat were incorporated into a new GIS file that was then overlaid with secondary habitat to create a file of secondary habitat adjacent to primary habitat. The KSC vegetation map was recorded to develop a file of ruderal habitat. Overlay analysis was used to overlay the ruderal habitat file with a file of all pixels within 110 m of primary habitat (110 m is the closest search distance possible to 100 m given the pixel size) to develop a file of ruderal habitat adjacent to scrub oak vegetation (Figure 2, Step 13). A preliminary file of all population centers was developed by combining primary habitat, adjacent secondary habitat, and adjacent ruderal habitat into one file. Contiguity analysis was used to delete isolated pixels classified as population centers that were assumed to be too small. This was done by clumping all pixels classified as population centers that were connected to each other, and then eliminating regions that were only one pixel in size (0.05 ha).

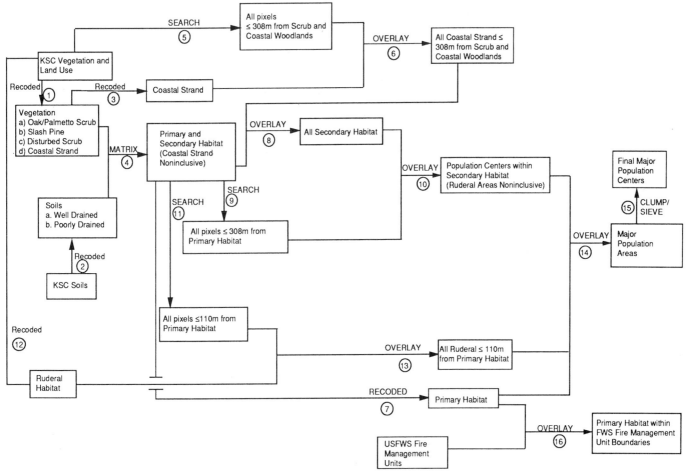

FIG. 2. Florida scrub jay GIS habitat mapping model. The overlay of well drained soils with scrub and slash pine was used to identify primary habitat. The overlay of poorly drained soils with scrub and slash pine was used to identify secondary habitat within scrub and slash pine. Coastal strand adjacent to areas with scrub oaks was used to identify additional secondary habitat. Potential population centers were defined as all primary habitat and adjacent secondary and ruderal habitat greater than one pixel in size. An overlay of fire management unit boundaries and primary habitat was used to identify the acreage of primary habitat outside fire management units and the fire management units most important to the Florida Scrub Jay population.

Primary habitat within FMUs was identified by an overlay of primary habitat and a file of FMU boundaries.

FIELD STUDIES

Data for estimating map accuracy and the contribution of mapping classes (primary habitat, secondary habitat within population centers, secondary habitat outside population centers) was derived from a stratified random design of 73 stations located in slash pine, disturbed scrub, and oak/palmetto scrub (Breininger, 1989). Measurements of oak canopy cover collected from each station were used to identify the habitat as optimal, suitable (but not optimal), or marginal, based on the model in Figure 1. Percent oak cover was determined by a modification of the point intercept method (Mueller-Dombois and Ellenberg, 1974; Hayes *et al.*, 1981; Breininger *et al.*, 1988). Eight lines of four points each were radiated from a point at the center of each station. At every point, the presence or absence of oak was determined. The number of points having oak divided by the total number of points gave an estimate of oak cover.

The variable distance circular plot method (Reynolds *et al.*, 1980) was used to estimate Florida Scrub Jay densities for each station. Stations were sampled eight times between March 1986 and February 1987 (Breininger, 1989).

ACCURACY ASSESSMENT

The map accuracy of primary (potentially optimal habitat) and secondary habitat was determined using an error matrix (Card, 1982; Story and Congalton, 1986) where the reference data were based on stations having optimal (greater than 50 percent) oak cover or less than optimal oak cover as determined from field measurements. The classified data were derived from stations mapped as occurring in primary habitat or secondary habitat. Errors of commission for primary habitat were defined as the number of stations classified as primary habitat when they actually had oak cover that was less than 50 percent. Errors of omission were defined as stations not classified as primary habitat that had 50 percent or greater oak cover. Overall accuracy was determined as the number of correct classifications divided by 73.

RELATIVE IMPORTANCE OF HABITAT TYPES TO FLORIDA SCRUB JAYS

The total number of Florida Scrub Jays within primary habitat, secondary habitat within population centers, and secondary habitat outside population centers was determined by multiplying the average density for each habitat type by the acreage of the type to compare the contribution of each type to the total population.

The spatial heterogeneity of scrub oak cover and Florida Scrub Jay density was evaluated for each of the mapping classes to estimate how much of each type was important for Florida Scrub Jays. The proportion of the mapping class actually used by Florida Scrub Jays was estimated from the proportion of stations where at least one Florida Scrub Jay was sighted during at least one of eight visits to the station. Oak cover field measurements collected from the stations were used to classify each station as optimal, suitable but not optimal, or marginal (Figure 1). The proportion of stations classified in each of these habitat suitability classes was determined for each habitat type.

Statistics were used (SPSS, 1988) to test whether oak cover and Florida Scrub Jay densities were different between primary and secondary habitat and between secondary habitat inside and outside population centers. An alpha level of 0.05 was used for all statistical tests. The Kolmogorov-Smirnov goodness of fit test determined whether oak cover and Florida Scrub Jay densities had a normal distribution. Oak cover was normally distributed, and t-tests were used to test for oak cover differences.

Variance was not significantly different between classes at the 95 percent level; pooled variance estimates were used for comparisons between primary and secondary habitat and for comparisons between secondary habitat inside and outside population centers. Florida Scrub Jay densities were not normally distributed and nonparametric Mann-Whitney U-Wilcoxon rank sum tests were used to test for differences between primary and secondary habitats and between secondary habitat inside and outside population centers.

RESULTS AND DISCUSSION

Primary habitat comprised only 2 percent of all KSC lands and 15 percent of all scrub and slash pine, but 57 percent of the total KSC Florida Scrub Jay population was accounted for within this habitat type (Table 1). Plate 1 shows that these well drained areas were interspersed with poorly drained areas. Areas mapped as potential population centers contained 86 percent of the population and 44 percent of all scrub and slash pine (Figure 3). Primary habitat had significantly higher Florida Scrub Jay densities and oak cover than secondary habitat.

Approximately 69 ha of coastal strand were within areas classified as secondary habitat. The estimate of the total number of Florida Scrub Jays maintained by this habitat was 14, derived by multiplying this acreage by 0.20 jays per hectare, which is a density estimate for this habitat type (Breininger, 1981).

Sixty-five stations were classified correctly, resulting in an

TABLE 1. SPATIAL HETEROGENEITY OF HABITAT AND CONTRIBUTION OF MAPPING CLASSES TO THE FLORIDA SCRUB JAY POPULATION ON JOHN F. KENNEDY SPACE CENTER.

| | | Secondary habitat | |
Characteristics	Primary Habitat	Within population centers	Outside population centers
Acreage (ha)	1600	3185	5986
Percent of scrub and slash pine[a]	15	30	55
Average Florida Scrub Jay density[b]	31[c]	8[d]	2
Population estimate	1240	637	299
Percent of population[e]	57	29	14
Number of stations	16	29	28
Mean oak cover (%)	72[f]	23[g]	25
Percent of habitat occupied by Florida Scrub Jays	94	62	25
Percent of habitat with opitmal oak cover[h]	69	7	4
Percent of habitat with suitable oak cover[i]	19	38	46
Percent of habitat with marginal oak cover[j]	12	55	50

[a]Acreage of habitat divided by the acreage of all scrub and slash pine (10,771 ha) multiplied by 100
[b]Birds/40 ha
[c]Primary habitat had a significantly higher ($p \leq 0.05$) density than all secondary habitat
[d]Secondary habitat within population centers had a significantly higher ($p \leq 0.05$) density than secondary habitat outside population centers
[e]Population estimate for the habitat type divided by the total population for scrub and slash pine (2,176 birds)
[f]Oak cover was significantly greater ($p \leq 0.05$) in primary habitat that secondary habitat
[g]Oak cover was not significantly different between the two classes of secondary habitat
[h]Greater than or equal to 50% oak cover
[i]30–49% oak cover
[j]Less than 30% oak cover

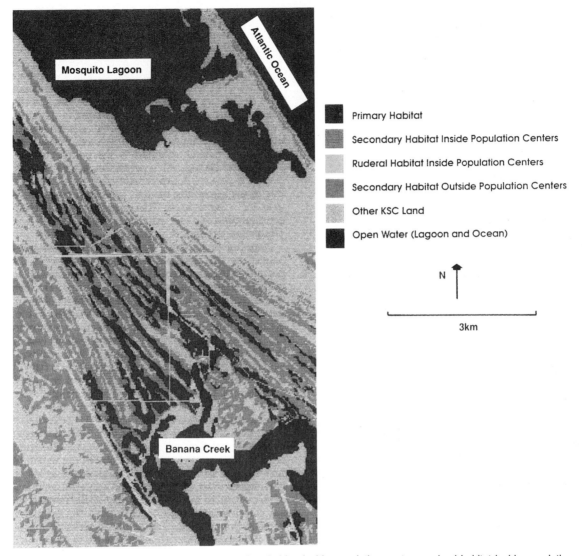

PLATE 1. Primary Florida scrub jay habitat, secondary habitat inside population centers, ruderal habitat inside population centers, and secondary habitat outside population centers. Horizontal and vertical lines are roads.

overall mapping accuracy of 89 percent (Table 2). This is similar to accuracy estimates obtained for maps of kestrel habitat (Lyon, 1983) and wood stork foraging habitat (Hodgson *et al.*, 1988). Errors of omission for optimal habitat were due to three stations with high scrub oak cover that occurred in poorly drained areas instead of primary habitat. Their vegetation and surface soil characteristics were similar to primary habitat, but these patches were small. Soil inclusions are often not treated as distinct soils mapping units because of their small size; they can significantly contribute to mapping errors in GIS applications (Walsh *et al.*, 1987). Errors of commission within primary habitat were associated with five stations that occurred in recently burned areas (less than three years post-fire). Oak cover is reduced for at least three years after fire (Schmalzer and Hinkle, 1987). We believe that all stations located within primary habitat were correctly classified as having potential to be optimal and that all primary habitat is potentially important to Florida Scrub Jays. Only one station within primary habitat was unoccupied by Florida Scrub Jays; this area was unburned for at least 25 years.

Scrub oak cover was not significantly different at the 95 percent level between the two types of secondary habitat (Table 1). Proximity to primary habitat may explain why Florida Scrub

Jay densities were significantly higher at the 95 percent level in secondary habitat within population centers than densities outside population centers. Secondary habitat should provide a buffer to primary habitat, enhancing the opportunity for fires to burn into primary habitat. Corridors of secondary habitat that connect population centers are especially important given the poor dispersal abilities of the Florida Scrub Jay (Woolfenden, 1970; Woolfenden and Fitzpatrick, 1984).

Almost half of the secondary habitat had oak cover that was either suitable or optimal and was capable of supporting Florida Scrub Jays. Secondary habitat provides for a population that is larger than would be maintained by primary habitat alone; larger populations are less susceptible to catastrophic events, epidemics, and inbreeding (Soule, 1987). It is not known how long Florida Scrub Jay populations would persist if no primary habitat were available. Animal populations often include population sinks (areas where mortality rates exceed net reproduction), but long-term persistence of these populations is dependent on source areas (where reproduction exceeds mortality) that provide individuals to subsidize the sink (Howe *et al.*, in press; Pulliam and Danielson, in press). The identification of sources and their management is crucial to persistence of populations;

255

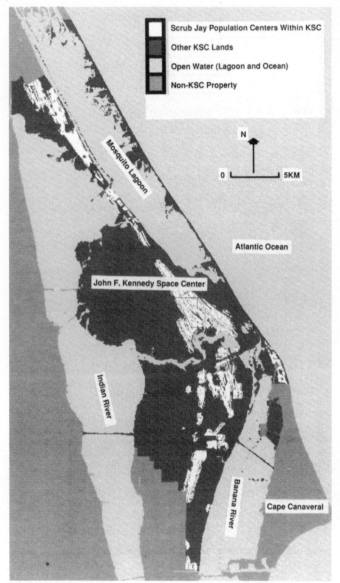

FIG. 3. Potential population centers of the Florida Scrub Jay on John F. Kennedy Space Center. Horizontal and vertical lines are roads.

TABLE 2. ERROR MATRIX FOR MAPPING PRIMARY AND SECONDARY HABITAT.[a]

	Map Category		
True Category[b]	Primary Habitat	Secondary Habitat	Totals
Greater Than or Equal to 50%			
Oak Cover	11	3	14
Less Than 50%			
Oak Cover	5	54	59
Totals	16	57	73

[a]Overall mapping accuracy = 89% [the number of stations classified correctly as primary habitat (11) plus the number of stations correctly classified as secondary habitat (54) divided by the total number of stations (73) multiplied by 100]
[b]Based on field measurements of 73 stations

this is an important consideration for habitat mapping applications.

This GIS application provides a map of potential Florida Scrub Jay population centers that can be used to minimize human disturbance to areas important for sustaining the Florida Scrub Jay population. Cumulative impacts across the landscape can also be evaluated using GIS applications (Johnston et al., 1988). Habitat lost to construction can be digitized to assess the impact from individual projects relative to the total habitat available. Files of many projects can be combined to quantify cumulative losses. Wildlife management problems arise when entire populations are maintained by source areas that are small, relative to the total habitat occupied by the population (Pulliam, 1988; Pulliam and Danielson, in press), but are not treated as separate mapping classes. A project site may appear insignificant, relative to the remaining habitat, but could be a source of individuals for a large area. This may be an especially important consideration for rare patches of good habitat located outside population centers.

Planning of habitat management practices can also be enhanced by GIS applications (Heinen and Mead, 1984). Eleven percent of primary habitat was found outside FMUs; this habitat is likely to become unsuitable if not burned. Thirteen of 33 FMUs that included scrub contained 96 percent of all the primary habitat. The FMUs are responsible for the viability of the KSC Florida Scrub Jay population and should be managed accordingly. The GIS analysis also found that primary habitat was typically less than one-third of the areas within an FMU and was adjacent to vegetation types such as marsh and palmetto flats that are more flammable. Controlled burn prescriptions will need to be written carefully to avoid burning primary habitat too frequently.

Remote sensing and GIS applications can be used to monitor habitat changes (Hodgson et al., 1988; Leckenbey et al., 1985). Fires, pine cover, and openings in the shrub layer are examples of parameters that can be mapped, but evaluating their effects on Florida Scrub Jays requires other remote sensing applications and a better understanding of habitat influences on reproduction and survival. Long-term study of reproduction and survival of color-banded birds is necessary to distinguish between habitat conditions suitable or unsuitable for maintenance of sustainable populations. The ability to develop maps of features that influence habitat suitability is likely to proceed at a faster pace than the ability to quantify how reproductive success and survival of Florida Scrub Jays varies with these features. The combination of demographic studies, remote sensing, and GIS applications provide an enhanced opportunity to test and refine habitat mapping.

ACKNOWLEDGMENTS

This study, funded by NASA, was enhanced by the cooperation of W. M. Knott, III, of the NASA Biomedical Operations and Research Office, John F. Kennedy Space Center under NASA contracts NAS10–10285 and NAS10–11624. Helpful comments on the analysis or manuscript were provided by B. W. Duncan, C.R. Hall, C.R. Hinkle, J.R. Jensen, J.L. Mailander, P.A. Schmalzer, and several anonymous reviewers.

REFERENCES

Agee, J. K., S. C. F. Stitt, M. Nyquist, and R. Root, 1989. A geographic analysis of historical grizzly bear sightings in the North Cascades. Photogrammetric Engineering & Remote Sensing 55:1637–1642.

Baldwin, R., C. L. Bush, R. B. Hinton, H. F. Huckle, P. Nichols, F. C. Watts, and J. A. Wolfe, 1980. Soil Survey of Volusia County, Florida. USDA Soil Conservation Service, Washingotn, D.C., 308 p.

Barnard, T., R. J. MacFarlane, T. Neraasen, R. P. Mroczynski, J. Jacobson, and R. Schmidt, 1981. Waterfowl habitat inventory of Alberta, Saskatchewan and Manitoba by remote sensing. Proceedings of the 7th Canadian Symposium on Remote Sensing, Winnipeg, Manitoba, pp. 150–158.

Berry, J. K., 1987. Computer-assisted map analysis: potential and pitfalls. *Photogrammetric Engineering & Remote Sensing* 53:1405–1410.

Breininger, D. R., 1981. *Habitat Preferences of the Florida Scrub Jay (Aphelocoma coerulescens coerulescens) on Merritt Island National Wildlife Refuge, Florida*. M.S. thesis, Florida Institute of Technology, Melbourne, Florida, 159 p.

———, 1989. A new population estimate for the Florida Scrub Jay on Merritt Island National Wildlife Refuge. *Florida Field Naturalist* 17:25–31.

Breininger, D. R., and P. A. Schmalzer, 1990. Effects of fire and disturbance on vegetation and bird communities in a Florida oak/palmetto scrub. *American Midland Naturalist* 123:64–74.

Breininger, D. R., P. A. Schmalzer, D. A. Rydene, and C. R. Hinkle, 1988. *Burrow and Habitat Relationships of the Gopher Tortoise in Coastal Scrub and Slash Pine Flatwoods on Merritt Island, Florida*. Florida Game and Fresh Water Fish Commission, Nongame Wildlife Program Final Report. 238 p.

Breininger, D. R., and R. B. Smith, 1989. Relationships between habitat characteristics and territory size of the Florida Scrub Jay (*Aphelocoma c. coerulescens*). Abstract, *Bulletin of the Ecological Society of America* 70:69.

Burrough, P. A., 1986. *Principles of Geographical Information Systems for Land Resources Assessment*. Clarendon Press, Oxford, England, 194 p.

Cannon, R. W., F. L. Knopf, and L. R. Pettinger, 1982. Use of Landsat data to evaluate lesser prairie chicken habitats in western Oklahoma. *Journal of Wildlife Management* 46:915–922.

Card, D. H., 1982. Using known map category marginal frequencies to improve estimates of thematic map accuracy. *Photogrammetric Engineering & Remote Sensing* 48:431–439.

Cole, C. A., and R. L. Smith, 1983. Habitat suitability indices for monitoring wildlife populations—An evaluation. *48th North American Wildlife Conference*, pp. 367–375.

Cox, J. A., 1984. *Distribution, Habitat, and Social Organization of the Florida Scrub Jay, with a Discussion of the Evolution of Cooperative Breeding in New World Jays*. Ph.D. dissertation, University of Florida, Gainesville, Florida, 259 p.

Craighead, J. J., F. L. Craighead, and D. J. Craighead, 1986. Using satellites to evaluate ecosystems as grizzly bear habitat. *Proceedings, Grizzly Bear Habitat Symposium*, Missoula, Montana, pp. 101–112.

Davis, F. W., D. M. Stoms, J. E. Estes, J. Scepan, and J. M. Scott, 1990. An information systems approach to the preservation of biological diversity. *International Journal of Geographical Information Systems* 4:55–78.

ERDAS, 1987. *ERDAS Users Guide*, ERDAS, Inc., Atlanta, Georgia.

Hayes, R. L., C. Summers, and W. Seitz, 1981. *Estimating Wildlife Habitat Variables*. U.S. Department of the Interior, Fish and Wildlife Service, FSW/OBS-81/47.

Heinen, J. T., and J. G. Lyon, 1989. The effects of changing weighting factors on wildlife habitat index values: a sensitivity analysis. *Photogrammetric Engineering & Remote Sensing* 55:1445–1447.

Heinen, J. T., and R. A. Mead, 1984. Simulating the effects of clearcuts on deer habitat in the San Juan National Forest, Colorado. *Canadian Journal of Remote Sensing* 10:17–24.

Hobbs, N. T., and T. A. Hanley, 1990. Habitat evaluation: do use/availability data reflect carrying capacity? *Journal of Wildlife Management* 54:515–522.

Hodgson, M. E., J. R. Jensen, H. E. Mackey, Jr., and M. C. Coulter, 1988. Monitoring wood stork foraging habitat using remote sensing and geographic information systems. *Photogrammetric Engineering & Remote Sensing* 54:1601–1607.

Howe, R. W., G. J. Davis, and V. Mosca, In press. The demographic significance of "sink" populations. *Biological Conservation*.

Huckle, H. F., H. D. Dollar, and R. F. Pendleton, 1974. *Soil Survey of Brevard County, Florida*. U.S. Department of Agriculture Soil Conservation Service, Washington, D.C., 230 p.

Johnston, C. A., N. E. Detenbeck, J. P. Bonde, and G. J. Niemi, 1988. Geographic information systems for cumulative impact assessment. *Photogrammetric Engineering & Remote Sensing* 54:1609–1615.

Lancia, R. A., S. D. Miller, D. A. Adams, and D. W. Hazel, 1982.

Validating habitat quality assessment: An example. *47th North American Wildlife Conference*, pp. 96–110.

Leckenby, D. A., D. L. Isaacson, and S. R. Thomas, 1985. Landsat application to elk habitat management in northeast Oregon. *Wildlife Society Bulletin* 13:130–134.

Lyon, J. G., 1983. Landsat-derived land-cover classifications for locating potential kestrel nesting habitat. *Photogrammetric Engineering & Remote Sensing* 49:245–250.

McGowan, K. J., and G. E. Woolfenden, 1989. A sentinel system in the Florida scrub jay. *Animal Behavior* 37:1000–1006.

Miller, K. V., and M. J. Conroy, 1990. Spot satellite imagery for mapping Kirtland's warbler wintering habitat in the Bahamas. *Wildlife Society Bulletin* 18:252–257.

Mueller-Dombois, D., and H. Ellenberg, 1974. *Aims and Methods of Vegetation Ecology*. John Wiley and Sons, Inc., New York, 547 p.

O'Conner, R. J., 1986. Dynamical aspects of avian habitat use. *Modeling Habitat Relationships of Terrestrial Vertebrates* (J. Verner, M. L. Morrison, and C. J. Ralph, eds.), University of Wisconsin Press, Madison, Wisconsin, pp. 235–240.

O'Neil, L. J., T. H. Roberts, J. S. Wakeley, and J. W. Teaford, 1988. A procedure to modify habitat suitability index models. *Wildlife Society Bulletin* 16:33–36.

Ormsby, J. P., and R. S. Lunetta, 1987. Whitetail deer food availability maps from thematic mapper data. *Photogrammetric Engineering & Remote Sensing* 53:1081–1085.

Payne, B. S., and K. S. Long, 1986. *Airborne Sensor Potential for Habitat Evaluation Procedures (HEP)*. Technical Report EL-86-3, U.S. Army Engineer Waterways Experiment Station, Vicksburg, Mississippi, 197 p.

Provancha, M. J., P. A. Schmalzer, and C. R. Hinkle, 1986. *Vegetation Types (Maps)*. NASA, Biomedical Operations and Research Office, John F. Kennedy Space Center, Florida.

Pulliam, H. R., 1988. Sources, sinks, and population regulation. *American Naturalist* 132:652–661.

Pulliam, H. R., and B. J. Danielson, In press. Sources, sinks and habitat selection: a landscape perspective on population dynamics. *American Naturalist*.

Reynolds, R. T., J. M. Scott, and T. A. Nussbaum, 1980. A variable circular-plot method for estimating bird numbers. *Condor* 82:309–313.

Scepan, J., F. Davis, and L. L. Blum, 1987. A geographic information system for managing California condor habitat. *Second Annual International Conference, Exhibits and Workshops on Geographic Information Systems*, San Francisco, California, pp. 476–486.

Schmalzer, P. A., and C. R. Hinkle, 1987. *Effects of Fire on Composition, Biomass, and Nutrients in Oak Scrub Vegetation on John F. Kennedy Space Center, Florida*. NASA Technical Memorandum No. 100305, Kennedy Space Center, Florida, 134 p.

Shaw, D. M., and S. F. Atkinson, 1990. An introduction to the use of geographic information systems for ornithological research. *The Condor* 92:564–570.

Simon, D. M., 1986. *Fire Effects in Coastal Habitats of East Central Florida*. National Park Service, Cooperative Park Studies Unit Technical Report 27. 139 p.

Soule, M. E., 1987. *Viable Populations for Conservation*. University Press, Cambridge, England, 189 p.

SPSS, 1988. SPSS/DC + V2.0 Base Manual, SPSS, Inc., Chicago, Illinois, 613 p.

Stenback, J. M., C. B. Travlos, R. H. Barrett, and R. G. Congalton, 1987. Application of remotely sensed digital data and a GIS in evaluating deer habitat suitability on the Tehama Deer winter range. *Second Annual International Conference, Exhibits and Workshops on Geographic Information Systems*, San Francisco, California, pp. 440–445.

Story, M., and R. G. Congalton, 1986. Accuracy assessments: A user's perspective. *Photogrammetric Engineering & Remote Sensing* 52:397–399.

Stout, I. J., 1980. *A Continuation of Base-Line Studies for Environmentally Monitoring Space Transportation Systems (STS) at John F. Kennedy Space Center*. Vol. 1, Terrestrial Community Ecology. NASA Contract No. NAS10–8986, 603 p.

Sweet, H. C., J. E. Poppleton, A. G. Shuey, and T. O. Peeples, 1980. Vegetation of central Florida's east coast: the distribution of six vegetational complexes on Merritt Island and Cape Canaveral Peninsula. *Remote Sensing of Environment* 9:93–108.

Van Horne, B., 1983. Density as a misleading indicator of habitat quality. *Journal of Wildlife Management* 47:813–901.

Verner, J., M. L. Morrison, and C. J. Ralph, 1986. Wildlife 2000, *Modeling Habitat Relationships of Terrestrial Vertebrates*. The University of Wisconsin Press, Madison, Wisconsin.

Walsh, S. J., D. R. Lightfoot, and D. R. Butler, 1987. Recognition and assessment of error in geographic information systems. *Photogrammetric Engineering & Remote Sensing* 53:1423–1430.

Webber, H. J., 1935. The Florida scrub, a fire-fighting association. *American Journal of Botany* 22:344–361.

Westcott, P. A., 1970. *Ecology and Behavior of the Florida Scrub Jay*. Ph.D. dissertation, University of Florida, Gainesville, Florida. 84 p.

Wiens, J., and J. Rotenberry, 1981. Censusing and the evaluation of avian habitat occupancy. *Studies in Avian Biology, Estimating Numbers of Terrestrial Birds* (C. J. Ralph and J. M. Scott, eds.) 6:522–532.

Williams, G. L., 1988. An assessment of HEP (habitat evaluation procedures) applications to bureau of reclamation projects. *Wildlife Society Bulletin* 16:437–447.

Woolfenden, G. E., 1974. Nesting and survival in a population of Florida scrub jays. *Living Bird* 12:25–49.

Woolfenden, G. E., and J. W. Fitzpatrick, 1984. *The Florida Scrub Jay: Demography of a Cooperative-Breeding Bird*. Monographs in Population Biology No. 20, Princeton University Press, Princeton, New Jersey. 407 p.

Young, T. N., J. R. Eby, H. L. Allen, M. J. Hewitt III, and K. R. Dixon, 1987. Wildlife habitat analysis using landsat and radiotelemetry in a GIS with application to spotted owl preference for old growth. *Second Annual International Conference, Exhibits and Workshops on Geographic Information Systems*, San Francisco, California, pp. 595–600.

GIS-Based Habitat Modeling Using Logistic Multiple Regression: A Study of the Mt. Graham Red Squirrel

*José M. C. Pereira** and *Robert M. Itami*
School of Renewable Natural Resources, University of Arizona, Tucson, AZ 85721

ABSTRACT: Multivariate statistical techniques were applied to the development of habitat suitability models for the Mt. Graham red squirrel, an endangered species. A digital map database and a Geographic Information System (GIS) were used to support the analysis and provide inputs for two logistic multiple regression models. The models attempted to predict squirrel presence or absence, the dichotomous dependent variable. Independent variables were a set of environmental factors in the first model, and locational coordinates in the second case, where a logistic trend surface was developed. Bayesian statistics were then used to integrate the models into a combined outcome. Potential habitat losses resulting from development of an astronomical observatory were assessed using the environmental model and were found to represent about 3 percent of the currently available habitat.

INTRODUCTION

THE MOUNT GRAHAM AREA, in the Pinaleno Mountains of Graham County, Arizona, 200 km northeast of Tucson, is the third highest mountain in the state, having a maximum elevation of 3278 m at High Peak (Figure 1). The USDA Forest Service is responsible for land management of the area, a part of Coronado National Forest. In 1984 the University of Arizona's Steward Observatory concluded a nationwide search for a site on which to build a new astronomical observatory by identifying Mt. Graham as its preferred location (Columbus Project Science Advisory Committee, 1987). Subsequently, the University submitted an astrophysical site and facility development proposal to Coronado National Forest.

Mt. Graham is an exceptionally interesting mountain from a biogeographic and ecological standpoint. Its steep relief creates the sharpest ascent from desert grassland to spruce-fir forest in Arizona. Chaparral, oak woodland, ponderosa pine, and mixed conifer occur as intermediate life zones. Floristic composition of vegetation communities is influenced by both Neartic and Neotropical floras: the spruce-fir forest is the southernmost pure stand in North America and, at the life zone immediately below, Chihuahuan and Mexican white pines of the mixed conifer zone are at the northern extreme of their distribution area. Biogeographic isolation of the Pinalenos in general, and Mt. Graham in particular, restricts gene flows of several species, giving the mountain a "sky-island" character that facilitates the evolution of endemisms among both plants and animals. One of these is an endangered sub-species of red squirrel, Tamiasciurus hudsonicus grahamensis, the Mt. Graham red squirrel (U.S. Forest Service, 1986).

Concern over the preservation of Mt. Graham's unique ecological values led Coronado National Forest to conclude that Steward Observatory's initial proposal was unacceptable due to its potential negative environmental impacts. Long-term survival of the red squirrel was of paramount importance because part of the proposed development would affect the species' prime habitat. An extensive environmental impact assessment study was initiated by the Forest Service (U.S. Forest Service, 1986), while Steward Observatory revised its proposal, eliminating some of the buildings. The revised project will have two phases. The first will include construction

of a new road, facilities for three telescopes, and logistic support structures. The second phase will involve adding three more telescopes, one support building, and a movable interferometer array.

Considering the complex, multidisciplinary character of the resource management problem posed by Steward Observatory's proposal, the U.S. Forest Service Coronado National Forest funded an independent study of habitat for the Mt. Graham red squirrel through the University of Arizona's School of Renewable Natural Resources. That analysis represented a small part of the impact assessment process implemented by the U.S. Forest Service and was meant to determine habitat suitability using quantitative, georeferenced data and assess potential red squirrel habitat and population losses due to project implementation. It was designed to assist U.S. Forest Service personnel with evaluating impacts of observatory facilities and access road locations.

This paper describes the core of the study. The specific objectives were to predict the probability of red squirrel pres-

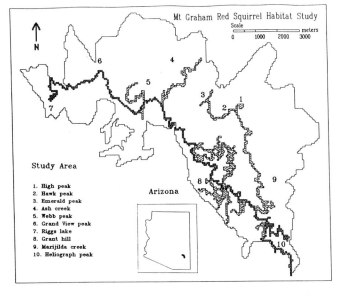

FIG. 1. Map of the study area.

---

*Presently with the Departamento de Engenharia Florestal, I. S. Agronomia, Tapada da Ajuda, P-1399 Lisboa, Portugal.

PHOTOGRAMMETRIC ENGINEERING & REMOTE SENSING,
Vol. 57, No. 11, November 1991, pp. 1475–1486.

0099-1112/91/5711–1475$03.00/0
©1991 American Society for Photogrammetry and Remote Sensing

ence or absence, based on a series of environmental and locational descriptor variables. We hypothesized that these variables could explain the spatial patterns of red squirrel habitat use as observed in the U.S. Forest Service's 1986/87 winter survey. It was assumed that probability of squirrel presence could be taken as a measure of habitat suitability, and that habitat losses would be used as a proxy indicator of potential population losses.

The Habitat Evaluation Procedures/Habitat Suitability Indices (HEP/HSI) (U.S. Fish and Wildlife Service, 1980,1981), a structured framework for habitat evaluation developed in the mid-1970s by the U.S. Fish and Wildlife Service, was used in the analysis. Lancia et al. (1982) remark that HEP/HSI models are often left untested, or are tested with inappropriate criteria. One of the most frequently used validation methods relies on consulting with experts on the species of concern, who are asked to examine model predictions and judge whether they are satisfactory. Because these models are usually built in a deductive manner, based also on expert knowledge, the entire process becomes highly circular. Multivariate statistical models, being inductive, empirical models, when appropriately tested against real habitat use data (Schamberger and O'Neil, 1986) offer the potential to minimize validation problems and were therefore the approach selected for the present study.

BACKGROUND

Red Squirrel Ecology

The Mt. Graham red squirrel study area, as designated by the U.S. Forest Service (U.S. Forest Service, 1988), covers approximately 6460 hectares of the upper part of the mountain. This site ranges in elevation from 2275 m to 3278 m and is characterized by a series of rolling areas surrounded by steep edges and narrow canyons, especially along the northern and eastern edges. Major land-cover types are conifer forests (spruce-fir, mixed, and ponderosa pine), small patches of aspen, meadows, cienegas, and rock outcrops (U.S. Forest Service, 1986). The relationships between the endangered red squirrel and its environment are primarily shaped by the need for appropriate food sources and cover conditions.

The Mt. Graham red squirrel's diet is not well known, except for the importance of conifer seeds from closed cones and limited evidence indicating that at least eight species of mushrooms are also consumed (U.S. Forest Service, 1988). Seed productivity of Mt. Graham conifers was ranked by Jones (1974), with Douglas-fir as the most productive species, followed by Engelmann spruce, corkbark fir, and lastly Ponderosa pine and White pine. Engelmann spruce and corkbark fir are considered the main suppliers of food to the red squirrel (U.S. Forest Service, 1988).

Red squirrels are territorial animals, very aggressive toward both conspecifics and other species of tree squirrels (Flyger and Gates, 1982). Size estimates of the average activity area vary between 0.5 and 1.0 hectares. Territoriality is expressed as central place foraging behavior, meaning that harvested cones are carried to a central place of the territory or activity area, where they are piled up or buried for winter and the following year's supply (U.S. Forest Service, 1988). These piles, or middens, consist not only of cones but also scales, cone cores, and sometimes needles (Hoffmeister, 1986). It is critical that cones remain humid; otherwise, they crack open and the seeds become susceptible to theft by other animals. Therefore, red squirrels look for damp, shaded spots (Rothwell, 1979), requirements that make obvious the role of tree cover and topography in habitat selection.

Favorable environmental conditions are especially necessary for the Mt. Graham sub-species because the Pinaleno Mountains, located at 32° N latitude, are the southernmost situation for both a continuous spruce-fir forest and a red squirrel population in North America. Therefore, more solar radiation reaches the top of the canopy layer here than anywhere else on the red squirrel's distribution range, and good habitat at the forest floor level can only be created when tree crowns intercept a large part of the incoming radiation. This seems to be in agreement with observations that the Mt. Graham red squirrel is very selective in choosing locations, not only for midden placement but also for general activity areas (U.S. Forest Service, 1988).

GIS in Wildlife Habitat Studies

Given the explicit importance of spatial habitat parameters in the Mt. Graham red squirrel ecology, it was decided to use Geographical Information Systems (GIS) technology as an aid to data management and analysis. A brief review of applications of GIS in wildlife habitat analysis work is provided, in order to set this paper in the broader context of a rapidly growing research field.

Lancia et al. (1986), Davis and DeLain (1986), and Ormsby and Lunetta (1987) used GIS in wildlife habitat studies, following the U.S. Fish and Wildlife Service Habitat Evaluation Procedures/Habitat Suitability Indices framework. Lancia et al. (1986) developed spatial models to assess habitat quality for three bird species, using georeferenced environmental data to create habitat suitability maps. These maps were validated by comparison with maps of observed frequency of habitat use. Better results were obtained for common, range restricted, or more specialized species, than for rare, wide-ranging, and/or more generalized forms.

Davis and DeLain (1986) used a GIS database as the key element to linkup wildlife habitat models with the ECOSYM forest planning system. They developed arithmetic HSI for the spotted owl in two spatial databases, and included habitat suitability maps in a cost-benefit analysis of timber management alternatives.

Lyon et al. (1987) presented three spatial habitat analysis models, one of which was supported by a multiple variable GIS database. They analyzed habitat suitability for the wood duck (Aix sponsa) in a forested wetland using topographic, vegetation, hydrologic, and infrastructure data. Model calibration, verification, and parameter sensitivity analysis are emphasized as necessary requirements of habitat modeling. These tasks are performed for a kestrel falcon non-GIS habitat model, whose performance was evaluated by comparison with both expert opinions and field habitat use and population data.

Ormsby and Lunetta (1987) developed whitetail deer food availability maps from Thematic Mapper land-cover digital data. These data were integrated with other cartographic information in a GIS and provided input to an arithmetic, expert-based habitat suitability model. Palmeirim (1988) used Landsat TM remote sensing data and a geographic information system to map avian species habitat, considering not only land-cover types but also habitat spatial characteristics, such as minimum patch size and distance to edge. These data were combined with bird counts to automatically generate distribution, suitability, and density maps, and to produce estimates of population size.

Broschart et al. (1989) used a stepwise multiple regression model to predict the density of beaver colonies in boreal landscapes, by relating vegetative and hydrologic landscape patches resulting from beaver impoundments with beaver presence/absence. They emphasize the usefulness of their results to estimate beaver abundance and determine historical and present population trends.

Hodgson et al. (1988) inventoried and analyzed availability of wetland foraging habitat for the wood stork, and its variability between wet and dry years.

METHODS

THE DIGITAL DATABASE

Figure 2 summarizes the overall analysis procedure followed in this study, from the selection of environmental variables and database development, to habitat suitability analysis and impact assessment. Detailed descriptions of the steps represented in this flowchart are provided throughout the text.

Digital cartographic data capable of supporting analysis and decision making, and based on previously collected information, were assembled. Elevation (Figure 3a) and road network (Figure 3e), as well as project location data (Figure 4f), were digitized from USGS 7-1/2 minute quadrangles. Vegetation data (Figures 4a to 4d) and squirrel activity data (Figure 3d) were digitized from a U.S. Forest Service stands map and a U.S. Forest Service survey map, respectively. The study area boundary was delineated by Coronado National Forest personnel while censusing the red squirrel population and habitat and does not correspond to any political or administrative units. Topography, vegetation, and road network are the major determinants of the study area shape. All maps were referenced to the UTM rectangular coordinate system and were available at a scale of 1:24,000 (Pereira, 1989). Digitization was performed with the CADGRID software package (Itami, 1988).

The elevation, road network and project location, vegetation, and squirrel activity data were transfered to the Map Analysis Package (MAP) (Tomlin, 1986), a PC-based raster geographic information system. MAP was used to develop a set of nine other layers using various GIS operations. Slope and aspect maps were derived using the DIFFERENTIATE and ORIENT operations, respectively. Both maps contain continuous interval data, with slope measured in percent values and aspect in degrees azimuth, but were categorized for display purposes (Figure 3b and 3c). Because aspect refers to angular data, this variable was transformed to a format suitable for conventional statistical analysis by decomposing the information for each cell into a north-south and an east-west component (Pereira, 1989).

The vegetation-related maps, land-cover types, canopy closure, food productivity, and tree diameter at breast height (d.b.h.) were obtained using the RECODE operation on the original Forest Service stands map. The first of these maps contains nominal information, while the others use ordinal scales (Figures 4 to 4d). The roads map (Figure 3e) was combined with the canopy closure map (Figure 4c) to produce the distance to openings map (Figure 4e). The squirrel activity map (Figure 3d) is a binary presence/absence map, and the project location map (Figure 4f) simply displays the location of project phases 1 and 2.

A cell size of 0.5 ha, corresponding to a length of 70.7 m on a side, was selected, resulting in a minimal bounding rectangle of 164 rows by 193 columns, for a total of 31,652 grid cells. Of these, 12,920 are contained within the study area and 18,732 outside of it. Three reasons dictated the choice of a cell size of 0.5 ha. First, it corresponded approximately to the smaller sizes of the range of red squirrel activity areas, which was the basic unit of analysis of the study. Second, mapping accuracy in the original map of activity areas provided by the Forest Service made it unadvisable to use a smaller cell size. Third, there were software limitations imposed by MAP. It cannot handle arrays larger than 32,767 grid cells, very close to the total actually used for the Mt. Graham data base (Pereira, 1989).

STUDY DESIGN

Given the binary nature of squirrel activity data, logistic regression or discriminant analysis are suitable modeling techniques but, because available data on some of the independent variables (e.g., food productivity, canopy closure, d.b.h.) are

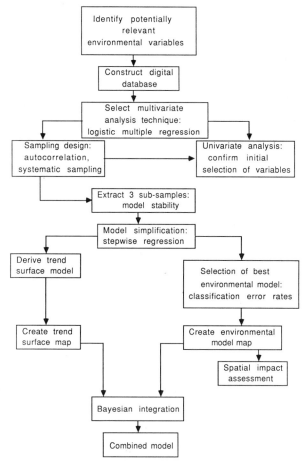

FIG. 2. Flowchart of the study design and data analysis strategy.

qualitative and non-multivariate normal, logistic regression was considered as more appropriate (Press and Wilson, 1978).

Kvamme (1985) used univariate statistical tests to assess the validity of individual model variables and obtained a better understanding of each variable's role before proceeding with global model development and testing, a procedure that is also recommended by Schamberger and O'Neil (1986). It is necessary to find out whether red squirrels actually discriminate among sites based on environmental factors considered relevant on an *a priori* basis. If they do, mean values of environmental variables at locations that squirrels have selected as favorable habitat should differ from mean values obtained from locations taken randomly from the background environment, as well as habitats they avoided. Additionally, the variance of the data would be smaller for selected locations than for the background environment (Kvamme, 1985).

Identification of such an active, non-randomly patterned habitat selection process requires the establishment of a control group, randomly selected from the population of all available sites avoided by squirrels, against which the data for selected habitat locations can be compared. The sample data for both univariate and multivariate statistical analyses were taken from digital database maps. Henceforth, database grid cells where squirrel activity is present will be refered to as "sites" or "active cells," while those from where squirrels are absent will be called "non-sites" or "inactive" cells. The sample data can be conceptualized as a two-way table or matrix, with observations (grid cells) as rows and cell descriptors as columns. These descriptors include environmental variables of the data base overlays, the

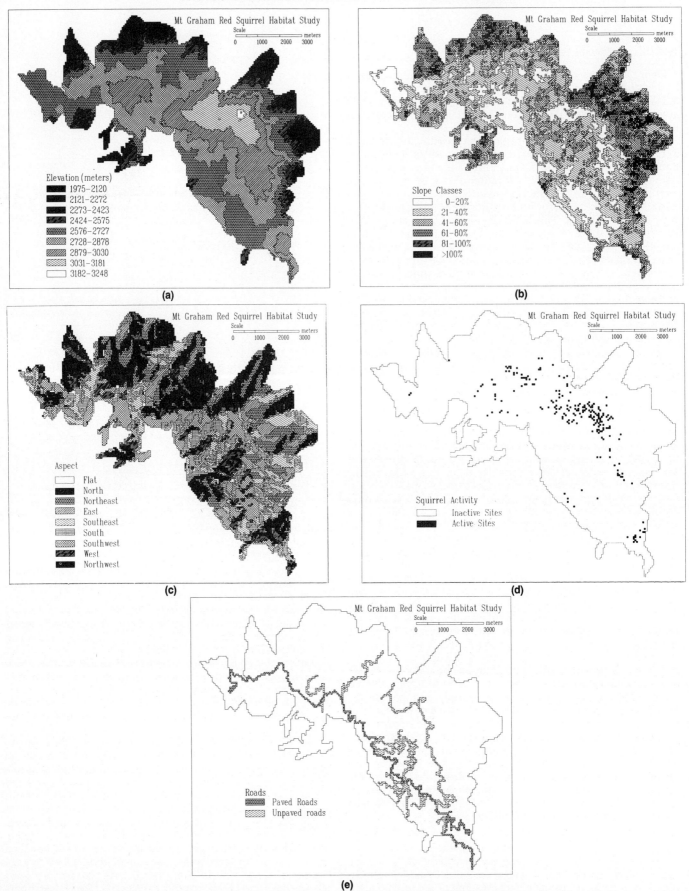

FIG. 3. Database maps of (a) elevation, (b) slope, (c) aspect, (d) squirrel activity, and (e) road network.

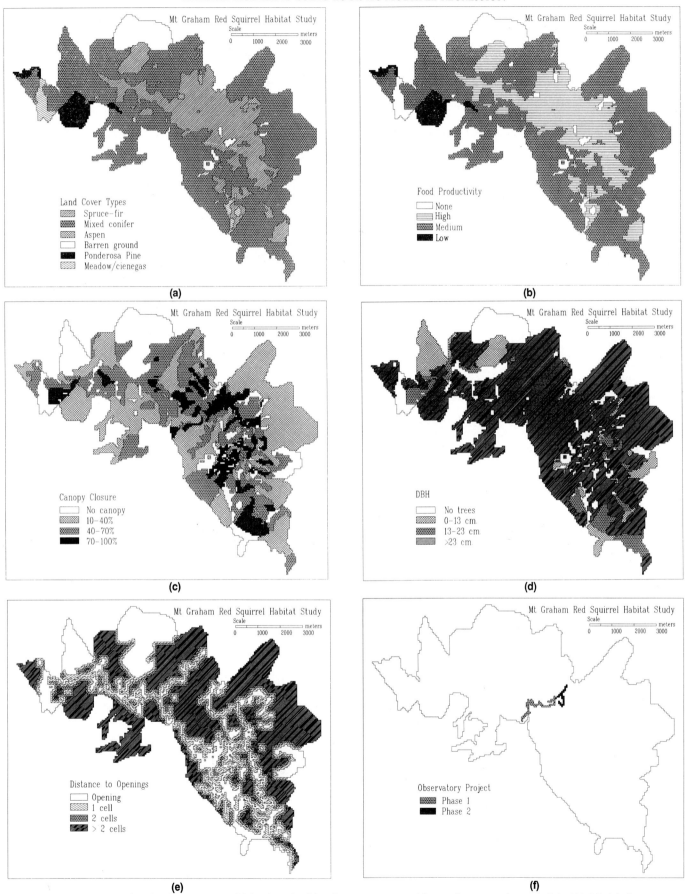

FIG. 4. Database maps of (a) land-cover types, (b) food productivity, (c) canopy cover, (d) tree diameter at breast height (d.b.h.), (e) distance to clearings, and (f) project location.

cells' x and y coordinates, and an indication of presence (1) or absence (0) of squirrel activity.

Two major considerations affected sampling design. Because non-site locations correspond to the vast majority of the study area (Figure 3d), larger variation is expected in environmental attributes for this group. A ratio of non-sites to sites larger than one is therefore desirable (Kvamme, 1985). There are 212 active cells in the database and, therefore, the sample should include a value larger than that for inactive cells. On the other hand, the spatial autocorrelation structure in the independent variables had to be considered in order to assess how to minimize it through systematic sampling (Haining, 1980). Moran's I coefficient (Cliff and Ord, 1981; Upton and Fingleton, 1985), as implemented in the AUTOCORR procedure of the IDRISI GIS package (Eastman, 1987), showed that, for a first-order lag, spatial autocorrelation values for each independent variable were close to unity, but when a seventh order lag was reached, Moran's I had dropped to values between 0.34 for the elevation overlay, down to 0.16 for the slope overlay. A systematic sampling scheme was then followed, where each seventh cell in the database was selected, in both row and column directions. This yielded a sample of 259 non-site cells.

Environmental Model

Two kinds of logistic multiple regression models were developed, one using environmental factors as explanatory variables, and the other a logistic trend surface model, a simple interpolation procedure that uses row and column cell values as independent variables. The categorical nature of the vegetation descriptors (food productivity, canopy closure, and d.b.h.) requires their recoding as dummy variables prior to inclusion in any regression model. Each one of these variables has four categories and must then be recoded to three dichotomous dummy variables (Wrigley, 1985), for a total of nine new variables.

The full environmental model includes these nine variables plus elevation, slope, aspect N-S, aspect E-W, and distance to clearings, for a total of 14 variables. Concern over model stability, which requires a high ratio of number of observations to number of variables, led to the use of three random sub-samples of the original data matrix. Out of each sub-sample, 75 percent of the data were used for training purposes, and 25 percent were left out for independent model validation. Each sub-sample was subjected to stepwise regression in order to simplify the full specification and generate more parsimonious models. Both backward ("p-to-leave" = 0.00) and forward ("p-to-leave" = 1.00) procedures were applied, resulting in a total of six environmental models.

Classification error rates, used to evaluate how well a model fits new samples of data from the same or similar populations, test the percentage of correct predictions on an independent sample. In order to do this, the interval-scaled outputs of the logistic regression model, measuring probability of success (i.e., probability of a sample cell being suitable habitat), are converted to dichotomous 0-1 data through specification of cut-off point. Any cells with values below a given cut-off are considered unsuitable while all above become suitable. This test measures what percentage of cells predicted to be suitable actually contain squirrel activity and, conversely, the percentage of cells predicted to be unsuitable from where squirrels are indeed absent. Moving the cut-off points along the [0,1] probability interval allows estimates of optimal cut-off points to be made by identifying the values for which most successes are correctly classified, while minimizing the number of failures.

Trend Surface Model

The trend surface model (Wrigley, 1976) for habitat suitability analysis is a multiple logistic regression model that uses a fourth-order polynomial of the x (column) and y (row) coordinates of the grid cells as explanatory variables. The polynomial's order determines the complexity (number of "bends") in the resulting probability surface and therefore controls how closely the model will fit the data. A fourth-order polynomial was deemed adequate to describe the general nature of the locational trend in squirrel habitat use, and the trend surface was developed using the same sample of data that yielded the best environmental model.

Bayesian Integrated Model

The environmental and trend surface models were combined using Bayesian statistical inference techniques. This is a technique commonly used in remote sensing where, for example, topographic information provides prior probabilities of a pixel containing a given vegetation type, and then spectral information is used to revise these probabilities, resulting in improved vegetation cover classification accuracy (Strahler et al., 1978; Strahler, 1980). For the Mt. Graham habitat suitability analysis, the trend surface was treated as the generator of prior probabilities and the environmental model as a source of additional information used to revise these probabilities. The mathematical formulation of the procedure is (Maynard, 1981)

$$Pnew = \frac{1}{1 + e[\log(1 - Penv/Penv) - \log(Ptrend/1 - Ptrend)]}$$

where Pnew is the new, revised probability estimate, and Penv and Ptrend are the probability estimates of the environmental and trend surface models, respectively.

RESULTS AND DISCUSSION

Univariate Analysis

Descriptive statistics for the interval-scaled variables are given in Table 1. Cumulative frequency graphs for the interval variables and the categorical variables are shown in Figure 5. The p-values given in Figure 5 were derived from two-sample t-tests (for the continuous variables) or from chi-square difference in proportion tests (for the categorical variables).

The univariate analysis confirms most expectations regarding the role of individual variables. Active cells are located at significantly higher elevations and gentler slopes. The north-south component of aspect was not a significant discriminator between suitable and unsuitable habitat, but cooler east-facing sites were preferred along the east-west component of aspect. Regarding vegetation characteristics, favorable habitat includes

TABLE 1 SAMPLE MEANS, MEDIANS, VARIANCES, AND COEFICIENTS OF VARIATION OF THE MT GRAHAM DATA

| Variables | \multicolumn{4}{c}{Active Sites (n = 212)} |
	Mean	Median	Variance	CV*
Elevation	9954.3	10170.0	269834.0	0.05
Slope	25.6	23.5	214.4	0.57
Aspect (E-W)	97.6	97.0	2605.2	0.52
Aspect (N-S)	94.3	90.0	2419.5	0.52
Distance	2.2	2.0	1.9	0.79

| Variables | \multicolumn{4}{c}{Inactive Sites (n = 259)} |
	Mean	Median	Variance	CV*
Elevation	9020.6	9080.0	583536.0	0.08
Slope	44.0	39.0	884.8	0.68
Aspect (E-W)	85.0	80.0	2411.7	0.58
Aspect (N-S)	88.0	89.0	2431.2	0.56
Distance	4.0	2.0	33.2	1.43

*CV = Variance ½ × 100/Mean

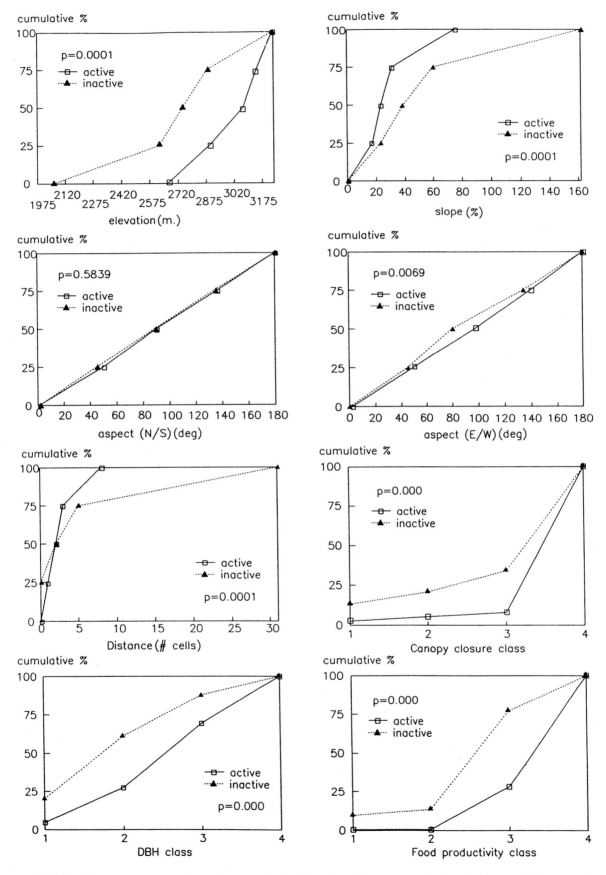

Fig. 5. Cumulative frequency graphs for model variables. For interval-scaled variables (elevation, slope, aspect (E-W), aspect (N-S), and distance to clearings) p-values are significance levels for t-tests of differences between mean values of site (active) and non-site (inactive) cells. For ordinal-scaled variables, p-values are significance levels for chi-square tests.

the more productive conifer cone vegetation types, as well as high d.b.h. and canopy closure classes (Figure 5).

Distance to openings was also a significant discriminator, but in the opposite direction to what was expected, i.e., the active cells are located closer to openings in the forest canopy than the overall environment. Because proximity to openings means more solar radiation and wind affecting the forest ground floor, creating dry, unfavorable conditions for cone storage, this result was apparently paradoxical.

Two explanations were plausible for this effect. It was possible that the negative impact of clearings decays so fast with distance that a cell size of 70.7 m on the side fails to capture it, but then this variable should not show up as an effective discriminator. The other likely explanation involves considering inter-variable correlations: the gentle slopes and high elevations favored by red squirrels were associated with the presence of roads that were built to provide access to the higher parts of the mountain and follow preferentially flat terrain. Most forest clearings in the areas of denser squirrel activity are road corridors and, therefore, the apparent preference of squirrels for clearings simply reflects the co-occurrence of squirrels and road corridors at high elevations on gentle slopes.

Environmental Model

Three models converged on formulations including elevation, slope, aspect E-W, and canopy closure as the statistically significant variables. The best of these models, at an optimum probability cut-off level of 0.4, correctly identifies 90 percent of the squirrel activity; at the same time only about 27 percent of the inactive areas are misclassified (Figures 6a and 6b), resulting in a model that would cover approximately 27 percent of the study area if it were mapped cell by cell. This represents a 63 percent improvement of predictive power over chance, because a worthless model that covers 27 percent of the landscape should only predict 27 percent of the sites correctly by chance; the fact that 90 percent are correctly predicted yields the 63 percent improvement over chance figure. The logistic model was represented by the equations

$$Y = 0.002 \times \text{elevation} - 0.228 \times \text{slope} + 0.685 \times \text{canopy1} + 0.443 \times \text{canopy2} \qquad (1) + 0.481 \times \text{canopy3} + 0.009 \text{ aspectE-W}$$

and

$$p = 1/(1 + \exp(-Y)) \qquad (2)$$

is the estimated probability of success, i.e., the probability of squirrel presence at a given cell. A habitat suitability map for the red squirrel was created by applying Equations 1 and 2 to the map overlays representing model variables. The result is a map of continuous probability values that was discretized into five categories and overlaid with the activity areas map to facilitate comparisons between observed spatial patterns of squirrel activity and model predicted suitability (Figure 7a).

The agreement between observations and predictions was very good, especially at the largest concentration of middens, on the highest part of the study area, around High, Hawk, and Emerald peaks (see Figure 1), and along the ridge extending south from High Peak. It was also very good around Heliograph Peak, in the southeastern edge of the study area, and at the headwaters of the northern branch of Marijilda Creek, north of Heliograph Peak and west of the main north-south ridge. Much moderate quality, and also some high quality habitat, was identified northeast of Webb Peak and around the headwaters of Ash Creek, but the agreement with habitat use was not as good as for the areas mentioned above. Besides these major clusters, the model also identified good quality habitat in the Grant Hill/

Hospital Flat area and near Grand View Peak, where there is an isolated squirrel midden.

One of the most obvious differences between model predictions and observed activity can be seen at the northwest edge of the study area, near Riggs Lake, where two isolated activity areas are present in what the model predicts to be poor quality habitat. However, one of these areas corresponds to an inactive (temporarily or permanently abandoned) midden and the location is actually believed to provide poor habitat conditions (Randall Smith, pers. comm.).

It is interesting to notice how the environmental suitability map (Figure 7a) shows tight clustering of activity, with squirrels inhabiting contiguous cells in some high density areas that are, however, surrounded by unused regions of predicted high quality habitat. This may reveal the influence of factors undetectable at the present spatial scale of analysis, but that let squirrels discriminate within what the model considers equally suitable areas. According to Vahle and Patton (1983), d.b.h. may be such a variable but this could only be confirmed by higher resolution mapping and measurement of d.b.h. at higher precision.

Trend Surface Model

Results of the trend surface model are shown in Figure 7c. Classification error rates (Figures 6c and 6d) show a maximum improvement over chance in predictive power of 57 percent at the 0.4 cut-off point, represented in the binary map of Figure 7d.

The high predictive power of the trend surface model may be due to the squirrel's tendency to form clusters in relatively well defined areas of good habitat. If intraspecific behavioral interactions account even partially for this clustering, then the trend surface captures an aspect of squirrel habitat use that is ignored by the environmental model.

Bayesian Model

Model performance statistics (Figures 6e and 6f) show that a probability level of 0.5 is the optimal cut-off point for a binary model, capable of correctly classifying 87 percent of the sites while covering only 24 percent of the study area, for a predictive improvement over chance of 63 percent. Although the Bayesian integration model has exactly the same predictive power as the environmental model alone, there are some differences among the two that are made clearer by comparing Figures 7a and 7b with Figures 7e and 7f. A Bayesian binary model defined at the optimum cut-off point captured a slightly smaller number of sites than an optimum binary environmental model, but also covers a proportionately smaller part of the study area. The shape of the Bayesian model revealed the influences of component models, with a clear smoothing of the higher probability areas of the central part of the study area due to the trend surface model. Transitions between lower suitability classes remain jagged and complex, primarily under control of the environmental model.

Spatial Impact Assessment

One of the goals of this study was to assess the amount and quality of red squirrel habitat that will be lost due to development of the astronomical observatory, with the underlying assumption that habitat losses can be used as a proxy measure for impact on long-term survival of the population. Squirrel habitat equivalents (U.S. Forest Service, 1988) is the concept that translates measurements of affected area into population impacts. Squirrel habitat equivalents equal the number of red squirrels that could be supported by a given habitat acreage, and are calculated by overlaying the project location areas (Figure 4f) on the environmental habitat suitability map (Figure 7a).

This determines the number of cells, or acreage lost in each suitability class.

Density of squirrel activity areas by suitability class was calculated by overlaying the squirrel activity map (Figure 3d) on the habitat suitability map and dividing the number of activity areas in each suitability class by the number of cells in that class. The number of squirrel habitat equivalents lost in each suitability class was given by the product of density of activity times acreage lost. Summation over all suitability classes determines the overall losses.

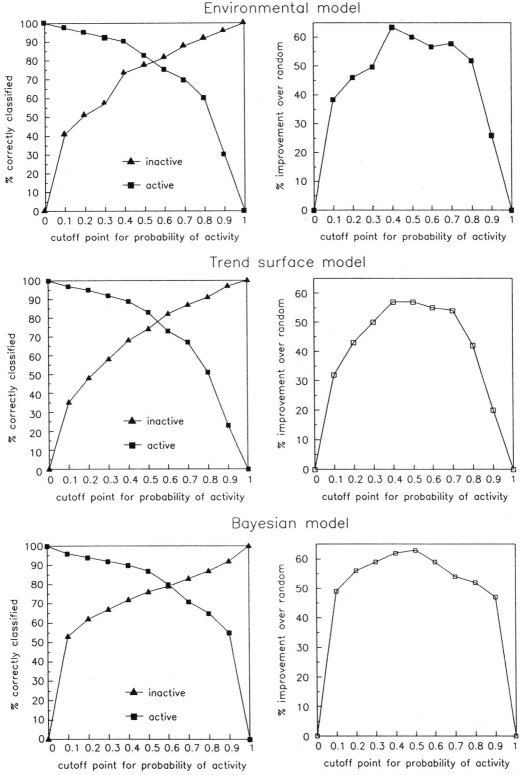

FIG. 6. Classification error rates and predictive improvement over random habitat classification for environmental, trend surface, and Bayesian combined models.

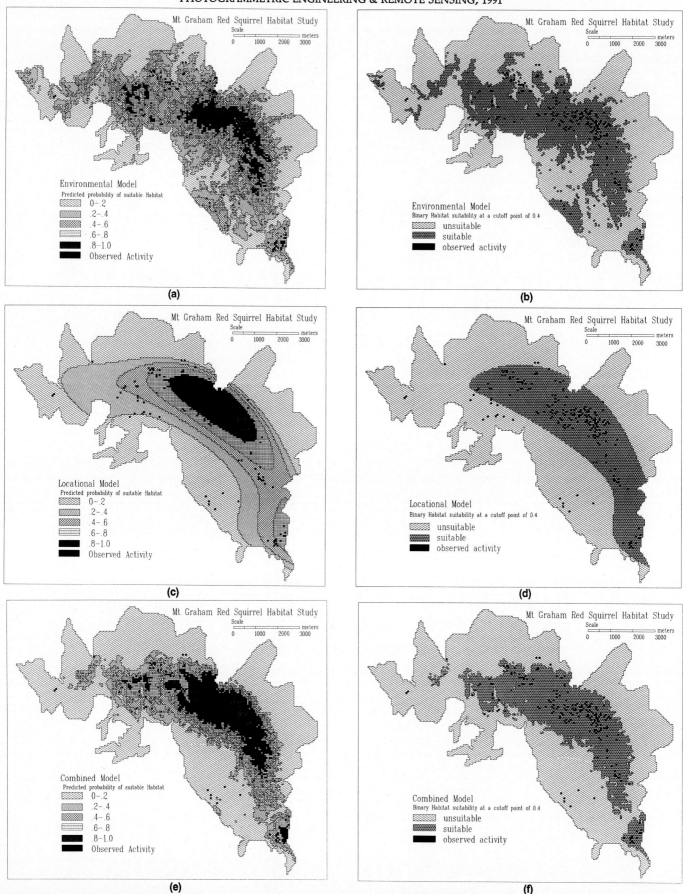

FIG. 7. Five class map representation of (a) environmental, (c) trend surface, and (e) Bayesian models, and binary habitat classification at optimal cut-off points for (b) environmental, (d) trend surface, and (f) Bayesian models.

Squirrel habitat equivalents lost to development were calculated using the data in Table 2. Phase 1 of the observatory project will cause the most impact, leading to the loss of 3.5 units while phase 2 is estimated to impact 3.2 habitat equivalents. A fully developed observatory would have an impact of 6.7 squirrel habitat equivalents, or approximately 3 percent of the 212 activity areas identified in the 1986-87 census and taken as a base population level for this study. These impact magnitude estimates assume that all habitat will be lost in a 70.7-m wide corridor, which is the best approximation to the true impact permitted by the grid-cell resolution. This value may overestimate the direct spatial impact of developing the observatory but it should be a better estimate of overall impact that includes clearcutting, paving, construction, and other negative effects of human presence, such as noise, smells, and movement.

It should be emphasized that habitat area lost is a proxy measure of the project impact on population size. The Mt. Graham red squirrel is in danger of extinction, and preservation of its habitat is a necessary, if not sufficient, condition for long-term survival. However, even though impact magnitude can be estimated, it is much harder to determine what will be the importance of a given impact, that is, how will it influence the attainment of the desired goal of maintaining a viable red squirrel population. Continued monitoring of population dynamics and habitat status will be needed in order to make sure that the various uses sought for the mountain can be reconciled and are not ultimately incompatible.

SUMMARY AND CONCLUSIONS

A GIS-based statistical habitat suitability model for the Mt. Graham red squirrel was developed, and impact assessment of the observatory project was accomplished. Selection of cell size, a critical decision in database development (Laymon and Reid, 1986), was successful because most of the original data were preserved and species-habitat relationships were clearly identified.

The univariate analysis was very informative and effectively demonstrated the role of different environmental variables as dimensions of habitat selection, and facilitated comparisons with previous expectations. Good results were also obtained in the development of predictive multivariate models. The visual impression of acceptable agreement between model predictions and field observations conveyed by the environmental, trend surface, and combined maps is confirmed by model performance statistics. Predominance of terrain variables in the model selected for impact assessment should not be attributed to biological irrelevance of vegetation factors, but probably stems from the coarse character of categorical information and to correlations with variables measured in higher resolution interval scales. This seems to explain the selection of elevation instead of food productivity, whose inter-correlation is quite clear (Figures 3a and 4b). Data coarseness alone may be responsible for the ineffectiveness of d.b.h., obviously too homogeneous throughout the entire study area to be a good discriminator (Figure 4d).

It is possible that different sets of variables dominate the habitat selection procedure of Mt. Graham red squirrels at different spatial scales: terrain variables would be more important at the overall landscape level, while vegetation characteristics dominate at a finer resolution. This hypothesis could be tested by developing habitat suitability models for smaller areas of more homogeneous terrain and using higher resolution mapping and more discriminating scales for the measurement of vegetation factors.

Finally, it is important to recall that the habitat use data from which the model was developed correspond to a single year, and may be insufficient for long-term management purposes, especially when the species of concern is an endangered one. This limitation can be removed by linking the static suitability model presented in this paper with a forest succession model capable of simulating habitat suitability changes as a function of landscape dynamics. Several examples of this type of work are given in the *Proceedings of the Wildlife 2000 Symposium* (see Section V: "Linking wildlife models with models of vegetation succession"). Validation of such an integrated system would require continued monitoring of the population and re-testing of the models on a longer time-series of data, considering also the need to develop distinct habitat suitability models for "boom" and for "bust" years, typical of rodent population dynamics in general and also, it is believed, of Mt. Graham red squirrels. Further research should also consider developing quantitative measures of squirrel habitat use, based on variables such as midden diameter or midden biomass.

ACKNOWLEDGMENTS

We are grateful to Dr. Kenneth L. Kvamme, Arizona State Museum, for his methodological support in the design and analysis of this study. The USDA Forest Service, Coronado National Forest, funded the "Mt. Graham Red Squirrel Geographic Information System" project. They also provided expert information regarding Mt. Graham and the red squirrel, mainly through Mark Kaplan, Randy Smith, and Jerry Connors, to whom we are very thankful. This paper was significantly improved by the constructive criticisms and valuable recommendations of three anonymous reviewers.

TABLE 2. SPATIAL IMPACT ASSESSMENT

Suitability Class	Activity Density	Number of cells Lost		Number of Habitat Equivalents Lost	
		Phase 1	Phase 2	Phase 1	Phase 2
0-0.1	0.000	0	0	0	0
0.1-0.2	0.004	0	0	0	0
0.2-0.3	0.005	0	0	0	0
0.3-0.4	0.009	0	0	0	0
0.4-0.5	0.017	2	1	0.034	0.017
0.5-0.6	0.025	8	1	0.200	0.025
0.6-0.7	0.019	19	1	0.361	0.019
0.7-0.8	0.028	11	4	0.308	0.028
0.8-0.9	0.089	12	5	1.068	0.445
0.9-1.0	0.150	10	18	1.500	2.700
Total	-	62	31	3.471	3.234

REFERENCES

Broschart, M. R., C. A. Johnston, and R. J. Naiman, 1989. Predicting beaver colony density in boreal landscapes. *Journal of Wildlife Management*, 53(4):929–934.

Cliff, A. D., and J. K. Ord, 1981. *Spatial Processes: Models and Applications*. Pion Press, London, 266 p.

Columbus Project Science Advisory Committee, 1987. *Scientific Justification for the Mt. Graham Observatory*. Preprints of the Steward Observatory, Rep. No.TBA (draft). University of Arizona, Tucson, Arizona.

Davis, L. S., and L. I. DeLain, 1986. Linking wildlife-habitat analysis to forest planning with ECOSYM. *Wildlife 2000* (J. Verner, M. L. Morrison, and C. J. Ralph, editors), The University of Wisconsin Press, Madison, Wisconsin, pp. 361–370.

Eastman, J. R., 1988. *Idrisi: A Grid-Based Geographic Analysis System*. Clark University School of Geography, Worcester, Massachussets.

Flyger, V., and J. E. Gates, 1982. Pine Squirrels. *Wild Mammals of North America* (J. A. Chapman and G. A Feldhamer, editors), The Johns Hopkins University Press, Baltimore, Maryland, pp. 230–238.

Haining, R., 1980. Spatial autocorrelation problems. *Geography and the Urban Environment* (D. T. Herbert and R. J. Johnston, editors), Vol. 3, pp. 1–43.

Hodgson, M. E., J. R. Jensen, H. E. Mackey, Jr., and M. C. Coulter, 1988. Monitoring wood stork foraging habitat using remote sensing and geographic information systems. *Photogrammetric Engineering & Remote Sensing*, 54(11):1601–1607.

Hoffmeister, D. F., 1986. *Mammals of Arizona*. University of Arizona Press, Tucson, Arizona.

Itami, R. M., 1988. *CADGRID User's Manual*. University of Arizona, Tucson, Arizona.

Jones, J. R., 1974. *Silviculture of Southwestern Mixed Conifers and Aspen: The Status of Our Knowledge*. U.S.D.A. Forest Service, Research Paper RM-122. Rocky Mountain Forest and Range Experiment Station, Fort Collins, Colorado.

Kleinbaum, D. G., L. L. Kupper, and K. E. Muller, 1988. *Applied Regression Analysis and other Multivariable Methods*. PWS-Kent, Boston, 718 p.

Kvamme, K. L., 1985. Determining empirical relationships between the natural environment and pre-historic site locations: a hunter-gatherer example. *For Concordance in Archeological Analysis* (C. Carr, editor), Wesport Publishers, Kansas City, Kansas, pp. 208–238.

Lancia, R. A., S. D. Miller, D. A. Adams, and D. W. Hazel, 1982. Validating habitat quality assessment: an example. *Transactions of the North American Wildlife and Natural Resources Conference*, 47:96–110.

Lancia, R. A., D. A. Adams, and E. M. Lunk, 1986. Temporal and spatial aspects of species-habitat models. *Wildlife 2000* (J. Verner, M. L. Morrison, and C. J. Ralph, editors), The University of Wisconsin Press, Madison, Wisconsin, pp. 177–182.

Laymon, S. A., and J. A. Reid, 1986. Effects of grid-cell size on tests of a spotted owl HSI model. *Wildlife 2000* (J. Verner, M. L. Morrison, and C. J. Ralph, editors), The University of Wisconsin Press, Madison, Wisconsin, pp. 177–182.

Lyon, J. G., J. T. Heinen, R. A. Mead, and N. E. G. Roller, 1987. Spatial data for modeling wildlife habitat. *Journal of Surveying Engineering*, 113(2):88–100.

Maynard, P. F., 1981. *The Logit Classifier: A General Maximum Likelihood Discriminant for Remote Sensing Applications*. Unpublished M.A. Thesis, Department of Geography, University of California, Santa Barbara, California.

Ormsby, J. P., and R. S. Lunetta, 1987. Whitetail deer food availability maps from Thematic Mapper data. *Photogrammetric Engineering & Remote Sensing*, 53(8):1081–1085.

Palmeirim, J. M., 1988. Automatic mapping of avian species habitat using satellite imagery. *Oikos* 52(1):59–68.

Pereira, J. M. C., 1989. *A Spatial Approach to Statistical Habitat Suitability Modeling: The Mt. Graham Red Squirrel Case Study*. Unpublished Ph.D. Dissertation, School of Renewable Natural Resources, University of Arizona, Tucson, Arizona. 151 p.

Press, S. J., and S. Wilson, 1978. Choosing between logistic regression and discriminant analysis. *Journal of the American Statistical Association*, 73(364):699–705.

Rothwell, R., 1979. Nest sites of red squirrels (Tamiasciurus hudsonicus) in the Laramie range of southeastern Wyoming. *Journal of Mammalogy*, 60(2):404–405.

Schamberger, M. L., and L. J. O'Neil, 1986. Concepts and constraints of habitat-model testing. *Wildlife 2000* (J. Verner, M. L. Morrison, and C. J. Ralph, editors), The University of Wisconsin Press, Madison, Wisconsin, pp. 177–182.

Short, H. L., and S. C. Williamson, 1986. Evaluating the structure of habitat for wildlife. *Wildlife 2000* (J. Verner, M. L. Morrison, and C. J. Ralph, editors), The University of Wisconsin Press, Madison, Wisconsin, pp. 97–104.

Steward Observatory, 1986. *Proposed Site Development Plan for the Mt. Graham International Observatory, Pinaleno Mountains, Graham County, Arizona*. University of Arizona, Tucson, Arizona.

Strahler, A. H., 1980. The use of prior probabilities in maximum likelihood classification of remotely sensed data. *Remote Sensing of Environment*, 10:135–163.

Strahler, A. H., T. L. Logan, and N. A. Bryant, 1978. Improving forest cover classification accuracy from LANDSAT by incorporating topographic information. *Proceedings of the Twelfth International Symposium on Remote Sensing of Environment*, ERIM, Ann Arbor, Michigan, pp. 927–942.

Thomas, J. W., 1982. Needs for and approaches to wildlife habitat assessment. *Transactions of the North American Wildlife and Natural Resources Conference*, 47:35–46.

Tomlin, C. Dana, 1986. *The IBM Personal Computer Version of the Map Analysis Package*. GSD/IBM AcIS Project, Report No. LCGSA-85-16 Laboratory for Computer Graphics and Spatial Analysis. Graduate School of Design, Harvard University. 60 p.

Upton, G. J. G., and B. Fingleton, 1985. *Spatial Data Analysis by Example. Volume 1: Point Pattern and Quantitative Data*. Wiley, New York, 409 p.

U.S. Fish and Wildlife Service, 1980. *Habitat Evaluation Procedures (HEP)*. Ecological Services Manual 102. U.S. Department of Interior, Fish and Wildlife Service, Division of Ecological Services. Government Printing Office, Washington, D.C., 84 p. plus appendices.

———, 1981. *Standards for the Development of Suitability Index Models*. Ecological Services Manual 103. U.S. Department of Interior, Fish and Wildlife Service, Division of Ecological Services. Government Printing Office, Washington, D.C., 68 p. plus appendices.

U.S. Forest Service, 1986. *Draft Environmental Impact Statement, Proposed Mt. Graham Astrophysical Area, Pinaleno Mountains*. Coronado National Forest, Tucson, Arizona, 217 p.

———, 1988. *Mount Graham Red Squirrel — An Expanded Biological Assessment*. Coronado National Forest, Tucson, Arizona, 130 p.

Vahle, J. R., and D. R. Patton, 1983. Red squirrel cover requirements in Arizona mixed conifer forests. *Journal of Forestry*, 81:14–15,22.

Wrigley, N., 1976. An introduction to the use of logit models in geography. *Concepts and Techniques in Modern Geography*, 10. Geo Abstracts, Norwich.

———, 1985. *Categorical Data Analysis for Geographers and Environmental Scientists*. Longman, London, 392 p.

Sensitivity of Wildlife Habitat Models to Uncertainties in GIS Data

David M. Stoms, Frank W. Davis, and Christopher B. Cogan
Department of Geography, University of California, Santa Barbara, CA 93106

ABSTRACT: Decision makers need to know the reliability of output products from GIS analysis. For many GIS applications, it is not possible to compare these products to an independent measure of "truth." Sensitivity analysis offers an alternative means of estimating reliability. In this paper, we present a GIS-based statistical procedure for estimating the sensitivity of wildlife habitat models to uncertainties in input data and model assumptions. The approach is demonstrated in an analysis of habitat associations derived from a GIS database for the endangered California condor. Alternative data sets were generated to compare results over a reasonable range of assumptions about several sources of uncertainty. Sensitivity analysis indicated that condor habitat associations are relatively robust, and the results have increased our confidence in our initial findings. Uncertainties and methods described in the paper have general relevance for many GIS applications.

INTRODUCTION

GEOGRAPHIC INFORMATION SYSTEMS (GIS) are playing an increasingly important role in conservation biology and wildlife management because they provide an efficient means for modeling potential distributions of species and habitats (Davis et al., 1990). The usefulness of GIS technology is now limited more by data availability and quality and by the reliability of habitat preference models than by technological obstacles. Because expensive and politically sensitive decisions are being based on GIS analysis, it is important to have a means of characterizing the uncertainty of GIS output products. Analytical models of spatial error propagation are often not applicable in such cases. Sensitivity analysis has been recommended as an alternative means of estimating reliability (Lyon et al., 1987; Openshaw, 1989; Lodwick et al., 1990). Whereas error analysis compares output data with an independent measure of "truth," GIS sensitivity analysis compares the initial output product to alternative results derived from data that have been perturbed in some controlled, systematic way (Lodwick et al., 1990). The goal is to determine whether the output seems valid over a set of reasonable assumptions about the nature of uncertainty (Openshaw, 1989).

The objective of this paper is to describe a sensitivity analysis of derived habitat associations to typical uncertainties in GIS observation and habitat data. We begin with a brief review of GIS habitat modeling and how sensitivity to typical uncertainties has been evaluated. Next we describe a habitat analysis of historical observations of the endangered California condor (*Gymnogyps californianus*). The two key GIS layers in the database and their potential errors are summarized. Then we describe the methods used to derive baseline habitat associations and the data manipulation that generated alternative data sets for the sensitivity analysis. Although the context is habitat modeling, the uncertainties encountered are typical of many GIS applications, and the sensitivity analysis methods can be employed both for management decision making and for scientific research.

HABITAT MODELING AND SENSITIVITY ANALYSIS

GIS modeling of species' habitat associations is one form of land suitability analysis. Two approaches have generally been utilized, depending on objectives and data availability. The deductive approach extrapolates known habitat requirements to the spatial distributions of habitat factors. If more than one spatial data layer is involved, they are usually combined by either logical or arithmetic map overlay operations (e.g., Davis and Goetz, 1990). A habitat suitability index can also be calculated from the spatial configuration of a single data layer (Mead et al., 1981). The GIS output product of the deductive approach is a map depicting levels of habitat suitability. This map can guide decisions regarding land acquisition or habitat preservation priorities, land management practices, or sites for reintroduction of endangered species. It should be noted that the model only identifies "potential" habitat, but does not imply that the species is actually present at a given location.

In many situations, the habitat requirements are not well-known, and a GIS is used to induce them from a sample of observations of the species georeferenced to one or more resource factor maps. Output in the inductive case is a tabular or textual summary describing the factors most significantly associated with the observed distribution of the species. Associations can be derived either from univariate or multivariate statistical analysis such as classification trees (Walker and Moore, 1988; Davis and Dozier, 1990). This inductive approach is more common in scientific research designed to increase our understanding of species distributions (Walker and Moore, 1988; Ferrier and Smith, 1990), but the results can be extrapolated to predict the spatial distribution of suitable habitat using the deductive method for habitat management purposes (Agee et al., 1989).

In both approaches, there will always be uncertainty in the GIS output product due to errors and uncertainties in data inputs. Quality of the outputs is affected by the accuracy of the maps of habitat factors, which is influenced by the interaction of minimum mapping unit (MMU) size, resolution of source data, map generalization, analyst skill, and many other factors (Lodwick et al., 1990). Tracking the propagation of errors as several map layers are combined into a habitat suitability map is often beyond our capabilities. The description of habitat preferences in the deductive approach can be inaccurate, usually to an unknown degree, and even the best model can only take into account a simplified set of factors that determine species' distributions. Stochastic processes, such as disturbance, weather fluctuations, or population dynamics, can prevent otherwise suitable habitat from being occupied. Similarly, field sampling to assess the accuracy of a habitat suitability map is hindered by the relatively small sample units of short duration in relation to the scale and assumptions of the map. Observation data used in the inductive approach are also subject to many sources of uncertainty, such as the accuracy of their locational coordinates. These data often cannot be tested because they record an event that occurred in the past. For the same reasons described above, it is difficult to assess the accuracy of the output description of

PHOTOGRAMMETRIC ENGINEERING & REMOTE SENSING,
Vol. 58, No. 6, June 1992, pp. 843–850.

0099-1112/92/5806–843$03.00/0
©1992 American Society for Photogrammetry
and Remote Sensing

habitat preferences because of problems with field sampling (Raphael and Marcot, 1986).

There are two approaches to comprehensive error analysis of habitat modeling. In one approach, knowing the accuracy of input layers and having a model of how error propagates through GIS processing, errors in the output can be deduced. Conversely, the error propagation model and accuracy of the output can be used to deduce the magnitude of errors in the inputs. In habitat modeling, neither the input or output layer accuracies nor the theoretical error propagation model can be known, forcing analysts to either express caveats about their results or to turn to alternative methods of evaluating uncertainty.

Perhaps the most promising alternative is sensitivity analysis. Lodwick et al. (1990, p. 413) define geographical sensitivity analysis as "the study of the effects of imposed perturbations (variations) on the inputs of a geographical analysis on the outputs of that analysis." Input data are perturbed in systematic ways, such as degrading spatial resolution by a sequence of scale factors. Perturbations represent the range of reasonable assumptions about the nature of uncertainty in each data layer. A GIS output is considered sensitive to variation in a given input if the resulting sensitivity measure exceeds a predetermined significance level. Greater care should be taken in compiling inputs whose perturbations produce the greatest effect on the outputs. Because the exact nature of uncertainties can seldom be expressed by mathematical functions, geographical sensitivity analyses are usually conducted empirically.

Objectives for sensitivity analysis in habitat modeling differ somewhat for the deductive versus the inductive methods. For deductive habitat modeling, the output is a map of potential distribution of habitat suitability. As this approach is common in a management decision or policy making context, the critical concern is whether the map is so sensitive to variation in inputs that a different decision would be reached with a different realization of the inputs. In the inductive approach, the issue is how confident we are in the derived habitat preferences.

While relatively common practice in fields such as planning (e.g., Alexander, 1989), sensitivity analysis is seldom employed in GIS applications. Recent examples of GIS sensitivity analysis include testing the effects of classification errors (Ramapriyan et al., 1981; Lyon et al., 1987), grid cell size (Laymon and Reid, 1986; Lyon et al., 1987; Turner et al., 1989), map extent (Turner et al., 1989), the number of thematic classes (Lyon et al., 1987), and subjective weighting factors (Heinen and Lyon, 1989). For an excellent description of the types of sensitivities in spatial analysis, measures of sensitivity, and a mathematical treatment of geographical sensitivity analysis, the reader is referred to Lodwick et al. (1990).

CONDOR GIS DATABASE

The endangered California condor most recently inhabited the mountainous regions of southern and central California (Figure 1), feeding primarily in open woodland and grasslands. Since 1987, the species survives only in captivity. A breeding program is underway to restore the population to a viable level, with the eventual goal of reintroducing condors into the wild. We collaborated with the California Department of Fish and Game, the U.S. Fish and Wildlife Service, and the National Audubon Society to study historical patterns of habitat use by the species and to aid in identifying suitable sites for future release of captively reared birds (Scepan et al., 1987). The GIS is being used to store and analyze the set of observations of wild condors over the past century and a map of land-use/land-cover (LU/LC) types, described briefly below. When completed, the database will cover the entire historic range. For this analysis, we only used the 1:250,000-scale Los Angeles quadrangle portion (see Figure 1), where 75 percent of the sightings occurred.

Condor Sighting Data

Beginning in 1966, researchers with the National Audubon Society, the U. S. Forest Service, and the U. S. Fish and Wildlife Service compiled visual sighting records from a network of field biologists, fire lookout personnel, ranchers, and other interested members of the public (Wilbur et al., 1972). These 7,341 sighting records were incorporated as a point coverage into the ARC/INFO GIS database, and include attributes such as the date

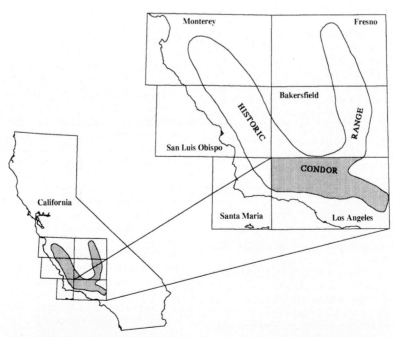

FIG. 1. Map of the historical range of the California condor. The index of 1:250,000-scale USGS quadrangle maps is also shown. The shaded region in the larger scale inset map shows the study area in the Los Angeles quadrangle.

of the observation and the bird's activity. The few scattered observations outside the historic range boundaries were not considered in the habitat association modeling. For this sensitivity analysis, the 508 feeding observations in the Los Angeles quadrangle were used.

Potential sources of uncertainty in the sighting data include errors in the recorded location and sampling bias. Locations were originally coded with 500-metre precision. Further, when the data were converted to GIS format, the transformation to UTM coordinates potentially introduced additional positional error. Observers may also have had difficulty in accurately mapping their location and that of the bird, especially given that condors can be identified at a distance of several kilometres (Johnson *et al.*, 1983). If the recorded location is displaced from the true location, it is conceivable that GIS analysis will associate the observation with a habitat type different from that which the condor actually used. The effect of positional error would be to lower the strength of the habitat model, indicating that habitat utilization was more random than was actually the case (White and Garrott, 1986).

Sightings of rare species tend to be located in places where they are expected to be seen (e.g., Snyder and Johnson, 1985) and that are most accessible to observers, such as near roads, trails, or other observation points. The condor sightings are certainly suspect in this regard, as much of the historic range is in remote, rugged terrain. The implication of biased sampling is that it may say more about the preferences of the observers than of the wildlife.

Condor Habitat Map

Land use and condor habitat were mapped over the 2.5 million ha range by photointerpretation of 1986 Landsat Thematic Mapper (TM) imagery (see Davis *et al.* (1988) for details). The classification system for mapping LU/LC was specifically designed to discriminate land surfaces that differ in quality as condor habitat. Based on field reconnaissance, we employed an MMU of 10 ha in an attempt to capture small grassland feeding habitats (potreros) that condor biologists considered important to the species. Thematic accuracy of the land-use/land-cover map was estimated at 76 percent for the Los Angeles quadrangle (Davis *et al.*, 1989). The relatively low accuracy reflects the complexity of topography and vegetation in the study area and the difficulty in capturing that complexity at a relatively small map scale.

At least four aspects of the habitat map can be a source of uncertainty: (1) loss of detail from spatial generalization, (2) similar loss of detail due to the level of precision of the classification system, (3) errors in class label or boundary location, and (4) choosing a study area that is unrepresentative of the entire range. Here we concentrate on the first and fourth aspects.

METHODS

Basic Habitat Associations Procedure

Using the inductive approach of habitat modeling, we overlaid point observation data and LU/LC maps for the Los Angeles quadrangle. A database program was written to generate contingency tables of land-cover types and condor activities. We then used a statistical package to compute the Chi-square statistic as a measure of the strength of association between cover types and observed condor activities. The null hypothesis proposes that condors utilize habitats in their range randomly. The expected frequency for each cover type was calculated by multiplying the total number of feeding observations by the proportion of the total area occupied by that cover type in the study area. The relative strength of association between condor activ-

ities and individual vegetation types was measured using the Bonferroni normal statistic approach described by Neu *et al.* (1974).

To simplify presentation of results, we have classified the measures of association into "positive," "negative," or "nonsignificant" levels based on the 90th percentile confidence intervals for an alpha significance level of 0.10. Positive association means condors appear to preferentially feed in that cover type. Negative association shows the birds selectively avoiding the cover type. A nonsignificant level of association occurs when the proportion of sightings in a cover type is similar to the proportion of area of that type. We emphasize that these levels are used only to facilitate the interpretation of a complex set of numerical comparisons, but should not be construed as formal significance testing based on independent random samples. The output product of this inductive procedure is a table listing the level of association of condor feeding with each LU/LC type.

Alternative Data Sets for Sensitivity Analysis

To test the sensitivity of condor habitat associations to uncertainty about sighting locations, sampling bias, map generalization, and map extent, we generated six alternative data sets of sighting data, which are summarized in Table 1.

Errors in location of the sightings could place them into a different map polygon, with a higher probability of being in the wrong class for classes characterized by small polygons. A GIS

TABLE 1. CHARACTERISTICS OF ORIGINAL AND ALTERNATIVE DATA SETS USED IN THE SENSITIVITY ANALYSIS OF CONDOR HABITAT ASSOCIATIONS. EACH DATA SET CONTAINS THE MAPPED LAND-USE/LAND-COVER TYPE AT THE LOCATION OF EACH CONDOR SIGHTING.

Data Set	Characteristics
	BASELINE
A	Original Data. 508 feeding observations at their coded locations.
	LOCATIONAL UNCERTAINTY
B	Location Precision. As in A, but northing and easting coordinates are displaced by distances from a uniform random distribution with a maximum of 250 m. Based on the limits of precision of the coded coordinates.
C	Location Error. As in B, but displacement based on a normal random distribution with 95 percent of sightings within 1 km of their coded position. Assumes greater uncertainty in locations than B.
D	Location Error. As in C, but 95 percent of sightings within 2 km. 505 sightings used.
	SAMPLING BIAS
E	Unique Locations. Subset of A with 137 observations such that, for each activity, locations where condors were sighted were only counted once.
	MAP GENERALIZATION
F	Minimum Mapping Unit. Same as A, except the primary land-use/land-cover map polygons less than 20 ha on the original map were dissolved into larger neighboring polygons.
	MAP EXTENT
G	Larger Sampling Domain. Same as A, except the primary land use/land cover and 77 feeding sightings for the Bakersfield 1:250,000-scale quadrangle were added to the analysis.

query reported the mean distance from sightings to the nearest polygon boundary in the study area to be about 500 m, ranging from 5 to 3100 m. In evergreen shrubland polygons, the average distance is over 800 m, so we would expect sightings in this class to be least affected by locational uncertainty. Grassland sightings were, on average, 400 m from boundaries, and all other classes averaged less than 250 m distance. Consequently, the deciduous shrubland and the forest sightings are most uncertain as to their true type.

Data Sets B, C, and D test the sensitivity of measured habitat association to locational uncertainty by displacing the coordinates. Displacements were randomly selected from two probability distributions (Figure 2) in the statistical software, and added to the original coordinates, from which new point coverages were generated. In Data Set B, sighting coordinates were randomly displaced by assuming errors are uniformly distributed up to 250 m in both UTM eastings and northings, reflecting the level of precision of the coded locations. In Data Sets C and D, coordinates have been displaced by assuming that locational errors are normally distributed around the recorded locations (White and Garrott, 1986). Set C assumes that 95 percent of the true locations occurred within 1 km of the encoded coordinates, whereas Set D assumes that 95 percent of the true locations were within 2 km. Only one realization of random error was tested for each model. In a more rigorous analysis, multiple realizations could be generated in a Monte Carlo simulation to determine the significance level at which effects were not different. For our purposes of exploratory analysis, we believe that the number of observations in each case (more than 500) was sufficiently large to provide a reasonable indication of the sensitivity of the habitat associations.

For Data Set E, we retained only one sighting at each location to reduce the effects of possible bias from frequent observations at fixed locations such as fire lookouts (see Figure 3). This reselection of points, retaining only one feeding observation within a buffer of 250 m radius centered on the coded locations, reduced the data set to 137 points. Observations made at sites where biologists placed animal carcasses for supplemental feeding of condors were excluded from all data sets.

Data Set F was created by increasing the MMU size of the LU/LC map in order to assess the effects of the level of generalization. LU/LC polygons less than 20 ha, such as small potreros, were dissolved into larger neighboring classes, reducing the number of map polygons from 1,763 to 1,186. As with distance to boundaries, polygon size is also a function of LU/LC type. Average polygon size in the Los Angeles quadrangle is 520 ha. Average size of evergreen shrubland polygons is over twice the average of all types combined. Forest types tend to occur in smaller patches so sightings in the latter classes are more likely to change types as MMU increases.

The condor GIS database is being completed in stages, so a comprehensive habitat association analysis cannot yet be conducted. We recognized that the Los Angeles study area may not accurately represent the proportions of habitat availability for the condor range as a whole. Data Set G was produced by extending the analysis to include sighting and LU/LC data for both the Los Angeles and Bakersfield 1:250,000-scale quadrangles. The Bakersfield quadrangle contains a transition from the coastal Transverse Ranges of the Los Angeles quadrangle into the southern Sierra Nevada and San Joaquin Valley. Including this portion of the range greatly increases the proportion of grassland, agriculture, and woodland types while the prominence of shrub types diminishes. Only 77 sightings were added from the Bakersfield quadrangle, however, despite a 75 percent increase in total area.

Output data from the baseline habitat associations and the alternative data sets included tabulations of numbers of sight-

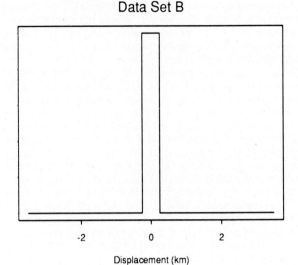

Data Set B

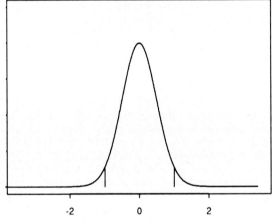

Data Set C

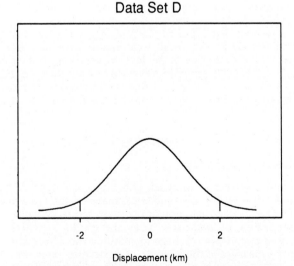

Data Set D

FIG. 2. Diagram of the random probability distributions used to displace locations of condor feeding sightings. For each sighting, a value was sampled from the probability distribution for both its easting and northing coordinate. These displacements were added to the coordinates to generate a new coverage.

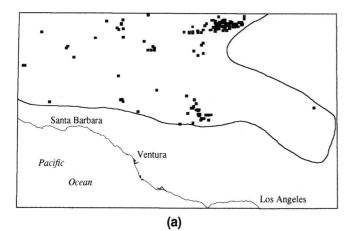

(a)

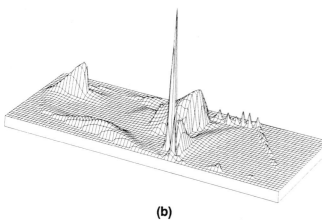

(b)

FIG 3. Map of condor feeding observations in the Los Angeles quadrangle: (a) distribution of sightings, and (b) number of sightings at each location represented by the height of peaks. The highest peak corresponds to 101 observations at a single site. This perspective is viewed from the southeast.

TABLE 2. FEEDING OBSERVATIONS OF CALIFORNIA CONDOR IN THE LOS ANGELES QUADRANGLE AND ASSOCIATIONS WITH PRIMARY LAND USE. CRITICAL VALUE OF CHI-SQUARE STATISTIC = 27.7, FOR α = 0.01, AND 13 DEGREES OF FREEDOM. EXPECTED OBSERVATIONS COMPUTED BY MULTIPLYING THE PROPORTION OF TOTAL AREA IN LAND-COVER TYPE BY TOTAL NUMBER OF OBSERVATIONS. LEVEL: '+' MEANS LAND-COVER TYPE IS SIGNIFICANTLY SELECTED BY THE CONDOR MORE THAN THE HABITAT'S AVAILABILITY IN THE LANDSCAPE; '−' MEANS LAND-COVER TYPE IS SIGNIFICANTLY AVOIDED; AND '0' MEANS USE IS NOT SIGNIFICANTLY DIFFERENT FROM RANDOM. SIGNIFICANCE LEVEL α = 0.1, 90 PERCENT FAMILY OF CONFIDENCE INTERVALS FOR k = 14 CLASSES (NEU *et al.*, 1974).

Primary Land Cover	Proportion of Total Area	Feeding Data Observed	Feeding Data Expected	Level
Agriculture	0.041	0	20.8	−
Water	0.005	0	2.5	−
Bare Land	0.013	0	6.6	−
Grassland	0.228	215	115.6	+
Evergreen Shrubland	0.412	193	208.9	0
Deciduous Shrubland	0.199	15	100.9	−
Conifer Woodland	0.050	3	25.4	−
Mixed Woodland	0.015	21	7.6	0
Broadleaf Woodland	0.008	7	4.1	0
Conifer Forest	0.001	0	0.5	−
Mixed Forest	0.009	30	4.6	+
Broadleaf Forest	0.008	24	4.1	+
Savanna	0.002	0	1.0	−
Urban	0.011	0	5.6	−
Total	1.000	508	508.0	
Calculated Chi-square		482.1		

ings by LU/LC types, and the positive, non-significant, and negative levels of association. Each data set was summarized with the calculated Chi-square statistic (based on the expected number of observations by class), the number of LU/LC classes that changed in level of association between each alternative data set and Data Set A, the percent area of each level of association, and an area sensitivity measure (Lodwick *et al.*, 1990). This last measure is a sum of the proportion of map area that changed from one level to another.

RESULTS

BASELINE ASSOCIATION OF CONDOR SIGHTINGS WITH MAPPED HABITATS

The distribution of sightings among cover types differ greatly from that expected in a random distribution (Table 2). Extrapolation of these levels of association of habitats are portrayed graphically in Figure 4. Some of the associations are what one would predict based on known life history attributes. For example, feeding observations occur with strong positive association in grassland and with strong negative association in agricultural areas. On the other hand, some feeding habitat preferences are unexpected, such as positive association with mixed forest and broadleaf forest. Even though 193 observations are associated with evergreen shrubland, this is actually slightly fewer than expected at random. Far fewer observations occur in deciduous shrubland than expected at random.

SENSITIVITY OF HABITAT ASSOCIATIONS

Results of the Chi-square analysis of the baseline and six alternative data sets are compared in Table 3. For condor feeding, the significance of use of each primary land-cover type is displayed. The "frequency" columns tabulate the number of data sets in which the levels of association for each cover type are positive, negative, or not significant.

Locational errors seem to be relatively unimportant. All three data sets with locational displacements produce results significantly different from random, and all are similar to the utilization pattern in Data Set A (Table 3). All changes are between adjoining levels, such as from significant to neutral, or vice-versa. The most noteworthy changes occur in association of condor feeding with grassland. Association is strongly positive in Data Sets A and B, but less in C. Recall that sightings in grassland habitat were closer to polygon boundaries than the average distance. In Data Set D, the association is negligible, such that the total area positively associated with condor feeding drops to less than three percent of the study site. These results suggest that the habitat associations are robust, if the assumption is true that the locational accuracy is better than one kilometre.

The 508 feeding observations in Data Set A occur at only 137 unique locations. Patterns of association between feeding activity and habitat based on unique locations are not much different than those based on all feeding observations (Table 3). The primary difference between E and A is that the extensive evergreen shrubland class becomes negatively associated in E. The area sensitivity measure is highest for this data set, indicating that while only two classes changed level, one (evergreen shrubland) was the largest class in the Los Angeles quadrangle.

The effect of larger MMU size, represented by Data Set F, was very minor. A net of 39 observations changed LU/LC class from grassland to evergreen shrubland as small potrero polygons were dissolved into the background chaparral mosaic. This shift

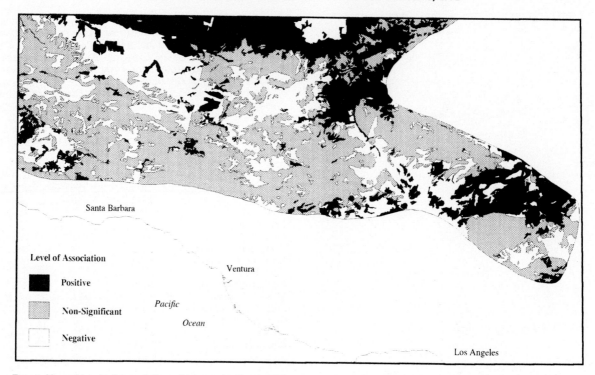

FIG. 4. Map of level of association of primary land cover types for feeding by condors in the Los Angeles quadrangle, based on Data Set A.

TABLE 3. COMPARISON OF SIGNIFICANCE OF UTILIZATION OF LAND-USE/LAND-COVER TYPES FOR FEEDING IN BASELINE AND ALTERNATIVE DATA SETS. CRITICAL VALUE OF CHI-SQUARE STATISTIC = 27.7, FOR α = 0.01, AND 13 DEGREES OF FREEDOM. LEVEL: SAME DEFINITIONS AS FOR TABLE 2.

Primary Land Cover	Data Set A Base	Data Set B 250m	Data Set C 1 km	Data Set D 2 km	Data Set E Unique	Data Set F MMU	Data Set G Extent	Frequency +	0	−
Agriculture	−	−	−	−	−	−	−	0	0	7
Water	−	−	−	−	−	−	−	0	0	7
Bare Land	−	−	−	0	−	−	−	0	1	6
Grassland	+	+	+	0	+	+	+	6	1	0
Evergreen Shrubland	0	0	0	0	−	0	0	0	6	1
Deciduous Shrubland	−	−	−	−	−	−	−	0	0	7
Conifer Woodland	−	−	−	−	0	−	−	0	1	6
Mixed Woodland	0	+	+	0	0	0	+	3	4	0
Broadleaf Woodland	0	0	0	+	0	0	0	1	6	0
Conifer Forest	−	−	−	−	−	−	−	0	0	7
Mixed Forest	+	+	+	+	+	+	+	7	0	0
Broadleaf Forest	+	+	+	+	+	+	+	7	0	0
Savanna	−	−	−	−	−	−	−	0	0	7
Urban	−	−	−	−	−	−	−	0	0	7
Changes from Set A		1	1	3	2	0	1			
Calculated Chi-square	482.1	454.2	527.6	481.4	359.0	426.3	397.5			
% Area + association	24.5	26.0	26.0	2.5	24.5	24.4	39.0			
% Area 0 association	43.5	42.0	42.0	66.8	7.3	43.6	30.3			
% Area − association	32.2	32.2	32.2	30.9	68.4	31.9	30.7			
Area sensitivity	0.000	0.015	0.015	0.249	0.462	0.000	0.015			

was not enough, however, to change the level of association for any land-cover class.

Including additional historic range in the analysis of Data Set G likewise made little difference in the level of association. Only the mixed woodland type became positively associated because of a large number of sightings in this map class in the Bakersfield quadrangle. The two largest types did, however, shift to the brink of changing levels. Grassland, with its large gain in area, nearly became nonsignificant, while evergreen shrubland almost became positively associated as its proportional area declined.

DISCUSSION

Some end users of GIS analysis accept output products uncritically. Others assume a more pessimistic view that uncertainties are so overwhelming that GIS outputs simply can not be trusted. Acknowledging the uncertainties in the condor database, we sought a middle ground by conducting a sensitivity analysis of habitat associations. The results have increased our confidence that GIS-based analysis provides a reasonable model of condor feeding habitat. Generally speaking, the habitat associations are relatively robust across the set of sensitivity analyses shown in Table 3. For the three most extensive or most heavily used cover types—i.e., grassland and evergreen and deciduous shrubland—the associations are particularly consistent. Of all the data sets, Set D, with the greatest locational displacements, has the highest number of changes in association level. Set E, using only unique locations, is most sensitive in terms of area affected, as indicated by the largest area sensitivity measure (Table 3).

Of course, there is no guarantee that sensitivity analysis will support the initial GIS results, as seen in several published studies. White and Garrott (1986) simulated the effects of locational errors in radio-tracking data and found that such errors could seriously decrease the predicted importance of preferred habitat. When computer simulation indicates significant sensitivity to locational accuracy, the wildlife biologist can reduce the effects either by improving the accuracy of the telemetry system or by increasing sample size of observations (White and Garrott, 1986). Where sample size is sufficiently large, observations close to boundaries between habitat polygons can be dropped from the habitat modeling to minimize uncertainty (White and Garrott, 1990). Condor habitat associations were probably not very sensitive to locational uncertainty, in part, because of the large number of feeding observations in our GIS database.

Other authors have found significant effects on habitat suitability indices as spatial resolution is degraded and small or rare habitats drop out (Laymon and Reid, 1986; Lyon et al., 1987; Turner et al., 1989). We tested the effects of coarser spatial resolution by eliminating polygons that are less than 20 ha, approximately one-third of the total number. Although nearly 8 percent of the feeding observations change from grassland to evergreen shrubland through this procedure, we observed no significant effects on the levels of association from changing MMU size over the small range of sizes we tested. This finding might suggest that the land-cover map is more detailed than necessary for modeling condor habitat. We believe, however, that the finer resolution of the original land-cover map will still be valuable for other GIS analysis, such as identifying potential release sites. Further generalization could determine at what MMU the habitat associations break down, but this has not been done.

Lyon et al. (1987) found that even a 5 percent change in classification accuracy of a land-cover map made a significant difference in levels of a habitat suitability index. Their results have strong implications for GIS habitat modeling with land cover maps, which always contain some degree of misclassification. We have not yet tested the sensitivity of condor habitat associations to assumptions about classification error. Such a test would be useful in determining the critical threshold of classification accuracy above which habitat associations would be reliable.

Any choice of study area boundaries is relatively arbitrary, yet it can affect analytical results (Wiens, 1986). Turner et al. (1989) observed that, as map extent expanded, more cover types were incorporated and their landscape indices increased in value. In our study, the baseline map extent was restricted to the historic condor range of the Los Angeles quadrangle map. Our results were only slightly different when we analyzed habitat associations over a larger portion of the range. When the database is completed, it will be possible to test the sensitivity of the derived associations for the entire range. It should be noted that the estimated associations may have been significantly stronger if habitat outside the historic range such as the Mojave Desert were also included in the analysis. This would have the

effect of increasing the number of cover types, decreasing the expected number of observations in cover types preferred by condors, and thereby inflating the calculated Chi-square statistic. While producing greater statistical significance, little if anything would be added to our knowledge of condor behavior, and we could even conclude erroneously that some cover types are more critical to condor survival than may actually be the case. The risk of such a mistake when considering the reintroduction of an endangered species could be catastrophic.

All previous examples of GIS sensitivity analysis we have seen were done with raster format data. Using grid cells has many advantages for sensitivity analysis, such as the relative ease of changing resolution or systematically adding error to a thematic map (Goodchild, 1990). Our study used vector format, including point data for the observations. This allowed us to test the effects of locational precision and accuracy that would not have been possible in a raster format unless grid cell size had been prohibitively small.

Sensitivity analysis should be considered in any GIS analysis where absolute truth cannot be determined and where the management decision could be controversial. If conducted at the pilot study stage, sensitivity analysis can be used to determine critical levels of resolution and accuracy needed to achieve the objectives of the database. It need not be technically difficult; the application demonstrated here used only standard GIS and statistical routines. Someday, a sensitivity analysis capability may even be a generic GIS function (Openshaw, 1989). Sensitivity analysis has the advantage that sources of error and their propagation do not need to be known exactly. The analyst need only make reasonable assumptions about data uncertainties. The risk in sensitivity analysis is in potentially adopting a "black box" view of the model, ignoring important questions about error propagation in GIS analyses. The benefit of sensitivity analysis would be in providing a measure of reliability of GIS output products to decision makers.

ACKNOWLEDGMENTS

The GIS database development was funded by California Department of Fish and Game (CDF&G) Contract C-2077. The senior author was supported by NASA Grant NAGW-1743 during the writing of the paper. We would like to thank Ron Jurek and Sherry Teresa of CDF&G, Linda Blum of the National Audubon Society, and the staff of the U. S. Fish and Wildlife Service office in Ventura, California, for their collaboration in this project. Much of the data input (drafting, digitizing, labeling, and editing the land-use/land-cover maps) was performed by a large number of undergraduate interns at UCSB. Joe Scepan, Marco Painho, and Brean Duncan played key roles in the design and development of the condor GIS database. Their collective efforts are warmly appreciated. Our thanks also to Mike Goodchild for thoughtful comments on the manuscript.

REFERENCES

Agee, J.K., S.C.F. Stitt, M. Nyquist, and R. Root, 1989. A geographic analysis of historical grizzly bear sightings in the North Cascades. *Photogrammetric Engineering & Remote Sensing*, 55:1637–1642.

Alexander, E. R., 1989. Sensitivity analysis in complex decision models. *Journal of the American Planning Association*, 55:323–333.

Davis, F. W., J. E. Estes, J. Scepan, M. Painho, and D. Stoms, 1988. *California Condor Database Project*. Final Report-Year 1, California Department of Fish and Game Contract C-2077, Sacramento.

Davis, F. W., J. Scepan, M. Painho, D. Stoms, B. Duncan, and C. Cogan, 1989. *California Condor Database Project*. Final Report-Year 2, California Department of Fish and Game Contract C-2077, Sacramento.

Davis, F. W., and J. Dozier, 1990. Information analysis of a spatial database for ecological land classification. *Photogrammetric Engineering & Remote Sensing*, 56:605–613.

Davis, F. W., and S. Goetz, 1990. Modeling vegetation pattern using digital terrain data. *Landscape Ecology*, 4:69–80.

Davis, F. W., D. M. Stoms, J. E. Estes, J. Scepan, and J. M. Scott, 1990. An information systems approach to the preservation of biological diversity. *International Journal of Geographical Information Systems*, 4:55–78.

Ferrier, S., and A. P. Smith, 1990. Using geographical information systems for biological survey design, analysis, and extrapolation. *Australian Biologist*, 3:105–116.

Goodchild, M. F., 1990. Modeling error in spatial databases, *Proceedings of GIS/LIS'90*, Anaheim, California, 7-10 November 1990, American Society for Photogrammetry and Remote Sensing and American Congress on Surveying and Mapping, Bethesda, Maryland, pp. 154–162.

Heinen, J. T., and J. G. Lyon, 1989. The effects of changing weighting factors on wildlife habitat index values: A sensitivity analysis. *Photogrammetric Engineering & Remote Sensing*, 55:1445–1447.

Johnson, E. V., D. L. Aulman, D. A. Clendenen, G. Guliasi, L. M. Morton, P. I. Principe, and G. M. Wegener, 1983. California condor: Activity patterns and age composition in a foraging area. *American Birds*, 37: 941–945.

Laymon, S. A., and J. A. Reid, 1986. Effects of grid-cell size on tests of a Spotted Owl HSI model, *Wildlife 2000: Modeling Habitat Relationships of Terrestrial Vertebrates* (Jared Verner, Michael L. Morrison, and C. John Ralph, editors), The University of Wisconsin Press, Madison, Wisconsin, pp. 93–96.

Lodwick, W. A., W. Monson, and L. Svoboda, 1990. Attribute error and sensitivity analysis of map operations in geographical information systems. *International Journal of Geographical Information Systems*, 4:413–428.

Lyon, J. G., J. T. Heinen, R. A. Mead, and N. E. G. Roller, 1987. Spatial data for modeling wildlife habitat. *Journal of Surveying Engineering*, 113:88–100.

Mead, R. A., T. L. Sharik, S. P. Prisely, and J. T. Heinen, 1981. A computerized spatial analysis system for assessing wildlife habitat from vegetation maps. *Canadian Journal of Remote Sensing*, 7:395–400.

Neu, C. W., C. R. Byers, and J. M. Peek, 1974. A technique for analysis of utilization-availability data. *Journal of Wildlife Management*, 38:541–545.

Openshaw, S., 1989. Learning to live with errors in spatial databases, *The Accuracy of Spatial Data Bases* (Michael Goodchild and Sucharita Gopal, editors), Taylor & Francis, London, pp. 263–276.

Ramapriyan, H. K., R. K. Boyd, F. J. Gunther, and Y. C. Lu, 1981. Sensitivity of geographic information system outputs to errors in remotely sensed data, *Proceedings of Machine Processing of Remotely Sensed Data Symposium*, pp. 555–566.

Raphael, M. G., and B. G. Marcot, 1986. Validation of a wildlife-habitat relationships model: Vertebrates in a douglas-fir sere, *Wildlife 2000: Modeling Habitat Relationships of Terrestrial Vertebrates* (Jared Verner, Michael L. Morrison, and C. John Ralph, editors), The University of Wisconsin Press, Madison, Wisconsin, pp. 129–138.

Scepan, J., F. Davis, and L. L. Blum, 1987. A geographic information system for managing California condor habitat, *Proceedings of GIS'87*, 26-30 October 1987, San Francisco, California, American Society for Photogrammetry and Remote Sensing and American Congress on Surveying and Mapping, Falls Church, Virginia, pp. 476–486.

Snyder, N. F. R., and E. V. Johnson, 1985. Photographic censusing of the 1982-1983 California condor population. *The Condor*, 87: 1–13.

Turner, M. G., R. V. O'Neill, R. H. Gardner, and B. T. Milne, 1989. Effects of changing spatial scale on the analysis of landscape pattern. *Landscape Ecology*, 3: 153–162.

Walker, P. A., and D. M. Moore, 1988. SIMPLE: An inductive modelling and mapping tool for spatially-oriented data. *International Journal of Geographical Information Systems*, 2:347–363.

White, G. C., and R. A. Garrott, 1986. Effects of biotelemetry triangulation error on detecting habitat selection. *Journal of Wildlife Management*, 50: 509–513.

———, 1990. *Analysis of Wildlife Radio-Tracking Data*. Academic Press, Inc., San Diego.

Wilbur, S. R., W. D. Carrier, J. C. Borneman, and R. W. Mallette, 1972. Distribution and numbers of the California condor, 1966-1971. *American Birds*, 26: 819–823.

Wiens, J. A., 1986. Spatial scale and temporal variation in studies of shrubsteppe birds, *Community Ecology* (Jared Diamond and Ted J. Case, editors), Harper & Row, New York, pp. 154–172.

SECTION 8

Land Use

Overview

Berry starts this section by illustrating the use of a GIS conflict resolution model for conservation, research, and development land use types in Botany Bay. In the next paper, Lo and Shipman discuss using image overlaying and binary masking to quantitatively reveal land use change dynamics in Hong Kong. The final article by Trietz et al. combines satellite, GIS, and Global Positioning System (GPS) technologies to map land use in the rural-urban fringe of Toronto, Canada.

Suggested Additional Reading

De Brouwer, H., C. Valenzuela, L. Valencia, and K. Sijmons, 1990. Rapid Assessment of Urban Growth Using GIS-RS Techniques. ITC Journal. 1990(3):233-235.

Dueker, K. J., and P. B. DeLacy, 1990. GIS in the Land Development Planning Process: Balancing the Needs of Land Use Planners and Real Estate Developers. Journal of the American Planning Association. 56:483-491.

Levine, J., and J. D. Landis, 1989. Geographic Information System for Local Planning. Journal of the American Planning Association. 55:209-220.

Nellis, M. D., K. Lulla, and J. Jensen, 1990. Interfacing Geographic Information Systems and Remote Sensing for Rural Land-Use Analysis. Photogrammetric Engineering and Remote Sensing. 56(3):329-331.

Tan, Y. R., and S. F. Shih, 1990. GIS in Monitoring Agricultural Land Use Changes and Well Assessment. Transactions of the ASAE. 33:1147-1152.

GIS Resolves Land Use Conflicts: A Case Study

BY JOSEPH K. BERRY

This article is based on an application sponsored by MacArthur Foundation under the direction of the Tropical Resources Institute, Yale University. It demonstrates the important concepts in the development and analysis of a spatial database for the Botany Bay vicinity, St. Thomas, U.S. Virgin Islands. Its objective is to familiarize readers with the practical considerations and potential capabilities of computer-assisted map analysis in resource planning and management. All of the analyses presented are academic and do not represent actual plans under consideration — the material is presented for demonstration purposes only.

Maps traditionally have provided precise placement of physical features, primarily for navigation through unfamiliar terrain and seas. More recently, analysis of mapped data for decision making has become an important part of resource planning. During the 1960s, manual analytic procedures for overlaying maps were popular. These techniques mark an important turning point in the use of maps — from emphasizing physical description of geographic space to spatially prescribing appropriate management actions.

The movement from descriptive to prescriptive mapping has set the stage for revolutionary concepts of map structure, content and use. GIS technology provides the means for bringing about such a transition. In one sense, GIS technology is similar to conventional map processing involving map sheets and drafting aids such as pens, rub-on shading, rulers, planimeters, dot grids and acetate sheets for light-table overlays. In another sense, the systems provide a vast array of analytic capabilities enabling managers to address complex issues in entirely new ways.

GIS technology has several roles in spatial information processing. First, it is viewed as a tool for computer mapping, emphasizing the creation and update of traditional map products. From this perspective, GIS is a purely descriptive graphical output of information provided by the user. GIS then became viewed as a technology for spatial database management, providing a linkage between descriptive attributes and geographic locations. From this perspective, GIS still is purely descriptive — graphical summaries of spatial data queries.

More recently, the roles of GIS as a map production tool and a database technology evolved to one of a "revolution" in which capabilities for interpretation of mapped data are part of the GIS — map analysis procedures addressing prescriptive applications. Within this context, the interrelationships among mapped data become the focus. Entirely new spatial information is created as users derive and interpret landscape factors for specific management activities. As a means of demonstrating GIS technology in resource planning, a demonstration database and sample analyses are described in detail here.

Database Development

The western portion of St. Thomas, U.S. Virgin Islands, comprises the demonstration site. A nested database centered on Botany Bay and consisting of three resolution windows was developed (Figure 1). Several primary data planes were digitized from two adjacent U.S Geological Survey (USGS) topographic sheets. The data layers included island boundaries, elevation, roads, geographic points and cultural features. Ocean depth was digitized from a combination of National Oceanic and Atmospheric Administration and locally produced navigational charts. A data plane indicating neighborhood districts was

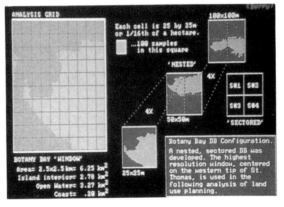

Figure 1.

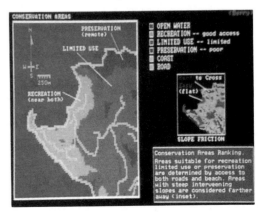

Figure 2.

See page 376 for color plates of Figures 1, and 2.

Figure 3.

See page 376 for color plates of Figure 3.

obtained from a tourist map published by the local Merchants' Association. The digitized data then were converted to the three resolution windows and stored as separate databases. These encoded data were used to derive maps of slope, aspect, proximity to road, proximity to coast, watersheds, "coastalsheds" and visual exposure to coastline.

Map Analysis

Four analyses were performed using the high-resolution Botany Bay vicinity database. The first analysis investigates the best areas for conservation uses including recreation, limited use and preservation. The rankings are based on relative accessibility to both existing roads and the coastline. The second model identifies the best areas for ecological research by characterizing watershed conditions and the "coastalsheds" they influence. The third analysis determines the best locations for residential development considering several engineering, aesthetic and legal factors. The final model addresses the best allocation of land, simultaneously considering all three potential landscape uses. The analyses presented are hypothetical and do not represent actual plans under consideration.

Defining Conservation Areas

A map of accessibility to existing roads and the coastline forms the basis of the Conservation Areas Model. In determining access, the slope of the intervening terrain is considered. The "slope-weighted" proximity from the roads and from the coastline were calculated. In these calculations, areas that appear geographically near a road actually may be much less accessible. For example, the coastline may be a

"stone's throw away" from the road, but if it's at the foot of a cliff, it may be inaccessible for recreation.

The two weighted-proximity maps from both the roads and the coast were combined into an overall map of accessibility. The final step involved interpreting relative access into conservation uses (Figure 2). Recreation was identified for areas near both roads and the coast. Intermediate access areas were designated for limited use. Areas half of a kilometer or more away from both were designated as preservation areas.

Defining Ecological Research Areas

The characterization of the Botany Bay area for ecological research involved several submodels. The first uses the elevation map to identify individual watersheds. The Target Rock, Botany Bay and Sandy Bay watersheds were elected because of the researchers' requirements that they be relatively large, totally contained areas. Another submodel develops a summary table of watershed characteristics, such as accessibility and terrain conditions, which is valuable in planning ecological experiments and control areas. The final submodel used the prevailing southerly current to identify and then summarize the coastal areas influenced by each of the three research watersheds.

Defining Areas for Development

To determine the "best" development locations, several maps describing engineering, aesthetic and legal factors were considered. The following is an outline of these factors:
• Engineering
  – gentle slopes
  – close to roads
• Aesthetics
  – close to coast
  – good view of coast
  – westerly aspect
• Legal constraints
  – 100-meter set-back from coast

  – no slopes greater than 50 percent

The engineering and aesthetic considerations were treated as gradients. This approach interprets the data as relative rankings, or preferences, for development. For example, an area viewing twice as much shoreline as another location is ranked twice as desirable. On the other hand, legal constraints were treated as critical factors. For example, an area within the 100-meter set-back is considered unacceptable, regardless of its aesthetic or engineering rankings.

Figure 4 is a flowchart of the Development Areas Model. The "boxes" represent maps, and the "lines" represent processing operations. The schematic maps on the left identify encoded data, termed Primary Maps. These data are transformed into Derived Maps, which are physical and can be measured, but are more easily calculated. The Interpreted Maps are an abstraction of the physical maps indicating the relative preference of conditions for an intended-use residential development in this case. The final level of abstraction is the Prescriptive Map, created by combining the individual preference expressions into a single map. This general approach of moving from encoded data through increasing levels of abstraction is common to all prescriptive models. The user conceptualizes the important relationships involved in a spatial decision, then uses GIS analytical tools to express them.

To incorporate the engineering considerations, a slope map was created from the encoded map of elevation. The slope map was interpreted on a scale of 0 to 10, as:
• 10 - best (0-5 percent slope)
• 8 - (6-15)

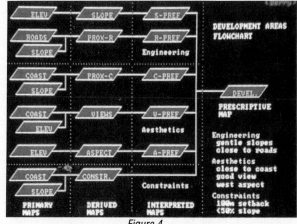

Figure 4.

See page 377 for color plate of Figure 4.

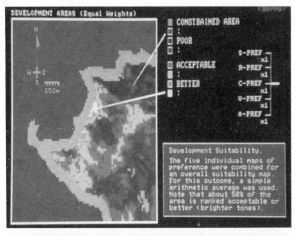

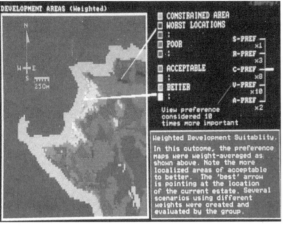

Figure 5.

- 6 - (16-25)
- 3 - (26-40)
- 0 - worst (greater than 40)

These criteria recognize the increased site preparation and building costs on steeper slopes. A related concern characterizes the preference for proximity to existing roads, in recognition of the increased costs of environmental disturbance and driveway construction as a function of distance. The map of effective proximity to roads was interpreted on a similar "0 to 10 goodness scale."

The aesthetics consideration used in this model favored being near the coast and having a good view. A slope-weighted proximity-to-coast map was created, then interpreted as:

- 10 - best (0-100 effective units away)
- 9 - (101-150)
- 8 - (151-200)
- 6 - (201-300)
- 4 - (301-400)
- 3 - (401-600)
- 1 - worst (more than 600)

To determine the visual aesthetics, the shoreline's "viewshed" was generated by computing the lines of sight in all directions over the eleva-

tion map from all of the shoreline locations. The procedure is similar to standing on the shore and noting all the locations you can see, then moving down the beach 25 meters and again noting the visual connections. When all shore locations have been considered, a "visual exposure" map is formed, with each inland location assigned a value equal to the number of times it was seen from the shoreline. The locations with high visual exposure values are interpreted as having the best views.

The last consideration indicates the preference for west-facing slopes. Such orientation allows a greater chance to view the setting sun. Easterly orientations were ranked next best as they provide inspiring sunrises for energetic individuals.

To determine legal constraints to development, simple proximity to coast and steepness were considered. Maps of distance to coast and slope were interpreted as:

- 0 - unsuitable (less than 100 meters from coast)
- 0 - unsuitable (greater than 50 percent slope)

Figure 5a shows a composite map containing the simple arithmetic average of the five separate preference maps. Environmentally constrained locations mask these results and are shown as light grey (values within constrained areas are assigned the preference value of 0). Note that approximately half of the land area is ranked "acceptable" or better (warmer tones). When averaging the five preference maps, all criteria were considered equally important.

The analysis was extended to generate a weighted suitability map favoring certain criteria, such as:

- view preference times-10 (most important)
- coast proximity times-8
- road proximity times-3
- aspect preference times-2
- slope preference times-1 (least important)

The resulting map of the weighted composite is presented in Figure 5b. Note that a smaller portion of the land is ranked as "acceptable" or better. Also note the spatial distribution of these prime areas are localized to three distinct clusters.

Three important cartographic modeling aspects are illustrated in the Development Areas Model — dynamic simulation, concise expression and flexibility. By changing parameters (preference values for slope, proximity, visual exposure and orientation), a user can simulate numerous alternatives and gain insight into the sensitivity of the planned activity to the actual spatial patterns of the various factors. It is important to note that the decision maker is interactively interrogating the model as new maps are progressively generated.

The quantitative nature of GIS technology provides an effective framework for concise expression of complex spatial relationships. The processing flowchart shown in Figure 4 is an example. The process uses a series of successive map operations to derive intermediate maps, and ultimately creates a final map of development suitability. The flowchart establishes a succinct format for communicating the logic, assumptions and relationships embodied in the analysis.

Finally, the GIS approach encourages decision makers to change the

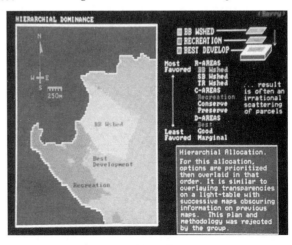

Figure 6.

See page 377 for color plates of Figures 5, and 6

model as new conditions or insights are developed. For example, the effect of a proposed road could be incorporated. The proposed route would be digitized and added to the existing road map. The model can be rerun using the revised road map and a new suitability map can be generated. Thus, a decision maker becomes an active participant in the analysis rather than choosing among a few alternatives provided by the analyst.

Conflict Resolution Model

The previous three analyses determined the best use of the Botany Bay area considering conservation, research or development criteria in a unilateral manner. However, most land use decisions require resolution of competing uses. Three approaches to resolving conflicts include "hierarchical dominance," "multiple use" and "tradeoff." Hierarchical dominance assumes certain land uses are more important and, therefore, supersede all other uses. Multiple use, on the other hand, identifies compatible uses and assigns several uses to a single location. Tradeoff recognizes conflicting uses at individual locations and attempts to develop the best mix of uses by choosing one over the others on a parcel-by-parcel basis. Effective land use decisions involve elements of each of these approaches.

From a map processing perspective, the hierarchical approach is easily expressed in a quantitative manner and results in a deterministic solution. Once the political system identifies a superseding use, it is relatively easy to map these areas and assign a value indicating the desire to protect them from other uses. Multiple use also is technically simple from a map analysis context, though often difficult from a policy context. When compatible uses are identified, a unique value identifying both uses is assigned to all areas with the joint condition.

Conflict occurs when the uses are not entirely compatible. In these instances, quantitative solutions to the allocation of land use are difficult, if not impossible, to implement. The complex interaction of the frequency and juxtapositioning of several competing uses is still most effectively dealt with by human intervention. GIS technology assists in these instances by deriving a "conflict" map that indicates

alternative uses for each location. Once in this visual form, the decision maker can assess the patterns of conflicting uses and determine land use allocations.

Hierarchical consideration of all three uses for the Botany Bay vicinity was performed. A map identifying the best development areas was isolated from the Development Areas Map. Similarly, maps of just the recreation areas and the research areas were isolated from the Conservation and Research Areas maps, respectively. Figure 6 shows the result of a hierarchical combination of these data. For this composite, development was least favored, recreation next, with the Botany Bay watershed taking final precedence. Note that the resultant map contains very little area for development and is fragmented into disjointed parcels — infeasible for development. The hierarchical approach often results in such infeasible solutions. What is clear in "policy space" is frequently muddled in the complex reality of geographic space.

An alternate approach is to create a map indicating all potential land uses for each location in a project area — a comprehensive "conflicts" map. Figure 7a is such a map. Note that most of the Botany Bay area does not have competing uses (dark green). In most applications, this counter-intuitive condition exists. However, interested parties and decision makers assume conflict is everywhere. In the absence of the spatial guidance of a conflicts map, proponents attempt to convince others that their opinion is best. With a conflicts map, attention is quickly focused on possible tradeoffs affording enlightened compromise.

Figure 7b presents one interpretation of the information on the Botany Bay conflict map. This "best" allocation involved several

Figure 7.

individuals' subjective tradeoffs among areas of conflict, with research receiving the greatest consideration. It was decided that the Target Rock and Sandy Bay watersheds should remain intact. These watersheds have less use conflict than the Botany Bay watershed.

The remaining good development areas were set aside, insuring that all development was contained within the Botany Bay watershed. In fact, this constraint would provide a third research setting to investigate development, with the other two watersheds serving as a control. Structures would be constrained to the approximately 20 contiguous hectares identified as best for development. The limited use area between the development cluster and the coast would be for the exclusive use of the residents. The Sandy Bay and Target Rock research areas would provide additional buffering and open space.

Conservation uses then received the group's attention. This step was easy because the area extending from St. Thomas Point along the southern coast was identified for recreation with minimal conflict. Finally, the remaining small "salt

See page 377 for color plate of Figure 7.

and pepper" parcels were absorbed by their surrounding "limited or preservation use" areas. In all, this provided a fairly rational land use allocation result.

The last step in the analysis may seem anticlimactic. After a great deal of "smoke and dust raising" about computer processing, the final assignment of land uses involved a large amount of subjective interpretation. This point highlights the capabilities and limitations of GIS technology. GIS provides significant advances in how we manage and analyze mapped data. It rapidly and tirelessly allows us to assemble detailed spatial information. It also allows us to incorporate sophisticated and realistic landscape interpretations, such as visual exposure and weighted distance. GIS doesn't, however, provide an artificial intelligence for land use decision making. GIS technology greatly enhances our decision-making capabilities, but does not replace them.

Management of land has always required spatial information as its cornerstone. However, purely descriptive landscape maps are not enough. They must be translated into prescriptive maps expressing the interrelationships among mapped data in terms of the decision at hand. GIS technology provides the means to more fully integrate these mapped data into resource and land use decision making. 🌐

Joseph K. Berry is a principal in Berry & Associates and a senior associate in Training and Professional Development for GIS World, Inc. He can be reached at 19 Old Town Square, Fort Collins, CO 80524, USA.

Editor's Note: This article is based on a chapter in *Geographical Information Systems: Principals and Applications*, Vol 2. Longman, London, pp. 285-295.

References

Berry, J.K., et. al. 1989. *Development and Analysis of a Spatial Data Base for the Botany Bay Vicinity*, Vol. 2. Final report entitled *Natural and Cultural Resources in the United States Virgin Islands: Research, Education and Management Needs.* Tropical Resources Institute, Yale University.

SIS. 1986. *pMAP User's Guide and Technical Reference, Professional Map Analysis Package (pMAP)*, Spatial Information Systems, Inc., Springfield, Virginia, USA.

A GIS Approach to Land-Use Change Dynamics Detection

C. P. *Lo* and *Robert L. Shipman*
Department of Geography, University of Georgia, Athens, GA 30602

ABSTRACT: A Geographic Information Systems (GIS) approach was applied to assess the impact of new town development in Tuen Mun, New Territories, Hong Kong, on the environment through integrating past and current aerial photographic data of land use with topographic and geologic data. The image overlaying and binary masking techniques were found to be particularly useful in revealing quantitatively the change dynamics in each category of land use which was impossible to accomplish by the conventional change detection technique. The same method was applied to assess the impact of such terrain attributes as slopes, surface hydrology, and geology on these land-use changes. It was revealed that the government had some successes in controlling the spread of eroded badland with reforestation as the intensity of urban land use increased, although the reforestation was hampered by rapid surface runoff on steep slopes. The GIS approach was evaluated to be accurate and capable of providing the planners with more insightful assessment of the impact of their actions on the environment.

INTRODUCTION

SEQUENTIAL AERIAL PHOTOGRAPHS have been commonly employed by planners to detect land-use change over a period of time in a region (e.g., Avery, 1965; Faulkner, 1968; Richter, 1969; Adeniyi, 1980; Campbell, 1983; and Lo and Wu, 1984). The method involves manually interpreting land-use categories from aerial photographs for each period of time and measuring their areas using a dot grid, planimeter, or digitizer. By comparing the area data between two or more periods of time, the predominant land-use changes in the region can be detected. However, this type of land-use change data generated is static, and cannot reveal the processes of changes that have occurred in space for each category of land use, i.e., the dynamics of land-use change, without going further into a laborious cross-referencing of each category of change in its spatial location

The recent advancement in microcomputer-based Geographic Information System (GIS) technology has availed the planners of a powerful tool which, by integrating spatial data collected from different sources and in different formats, allows overlaying of two or more maps to be carried out with ease (e.g., Williams, 1985; Wheeler and Ridd, 1985; Johnston et al., 1988; Lindhult et al., 1988; Hathout, 1988; Berry and Berry, 1988). In this paper, the use of a low-cost microcomputer-based GIS — IDRISI (Eastman, 1988a, 1988b) in land-use change detection from sequential aerial photographs is explained. In particular, the usefulness of the binary masking method in revealing the dynamics of land-use change and the impact of the change on the physical environment will be demonstrated. Finally, the accuracy of the GIS approach for change detection will also be evaluated.

THE STUDY AREA

The site selected for this application is East Teun Mun in West New Territories of Hong Kong, which is dominated by a rapidly developing new town called Tuen Mun (Figure 1). Hong Kong, which is a British Colony with a total land area of a mere 1,000 km² located on the South China coast, has experienced large population increases accompanied by dramatic economic growth since 1949. Most of its population was concentrated on a small metropolitan area occupying only 12 percent of the land area of Hong Kong. In order to decentralize population growth, the Hong Kong Government has, since the early 1960s, started building new towns in the suburban and rural areas. These new towns are self-contained and are characterized by a mixture of

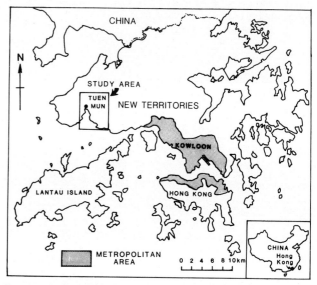

FIG. 1. Location map of the study area: East Tuen Mun, New Territories, Hong Kong.

residential, commercial, and industrial uses. Residential use is dominated by high-density low-cost public housing planned and operated by the government. Today, as the level of affluence of the population increases, the government's new town objective has also shifted to emphasize higher quality public housing and a better planned urban environment (Leung, 1986). Teun Mun is a typical example of this new generation of new towns under development since 1975 (New Territories Development Department, 1977).

The Tuen Num region, however, is restricted in growth by some physical constraints. These include limited land areas with gentle slopes and high erosion potential of the surrounding areas. The new town itself, which is sandwiched between two plateaux, was built on deposits of alluvium and colluvium of Tuen Mun Valley and on land reclaimed from Castle Peak Bay (Figure 2). According to the survey conducted by the Geotechnical Control Office (1987), the Tuen Mun valley is thought to be a fault controlled "graben" structure with a thrust fault forming the western plateau which rises to a height of 583 metres. The

PHOTOGRAMMETRIC ENGINEERING & REMOTE SENSING,
Vol. 56, No. 11, November 1990, pp. 1483–1491.

FIG. 2. Stereogram of East Tuen Mun study area 5 January 1987 (original photographic scale 1:40,000). A = Low Density Urban; B = High Density Urban; C = Transportation; D = Cultivated Land; E = Argicultural/Residential; F = Mixed Woodland; G = Reservoir; H = Bays; I = Eroded Badland; J = Barren Land; and K = Transitional (Copyright: Hong Kong Government).

eastern plateau reaches an elevation of 511 metres with a substantial part of the area above 300 m. The two plateaux are made up mainly of granites with essentially similar mineralogy, which exhibit distinct rock jointing. There are also numerous faults criss-crossing the area, the most dominat of which trend north to south with a lesser curvilinear series trending east northeast to west southwest. The combination of geology, slope, and a monsoonal climate favors weathering and erosion in these plateau areas. The granite ridgecrests and sideslopes are often weathered to a depth of at least 20 m. Sheet erosion, rill erosion, and gully erosion were found to occur in different parts of the study area, thus accounting for a significant level of soil loss which, in turn, results in thin vegetation cover dominated by grass and shrubs. All these have given rise to slope instability. The new town itself is bisected into two halves by a north-south trending ditch of 80-metre width, which is really an artifically channelled Tuen Mun River for the purpose of accommodating the very rapid runoff from the surrounding hill slopes in order to avert flooding during periods of heavy rainstorms. The study site is, therefore, an environmentally sensitive area, the use of which requires careful planning.

DATA AND METHODOLOGY

The best source of land-use and land-cover information at different times is aerial photographs, for which Hong Kong has excellent coverage. Two sets acquired on 23 November 1976 and 5 January 1987 at a nominal scale of 1:25,000 and 1:40,000, respectively, were selected for this study because the year 1976 marked the beginning of visible new town development in Tuen Mun while the year 1987 signified the maturing of the new town

after 11 years. Full technical details of these aerial photographs are shown in Table 1. A total of seven photographs was employed for this research—four for 1976 and three for 1987 (Figures 2 and 3).

Complementing these aerial photographs are topographic and geologic maps of the study site at 1:50,000 scale, from which terrain attributes relating to elevation, slope, aspect, surface hydrology, watershed, geology, and transportation were extracted (Table 2).

The methodology for land-use change dynamics detection involves five stages: (1) data extraction, (2) data capture, (3) data integration, (4) data analysis, and (5) output of results.

TABLE 1. TUEN MUN AERIAL PHOTOGRAPHIC INFORMATION.

	1976 Photographs	1987 Photographs
Date of acquisition	23 November 1976	5 January 1987
Time of acquisition	2:10 P.M. local time	11:42 A.M. local time
Scale	1:25,000	1:40,000
Focal length	152.53 mm	152.12 mm
Flying height	3,810 m	6,096 m
Camera type	Wild RC10	Wild RC10A
Frame numbers	16511-16514	A08422-A08424
Film format	23 × 23 cm	23 × 23 cm
Endlap	70%	64%
Quality	very good	good
Agency	Surveying and Mapping Office, Hong Kong Goverment	Surveying and Mapping Office, Hong Kong Government

FIG. 3. Stereogram of East Tuen Mun study area, 23 November 1976 (original photographic scale 1:25,000). The annotations are the same as in Figure 2. (Copyright: Hong Kong Government).

TABLE 2. DATABASE ATTRIBUTES AND MAP SOURCES.

Attribute	Source
Elevation	Hong Kong 1:25,000-scale topographic map: Sheet 5, Castle Peak; Sheet 6, Yuen Long. Hong Kong Government, 1969.
Slope	derived from elevation data
Aspect	derived from slope data
Surface Hydrology	Map of the Territory of Hong Kong, 1:50,000-scale: Sheet 1 of 2. Hong Kong Government, 1986.
Watershed	derived from aspect data
Geology	Geological Map of Hong Kong, Kowloon, and the New Territories, 1:50,000-scale: Sheet 1 of 2. Hong Kong Government, 1972.
Transportation	Map of the Territory of Hong Kong, 1:50,000-scale: Sheet 1 of 2. Hong Kong Government, 1986.

TABLE 3. MODIFIED U.S.G.S. LAND-USE/LAND-COVER CATEGORIES.

U.S.G.S. Level II Code Equivalent	Description	Code
11,16	Low Density Urban	11
12-15	High Density Urban	12
14	Transportation	14
21	Cultivated Land	21
None	Agricultural/Residential	24
43	Mixed Woodland	43
53	Reservoirs and Ponds	53
54	Bays and Estuaries	54
None	Eroded Badland	70
74	Barren Land	74
76	Transitional Land	76

DATA EXTRACTION

The primary data extraction is manual interpretation of the aerial photographs for land-use/land-cover information of the study area based on a modified Level II classification scheme (Table 3). Because of the high degree of intermixing between residential, commercial, and industrial uses, two general categories of urban use, namely, low-density and high-density, were identified. The area, being rural in nature, was also characterized by the occurrence of village clusters and their associated agricultural activities. Manual interpretation was aided

by collateral materials from Tuen Mun supplied by New Territories Development Department (1977) and Geotechnical General Office (1988) as well as generalized land-use maps of Hong Kong produced by the Lands Department, Hong Kong Government in 1977 and 1982. All these efforts ensured that the interpretation accuracy met the minimum 85 per cent required by the U.S. Geological Survey's classification scheme (Andersen et al., 1976).

The land-use catergories were delineated onto clear mylar overlays for the aerial photographs of each year. This was executed both stereoscopically with the aid of a mirror stereoscope (3 times to 6 times magnification) and monoscopically with a hand-held 2 times magnifying glass. The land-use categories delineated on the mylar overlays were then transferred to a

1:25,000-scale base map using a Bausch and Lomb Zoom Transferscope based on common control points between the maps and the aerial photographs. The result was land-use maps of the study area for two different years, which could be *accurately* registered together (Figure 4).

Data Capture

Data capture refers to the digitizing process by which map data are transformed to digital format for storage in the computer. For this project, a Summagraphics Microgrid II digitizer(with an accuracy of ±0.254 mm and a resolution of 40 lines per mm) connected to an IBM personal computer and a computer program called CAPTURE were employed for encoding. The digitized

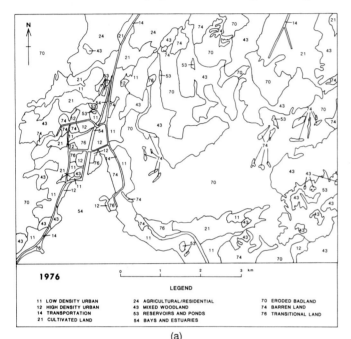

1976

LEGEND

11 LOW DENSITY URBAN	24 AGRICULTURAL/RESIDENTIAL	70 ERODED BADLAND
12 HIGH DENSITY URBAN	43 MIXED WOODLAND	74 BARREN LAND
14 TRANSPORTATION	53 RESERVOIRS AND PONDS	76 TRANSITIONAL LAND
21 CULTIVATED LAND	54 BAYS AND ESTUARIES	

(a)

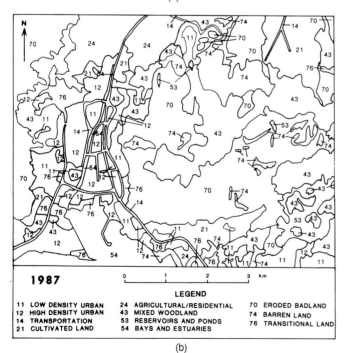

1987

LEGEND

11 LOW DENSITY URBAN	24 AGRICULTURAL/RESIDENTIAL	70 ERODED BADLAND
12 HIGH DENSITY URBAN	43 MIXED WOODLAND	74 BARREN LAND
14 TRANSPORTATION	53 RESERVOIRS AND PONDS	76 TRANSITIONAL LAND
21 CULTIVATED LAND	54 BAYS AND ESTUARIES	

(b)

FIG. 4. Land-use maps of East Tuen Mun as interpreted from aerial photographs for the years (a) 1976 and (b) 1987.

coordinates of points from the map were then transformed into Universal Transverse Meractor (UTM) coordinates using four to five ground control points in UTM coordinates and an affine transformation program. Each land-use map of the study area was individually digitized and transformed into UTM coordinates. The resultant root mean square error in planimetry ($RMSE_{xy}$) at the 1:25,000 map scale was found to be ± 6.0 metres at 90 percent level of confidence, which is better than the ±7.5 metres planimetric error permitted by the U.S. National Map Accuracy Standards.

Other maps of varying scales that have been digitized and transformed in the same manner included elevation, geology, and surface hydrology. A digital terrain model (DEM) was created by digitizing over 800 sampled elevations from the topographic map.

Data Integration

Data integration is the process by which all "layers" of the digital data are made to conform in format and geographic reference. Because the GIS software (IDRISI) employs a grid-based or raster format, all the digitized maps obtained in the data capture stage, which are in vector format, have to be converted to raster format using the rasterizing algorithm supplied by IDRISI. The grid size selected was 20 by 20 metres, which is compatible with the scale and resolution of the aerial photographs used in a Level II land-use classification. The grid size is further constrained by the storage capacity of the microcomputer. After the vector-to-raster conversion of the map data, a 3 by 3 mode filter was passed over each data layer to eliminate any "slivers" which tended to occur between digitized polygons sharing common boundaries (Figure 5). Finally, each data layer was registered to a common grid system or map projection. For this application, the UTM (Universal Transverse Mercator) projection was used.

Data Analysis

The basic data analysis techniques employed for land-use change dynamics detection and impact assessment are image overlaying and binary masking (Pilon *et al.*, 1988). Each pixel value for the 1976 land-use image was subtracted from its corresponding pixel location on the 1987 land-use image. The result was a new image made up of positive, negative, and zero values. Zero values denoted pixels where no change has occurred, while positive and negative values represented pixels where change has taken place. The positive and negative values were reclassified to 1, leaving unchanged the zero values. The resultant image was a binary change mask consisting only of "zeros" and "ones" (Figure 6). Values of "ones" represent areas which have undergone change in land use since 1976. "Zeros" represent areas where no change in land use has occurred. The binary change mask was then multiplied to each of the original land-use images, thus giving rise to a masked classification image for 1976 and 1987 individually. The masked 1976 image indicated spatial locations of those land-use categories that would be lost, while the masked 1987 image indicated the corresponding spatial locations of those land-use categories that had been gained (Figure 7). Quantitative areal data of the overall land-use changes as well as the gains and losses in each category of land use between 1976 and 1987 could be compiled for the study area. In addition, land-use change maps could also be produced.

The next stage of data analysis was to assess the relationship between the changed land-use categories and the physical environment. Only three terrain characteristics were used: slope, geology, and surface hydrology. From the digital elevation model obtained in the data capture stage, a slope map was produced by applying a second interpolation function of the IDRISI program. The binary land-use change mask was multiplied to each of the

Fig. 5. Rasterized land-use map of East Tuen for the years (a) 1976 and (b) 1987. Key: --- Bays, = = = Transportation, * Low Density Urban, % High Density Urban, & Barren Land, # Transitional Land, $ Eroded Badland, 0 Cultivated Land, 1 Agricultural/Residential, 2 Mixed Woodland, and 4 Reservoirs.

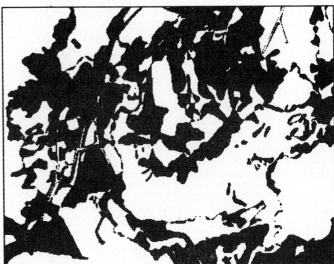

Fig. 6. Map of Binary change mask showing areas which have undergone land-use changes between 1976 and 1987 (black), and areas where no land-use changes have occurred (white).

RESULTS OF ANALYSIS

CHARACTERISTICS OF LAND USE OF THE STUDY AREA AS INTERPRETED FROM AERIAL PHOTOGRAPHS

The land use of East Tuen Mun was characterized by a mixture of urban and rural activities which were readily interpretable from the aerial photographs. Major urban land uses were concentrated in the new town where *High Density Urban Land Use* (12) tended to predominate. This occurred in the form of high-rise buildings which were distinctly identifiable from the stereo-pair of aerial photographs (Figure 2). This class represented an amalgamation of high density residential, commercial and services, and industrial land uses. *Low Density Urban Land Use* (11), on the other hand, was exhibited as low-rise buildings on the aerial photographs, which occurred along the lower hillslopes flanking the new town. These buildings comprised squatter structures, bungalows, and other detached houses. Development of a new town in a rural area required the contruction of highways and roads to link it to the major metropolitan area of Hong Kong. *Transportation* (14), therefore, appeared as a very important form of land use in the study area, which was distinguished by its light tone and narrow linear and curvilinear shape. *Cultivated Land* (21) could still be found along Tuen Mun River and its tributaries with specialization in vegetables and other high-value market gardening crops. Another interesting land use was *Agricultural/Residential* (24), which described the intermixture of village house clusters and small cultivated fields. These represented the sites of villages of the original rural inhibitants in the area. These were found to the north of the new town along Tuen Mun River in close association with the *Cultivated Land* (21). On the mountain areas to the east and west of the new town, *Mixed Woodland* (43) occurred. This composed both deciduous and coniferous tree species. On the aerial photographs, this class of land use was distinguished by very dark tones and fine texture, and was associated frequently with the foothills of the mountainous eroded areas. *Reservoirs and Ponds* (53) were found both in the river plain and the mountain area. In the plain, these were mainly fish ponds associated with the agricultural activities and/or for decorative purpose. In the mountains, they are reservoirs which supply drinking water to the population of Hong Kong. Tai Lam Chung Reservoir, which occupies the drainage basin of Tai Lam River, is the largest

three terrain characteristics maps. In this way, spatial locations of land-use change were correlated with individual terrain characteristics. In order to evaluate the impact of steep slopes on land use in 1976 and 1987, a binary steep slope mask was developed, which distinguished slopes of 24 percent and above. The criterion of 24 percent as the lower limit of steep slopes was suggested on civil engineering grounds by the Geotechnical Control Office in Hong Kong (1988), which regarded slopes of more than 24 percent neither safe nor economical to develop. This binary steep slope mask was multiplied individually to the 1976 and 1987 land-use images in the GIS.

OUTPUT OF RESULTS

The GIS approach permits the results of the analysis to be displayed in maps and table forms. The IDRISI program allows hard copies of maps to be produced in color by the Hewlett-Packard PaintJet Color Graphics Printer. However, because of the cost of color reproduction, only black-and-white pattern maps are used throughout this paper.

290

FIG. 7. Rasterized land-use maps displaying land use categories where changes have occurred: (a) 1976 (losses) and (b) 1987 (gains). For symbol key, see, Figure 5.

photographs and were somewhat darker and more regularly shaped than *Barren Lands* (74) (Figures 2 and 3).

LAND USE CHANGE DYNAMICS

The initial analysis of the 1976 and 1987 land-use map images (Figure 5) by the GIS approach generated Table 4 which displayed the static land-use data of the study area for the two years. It is clear that for both years Eroded Badland was most dominant, followed by Mixed Woodland. However, a comparison of the statistics revealed a decline in Eroded Badland from 36.5 percent to 29.8 percent, and an increase in Mixed Woodland from 20.1 percent to 21.6 percent, while High Density Urban use has jumped dramatically from 1.4 percent to 7.9 percent during this period. Subsequent analyses using the image overlaying and binary masking techniques as explained previously generated Figure 7 and Table 5. Figure 7 pinpointed the spatial locations where land-use changes have taken place. Figure 7(a) indicated the locations of the original land use categories in 1976 which would be changed while Figure 7(b) indicated what the new land-use categories were for the same locations by 1987. Table 5 summarized these changes in terms of "losses" and "gains," and one clearly sees a net gain (+ 6.5 percent) of High Density urban use and a net loss (− 6.7 percent) of Eroded Badland. By comparing the before-change and after-change maps (figure

TABLE 4. LAND USE IN EAST TUEN MUN, 1976 AND 1987.

	1976		1987	
Land Use Class	Pixels*	% of Total	Pixels*	% of Total
11 Low Density Urban	11,049	9.2	7,323	6.1
12 High Density Urban	1,645	1.4	9,480	7.9
14 Transportation	1,396	1.2	3,574	3.0
21 Cultivated Land	11,191	9.3	9,130	7.6
24 Agricultural/ Residential	5,130	4.3	7,976	6.6
43 Mixed Woodland	24,054	20.1	25,934	21.6
53 Reservoirs and Ponds	3,272	2.7	3,027	2.5
54 Bays and Estuaries	10,732	8.9	7,172	6.0
70 Eroded Badland	43,826	36.5	35,774	29.8
74 Barren Land	6,106	5.1	7,517	6.3
76 Transitional Land	1,599	1.3	3,093	2.6
TOTAL	120,000	100.0	120,000	100.0

*Each pixel is a 20 × 20 m cell or 0.04 hectare.

reservoir in this area for this purpose. Tuen Mun new town is located on a bay (Castle Peak Bay) which is being artificially reclaimed southward to provide more land for the new town to develop, hence the category of land use, *Bays and Estuaries* (54). As has already been mentioned, the mountain areas flanking the new town are very susceptible to weathering and erosion, especially along the ridgecrests and sideslopes. The erosion was so well developed that the term "badland" was given to them hence the land-use class *Eroded Badland* (70), which could be distinguished by the light tone on the aerial photographs and its association with ridgecrests and steep slopes. Indeed, gullies could also be detected in areas of intense erosion by stereoscopic examination of the aerial photographs (Figure 2 and 3). The study area also showed *Barren Land* (74), which included rock quarries, highly eroded localized areas where bare rock was evenly exposed, and areas where reclamation or excavation has been undertaken but no development existed. Finally, inside the reclaimed areas of the new town, *Transitional Land* (76) tended to occur. In this class of land use, some type of development was underway, such as in paving or construction. Transitional lands displayed light to medium grey tones on the aerial

TABLE 5. LAND-USE CHANGE IN EAST TUEN MUN 1976-1987. SHOWN ARE THE NUMBER OF PIXELS IN EACH LAND-USE CATEGORY BEFORE (1976) AND AFTER (1987) CHANGES HAVE OCCURRED.

	1976 (Losses)		1987 (Gains)		1976-1987
Land Use Class	Pixels*	% of Total	Pixels*	% of Total	Net Change%
11 Low Density Urban	7,714	6.4	3,988	3.3	−3.1
12 High Density Urban	619	0.5	8,454	7.0	+6.5
14 Transportation	846	0.7	3,024	2.5	+1.8
21 Cultivated Land	4,478	3.7	2,417	2.0	−1.7
24 Agricultural/ Residential	294	0.2	3,140	2.6	+2.4
43 Mixed Woodland	12,146	10.1	14,026	11.7	+1.6
53 Reservoirs and Ponds	248	0.2	3	0.0	−0.2
54 Bays and Estuaries	4,125	3.4	565	0.5	−2.9
70 Eroded Badland	16,886	14.1	8,834	7.4	−6.7
74 Barren Land	5,120	4.3	6,531	5.4	+1.1
76 Transitional Land	1,599	1.3	3,093	2.6	+1.3
Unchanged	65,925	54.9	65,925	54.9	0
TOTAL	120,000	99.8	120,000	99.9	

*Each pixel is a 20 × 20 m cell or 0.04 hectare.

TABLE 6. LAND-USE CHANGE DYNAMICS IN EAST TUEN MUN, 1976-1987*.

Land Use Class	11	12	14	21	24	43	53	54	70	74	76	Total (1987)
11 Low Density Urban	0	304	70	271	0	1,195	75	114	1,203	620	136	3,988
12 High Density Urban	1,842	0	432	857	2	426	81	2,725	267	973	849	8,454
14 Transportation	892	182	0	346	169	109	10	301	105	796	114	3,024
21 Cultivated Land	815	29	21	0	24	765	0	0	341	147	275	2,417
24 Agricultural/Resid.	701	0	119	1,130	0	408	79	0	589	114	0	3,140
43 Mixed Woodland	1,064	0	58	408	99	0	3	20	10,657	1,617	100	14,026
53 Reservoirs and Ponds	0	0	0	0	0	3	0	0	0	0	0	3
54 Bays and Estuaries	217	95	127	2	0	0	0	0	6	5	113	565
70 Eroded Badland	360	0	0	758	0	6,917	0	0	0	787	12	8,834
74 Barren Land	569	0	0	25	0	2,142	0	167	3,628	0	0	6,531
76 Transitional Land	1,254	9	19	681	0	181	0	798	90	61	0	3,093
TOTAL	7,714	619	846	4,478	294	12,146	248	4,125	16,886	5,120	1,599	54,075

*All values are given in numbers of pixels. Each pixel is a 20 × 20 m cell or 0.04 hectares.

7) category by category using the same binary masking method, a picture of the land-use change dynamics in the study area was obtained. Table 6 displayed the constituent components of losses and gains in each category of land use undergoing change. Thus, one knows from Table 5 that 7,714 pixels of Low Density Urban Land were lost. But from Table 6 one finds that, of these 7,714 pixels, 1,842 pixels (or 23.9 percent) were lost to High Density Urban Land, 892 pixels (or 11.6 percent) to Transportation, 815 pixels (or 10.6 percent) to Cultivated Land, 1,064 pixels (or 13.8 percent) to Mixed Woodland, 1,254 pixels (or 16.3 percent) to Transitional Land, and so on. On the other hand, 3,988 pixels of Low Density Urban Land were gained from 304 pixels (7.6 percent) of High Density Urban Land, 70 pixels (1.7 percent) of Transportation, 271 pixels (6.8 percent) of Cultivated Land, 1,195 pixels (30.0 percent) of Mixed Woodland, 1,203 pixels (30.2 percent) of Eroded Badland, and so on (Table 6).

Based on a careful interpretation of the land-use change dynamics revealed in Table 6, one can make the following generalizations:

(1) There was quite a substantial increase in High Density Urban Land at the expense of Low Density Urban Land, probably resulting from clearing the squatter areas (catergorized as Low Density Urban) on the lower hillslopes flanking the new town.

(2) There was a dramatic reduction in Eroded Badland, most of which was converted to Mixed Woodland by 1987. But a very small area of Eroded Badland had also become Low Density Urban Land, with the implications that *either* new squatters continued to spread *or* the government had developed the land.

(3) The Mixed Woodland had increased in area.

(4) In the Reservoirs and Ponds category, a great loss had occurred, apparently resulting from filling up the fish ponds in the cultivated area immediately to the north edge of the new town.

(5) As expected, there was a great loss in Cultivated Land, especially in the area adjacent to the new town where most of the Cultivated Land was converted into urban use. But a large area of Cultivated Land had also become Agricultural/Residential use, probably resulting from Chinese immigrant farmers building their own houses on the cultivated land.

(6) The development of the new town was still in progress even by 1987 because a great increase in Transitional Land occurred.

(7) The fact that much of the new town was built on land reclaimed from the sea was reflected by a great loss in the area of the Bays and Estuaries category.

(8) There was also a great increase in Barren Land resulting from an increase in the number and size of quarries necessitated by the intense building activities in the new town.

RELATIONSHIP BETWEEN LAND-USE CHANGE AND TERRAIN CHARACTERISTICS

Tables 7 and 8 displayed the relationship between land-use change and the three terrain characteristics of steep slopes, surface hydrology, and geology employed for this study, made possible by the same binary masking technique. It is clear from Table 7 that High Density Urban use, which shunned the steep slopes and high surface drainage areas in 1976, established itself on steep slopes and high surface drainage areas by 1987. On the other hand, Eroded Badland located on steep slopes and high surface drainage areas appeared to have decreased in area by 1987, and Mixed Woodland located on steep slopes was also drastically reduced in area by 1987. From Table 8 one sees that steep slopes tended to occur in Sung Kong Granite (medium-grained), Cheung Chau Granite, and Needle Hill Granite (both fine-grained and medium-grained), where, in addition to Colluvium Deposit, Undifferentiated Alluvium, and Reclaimed Land, most of the land-use change during this period was also found. Clearly, the new town development has encroached on steeper slopes and the coastal zone as urban development intensified. While Eroded Badland has decreased and Mixed Woodland has increased in area during this period when the government attempted to stabilize the slopes with reforestation,

TABLE 7. SUMMARY OF TERRAIN ATTRIBUTES PERTAINING TO LAND-USE CHANGES, 1976 AND 1987 CATEGORIES.

	1976		1987	
	Pixels*		Pixels*	
Land Use Category	Steep Slopes (>24%)	Surface Hydrology	Steep Slopes (>24%)	Surface Hydrology
11 Low Density Urban	752	328	987	319
12 High Density Urban	0	59	248	108
14 Transportation	82	28	183	132
21 Cultivated Land	979	499	976	438
24 Agricultural/ Residential	28	111	177	234
43 Mixed Woodland	7,994	1,317	43	1,451
53 Reservoirs and Ponds	42	28	42	28
54 Bays and Estuaries	84	0	115	3
70 Eroded Badland	18,395	3,066	16,671	2,534
74 Barren Land	1,369	232	2,901	418
76 Transitional Land	128	29	141	32
TOTALS	29,853	5,697	29,853	5,697

*Each pixel is a 20 × 20 m cell or 0.04 hectare.

TABLE 8. LAND-USE CHANGES RELATED TO GEOLOGY AND STEEP SLOPES, 1987.

	Number of Pixels*		
Geologic Unit	1987 Total	Total in Changes	Total in Steep Slopes (>24%)
Undifferentiated Alluvium	10,181	5,401	124
Raised Alluvium	1,606	224	8
Colluvium Deposit	12,237	5,705	1,501
Reclaimed Land	5,709	4,978	64
Marine Sediments	99	93	0
Repulse Bay Formation	8,916	4,791	1,762
Lok Ma Chau Formation	1,542	921	267
Needle Hill Granite (fine-grained)	10,432	5,944	3,125
Needle Hill Granite (medium-grained)	15,544	5,768	3,165
Cheung Chau Granite	19,065	10,857	8,138
Sung Kong Granite (fine-grained)	1,423	634	312
Sung Kong Granite (medium-grained)	22,667	7,523	11,277
Reservoir	2,895	3	1
Bay	7,684	1,233	109
TOTAL	120,000	54,075	29,853

*Each pixel is a 20 × 20 m cell or 0.04 hectares.

steep slopes with abundant surface drainage developed in granite area remained difficult to be forested.

ACCURACY OF ANALYSIS

The accuracy of the results of land-use change dynamics analysis using the GIS approach depends on the reliability of the spatial databases and the precision with which each layer can be registered together in the raster format. The reliability of the spatial database depends on the data sources and the procedures of data extraction, which, in the present case, involved interpretation of aerial photographs and existing topographic and geologic maps. The accuracy of the land-use interpretation from aerial photographs met the 85 percent minimum standard for Level II details based on checking with existing land-use maps and other collateral materials. On the other hand, the precision of registration of map layers depends on how accurately the maps can be rasterized and incorporated with the GIS databases under the data integration stage. In turn, this determined the accuracy of image overlaying and the developed binary masks. For the present project, all maps were rasterized to 20-m by 20-m grid cells which represent the pixel size. In order to quantitatively evaluate the accuracy of map rasterization, 16 check points on the boundaries of land-use polygons common to both the original line map and the rasterized map of the same year were selected, and using five additional evenly distributed points as control, an affine transformation with a least-squares adjustment was performed. It was found that, for both the 1976 and 1987 rasterized land use maps, the RMSE for planimetry were determined to be ± 24.5 metres and ± 25.8 metres at map scale, respectively, which were slightly over one pixel size. The accuracy was obviously determined by the precision of the digitizer used and the size of the grid cell selected for rasterization. Subjected to these limitations, the rasterized maps were therefore shown to be capable of retaining quite accurately the positions of the boundaries of the land-use polygons of the original maps. In order to determine quantitatively how accurately rasterized land-use maps of two different years could be registered, the coor-

dinates of the four corner points of one map (which delimited the areal extent of the study area) were mathematically transformed to those of the other map. The resultant RMSE in planimetry was found to be ± 13.2 metres which is slightly larger than half a pixel size. Thus, the overall conclusion is that the GIS developed for land-use change and environmental impact analysis for this project is accurate within 1/2 pixels. This accuracy can be improved if a digitizer with better resolution and higher accuracy (say, an accuracy of ± 0.127 mm and a resolution of 80 liner per mm) is used.

CONCLUSIONS

It has been demonstrated in this research that the GIS approach is most powerful in detecting land-use change dynamics and assessing the impact of these changes to the environment. Such an approach permits the incorporation of aerial photographic data of current and past land-use data with other map data. The operation of the GIS for this application is characterized by the use of image overlaying and the binary masking technique in extracting and quantifying changes and terrain impacts. A major contribution of the technique is its capability to understand land-use change dynamics. Hard copies of color maps displaying land-use losses and gains and their impacts can be produced for documentation and visual analysis. All these can be carried out speedily, accurately, and at low-cost with the microcomputer.

The analysis conducted for East Tuen Mun for the period of 1976 and 1987 revealed that, despite careful government planning in the development of the new town (such as in flood control and slope stabilization), high density urban use had encroached on steep slopes as the new town developed. The combination of extensive granite rock and monsoonal climatic condition made this area most susceptible to soil erosion with the production of gullies and badland in areas of steep slope and abundant surface drainage. Efforts to reforest the hillslopes took place and some success was seen in the increase in the area of mixed woodland, while the steep slopes continued to be difficult to reforest. Thus, the analysis undertaken with the GIS approach allows the planners to update quickly their land-use data and to make decisions for new town development and environmental protection in a physically constrained environment.

REFERENCES

Adeniyi, P. O., 1980. Land-use change analysis using sequential aerial photography and computer techniques. *Photogrammetric Engineering & Remote Sensing*, 46:1447–1464.

Anderson, J. R., E. E. Hardy, J. T. Roach, And R. E. Witmer, 1976. *A Land Use and Land Cover Classification Scheme for Use with Remote Sensor Data*, United States Government Printing Office, Washington, D.C.

Avery, T. E., 1965. Measuring land use changes on USDA photographs. *Photogrammetric Engineering*, 31:620–624.

Berry, J. K., and J. K. Berry, 1988. Assessing spatial impacts of land use plans. *Journal of Environmental Management*, 27:1–9.

Campbell, J. B., 1983. *Mapping the Land: Aerial Imagery for Land Use Information*, Resource Publications in Geography, Association of American Geographers, Washington, D.C.

Eastman, J. R., 1988a. *IDRISI: A Grid-Based Geographic Analysis System*, Clark University Graduate School of Geography, Worchester, Massachusetts.

———, 1988b. IDRISI: a collective geographic analysis system project. *Proceedings of the 8th International Symposium on Computer-Assisted Cartography*. American Society for Photogrammetry and Remote Sensing and American Congress on Surveying and Mapping, Falls Church, Virginia, pp. 421–430.

293

Faulkner, E., 1968. Land use changes in Parkway School District. *Photogrammetric Engineering*, 34:52–57.

Geotechnical Control Office, 1987. *Geotechnical Area Studies Programme-West New Territories,* The Government Printer, Hong Kong.

Hathout, S., 1988. Land use change analysis and prediction of the suburban corridor of Winnipeg, Manitoba. *Journal of Environmental Management*, 27:325–335.

Johnston, C. A., N. A. Detenbeck, J. P. Bondee, and G. J. Niemi, 1988. Geographic information systems for cumulative impact assessment. *Photogrammetric Engineering & Remote Sensing*, 54:1609–1615.

Leung, W. T., 1986. The new towns programme, *A Geography of Hong Kong* (T. N. Chui and C. L. So, eds), Oxford University Press, Hong Kong, p. 251–278.

Lindhult, M. S., J. Fabos, P. Brown, and N. Price, 1988. Using geographic information systems to assess conflicts between agricultural and development. *Landscape and Urban Planning*, 16:333–343.

Lo, C. P., and C. Y. Wu, 1984. New town monitoring from sequential aerial photographs. *Photogrammetric Engineering & Remote Sensing*, 50:1145–1158.

New Territories Development Department, 1977. *Hong Kong's New Towns Tuen Mun*, The Government Printer, Hong Kong.

Pilon, P. G., P. J. Howarth, R. A. Bullock, and P. O. Adeniyi, 1988. An enhanced classification approach to change detection in semi-arid environments. *Photogrammetric Engineering & Remote Sensing*, 54:1709–1716.

Richter, D. M., 1969. Sequential urban change. *Photogrammetric Engineering*, 35:764–770.

Wheeler, D. J., and M. K. Ridd, 1985. A geographic information system for resource managers based on multi-level remote sensing data. *Technical Papers, 51st Annual Meeting of American Society of Photogrammetry, Washington, D.C.,* American Society of Photogrammetry, Falls Church, Virginia, pp. 528–537.

Williams, T. H. L., 1985. Implementing LESA on a geographic information system-a case study. *Photogrammetric Engineering & Remote Sensing*, 51:1923–1932.

(Received 14 December 1989; revised and accepted 5 May 1990)

294

Application of Satellite and GIS Technologies for Land-Cover and Land-Use Mapping at the Rural-Urban Fringe: A Case Study

Paul M. Treitz, Philip J. Howarth, and *Peng Gong*
Earth-Observations Laboratory, Institute for Space and Terrestrial Science, Department of Geography, University of Waterloo, Waterloo, Ontario N2L 3G1, Canada

ABSTRACT: SPOT HRV multispectral and panchromatic data were recorded and co-registered for a portion of the rural-urban fringe of Toronto, Canada. A two-stage digital analysis algorithm incorporating a spectral-class frequency-based contextual classification of eight land-cover and land-use classes resulted in an overall Kappa coefficient of 82.2 percent for training-area data and a Kappa coefficient of 70.3 percent for test-area data. A matrix-overlay analysis was then performed within the geographic information system (GIS) to combine the land-cover and land-use classes generated from the SPOT digital classification with zoning information for the area. The map that was produced has an estimated interpretation accuracy of 78 percent. Global Positioning System (GPS) data provided a positional reference for new road networks. These networks, in addition to the new land-cover and land-use map derived from the SPOT HRV data, provide an up-to-date synthesis of change conditions in the area.

INTRODUCTION

REGIONAL AND MUNICIPAL PLANNERS require up-to-date information to effectively manage land development and plan for change. In urban areas, particularly at the rural-urban fringe, this change is very rapid. As a result, it is difficult to maintain up-to-date information on new housing and industrial/commercial developments. This is particularly true for regional municipalities whose jurisdictions cover large areas.

The land-use map, as a source of thematic information, has been an important component of urban and regional planning for many years. In areas where change is marginal or very slow, land-use maps that are considered relatively old (i.e., 10 to 20 years) may continue to portray adequately current conditions, and thus provide useful information. However, this is not the case in areas of rapid change, such as the rural-urban fringe, where the entire landscape can change over a short period of time. Here, fields and open areas are converted to residential subdivisions and commercial/industrial plazas. In such areas, the most recent map may be of little value to the person requiring up-to-date information.

Even with the availability of satellite imagery and computer storage of information, the stage has not yet been reached where up-to-date information can be rapidly and easily provided. However, steps are being taken to achieve this. In Ontario, for example, data obtained as part of the Ontario Basic Mapping (OBM) program are being digitized and input to geographic information systems. This provides baseline information for an area, but the information is only as up-to-date as the aerial photographs from which it was mapped. In practical terms, there has been a great deal of improvement in recent years in data collection, storage, and presentation. However, much information on land cover and land use is still five to ten years out of date and for many areas is too old for operational use. For example, for the Town of Markham at the rural-urban fringe of Metropolitan Toronto, the latest OBM maps were published in 1984. Thus, the land use shown for many areas is now incorrect. For a variety of planning purposes, it would be beneficial to have up-to-date information. The question is, how can this be provided rapidly and economically?

Remote sensing has been recognized as a useful means of supplying up-to-date information on activities within the urban environment, including the rural-urban fringe (Ehlers *et al.*, 1990; Forster, 1985; Jensen and Toll, 1982). However, it is felt that the interfacing of GIS technology with remote sensing will provide the maximum information content and analysis capabilities and thus be of benefit to land-use planners (Nellis *et al.*, 1990). It has been recognized (e.g., Quarmby and Cushnie, 1989; Forster, 1985; Welch, 1985) that there are many advantages to combining remotely sensed data with existing spatial, image, and statistical data, thereby maximizing the information upon which responsible decisions for land-use planning can be made. Geographic information systems (GIS) technology provides the medium for this integration of spatial data, and at the same time provides a powerful tool for the quantitative analysis of land-use change and map revision (Welch *et al.*, 1988). However, while GIS technology has grown exponentially, implementation of this technology for management applications has only experienced linear growth (Johnston, 1987).

Research is ongoing into the potential for digital image processing of high resolution imagery for mapping areas of rapid change (Gong and Howarth, 1991; 1990a; 1990b; Swann *et al.*, 1988). However, it remains difficult to map some point and linear features, particularly digitally, due to the fact that they are not always recognizable at the spatial resolution of the data, nor are they represented at their "true" location due to sensor and-panoramic distortions inherent in satellite data collection. It has also proven difficult to digitally separate linear features such as road networks from surrounding land cover and land use (Schanzer *et al.*, 1990; O'Brien, 1988; Nevatia and Babu, 1980). This is largely due to the complexity of pattern recognition procedures required for tracing specific cultural edge features. Global Positioning System (GPS) data, on the other hand, are static and provide positional information for newly developed, presently unmapped features such as new roads.

Earlier work has examined visual and digital techniques for classifying SPOT HRV data for integration into a geographic information system with various types of digital data (Treitz *et al.*, 1990a; 1990b). The aim of this paper is to present a procedure whereby SPOT HRV imagery, GPS data, and land-use zoning information can be used in conjunction with existing OBM data to provide updated, intermediate map products that the planner can use between official survey-grade updates to the database. Accuracies of the procedure are evaluated.

PHOTOGRAMMETRIC ENGINEERING & REMOTE SENSING,
Vol. 58, No. 4, April 1992, pp. 439–448.

0099-1112/92/5804-439$03.00/0
©1992 American Society for Photogrammetry and Remote Sensing

PLATE 1. A 10 m resolution color composite of the Markham study area. The area shown is approximately 4 km by 4 km.

STUDY SITE

The Town of Markham, located at the northeastern fringe of Metropolitan Toronto, Canada, has been the location of research concerned with mapping the changing conditions at the rural-urban fringe (e.g., Treitz *et al.*, 1990a; 1990b; Gong and Howarth, 1990a; 1990b; Martin *et al.*, 1988). The study location is centered on latitude 43° 53′ N, longitude 79° 18′ W and covers an area of approximately 200 sq km. The landscape is relatively flat and, with close proximity to Toronto, is subject to "urban sprawl." Typical of large North American cities, farmland and natural land are rapidly being converted to residential, industrial and commercial uses.

A study site measuring 16 sq km that contains a wide variety of land uses and land covers, as well as exhibiting significant change, was selected for detailed analysis and testing of the techniques (Plate 1). The area is representative of the environment within the region and has undergone significant change over the last ten years. Discussions with planners in the region revealed that it has been difficult to collect timely information on land-use change necessary to devise and implement land-development policies.

DATA DESCRIPTION

The SPOT HRV XS (multispectral mode) and P (panchromatic mode) data were recorded by the Canada Centre for Remote Sensing (CCRS) on 18 August 1989 at 1622 GMT for the Markham study area (Scene K615/J262). A summer scene was requested to optimize the spectral contrast between vegetated surfaces and cultural surfaces such as pavement, bare soil, construction areas, and buildings. The sun elevation and azimuth at the image center were 57° and 153°, respectively. The satellite sensor data were processed by CCRS using the MOSAICS system which corrects for Earth rotation, Earth curvature, off-nadir viewing, sensor alignment on the satellite, and satellite position, velocity, and attitude variations.

Global Positioning System (GPS) data were collected on 24 October 1989 using a Trimble Advanced Navigation Sensor (TANS) incorporated into the Trimble Pathfinder System. TANS is a two-channel sequencing GPS Navigation Sensor; it receives the L Band in C/A code which is broadcast by the NAVSTAR GPS satellites. By means of an automobile driven around the roads of the study site, data were collected at one-second intervals for approximately two hours using a single receiver in autonomous position mode. In this mode, the absolute accuracy of the GPS data is approximately 12 m CEP[1] (Lange, 1990). The receiver

---

[1]CEP stands for Circular Error Probability and equates horizontal, two-dimensional accuracy to a median: 50 percent of the collected points will be inside a circle with radius 12 m and 50 percent of the points will be outside that radius. CEP is the horizontal accuracy standard adopted by the U.S. Department of Defense for radionavigation systems (U.S. Department of Defense, 1984).

antenna was attached to the roof of the automobile with a magnetic mount, and driving speeds ranged from 0 to 60 km per hour in the area covered. Data collection was limited to a time window between 1200 and 1830 GMT. During this time interval, no less than three GPS satellites were "in view" above the horizon, a requirement for two-dimensional coordinate positioning by triangulation. It is estimated that by mid-1991 sufficient satellites will be in orbit to provide 24-hour-a-day global coverage in two dimensions, and by mid-1992, full coverage will be available in three dimensions (Lange, 1990).

Generalized zoning data for Lots 11 to 15 of Concession 4 were digitized into the GIS from a map sheet produced by the Town of Markham (Scale 1:4,000). It should be noted that, although the zoning by-law information on these maps is kept up-to-date, the positions of parcel boundaries are not based on survey data, but are estimated from lot and concession coordinates from the original basemap. The zoning information was generalized to a level compatible with the satellite data and the land-cover and land-use classification scheme. For example, individual residential lots were not digitized separately, but were incorporated into a residential-land-use zone.

Digital OBM data of the study site were not yet available from the Ontario Ministry of Natural Resources. Instead, the data were obtained by digitizing original OBM map transparencies (1:10,000 scale) to OBM specifications and then importing them into the ARC/INFO environment. OBM specifications dictate that 90 percent of all well-defined features, with the exception of those unavoidably displaced by symbolization, shall be located within 0.5 mm of their true planimetric locations; 5 m at 1:10,000 scale. These specifications are comparable to the circular map accuracy standard (CMAS) (Maling, 1989). The OBM map of the area was published in 1984 and was based on 1982 aerial photography.

Supplementary data, used as ground confirmation for accuracy assessment, included photomaps at 1:5,000 scale produced from aerial photographs (1:8,000 scale) acquired in April 1987. Field reconnaissance data were also collected in September 1989.

METHODOLOGY

The study involved the combination and analysis of XS and P data from the HRV sensor on the SPOT satellite, GPS data, land-use zoning maps, and OBM data. An outline of the procedures used in this study is presented in Figure 1.

PREPROCESSING

Preprocessing of the SPOT HRV data was performed using a Dipix ARIES III Image Analysis System, as well as software developed at the University of Waterloo on a VAX 11/785 computer in FORTRAN 77. SPOT HRV XS and P data were combined to preserve the spatial and spectral information of the two data sets (Holder, 1990). First, SPOT HRV P data were resampled to 20 m and co-registered with SPOT HRV XS data using a first-order polynomial transform and nearest-neighbor resampling algorithm. The residual errors were 4.6 m in both the x and y direction (0.23 pixels, 0.23 lines, ten ground control points (GCPs)) and are well within the spatial resolution of the image data sets.

Second, the corrected SPOT HRV XS data were resampled to 10-m spatial resolution using a nearest-neighbor resampling routine. As a result, the SPOT HRV XS data possess similar spatial and geometric characteristics to the original SPOT HRV P data. The nearest-neighbor resampling algorithm was used to preserve the statistical properties of the data.

Third, the SPOT HRV data were geometrically corrected to the Universal Transverse Mercator (UTM) coordinate system. GCPs were identified on OBM 1:10,000-scale map sheets and on the SPOT HRV image data (line and pixel coordinates). A first-order polynomial transform was calculated to model the geometric

distortions in the SPOT HRV data. Finally, a nearest-neighbor resampling algorithm was applied to the SPOT HRV data to produce the geometrically corrected image. The residual errors were 2.5 and 2.1 m in the x and y directions, respectively (0.25 pixels, 0.21 lines, ten GCPs). The registration error for the rectified 10-m SPOT data can also be stated as 4.9 m based on the circular mapping accuracy standard (CMAS) (Maling, 1989). This estimate falls within the accuracy levels of the OBM data before digitization.

Correlation coefficients were calculated for the digital values of the SPOT HRV XS and P data. High values were observed between the panchromatic and the red band (0.950) and the panchromatic and the green band (0.954). A negative correlation coefficient (−0.183) was observed between the panchromatic and infrared bands. To avoid data duplication or redundancy, the SPOT HRV infrared band at 10-m spatial resolution was used with the SPOT HRV panchromatic band for subsequent classification. For visual interpretation, an edge enhancement in the form of a high-pass filter was applied to the data to enhance the boundaries between cover types, while at the same time smoothing some of the internal heterogeneities within cover types (Holder, 1990). A three-band color composite with a spatial resolution of 10 m was produced consisting of an infrared band, an edge-enhanced panchromatic band, and the panchromatic band (Plate 1).

GPS data were initially downloaded into ARC/INFO and a point-to-vector conversion was applied to the raw data. Many anomalous vectors occurred where the vehicle (receiver) became stationary (e.g., at intersections) or when a road was traveled more than once (Figure 2). The data were edited in order to produce a single-line road network map. GPS vector coverage was processed to build polygon topology, and an associated polygon attribute table was produced. The topology that resulted was necessary for the CLEAN command with its "poly" option to collapse the small elongate polygons which existed in the coverage (ESRI, 1989)(Figure 2).

The GPS data were cleaned using a fuzzy tolerance of 10.5 (m) to collapse small unwanted polygons (e.g., cul-de-sacs and double-line road networks) without changing the overall representation of the area. The fuzzy tolerance determines the resolution of the output coverage because no two coordinates in the output coverage resulting from the clean operation will be within this distance of one another (ESRI, 1989). The remaining unwanted arcs were visually identified and recoded to an identification value of 500 so that they could be distinguished from the wanted arcs. All arcs with a value less than 500 were extracted from the coverage and stored in another coverage using the RESELECT command in ARC. This was done through the use of a set of logical criteria which were applied to the feature attributes. Finally, additional editing was required to delete and connect a few remaining arcs/polygons (Figure 3). The final coverage that resulted was exported to TYDAC SPANS.

Land-use zoning information was digitized using TYDAC's TYDIG module, and was then imported into the SPANS environment. Zoning information classes of interest include floodplain, public/institutional, residential, industrial/commercial, local commercial, and utilities (Figure 4). OBM data (1:10,000 scale) were digitized and edited using ARC/INFO software, and exported to TYDAC SPANS.

CLASSIFICATION

Standard per-pixel classification algorithms are based on the assumption that the distribution of spectral values for the land-use classes of interest demonstrate a normal or Gaussian distribution and are separable. This assumption is rarely true in an urban environment where land-use classes possess a wide range of spectral reflectance values that overlap in spectral space, and thereby confound the probabilistic decision rules com-

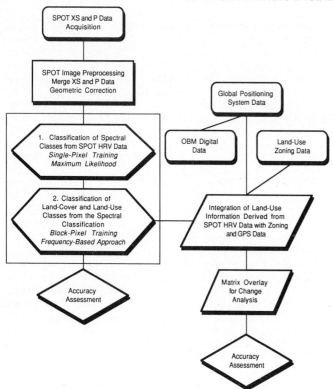

FIG. 1. Flow chart depicting the procedures followed in this study.

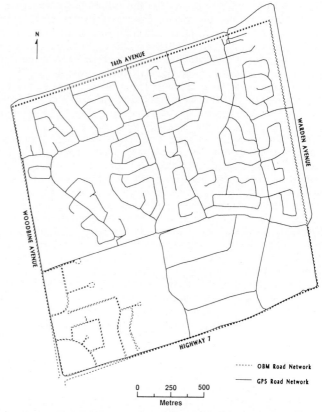

FIG. 3. Final edited version of the GPS road network overlain with OBM road data.

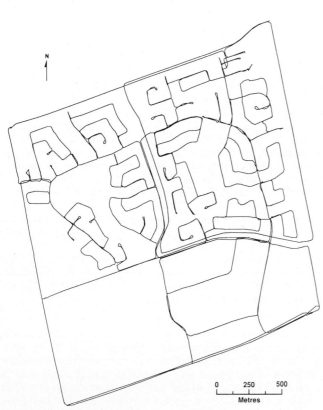

FIG. 2. Global Positioning System data after point-to-vector conversion.

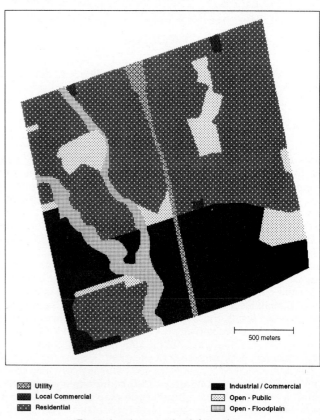

FIG. 4. Land-use zoning information.

298

monly used in per-pixel classifiers (Jensen and Hodgson, 1987; Khorram *et al.*, 1987; Haack *et al.*, 1987; Toll, 1985). In this study, an indirect classification approach was used for an area of approximately 16 sq km (Gong and Howarth, 1991).

The first stage in the classification procedure involved classifying the SPOT HRV XS and P data into eight spectral classes using the conventional supervised maximum-likelihood classification. The eight spectral classes used were bare and dry soil, forest and trees, grassland, crop land, pavement, fallow land, industrial roofs, and residential roofs. These spectral classes were selected on the assumption that they possess a minimal amount of intra-class variability. In defining the spectral classes, single-pixel training was used to ensure that the training data sampled this low intra-class variability. A minimum of 45 pixels was identified for each spectral class. This satisfies the requirement for a representative sample, as recommended by Swain and Davis (1978). During a second stage, a frequency-based method was used to classify the land-cover and land-use classes from the results of the spectral classification (Gong and Howarth, 1991; Zhang *et al.*, 1988; Wharton, 1982)(Figure 1).

The land-cover and land-use classes identified for the rural-urban fringe are outlined in Table 1 (Martin *et al.*, 1988). The main components of the industrial/commercial class are large industrial parks and shopping plazas with low-rise buildings and large associated parking areas. Smaller commercial areas (i.e., local commercial, as identified in the zoning data) are also incorporated into this class. Industrial and commercial land uses are grouped together due to their spectral, locational and functional similarities (Martin and Howarth, 1989). The open space class consists of cultivated farmland and parkland. Rough, pasture-like terrain is also a component of this class (Martin and Howarth, 1989). The purpose of this study was to identify the current land cover and land use for an area undergoing rapid urban growth. This includes the identification of land conversion activities. It should be noted that, as an area evolves from an existing land cover (e.g., natural vegetation) to a fully developed cultural class (e.g., residential), a variety of changes occur in the spectral reflectance. As a result, several stages in the land conversion were aggregated into two classes: "cleared land" (e.g., clearing, subdivision) and "under construction" (e.g., transportation, building, and landscaping) (Martin *et al.*, 1988; Jensen and Toll, 1982). Cleared land exhibits high uniform spectral reflectance, characteristic of bare soil, while sites under construction possess a more varied high reflectance resulting from building foundations and superstructures, construction materials, and partially installed roads and utilities (Martin *et al.*, 1988).

In the second stage, the eight land-cover and land-use classes listed in Table 1 were classified from the results of the spectral classification of the SPOT HRV data using a frequency-based approach (Gong and Howarth, 1991; Zhang *et al.*, 1988; Wharton, 1982). This procedure involved three steps. First, an 11- by 11-pixel window was moved over the classified image. The 11- by 11-pixel window was selected because it provided the optimum classification accuracy in tests of window sizes ranging from 3

by 3 to 21 by 21 (Gong and Howarth, 1991). Within each particular 11- by 11-pixel window, the frequencies of all eight spectral classes were counted and assigned to the center pixel of the window as spatial features for the final classification of this pixel. For example, the 121 pixels in an 11- by 11-pixel window in a residential area will consist of a certain proportion of each of the eight spectral classes. Second, mean frequencies for the eight spectral classes were extracted from the frequency features for each land-cover and land-use class using a block training (i.e., contiguous pixel) sampling strategy (Gong and Howarth, 1991). As a result, the average proportion of each spectral class contained within a specific land-cover/land-use class was calculated. Finally, the frequency features for each pixel were classified, according to the mean frequencies, using a minimum-distance classifier. The result is shown in Figure 5.

CLASSIFICATION ACCURACY ASSESSMENT

The accuracy of the SPOT HRV classified image was assessed first by examination of the training-area pixels, and second by independent test-area samples. Test areas (i.e., pixels independent of the maximum-likelihood decision rules) consisted of a series of 5- by 5-pixel blocks, and were selected randomly from a color composite of the study area. A minimum of 100 pixels was selected for all classes, regardless of abundance in the study area. "Classification accuracy" refers to the agreement between the training-area pixels and the ground-truth information, while "interpretation accuracy" refers to the agreement between the test-area pixels and the ground-truth information. Accuracy assessments, expressed in percent, are reported for each class along with a mean estimate for the study site. Kappa coefficients were calculated for each class, and for the digital classification as a whole (Cohen, 1960). Rosenfield and Fitzpatrick-Lins (1986) identified the Kappa coefficient as a suitable accu-

TABLE 1. LAND-USE AND LAND-COVER CLASSIFICATION SCHEME FOR DIGITAL CLASSIFICATION OF SPOT HRV DATA.

Class	Abbreviation
Low-Density Residential	LDR
Cleared Land	CL
Under Construction	CS
Industrial/Commercial	I/C
Open Space	OS
Woodland	W
Cropland	C
Fallow Land	FL

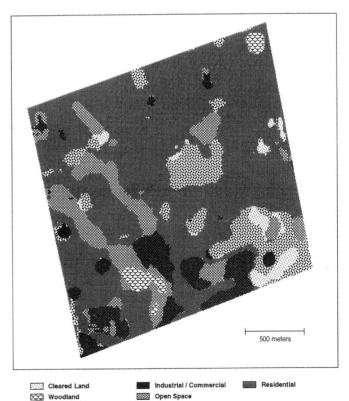

FIG. 5. SPOT HRV digital classification.

racy measure in thematic classification for representing class accuracy. Its strength lies in the fact that it takes all the elements of the confusion matrix into consideration, in contrast to the overall accuracy measures which only consider the diagonal elements of the matrix.

DATA INTEGRATION

The data sets (SPOT HRV digital classification, GPS road network data, zoning data, and OBM data) of various forms (raster and vector) were imported into a TYDAC SPANS geographic information system. A matrix-overlay analysis was performed to construct a map containing the significant information from the land-use zoning information and the land-cover and land-use classification derived from the SPOT HRV data (Table 2 and Plate 2). A matrix overlay allows the analyst to select only those class combinations, arising through the combination of the source data sets, that are relevant to the study. The objective here was to incorporate up-to-date land-cover information into the known zoning information. SPOT HRV data were able to show the changes that were occurring within the zones in terms of development stage (e.g., cleared, under construction). Additional overlay techniques were used to integrate GPS data with the matrix-overlay map. The GPS data provided a simple means of mapping the new road networks, with accuracy levels comparable to the resolution of the SPOT HRV data. Together, the three data sets provide a good information source for land use and land cover, as well as development activities, at the time of SPOT HRV data acquisition. A hardcopy map containing the most up-to-date information from the three data sets was then output on a color plotter. This map provides an intermediate information source between provincial updates of OBM data.

MAP OVERLAY ACCURACY

Currently, there is no reliable method for comparing map data when both maps may contain error. In this study, it was desirable to determine the accuracies for each of the 19 classes generated by the combination of data from the land-use zoning data and the digital classification through the matrix-overlay analysis. The first six classes listed in Table 2 represent the classes derived from the land-use zoning map produced by the Planning Department of the Town of Markham. Even though the zoning boundaries are not based on survey data, it was assumed that the identification or classification of the polygons is correct. Therefore, the generalized zoning classes were assumed to have an accuracy of 100 percent. It was difficult to

assess boundary-location accuracy because no accuracy measure was attached to the zoning map.

However, when the zoning classes occurred in combination with classes derived from the SPOT HRV digital classification (i.e., the remaining 13 classes), the interpretation accuracies of the SPOT HRV-derived classes were used as a measure of those class accuracies. In this sense, the SPOT HRV classification served as the ground truth or prime reference for the resulting class combinations. This method follows the assertion by Newcomer and Szajgin (1984) that the highest accuracy achievable for any GIS output product is restricted to the least accurate data plane in the source data. Therefore, the interpretation accuracy of each theme in the SPOT HRV classification represents the limiting factor for the resulting class accuracies. These accuracies were then averaged to provide an estimate for the overall interpretation accuracy of the map.

RESULTS

SPOT HRV DIGITAL CLASSIFICATION

The overall Kappa coefficients for the training- and test-area data were 82.2 percent and 70.3 percent, respectively (Tables 3 and 4). The highest Kappa values for training-area data were achieved for woodland (100 percent), low-density residential (93.1 percent), industrial/commercial (87.8 percent), cropland (80.9 percent), and fallow land (80.4 percent) (Table 3). High Kappa values for test-area data included cleared land (100 percent), cropland (100 percent), and low-density residential (83.3 percent) (Table 4). It should be noted that Kappa coefficients were higher for test area data than training area data for cleared land, construction sites, and cropland (Tables 3 and 4). This is probably a function of the block-sampling technique used for

TABLE 2. LAND-USE AND LAND-COVER CLASSIFICATION SCHEME FOR THE GIS MATRIX OVERLAY.

Floodplain
Public/Institutional (parkland, schools, church lands)
Residential (single-family dwelling)
Industrial/Commercial
Local Commercial
Utility (hydro corridor)
Floodplain/Open Space
Floodplain/Woodland
Public/Institutional/Cleared Land
Public/Institutional/Construction
Public/Institutional/Open Space
Public/Institutional/Woodland
Residential/Cleared Land
Residential/Construction
Industrial/Commercial/Cleared Land
Industrial/Commercial/Construction
Industrial/Commercial/Open Space
Local Commercial/Cleared Land
Local Commercial/Construction

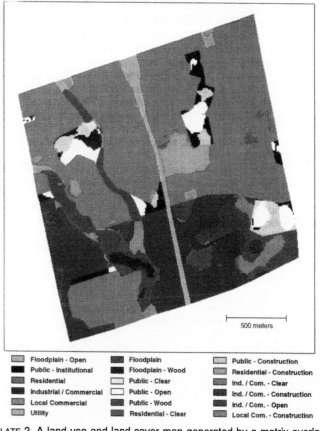

PLATE 2. A land-use and land-cover map generated by a matrix-overlay analysis combining zoning information with the digital classification.

TABLE 3. CONFUSION MATRIX AND SUMMARY STATISTICS FOR TRAINING-AREA DATA*

	Classified Results								Total	Omission errors(%)	Classification accuracy(%)	Kappa coefficient(%)
	LDR	CL	CS	I/C	OS	W	C	FL				
LDR	2350				33			57	2440	3.7	96.3	93.1
CL	7	43	25						75	42.7	57.3	55.3
CS		186	378						564	33.0	67.0	63.7
I/C			59	472					531	11.1	88.9	87.8
OS	9				241			101	351	31.3	68.7	65.6
W						70			70	0.0	100.0	100.0
C					129		642		771	16.7	83.3	80.9
FL	4				48			235	287	18.1	81.9	80.4
Total	2370	229	462	472	451	70	642	393	5089	12.9		
Commission errors (%)	0.8	81.2	18.2	0.0	46.6	0.0	0.0	40.2	12.9			

Mean classification accuracy = 80.5%
Overall classification accuracy = 87.1%
Overall Kappa coefficient = 82.2%
Percent unclassified pixels = 0.0%

*The abbreviated classes are listed in Table 2.
Mean classification accuracy refers to the average of all class accuracies.
Overall classification accuracy refers to the total correctly classified pixels.

TABLE 4. CONFUSION MATRIX AND SUMMARY STATISTICS FOR TEST-AREA DATA*

	Classified Results								Total	Omission errors(%)	Interpretation accuracy(%)	Kappa coefficient(%)
	LDR	CL	CS	I/C	OS	W	C	FL				
LDR	175							25	200	12.5	87.5	83.3
CL		100							100	0.0	100.0	100.0
CS		25	75						100	25.0	75.0	72.6
I/C	25		4	71					100	29.0	71.0	68.5
OS					25			75	100	25.0	25.0	18.2
W					50	50			100	50.0	50.0	47.1
C							100		100	0.0	100.0	100.0
FL	26							74	100	26.0	74.0	67.8
Total	226	125	79	71	75	50	100	174	900	25.6		
Commisssion errors (%)	22.6	20.0	5.1	0.0	66.7	0.0	0.0	57.5	25.6			

Mean interpretation accuracy = 72.8%
Overall interpretation accuracy = 74.4%
Overall Kappa coefficient = 70.3%
Percent unclassified pixels = 0.0%

*The abbreviated classes are listed in Table 2.
Mean interpretation accuracy refers to the average of all class accuracies.
Overall interpretation accuracy refers to the total correctly classified pixels.

the test-area definition, where test areas were collected as 25-pixel blocks.

Significant confusion occurred between cleared land and construction, as evidenced by high classification omission errors (42.7 percent and 33.0 percent, respectively) and commission errors (81.2 percent and 18.2 percent, respectively) (Table 3). This is not surprising because cleared areas occur within construction sites as part of the spectral make-up of that class. There was also confusion in class assignment for the vegetated classes: open space, cropland, and fallow land (Table 3). The spectral characteristics of these classes are similar because they contain the same cover type in the form of grasses. For test-area data, residential, open space, and fallow land exhibited some confusion, as did open space and fallow, and woodland and open space (Table 4).

SPOT HRV / ZONING DATA OVERLAY

The average interpretation accuracy for the land-cover and land-use map produced through the matrix overlay of the zoning information and the SPOT digital classification was 78 percent (Table 5). As explained below, this is indicative of the individual com-

ponents from each of the two source maps, and should be considered only as an estimate of the map's accuracy.

DISCUSSION

Welch (1982) stated that medium- to large-scale aerial photographs with ground resolutions ranging from 0.5 to 3 m are required for urban land-use mapping for Levels II and III of the four-level classification hierarchy proposed by Anderson et al. (1976). This was supported by Konecny et al. (1982) who demonstrated that a resolution of 5 m or less is required for urban cartographic mapping. However, these types of resolutions may not be necessary for thematic mapping, where detection of themes is more important than identification (Forster, 1985). For example, Welch (1982) considered that a minimum of four pixels is necessary to identify basic land parcels reliably, and that a sensor with an instantaneous field of view of 30 m may be adequate for urban centers in North America. Although the results are inconclusive, SPOT HRV XS and P data may be more amenable to urban monitoring through the improved detection of high frequency targets resulting from the finer spatial resolution.

Satellite remote sensing is capable of providing information

TABLE 5. LAND-USE AND LAND-COVER CLASSIFICATION ACCURACY FOR THE GIS MATRIX OVERLAY.

Floodplain	100%
Public/Institutional (parkland, schools, etc.)	100%
Residential (single-family dwelling)	100%
Industrial/Commercial	100%
Local Commercial	100%
Utility (hydro corridor)	100%
Floodplain/Open Space	25%
Floodplain/Woodland	50%
Public/Institutional/Cleared Land	100%
Public/Institutional/Construction	75%
Public/Institutional/Open Space	25%
Public/Institutional/Woodland	50%
Residential/Cleared Land	100%
Residential/Construction	75%
Industrial/Commercial/Cleared Land	100%
Industrial/Commercial/Construction	75%
Industrial/Commercial/Open Space	25%
Local Commercial/Cleared Land	100%
Local Commercial/Construction	75%
Average Interpretation Accuracy	78%

on development activities in the rural-urban fringe (Forster, 1985; Jensen and Toll, 1982). For example, it has been found that a great deal of spatial detail can be extracted both visually and digitally from SPOT data (Treitz et al., 1990a; 1990b; Ehlers et al., 1990; Gong and Howarth, 1990b; Li et al., 1989; Martin et al., 1988). The spatial resolution of SPOT HRV XS and P data (20 m and 10 m, respectively) is able to sample high-frequency land-use parcels characteristic of a typical North American urban environment (Stromquist et al., 1988; Welch, 1985). As a result, there are fewer mixed pixels resulting in sharper boundaries in a heterogeneous environment such as the rural-urban fringe.

The two-stage classification algorithm applied in this study was relatively successful in identifying residential and industrial/commercial land use from SPOT HRV XS and P data. This is due to the ability of the algorithm to model the spectral and spatial characteristics of these classes (Gong and Howarth, 1991). Of particular interest in land-change analysis is the detection of land being converted from an existing land cover to either residential or industrial/commercial land use. Here, the classifier had some difficulty separating cleared land from land under construction, as exhibited by Kappa coefficients of 55.3 percent and 63.7 percent, respectively, for training area data, and 100 percent and 72.6 percent for test area data. This is understandable because their spectral characteristics are very similar and large areas of cleared land will occur within a construction site. However, more detailed spectral class components may be needed to model these land-cover and land-use classes. The confusion between woodland and open space for the test-area data may be explained by the fact that areas of sparse tree cover were sampled in the test-area data.

The matrix-overlay analysis technique is a convenient method of combining land-cover and land-use classes from two separate data sets. In fact, combining data from a variety of sources can actually enhance the value of the information contained in the individual layers (Chrisman, 1987). Here, the important information from the digital classification of the SPOT HRV data and the zoning data were identified within the matrix to create new land-cover and land-use classes that portrayed the changing conditions at the rural-urban fringe. For example, cleared land and construction areas could be identified within residential and industrial/commercial areas to provide data on the extent of development within those land-use classes. However, it is difficult assigning an accuracy measure to the new data when

one or more of the data sets cannot be assumed to be 100 percent correct.

GIS products must be examined with reference to the quality of the source data, as well as the decision criteria used in the analysis. A number of authors have examined the concepts of accuracy and error in geographic information systems (Foody, 1988; Walsh et al., 1987; Drummond, 1987; Chrisman, 1987; Newcomer and Szajgin, 1984; Vitek et al., 1984). Even though it is recognized that error statements or evaluation matrices are required for data input to a GIS or generated within a GIS (Dicks and Lo, 1990; Story and Congalton, 1986; Vitek et al., 1984), there is no standard method by which to derive this assessment. As a result, GIS products rarely possess a quality indicator. This is particularly true for boundary maps of discontinuous themes (Drummond, 1987). Foody (1988) expressed a need to include more than a single accuracy measure for a classified remotely sensed image in order to account for the spatial variability of spectral response, and hence accuracy, as a function of viewing geometry. However, due to the narrow field of view experienced for the coverage in this study, it was felt that this precaution was unnecessary.

Hord and Brooner (1976) identified three components that determine the quality of a thematic map product. These are errors in boundary location, map geometry, and classification. These types of errors in source documents are compounded during overlay analysis. Two types of errors affect the accuracy of products generated by a geographic information system. These are inherent errors, or errors present in the source data, and operational errors that arise from data capture and manipulation within the GIS (Walsh et al., 1987). Operational errors may further be categorized as positional and identification errors, and in combination are a component of every thematic overlay (Newcomer and Szajgin, 1984). The authors add that the accuracy of products generated through GIS manipulation is a function of the number of layers involved in the analysis, the accuracy of the individual layers, and the frequency of coincident errors at similar locations within several map layers.

To date, there is no clear consensus on how to assess the accuracy of a map that has been created by combining selected classes from two maps using a matrix-overlay technique. The primary question that comes to mind is "what is to be used as the reference or ground truth for the new map product?" One method of obtaining an accuracy measure would be the acquisition of in-depth ground information obtained for the area that corresponds to the SPOT HRV data acquisition and land-use zoning information. For a proper accuracy assessment, a knowledge of the class combinations derived from the matrix overlay must be anticipated in advance. This is difficult, if not impossible. However, it may be proven over time that certain land-cover and land-use classes are useful and these will become the reference for ground truth data collection. At any rate, accuracy assessment for this type of map product, where data components are selected from a variety of sources and then integrated, needs to be addressed in future studies.

Other features of importance for rural-urban fringe monitoring include road networks because these provide the framework for land-use change and development (Forster, 1985). Although algorithms are being developed to extract these types of linear features from SPOT HRV data, GPS data provide an attractive method by which linear features can be mapped quickly and accurately. GPS data can potentially provide the positional information required for the location of new road networks within the spatial context of the SPOT HRV data, while the SPOT HRV XS and P data provide the spatial information for the thematic data. Because GPS data are collected as digital point data, they are suited to data integration within a GIS environment. To achieve positional accuracies comparable to OBM accuracy specifications, however, it is recommended that GPS data be collected in differential mode in which two GPS receiver/recorders are used.

An integrated approach is optimal in providing the land-use planner with the maximum information content and benefit. This integrated approach maximizes the spatial information content and positional accuracy of land-use change detection. While SPOT HRV data provide a means of monitoring the rate of change with respect to land-cover conversion and construction activities, other forms of digital data provide the positional reference for new and existing land covers and land uses. Through the integration of varied data sets, the land-use planner is able to make responsible decisions based on existing information within the digital database, as well as create new information through various spatial analysis techniques. In this study, the SPOT HRV, GPS, and land-use zoning data complement the existing OBM data and provide a means for land-use planners to monitor development in the rural-urban fringe.

GIS technology provides a suitable environment for the integration and analysis of image, spatial, and statistical data. However, certain editing and analysis procedures are more suited to particular GIS platforms. This is particularly due to the fact that certain systems handle vector or raster data more efficiently. For this reason, ARC/INFO was selected for handling a majority of the vector processing, whereas TYDAC SPANS was selected for the overlay analysis. ARC/INFO currently provides extensive vector editing functions, whereas SPANS, a raster/quadtree based system, provides effective overlay analysis capabilities.

CONCLUSIONS

This study provides a natural extension of current research in rural-urban fringe monitoring using SPOT HRV data. The ability to extract land-use information from spectral data has long been a problem faced by remote sensing scientists. The classification results described here for land-cover extraction from SPOT HRV data are encouraging. A two-stage digital analysis algorithm incorporating a spectral-class frequency-based contextual classification of eight land-cover and land-use classes achieved an overall Kappa coefficient of 82.2 percent for training-area data and a Kappa coefficient of 70.3 percent for test-area data. This type of approach, where contextual information is incorporated into the digital decision rules, is necessary for classification of high-resolution data such as from the SPOT HRV system. It is evident that SPOT HRV XS and P data provide sufficient detail to routinely update map information at scales as large as 1:10,000. This can be attributed to the incorporation of spectral classes within the image, as well as structural information within the land-use classes.

In this study, it was demonstrated that classified digital image data can enhance the information portrayed on a land-use zoning map. Because SPOT HRV data records timely land-cover information, the stages of development that are occurring on the ground can be monitored. Through the integration of zoning information, and land-cover and land-use information obtained through the digital classification of SPOT HRV data, an intermediary map product for monitoring the changing landscape within large areas (e.g., regional municipalities) can be produced. This is particularly true for areas of rapid change such as the rural-urban fringe. As digital classification techniques for the identification of land-use classes improve, and GIS and image analysis systems (IAS) become more fully integrated, this technique will provide a valuable method by which planners can monitor the activities within their jurisdictions.

Significant research is still required in the area of accuracy assessment where a variety of data sources are integrated to create new information. This is of particular importance when information extraction from the source documents is selective,

rather than complete. Accuracy measures must be made available for source data, as well as for new information created through spatial analysis techniques within a geographic information system environment.

ACKNOWLEDGMENTS

This research was funded by a Centre of Excellence Grant from the Province of Ontario to the Institute for Space and Terrestrial Science. The authors would like to thank the Urban and Regional Information Systems Group at the University of Waterloo for access to the ARC/INFO facilities, and C. Allan Greatrex of SURNAV Corporation in Ottawa for providing the Trimble Pathfinder System for GPS data collection. Also, thanks to Denis Gratton for his assistance with the GPS data formatting and conversion, and to M. Lynne Elliot for editing the GPS data.

REFERENCES

Anderson, J., E.E. Hardy, J.T. Roach, and R.E. Witmer, 1976. *A Land Use and Land Cover Classification System for Use with Remote Sensor Data*. Professional Paper 964, United States Geological Survey, Washington, D.C., 28 p.

Chrisman, N.R., 1987. The Accuracy of Map Overlays: A Reassessment. *Landscape and Urban Planning*, 14:427–439.

Cohen, J., 1960. A Coefficient of Agreement for Nominal Scales. *Educational and Psychological Measurement*, 20(1):37–46.

Dicks, S.E., and T.H.C. Lo, 1990. Evaluation of Thematic Map Accuracy in a Land-Use and Land-Cover Mapping Program. *Photogrammetric Engineering & Remote Sensing*, 56(9):1247–1252.

Drummond, J., 1987. A Framework for Handling Error in Geographic Data Manipulation. *ITC Journal*, 1987(1):73–82.

Ehlers, M., M.A. Jadkowski, R.R. Howard, and D.E. Brostuen, 1990. Application of SPOT Data for Regional Growth Analysis and Local Planning. *Photogrammetric Engineering & Remote Sensing*, 56(2):175–180.

ESRI, Inc., 1989. *Users Guide, ARC/INFO, Volume 2, Command Reference, The Geographic Information System Software*, Environmental Systems Research Institute, Inc., Redlands, California.

Foody, G.M., 1988. Incorporating Remotely Sensed Data into a GIS: The Problem of Classification Evaluation. *Geocarto International*, 3:13–16.

Forster, B.C., 1985. An Examination of Some Problems and Solutions in Monitoring Urban Areas from Satellite Platforms. *International Journal of Remote Sensing*, 6(1):139–151.

Gong, P., and P.J. Howarth, 1989. Performance Analyses of Probabilistic Relaxation Methods for Land-Cover Classification. *Remote Sensing of Environment*, 30:33–42.

———, 1990a. The Use of Structural Information for Improving Land-Cover Classification Accuracies at the Rural-Urban Fringe. *Photogrammetric Engineering and Remote Sensing*, 56(1):67–73.

———, 1990b. An Assessment of Some Factors Influencing Multispectral Land-Cover Classification. *Photogrammetric Engineering and Remote Sensing*, 56(5):597–603.

———, 1991. Land-use Classification of SPOT HRV Data Using a Cover-Frequency Method. *International Journal of Remote Sensing*, (in press).

Haack, B., N. Bryant, and S. Adams, 1987. An Assessment of Landsat MSS and TM Data for Urban and Near-Urban Land-Cover Digital Classification. *Remote Sensing of Environment*, 21(2):201–213.

Holder, G.H., 1990. *A Structural Analysis of SPOT Data for the Identification of Residential Land-Use at the Toronto Rural-Urban Fringe*. Unpublished Ph.D. Thesis, University of Waterloo, Waterloo, Ontario, Canada, 263 p.

Hord, R.M., and W. Brooner, 1976. Land-Use Map Accuracy Criteria. *Photogrammetric Engineering & Remote Sensing*, 42(5):671–677.

Howarth, P.J., L.R.G. Martin, G.H. Holder, D.D. Johnson, and J. Wang, 1987. SPOT Imagery for Detecting Residential Expansion on the Urban-Rural Fringe of Toronto, Canada. *SPOT 1: Image Utilization, Assessment, Results* (CNES, editors). Cepadues-Editions, Toulouse, France, pp. 491–498.

Jensen, J.R., and M.E. Hodgeson, 1987. Interrelationships Between Spatial Resolution and Per-Pixel Classifiers for Extracting Information Classes, Part 1: The Urban Environment. *Technical Papers of the ASPRS-ACSM Annual Convention*, Vol. 1, pp. 121–129.

Jensen, J.R., and D.L. Toll, 1982. Detecting Residential Land-Use Development at the Urban Fringe. *Photogrammetric Engineering & Remote Sensing*, 48(4):629–643.

Johnston, K., 1987. Natural Resource Modeling in the Geographic Information System Environment. *Photogrammetric Engineering & Remote Sensing*, 53(10):1411–1415.

Khorram, S., J.A. Brockhaus, and H.M. Cheshire, 1987. Comparison of Landsat MSS and TM Data for Urban Land-Use Classification. *IEEE Transactions on Geoscience and Remote Sensing*, 25(2):238–243.

Konecny, G., W. Schuhr, and J. Wu, 1982. Investigations of Interpretability of Imagery by Different Sensors and Platforms for Small Scale Mapping. *Proceedings, International Symposium on Primary Data Acquisition*, Commission I, ISPRS, Canberra, pp. 11–22.

Lange, A.F., 1990. GPS, A Revolutionary Tool for GIS. *Proceedings, 10th Annual ESRI User Conference*, Vol. 1, Environmental Systems Research Institute, Inc., Redlands, California.

Li, L., G. Deeker, K. Yurach, and J. Seguin, 1989. Updating Urban Street Network Files with High Resolution Satellite Imagery. *Proceedings, Auto-Carto IX Symposium*, ASPRS/ACSM, Baltimore, Maryland.

Maling, D.H., 1989. *Measurements from Maps: Principles and Methods of Cartometry*, Pergamon Press, New York, 577 p.

Markham, B.L., and J.R.G. Townshend, 1981. Land Cover Classification Accuracy as a Function of Sensor Spatial Resolution. *Proceedings, 15th International Symposium on Remote Sensing of Environment*, Environmental Research Institute of Michigan, Ann Arbor, Michigan, pp. 1075–1090.

Martin, L.R.G., and P.J. Howarth, 1988. The Use of Satellite Imagery in Rural Planning. *International Yearbook of Rural Planning, 1988* (A. W. Gilg, editor), Elsevier Applied Science, New York, pp. 212–232.

———, 1989. Change-Detection Accuracy Assessment Using SPOT Multispectral Imagery of the Rural-Urban Fringe. *Remote Sensing of Environment*, 30:55–66.

Martin, L.R.G., P.J. Howarth, and G.H. Holder, 1988. Multispectral Classification of Land Use at the Rural-Urban Fringe Using SPOT Data. *Canadian Journal of Remote Sensing*, 14(2):72–79.

Nellis, M.D., K. Lulla, and J. Jensen, 1990. Interfacing Geographic Information Systems and Remote Sensing for Rural Land-Use Analysis. *Photogrammetric Engineering & Remote Sensing*, 56(3):329–331.

Nevatia, R., and K.R. Babu, 1980. Linear Feature Extraction and Description. *Computer Graphics and Image Processing*, 13:257–269.

Newcomer, J.A., and J. Szajgin, 1984. Accumulation of Thematic Map Error in Digital Overlay Analysis. *The American Cartographer*, 11(1):58–62.

O'Brien, D., 1987. Road Network Extraction from SPOT Panchromatic Data. *Proceedings, International Symposium on Topographic Applications of SPOT Data*, Canadian Institute of Surveying and Mapping, Sherbrooke, Quebec, Canada pp. 273–287.

Quarmby, N.A., and J.L. Cushnie, 1989. Monitoring Urban Land Cover Changes at the Urban Fringe from SPOT HRV Imagery in South-East England. *International Journal of Remote Sensing*, 10(6):953–963.

Rosenfield, G.H., and K. Fitzpatrick-Lins, 1986. A Coefficient of Agreement as a Measure of Thematic Classification Accuracy. *Photogrammetric Engineering & Remote Sensing*, 52(2):223–227.

Schanzer, D.L., Plunkett, G.W., and D. Wall, 1990. Filters for Residential Road Delineation from SPOT PLA Imagery. *Proceedings, GIS For the 1990s, Second National Conference on GIS*, Ottawa, Ontario, Canada, pp. 801–815.

Story, M., and R.G. Congalton, 1986. Accuracy Assessment: A User's Perspective. *Photogrammetric Engineering & Remote Sensing*, 53(3):397–399.

Stromquist, L., R.A. Larsson, and M. Bystrom (editors), 1988. *An Evaluation of the SPOT Imagery Potential for Land Resources Inventories and Planning: A Lesotho Case Study*. UNGI Rapport Nr. 68, Swedforest Consulting AB and Swedish Space Corporation, 43 p.

Swain, P.H., and S.M. Davis (editors), 1978. *Remote Sensing: The Quantitative Approach*. McGraw-Hill, New York, 396 p.

Swann, R., D. Hawkins, A. Westwell-Roper, and W. Johnstone, 1988. The Potential for Automated Mapping from Geocoded Digital Image Data. *Photogrammetric Engineering & Remote Sensing*, 54(2):187–193.

Toll, D., 1985. Effect of Landsat Thematic Mappers Sensor Parameters on Land Cover Classification. *Remote Sensing of Environment*, 17:129–140.

Treitz, P.M., P.J. Howarth, D.J. Gratton, G.H. Holder, and C.A. Greatrex, 1990a. GPS and SPOT Data for Map Revision in the Rural-Urban Fringe. *Proceedings, GIS For The 1990s, Second National Conference on GIS*, Ottawa, Ontario, Canada, pp. 1539–1545.

Treitz, P.M., P.J. Howarth, P. Gong, and D.J. Gratton, 1990b. Integrating Remote Sensing Data within a GIS Environment for Mapping the Changing Landscape at the Rural-Urban Fringe, *Proceedings, 13th Canadian Symposium on Remote Sensing*, Fredericton, N.B., Canada, pp. 448–459.

U.S. Department of Defense, 1984. *Federal Radionavigation Plan*. Technical Report, No. DOD-4650.4, U.S. Department of Defense, 204 p.

Vitek, J.D., S.J. Walsh, and M.S. Gregory, 1984. Accuracy in Geographical Information Systems: An Assessment of Inherent and Operational Errors. *Proceedings, PECORA IX, Symposium*, pp. 296–302.

Walsh, S.J., D.R. Lightfoot, and D.R. Butler, 1987. Recognition and Assessment of Error in Geographic Information Systems. *Photogrammetric Engineering & Remote Sensing*, 53(10):1423–1430.

Welch, R., 1985. Cartographic Potential of SPOT Image Data. *Photogrammetric Engineering & Remote Sensing*, 51(8):1085–1091.

———, 1982. Spatial Resolution Requirements for Urban Studies. *International Journal of Remote Sensing*, 3(2):139–146.

Welch, R., M.M. Remillard, and R.B. Slack, 1988. Remote Sensing and Geographic Information System Techniques for Aquatic Resource Evaluation. *Photogrammetric Engineering & Remote Sensing*, 54(2):177–185.

Wharton, S.W., 1982. A Contextual Classification Method for Recognizing Land Use Patterns in High Resolution Remotely Sensed Data. *Pattern Recognition*, 15(4):317–324.

Zhang, Z., H. Shimoda, K. Fukue, and T. Sakata, 1988. A New Spatial Classification Algorithm for High Ground Resolution Images. *Proceedings, IGARSS88, International Geoscience and Remote Sensing Symposium*, Edinburgh, UK, pp. 509–512.

SECTION 9

Biological Diversity

Overview

Davis et al., in the first article, outline a comprehensive national biodiversity information system which uses GIS to identify gaps in the network of nature reserves. In the second paper, Ahearn et al. describe a biodiversity database which is based on the technologies of digital imaging, remote sensing, GIS, global positioning systems, and various types of software. In the last article, Skole and Tucker describe their use of satellite data to study deforestation, fragmentation, and biodiversity in the Amazon region of Brazil.

Suggested Additional Reading

Miller, R. I., S. M. Stuart, and K. M. Howell, 1989. A Methodology for Analyzing Rare Species Distribution Patterns Utilizing GIS Technology: The Rare Birds of Tanzania. Landscape Ecology. 2(3):173-189.

Scott, J. M., F. Davis, B. Csute, R. Noss, B. Butterfield, C. Groves, H. Anderson, S. Caicco, F. D'Erchio, T. C. Edwards, Jr., J. Ulliman, and R. G. Wright. 1993. Gap Analysis: A Geographic Approach to Protection of Biological Diversity. Wildlife Monographs, 57, 1-41.

Stoms, D. M., and J. E. Estes. 1993. A Remote Sensing Research Agenda for Mapping and Monitoring Biodiversity. International Journal of Remote Sensing. 14(10):1839-1860.

Twery, M. J., 1991. Scientific Exploration with an Intelligent GIS: Predicting Species Composition from Topography. AI Applications. 5(2):45-58.

INT. J. GEOGRAPHICAL INFORMATION SYSTEMS, 1990, VOL. 4, NO. 1, 55–78

An information systems approach to the preservation of biological diversity

FRANK W. DAVIS, DAVID M. STOMS, JOHN E. ESTES
and JOSEPH SCEPAN

Department of Geography, University of California,
Santa Barbara, California 93106, U.S.A.

and J. MICHAEL SCOTT

U.S. Fish and Wildlife Service,
Idaho Cooperative Fish and Wildlife Research Unit,
College of Forestry, University of Idaho, Moscow, Idaho 83843, U.S.A.

Abstract. Although biological diversity has emerged in the 1980s as a major scientific and political issue, efforts at scientific assessment have been hampered by the lack of cohesive sets of data. We describe, in concept, a comprehensive national diversity information system, using geographical information system (GIS) techniques to organize existing data and improve spatial aspects of the assessment. One potential GIS analysis, to identify gaps in the network of nature reserves for California, is discussed in greater detail. By employing an information systems approach, available data can be used more effectively and better management strategies can be formulated.

1. Introduction

Alarm over the accelerating rate of extinctions of plant and animal species and the destruction of ecosystems has prompted a call to the scientific community to make a comprehensive assessment of the status and trend of biological diversity (biodiversity) and recommend strategies for conservation (Wilson 1988, U.S. Congress Office of Technology Assessment 1987). In the United States, proposed legislation (H.R. 1268) would establish a National Center for Biological Diversity and Environmental Research to co-ordinate a national assessment. A wide variety of biological, ecological and cultural information is required to make such an assessment. Unfortunately, data relevant to the preservation of biodiversity have often been acquired without the guidance of a co-ordinated information management goal, are scattered among different institutions in incompatible formats and, as such, are often difficult to locate (U.S. Congress Office of Technology Assessment 1987, Tangley 1985). Holes in the knowledge base remain, both for geographical and taxonomic coverage. Because many experts believe that the threat to biological diversity has reached a crisis stage (Wilson 1988, Lovejoy 1988), it is our opinion that it is unrealistic to postpone action on preserving biodiversity until 'complete' information is collected. Rather, we must make effective use of what we already know, while systematically organizing and expanding our knowledge base.

Herein, we present our concept for the development of a comprehensive biological diversity information system. Outlined is a geographical information system (GIS) approach in which existing information can be input, managed and analysed, while needs for additional information can be identified. The system envisaged is multi-leveled, encouraging information flow from local up to international levels and vice versa, including key components at national centres. Our intent in presenting this material now, prior to the establishment of the National Center for Biological Diversity, is two-fold. First, we wish to notify the GIS community of the need for their skills in addressing this international problem of declining biodiversity. Second, we want to stimulate discussion on a GIS for handling biodiversity data, so that implementation can be expedited if and when the enabling legislation is enacted. It should be emphasized that the design for a national biodiversity information system presented here is not meant to be the definitive solution; it is, we hope, one valid approach to a problem of significant local, national and international concern. While the tropics are acknowledged to contain far greater diversity (and greater risk of mass extinctions) than temperate regions, all nations need to manage their development within ecologically sustainable limits (Lovejoy 1988). A GIS-based assessment can be one component in an overall strategy.

Diversity is a complex concept and the term is used in many ways. Most generally, diversity refers to the total number of species inhabiting an area. We use the term 'species richness' to convey this meaning. Individual ecosystems, defined by combinations of biological and abiotic factors, have both structural and functional diversity. The terms 'biological diversity' or 'biodiversity' will be used when we mean 'the variety and variability among living organisms, and the ecological complexes in which they occur' (U.S. Congress Office of Technology Assessment 1987, p. 3), incorporating alpha, beta and gamma diversity as traditionally used by ecologists (Whittaker 1975). Conservation strategies should address the range of diversity from the molecular level of genetic material to species and ecosystems. A diversity information system should support the assessment process by providing the data needed to describe current environmental baseline conditions, identify species and habitats at greatest risk, guide land management decisions and model the effects of alternative conservation policies.

In the past, environmental data were often collected and organized for a single, limited purpose. Further use of these data may require reformatting, or even recollecting. Given the increasing demand for information on the status of biological diversity, many are realizing the need for improved information systems (Scott *et al.* 1987 a, Pellew and Harrison 1988, Mooneyhan 1988, U.S. Congress Office of Technology Assessment 1987). Marble (1986) has described a number of the shortcomings of existing species databases (e.g., lack of a consistent data dictionary and updating procedures). To accomplish our goal of developing an overall species diversity information system, we must broaden our perspective and consider the overall flow from data capture to analysis and management and not just the content of the GIS database *per se* (Estes 1985). In the following discussion the types of data available, how they are typically used in a non-GIS context and the limitations of that approach are described. Next, we outline a generic information system for integrating data which are essential to the assessment of biological diversity. Although the system is described in the context of a National Center for the United States, the basic concepts could be readily adapted by other nations and institutions. Finally, we propose a process to address one specific component of a conservation programme, the search for biotic communities and species in need of preservation management (gap analysis).

2. Background

An idealized set of data for assessing the status and for projecting trends in biological diversity includes the distribution of taxa, ecological factors that characterize their habitats and human activities that affect their habitats (table 1). These data are

Table 1. Taxonomic, ecological and cultural variables required for assessment of biological diversity and their corresponding information scale.

Information scale, areal extent (km²) and suggested map scale	Taxon distribution	Habitat factors	Cultural features
Biogeographic 10^4–10^6 1:2500000–1:10000000	Species range (historical and modern)	Climate type Physiography Vegetation formation Soil order	Dominant land use Administrative boundaries
Regional 10^2–10^4 1:100000–1:2500000	Species and subspecies range (historical and modern) Population occurrences (notably rare, endangered and indicator species)	Climate provinces Landform Vegetation series Surface geology Soil order Community interactions	Land use Prime farmlands Land capability Energy/mineral resources Transportation corridors Air/water quality Land ownership Nature reserves
Local 10^{-2}–10^2 1:10000–1:100000	Narrowly endemic species Population occurrences Observation data	Microclimate Topography Vegetation association Surface geology Soil series Hydrography Community interactions	Land use Zoning Primary/secondary roads Air/water quality

inherently spatial attributes and thus can be stored in map (or graphic), tabular and textual format. Here we describe the nature of these attributes, how they are mapped, how they have been used in assessments of biodiversity and conservation planning, and the limitations of those methods, especially when GIS technology has not been used. Table 1 considers only the terrestrial biota, although some of the ideas also apply to aquatic species and ecosystems.

We arbitrarily distinguish three levels of spatial scale, recognizing the difference in biological and ecological variables that most influence distribution at each scale. The broadest level is the biogeographic scale and corresponds to areas roughly 10^4 to 10^6 km^2, the magnitude of the range of many species. At the next level down in the hierarchy is the regional scale. A region can be an area ranging from 10^2 to 10^4 km^2, in which the climatic type, physiography and dominant vegetation are relatively uniform. Ranges of subspecies and varieties are often of these dimensions. The local scale applies to homogeneous ecosystems of the order of 10^{-2} to 10^2 km^2 in size, at which distributions of rare species, populations and associated microhabitat factors can be delineated. Integration across scales should be possible, but has been difficult in practice in ecology (Allen and Starr 1982). Translating across scales has not just been a scientific problem—management of biodiversity must intervene at all ecological scales, requiring the co-operation of all levels of jurisdiction.

2.1. *Geographical distribution of taxa*

Data on the range and abundance of species are of fundamental importance for ecological studies. Abundance data are more difficult to collect than range data, since the former requires more intensive sampling. As a result, such information is available only for the most thoroughly studied taxa such as game species, pests and endangered species. Realistically, then, assessments of biodiversity will be based essentially on data on the range of species. Even range data tend to be of low quality. The spatial sampling frequencies often vary from one taxon to the next, or even over the range of a single taxon. Furthermore, ranges are dynamic in response to environmental fluctuations or trends, such as the global warming predicted in the coming decades. Consequently, conclusions from assessments of biodiversity should be qualified by the limitations of the data.

Range has been defined in its simplest form as 'the area occupied by a given species' (Rapoport 1982, p. 3) and is used synonymously with distribution area. The term can be applied to either modern or historical distributions and the intended usage should be indicated with range data. To determine what area is occupied, field biologists collect specimens or record observations, noting the geographical locations. From a collection of point observations, a map can be rendered of a species range, using one of three basic techniques. As can be seen in figure 1 (*a*)–(*c*), each technique renders a different view of a species' range.

The most straightforward technique is to plot the points on a base map, making no specific inferences about the occupancy of the intervening areas. Figure 1 (*a*) shows an example of this method for historical observations of the California condor (*Gymnogyps californianus*), an endangered bird species currently surviving only in captivity. This technique has also been used for encoding specimens collected for herbaria or museums. Precise plotting of each observation may be somewhat tedious, because the original specimen labels are usually coded with a geographical place name and not with consistent spatial coordinates (McGranaghan and Wester 1988). A greater problem with observational data is the strong locational bias, with denser sampling in the most accessible sites.

Another common method of displaying range data is what Morse *et al.* (1981) call the 'synthetic approach'. Here observation data are displayed as choropleth maps, based on artificial boundaries with either vector or raster data structures. County boundaries are commonly used and the presence of a species is indicated by shading the entire polygon or as shown in figure 1 (*b*), again using condor data. Some non-GIS databases, such as TROPICOS (Crosby and Magill 1988), Geoecology (Olson *et al.* 1983), or the International Union for Conservation of Nature and Natural Resources (IUCN) Conservation Monitoring Centre database (Pellew and Harrison 1988), code ranges as attributes of political or ecological areas. Alternatively, a synthetic grid or raster system can be used (e.g., Perring and Walters 1962). An example of a grid map for the condor is shown in figure 1 (*c*). Despite differences in data structure, the synthetic methods depicted in figures 1 (*b*) and (*c*) both generalize data to units that have little or no ecological meaning, and the locational precision of the original observations is lost to a greater or lesser extent through the process of generalization.

In the third technique, point observations are enclosed in a boundary separating range from non-range in a simple thematic map. The map in figure 1 (*a*) of the historical range of the California condor includes an interpreted boundary around the set of points. Rapoport (1982) identifies eight different areographic criteria for bounding a polygonal range from a set of points. Each bounding method produces quite different results from the same data points.

Range maps are frequently stored in a database consisting of a published atlas for a particular taxonomic group with supplemental maps of ecological factors. This format is designed for simple queries on the range of a single species, but is completely inappropriate for identifying where the most species occur or which multivariate factors are related to species richness (Marble 1986).

2.2. Habitat factors

For a comprehensive assessment of biodiversity, habitat factors must be considered for two reasons. First, the combination of factors constitute types of ecosystem that are as important a component of biodiversity as species. Second, species ranges and richness are often correlated with these factors and thus may be predicted for areas where reliable range maps do not exist.

In general, the primary environmental factors that limit the range of species include climate, physiography, vegetation, soils and geology (table 1). Sometimes these variables are combined into synthetic maps of ecoregions at the biogeographic scale (e.g., Bailey 1976, Omernik 1987). Climate is generally regarded as the dominant control over the potential range of taxa. At the biogeographic scale, climatic variables have been expressed and mapped as simple classifications (e.g., Holdridge 1947, Thornthwaite 1948). Ranges of species are sometimes restricted, not by the average conditions used in such classifications, but by bioclimatic factors such as absolute minimum temperature, annual temperature range, conditions during critical phases of a species' life cycle, or the frequency of extreme events that limit further range expansion (Tuhkanen 1980). Maps of climate, bioclimate, physiography and so on are typically available, but in many areas those of limiting factors are not.

Vegetation is an important synthetic variable that incorporates a characteristic set of plant species and also defines, in part, habitat for animal species. Vegetation is also an easily identifiable feature representing the integration of many less visible ecological

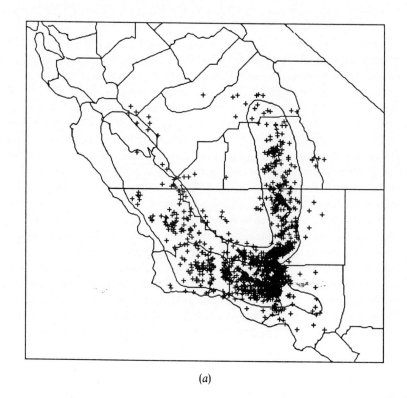

(*a*)

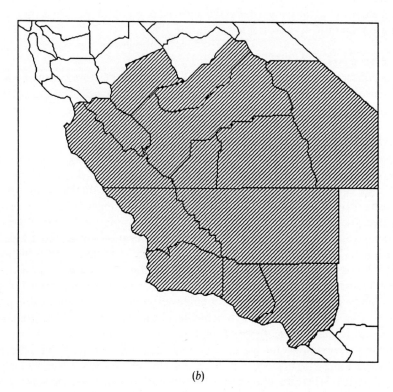

(*b*)

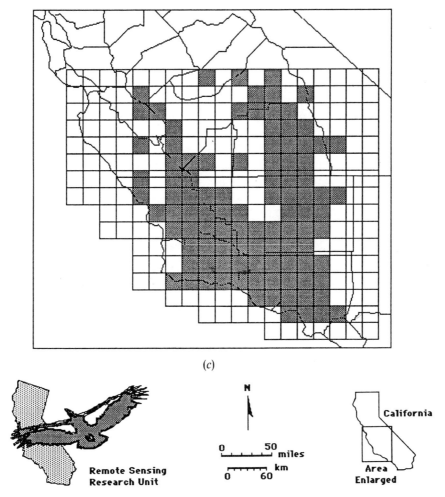

(c)

Figure 1. Historical distribution of the California condor. Range is displayed with various cartographic techniques: (*a*) locations of approximately 7000 observations (each cross represents one sighting, although many overlap) and with one possible polygonal representation of the inferred range boundary (Scepan *et al.* 1987); (*b*) a synthetic approach with hatch in counties where observations occurred, and (*c*) another synthetic approach where observations are aggregated to grid cells. Each technique clearly generates a different cartographic product from the same set of observations.

factors. Classification schemes for mapping vegetation communities, however, depend on the objectives (and scale) for which they are created, and hence many different schema exist (Küchler 1967). Vegetation is a dynamic phenomenon, so that maps can quickly become dated. Where boundaries between classes are visible, mapping can be performed by interpreting aerial photography or digital satellite imagery, supplemented by appropriate field verification. In some cases, however, one class may grade into another, in which case a map of vegetation classes provides a somewhat inaccurate model of vegetation cover. Some small, patchy vegetation communities are disproportionately valuable for conservation relative to their areal extent. These sites, such as

313

riparian areas and wetland ecosystems, are often not mapped except at large scales or are plotted only as point data.

An alternative to mapping actual vegetation is to infer potential natural vegetation cover from other ecological variables (e.g., Küchler 1964). Human impacts such as agricultural land use are replaced on the map with the vegetation that would presumably occur naturally. Figure 2 illustrates the differences between actual vegetation as mapped by photo-interpretation from Landsat Multispectral Scanner images (Matyas and Parker 1980) and potential vegetation (Küchler 1977) over a region of California. While there are similarities in the vegetation pattern of Coast live oak forest in these two maps, the fragmentation and modification of this habitat is clear.

Because range mapping is so labour-intensive, indirect methods are often used to infer range from the distribution of the habitat requirements of the species and constraints that are often easier to map than the species themselves. On the assumption that a strong correlation exists between habitat parameters and the ecological requirements of a species, maps can be produced by this method which represent potential range (e.g., Busby 1988). Historical, stochastic and additional biological and ecological factors may still limit the actual range relative to the potential range. Species richness may also be predicted from ecological factors (e.g., Richerson and Lum 1980, Miller *et al.* 1989).

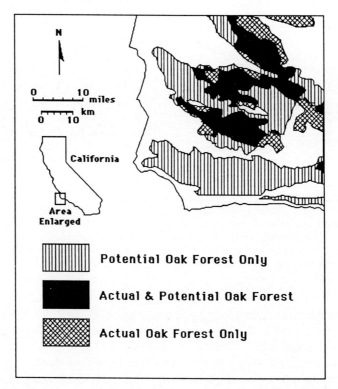

Figure 2.   Potential versus actual vegetation in a region of California. Potential natural vegetation (Küchler 1977); actual vegetation mapped from Landsat Multispectral Scanner imagery as part of CALVEG project (Matyas and Parker 1980). The figure illustrates the fragmentation and conversion of Coast live oak forest to urban and agricultural land uses as well as differences in interpretation.

2.3. *Cultural features*

In an assessment of the trends in biological diversity, we also need to know where habitats are being or will soon be modified by human activities. Perhaps because biologists and ecologists have led the assessments of diversity, cultural aspects of the biodiversity issue are frequently ignored (U.S. Congress Office of Technology Assessment 1987). Remote sensing techniques have proven effective for mapping land use and monitoring changes, especially where existing maps are out of date (Estes 1983). Digital cartographic boundaries of administrative units, as well as Federal and state land ownership and locations of existing nature preserves, are generally available as part of public land management and other programmes. In setting conservation priorities, policy makers also need to be advised of potential conflicts between biodiversity and other resources. Land capability and suitability for natural resources, such as prime farmlands, forestry, recreation, grazing and energy and minerals extraction have been effectively modelled from maps of environmental factors (McHarg 1969).

2.4. *Current methods and their limitations*

Several types of assessment of biodiversity have previously been performed, based on either species or communities. One approach to assessment is to evaluate the degree that each type of vegetation community has been preserved. For instance, the U.S. Forest Service investigated how well each Bailey ecoregion (1976) is represented in the existing wilderness system as one criterion for recommending new areas for formal designation by Congress (Olson *et al.* 1983). Crumpacker *et al.* (1988) conducted a GIS analysis of the United States by intersecting Küchler's potential vegetation map (Küchler 1964) with Federal and Indian lands. They found many terrestrial and wetland ecosystems under-represented on these lands. Basing conservation strategies on potential vegetation should be approached cautiously, however. As Scott *et al.* (1988) observe, disturbed areas such as the prairies in the U.S. Great Plains may never revert to their potential cover, even if agricultural activity ceased. The Crumpacker assessment also begs the question of whether each potential vegetation type on Federal land is actually preserved, since not all agencies manage land specifically to maintain biodiversity. The Nature Conservancy (TNC), which has been a leader in this field, also employs a community-level assessment of preservation status to identify candidate communities for preservation. TNC believes that preserving the best representatives of natural communities, which TNC refers to as a 'coarse filter' method, can assure the long-term survival of perhaps 85–90 per cent of all species (Noss 1987, Jenkins 1988). Species at greatest risk of extinction, however, may not be found in the representative communities and common species may be overlooked until they too are in jeopardy.

To overcome this potential oversight, TNC also employs a fine filter method to identify habitats of species that are threatened, endangered, rare or otherwise of biological interest. Thus, any critical species not protected in the community reserves can be managed individually, but only when their geographical occurrences are known. Species that are relatively common now are not considered, so that if the fine filter approach were used exclusively, their habitat could decline from human development. More importantly, until we conduct an unbiased survey of biological diversity at the appropriate level of resolution, we simply do not know what percentage of biodiversity is protected nor what remains to be done.

An alternative approach that combines species and community perspectives involves monitoring a species that is characteristic of a particular habitat, as a measure

315

of the condition of an entire community. An example of such an indicator species is the spotted owl (*Strix occidentalis*), used because it is sensitive to disturbance to its habitat in old-growth conifer forest in the Pacific Northwest (Simberloff 1987). Maintaining an adequate habitat for an indicator can presumably preserve all, or at least most, other species dependent upon the same habitat.

Simpson (1964) investigated species richness by counting occurrences in very large grid cells from range maps. His initial approach, based on simple visual interpretation of the resulting richness map, has been extended to include quantitative models of ecological relationships (e.g., Richerson and Lum 1980, Miller *et al.* 1989). Centres of species richness, identified from ranges of small subsets of all species, have occasionally been recommended as nature reserves. For instance, in a gap analysis for Ecuador and Columbia, Terbough and Winter (1983) mapped richness of endemic birds and recommended the richest sites as nature reserves. They explicitly assumed that centres of richness for all other taxa coincide with those of endemic birds. Scott *et al.* (1987 b) have demonstrated the power of GIS by comparing the species richness of endangered forest birds in Hawaii with existing reserve boundaries. Assessments have seldom, if ever, been based on a systematic survey of all elements of diversity within an entire biogeographic province or political jurisdiction. Instead, the analysis has usually been based on a simplified set of factors, focusing on rarity or usefulness to humanity. Cultural and political considerations have also limited the search to selected areas or species.

These examples illustrate many of the difficulties confronting an assessment of the status and trends of biodiversity. The first is data quality, in terms of low spatial resolution, uneven spatial coverage, currency of dynamic features and map accuracy. Besides this cartographic uncertainty, the ecological relationships of species and their habitat requirements are often poorly understood. Another problem is locating and consolidating the large volume of data required and then integrating the various data structures. Sometimes data that are aggregated to different political and ecological units must be transformed to a common system. Once the data are organized, there is still the problem of manipulating very large numbers of map sheets, analysing their contents and reducing the results to an effective display. All too commonly, the next researcher must rebuild the database for a new purpose. A GIS is definitely not a panacea for all these difficulties. Certainly, data in a GIS database can be of no higher quality than the source material. Nor are the issues of data transformation, manipulation and analysis trivial ones. Map errors, for instance, can propagate and multiply through overlay operations. We maintain, however, that digital GIS can be a more effective approach than either manual methods or non-spatial automated means of making an assessment of biodiversity.

3. Conceptual design of a biodiversity information system

As suggested above, the design of an information system involves the articulation of the entire process of data flow. The flow of information, shown diagrammatically in figure 3, includes the five basic components of a GIS: (1) encoding, (2) management, (3) retrieval, (4) manipulation and analysis, and (5) display of data (Smith *et al.* 1987). The system design described here is meant to be generic, whether in the context of a National Center for Biological Diversity and Environmental Research or of that of an existing agency or organization.

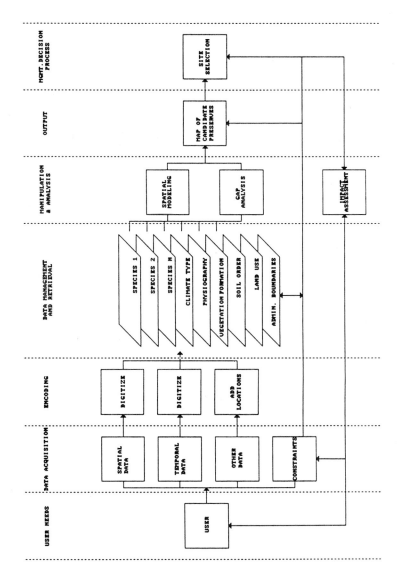

Figure 3. An example of an information flow in a biodiversity database. Headings along the top indicate the sequential steps in the design, construction and application of the database. Squares represent information produced at each step of a gap analysis. Arrows indicate the flow of information between steps and of feedback loops in the process.

Database construction, including correcting errors and standardizing information, generally requires a substantial investment of resources (Dangermond 1988). It is not enough simply to observe that data need to be digitized. As discussed in § 2, data comes from many sources that may conflict in the way they represent geographical features, e.g., coastlines. Thus, techniques have been developed to improve map accuracy before, during and after the digitization process. Tabular data may also need to be restructured and related to spatial coordinates.

An effective GIS needs software tools for efficient data management and retrieval. By data management, we include (1) the ability to support multiple users, (2) efficient data storage, retrieval and updating, (3) non-redundancy of data and (4) data independence, security and integrity (Estes 1986). The information system must also support the two most fundamental types of database query: what attributes occur at a specific location, and where do specific attributes occur? (Smith *et al.* 1987). By integrating a relational database management system into the biodiversity GIS, queries on subsets of the data would be possible. For instance, data on all species endemic to a region could be readily accessed and displayed.

The power of GIS comes from its ability to manipulate spatial objects and their attributes to generate new information which is not explicitly stored in the database. It is beyond our intent to enumerate all analytical operations performed by a GIS (see Smith *et al.* 1987 for a summary), but map overlay, point in polygon, buffer and area measurement are among the most important functions envisaged for a biodiversity GIS. In addition, the GIS should be capable of shipping data to analytical models used by ecologists, biologists and natural resource managers, and then re-importing the model outputs for display as maps, tables or graphs (Dangermond 1989).

Whereas the direction of information flow runs from input to output (figure 3), the process of system design should begin with the information products that users expect from the GIS, and then work backwards to the requirements of source data.

3.1. *User needs and information products*

An important initial phase in the design an information system is to identify that set of users to be supported and to assess their information needs. Often the calls for a biodiversity assessment have not been very specific as to the form of its outputs. Would it generate a map of species richness, of conservation hot spots (i.e., biologically significant areas facing imminent degradation), or would it generate lists of species and biotic communities in decline? Would the database be continuously queried interactively by users or only used periodically for major updates of the assessment? A formal assessment of user needs should be performed prior to development of any database. Consequently, the discussion that follows should be viewed as preliminary, based on our experience with the biodiversity issue to date. Potential users of the proposed information system would certainly include public policy makers, natural resource managers, research scientists, conservation organizations, natural resource industries and public utilities, international development organizations and educators. Multiple uses of a small-scale GIS database help to justify the massive effort required to construct it (e.g., Cocks *et al.* 1988). On the other hand, satisfying a complex set of users' needs is generally more difficult than with single-purpose databases (Rhind and Green 1988).

A biodiversity information system should address the following kinds of questions:

- what is the range of a given species or community type?
- which species are at greatest risk?
- which sites have greatest species richness?
- which biologically important sites are at greatest risk (i.e., hot spots)?
- which ecosystems are adequately protected?
- what environmental factors are related to sites of greatest biodiversity? Can diversity be predicted on the basis of these factors?
- where can ecologically sustainable development occur with acceptable impacts on biodiversity?
- what are the trends over time in species and ecosystem diversity?

3.2. *Database applications and functions*

Based on our preliminary assessment of user needs, we have identified four primary applications of a biodiversity information system: the baseline assessment of biodiversity and subsequent updates, identification of gaps in the nature reserve network, environmental impact assessment of proposed development projects and a wide range of scientific research. These applications are described briefly in the following paragraphs, including the data retrieval and analysis functions needed to perform them.

3.2.1. *Biodiversity assessment*

The fundamental assessment would consist of several components. The manual overlay method of determining species richness (e.g., Simpson 1964) could be automated. Range maps can be refined by incorporating data about the distribution of habitat factors. The area of communities is automatically computed and can be used to identify rare types. Both the species richness map and the vegetation map could be compared to maps of existing land use and land suitability in order to determine the extent of current and potential loss of biodiversity. Where maps of land suitability do not exist, GIS methods have been effectively used to derive them for many resources based upon the relationships of mapped environmental variables (Dangermond 1989). The objective of this application is to produce a map of the spatial location of the richest and rarest components of biodiversity and an indication of which are at greatest risk.

Of particular concern, especially in the less developed nations, is the lack of primary biological data; GIS can also be used in such situations for sample design. One approach is to analyse the degree of uncertainty, say in a species richness map, as a function of spatial location. Sites with greatest uncertainty are the highest priority for field sampling. Alternatively, if the relationship between richness and ecological factors is known, modelling can predict where richness is likely to be greatest, and thus where surveys are most urgently needed.

3.2.2. *Conservation gap analysis*

One widely-used strategy for preserving biological diversity is to allocate lands for nature reserves. Some sites are managed exclusively for preservation and research, while public recreation and low intensity resource utilization are permitted on others, depending on the objective of the responsible agency or organization. Candidate sites for new reserves can be identified and evaluated by some form of gap analysis (Scott *et al.* 1988) that identifies species or habitats not permanently preserved from human impacts. The output of a gap analysis is a map of candidate sites of high conservation value and tables of communities which are not currently represented (or are under-represented) in a network of reserves. Diversity elements which are not found in reserves face greater risk of extinction and thus represent gaps in the conservation strategy. A process to identify gaps in the network of reserves is discussed by Scott *et al.* (1988) and in § 4 of this paper.

3.2.3. *Impacts of proposed developments*

An important use of a national biodiversity information system would be to aid in the evaluation of the effects on biological diversity in the environmental impact assessment process and any subsequent attempts at mitigation. The information system can be the point of contact for data on critical elements of diversity that may be affected by a given project. This transaction involves overlay of the project boundary with the data layers of observations of endangered species, species richness and communities, resulting in a map of locations of critical elements of diversity potentially affected.

3.2.4. *Scientific research*

A comprehensive biodiversity information system would be an invaluable asset to scientific researchers, whose time could be spent analysing data and testing theories, rather than locating, verifying and reformatting data. To enhance the accessibility to the data maintained within the system, we suggest a computerized directory of data sources and nature reserves, similar to one for digital satellite data under development by the U.S. National Aeronautics and Space Administration (Estes and Bredekamp 1988).

Research, by its nature, involves exploration of new methods of data analysis, including functions of spatial analysis, making it difficult to design an information system (Rhind and Green 1988). Rather than attempting an exhaustive enumeration of the potential roles for GIS in biodiversity research, here we suggest a few potential applications.

Optimal conservation strategies for selecting sites for reserves and establishing boundaries have been a continuing theoretical issue for many years (e.g., MacArthur and Wilson 1967, Zimmerman and Bierregaard 1986). While it is not our intent to elaborate on this debate here, many of the variables involve size of habitat islands in disturbed landscapes and distances between them or the association of ecological factors, and GIS, as discussed above, are well-suited to the analysis of spatial and multivariate properties.

GIS can also provide data management and display capabilities for ecological modelling. Predictive modelling of species ranges is described above. In addition, researchers are using spatial data to explore issues of global change and its effects on biodiversity. Examples include projecting the future distributions of species and communities under the greenhouse effect (Busby 1988) and future levels of land-use activities (Esser 1989).

3.3. *Database contents*

Based upon the preceding discussion of user needs and GIS applications, we can now tentatively identify the data inputs to a national assessment of biodiversity. Even though having all of the factors listed in table 1 would be ideal, as a practical matter, priorities must be set for the sequence of data encoding. The most urgently needed data layers, we suggest, are

(1) existing range maps for vertebrate species,
(2) an ecoregions map, integrating many habitat factors,
(3) a map of large nature reserves (e.g., wilderness areas),
(4) sites of rare and endangered species and communities, and
(5) major human land uses and potential land conversions (e.g., for energy and mineral development).

For the initial assessment, these data would be assembled at a small scale. Over time, as museum and herbaria collections become computerized, as range maps are revised through more current observations, as remotely-sensed imagery is used to record recent-land-use changes, and so on, the database can be refined and enlarged.

The authors believe that a National Center should not attempt to be the repository for all biological data, but instead should implement a central directory while planning for a distributed database system over the longer term. This recommendation is consistent with that of the National Academy of Sciences (Committee on Data Management and Computation 1986), which endorses the concept of networked distributed data centres, with the data residing in close proximity to the most active user community.

3.4. *Development of standards*

A data dictionary is the vehicle for establishing standards for the contents of the database and documenting their definitions and attributes (Marble 1986). Other aspects of the definitions include their source, resolution, standardized geographical coordinate system (for spatial data), their required quality, precision and legitimacy (objectivity, reproducibility, accuracy and authority), the definitions of each variable and its legitimate values and the schedule for updates or revisions. Too often, a dictionary is not formally prepared, leaving users of the system with data sets of unknown origin and relevance.

Although it is known that data coverage is not uniform for all species and habitats and for all geographical regions in the U.S.A., no systematic survey of existing biodiversity data sets has ever been made (Tangley 1985). Creating the data dictionary systematically determines which data sets meeting the required standards already exist, and which must still be collected. The process of designing the GIS database naturally forms the basis for a first comprehensive assessment of the knowledge base of biodiversity.

4. The process of conservation gap analysis

In this section, we examine one of the most complex applications in a biodiversity information system, gap analysis, in greater detail. Scott *et al.* (1988) have previously outlined the basic procedure and discussed the biological rationale. Here we demonstrate the feasibility of this procedure by verifying that the required data and

321

GIS functions are typically available. For illustration, we have chosen the State of California, U.S.A., where a pilot analysis is being contemplated (K. Smith, personal communication, 1989).

California, covering approximately 411 000 km², is an extremely heterogenous environment, hosting a diverse flora and fauna in five biogeographic provinces (Udvardy 1975). Although 11 per cent of the State is already under some form of preservation management, many important habitats and species are still not adequately protected (Klubnikin 1980). Experts estimate that 220 animal and 600 plant species, and 200 types of natural community are experiencing severe reduction or extinction in California (Jones and Stokes Associates 1987).

Three biodiversity components of a gap analysis include geographical centres of species richness of animals, habitats of all special interest species and endangered communities and representatives of all vegetation communities. Tentative sources of data to be used in the California gap analysis are listed in table 2. We suggest that an acceptable first approximation of species richness could be determined by overlaying range maps of approximately 700 vertebrates (i.e., mammals, birds, fish, reptiles and amphibians), recently updated and digitized by the California Department of Fish and Game (CDF&G) at a scale of approximately 1:3 400 000. Current gap analysis programmes in Idaho and Oregon have produced their range maps by masking out land-use categories and vegetation types that are not used by the species (B. Csuti, personal communication, 1989). The ranges of the 5000 native vascular plants and 28 000 insect species that inhabit the State are less well known than those of the vertebrates and are not recommended for gap analysis. Butterflies were also recommended by Scott *et al.* (1988) as representatives of invertebrates, but maps of their ranges are not yet available for California.

The locations of populations of nearly 1100 rare, threatened, endangered and special interest species and communities are available in digital format in the Natural Diversity Data Base (NDDB) of the CDF&G (Jones and Stokes Associates 1987). Because the NDDB is not a GIS, the specimen locations must be reformatted into the GIS data structure. Known locations of rare and endangered species can be

Table 2. Data layers required to identify gaps in the reserve network of California.

Data category	Data source	Published scale
Biogeographic provinces	Udvardy (1975)	~1:50 million
Vertebrate range maps	California DF&G	1:3·4 million
Special interest species and communities	California DF&G (NDDB)	Tabular
Ecological factors		
Climate	Various	Various
Elevation	USGS†	1:250000
Vegetation associations	CALVEG	1:250000
Geology	California Division of Mines	1:250000
Soil associations	USDA SCS‡	1:250000
Existing reserves	Various	Various

† U.S. Geological Survey.
‡ U.S. Department of Agriculture Soil Conservation Service.

supplemented by predictive modelling of species range or richness from ecological variables, including climate, topography, vegetation, soils and geology. Habitat factors known to produce rare and unusual species, such as vernal pools or serpentine soils (Jones and Stokes Associates 1987) could also be used to delineate biologically significant areas. The vegetation layer is needed both for modelling and to portray vegetation communities as the third component of the gap analysis. Only one map of actual vegetation currently exists for the entire state at an appropriate scale, the CALVEG map produced by the U.S. Forest Service (Matyas and Parker 1980).

A map depicting the boundaries of existing nature reserves (both public and private) is needed to identify species and ecosystems already protected. Defining what land management constitutes preservation may be politically sensitive, since a management prescription may preserve some species and not others. The data dictionary described earlier must establish clear criteria as to what areas are to be included. A preliminary selection of sites that qualify as nature reserves is given in table 3, including Federal research natural areas, and wilderness areas, national parks and wildlife refuges, state parks and reserves, the 27 sites of the University of California Natural Reserve System and lands owned or leased by TNC and other private conservation groups. Although state and national parks are included in this initial list, their primary objective is to preserve outstanding scenic and recreational areas, and therefore they do not

Table 3.   Area of lands in California in existing nature reserves. Source: Jones and Stokes Associates 1987.

Administration	Programme	Area (ha)
Federal ownership		
U.S. Forest Service	Research natural areas	10438
	Special interest areas	32788
	Wilderness areas	1561301
Bureau of Land Management	Research natural areas	32327
	Areas of critical environmental concern	292459
	Outstanding natural areas	45198
National Park Service	Parks, monuments, seashores	2109352
U.S. Fish and Wildlife Service	National Wildlife Refuges	118575
State ownership		
California State Parks	State parks	371706
	State reserves	10672
	Other natural preserves	853
California DF&G	Ecological reserves	21698
	Wildlife areas	123721
University of California	Natural Reserve System	27094
Private ownership		
The Nature Conservancy	Preserves	48562
National Audubon Society	Preserves	2809
Sierra Club		324
National Wildlife Federation		1119
Total area of reserves		4720996
Total area of California		41101300

Although state and national parks are included in this list, developed recreation sites within parks may not adequately preserve natural habitats. Other lands not in this list may currently be in a natural condition due to lack of access or resource potential, but future status is not assured.

necessarily preserve biodiversity. Park areas outside of developed recreation facilities, however, often preserve natural ecosystems and should be considered in this inventory. Regional parks, perhaps, should also be considered.

The original data will not be in a form where gaps in the reserve network can be easily detected. The process of synthesis and reduction of data in the GIS is illustrated schematically in figure 4 and represents a more detailed portrayal of part of figure 3. Part of the challenge is integrating small-scale data on species range (e.g., 1 : 3 400 000) with medium-scale maps of vegetation communities and rare and endangered species (e.g., 1 : 250 000). Species richness will be derived by overlaying the vertebrate range maps, and then be stratified by the map of biogeographic provinces (e.g., Udvardy 1975) to identify centres of greatest richness. It would be naïve to think that a GIS-based gap analysis would identify areas of high species richness precisely, because small-scale range maps are inherently crude representations of the area actually occupied by species. At best a map of vertebrate species richness could indicate sites that should be investigated in greater detail. Manual methods of gap analysis would be prone to the same problems and would be extremely tedious in comparison to a digital GIS approach.

Known and modelled locations of all special-interest species and natural communities from the NDDB would be composited for the State and intersected with the map of centres of species richness and the map of existing nature reserves. Biologically rich areas and areas of special interest outside existing reserves would be candidates for designation as new nature reserves.

Next, the map of existing nature reserves would be compared with the CALVEG maps of vegetation associations, quantifying the area of each association within reserves and identifying communities that are preserved nowhere (or rarely) in the State. Determining the extent to which vegetation communities are represented in the preserve network is probably most effectively done by examining a tabular listing. An example of such a table for potential vegetation, excerpted from Klubnikin (1980), is presented in table 4. From such a table, priorities can be set for the most critical community types and a search of the GIS database for the best examples of each type can be initiated.

Conducting a comprehensive gap analysis as described here is clearly an ambitious undertaking. It appears technically feasible to do, however, for an area such as California, where reasonably good quality data already exist. The volume of data is large but not beyond the capacity of modern minicomputer disk drives. As a rough approximation for our example, we estimate 750 data layers, most of which are species range maps (and could therefore be simple bit maps). Even using a raster data structure, with 1 km^2 cells and 1 b per cell, the data volume for California would be of the order of 300 Mb (which could be reduced significantly with a more efficient data structure or lower resolution). Gap analysis primarily involves overlay, reclassification and topographic functions that are all routine capabilities in most commercial GIS. Even modelling is possible with a GIS database (e.g., Miller *et al.* 1989). For a gap analysis to be accepted by decision makers, the issues of cartographic error and its propagation through the analysis process must be addressed. The species richness map and model predictions must be validated with field data. The analysis procedure must also overcome the implicit assumption of preservation management that the ranges of species are static. Concerns have recently grown, for instance, about the potential impacts on nature reserves and their resident species if global warming occurs (Peters and Darling 1985).

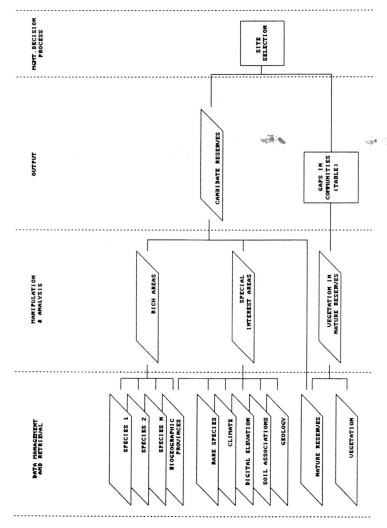

Figure 4. Conservation gap analysis data flow. This diagram expands the detail of the data storage, manipulation and analysis, and output stages of the overall information flow of figure 3 for a gap analysis as one specific application.

Table 4. Example of tabular listing from GIS of the area of vegetation type preserved in California (after Klubnikin 1980). Potential natural vegetation types, based on Küchler (1977), were aggregated into the types shown here.

Potential natural vegetation type	Area preserved (in ha)	Proportion of type preserved (per cent)	Abundance of vegetation (percentage of State's area)
Creosote bush scrub	902789	11·9	18·4
Subalpine forest	531344	33·7	3·8
Wet coniferous forest	440080	9·6	11·0
Alpine community	225291	76·5	0·7
Saltbush	164503	8·9	4·5
Juniper pinyon woodland	132076	7·6	4·2
Chaparral	111102	5·2	5·1
Blue oak-digger pine forest	96023	1·0	9·7
Mixed evergreen forest	93081	30·3	7·4
Yellow pine forest	87804	5·1	4·1
Joshua tree scrub	70563	15·2	1·1
Great Basin subalpine forest	59783	37·7	0·4
Sagebrush steppe	53655	2·1	6·3
Mixed hardwood and redwood forest	36536	61·2	0·1
California prairie	35375	0·9	9·9
Coastal prairie and scrub mosaic	28115	8·2	0·8
Coastal saltmarsh	26437	25·7	0·3
Tule marsh	12706	1·6	1·9
Southern oak forest	8515	1·0	2·0
Coastal sagebrush	7849	0·8	2·5
Coastal cypress and pine forest	6683	8·2	0·2
Northern seashore community	5029	16·0	0·1
Coulter pine forest	5010	15·7	0·1
Alkaline scrub woodland	3729	13·4	0·1
Riparian forest	2571	0·5	1·3
Savanna	1952	0·2	2·3
Mojave montane forest	64·8	2·4	0·01
Blackbush scrub	64·8	0·02	0·8
San Benito forest	0	0	0·01
Oregon oak forest	0	0	0·8
Southern seashore communities	0	0	0·1

5. Conclusions

Although a comprehensive assessment of the trend of biological diversity has been beyond the capabilities of the scientific community, case studies from around the world show that diversity is being reduced at a disturbing rate. To formulate biologically defensible reponses to this crisis, we must garner the best data we have on species, their habitats and human land uses that affect habitats. Many efforts to collect and manage data on biological diversity are under way (e.g., TNC's Heritage Data Base programme and IUCN's Conservation Monitoring Centre) or under discussion (e.g., the National Center for Biological Diversity and Environmental Research proposed in H.R. 1268).

In this paper, we have proposed a concept for a comprehensive diversity information system that builds on this strong foundation. The conceptual information system we propose, based on a GIS approach, is integrative in three important ways. First, data from many disciplines are brought together in a single database, essentially for the first time. This contrasts with existing databases which are typically structured around a single theme or a small subset of biological species. Bringing together data on the distribution of areas of high biological interest and sensitivity with data on potential resource development can encourage a preventative rather than a reactive approach to conflicts. Because the data needed by a diversity information system overlap with the needs of a wide variety of resource management agencies, horizontal integration across departmental lines is also imperative. The difficulties in obtaining agreement between the players on the data dictionary and other issues is acknowledged. However, there seems to be a growing acceptance within the U.S. Federal establishment of the need for inter-agency co-ordination in data management. Secondly, the system encourages the vertical flow of spatially-distributed information. Data from lower levels can be aggregated and generalized for use at higher levels, which in turn can serve as clearinghouses to disseminate information about gaps in data and reserves, and about experience in other jurisdictions. Thirdly, the system could provide information to a wide variety of users, including policy makers, development interests, researchers and the public. We predict that the function of the directory will be especially useful to those trying to locate data.

We have specifically outlined this information system in the context of a National Center for the United States, as stated in H.R. 1268. Similarly, our proposed process for conservation gap analysis is for the State of California and is based on ecological factors and data sets specific to the area. However, as stated by Scott *et al.* (1987 a, 1988), the system concept presented and the process involved in the development and the functions of the system are generic enough to be adapted to the needs of other nations and states. It is recognized that the less developed countries will be the most hampered in their database development, due to the lack of data and of the infrastructure to maintain advanced information systems. Indeed, all nations will be confronted by a combination of the cartographic uncertainty of their primary data and the ecological uncertainty about the relationships between biodiversity and environmental factors. Through pilot studies, these relationships can be better understood. From environmental maps, nations can begin systematically to determine priorities for field surveys and for conserving their natural heritage while developing their resources.

Leon *et al.* (1985) observed that no database in and of itself has saved a single species (at least in the case of Mediterranean plants, to which they were referring). Information systems make no guarantee that they will be used to make wise decisions. However, we have all seen the price paid for decisions made without good information, species after species driven to extinction by both wilful and inadvertent human disruption of critical habitats, or species saved only through heroic (and expensive) recovery programmes. If the quality of land-use decisions can be improved by incorporating a better understanding of the location of the important elements of diversity and of our effects upon them, ecologically sustainable development of the biosphere may succeed.

Acknowledgments

The authors would like to thank Blair Csuti, Ron Miller, Rich Walker and Chuck Paul for reviewing drafts of this article. The condor sighting data used in figure 1 were provided by the U.S. Fish and Wildlife Service and the National Audubon Society. Figures 1 and 2 were produced with the assistance of Marco Painho and Josh Pritikin. The Idaho Cooperative Fish and Wildlife Research Unit is supported by the Idaho

Department of Fish and Game, University of Idaho, U.S. Fish and Wildlife Service and the Wildlife Management Institute. This article is contribution number 467 from the University of Idaho Forestry and Wildlife Resources Experiment Station.

References

ALLEN, T. F. H., and STARR, T. B., 1982, *Hierarchy: Perspectives for Ecological Complexity* (Chicago: University of Chicago Press).

BAILEY, R. G., 1976, *Ecoregions of the United States* (Ogden, Utah: USDA Forest Service).

BUSBY, J. R., 1988, Potential impacts of climate change on Australia's flora and fauna. In *Greenhouse: Planning for Climate Change*, edited by G. I. Pearman (Melbourne: CSIRO Australia), pp. 387–398.

COCKS, K. D., WALKER, P. A., and PARVEY, C. A., 1988, Evolution of a continental-scale geographical information system. *International Journal of Geographical Information Systems*, **2**, 263.

COMMITTEE ON DATA MANAGEMENT AND COMPUTATION, 1986, *Issues and Recommendations Associated with Distributed Computation and Data Management Systems for the Space Sciences* (Washington, D.C.: National Academy Press).

CROSBY, M. R., and MAGILL, R. E., 1988, *TROPICOS: A Botanical Database System at the Missouri Botanical Garden* (St Louis: Missouri Botanical Garden).

CRUMPACKER, D. W., HODGE, S. W., FRIEDLEY, D., and GREGG, W. P., JR, 1988, A preliminary assessment of the status of major terrestrial and wetland ecosystems on Federal and Indian lands in the United States. *Conservation Biology*, **2**, 103.

DANGERMOND, J., 1988, A review of digital data commonly available and some of the practical problems of entering them into a GIS. In *Technical Papers of the 1988 ACSM-ASPRS Annual Convention*, Vol 5, St. Louis, Missouri, 13–18 March 1988 (Falls Church, Virginia: American Congress on Surveying and Mapping and American Society for Photogrammetry and Remote Sensing), pp. 1–10.

DANGERMOND, J., 1989, The maturing of GIS and a new age for geographic information modeling (GIMS). *Proceedings of the International Geographic Information Systems Symposium (IGIS): The Research Agenda*, Vol. 2, Arlington, Virginia, 15–18 November 1987 (Washington, D.C.: National Aeronautics and Space Administration), pp. 55–66.

ESSER, G., 1989, Global land-use changes from 1860 to 1980 and future projections to 2500. *Ecological Modelling*, **44**, 307.

ESTES, J. E., 1985, The need for improved information systems. *Canadian Journal of Remote Sensing*, **11**, 124.

ESTES, J. E., 1986, A perspective on the use of geographic information systems for environmental protection. *Proceedings of the Workshop on Geographic Information Systems for Environmental Protection*, Las Vegas, Nevada, 22–23 January 1986 (Las Vegas: University of Nevada, Las Vegas), pp. 3–23.

ESTES, J. E., and BREDEKAMP, J. H., 1988, Activities associated with global databases in the National Aeronautics and Space Administration. In *Building Databases for Global Science*, edited by Helen Mounsey (London: Taylor & Francis), pp. 251–269.

ESTES, J. E. (editor), 1983, *Manual of Remote Sensing*, Vol 2 (Falls Church, Virginia: American Society of Photogrammetry).

HOLDRIDGE, L. R., 1947, Determination of world plant formations from simple climate data. *Science, New York*, **105**, 367.

JENKINS, R. E., 1988, Information management for the conservation of biodiversity. In *Biodiversity*, edited by E. O. Wilson (Washington, D.C.: National Academy Press), pp. 231–239.

JONES AND STOKES ASSOCIATES, 1987, *Sliding Toward Extinction: The State of California's Natural Heritage, 1987* (San Francisco: The California Nature Conservancy).

KLUBNIKIN, K., 1980, A distributional analysis of preserves relative to vegetation types in California. Unpublished paper presented at *The Second Conference on Scientific Research in the National Parks*, San Francisco, California, 26–30 November 1979.

KÜCHLER, A. W., 1964, *Potential Natural Vegetation of the Conterminous United States*, Special Publication Number 36 (New York: American Geographical Society).

KÜCHLER, A. W., 1967, *Vegetation Mapping* (New York: Ronald Press Company).

KÜCHLER, A. W., 1977, A map of the natural vegetation of California. In *Terrestrial Vegetation of California*, edited by M. G. Barbour and J. Major (New York: John Wiley & Sons), pp. 909–938.

LEON, C., LUCAS, G., and SYNGE, H., 1985, The value of information in saving threatened Mediterranean plants. In *Plant Conservation in the Mediterranean Area*, edited by C. Gomez-Campo (Dordrecht: Dr W. Junk Publishers), pp. 177–196.

LOVEJOY, T. E., 1988, Will unexpectedly the top blow off? *BioScience*, **38**, 722.

MACARTHUR, R. H., and WILSON, E. O., 1967, *The Theory of Island Biogeography* (Princeton, New Jersey: Princeton University Press).

MARBLE, D., 1986, Geographic information systems as a tool to assist in the preservation of biological diversity. In *Technologies to Maintain Biological Diversity*, Vol. 2, Contract Papers, Part C: Natural Systems—United States (Washington, D.C.: U.S. Congress Office of Technology Assessment), pp. 85–132.

MATYAS, W. J., and PARKER, I., 1980, *CALVEG: Mosaic of Existing Vegetation of California* (San Francisco: U.S. Forest Service Regional Ecology Group).

MCGRANAGHAN, M., and WESTER, L., 1988, Prototyping an herbarium collection mapping system. *Technical Papers of the 1988 ACSM–ASPRS Annual Convention*, Vol. 5, St. Louis, Missouri, 13–18 March 1988 (Falls Church, Virginia: American Congress on Surveying and Mapping and American Society for Photogrammetry and Remote Sensing), pp. 232–238.

MCHARG, I. L., 1969, *Design with Nature* (Garden City, New York: The Natural History Press).

MILLER, R. I., STUART, S. N., and HOWELL, K. M., 1989, A methodology for analyzing rare species distribution patterns utilizing GIS technology: the rare birds of Tanzania. *Landscape Ecology*, **2** (in the press).

MOONEYHAN, D. W., 1988, Applications of geographical information systems within the United Nations Environment Programme. In *Building Databases for Global Science*, edited by Helen Mounsey (London: Taylor & Francis), pp. 315–329.

MORSE, L. E., HENIFIN, M. S., BALLMAN, J. C., and LAWLER, J. I., 1981, Geographical data organization in botany and plant conservation: a survey of alternative strategies. In *Rare Plant Conservation: Geographical Data Organization*, edited by Larry E. Morse and Mary Sue Henifin (Bronx, New York: The New York Botanic Garden), pp. 9–29.

NOSS, R. F., 1987, From plant communities to landscapes in conservation inventories: a look at The Nature Conservancy (USA). *Biological Conservation*, **41**, 11.

OLSON, R. J., KLOPATEK, J. M., and EMERSON, C. J., 1983, Regional environmental analysis and assessment utilizing the Geoecology data base. In *Computer Graphics and Environmental Planning*, edited by Eric Teicholz and Brian J. L. Berry (Englewood Cliffs, New Jersey: Prentice-Hall), pp. 102–118.

OMERNIK, J. M., 1987, Ecoregions of the conterminous United States. *Annals of the Association of American Geographers*, **77**, 118.

PELLEW, R. A., and HARRISON, J. D., 1988, A global database on the status of biological diversity: the I.U.C.N. perspective. In *Building Databases for Global Science*, edited by Helen Mounsey (London: Taylor & Francis), pp. 330–339.

PERRING, F. H., and WALTERS, S. M., 1962, *Atlas of British Flora* (London: Nelson and Sons).

PETERS, R. L., and DARLING, J. D. S., 1985, The greenhouse effect and nature reserves: global warming would diminish biological diversity by causing extinctions among reserve species. *BioScience*, **35**, 707.

RAPOPORT, E. H., 1982, *Areography: Geographical Strategies of Species* (Oxford: Pergamon Press).

RHIND, D. W., and GREEN, N. P. A., 1988, Design of a geographical information system for a heterogeneous scientific community. *International Journal of Geographical Information Systems*, **2**, 171.

RICHERSON, P. J., and KWEI-LIN LUM, 1980, Patterns of plant species diversity in California: relation to weather and topography. *American Naturalist*, **116**, 504.

SCEPAN, J., DAVIS, F., and BLUM, L. L., 1987, A geographic information system for managing California condor habitat. *Proceedings of GIS '87—Second Annual International Conference, Exhibits and Workshops on Geographic Information Systems*, San Francisco, California, 26–30 October 1987 (Falls Church, Virginia: American Society for Photogrammetry and Remote Sensing and American Congress on Surveying and Mapping), pp. 476–486.

SCOTT, J. M., CSUTI, B., JACOBI, J. D., and ESTES, J. E., 1987 a, Species richness: a geographic approach to protecting future biological diversity. *BioScience*, **37**, 782.

SCOTT, J. M., CSUTI, B., SMITH, K., ESTES, J. E., and CAICCO, S., 1988, Beyond endangered species: an integrated conservation strategy for the preservation of biological diversity. *Endangered Species Update*, **5**, 43.

SCOTT, J. M., KEPLER, C. B., STINE, P. A., LITTLE, H., and TAKETA, K., 1987 b, Protecting endangered forest birds in Hawaii: the development of a conservation strategy. *Transactions of the 52nd North American Wildlife and Natural Resources Conference*, Quebec City, Quebec, Canada, 20–25 March 1987, edited by R. E. McCabe (Washington, D.C.: Wildlife Management Institute), pp. 348–363.

SIMBERLOFF, D., 1987, The spotted owl fracas: mixing academic, applied, and political ecology. *Ecology*, **68**, 766.

SIMPSON, G. G., 1964, Species density of North American recent mammals. *Systematic Zoology*, **13**, 57.

SMITH, T. R., MENON, S., STAR, J. L., and ESTES, J. E., 1987, Requirements and principles for the implementation and construction of large-scale geographic information systems. *International Journal of Geographical Information Systems*, **1**, 13.

TANGLEY, L., 1985, A national biological survey. *BioScience*, **35**, 686.

TERBOUGH, J., and WINTER, B., 1983, A method for siting parks and reserves with special reference to Columbia and Ecuador. *Biological Conservation*, **27**, 45.

THORNTHWAITE, C. W., 1948, An approach towards a rational classification of climate. *Geographical Review*, **38**, 55.

TUHKANEN, S., 1980, *Climatic Parameters and Indices in Plant Geography*, Acta Phytogeographica Suecica Series (Uppsala, Sweden: Almqvist and Wiksell International).

U.S. CONGRESS OFFICE OF TECHNOLOGY ASSESSMENT, 1987, *Technologies to Maintain Biological Diversity* (Washington, D.C.: U.S. Government Printing Office).

UDVARDY, M. D. F., 1975, *A Classification of the Biogeographical Provinces of the World* (Morges, Switzerland: International Union for Conservation of Nature and Natural Resources).

WHITTAKER, R. H., 1975, *Communities and Ecosystems* (New York: MacMillan).

WILSON, E. O. (editor), 1988, *Biodiversity* (Washington, D.C.: National Academy Press).

ZIMMERMAN, B. L., and BIERREGAARD, R. O., 1986, Relevance of the equilibrium theory of island biogeography and species–area relations to conservation with a case from Amazonia. *Journal of Biogeography*, **13**, 133.

Framework for a Geographically Referenced Conservation Database: Case Study Nepal

Sean C. Ahearn*
Remote Sensing Laboratory, University of Minnesota, 1530 N. Cleveland Ave., St. Paul, MN 55108
James L. David Smith
Department of Fisheries and Wildlife, University of Minnesota, 1980 Folwell Ave., St. Paul, MN 55108
Catherine Wee
Remote Sensing Laboratory, University of Minnesota, 1530 N. Cleveland Ave., St. Paul, MN 55108

ABSTRACT: Many national governments and most international development organizations are attempting to integrate conservation and sustainable development goals. To do so they need biological diversity information in a readily accessible form. Currently available conservation databases are constrained by reliance on paper map products as repositories for spatial information and an inability to quickly obtain information and integrate it with other map layers. A framework for developing a conservation database using the convergence of technological developments in digital imaging, remote sensing, micro-computers, database management, geographic information systems, global positioning systems, communications and user interface software is proposed. We also describe a pilot project in which we developed the software for a geographically referenced visual/tabular conservation database for the lowlands of Nepal.

INTRODUCTION

WORLDWIDE CONCERN FOR LESS OF BIOLOGICAL DIVERSITY has resulted in a variety of policy and program initiatives to slow the high rate of species loss. Miller *et al.* (1989) argue that it is time to shift from a defensive role of stemming the loss of species to an offensive position of integrating conservation goals with sustainable development and the needs of indigenous people. Current biological diversity information, that can be accessed easily, is needed by national governments and international development agencies as they attempt to integrate conservation and sustainable development goals. At present, conservation databases are limited because they lack geo-referenced data or the ability to rapidly access information and integrate it with other spatial data.

While movement is underway to automate conservation databases, a framework for doing so needs to be established. The convergence of technological advancements in digital imaging, remote sensing, micro-computers, database management, geographic information systems (GIS), global positioning systems (GPS), communications, and user interface software will have a profound effect on the nature of this framework. Recent developments in these technologies can help solve existing problems as well as provide new forms of information previously ignored. These technologies are impacting the development of conservation databases in the following ways: locational information is gathered more easily through GPS; data access is enhanced through the use of database management systems; geographically referenced visual catalogues of flora, fauna, and habitats are being developed through the use of imaging technologies (Hamilton *et al.*, 1989); and remote sensing enables the creation of image maps that will greatly enhance data input, interpretation of data, and data output products for decision makers.

In this paper we propose a framework for developing a conservation database founded on these new technologies. We also describe a pilot project in which we developed the software for a geographically referenced visual/tabular conservation database. It is not the intent of this paper to give a definitive statement or framework for a global conservation database; our objective is to begin development of the adumbrations for one in the context of today's relevant technological developments. The study site for demonstrating this software is the lowlands of Nepal.

CONSERVATION DATABASES

From the 1970s to the mid-1980s, the central clearing houses for endangered species information have been institutions such as the International Union for the Conservation of Nature's (IUCN) Survival Species Commission (SSC) which issues the Red Data Books, and The Nature Conservancy (TNC) which developed the Natural Heritage Data Base (NHDB). The SSC's Red Data Book has grown from a part-time effort relying on a network of volunteer wildlife experts to a separate institution, the World Conservation Monitoring Center (WCMC), Cambridge, which brought together bird, mammal, and protected area databases (Thornback and Jenkins, 1982). The present system has massive volumes of gray literature that are stored in files and periodically summarized in the Red Data Books or in specialized products based on individual requests. WCMC has recently undertaken a GIS project to develop an atlas of tropical forests (Mark Collins, pers. comm.) and is seeking input from the scientific and conservation community in developing new approaches to conservation databases. (Robin Pellew, pers. comm.).

The Nature Conservancy's Natural Heritage Data Base originated in 1974 as a cooperative effort between TNC and South Carolina to develop a state-wide conservation database (Jenkins, 1988). This original system has continually been improved, and the format has been adopted by all states. The key to its success is the highly standardized methodology that provides efficient communication and exchange of information as well as the economy of having TNC act as system administrator and developer. With the recent establishment of Latin American Conservation Data Centers in several South and Central American countries, the system is expanding throughout the western hemisphere. The data are used both internally by the TNC and state and national agencies and externally as products these agencies prepare for other organizations. Internal uses include products such as inventories and monitoring, setting of conservation priorities, preserve selection and design, and element management (an element is a species, a community type, or

*Presently at the Department of Geology and Geography, Hunter College - City University of New York, 695 Park Avenue, New York, NY 10021.

PHOTOGRAMMETRIC ENGINEERING & REMOTE SENSING,
Vol. 56, No. 11, November 1990, pp. 1477-1481.

0099-1112/90/5611–1477$03.00/0
©1990 American Society for Photogrammetry and Remote Sensing

some other feature or phenomenon of special interest to conservationists)(Jenkins, 1988). In addition, external products are generated for other government agencies and research, conservation, and development institutions for development planning, environmental impact analysis, and predictive modeling (Jenkins, 1988).

Despite their tremendous strengths, the NHDB and the WCMC have the following weaknesses that derive from the fact that their maps are not digitally based:

- During data entry, obtaining geo-referencing is time consuming and prone to small scale generalizations as well as occasional large errors.
- For most users it is critical to know an element's location and spatial context. However, with the present systems it is difficult to generate map-based products with this information.
- These systems do not provide photographic or image products. The adage, a picture is worth a thousand words, is not trivial when trying to describe habitats or species or to create the emotional impact that motivates decision makers.
- It is not easy to create data layers that are needed for sophisticated spatial analysis in a GIS environment; the layers must be compatible in format, spatial content and quality.

FRAMEWORK FOR PROPOSED SYSTEM

The importance of conservation databases depends in part on how well they contribute to the making of informed decisions regarding the potential impact land uses may have on biological systems. With greater tendencies toward the use of GIS to make such decisions, it is critical that conservation databases be in a form that easily can be integrated into the GIS environment. However, when a GIS has not been developed for a region, the conservation database should stand on its own as a tool for sound environmental decision making. A conservation database can be thought of as a specialized subset of a generic GIS. The distinction between the systems concern their analytic capabilities and the data requirements of each system. The spatial operations necessary for a conservation database are confined largely to point in polygon and distance computations. It also is necessary to support combined spatial/attribute queries (i.e., find all tigers within a specified polygon in lowland forests. In contrast, GIS are multi-layered databases that have a wealth of spatial operations involving single and multiple layers.

It is also necessary for conservation databases to communicate more than just text information regarding elements. A visual component can turn the species cataloged in the database from an abstract to a tangible entity. An image provides habitat quality information that cannot be readily communicated in a text form. The technology is available to develop conservation databases to meet these requirements and a diversity of individuals and institutions (e.g., Conservation International; International Council for Bird Preservation; WCMC) have begun to develop such systems.

The wide range of computer expertise in the user community necessitates a system that is very simple for both data input and data access. For any database system the primary costs and impediments to a functional system are usually associated with data input. Therefore, it is necessary to minimize the time and expertise needed for the local input of data as well as to provide a means to regionalize and centralize the information.

DATA STRUCTURE

Conservation data sets do not form a continuous, topologically complete layer of geographic information but consist of a set of points or polygons that designate the location of elements. Associated with this spatial information is the attribute information that describes the nature and significance of the element. The attributes for a conservation database should include both structured and unstructured data. Both spatial and attribute

information can be managed using a relational database. The cartographic base linked to the conservation data can be raster, vector, or both. While a raster system is easy to implement, it is limited in its ability to link the cartographic information with the conservation data. In contrast, a vector structure facilitates the linking of the cartographic data and its associated attributes with element data. For example, it might be desirable to find a specific element type within a particular political unit (i.e., a panchyat in Nepal). This could only be done with a topologically complete cartographic layer. Digital cartographic information is becoming more prevalent and is now available for the entire world at 1:1,000,000 (MundoCart, 1989). Digital line graphs (DLG) also are available for much of the United States at scales ranging from 1:24,000 to 1:2,000,000 (USGS, 1987). Digital images of the Earth's surface can be obtained at resolutions as low as 10 metres in Pancromatic mode to 20, 30, 80, and 1100 metres multispectral. These images can be geo-referenced and overlayed with cartographic information to create image maps (Colvocoresses, 1986). The advantage of the image map is the additional information it contains pertaining to cover types and topographic conditions. The image map is very useful for orientation purposes during data input and access as well as for data presentation. We suggest that the optimal spatial framework is a digital image map that maintains the cartographic data in vector form and images in raster. This linkage is essentially the approach used in TYDAC'S SPANS and in the ARCINFO/ERDAS Live Link. The approach has all the advantages of an image map while retaining the topological relationships necessary to access features within their spatial context. The types of spatial operations needed in a conservation database are relatively simple in comparison to a GIS. Spatial queries include proximity to a point, line, or polygon and point in polygon operations. These spatial queries are modified by searches for particular element types or sub-attributes of the elements.

DATA INPUT

A conservation database must be capable of ingesting both existing and new conservation data. Existing data in ASCII format can easily be incorporated by means of a data conversion routine. Written data sets need to be manually entered. An automated check on the validity of the geographic coordinates for all written and digital data sets is a requisite function of the system. This check is for major blunders such as the identification of data points that occur outside the state or region in which they are supposed to be contained. The specificity with which these checks can be made depends on the level of detail that is contained in the cartographic/image database used by the system. Manual checks of spatial location can also be made by the person entering the data. This is done by displaying the points or polygons on the cartographic/image base as a test for consistency with the element's location as defined by its political or geographic location. The coordinates for new elements can be derived from two possible sources: (1) GPS receivers or (2) images, maps, or image-maps in either hardcopy or digital form. GPS enables the recording of locational information while data are collected from the ground. Ground GPS systems have been found to be very useful even in the most demanding of conditions (Wilke, 1989) and can provide very accurate vertical and horizontal coordinates during field examination. Screen digitization on digital cartographic or image maps automatically records the geographic coordinates for the elements entered. Elements located on the paper products can be electronically digitized after map registration. The cover type information interpretable on an image-map can be used to guide the person to the location of a particular point or help identify regions that may contain elements that need to be recorded. This is of particular importance in areas with few cultural or natural features.

is used to formulate a query to retrieve information from the database. Table 2 gives an example of how DML can retrieve all tiger locations in Nepal. Because the general purpose programming language used is C, all the above DML are used in conjunction with this general purpose programming language by imbedding SQL calls within the C language program.

For the prototype a raster image map referenced to the UTM coordinate system is used as the cartographic base on which new element locations can be designated for input into the database or existing elements retrieved.

DATA INPUT AND RETRIEVAL

New data are input by entering geo-coordinates for the element occurrence or by digitizing its location on the digital image map which automatically places geo-coordinates in the appropriate field of the new element occurrence. A window will then open that contains the attribute template for the element. If free form text and pictorial image files also are to be included, the file names are entered in the appropriate fields. Input of text and image capture can occur by starting a new session in a separate window. Data can be retrieved by attribute for a given geographic location which can be typed in or selected on the image map. A radius about a point or a search within a defined polygon can be chosen. These searches result in the display of a summary data form stating the number of occurrences, the locations of all records that fit the search criteria as displayed on the image map, and a typical example (digital picture) of the element of interest. Information for a selected element is displayed in various windows. Icons indicate if additional free form text or images are associated with a given site. Map and image data for the given location can then be displayed or printed (Plate 1).

TABLE 2. IN THIS EXAMPLE, table3 IS USED TO OBTAIN THE CORRESPONDING INDEX FOR TIGER. USING THIS INDEX, ALL LOCATIONS OF TIGER ARE RETRIEVED FROM table1. USING THESE LOCATIONS, THE IMAGE OF THESE LOCATIONS CAN BE PRODUCED FROM table2.

```
EXEC SQL

DECLARE cursor1 CURSOR FOR
    SELECT SPECIES_INDX, VIDEO_FILENAME
        FROM table3
    WHERE SPECIES_NAME = "tiger".


EXEC SQL
    DECLARE cursor2 CURSOR FOR
        SELECT X_POSITION, Y_POSITION, OBSERVER_NAME,
        OBSERVE_INDX,HABITAT_INDX,LANDUSE_INDX,
        TEXT_FILENAME
        FROM table1
        WHERE SPECIES_INDX = :species_indx.

EXEC SQL
    DECLARE cursor3 CURSOR FOR
        SELECT VIDEO_FILENAME
            FROM table2
        WHERE (X_POSITION = :x_position and
            Y_POSITION = :y_position).
```

CONCLUSIONS

As conservation and development programs increasingly require decisions at local, regional, and global levels, the success of conservation efforts will depend on the establishment of an international network of conservation data centers. The WCMC and TNC recognize the need for these networks and currently are developing them. If we are going to martial the information in conservation databases to realistically integrate conservation and sustainable development goals, we need to combine databases such as those maintained by the WCMC and TNC to eliminate costly duplication of effort and maximize use of information stored in these systems.

The system described in this paper is a pilot system for concept exploration. Some advantages of the system are: it is geographically based, it is easy to input existing and new data, and it generates a wide array of output products. Because the system incorporates digital maps and requires and facilitates georeferencing, it provides spatial output products that currently are not readily available (e.g., hard copy maps, GIS data layers). Instant access to maps, visual images, and text make our system an excellent medium for communication.

ACKNOWLEDGMENTS

We thank P. Lau for his contribution to software development, F. Cuthbert, and two anonymous reviewers for comments on the manuscript and R. Jenkins and staff at TNC for discussions on conservation databases. The manuscript was developed while Ahearn and Smith were supported by funds from the Minnesota Agricultural Experiment Station.

REFERENCES

Colvocoresses, A.P., 1986. Image Mapping with the Thematic Mapper, *Photogrammetric Engineering & Remote Sensing*, Vol. 52, No. 9, pp. 1499–1505.

Elmasri, R., and S.B. Navathe, 1989. *Fundamentals of Database Systems*, The Benjamin/Cummings Publishing Company, Inc.

Hamilton, M.P., L.A. Salazar, and K.E. Palmer, 1989. Geographic information system: providing information for wildland fire planning. *Fire Technology*, Vol. 25, pp. 5–23.

Jenkins, R.E., 1988. Information Management for the Conservation of Biodiversity. *Biodiversity* (E.O. Wilson, ed.) National Academy Press, Washington, D.C., pp. 231–239.

Miller, K.R., W. Reid, and J. McNeely, 1989. A Global Strategy for Conserving Biodiversity. *Diversity*, Vol. 5, pp 4–7.

MundoCart, 1989. Chadwyck-Healey LTD, Cambridge Place, Cambridge, CB2 INR.

Smith, J.L.D., C. Wemmer, and H.R. Mishra, 1987. A tiger geographic information system: the first step in a global conservation strategy. *Tigers of the World: the Biology, Biopolitics, Management and Conservation of an Endangered Species* (R.L. Tilson and U.S. Seal, eds.). Noyes Publ., Park Ridge, N.J., pp. 464–474.

Thornback, J., and M. Jenkins, 1982. *The IUCN Mammal Red Data Book*

USGS, 1987. *United States Geological Survey, Digital Line Graph Users Guides*, Branch of Technical Management, USGS, 507 National Center, Reston, Virginia 22092

Wilke, D.S., 1989. Performance of a Backpack GPS in a Tropical Rain Forest. *Photogrammetric Engineering & Remote Sensing*. Vol. 55, No. 12, pp. 1669–1812.

Tropical Deforestation and Habitat Fragmentation in the Amazon: Satellite Data from 1978 to 1988

David Skole and Compton Tucker

Landsat satellite imagery covering the entire forested portion of the Brazilian Amazon Basin was used to measure, for 1978 and 1988, deforestation, fragmented forest, defined as areas less than 100 square kilometers surrounded by deforestation, and edge effects of 1 kilometer into forest from adjacent areas of deforestation. Tropical deforestation increased from 78,000 square kilometers in 1978 to 230,000 square kilometers in 1988 while tropical forest habitat, severely affected with respect to biological diversity, increased from 208,000 to 588,000 square kilometers. Although this rate of deforestation is lower than previous estimates, the effect on biological diversity is greater.

Deforestation has been occurring in temperate and tropical regions throughout history (1). In recent years, much attention has focused on tropical forests, where as much as 50% of the original extent may have been lost to deforestation in the last two decades, primarily as a result of agricultural expansion (2). Global estimates of tropical deforestation range from 69,000 km² year⁻¹ in 1980 (3) to 100,000 to 165,000 km² year⁻¹ in the late 1980s; 50 to 70% of the more recent estimates have been attributed to deforestation in the Brazilian Amazon, the largest continuous region of tropical forest in the world (2, 4, 5).

The area and rate of deforestation in Amazonia are not well known, nor are there quantitative measurements of the effect of deforestation on habitat degradation. We used 1:500,000 scale photographic imagery from Landsat Thematic Mapper data and a geographic information system (GIS) to create a computerized map of deforestation and evaluate its influence on forest fragmentation and habitat degradation. Areas of deforestation were digitized into the GIS and the forest fragments and edge effects that result from the spatial pattern of forest conversion were determined.

Background

Tropical deforestation is a major component of the carbon cycle and has profound implications for biological diversity. Deforestation increases atmospheric CO_2 and other trace gases, possibly affecting climate (6, 7). Conversion of forests to cropland and pasture results in a net flux of carbon to the atmosphere because the concentration of carbon in forests is higher than that in the

agricultural areas that replace them. The paucity of data on tropical deforestation limits our understanding of the carbon cycle and possible climate change (8). Furthermore, while occupying less than 7% of the terrestrial surface, tropical forests are the home to half or more of all plant and animal species (9). The primary adverse effect of tropical deforestation is massive extinction of species including, for the first time, large numbers of vascular plant species (10).

Deforestation affects biological diversity in three ways: destruction of habitat, isolation of fragments of formerly contiguous habitat, and edge effects within a boundary zone between forest and deforested areas. This boundary zone extends some distance

into the remaining forest. In this zone there are greater exposure to winds; dramatic micrometeorological differences over short distances; easier access for livestock, other nonforest animals, and hunters; and a range of other biological and physical effects. The result is a net loss of plant and animal species in the edge areas (11).

There is a wide range in current estimates of the area and rate of deforestation in Amazonia. Scientists at the Instituto Nacional de Pesquisas Espaciais (12–15) estimated a total deforested area of 280,000 km² as of 1988 and an average annual rate of 21,000 km² year⁻¹ from 1978 to 1988. Other studies (2, 4, 5) have reported rates that range from 50,000 to 80,000 km² year⁻¹ (Table 1). Additional deforestation estimates have been made for geographically limited study areas in the southern Amazon Basin of Brazil with Landsat and meteorological satellite data (16–20).

The Amazon Basin of Brazil has been defined by law to include the states of Acre, Amapá, Amazonas, Pará, Rondônia, and Roraima plus part of Mato Grosso, Maranhão, and Tocantins and is referred to as the Legal Amazon (21). It covers an area of

Fig. 1. Landsat Thematic Mapper color composite image of southern Rondônia state, Brazil, for path 230 and row 69 acquired on 5 June 1988. Areas of tropical forest, deforestation, regrowth, and isolated forest are labeled. The area identified as isolated forest is about 3 km by 15 km in size.

D. Skole is with the Institute for the Study of Earth, Oceans, and Space, University of New Hampshire, Durham, NH 03824. C. Tucker is with the Laboratory for Terrestrial Physics, NASA Goddard Space Flight Center, Greenbelt, MD 20771.

Reprinted by permission of the publisher Institute for the Study of Earth, Oceans, and Space, *Science*, Vol. 260, 25 1993 Ju

See page 378 for color plate of Figure 1.

Table 1. Tropical forest area (3) and reported tropical deforestation rates by country. The deforestation rates from the 1970s are from the Food and Agriculture Organization (FAO) (3). The 1980s data are from Meyers (2) and the World Resources Institute (WRI) (5).

Country	Total forest area (km^2)	Percent of world total	Deforestation rate, 1970s (km^2)	Percent of world total	Deforestation rates, late 1980s			
					Myers (km^2)	Percent of world total	WRI (km^2)	Percent of world total
Brazil	3,562,800	30.7	13,600	19.7	50,000	36.1	80,000	48.4
Indonesia	1,135,750	9.8	5,500	8.0	12,000	8.7	9,000	5.4
Zaire	1,056,500	9.1	1,700	2.5	4,000	2.9	1,820	1.1
Peru	693,100	6.0	2,450	3.6	3,500	2.5	2,700	1.6
Columbia	464,000	4.0	8,000	11.6	6,500	4.7	8,200	5.0
India	460,440	4.0	1,320	1.9	4,000	2.9	15,000	9.1
Bolivia	440,100	3.8	650	1.0	1,500	1.1	870	0.5
Papua, New Guinea	337,100	2.9	210	0.3	3,500	2.5	220	0.1
Venezuela	318,700	2.7	1,250	1.8	1,500	1.1	1,250	0.8
Burma	311,930	2.7	920	1.3	8,000	5.8	6,770	4.1
Others*	2,829,930	24.4	33,300	48.3	44,100	31.8	39,610	23.9
Total	11,610,350	100.0	68,900	100.0	138,600	100.0	165,440	100.0

*Sixty-three other countries.

~5,000,000 km^2, of which ~4,090,000 km^2 is forested, ~850,000 km^2 is cerrado or tropical savanna, and ~90,000 km^2 is water (Table 2). Confusion has arisen among researchers regarding the stratification of the Brazilian Amazon into forest, cerrado, and water strata. A Food and Agriculture Organization (FAO)–United Nations Environmental Program (UNEP) study (3) found 3,562,800 km^2 of forest, whereas Fearnside and co-workers claim there is 4,195,660 km^2 of forest, 793,279 km^2 of cerrado (17), and 4,906,784 km^2 total (13). Meanwhile, an IBGE study (22) found 20,972 km^2 of water, 3,793,664 km^2 of forest, and 1,149,943 km^2 of cerrado for a total of 4,964,920 km^2. These differences prevent comparison of different deforestation studies.

The use of satellite data and the GIS make it possible to explicitly stratify Amazonia on the basis of cover types (22), thereby providing a means of comparison with other studies. This approach is also necessary for spatial analysis of habitat fragmentation and edge effects of deforestation. Finally, GIS provides a data management tool with which we could manage large amounts of spatial data and precisely merge and geocode information from the more than 200 satellite images used in this study.

Remote Sensing

The large area of the Brazilian Amazon necessitates a straightforward and accurate method of measurement. Landsat Thematic Mapper photo products are inexpensive and of sufficient spatial and spectral resolution for the determination of deforestation. Analysis with visual interpretation techniques produces quantitative results similar to digital processing of full-resolution, multispectral data from the Thematic Mapper and SPOT (23).

We acquired 210 black and white photo-

Table 2. Predeforestation water, forest, and cerrado land cover for the Brazilian Amazon by state as used in this study. The values determined in this study were based on the IBGE vegetation map and by interpretation of satellite data (22). Areas obscured by clouds were excluded from deforestation and affected forest habitat analyses (97% of the cloud-affected data were over tropical forest).

State	Water area (km^2)	Forest area (km^2)	Cloud total (km^2)	Cerrado area (km^2)	Total area (km^2)
Acre	393	152,394	0	0	152,787
Amapá	1,188	137,444	53,566	978	139,610
Amazonas	29,842	1,531,122	94,058	14,379	1,575,343
Maranhão	1,344	145,766	13,444	114,675	261,785
Mato Grosso	4,212	527,570	8,630	368,658	900,440
Pará	49,522	1,183,571	56,807	28,637	1,261,730
Rondônia	1,462	212,214	474	24,604	238,280
Roraima	1,817	172,425	15,232	51,464	225,706
Tocantins	2,914	30,325	0	244,005	277,244
Total	92,694	4,092,831	(242,211)	847,400	5,032,925

Table 3. Tropical deforestation, forest isolated or cut off by deforestation, and the area of forest adversely affected by a 1-km edge effect from adjacent areas of deforestation in the Brazilian Amazon. Areas that were obscured by clouds were omitted from this analysis. Parentheses following the edge effect entries contain the ratio between a 500-m buffer and a 1,000-m buffer.

State	Deforested (km^2)	Isolated (km^2)	Edge effect (km^2)	Total (km^2)
		1978		
Acre	2,612	18	4,511	7,141
Amapá	182	0	368	550
Amazonas	2,300	36	6,498	8,834
Maranhão	9,426	705	13,120	23,251
Mato Grosso	21,134	776	25,418	47,328
Pará	30,449	2,248	49,791	82,488
Rondônia	6,281	991	17,744	25,016
Roraima	196	4	812	1,012
Tocantins	5,688	337	6,584	12,609
Total	78,268	5,115	124,846	208,229
		1988		
Acre	6,369	405	23,686 (0.517)	30,460
Amapá	210	1	689 (0.537)	900
Amazonas	11,813	474	36,392 (0.582)	48,679
Maranhão	31,952	2,123	28,147 (0.626)	62,222
Mato Grosso	47,568	2,542	71,128 (0.580)	121,238
Pará	95,075	6,837	116,669 (0.633)	218,581
Rondônia	23,998	2,408	52,345 (0.657)	78,751
Roraima	1,908	1	5,236 (0.521)	7,145
Tocantins	11,431	1,437	6,760 (0.659)	19,628
Total	230,324	16,228	341,052 (0.610)	587,604

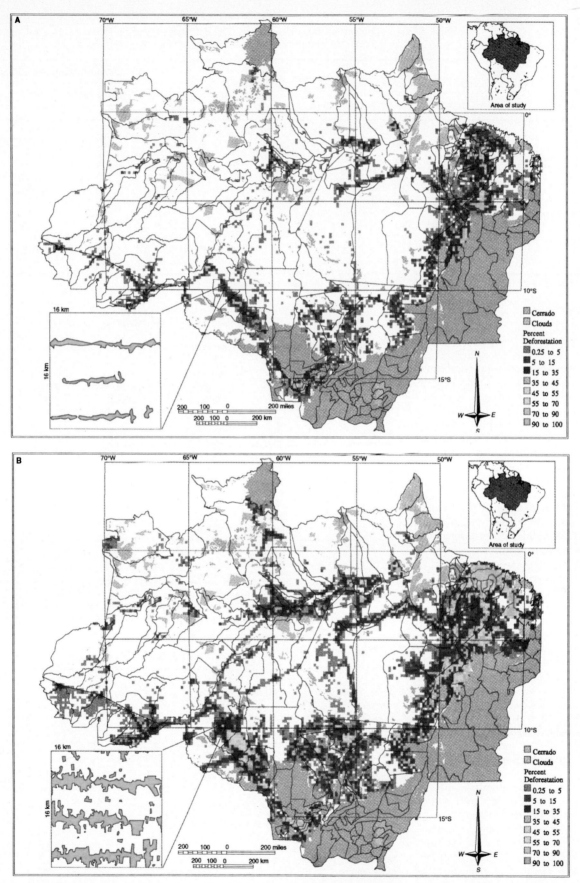

Fig. 2. Representation of deforestation in the Amazon of Brazil from (**A**) 1978 and (**B**) 1988. The deforestation represented in these figures is confined exclusively to the forest strata. The data were averaged into 16 km by 16 km grid cells.

See page 379 for color plate of Figure 2.

338

graphic images of the entire Brazilian Amazon. They were obtained with channel five of the Landsat Thematic Mapper (1.55 to 1.75 μm) at 1:500,000 scale and were primarily from 1988 (24). We digitized the deforested areas with visual deforestation interpretation and standard vector GIS techniques (Fig. 1). The digitized scenes were projected into equal-area geographic coordinates (latitude, longitude), edge matched, and merged in the computer to form a single, seamless data-set for the entire Brazilian Amazon.

Spatial analysis of the geometry of deforestation is critical to the estimation of forest fragmentation and the edge effect. If 100 km² of tropical deforestation occurs as a 10 km by 10 km square and we assume that the edge effect is 1 km, the total area affected is ~143 km². In contrast, if the 100 km² of deforestation is distributed as ten strips, each 10 km by 1 km, the affected area is ~350 km².

We extracted forest fragments <100 km² that were isolated by deforestation and computed edge effects for a zone of 1 km along the boundaries. All areas of closed-canopy tropical forest deforested by 1988 were delineated, including areas of secondary growth on abandoned fields and pastures where visible (Fig. 1). Areas of long-term forest degradation along river margins in central Amazonia were also included, as were scattered small clearings associated with rubber tappers, mining operations, airfields, and other small disturbances. All visible roads, power line right of ways, pipelines, and similar human-made features were also digitized into the GIS and treated as deforestation. We used 50 digital Landsat Multispectral Scanner (MSS) scenes from 1986 and 15 digital Thematic Mapper images from 1988 for detailed examination of Acre, Amazonas, Mato Grosso, Pará, and Rondônia.

To determine the extent of deforestation in 1978, we used the GIS to digitize maps of scale 1:500,000 from single-channel Landsat MSS data, produced jointly by the Instituto Brasiliero de Desenvolvimento Florestal (IBDF) and the Instituto de Pesquisas Espaciais (INPE) in the early 1980s (12, 23). These maps did not differentiate between forest and cerrado clearing. We compiled forest, cerrado, and water data by combining a vegetation map with analysis of Landsat images and meteorological satellite data (25). Our deforestation and affect-

Table 4. Spatial characteristics of isolated and remaining tropical forest within the Legal Amazon as determined by analysis of 1988 Landsat Thematic Mapper imagery. Isolated forest refers to areas of forest <100 km² surrounded by deforestation. Remaining forest refers to tropical forest that has not been deforested and includes both isolated and larger areas of forest. Many of the largest remaining areas of tropical forest are contiguous among states. Areas affected by clouds were omitted from this analysis.

State	Isolated forest		Undisturbed remaining forest		Range of areas (km²)	
	Area (km²)	Polygons (no.)	Area (km²)	Polygons (no.)	Minimum	Maximum
Acre	405	603	146,025	605	<1	139,215
Amapá	1	2	83,676	3	<1	83,675
Amazonas	474	464	1,425,253	465	<1	1,424,779
Maranhão	2,123	1,035	100,554	1,042	<1	70,057
Mato Grosso	2,542	2,016	478,619	2,027	<1	471,792
Pará	6,837	4,030	1,032,194	4,032	<1	1,021,263
Rondônia	2,408	1,587	187,743	1,588	<1	185,335
Roraima	1	2	155,326	6	<1	152,414
Tocantins	1,437	493	18,894	508	<1	6,982
Total	16,228	10,232	3,628,284	10,276		

Fig. 3. Map of the Brazilian Amazon Basin showing where biological diversity was adversely affected in 1988 by deforestation, isolation of forest, and the 1-km edge effect of deforestation. The largest contributor to the area of negative effects on biological diversity was the 1-km edge effect from adjacent areas of deforestation. Isolation of forest patches was not a large contributor to this problem. The affected-habitat data were averaged into 16 km by 16 km grid cells.

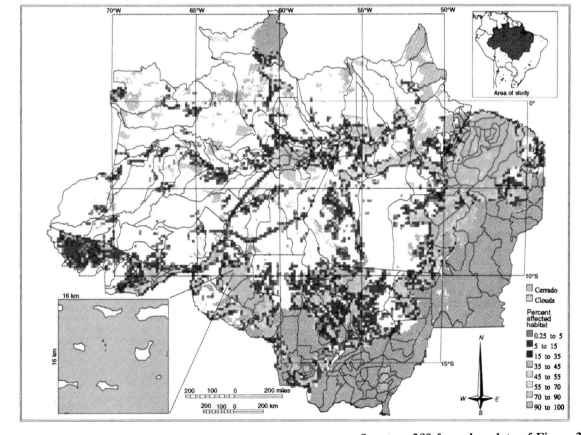

See page 380 for color plate of Figure 3.

T. A. Stone, R. F. Nelson, W. Kovalick, *J. Geophys. Res.* **92**, 2157 (1987).

20. A. W. Setzer and M. C. Pereira, *Ambio* **20**, 19 (1991); A. W. Setzer, *Relatorio INPE-4534-RPE/565* (Instituto Nacional de Pesquisas Espaciais, São José dos Campos, Brazil, 1988).

21. *Anuario Estatistico do Brasil 1991* (Fundacao Instituto Brasileiro de Geografia e Estatistica, Rio de Janeiro, Brazil, 1991), vol. 51, pp. 1–1024.

22. *Mapa de Vegetacão do Brasil* (Fundacão Instituto Brasileiro de Geografia e Estatistica, Rio de Janeiro, Brazil, 1988).

23. D. L. Skole, thesis, University of New Hampshire (1992).

24. Images: 7 from 1989, 175 from 1988, 8 from 1987, and 20 from 1986. All data from the Brazilian Landsat receiving station. The exact boundary between intact forest and deforested land was digitized in the Universal Transverse Mercator projection and then edited and error-checked with use of clear velum plots of the line-work overlaid on each photographic image. Each Landsat scene contained coordinate control points in decimal degree units, such that each scene could be geographically registered within precise tolerances and mosaicked together. For digitization, vertices were placed approximately every 50 m of ground position. Tests of positional accuracy in digitizing followed those of R. Dunn, R. Harrison, and J. C. White [*Int. J. Geograph. Inf. Syst.* **4**, 385 (1990)] and indicated encoding; hence, area-estimation errors were less than 3% (23). The variance associated with interpretation and delineation of boundaries between intact forest and deforested areas was less than 10% overall. Further accuracy assessment was made in test sites established in Rondonia, where fragmentation was very high. An explicit spatial comparison between our estimate of deforestation and the same derived from high-resolution (20-m resolution) SPOT satellite imagery was highly correlated ($r^2 = 0.98$; $y = 1.11x - 57.358$). Additional ground checking and verification was done in eastern Para state, north of Manaus, and along the Rio Negro, both in Amazonas.

25. Fundamental to our analysis was a specified representation for water, cerrado or savanna, and forest for the Brazilian Amazon. We used a vegetation map (23) that was augmented by Landsat Thematic Mapper and meteorological satellite imagery for more accurate depiction of cerrado and water. This GIS representation is available upon request.

26. R. B. Buschbacher, *BioScience* **36**, 22 (1986); C. Uhl, R. B. Buschbacher, E. A. S. Serrao, *J. Ecol.* **76**, 663 (1988); R. B. Buschbacher, C. Uhl, E. A. S. Serrao, *ibid.*, p. 682.

27. This work was supported by National Aeronautics and Space Administration's mission to planet Earth and the Eos Data Information System's Landsat Pathfinder Program. We acknowledge S. Tilford and W. Huntress for initiating this research, W. Chomentowski for assistance in developing the satellite and GIS database, and A. Nobre for his assistance in interpreting the satellite data. G. Batista, M. Heinicke, and T. Grant assisted with the GIS representation of forest, water, and cerrado.

GIS Applications Bibliography

Abkowitz, M., S. Walsh, and E. Hauser, 1990. Adaptation of Geographic Information Systems to Highway Management. Journal of Transportation Engineering. 116:310-327.

Agee, J. K., S. C. F. Stitt, M. Nyquist, and R. Root, 1989. A Geographic Analysis of Historical Grizzly Bear Sightings in the North Cascades. Photogrammetric Engineering and Remote Sensing. 55(11):1637-1642.

Ahearn, S.C., J. L. D. Smith, and C. Wee, 1990. Framework for a geographically referenced conservation database: Case study Nepal. Photogrammetric Engineering and Remote Sensing. 56(11):1477-1481.

Akinyede, J. O., 1990. A Geotechnical GIS Concept for Highway Route Planning. ITC Journal. 1990(3):262-269.

Al-Ankary, K. M., 1991. An Incremental Approach for Establishing a Geographical Information System in a Developing Country: Saudi Arabia. International Journal of Geographical Information Systems. 5(1):85-98.

Ali, C. Q., L. G. Ross, M. C. M. Beveridge, 1991. Microcomputer Spreadsheets for the Implementation of Geographic Information Systems in Aquaculture: A Case Study on Carp in Pakistan. Aquaculture. 1991(92):199-205.

Allen, T. R., and S. J. Walsh, 1993. Characterizing Multitemporal Alpine Snowmelt Patterns for Ecological Inferences. Photogrammetric Engineering and Remote Sensing. 59(10):1521.

Angus-Leppan, P., 1989. The Thailand Land Titling Project. First Steps in a Parcel-Based LIS. International Journal of Geographical Information Systems. 3(1):59-68.

Ansoult, M. M., and P. J. Soille, 1990. Mathematical Morphology: A Tool for Automated GIS Data Acquisition from Scanned Thematic Maps. Photogrammetric Engineering and Remote Sensing. 56(9):1263-1271.

Anys, H., F. Bonn, and A. Merzouk, 1994. Remote Sensing and GIS Based Mapping and Modeling of Water Erosion and Sediment Yield in a Semi-Arid Watershed of Morocco. Geocarto International. 9(1):31.

Astroth, J. H., Jr., J. Trujillo, and G. E. Johnson, 1990. A Retrospective Analysis of GIS Performance: The Umatilla Basin Revisited. Photogrammetric Engineering and Remote Sensing. 56(3):359-363.

Baker, W., and Y. Cai, 1992. The r.l.e. Programs for Multiscale Analysis of Landscape Structure Using the GRASS Geographical Information System. Landscape Ecology. 7(4):291-302.

Baker, C. P., and E. C. Panciera, 1990. A Geographic Information System for Groundwater Protection Planning. Journal of Soil and Water Conservation. 45(2):246-248.

Baskent, E.Z. and Jordan, G.A, 1991. Spatial Wood Supply Simulation Modelling. For. Chron. 67(6):610-621.

Berry, J. K., and J. K. Sailor, 1987. Use of a Geographic Information System for Storm Runoff Prediction from Small Urban Watersheds. Environmental Management. 11(1):21-27.

Bhaskar, N. R., W. James, and R. Devulapalli, 1992. Hydrologic Parameter Estimation Using Geographic Information System. Journal of Water Resource Planning and Management. 118(5):492-512.

Bocco, G., J. Palacio, and C. Valenzuela, 1990. Gully Erosion Modelling Using GIS and Geomorphic Knowledge. ITC Journal. 1990(3):253-261.

Bocco, E., and C. R. Valenzuela, 1988. Integration of GIS and Image Processing in Soil Erosion Studies Using ILWIS. ITC Journal. 1988(4):309-319.

Bolstad, Paul V., 1992. Geometric Errors in Natual Resource GIS Data: Tilt and Terrain Effects in Aerial Photographs. Forest Science. (38)(2):367-380.

Bolstad, P. V., and T. M. Lillesand, 1992. Improved Classification of Forest Vegetaton in Northern Wisconsin Through a Rule-based Combination of Soils, Terrain, and Landsat Thematic Mapper Data. Forest Science. 38(1):5-20.

Bolstad, P. V., and J. L. Smith, 1992. Errors in GIS. Journal of Forestry. 90(11):21-29.

Breininger, D., 1991. Mapping Florida Scrub Jay Habitat for Purposes of Land Use Management. Photogrammetric Engineering and Remote Sensing. 57(11):1467-1474.

Brinker, R. W., and B. D. Jackson, 1991. Using a Geographic Information System to Study a Regional Wood Procurement Problem. Forest Science. 1991(37):1614-1631.

Brown, N. J., and D. A. Norris, 1988. Early Applications of Geographical Information Systems at the Institute of Terrestrial Ecology. International Journal of Geographical Information Systems. 2(2):153-160.

Brown, S., L. R. Iverson, A. Prasad, and D. Liu, 1993. Geographical Distributions of Carbon in Biomass and Soils of Tropical Asian Forests. Geocarto International. 8(4):45.

Burke, I. C., D. S. Schimel, C. M. Yonker, W. J. Parton, L. A. Joyce, and W. K. Lauenroth, 1990. Regional Modeling of Grassland Biogeochemistry Using GIS. Landscape Ecology. 4(1):45-54.

Calkins, H. W., and N. J. Obermeyer, 1991. Taxonomy for Surveying the Use and Value of Geographical Information. International Journal of Geographical Information Systems. 5(3):341-352.

Cameron, G. N., and D. Scheel, 1993. A GIS Model of the Effects of Global Climate Change on Mammals. Geocarto International. 8(4):19-32.

Chou, Yue Hong, 1992. Management of Wildfires with a Geographical Informational System. International Journal of Geographical Informational Systems. (6)(2):123-140.

Chuvieco., E., 1993. Integration of Linear Programming and GIS for Land-use Modelling. International Journal of Geographical Information Systems. 7(1):71-84.

Chuvieco, E., and R. G. Congalton, 1989. Application of Remote Sensing and Geographic Information Systems to Forest Fire Hazard Mapping. Remote Sensing of the Environment. 29(2):147-159.

Clayton, I., 1991. Gulf of Maine GIS Database Aids Oceanographers, Resource Managers. Sea Technology. 32:29-31.

Cleynenbreugel, J. V., F. Fierens, P. Suetens, and A. Oosterlinck, 1990. Delineating Road Structures on Satellite Imagery by a GIS-Guided Technique. Photogrammetric Engineering and Remote Sensing. 56(6):893-898.

Cocks, K. D., P. A. Walker, and C. A. Parvey, 1988. Evolution of a Continental-Scale Geographical Information System. International Journal of Geographical Information Systems. 2(3):263-280.

Congalton, R.G., K. Green, and J. Teply, 1993. Mapping Old Growth Forests on National Forest and Park Lands in the Pacific Northwest from Remotely Sensed Data. Photogrammetric Engineering and Remote Sensing. 59(4):529-535.

Congalton, Russell G., and Kass Green, 1992. The ABCs of GIS: An Introduction to Geographic Information Systems. Journal of Forestry. (90)(11):13-21.

Cress, J. J. and R. R. P. Deister, 1990. Development and Implementation of a Knowledge-Based GIS Geological Engineering Map Production System. Photogrammetric Engineering and Remote Sensing. 56(11):1529-1535.

Curtis, E. W., C. H. Sham and B. Shaw, 1990. Comments on Selecting a Geographic Information System for Environmental Management. Environmental Management. 14(3):307-315.

Dangermond, J., 1991. Where is the Technology Leading Us? The Forestry Chronicle. 67(6):599-603.

Davis, F. W., D. A. Quattrochi, M. K. Ridd, N. Lam, S. Walsh, J. C. Michaelsen, J. Franklin, D. A. Stow, C. J. Johannsen, and C. A. Johnston, 1991. Environmental Analysis Using Integrated GIS and Remotely Sensed Data: Some Research Needs and Priorities. Photogrammetric Enginering and Remote Sensing. 57(6):689-697.

Davis, F. W., D. M. Stoms, J. E. Estes, J. Scepan, and J. M. Scott, 1990. An Informations Systems Approach to the Preservation of Biological Diversity. International Journal of Geographical Information Systems. 4(1):55-78.

Davis, F.W. and S. Goetz, 1990. Modelling Vegetation Patterns Using Digital Terrain Data. Landscape Ecology. 4(1):69-80.

de Brouwer, H., C. Valenzuela, L. Valencia, and K. Sijmons, 1990. Rapid Assessment of Urban Growth Using GIS-RS Techniques. ITC Journal. 1990(3):233-235.

DeMers, M. N., and P. F. Fisher, 1991. Comparative Evolution of Statewide Geographic Information Systems in Ohio. International Journal of Geographical Information Systems. 5(4):469-486.

Derenyi, E. and R. Pollock, 1990. Extending a GIS Support Image-Based Map Revision. Photogrammetric Engineering and Remote Sensing. 56(11):1493-1496.

Dueker, K. J., and P. B. DeLacy, 1990. GIS in the Land Development Planning Process: Balancing the Needs of Land Use Planners and Real Estate Developers. Journal of the American Planning Association. 56:483-491.

Eckhardt, D. W., and J. P. Verdin, 1990. Automated Update of an Irrigated Lands GIS Using SPOT HRV Imagery. Photogrammetric Engineering and Remote Sensing. 56(11):1515-1522.

Edralin, J. S., 1991. Conference Report. International Conference on Geographic Information Systems Applications for Urban and Regional Planning. International Journal of Geographical Information Systems. 5(1):147-154.

Eliasson, A. 1991. Integration of Satellite Remote Sensing in a Forestry Oriented GIS. Scandinavian Journal of Forest Research. 6(3):413-423.

Ellis, M. C., and R. Galeano, 1987. SISTERRA: The Spatial Information System for Terrain Evaluation Microcomputer Software for Geo Information Systems and Digital Image Processing. ITC Journal. 1987(2):165-168.

Evans, B. M., and W. L. Meyers, 1990. A GIS-based Approach to Evaluating Regional Groundwater Pollution Potential with DRASTIC. Journal of Soil and Water Conservation. 45(2):242-245.

Fabos, J., 1988. Computerization of Landscape Planning. Landscape and Urban Planning. 15:279-289.

Falcidieno, B., and M. Spagnuolo, 1991. A New Method for the Characterization of Topographic Surfaces. International Journal of Geographical Information Systems. 5(4):397-412.

Fernandez, R. N., and M. Rusinkiewicz, 1993. A Conceptual Design of a Soil Database for a Geographical Information System. International Journal of Geographical Information Systems. 7(6):525-540.

Fisher, P. F., 1991. Modelling Soil Map-Unit Inclusions by Monte Carlo Simulation. International Journal of Geographical Information Systems. 5(2): 193-208.

Ferris, J. S., and R. G. Congalton, 1989. Satellite and Geographic Information System Estimates of Colorado River Basin Snowpack. Photogrammetric Engineering and Remote Sensing. 55(11):1629-1635.

Fox, J. M., 1991. Spatial Information for Resource Management in Asia: a Review for Institutional Issues. International Journal of Geographical Information Systems. 5(1): 59-72.

Friedl, M. A., J. E. Estes, and J. L. Star, 1988. Advanced Information-Extraction Tools in Remote Sensing for Earth Science Applications: AI and GIS. AI Applications. 2(2-3):17-31.

Green, K., 1992. Spatial Imagery and GIS. Journal of Forestry. 90(11):32-36.

Greve, C. W., J. A. Kelmelis, R. Fegeas, S. C. Guptill, and N. Mouat, 1993. Investigating U.S. Geological Survey Needs for the Management of Temporal GIS Data. Photogrammetric Engineering and Remote Sensing. 59(10):1503-1508.

Grove, M., and M. Hohmann, 1992. Social Forestry and GIS. Journal of Forestry. 90(12):10-15.

Hall, Forrest G., Donald E. Strebel, and Piers J. Sellers, 1988. Linking Knowledge Among Spatial and Temporal Scales: Vegetation, Atmosphere, Climate, and Remote Sensing. Landscape Ecology. 2(1):3-22.

Hamilton, M. P., L. A. Salazar, and K. E. Palmer, 1989. Geographic Information Systems: Providing Information for Wildland Fire Planning. Fire Technology 25(1): 5-23.

Hastings, D. A., J. J. Kineman, and D. M. Clark, 1991. Development and Application of Global Databases: Considerable Progress, but more Collaboration Needed. International Journal of Geographical Information Systems. 5(1): 137-146.

Hastings, D. A., and D. M. Clark, 1991. GIS in Africa: Problems, Challenges, and Opportunities for Co-operation. International Journal of Geographical Information Systems. 5(1):29-40.

Hendrix, W. G., J. G. Fabos, and J. E. Price, 1988. An Ecological Approach to Landscape Planning using Geographic Information System Technology. Landscape and Urban Planning. 15:211-225.

Herr, A. M., and L. P. Queen, 1993. Crane Habitat Evaluation Using GIS and Remote Sensing. Photogrammetric Engineering and Remote Sensing. 59(10):1531.

Hock, J. C., 1986. Preliminary Report on the Development of Marine Geographic Information Systems. ITC Journal. 1986(2):156-163.

Hyde, R. F., 1991. The Feasibility of a Land Information System for Belize, Central America. International Journal of Geographical Information Systems. 5(1): 99-110.

Jackson, M. J., and D. C. Mason, 1986. The Development of Integrated Geo-Information Systems. International Journal of Remote Sensing. 7(6):723-740.

Jakubauskas, M. E., P. L. Kamlesh, and P. W. Mausel, 1990. Assessment of Vegetation Change in a Fire Altered Forest Landscape. Photogrammetric Engineering and Remote Sensing. 56(3):371-377.

Jensen, J. R., S. Narumalani, O. Weatherbee, K. S. Morris, Jr., and H. E. Macke, Jr., 1992. Predictive Modeling of Cattail and Waterlily Distribution in a South Carolina Reservoir. Photogrammetric Engineering and Remote Sensing. 58(11):1561.

Jensen, J. R., E. W. Ramsey III, J. M. Holmes, J. E. Michel, B. Savitsky, and B. A. Davis, 1990. Environmental Sensitivity Index (ESI) Mapping for Oil Spills Using Remote Sensing and Geographic Information System Technology. International Journal of Geographical Information Systems. 4(2):181-201.

Johnson, Lucinda B., 1990. Analyzing Spatial and Temporal Phenomena Using Geographical Information Systems: A Review of Ecological Applications. Landscape Ecology. 4(1):31-43

Johnston, C., 1990. GIS: More Than Just a Pretty Face. Landscape Ecology. 4(1):3-4.

Johnston, C. A., and J. Bonde, 1989. Quantitative Analysis of Ecotones Using a Geographic Information System. Photogrammetric Engineering and Remote Sensing. 55(11):1643-1647.

Johnston, C. A., and R. J. Naiman, 1990. The Use of a Geographic Information System to Analyze Long-Term Landscape Alteration by Beaver. Landscape Ecology. 4(1):5-19.

Karneili, A., 1991. Stepwise Overlay Approach for Utilizing a GIS with a Soil Moisture Accounting Model. ITC Journal. 1991(1):11-18.

Kim, K., and S. Ventura, 1993. Large-Scale Modeling of Urban Nonpoint Source Pollution Using a Geographic Information System. Photogrammetric Engineering and Remote Sensing. 59(10):1539-1544.

Kubo, S., 1987. The Development of Geographical Information Systems in Japan. International Journal of Geographical Information Systems. 1(3):243-252.

Lachowski, Henry, Paul Maus, and Bruce Platt, 1992. Integrating Remote Sensing with GIS: Procedures and Examples from the Forest Service. Journal of Forestry 90(12):16-21.

Lai, P., 1991. Issues Concerning the Technology Transfer of Geographic Information Systems. Environmental Management. 15(5):595-601.

LaGro, J., 1991, Assessing Patch Shape in Landscape Mosaics. Photogrammetric Engineering and Remote Sensing. 57(3):285-293.

Langran, G., 1989. A Review of Temporal Database Research and Its Use in GIS Applications. International Journal of Geographical Information Systems. 3(3):215-232.

Lee, J., 1994. Visibility Dominance and Topographic Features on Digital Elevation Models. Photogrammetric Engineering and Remote Sensing. 60(4):451-456.

Lee, J. K., J. C. Randolph, K. P. Lulla, and M. R. Helfert, 1993. Interfacing Remote Sensing and Geographic Information Systems for Global Environmental Change Research. Geocarto International. 8(4):7-18.

Lee, J., R. A. Park, and P. W. Mausel, 1992. Application of Geoprocessing and Simulation Modeling to Estimate Impacts of Sea Level Rise on the Northeast Coast of Florida. Photogrammetric Engineering and Remote Sensing. 58(11):1579-1586.

Lee, J., 1991. Analyses of Visibility Sites on Topographic Features. International Journal of Geographical Information Systems. 5(4):413-430.

Levine, J., and J. D. Landis, 1989. Geographic Information System for Local Planning. Journal of the American Planning Association. 55:209-220.

Lewis, S., 1990. Use of Geographical Information Systems in Transportation Modelling. ITE Journal. 60:34-38.

Lillesand, T. M., 1990. Remote Sensing and Geographic Information Systems. *In* Introduction to Forest Science, 2nd Ed., Wiley. Pp. 277-299.

Lindhult, M. S., J. Fabos, P. Brown, and N. Price, 1988. Using Geographic Information Systems to Assess Conflicts Between Agriculture and Development. Landscape and Urban Planning. 16:333-343.

Lo, C. P., and W. T. Hutchinson, 1991. Determination of Turbidity Patterns of the Zhujiang Estuarine Region, South China, Using Satellite Images and a GIS Approach. Geocarto. 6(3):27-38.

Lo, C. P., and R. L. Shipman, 1990. A GIS Approach to Land-Use Change Dynamics Detection. Photogrammetric Engineering and Remote Sensing. 56(11):1483-1491.

Loh, D, and E. Rykiel, 1992. Integrated Resource Management Systems: Coupling Expert Systems with Data Base Management and a GIS. Environmental Management. 16(2):167-178.

Loukes, D. K., and J. McLaughlin, 1991. GIS and Transportation: Canadian Perspective. Journal of Surveying Engineering. 117:123-133.

Lowell, K. E., 1991. Utilizing Discriminant Function Analysis with a Geographic Information System to Model Ecological Succession Spatially. International Journal of Geographical Information Systems. 5(2):175-192.

Lowell, K. E., 1990. Differences between Ecological Land Type Maps Produced Using GIS or Manual Cartographic Methods. Photogrammetric Engineering and Remote Sensing. 56(2):169-173.

Lowell, K. E., and J. H. Astroth, Jr., 1989. Vegetative Succession and Controlled Fire in a Glades Ecosystem. A Geographical Information System Approach. International Journal of Geographical Information Systems. 3(1):69-81.

Ludeke, A. K., R. C. Maggio, and L. M. Reid, 1990. An Analysis of Anthropogenic Deforestation Using Logistic Regression and GIS. Journal of Environmental Management. 31(3):247-260.

Maclean, A. L., T. P. D'Avello, and S. G. Shetron, 1993. Digital Soil Maps in a GIS. Photogrammetric Engineering and Remote Sensing. 59(2):239-244.

Maclean, Ann L., David D. Reed, Glenn D. Mroz, Gary W. Lyon, Thomas Edison, 1992. Using GIS to Estimate Forest Resource Changes: A Case Study in Northern Michigan. Journal of Forestry. Vol. 90. No. 12. Pp. 22-26.

Manore, M. J., and R. J. Brown, 1990. Remote Sensing/GIS Integration in the Canadian Crop Information System. Geocarto. 5(1):74-76.

Marsh, S. E., J. L. Walsh, and C. F. Hutchinson, 1990. Development of an Agricultural Land-Use GIS for Senegal Derived from Multispectral Video and Photographic Data. Photogrammetric Engineering and Remote Sensing. 56(3):351-357.

Matthews, E., 1993. Global Geographical Databases for Modelling Trace Gas Fluxes. International Journal of Geographical Information Systems. 7(2):125-142.

Meaille R., and L. Wald, 1990. A Geographical Information System for Some Mediterranean Benthic Communities. International Journal of Geographical Information Systems. 4(1):79-86.

Meijere, J. C., and R. A. van de Putte, 1987. The Role of Information Systems in Natural Resource Management. ITC Journal. 1987(2):129-133.

Miller, R. I., S. M. Stuart, and K. M. Howell, 1989. A Methodology for Analyzing Rare Species Distribution Patterns Utilizing GIS Technology: The Rare Birds of Tanzania. Landscape Ecology. 2(3):173-189.

Mohie el Deen, F. A., 1991. The Use of GIS, GPS, and Satellite Remote Sensing to Map Woody Vegetation in Kazgail Area, Sudan. ITC Journal. 1991(1):11-18.

Moore, D. M., 1991. A New Method for Predicting Vegetation Distribution Using Decision Tree Analysis in a GIS. Environmental Management. 15(1):59-72.

Morse, A., T. J. Zarriello, and W. J. Kramber, 1990. Using Remote Sensing and GIS Technology to Help Adjudicate Idaho Water Rights. Photogrammetric Engineering and Remote Sensing. 56(3):365-370.

Nag, P., 1987. A Proposed Base for a Geographical Information System for India. International Journal of Geographical Information Systems. 1(2):181-187.

Nellis, M. D., K. Lulla, and J. Jensen, 1990. Interfacing Geographic Information Systems and Remote Sensing for Rural Land-Use Analysis. Photogrammetric Engineering and Remote Sensing. 56(3):329-331.

Nielsen, G. A., J. M. Caprio, P. A. McDaniel, R. D. Snyder, and C. Montagne, 1990. MAPS: A GIS for Land Resource Management in Montana. Journal of Soil and Water Conservation. 45(4):450-453.

Niemann, O., 1993. Automated Forest Cover Mapping Using Thematic Mapper Images and Ancillary Data. Applied Geography. 13:86-95.

Nkambwe, M., 1991 (a). URBANIFE: A GIS for Monitoring Internal Developments in an African Traditional Urban Area. ISPRS Journal of Photogrammetry and Remote Sensing. 46(6):346-358.

Nkambwe, M., 1991 (b). Resource Utilization and Regional Planning Information Systems (RURPIS) in Botswana. International Journal of Geographical Information Systems. 5(1):111-122.

Oliver, J. J., 1990. Selecting a GIS for a National Water Management Authority. Photogrammetric Engineering and Remote Sensing. 56(11):1471-1475.

Olsen, E. R. R. D. Ramsey, and D. S. Winn, 1993. A Modified Fractal Dimension as a Measure of Landscape Diversity. Photogrammetric Engineering and Remote Sensing. 59(10):1517.

O'Neill, W. A., 1991. Developing Optimal Transportation Analysis Routes using GIS. ITE Journal. 61:33-36.

Parker, H. D., 1989. GIS Software 1989: A Survey and Commentary. Photogrammetric Engineering and Remote Sensing. 55(11):1589-1591.

Pastor, John, and Michael Broschart, 1990. The Spatial Pattern of a Northern Conifer-Hardwood Landscape. Landscape Ecology. 4(1):55-68.

Pereira, J. M. C., and L. Duckstein, 1993. A Multiple Criteria Decision-making Approach to GIS-based Land Suitability Evaluation. International Journal of Geographical Information Systems. 7(5):407-424.

Pereira, Jose M.C., and Robert M. Itami, 1991. GIS-Based Habitat Modeling Using Logistic Multiple Regression: A Study of the Mt. Graham Red Squirrel. Photogrammetric Engineering & Remote Sensing. 57(11):1475-1486.

Plummer, R. W., 1992. Using a Geographic Information System as a Tool in Mineral Exploration. CIM Buletin. 85:67-71.

Pochin, L., 1990. Feasibility of Geographic Information Systems Approach for Natural Resource Management. Environmental Management. 14(1):73-80.

Randolph, J. C., and J. K. Lee, 1994. Effects of Climate Change on Forests of the Eastern United States. Geocarto International. 9(1):15-30.

Rex, K., and G. Malanson, 1990. The Fractal Shape of Riparian Forest Patches. Landscape Ecology. 4(4):249-258.

Rhind, D., 1991. Geograhical Information Systems and Environmental Problems. International Social Science Journal. 43:649-668.

Rhind, D., 1987. Recent Developments in Geographical Information Systems in the U. K. International Journal of Geographical Information Systems. 1(3):229-241.

Ripple, W.J., G.A. Bradshaw, and T.A. Spies, 1991. Measuring Forest Landscape Patterns in the Cascade Range of Oregon. Biological Conservation. 57(1):73-88.

Robinson, V. B., A. U. Frank, and H. A. Karimi, 1987. Expert Systems for Geographic Information Systems in Resource Management. AI Applications. 1(1):47-57.

Rundquist, D., 1991. Statewide Groundwater Vulnerability Assessment in Nebraska Using the DRASTIC/GIS Model. Geocarto. 6(2):51-58.

Schetselaar, E., P. M. van Dijk, and Y. A. Al Fasatwi, 1990. Digital Processing of Geophysical Data Using a Raster-Based GIS. ITC Journal. 1990(3):248-252.

Schreier, H., G. Kennedy, and P. B. Shah, 1991. Food, Feed, and Fuelwood Resources in Nepal: A GIS Evaluation. Environmental Management. 15(6):815-822.

Schreier, H., G. Kennedy, and P.B. Shah, 1990. Evaluating Mountain Watersheds in Nepal Using Micro-GIS. Mountain Research and Development. 10(2):151-159.

Schulz, T. T., and L. Joyce, 1992. A Spatial Application of a Martin Habitat Model. Wildlife Society Bulletin. 20:74-83.

Shelstad, D., L. Queen, and D. French, 1991. Describing the Spread of Oak Wilt Using a Geographic Information System. Journal of Arboriculture. 17:192-199.

Shih, S. F., 1990. Satellite Data and Geographic Information System for Rainfall Estimation. Journal of Irrigation and Drainage Engineering. 116:319-331.

Siverton, A., L. E. Reinelt, and R. Castensson, 1988. A GIS Mehtod to Aid in Non-point Source Critical Area Analysis. International Journal of Geographical Information Systems. 2(4):365-378.

Skidmore, A. K., P. J. Ryan, W. Dawes, D. Short, and E. O'Loughlin, 1991. Use of an Expert System to Map Forest Soils from a Geographical Information System. International Journal of Geograhical Information Systems. 5(4):431-446.

Skidmore, A. K., 1990. Terrain Position as Mapped from a Gridded Digital Elevation Model. International Journal of Geographical Information Systems. 4(1):33-49.

Smith, J., J. Logan, and T. Gregoire, 1992. Using Aerial Photography and Geographical Information Systems to Develop Databases for Pesticide Evaluations. Photogrammetric Engineering and Remote Sensing. 58(10):1447-1452.

Solntseva, O, 1991. The Status of GIS in the USSR. ITC Journal. 1991(1):34-38.

Speed, V., 1990. Automating Water Resource Management. WATER/Engineering & Management. 137(8):28-30.

Stoms, D. M., 1992. Effects of Habitat Map Generalization in Biodiversity Assessment. Photogrammetric Engineering and Remote Sensing. 58(11):1587-1592.

Stoms, D. M., F. W. Davis, and C. B Christopher, 1992. Sensitivity of Wildlife Habitat Models to Uncertainties in GIS Data. Photogrammetric Engineering & Remote Sensing. 58(6):843-850.

Susilawati, S., and M. Weir, 1990. GIS Applications in Forest Land Management in Indonesia. ITC Journal. 1990(3):236-244.

Tan, Y. R., and S. F. Shih, 1990. GIS in Monitoring Agricultural Land Use Changes and Well Assessment. Transactions of the ASAE. 33:1147-1152.

Tappan, G. G., D. G. Moore, and W. I. Knausenberger, 1991. Monitoring Grasshopper and Locust Habitats in Sahelian Africa Using GIS and Remote Sensing Technology. International Journal of Geographical Information Systems. 5(1):123-136.

Tomlinson, R. F., 1987. Current and Potential Uses of Geographical Information Systems. The North American Experience. International Journal of Geographical Information Systems. 1(3):203-218.

Trotter, C. M., 1991. Remotely-sensed Data as an Information Source for Geographic Information Systems in Natural Resource Management: A Review. International Journal of Geographical Information Systems. 5(2):225-240.

Tudor, G. S., and L. J. Sugarbaker, 1993. GIS Orthographic Digitizing of Aerial Photographs by Terrain Modeling. Photogrammetric Engineering and Remote Sensing. 59(4):499-504.

Twery, M. J., G. A. Elmes, and C. B. Yuill, 1991. Scientific Exploration with an Intelligent GIS: Predicting Species Composition from Topography. AI Applications in Natural Resource Mangement. 5(2):45-58.

van Kleef, H. A., and Th. J. Linthorst, 1986. Geographic Information for Land-Use Management. Netherlands Journal of Agricultural Science. 34:329-338.

Vasile, C., D. Cristescu, and C. Savulescu, 1989. The Development and State of the Art of GIS in Romania. International Journal of Geographical Information Systems. 3(2):185-190.

Ventura, S. J., 1990. Conversion of Automated Geographic Data to Decision-Making Information. Photogrammetric Engineering and Remote Sensing. 56(9):511-516.

Ventura, S. J., B. J. Niemann, Jr., and D. D. Moyer, 1988. A Multipurpose Land Information System for Rural Resource Planning. Journal of Soil and Water Conservation. 43(3):226-229.

Wadge, G., 1988. The Potential of GIS Modelling of Gravity Flows and Slope Instabilities. International Journal of Geographical Information Systems. 2(2):143-152.

Walsh, S. J., J. W. Cooper, I. E. Von Essen, and K. R. Gallager, 1990. Image Enhancement of Landsat Thematic Mapper Data and GIS Data Integration for Evaluation of Resource Characteristics. Photogrammetric Engineering and Remote Sensing. 56(8):1135-1141.

Weir, M. J. C., 1989. More Advanced Technology Needed. Journal of Forestry. 87(7):20-25.

Welch, R., M. Remillard, and J. Alberts, 1992. Integration of GPS, Remote Sensing, and GIS Techniques for Coastal Resource Management. Photogrammetric Engineering and Remote Sensing. 58(11):1571-1578.

Westmoreland, S., and D. A. Stow, 1992. Category Identification of Changed Land-Use Polygons in an Integrated Image Processing/Geographic Information System. Photogrammetric Engineering and Remote Sensing. 58(11):1593-1600.

Wheeler, D. J., 1993. Commentary: Linking Environmental Models with Geographic Information Systems for Global Change Research. Photogrammetric Engineering and Remote Sensing. 59(10):1497-1501.

Williamson, S. C., and I. E. Lindauer, 1988. Assessing Rangeland Vegetation Mapping Alternatives for Geographic Information Systems. Photogrammetric Engineering and Remote Sensing. 54(5):615-618.

Xiang, W. N., 1993. A GIS Method for Riparian Water Quality Buffer Generation. International Journal of Geographical Information Systems. 7(1):57-70.

Yeh, A. G.-O., 1991. The Development and Applications of Geographic Information Systems for Urban and Regional Planning in the Developing Countries. International Journal of Geographical Information Systems. 5(1):5-28.

Young, J. A. T., 1986. Remote Sensing and an Experimental Geographic Information System for Environmental Monitoring, Resource Planning and Management. International Journal of Remote Sensing. 7(6):741-744.

Yue, L., L. Zhang, C. Ziaogang, and Z. Yingming, 1991. The Establishment and Application of the Geographic Mapping Database by City/County Unit in China. International Journal of Geographical Information Systems. 5(1):73-84.

Zack, J. A., and R. A. Minnich, 1991. Integration of Geographic Information Systems with a Diagnostic Wind Field Model for Fire Management. Forest Science. 37:560-573.

Zhou, H. J., K. B. MacDonald, and A. Moore, 1991. Some Cautions of the Use of GIS Technology to Integrate Soil Site and Area Data. Canadian Journal of Soil Science. 71:389-394.

Zhu, Z., and D. Evans, 1992. Mapping Midsouth Forest Distributions. Journal of Forestry. 90(11):27-30.

APPENDIX I

GEOGRAPHIC INFORMATION SYSTEMS:
SOME SOURCES OF INFORMATION

by

James W. Merchant
Center for Advanced Land Management Information Technologies
Conservation and Survey Division
Institute of Agriculture and Natural Resources
University of Nebraska-Lincoln
Lincoln, NE 68588-0517
(402) 472-7531

It is often difficult for persons wishing to explore geographic information systems (GIS) technology to identify good sources of information. The following list provides a brief selective guide to major books, conference proceedings and periodicals.

Books:

Allen, K.M.S., S.W. Green and E.B.W. Zubrow, eds. 1990.
Interpreting Space: GIS and Archaeology. Taylor and Francis, Inc., 1900 Frost Road, Suite 101, Bristol, PA 19007. (An excellent overview of GIS applications in archaeology).

Antenucci, J.C., K. Brown, P.L. Croswell and M.J. Kevany with Hugh Archer. 1991. Geographic Information Systems: A Guide to the Technology. Van Nostrand Reinhold, 115 Fifth Avenue, New York, NY 10003. (Especially good coverage of implementation, administrative, policy, economic and legal issues).

Aronoff, Stan. 1989. Geographic Information Systems: A Management Perspective. WDL Publications, P.O. Box 8457, Station "T", Ottawa, Ontario, CANADA, K1G 3H8. (An excellent introduction to GIS technology, implementation and applications).

Bernhardsen, T. 1992. Geographic Information Systems. Viak IT, Longum Park, P.O. Box 1699, Myrene, 4801 Arendal, NORWAY. (A basic introduction to GIS; Scandinavian emphasis).

Brown, P.M. and D.D. Moyer. 1989. Multipurpose Land Information Systems: The Guidebook. N/CG1x10/1 SSMC3, Station 9361, Coast and Geodetic Survey, 1315 East-West Highway, National Oceanic and Atmospheric Administration, Silver Spring, MD 20910. (Handbook dealing primarily with local level GIS, base mapping, standards, geodetic referencing).

Burrough, P.A. 1986. <u>Principles of Geographical Information Systems for Land Resources Assessment</u>. Monographs on Soil and Resources Survey No. 12. Clarendon Press/Oxford University Press, 200 Madison Avenue, New York, NY 10016. (A textbook for the more advanced GIS practitioner).

Castle, G.H. (ed.). 1993. <u>Profiting From a Geographic Information System</u>. GIS World, Inc., 155 East Boardwalk Drive, Suite 250, Ft. Collins, CO 80525. (An overview of GIS applications in business and industry).

Clarke, K.C. 1990. <u>Analytical and Computer Cartography</u>. Prentice Hall, Englewood Cliffs, NJ 07632. (Although not itself a GIS book, this volume has excellent sections on data structures, geocoding, terrain modelling, hardware and software and cartographic transformations).

Dahlberg, R.E., J.D. McLaughlin and B.J. Niemann, Jr. (eds.). 1989. <u>Developments in Land Information Management</u>. Institute for Land Information, 440 First Street, NW, 8th floor), Washington, DC 20001. (A compendium of articles focusing on GIS, land records systems and cadastral mapping).

Dueker, K.J. and D. Kjerne. 1989. <u>Multipurpose Cadastre: Terms and Definitions</u>. American Society for Photogrammetry and Remote Sensing, 5410 Grosvenor Lane, Suite 210, Bethesda, MD 20814-2160.

Environmental Systems Research Institute. 1990. <u>A Glossary of GIS and ARC/INFO Terms</u>. ESRI, 380 New York Street, Redlands, CA 92373. (Well illustrated, dictionary format - deals with GIS terminology).

Environmental Systems Research Institute. 1990. <u>Under-standing GIS-The ARC/INFO Method</u>. Understanding GIS-The ARC/ INFO Method. ESRI, 380 New York Street, Redlands, CA 92373. (A self instruction manual for ESRI's ARC/INFO software).

Federal Geographic Data Committee. 1992. <u>Manual of Federal Geographic Data Products</u>. Federal Geographic Data Committee Secretariat, U.S. Geological Survey, 590 National Center, Reston, VA 22092. (An illustrated guide to digital spatial data produced by federal agencies).

Goodchild, M. and S. Gopal (eds.). 1990. <u>Accuracy of Spatial Databases</u>. Taylor and Francis Publishing, 1900 Frost Road, Suite 101, Bristol, PA 19007-1598. (Addresses error and accuracy issues in GIS).

Guptill, Stephen C. (ed.). 1988. <u>A Process for Evaluating Geographic Information Systems</u>, U.S.G.S. Open File Report 88-105. U.S. Geological Survey/Federal Interagency Coordina-ting Committee on Digital Cartography, 590 USGS National Center, Reston, VA 22092. (A guide to selection of a GIS).

Huxhold, W.E. 1991. <u>An Introduction to Urban Geographic Information Systems</u>. Oxford University Press, 200 Madison Avenue, New York, NY 10016. (An introduction to urban, regional and land records information systems).

Keating, J.B. 1993. <u>Geo-Positioning Selection Guide for Resource Management</u> (Technical Note 389). U.S. Bureau of Land Management, BLM/PMDS SC, 657B, Building 41, Denver Federal Center, Denver, CO 80225-0045. (An excellent introductory guide to GIS, GPS and remote sensing).

Laurini, R. and D. Thompson. 1992. <u>Fundamentals of Spatial Information Systems</u>. Academic Press, San Diego, CA 92101. (An excellent treatment of advanced concepts in GIS).

Maguire, D.J., M.F. Goodchild and D.W. Rhind, eds. 1991. <u>Geographical Information Systems: Principles and Applications</u>. J. Wiley and Sons, Inc., 605 Third Avenue, New York, NY 10158. (A two-volume, sixty-chapter reference on GIS and applications of the technology).

Masser, I. and M. Blakemore, eds. 1991. <u>Handling Geograph-ical Information: Methodology and Potential Applications</u>. (Readings on GIS methods and applications; U.K. emphasis)

Montgomery, G.E. and H.C. Schuch. 1993. <u>GIS Data Conversion Handbook</u>. GIS World, Inc., 155 East Boardwalk Drive, Suite 250, Ft. Collins, CO 80525. (An introduction to alternatives for database generation).

Niemann, B.J., Jr., and D.D. Moyer (eds.). 1988. <u>A Primer on Multipurpose Land Information Systems</u>, Wisconsin Land Information Report 4. Institute for Environmental Studies, University of Wisconsin-Madison, 550 North Park Street, 15 Science Hall, University of Wisconsin-Madison, Madison, WI 53706. (Papers on recent advances in LIS and GIS).

Onsrud, H.J. and D.W. Cook (eds.). 1990. <u>Geographic and Land Information Systems for Practicing Surveyors</u>. American Congress on Surveying and Mapping, 5410 Grosvenor Lane, Bethesda, MD 20814. (A compendium of articles dealing primarily with GIS applications in land records management, cadastral mapping and legal issues related to GIS).

Peuquet, Donna J., and Duane F. Marble. 1990. <u>Introductory Readings in Geographic Information Systems</u>. Taylor and Francis, 1900 Frost Road, Suite 101, Bristol, PA 19007-1598. (Selected articles by a variety of authors).

Public Technology, Inc. 1991. <u>The Local Government Guide to Geographic Information Systems: Planning Implementation</u>. Public Technology, Inc., 1301 Pennsylvania Ave., Washington, DC 20004. (Excellent guide to county and municipal GIS implementation).

Rhind, David and Helen Mounsey. Expected early 1991. Understanding GIS. Taylor and Francis, 1900 Frost Road, Suite 101, Bristol, PA 19007-1598. (An introductory text).

Ripple, William J. (ed.). 1987. Geographic Information Systems for Resource Management: A Compendium. American Society for Photogrammetry and Remote Sensing, 5410 Grosvenor Lane, Suite 210, Bethesda, MD 20814-2160. (Selected reprints of articles on GIS; an introduction to GIS).

Ripple, William J. (ed.). 1989. Fundamentals of Geographic Information of Geographic Information Systems: A Compendium. American Society for Photogrammetry and Remote Sensing, 5410 Grosvenor Lane, Suite 210, Bethesda, MD 20814-2160. (A collection of articles on GIS issues and applications).

Rodcay, G.K. (ed.). 1994. The GIS Sourcebook. GIS World, Inc., 155 East Boardwalk Drive, Suite 250, Fort Collins, CO 80525. (A guide to software, hardware, and new developments in GIS).

Star, Jeffrey L. and John E. Estes. 1990. Geographic Information Systems: An Introduction. Prentice-Hall, Inc., Sylvan Avenue, Englewood Cliffs, NJ 07632. (An introductory text; gives special attention to the GIS/remote sensing interface).

Tomlin, C. Dana. 1990. Geographic Information Systems and Cartographic Modeling. Prentice-Hall, Inc., Sylvan Avenue, Englewood Cliffs, NJ 07632. (Especially good for users of the MAPs family of software).

Ventura, S.J. 1991. Implementation of Land Information Systems in Local Government - Steps Towards land Records Modernization in Wisconsin. Wisconsin State Cartographer's Office, University of Wisconsin, 155 Science Hall, 550 North Park St., Madison, WI 53706-1404. (An inexpensive, excellent overview of technical and institutional issues with applications far beyond Wisconsin).

Vonderohe, A.P., R.F. Gurda, S.J. Ventura and P.G. Thum. 1991. Introduction to Local Land Information Systems for Wisconsin's Future. Wisconsin State Cartographer's Office, University of Wisconsin, 155 Science Hall, 550 North Park St., Madison, WI 53706-1404. (A complement to Ventura's booklet; an inexpensive guide for all prospective governmental users of GIS).

Warnecke, L., J. Johnson, K. Marshall, and R. Brown. 1992. State Geographic Information Activities Compendium. Council of State Governments, Iron Works Pike, PO Box 11910, Lexington, KY 40578-1910. (An excellent overview of GIS activities in state governments).

Proceedings:

AutoCarto 9: Ninth International Symposium on Computer-Assisted Cartography. American Society for Photogrammetry and Remote Sensing, 5410 Grosvenor Lane, Suite 210, Bethesda, MD 20814- 2160. (Most recent in the AutoCarto series of symposia).

Automated Mapping/Facilities Management Conference Proceedings.
AM/FM International, 8775 East Orchard Road, Englewood, CO 80111. (Of special interest to GIS users in the public utilities).

GIS/LIS '93. American Society for Photogrammetry and Remote Sensing, 5410 Grosvenor Land, Suite 210, Bethesda, MD 20814-
2160. (Proceedings of annual conference co-sponsored with the American Congress on Surveying and Mapping, the Association of American Geographers and the Urban and Regional Information Systems Association; conferences were also held each year since 1986).

International Geographic Information Systems (IGIS) Symposium - 1987. Association of American Geographers, 1710 Sixteenth Street, NW, Washington, DC 20009. (Subsequent smaller conference was held in 1989).

International Symposia on Spatial Data Handling. International Geographical Union, Commission on Geographical Data Sensing and Processing, Department of Geography, The Ohio State University, Columbus, OH 43210. (Conferences held in 1984, 1986, 1988, and 1992).

Proceedings of the Annual Convention of the American Society for Photogrammetry and Remote Sensing and the American Congress on Surveying and Mapping. American Society for Photogrammetry and Remote Sensing or American Congress on Surveying and Mapping, 5410 Grosvenor Lane, Suite 210, Bethesda, MD 20814-2160.

Proceedings of the Annual Meeting of the Urban and Regional Information Systems Association (URISA). URISA, 900 Second Street, NE, Suite 304, Washington, DC 20002.

Periodicals:

Cartography and Geographic Information Systems. American Congress on Surveying and Mapping, 5410 Grosvenor Lane, Bethesda, MD 20814. (Emphasizes basic research on cartography and the cartographic-GIS interface).

Geo Info Systems. PO Box 7678, Riverton, NJ 08077-7678. (Magazine focusing on GIS applications).

GIS World. 155 East Boardwalk Drive, Suite 250, Fort Collins, CO 80525. (A magazine that provides software reviews, information on publications and applications; written for the GIS user).

International Journal of Geographical Information Systems. Taylor and Francis, 1900 Frost Road, Suite 101, Bristol, PA 19007-1598. (Research papers on GIS).

Journal of the Urban and Regional Information Systems Association (URISA). URISA, 900 Second Street, NE, Suite 304, Washington, DC 20002. (Emphasizes articles on urban applications and land records systems).

Photogrammetric Engineering and Remote Sensing. American Society for Photogrammetry and Remote Sensing, 5410 Grosvenor Lane, Suite 210, Bethesda, MD 20814-2160. (Frequent articles and news on GIS; annual special issues are devoted to GIS).

GPS World. PO Box 7677, Riverton, NJ 08077-7677. (Focus on global positioning system technology, GPS-GIS interface).

Note: Many other journals carry articles on GIS from time to time. These include, for example, the Journal of Soil and Water Conservation, Environmental Management, the Journal of Forestry, and the Journal of the American Planning Association. In addition, there are dozens of newsletters (many free) that deal with GIS.

Author Index

Color Plates

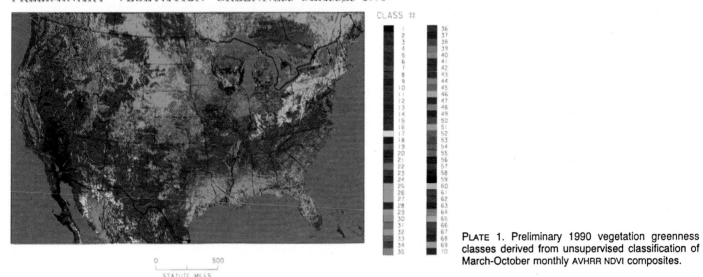

PLATE 1. Preliminary 1990 vegetation greenness classes derived from unsupervised classification of March-October monthly AVHRR NDVI composites.

See **"Development of a Land-Cover Characteristics Database for the Conterminous U.S."** Loveland, Merchant, Ohlen, and Brown. page 47.

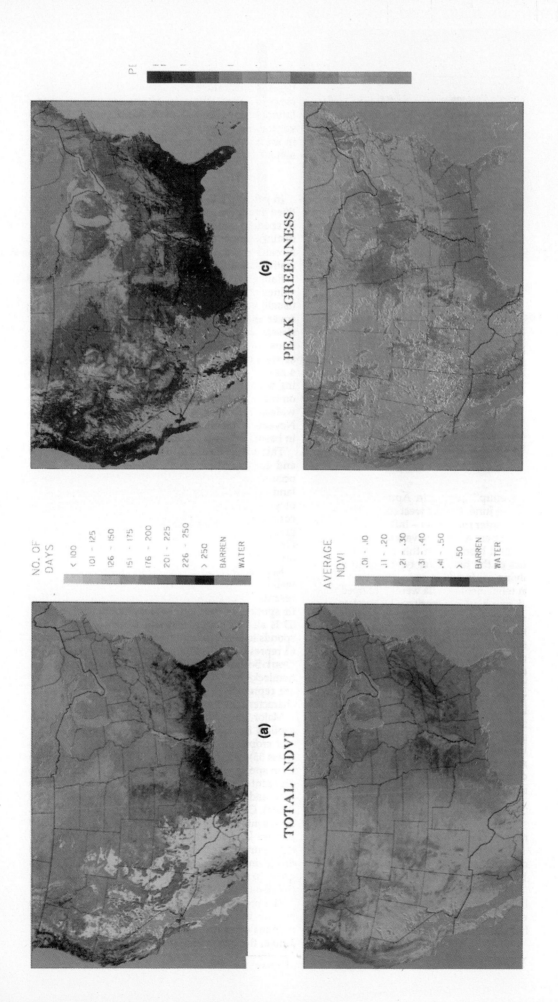

PLATE 2. Seasonal parameters calculated for preliminary vegetation greenness classes include (a) onset of greenness, (b) period of peak greenness, (c) duration of green period, and (d) total NDVI.

See "Development of a Land-Cover Characteristics Database for the Conterminous U.S." Loveland, Merchant, Ohlen, and Brown. page 48

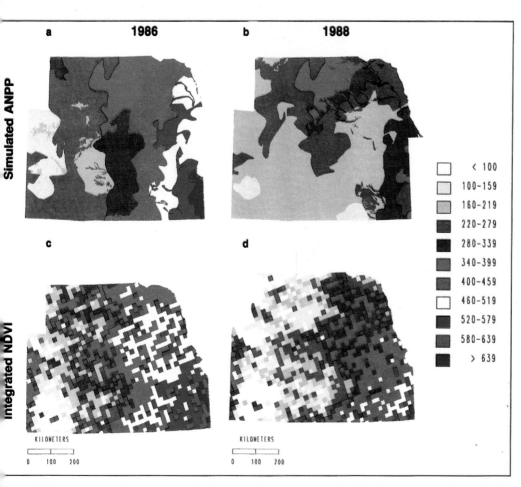

See "**Regional Analysis of the Central Great Plains**" Burke, Kittel, Lauenroth, Snook, Yonker, Parton. See page 74.

Figure 4. Simulated aboveground net primary production ($g \cdot m^{-2} \cdot y^{-1}$) for grasslands within the central Great Plains and adjacent Central Lowlands for (a) 1986 and (b) 1988. Annual integral of the normalized difference vegetation index (NDVI) for (c) 1986 and (d) 1988. Colors correspond to regression values of simulated ANPP, using the following equations. 1986: NDVI (in NDVI day) = [?].1 + 11/modeled ANPP (in g biomass $\cdot m^{-2}$); 1988: NDVI = 42.4 + 9.2/modeled ANPP. Both regressions were highly significant [?] < 0.0001).

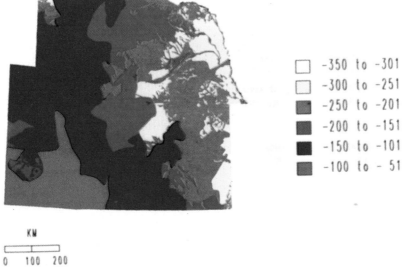

See "**Regional Analysis of the Central Great Plains**" Burke, Kittel, Lauenroth, Snook, Yonker, Parton. See page 76.

Figure 5. Simulated changes in ecosystem carbon storage (g/m^2) for grasslands within the central Great Plains and adjacent Central Lowlands in response to 50 years of global climate change.

369

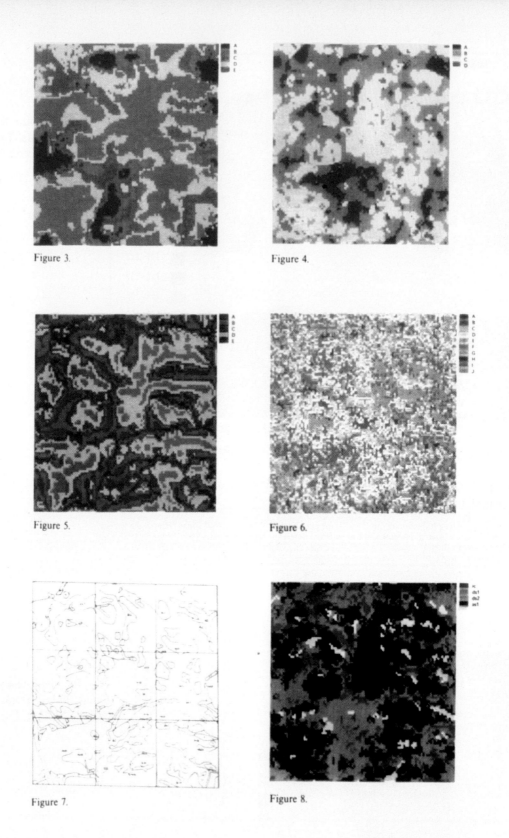

Figure 3.

Figure 4.

Figure 5.

Figure 6.

Figure 7.

Figure 8.

See **"Use of an Expert System to Map Forest Soils from a Geographical Information System"** Skidmore, Ryan, Dawes, Short, O'Loughlin. page 104.

370

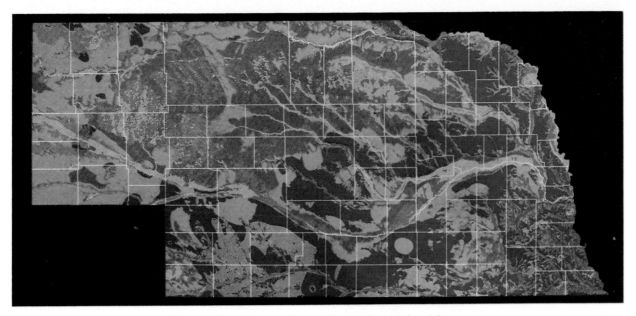

Figure 3 Statewide map of potential groundwater vulnerability

See "**Statewide Groundwater-Vulnerability Assessment in Nebraska Using the DRASTIC/GIS Model**"
Rundquist, Rodekohr, Peters, Ehrman, Di, and Murary. see page 121.

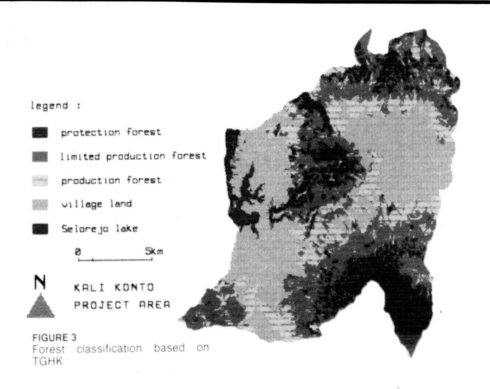

legend :

■ protection forest

■ limited production forest

■ production forest

■ village land

■ Selorejo lake

0   5km

N

KALI KONTO
PROJECT AREA

FIGURE 3
Forest classification based on
TGHK

See "**GIS Applications in Forest Land Management in Indonesia**" Susilawati, and Weir. See page 169.

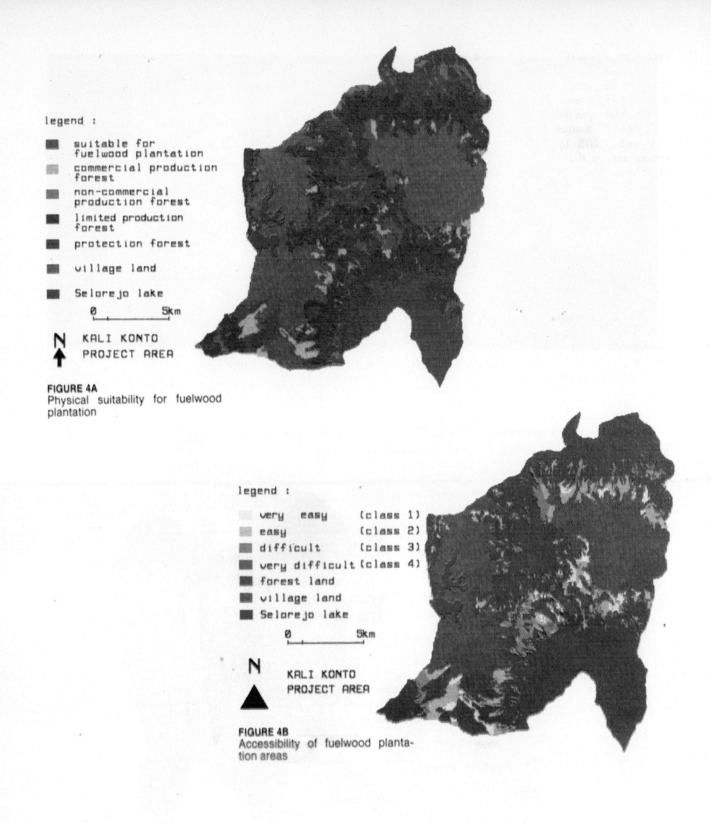

legend :

- suitable for fuelwood plantation
- commercial production forest
- non-commercial production forest
- limited production forest
- protection forest
- village land
- Selorejo lake

0 _____ 5km

N KALI KONTO PROJECT AREA

FIGURE 4A
Physical suitability for fuelwood plantation

legend :

- very easy (class 1)
- easy (class 2)
- difficult (class 3)
- very difficult (class 4)
- forest land
- village land
- Selorejo lake

0 _____ 5km

N KALI KONTO PROJECT AREA

FIGURE 4B
Accessibility of fuelwood planta-tion areas

See **"GIS Applications in Forest Land Management in Indonesia"** Susilawati, and Weir. See page 170.

372

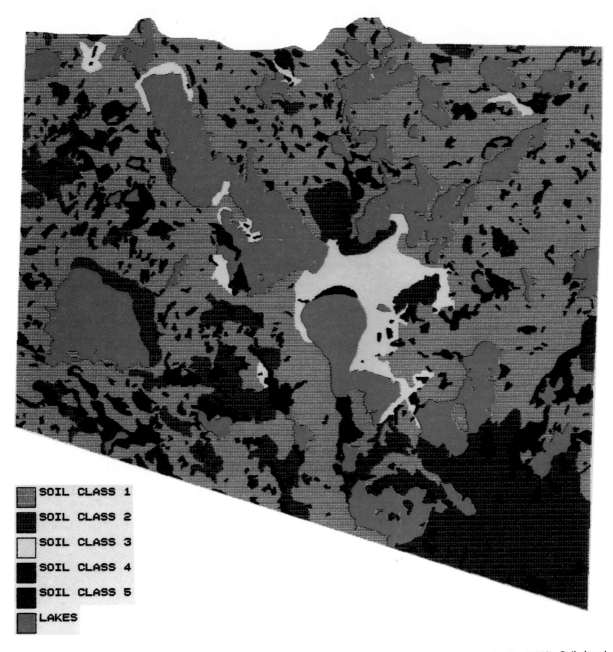

Fig. 1. Computer generated map of the soil types represented on the Sylvania Recreation Area, MI., from Jordan (1973). Soil class 1 was well-drained to moderately well-drained with coarse loamy textures and a moderate fragipan; soil class 2 was well-drained to moderately well-drained with sandy textures; soil class 3 was well-drained with sandy textures; soil class 4 was moderately well-drained with coarse silty textures; and soil class 5 was very poorly drained organic soils of strongly to slightly acid herbaceous and woody materials.

See **"The Spatial Pattern of a Northern Conifer-Hardwood Landscape"** Pastor and Broschart. See page 209.

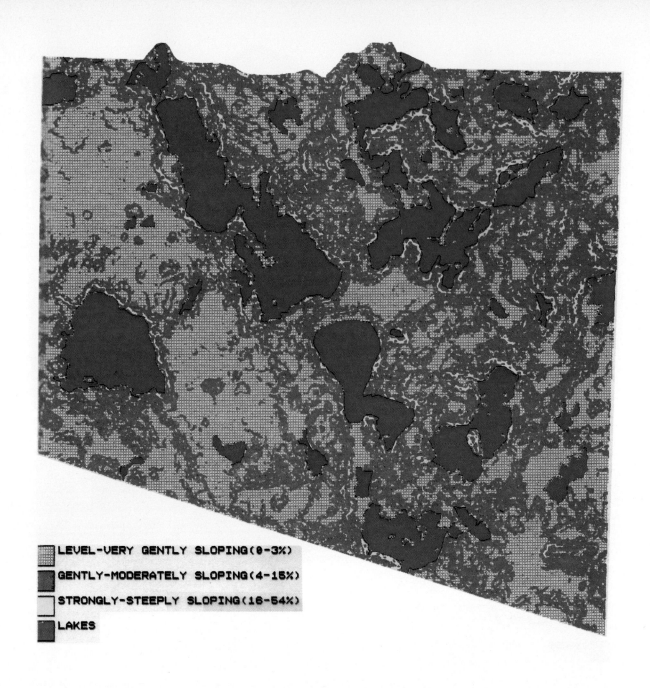

LEVEL-VERY GENTLY SLOPING(0-3%)

GENTLY-MODERATELY SLOPING(4-15%)

STRONGLY-STEEPLY SLOPING(16-54%)

LAKES

See "The Spatial Pattern of a Northern Conifer-Hardwood Landscape" Pastor and Broschart. See page 210.

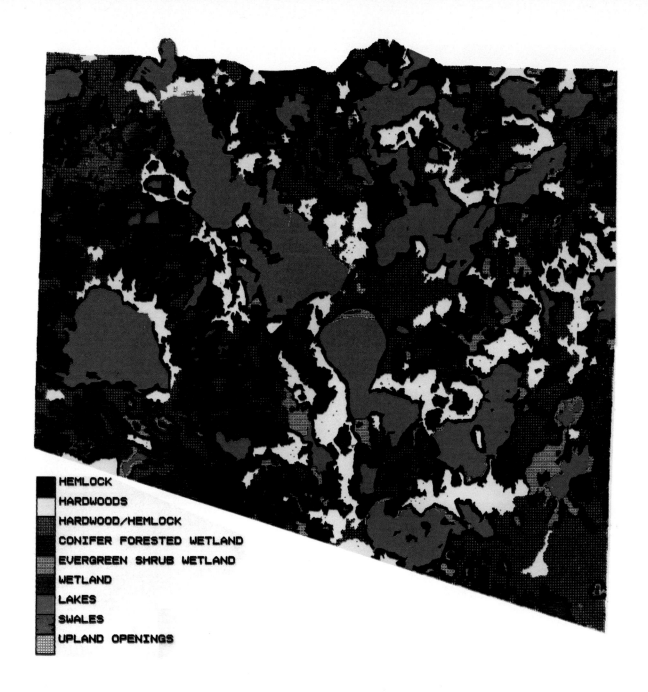

HEMLOCK
HARDWOODS
HARDWOOD/HEMLOCK
CONIFER FORESTED WETLAND
EVERGREEN SHRUB WETLAND
WETLAND
LAKES
SWALES
UPLAND OPENINGS

See "The Spatial Pattern of a Northern Conifer-Hardwood Landscape" Pastor and Broschart. See page 213.

Fig. 7. Predicted distribution of coast live oak forest based on geology, topography and insolation. Black areas are predicted vegetation other than oak forest. Colored areas are predicted oak forest sites on which mapped existing vegetation was oak forest (red), oak woodland (blue), coastal scrub (green), conifer (white) or other land cover types (yellow). Image orientation and area are as in Fig. 1.

See "Modeling Vegetation Pattern Using Digital Terrain Data Davis and Goetz. page 228.

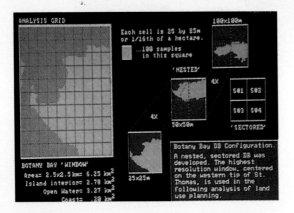

Figure 1.

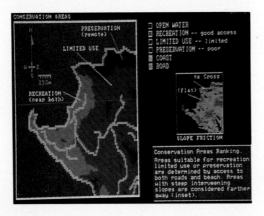

Figure 2.

Figure 3.

See "GIS Resolves Land Use Conflicts: A Case Study," Berry. pages 281 and 282.

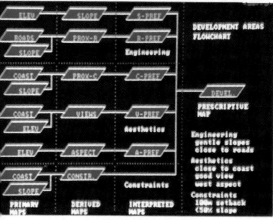

Figure 4.

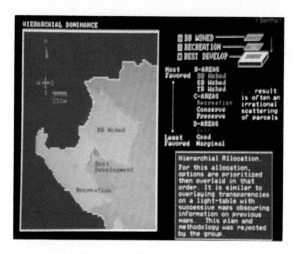

Figure 6.

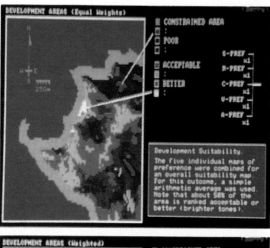

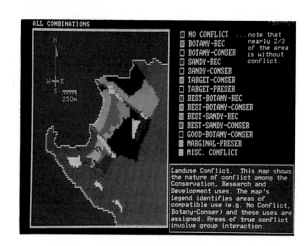

Figure 5.

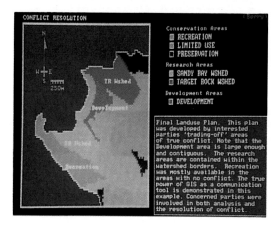

Figure 7.

See "GIS Resolves Land Use Conflicts: A Case Study" Berry. page 282, 283, and 284.

Fig. 1. Landsat Thematic Mapper color composite image of southern Rondônia state, Brazil, for path 230 and row 69 acquired on 5 June 1988. Areas of tropical forest, deforestation, regrowth, and isolated forest are labeled. The area identified as isolated forest is about 3 km by 15 km in size.

See **"Tropical Deforestation and Habitat Fragmentation in the Amazon: Satellite Data from 1978 to 1988"** Skole, and Tucker. page 336.

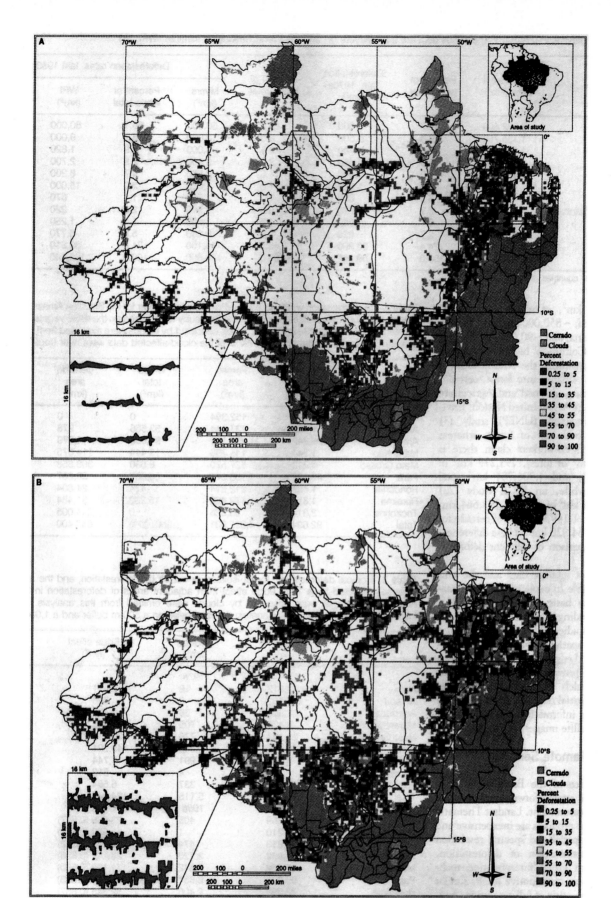

See "Tropical Deforestation and Habitat Fragmentation in the Amazon: Satellite Data from 1978 to 1988" Skole, and Tucker. page 338.

Fig. 2. Representation of deforestation in the Amazon of Brazil from (**A**) 1978 and (**B**) 1988. The deforestation represented in these figures is confined exclusively to the forest strata. The data were averaged into 16 km by 16 km grid cells.

Fig. 3. Map of the Brazilian Amazon Basin showing where biological diversity was adversely affected in 1988 by deforestation, isolation of forest, and the 1-km edge effect of deforestation. The largest contributor to the area of negative effects on biological diversity was the 1-km edge effect from adjacent areas of deforestation. Isolation of forest patches was not a large contributor to this problem. The affected-habitat data were averaged into 16 km by 16 km grid cells.

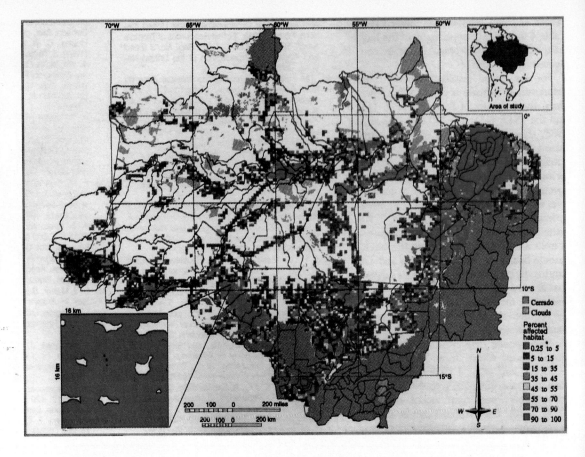

See "Tropical Deforestation and Habitat Fragmentation in the Amazon: Satellite Data from 1978 to 1988" Skole, and Tucker. page 339.